A SOCIAL HISTORY OF
TWENTIETH-CENTURY EUROPE

A Social History of Twentieth-Century Europe offers a systematic overview of major aspects of social life, including population, family and households, social inequalities and mobility, the welfare state, work, consumption and leisure, social cleavages in politics, and urbanization, as well as education, religion and culture. It also addresses major debates and diverging interpretations of historical and social research regarding the history of European societies in the past one hundred years.

Across ten thematic chapters, this book takes an interdisciplinary approach, making use of the methods and results of not only history, but also sociology, demography, economics and political science. Béla Tomka presents both the diversity and the commonalities of European societies looking not just to Western European countries, but to Eastern, Central and Southern European countries as well. An essential introduction for all students of European history.

Béla Tomka is Professor of Modern Social and Economic History, University of Szeged, Hungary. He is the author of thirteen books, including *Welfare in East and West* (2004), and editor of several other volumes. He is a co-founder and board member of the International Social History Association, Amsterdam.

A Social History of Twentieth-Century Europe

Béla Tomka

Routledge
Taylor & Francis Group

LONDON AND NEW YORK

First published 2013
by Routledge
2 Park Square, Milton Park, Abingdon, Oxon OX14 4RN

Simultaneously published in the USA and Canada
by Routledge
711 Third Avenue, New York, NY 10017

Routledge is an imprint of the Taylor & Francis Group, an informa business

British Library Cataloguing in Publication Data
A catalogue record for this book is available from the British Library

Library of Congress Cataloging in Publication Data
Tomka, Béla.
A social history of 20th century Europe / Béla Tomka.
pages cm
"Simultaneously published in the USA and Canada"--Title page verso.
Includes bibliographical references.
1. Europe--Social conditions--20th century. 2. Europe--Social life and
customs--20th century. I. Title. II. Title: Social history of twentieth
century Europe.
HN373.5.T66 2013
306.094--dc23
2012034241

ISBN: 978-0-415-62843-3 (hbk)
ISBN: 978-0-415-62845-7 (pbk)
ISBN: 978-0-203-37535-8 (ebk)

Typeset in Bembo
by Taylor & Francis Books

To Hartmut Kaelble and György Kövér

CONTENTS

LIST OF FIGURES

LIST OF TABLES

PREFACE

Not only do the many facets of the social history of twentieth-century Europe invite similarly diverse interpretations but the process of writing a book on the subject contains numerous and often intricate phases as well. In the case of this volume, although my fascination with the topic never faltered, at times the difficulties of collecting comparative material on a great number of societies seemed daunting, and a feeling of hopelessness even lingered about ever completing the work. As for the methodological issues and the style of the book, the most complicated set of choices concerned whether it should centre around an overarching narrative and survey those aspects of history dictated by it, or whether another framework for determining the areas considered could be found; if nation-states should be regarded as major units of the study, or if the discussion could move to other levels; which national societies were to be involved, and what weight should they be assigned in the analysis; what time period should be covered and how should temporal structures be introduced; and, finally, whether a more accessible and colourful style of presentation is to be preferred, or arguments are better to be advanced in as precise and learned a way as possible.

However, even when I faced the most troublesome, conflicting alternatives of how to structure the manuscript, I was aware that writing a volume on the social history of twentieth-century Europe was a unique experience. On the one hand, during my academic career thus far, problems of social diversity and unity in Europe, as well as the transfers and entanglements in the continent, have increasingly become the focus of my interest, and I have conducted research on different aspects of comparative social and economic history in modern and contemporary Europe. While writing this book I obviously relied on this skill, but the project also demanded that I systematize my knowledge in the more familiar scholarly fields and deepen it in less well-known areas; that is, however clichéd it might sound, the work was the source of great intellectual enjoyment. On the other hand, as someone who grew up in a country firmly isolated from a good part of the continent, I have strong empathy towards Europe and what is often called the European cultural heritage. The work enabled me to go beyond my occasionally almost naive ideas about the nature of these legacies, although my attachment became even more conscious and stronger in several respects. I hope that the latter attitudes did not affect the content of this volume, but that rather, the reader gains some insight into the complexity of European social history and its various interpretations.

One can hardly write any study on European societies without taking account of the first-hand academic and everyday experiences gained on the continent and, of course, beyond it. During the several years long work with sometimes lengthy interruptions, I have acquired a particularly strong amount of knowledge on my visits to various universities and academic institutions. These occasions and stays have enabled me to get acquainted with the relevant literature and those problems that particularly capture the interest of historians and other social scientists with regard to the social change of twentieth-century Europe. Thus, it is a satisfying pleasure that here I have the opportunity to express my gratitude to those collea-gues who have helped my work. Not only were they encouraging and dedicated when I was collecting the material and writing this book but also they supported other comparative research projects, the lessons of which I have used as well. To mention only a few colleagues among the many who supported and inspired me: the consultations with Hartmut Kaelble in Berlin were of particular importance for me; I learnt most of all from our conversations on historical comparisons and other scholarly issues, but his personality and scholarly attitude were a further inspiration for me. I also have to mention Philipp Ther in the *Berliner Kolleg für Vergleichende Geschichte Europas*, and in the International Institute of Social History, Amsterdam, Marcel van der Linden and Lex Heerma van Voss supported my research. The invitations of Bo Stråth to Florence, and the discussions with David Coleman in Oxford, were additional important sources of motivation for me. For ensuring the undisturbed and excellent conditions for the last phase of preparing the manuscript, I have to express my gratitude to my colleagues at the *Imre Kertész Kolleg* in Jena, and above all to Joachim von Puttkamer and Wlodzimierz Borodziej. At my home university in Szeged, Patrick Alexander, Zoltán Cora and Attila Kiss gave me indispensable assistance in the translation of the work. I owe a particular debt to György Kövér, Budapest, who has followed my career since the beginnings and also commented on the first version of this book. Gábor Gyáni not only helped with valuable pieces of advice but also encouraged the publishing of the book in Hungarian, for which gratitude is also due to the Osiris Publishing House, and especially to János Gyurgyák and Zsejke Nagy. Beyond those already mentioned, a number of additional institutions and organizations have supported my work in some form over the last years. Besides the University of Szeged, I have to name the Hungarian Scientific Research Fund and the 21st Century Institute, Budapest, as well as the *Alexander von Humboldt-Stiftung,* in Bonn. I also wish to express my gratitude to Eve Setch and Laura Mothersole, Editors at Routledge, for their guidance and careful preparation of the publication, and finally, to the three anonymous reviewers for their comments on the manuscript.

Szeged–Jena, May 2012
Béla Tomka

LIST OF ABBREVIATIONS

BBC	British Broadcasting Corporation
CDU	*Christlich Demokratische Union Deutschlands* (Christian Democratic Union of Germany)
CDA	*Christen-Democratisch Appèl* (Dutch Christian Democratic Party)
CSU	*Christlich-Soziale Union in Bayern* (Christian Social Union of Bavaria)
CVP	*Christlichdemokratische Volkspartei* (Swiss Christian Democratic People's Party)
DC	*Democrazia Cristiana* (Italian Christian Democratic Party)
DM	*Deutsche Mark*
ETA	*Euskadi Ta Askatasuna* (Basque Homeland and Freedom)
EVP	*Evangelische Volkspartei* (Swiss Evangelical People's Party)
FDJ	*Freie Deutsche Jugend* (Free German Youth of the GDR)
FDP	*Freie Demokratische Partei* (German Free Democratic Party)
FN	*Front National* (French National Front)
FPÖ	*Freiheitliche Partei Österreichs* (Austrian Freedom Party)
KF	*Konservative Folkeparti* (Danish Conservative People's Party)
KOR	*Komitet Obrony Robotników* (Polish Workers' Defence Committee)
KrF	*Kristelig Folkeparti* (Norwegian Christian People's Party)
KESK	*Keskustapuolue* (Finnish Centre Party)
ÖVP	*Österreichische Volkspartei* (Austrian People's Party)
PCE	*Partido Comunista de España* (Communist Party of Spain)
PCF	*Parti Communiste Français* (French Communist Party)
PCI	*Partido Comunista Italiano* (Italian Communist Party)
PDS	*Partei des Demokratischen Sozialismus* (German Party of Democratic Socialism)
PNV	*Partido Nacionalista Vasco* (Basque Nationalist Party)

PSB	*Belgische Socialistische Partij/Parti Socialiste Belge* (Belgian Social Democratic Party)
PPI	*Partito Popolare Italiano* (Italian People's Party)
PvdA	*Partij van de Arbeid* (Dutch Party of Work, Social Democratic Party)
PVV	*Partij voor Vrijheid en Vooruitgang* (Belgian Liberal Party)
SdP	*Sudetendeutsche Partei* (Sudeten German Party)
SED	*Sozialistische Einheitspartei Deutschlands* (East German Socialist Unity Party)
SFP	*Svenska Folkpartiet* (Swedish People's Party in Finland)
SGP	*Staatkundig Gereformeerde Partij* (Dutch Calvinist Party)
SKDL	*Suomen Kansan Demokraattinen Liitto* (Finnish People's Democratic League)
SKL	*Suomen Kristillinen Liitto* (Finnish Christian League)
SKP	*Suomen Kommunistinen Puolue* (Finnish Communist Party)
SPD	*Sozialdemokratische Partei Deutschlands* (German Social Democratic Party)
SPÖ	*Sozialistische Partei Österreichs* (Austrian Socialist Party) From 1991 *Sozialdemokratische Partei Österreichs* (Social Democratic Party of Austria)
SVP	*Schweizerische Volkspartei* (Swiss People's Party)
UN	United Nations

1

INTRODUCTION

During the last couple of decades, new social relations have emerged and strong ties have been established among people from different societies in Europe. Although economy has clearly been the most advanced part of the integration, very little of national social life has remained unaffected by intensive and often new forms of interaction across the continent. People travel not only for business purposes but also for vacation; they work and study abroad; they purchase food and other products and consume news, music and television programmes coming from abroad, which inform them about what is happening in other countries. It is without doubt that the growing contacts and cooperation do not equally influence all social groups and countries in Europe, and people from different countries largely maintain their own languages and cultures. Still, as a result of these comprehensive and intensive links and the high level of interdependence among European countries, Europe has become a major element of people's lives on the continent, and many citizens consider themselves as Europeans.[1] It falls upon historians to respond in their own ways to these changes and synergies by considering not only the past of national societies, but also by examining Europe as a whole, even if this endeavour clearly implies several pitfalls. This volume attempts to do this by covering most of the regions and major aspects of social life of twentieth-century Europe, as much as possible and plausible in a single-volume historical work.

In recent decades, surprisingly few studies have undertaken this or similar tasks, and those facing the challenge often covered the social history of twentieth-century Europe only from a particular point of view. Although several accomplished scholars have produced valuable research and insights regarding social changes in Europe, no publication exists that synthesizes these discrete aspects to give a comprehensive account of social developments in twentieth-century Europe. A brief overview of the most prominent related publications from the past two decades in English might illuminate the case in point. The books co-authored by Frank B. Tipton and Robert Aldrich are easily accessible to students, but do not provide a systematic overview of social history, because there are major topics (such as family, social mobility and social policy) that hardly surface in the two volumes.[2] The work published in 1989 by Gerold Ambrosius and William H. Hubbard is more comprehensive and also offers important textbook features, such as incorporating figures and tables that show key historical processes. That book discusses the social history of the continent by focusing primarily on integrating forces and conflicts in society and successfully considers those social developments in the individual societies of twentieth-century Europe that either contributed to social cohesion or resulted in social frictions. A further merit of the volume is that it includes Central and Eastern European countries in its analysis; nevertheless, its major emphasis lies on economic history and tracks changes only up to the 1970s.[3] Among the most renowned social histories of twentieth-century Europe is that written by the German historian Hartmut Kaelble, which centres around the problem of social integration on the Western half of the continent (his more recent volume covers most of Europe in the post-war era),[4] along with Göran Therborn's work, which mainly explores the historical meaning and significance of European modernity in the decades after 1945.[5] The list would not be complete without Colin Crouch's book that provides the most comprehensive analysis available of the social changes in post-war Western Europe.[6] These approaches are discussed later in detail.

There exist several other works offering introductions to distinct aspects of the social history of twentieth-century Europe, but they almost exclusively deal with Western and Southern Europe in the last decades of the century.[7] Besides monographs, related contributions include edited volumes as well.[8] Another major tool for students of social history is a multi-volume handbook covering European social history from 1350 to 2000 containing some two hundred distinct entries. However, in these articles, twentieth-century developments appear in a relatively subordinate position, and the selection altogether does not provide a coherent picture about the social history of Europe in the past one hundred years.[9] There are numerous reasons for this lack of overall accounts of the social history of the continent in the last hundred years. The poverty of appropriate sources and research in the case of several fields and societies, the circumstance that historians are still averse to cover more than one or a couple of societies, and the fact that political upheavals had a profound impact on the twentieth-century history of the European continent appear high on the list. Most importantly, the development of twentieth-century European societies was so diverse and complex that any synthesis necessarily simplifies these histories to a great extent and thus for many might seem a pointless endeavour.

The significance of Europe as a subject of historical analysis, as well as the relatively low number of systematic works and overall accounts on the continent's twentieth-century social history, together with their thematic, chronological and other limitations (and above all, the neglect of the first half of the century and an approach that might qualify for 'Western Europe-centrism') all seem to justify the ambition of writing a social history that attempts to offer insights into long-term social trends and devote attention to regions outside the Western half of the continent within a comprehensive overview of Europe. This is, therefore, our objective in the following chapters.

An undertaking like this poses intricate questions to be answered and forces the author to make hard choices while writing the book. Thus, a few further remarks seem necessary concerning the approach and the subject as well as the limitations of the current volume. A major concern in such a work is how to conduct the analysis and present the results. One option is to focus on Europe at a supranational level and, thus, to use references to the particular societies to illustrate general tendencies. This method, often applied in historical overviews, allows us to highlight and elaborate on social trends and phenomena that we consider most crucial. But in this case, the argumentation necessarily lacks convincing empirical evidence and is hardly adequate for illuminating differences within Europe. Therefore, we do not consider this method fully adequate for our purposes. Another approach aims at a systematic analysis of the developments in various segments of particular national societies and even regions in order to draw conclusions with regard to general trends of development, as well as similarities and differences. This latter approach basically implies the consistent application of the comparative method. We consider comparisons to be useful for writing a social history of Europe, and the topics as well as the questions discussed do provide space for, and even require, such perspectives. However, it is obvious that the systematic application of the comparative approach to many societies multiplies the difficulties and even pitfalls inherent in comparisons, and also requires considerable technical apparatus and space. The number of societies in Europe is well beyond the scope that can be handled effectively by systematic comparisons, all the more so because the results are to be conveyed to the readers in an accessible way. Thus, with these considerations in mind, we strongly rely on comparisons, but they often cannot be applied systematically in the volume. Accordingly, we aim at a kind of combination of, or rather compromise between, the two approaches referred to above.

The study largely focuses on national societies, which undoubtedly raises significant concerns. This approach cannot account for several developments taking place within regional boundaries. Other processes, quite on the contrary, are of a transnational or supranational nature, crossing borders and superseding the authority and domain of nation states and individual societies. Thus, they can be comprehended only by focusing on the interaction and interdependence of particular national societies. At the same time, the nation state had a decisive role in the formation of many social institutions in the twentieth century, and there also exist practical reasons for relying on it as an essential unit of analysis. Information on most of the social phenomena is available with regard to nation states: they do not apply to the entire continent, nor are they broken down into regional units. Furthermore, building up from the regional level, to see if nation states can really be considered social units, would overburden the text, and thus, cannot simply be performed in a single volume. Still, we are aware that primarily dealing with nation states, and, *nolens volens*, assuming that they are societies, it is an approach that cannot account for significant dimensions of social change.

Another major question that the author of a social history of the continent should answer concerns the spatial scope of the coverage. Geographical definitions and boundaries are of little help in this case. Historical works tend to select their objects of analysis on the basis of social patterns, rather than by relying on geographical criteria. Moreover, if we want to keep the volume manageable, it seems necessary to set up certain limits in terms of the range of societies and regions discussed. The most important among these is that we focus on Western Europe, in a wider sense, together with East Central Europe, but Southern Europe and the Balkans are also included in the analysis as much as possible.

The inclusion of Russia/the Soviet Union and the Baltic states would definitely be justified as well. However, Russia/the Soviet Union constituted a world of its own, with sizeable internal diversity throughout the twentieth century, the analysis of which would require a lot of space and would further increase the complexity of the argumentation and would strain the structure of the work. In addition, for these regions, we simply do not have sufficient and reliable comparative data and other information in several social areas. Thus, the Baltic States, the Soviet Union and its successor states are not covered. This self-constraint is not unique: neither of the major social histories of Europe considers Russia/the Soviet Union and often even more general histories of Eastern Europe fully neglect Russia/the Soviet Union and the Baltic states.[10] Nevertheless, we obviously do not intend to deny that the past of these regions constitutes an integral part of the history of Europe. Even within these constraints, a full coverage of European regions is not possible. Even if we intend to include as many societies as the availability of historical information permits, the logic and accessibility of argumentation also set limits, and we determine empirically, subject by subject, which societies are to be considered.

At this point, it is necessary to define the regions referred to in the volume. As a general rule, Western Europe includes North Western Europe (United Kingdom/Great Britain, France, the Netherlands, Belgium and Ireland), Central Europe (Germany/FRG, Switzerland, and Austria) and Scandinavia (Sweden, Denmark, Norway, and Finland). Southern Europe refers to Italy, Spain, Portugal, and Greece; East Central Europe involves Poland, Czechoslovakia and Hungary, and South-Eastern Europe coincides with the Balkan region without Greece. We are well aware that these regional conceptualizations are artificial in many ways, because they fail to fully represent the common characteristics of societies as well as their relations, which were moreover prone to change over the twentieth century. However, the length of the examined period and the diversity of themes did not allow the concepts of regions to be fully consistently applied. Most of all, this is prevalent in the case of Southern Europe; Italy and Greece are the countries in case. However, these altogether negligible alterations are indicated if necessary.

Interdisciplinarity, as a due extension to the methods already referred to, is intended to be one of the most important approaches emerging in the work, that is, the discussion relies on the methods and results of a number of disciplines. In addition to history, these branches include, above all, sociology, demography, economics and political science. The ambition to be comparative and interdisciplinary also presents itself in the mode of presentation. The most obvious consequence is that we analyse the trends of European social history by extensively making use of quantitative evidence. In the meantime, we have to keep it in mind, on the one hand, that they might entail shortcomings concerning the comparability of available data, and on the other hand, that formal and quantitative similarities or differences are often misleading in terms of social functions. Besides statistical material, it is obvious that we apply the relevant research literature of the related disciplines mentioned above, which is sometimes scarce, although in other cases incomprehensibly abundant for a single author. The unevenness of research obviously surfaces in the volume as well. Finally, because of the limits of the study, we can cover the diverging positions present in the scholarly literature or the controversies about particular research issues only in a highly selective manner.

When structuring the book and choosing the aspects and themes of social history for analysis, we have not been led by the concerns of a particular social theory or approach, but intended to pragmatically include aspects prominently present in international research. Even if it is far from obvious which subjects qualify for this status, a review of the major publications and conferences of social history clearly identifies the themes most frequented by social historians. As the list of the chapters and subchapters reveals, we failed to fully cover all the important aspects of social history. In some cases, the author's expertise was responsible for this, in other cases already written chapters fell victim to limits of space. Last but not least, the particular subjects also had to lend themselves to empirical and comparative study, which excluded some topics as well, most importantly some cultural aspects, including changes in values and mentalities.

Temporal change is obviously a major concern of every historical work. Social historians are more committed to studying the long-term processes rather than focusing on specific events, and tend to emphasize that various historical processes operate on diverging scales of historical time. As a result, they do not necessarily expect any close alignment of periods of social history and other branches of the discipline, most eminently including political history. Thus, periodization in social history is usually not a keystone of research and, thereby, while selecting the demarcations of the book, we adhered to expediency again. The period discussed primarily covers the era between the First World War and the end of the century, but we aim at addressing the most important antecedents, as well as (mostly in a separate sub-chapter) the developments around the turn of the millennium.

As it may have already become clear from the above mentioned concerns, covering the social history of twentieth-century Europe in a single volume by a single author is a challenging task for a number of reasons. The period covered is long, and (even if we focus on the Western European and East Central European regions, with the limitations discussed above), the number of societies involved in the study is high. These circumstances alone make certain reductions necessary in terms of the depth of the discussion. Therefore, we hardly have to emphasize that there are limits to our analysis, some of which are consciously observed, whereas others are unintended. As has already been suggested, we could obviously not make up for the deficits of the available literature. The most conspicuous imbalance is of a chronological nature: because of the lack of available sources, we could devote less attention than necessary to how social trends evolved in the interwar period. In a number of fields of social history, no sufficient research has been conducted about the entire continent or at least major regions with regard to the first half of the century.

There have been several diverse and imaginative attempts by historians and particularly by other social scientists to conceptualize the social development of Europe in the twentieth century. We obviously cannot offer an overview, however brief it may be, of the relevant interpretations, because their number and complexity are extremely high. Referring to the end of the twentieth century alone, the terms surfacing most often in research and the public discourse include post-industrial society,[11] network society,[12] multi-cultural society,[13] organizational society,[14] mass society,[15] leisure society,[16] risk society,[17] or the age of reflexive modernity,[18] the era of globalization and post-modernism.[19]

These concepts and theories clearly illuminate important social phenomena and directions of change; therefore, many of them appear in this volume. However, similarly to several other authors dealing with modern and contemporary European society, we do not consider any single social theory or approach applicable to the whole covered period and to the entire continent.[20] Thus, the volume also lacks a grand narrative or a strong central argument, which might be missed by some readers. Instead, we endeavoured to write a book that can be used as a first reference on specific subjects by students as well as scholars, and not exclusively historians, but also students of social sciences. This bifurcated aim determined the approach and the mode of presentation. An overarching narrative on the social history of a single region of Europe or on the post-war years can be convincing, but any grand narrative concerning the whole twentieth century and almost the whole of Europe might weaken the study as being less plausible. Moreover, in a post-paradigmatic world, opting for a grand narrative seemed to limit the usefulness of the book. This is not to say that we favour some kind of 'theoryless' history. We do not believe that history should resort to a mere description of relevant developments, or that such an account would be possible without theoretical guidance. On the contrary, we put a lot of emphasis on the theoretical approaches to specific issues of twentieth-century European social history. The demographic transition, the Kuznets curve, the typology of welfare states and several other conceptualizations and theories explaining and framing social developments in Europe occupy a considerable part of the volume and are treated probably in a more systematic manner than in many other works of similar nature. Thus, rather than resorting to a grand theory or interpretation encompassing, framing and explaining the entire twentieth-century history of European societies, we set out to interpret and explain the development of particular social historical phenomena. We intend to apply these approaches in a close semblance to what sociologists often refer to as 'the theory of middle-range', after Robert K. Merton. Also, we tried to assess the value of the existing overarching narratives that are outlined later, with new and more extensive empirical material: how they conform to the social reality of the entire twentieth century and not only to Western Europe but to other regions of the continent as well. Furthermore, we sought to present systematic information on diverse aspects of social change in twentieth-century Europe that cannot be found elsewhere. Consequently, a grand narrative would necessarily make much of the empirical material of the book obsolete.

The organization of the book primarily follows thematic principles. Chapter 2 offers an overview of twentieth-century population developments, tracing changes in such areas as fertility and mortality, as well as migration. Chapter 3 focuses on the major trends of family history, primarily by analysing marriage patterns and intrafamily relationships. Chapter 4 investigates the most important characteristics of social stratification and social mobility during the twentieth century in Europe. The history of the welfare state (or social policy) is the subject of Chapter 5. The following chapters deal with aspects of work, leisure, as well as consumption (Chapter 6), and the contact zones of society and politics (Chapter 7), and Chapter 8 discusses the historical paths that urbanization took in Europe. Selected aspects of culture with relation to twentieth-century Europe are introduced in Chapter 9. On the last pages (Chapter 10), we present the conclusions of the book, also addressing some of the major issues connected to the interpretation of the social history of Europe in the twentieth century.

The structure of various chapters differs slightly throughout the volume. Although we mostly prefer a thematic approach in the individual chapters, it seems reasonable in some cases to observe chronological considerations as well. One of the major objectives of the book is to introduce the causes and the determinants of social phenomena, which are most often discussed in separate passages, whereas in other chapters (where interpretations are less controversial or wide-ranging), they are integrated in the discussion of historical trends.

2

POPULATION

Population events are of significance at a variety of scales both in the life of individuals and in the evolution of societies. Childbirth, migration and death constitute turning points in the human life-course often marked by ceremonies, such as christening and funerals, which carry diverse societal and cultural meanings. Population occurrences considered together also have a great impact on the trajectory of societies. Births and immigration increase the size of population, whereas deaths and migration decrease it. In addition, population events taken in the aggregate induce shifts between the groups constituting societies. Fertility and migration usually exhibit considerable differentials between social strata and between ethnic groups; even the risk of death varies with social classes. Thus, the results of demographic processes greatly contribute to social dynamics. In turn, demographic events are themselves affected by the intricate interplay of contextual factors. Although the demographic behaviour of families is apparently determined by individual preferences and choices, in reality, the range of options available for them is considerably influenced by economic, social, cultural and political circumstances. For instance, established patterns in family size are among the crucial determinants of fertility, and migration can be constrained by legal frameworks, whereas mortality is often closely related to the living standard.[1]

The study of population change has an ancient history, however, and as a distinct field of research is usually traced back to the seventeenth century, when John Graunt and his followers developed the concept of life table, forecasting the longevity of members of a group based on the longevity of other members of the same group. The classical period of political economy in the eighteenth century and particularly the writings of Thomas Robert Malthus brought further advances in demography. He is well known for the thesis that population left unchecked would grow faster than the resources available for society. More importantly, the relationship between population characteristics, social change and economic conditions was considered in his works, and the path was set for further study of the relationship between demographic events in the nineteenth and twentieth century. Public and scholarly interest in population has alternated since then in Europe in terms of both intensity and focus. In the early decades of the twentieth century, for instance, the low fertility evident in many countries of Europe had a great impact on the development of population thought and discourse. At mid-century, in turn, rapid population growth in the less-developed world attracted the most attention from scholars and politicians.[2]

In the twentieth century, governments realized the importance of demography for social planning and increasingly relied on its contribution to government fore-casting. Demographers have developed a range of highly sophisticated, largely sta-tistical, models for investigating population change to meet this demand. One major theoretical advance was the concept of demographic transition, which refers to the historical conditions of population change and is discussed later in the chapter. A great surge in the institutionalization of historical demography took place in the 1950s, when the French demographer Louis Henry developed the method called family reconstitution. This method enabled researchers to follow the history of population events based on parish registers and then calculate birth, death and marriage rates. Parallel to these developments, demography tended to use distinct methods and sources and detached itself from historical research and sociology alike. Whereas demographers tended to disregard the social and cultural variables that mediate between population and the rest of the social setting, historians and sociologists have ignored demographic factors in social development. This mutual neglect between the disciplines has now improved with recent advances in scholarship, including the growing demand for interdisciplinary approaches. Major mediators of change are his-torical demography and historical sociology, which are greatly concerned with the effect of social conditions on major population developments and vice versa.

Another factor of rapprochement between demography and other branches of social studies has been the changing place of population issues in public discourse. Concerns over population decline in Europe emerged again towards the end of the twentieth century. Observers focused on three partly interrelated aspects of demographic change: the move to a smaller population, population ageing, and the prospect of ethnically less cohesive societies. Recent United Nations population estimates suggest that by the middle of the twenty-first century there will be about 10 percent fewer people living in the continent than there are today. The decrease of the total population would also mean a shrinking European share of the world population. The magnitude and effect of population ageing is highly discussed; however, it is widely assumed that it will generate difficulties for the social security systems and may create problems for public finances and economic productivity. Finally, mass migration filling the vacuum created by low fertility in Europe is feared to weaken cultural distinctiveness and identities, and thus undermine cohesion both on the national and European level, as well as fuel political radicalism.[3] Even though these worries about the demographic future of Europe will not necessarily materialize, they clearly placed population issues into the centre of public debates in Europe.

This chapter reviews the major trends of population change in twentieth-century Europe. In addition to describing the various aspects of transformation, insight into major causes of development is provided. Attention is first directed to population size and the model of demographic transition, while later sections focus specifically on major components of population change: fertility, mortality and migration. Finally, like in the other chapters of the book, recent developments in Europe are discussed.

Changes in population size: eras of demographic catastrophes, stepped growth and stability

If one examines the overall trends in population size in twentieth-century Europe as the basic context for detailed analysis of the specific areas of population movement in the following subchapters, the population of Europe significantly expanded in the course of the twentieth century compared with earlier historical periods.[4] For example, between 1920 and 2000 the increase was 51%, which greatly surpassed the growth of the whole nineteenth century. The growth was even faster in other continents, so the proportion of Europe in the global population actually diminished. In 1900, 19% of the world population lived in Europe, then 14.9% in 1950 and only 8.4% in 2000 (Table 2.1).[5]

The population of Europe grew despite the huge losses of lives in the two World Wars. In the First World War, about 6.6 million soldiers died in the continent.[6] The military loss of France and Germany was especially high, in both cases amounting to, excluding the wounded, 10% of the male labour force. Civilian victims of the First World War were in the same order of magnitude, about 5 million people. However, unlike the later civilian casualties of the Second World War, they did not die directly as a result of military action. Rather, they lost their lives during and especially after the war to malnutrition and epidemics. In the weakened population, many people fell victim to the Spanish flu in 1918–19. During the First World War, the number of marriages and births also plummeted, because so many couples were separated by war events. The number of missed births is estimated at 12.6 million. The deficit of births left a more striking mark on the population pyramid of most countries than the also devastating but more diffuse effect of the war victims. Fertility was still high enough in several countries to compensate for the losses of war, but there were others where population size decreased (Table 2.1).[7]

Despite the shrinking fertility figures in the 1920s and 1930s, the population of Europe significantly increased in each region, and especially in Southern, South-Eastern and East Central Europe. Then the Second World War brought on a demographic catastrophe even greater than that of the First World War, with victims reaching about 16.8 million. This equals 4% of the population, as opposed to the ca. 3.6% population loss of the First World War. In the Second World War, the loss of civilian lives (10.8 million) significantly surpassed that of military casualties (6 million) and most civilians perished in aggression directed at them, in genocide and in terror bombings. In addition, indirect population loss attributable to the war is estimated at 5–7 million. The Second World War affected mostly the countries of Central

TABLE 2.1 Population by country, 1900–2000 (in millions)

	1900	1913	1920	1930	1940	1950	1960	1970	1980	1990	2000	Change (%) 1900–2000	1920–2000
United Kingdom	41.2	43.0	43.5	45.7	47.8	50.6	52.5	55.4	55.9	57.5	59.5	+44	+37
France	40.6	41.7	39.0	40.8	41.3	41.7	45.7	50.8	53.7	56.7	59.4	+46	+52
Netherlands	5.1	6.3	6.8	7.8	8.9	10.1	11.5	13.0	14.1	15.0	15.9	+212	+134
Belgium	6.7	7.7	7.6	8.1	8.4	8.6	9.2	9.7	9.9	10.0	10.2	+52	+34
Ireland	4.5	2.9	2.9	2.9	2.9	2.9	2.8	2.9	3.4	3.5	3.8	-16	+31
Germany/FRG	54.4	58.5	59.9	64.7	69.3	49.9	55.3	60.7	61.6	79.4	82.2	+51	+37
GDR						18.9	17.9	17.1	16.7				
Austria	6.0	6.6	6.4	6.7	6.7	6.9	7.1	7.4	7.5	7.7	8.1	+35	+27
Switzerland	3.3	3.9	3.9	4.0	4.2	4.7	5.4	6.3	6.4	6.8	7.3	+121	+87
Sweden	5.1	5.6	5.8	6.1	6.3	7.0	7.5	8.1	8.3	8.6	8.9	+75	+53
Denmark	2.6	2.9	3.2	3.5	3.8	4.3	4.6	4.9	5.1	5.1	5.3	+104	+65
Norway	2.2	2.5	2.7	2.8	3.0	3.3	3.6	3.9	4.1	4.2	4.5	+105	+67
Finland	2.6	3.2	3.1	3.4	3.7	4.0	4.4	4.6	4.8	5.0	5.2	+100	+68
Italy	33.7	36.2	35.9	40.7	44.3	46.6	49.4	53.6	57.1	56.7	57.7	+71	+61
Spain	18.6	20.3	21.0	23.2	25.5	27.9	30.3	33.8	37.4	39.4	40.0	+115	+90
Portugal	5.4	6.0	6.4	6.7	7.6	8.4	8.8	9.6	9.9	9.9	10.0	+85	+56
Greece	5.0	5.4	5.7	6.3	7.2	7.6	8.3	8.8	9.6	10.2	10.6	+112	+86
Poland	24.8	30.7	29.4	31.1	34.9	24.8	29.7	32.6	35.6	38.1	38.6	+56	+31
Czechoslovakia	12.1	13.6	13.5	14.6	15.3	12.4	13.6	14.3	15.3	15.6			
Czech Republic											10.3		
Slovakia											5.4		

TABLE 2.1 (continued)

	1900	1913	1920	1930	1940	1950	1960	1970	1980	1990	2000	Change (%) 1900–2000	Change (%) 1920–2000
Hungary	7.1	7.9	7.9	8.6	9.2	9.3	10.0	10.3	10.7	10.4	10.1	+42	+28
Romania	11.0	16.2	15.9	18.2	20.0	16.3	18.4	20.2	22.2	22.9	22.4	+104	+41
Bulgaria	4.0	4.9	5.2	5.7	6.3	7.3	7.9	8.5	8.9	8.9	7.8	+95	+50
Yugoslavia	11.2	12.3	11.7	13.5	15.6	16.3	18.4	20.4	22.3	22.5	23.0		
Albania	0.8	0.9	0.9	1.0	1.1	1.2	1.6	2.2	2.7	3.3	3.5	+338	+289
Total	308.0					374.7					509.6	+65	
World population	1625					2519					6057	+273	
Europe's population as a % of world population	19.0					14.9					8.4		

Notes: The years 1900–1940 refer to 1923 borders; 1950–2000 to 1950 borders; FRG includes West Berlin, figures of GDR include East Berlin; Yugoslavia 2000: the sum of Yugoslavian successor states (Slovenia 2.0, Croatia 4.5, Macedonia 2.0, Bosnia–Herzegovina 3.8, Yugoslavia 10.7 million population).

Sources: Gerold Ambrosius and William Hubbard, *A Social and Economic History of Twentieth-Century Europe*, Cambridge, Ma.: Harvard University Press, 1989, 58–59 (Europe 1900–1980); Angus Maddison, *The World Economy*, Paris: OECD, 2003, 36–97 (Europe 1990–2000); Pál Demény, 'Európa népességpolitikai dilemmái a huszonegyedik század kezdetén', *Demográfia*, vol. XLVII. (2004), no. 1–2, 4–40 (World population); *OECD Factbook 2007. Economic, Environmental and Social Statistics*, Paris: OECD, 2007, 13 (Czech Republic and Slovakia 2000); UNICEF, *A Decade of Transition. Regional Monitoring Report 8*, Florence, UNICEF, 2001, 120 (Yugoslavia 2000).

and East Central Europe. Poland lost 18–20% of her pre-war population, Yugo-slavia 10% and Germany 7% – as has already been pointed out elsewhere in this volume, with the exclusion of the Soviet Union.[8]

The second half of the twentieth century saw no demographic crises similar to the World Wars and the population of the continent grew continually, albeit at differing paces by time and region. Population growth was especially significant in the 1950s and 1960s, when (except for East Germany, where the loss to migration could not be replaced by natural increase) populations in almost every country grew at a faster pace than between the two World Wars. The decade between 1961 and 1970 saw the most significant rise in population size in Europe (9.2%) in the whole century (Table 2.1). Afterwards, the pace of growth slowed down, and in the 1980s in several Western European countries, even the sluggish population growth resulted only from migration.

At the end of the century, depressing demographic conditions emerged in Germany, Spain, Italy and many East Central and South-Eastern European countries, where fertility dropped to extremely low levels. However, whereas in Western Europe the boom of immigration counterbalanced natural decrease, population size started to decrease in many former communist countries, which were less attractive to migrants and which, in addition, had poor mortality figures (e.g. Bulgaria, Hungary and Romania).[9]

All in all, the slowest population growth between 1920 and the end of the century was produced by Austria (27%) and Hungary (28%). Modest growth can be observed in Poland, Ireland, Belgium, Germany and the United Kingdom as well, although the causes behind this development differ from country to country. In contrast, the growth rate of the Netherlands and especially Albania was remarkable. Similarly, the population increased relatively significantly in Scandinavia and Southern Europe (Table 2.1).

The demographic transition: model and criticism

The population growth of Europe in the nineteenth and in a great part of the twentieth century was based on a process known as the demographic transition. The demographic transition is a long-term change, in the course of which the population moves between two relatively steady states: from one of high fertility and high mortality to one of low fertility and low mortality. Because of the timing difference between the mortality and fertility downswings, the population size increases significantly over a variable but usually long period.[10] Named *révolution démographique* by Adolphe Landry, who in 1934 first described the process in depth, this large-scale historical trend generated a huge literature that ultimately gave birth to the model after the Second World War, and it is now universally referred to as the demographic transition.[11] In its standard version, the transition takes place in a succession of four stages:

1. In the first stage, before the transformation process commences, fertility and mortality are equally high, the former not or hardly surpassing the latter. Therefore, the population is in a stationary state or is growing at a low rate. This is characteristic of societies often referred to as premodern.

2. Next, mortality starts to decline gradually, primarily because of improved nutrition and, later, because of advances in public health and sanitation. Birth rates remain high because they are regulated by customs, moral and religious rules as well as family arrangements, which do not lend themselves to change easily. The result is an acceleration of population growth.

3. In a new stage, the decrease in the rate of births sets in as a result of, for instance, urbanization, shifting marriage patterns, value changes, spreading use of birth control, etc., whereas the number of deaths remains at a relatively moderate level. Consequently, the rate of population growth is still significant but starts to slow down.

4. In the final stage of a demographically mature society, both birth and death rates tend to stabilize at similarly low levels. Hence a 'new demographic balance' is achieved, again with no or a small natural increase.[12] This stage is claimed to be reached in Europe, North America and a few other regions at some point in the twentieth century and expected to come as a result of modernization in the less developed countries of the world.

The demographic transition model has met serious criticism. First of all, it is questionable whether a permanently stationary state of population (stages 1 and 4) has existed or could ever be possible. Rather, we find that such balanced conditions are rare in the population history of Europe and have occurred basically only when the curves of birth and death rates crossed each other. The population of early modern and modern England, one of the most intensely researched subject areas of historical demography, shows strong fluctuations in both birth and death rates, i.e. in reality there exists no stationary state of population. Also, researchers have pointed out that, contrary to expectations, the last stage has not been observed anywhere. The population development of less industrialized countries is still at the phase of expansion, and there is no assurance that they will replicate the experience of Europe and its direct overseas offshoots. In most European countries, from the 1970s on, instead of balance setting in, natural increase has been decreasing below the net reproduction level.[13] Furthermore, one of the most fundamental lines of criticism concerns the connection made in the model between the decrease of fertility and what is called the modernization process. The largest comparative study on European population history to date (the Princeton European Fertility Project) did not identify an unambiguous relationship between modernization (the major aspects of which are industrialization and urbanization) and the decline of fertility.[14] Another line of criticism targets the suggestion by the model of fixed patterns and irreversible development, whereas in real life, demographic processes do not necessarily bear these characteristics. A good example here is the resumed increase of fertility after a period of decline in post-Second World War Western Europe, or the deteriorating mortality rates in communist countries from the 1960s that interrupted decades of improvement. These phenomena are discussed in detail later.

Taken at face value, demographic transition is a description of historical patterns of vital rates. However, description is interwoven with explanation of mortality and fertility changes, which proved to be especially controversial. Several proponents of the model suggest a strong association between the decline of mortality (especially infant mortality) and that of fertility. They argue that the fall in mortality leads to an increase in family size and thus in population size, which is a pressure for families and societies alike. Consequently, they would try to adapt to the new conditions by using birth control and decreasing their fertility. Therefore it is the decline of deaths that eventually causes a decrease in births. However, this single-factor explanation that considers only demographic factors (fertility and mortality) seems to be unsatisfactory. It fails to shed light on the differences in the twentieth-century population history of European countries, because, as is discussed later, shrinking birth rates have also been triggered by societal, cultural and other factors.

Considering all this, it is not surprising that in its standard form the transition has practically not been observed anywhere in Europe. The starting conditions (fertility and mortality levels before the transition), the commencement of the transition, and the dynamics of the process diverged from the model. Some of the stages may have been missing, or, at least, the length of phases seems varied in individual societies.

Mortality started to decline in the second half of the eighteenth century in Europe, and, as will be shown, this process has continued to the present day, first at an accelerating, then at a decelerating pace. Timing lags were significant even between the three pioneering countries, England-Wales, Sweden and France. In England and Sweden, disregarding short-term fluctuations, gains in life expectancy can be registered from around 1740, whereas in France, the starting point of the momentous change in mortality was around 1780. It took at least a century for the improvement initially achieved in North-West Europe to spread to the central, southern, and eastern regions of the continent. Considerable gains in life expectancy appear to have begun in about 1840 in the Netherlands, about 1880 in Italy and about 1900 in Spain.[15]

The later stages of demographic transition began in France, where birth rates had been plummeting since the 1790s. In other countries, fertility decline never truly started until the end of the nineteenth century, or, even more often, the early twentieth century. The starting points are the 1870s in Sweden and England, 1882 in Belgium, 1890 in Germany, 1895 in Switzerland and 1897 in the Netherlands. In the rest of Scandinavia (Denmark, Finland, Norway) and in Austria, this tendency began after the turn of the century, and in the Balkans, Southern Europe and Ireland only between the two World Wars. This means that those stages of the demographic transition, in which population growth is considerable, stretch well beyond the First World War in most European societies.[16]

In several countries, population growth commenced with a rise in fertility without a corresponding fall in mortality, as it did in the case of the Netherlands in the early nineteenth century. Hungary is another example where the pattern of low death and birth rates emerged in a manner considerably different from the predictions of the demographic transition model after 1880. Except for the short interval of 1880–86, what we find here is not a plunge in the mortality rate accompanied by stagnating, then decreasing fertility rates. Instead, these two demographic indicators declined almost parallel between the mid-1880s and the 1930s, then the decline of birth rates accelerated, as a result of which from the middle of the 1930s, natural increase reached a relatively low level, around six per mil.[17]

In summary, the research findings of the past decades have cast strong shadows on the validity of demographic transition as a population theory. However, despite the criticisms, the concept is still widely used in population history and demography alike, because even with its simplifications, it reveals important historical processes and offers a heuristic framework for discussion. First of all, demographic conditions altered thoroughly in all developed societies in the past centuries, the transformation leading to declining mortality and fertility, whereas, even if for a short period, population size significantly grew in several cases. Let us turn next to the detailed discussion of the factors playing a role in demographic transition and population change in general.

Main trends in fertility: from high to lowest-low

The demographic transition has brought significant changes in the reproductive structure of European societies in the twentieth century. Three tendencies in fertility deserve special attention:

1. Fertility was declining considerably, even though the pace of the decrease varied in different societies and periods. By the end of the century, birth rates reached below-replacement level in almost all societies.
2. In certain periods and countries, the declining tendency discontinued for a few years. In addition to these short-term fluctuations, a longer, one-and-a-half-decade period of rise can also be found in post-war Western Europe.
3. In Western and Southern Europe, differences between countries diminished in the course of the century, unlike in East Central Europe, where fluctuations in fertility make it difficult to recognize any tendencies of demographic integration.

1. Generally speaking, a great fertility decline took place in all European countries in the course of the twentieth century.[18] This is revealed by the simplest of indicators, the crude birth rate, but even more accurately by fertility rates that control for differences in gender and age distribution, which are therefore more appropriate for international comparisons as well (Table 2.2).

Although the fertility decline was common to all European countries, it did not occur everywhere simultaneously. When considering the total fertility rate, we find that Western Europe continued to be the region with the lowest family size until the end of the twentieth century, even though Ireland constituted a remarkable exception. In this region, the rank of the countries had often varied in terms of fertility; again, with the exception of Ireland. At the turn of the century, Austria, Germany and Ireland had the highest birth rates, and family size was the smallest in France. By 1950, Ireland was joined by Finland and the Netherlands in the group with the highest fertility, whereas West Germany, Austria and the United Kingdom comprised that of the lowest. By the end of the 1980s, Ireland, Norway, the United Kingdom and

TABLE 2.2 Total fertility rates for various European countries, 1900–2000

	1900	1910	1920	1930	1940	1950	1960	1970	1980	1990	2000
United Kingdom	2.89	2.92	3.08	1.95	1.79	2.18	2.66	2.41	1.89	1.83	1.65
France		2.56	2.67	2.27	2.00	2.93	2.73	2.48	1.95	1.78	1.88
Netherlands	4.53	3.94	3.89	3.03	2.67	3.06	3.12	2.57	1.60	1.62	1.72
Belgium				2.25	1.84	2.35	2.58	2.20	1.69	1.62	1.66
Ireland			3.20	2.92	2.90	3.28	3.76	3.87	3.23	2.12	1.89
Germany/FRG	4.77	3.52	2.62	1.88	2.40	2.09	2.37	2.02	1.44	1.45	1.38
Austria	4.93	4.67			1.54	2.09	2.65	2.31	1.65	1.45	1.34
Switzerland	3.82	3.01	2.43	1.96	1.83	2.40	2.44	2.09	1.55	1.59	1.50
Sweden	4.06	3.60	3.22	1.96	1.85	2.32	2.17	1.94	1.68	2.14	1.54
Denmark	4.40	3.60	3.29	2.30	2.23	2.58	2.54	1.95	1.55	1.67	1.77
Norway	4.37	3.82	3.61	2.19	1.95	2.53	2.83	2.51	1.72	1.93	1.85
Finland						3.16	2.71	1.83	1.63	1.78	1.73
Italy	4.43	4.28	3.90	3.38	3.07	2.47	2.41	2.43	1.69	1.29	1.23
Spain	4.71	4.43	4.14	3.68	3.09	2.16	2.86	2.84	2.22	1.30	1.24
Poland						3.71	2.98	2.20	2.25	2.04	1.34
Czechoslovakia						3.02	2.41	2.06	2.15	1.96	1.14/1.29
Hungary	5.28	4.67	3.74	2.84	2.48	2.62	2.02	1.97	1.92	1.84	1.32

Notes: United Kingdom 1910–1950: England and Wales; Czechoslovakia 2000: Czech Republic/Slovakia; Different years: France 1901; Netherlands 1901; Ireland 1926, 1936, 1941, 1951; Germany 1903, 1913, 1923; Austria 1903, 1908, 1937; Switzerland 1903, 1913, 1923, 1932; Sweden 1901; Denmark 1903, 1911; Norway 1901; Italy 1903, 1913, 1923; Spain 1901; Hungary 1900–1901, 1910–1911, 1920–1921, 1930–1931, 1940–1941.

Sources: Jean-Paul Sardon, 'Generation Replacement in Europe since 1900', *Population: An English Selection*, vol. 3 (1991), 19–20 (Western Europe 1900–1940); David Coleman, 'New Patterns and Trends in European Fertility: International and Sub-National Comparisons', in David Coleman, ed., *Europe's Population in the 1990s*, Oxford: Oxford University Press, 1996, 49–53 (Western Europe 1950–1990; Southern Europe 1950–1990; East Central Europe 1950–1990); Franz Rothenbacher, *The European Population, 1850–1945*, Houndmills: Palgrave, 2002, CD-ROM Publication (Denmark 1903; Spain 1901–1940); *OECD Factbook 2007. Economic, Environmental and Social Statistics*, Paris: OECD, 2007, 15 (Europe 2000); Ferenc Kamarás, 'A születési mozgalom és a termékenység jellegzetességei az elmúlt 125 évben', in József Kovacsics, ed., *Magyarország történeti demográfiája, 896–1995*, Budapest: KSH, 1997, 320 (Hungary 1900–1941); László Hablicsek, *Az első és a második demográfiai átmenet Magyarországon és Közép-Kelet-Európában*, Budapest: KSH, 1995, 41 (Hungary 1970–1990).

France had the highest total fertility rates, and West Germany along with Austria had the lowest ones (Table 2.2).[19] Not only France produced a remarkable turn in its relative position, but also two of the Southern European countries: Italy and Spain were among the societies with the highest fertility levels in a great part of the century, but by the new millennium they were among those with the 'lowest-low' birth rates, as the total fertility rate below 1.3 is sometimes referred to in the literature.[20]

At the beginning of the century, the fertility of East Central Europe and the Balkans was markedly high in a European context. In these regions, most reliable data are available for Hungary, where the crude birth rate figured around 39‰ and the total fertility rate around 5.3 in the early twentieth century. Both surpassed the corresponding figures of all Western European countries, just like the fertility ratios of Poland did in the interwar years. However, in the following decades, the countries of these regions showed considerably different paths of development.[21] In the post-war decades, Hungarian fertility was only medium level when compared with Western European countries, as shown by the total fertility rate of 1.84 in 1990 (Table 2.2). In contrast, Poland was considered one of the countries with the highest willingness for childbearing in the continent up until the end of the 1980s, to be surpassed only by South-Eastern Europe and Ireland. However, in the last decade of the twentieth century, fertility fell below the European mean not only in Poland and the other East Central European countries, but also in the Balkans, with the only exception of Albania.

2. Another phenomenon to emphasize is that fertility decline was not a continuous process, because it was occasionally interrupted by periods of rise. In the early decades of the century, the rapid decline of fertility was turned hectic by the fluctuations due to the First World War, the huge setbacks during, and the transitory rises after, the war. As a result of the decline, fertility decreased below the net reproduction level in most of Western Europe (the Netherlands and Ireland constituted exceptions) already in the interwar period.[22] Right after the Second World War, a short period of fertility rise can be observed, caused by family reunions and the rising number of marriages, then a period of lower fertility succeeded in the late 1940s and early 1950s in several countries. The following 'baby boom' similarly affected all Western European countries. Until the mid-1960s, birth rates increased remarkably everywhere and significantly surpassed the levels of the interwar period. The rise in fertility held out much longer and was on a larger scale than would be possible if its sole reason had been the usual rise in births after war (Figure 2.1). Furthermore, the collapse of the baby boom (known as 'baby bust') occurred at nearly the same time (around 1964) and in a similarly dramatic manner in most Western European countries. After this, fertility in most Western European societies declined to a great extent, a tendency that often further accelerated in the early 1970s. By 1975, fertility dropped below the level necessary for net reproduction in almost all Western European countries (e.g. in Sweden from 1968, in Denmark from 1969, in West Germany from 1970) and has not risen above it ever since.[23] After the mid-1970s, fertility remained at this low level. Southern European

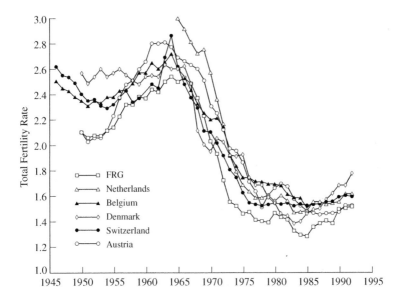

FIGURE 2.1 Total fertility rates in various Western European countries, 1945–1992
Source: David Coleman, ed., *Europe's Population in the 1990s*, Oxford: Oxford University Press, 1996, 49–53.

countries also showed considerable fertility decline from the 1960s on. In Western Europe, only Ireland remained an exception where fertility figured at a relatively high level, although even here, the 1970s and 1980s halved the total fertility rate. In most North Western European and Scandinavian countries, the number of births began to rise from the mid-1980s again. Among them, Sweden enjoyed the most significant gain, a phenomenon that can be plausibly explained by measures of family policy.[24] However, this was only a temporary rise everywhere and by the turn of the millennium the fertility data conformed to the declining trend observed throughout the century.

The East Central European societies experienced even more pronounced fluctuations in fertility. On the one hand, wars caused oscillations in births. Births tumbled during the First World War, and during the increase in fertility after the war reproductive capacity often failed to reach pre-First World War levels.[25] From the mid-1920s, there is again continuous decline, which then accelerated in the years of the Great Depression. The plunge in fertility was so rapid in Czechoslovakia that this country ended up below the levels of several Western European countries. That is, this was the first period in which the century-long tradition of East–West divide in fertility disappeared, leaving a zone of low fertility in Central and Northern Europe.[26]

After the short period of rise after the Second World War, the former trend of fertility recommenced in East Central and South-Eastern Europe, that is, the number of children per family decreased, and the pace of the process even accelerated. In these regions there was no baby boom in the 1950s like in many Western European countries and in North America; however, frequent and significant ups and downs in fertility developed. In fact, a major characteristic of the decades after the Second

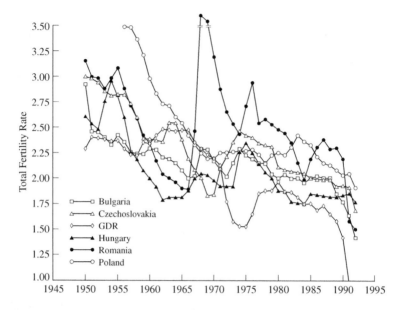

FIGURE 2.2 Total fertility rates in various East Central European countries, 1950–1992
Source: David Coleman, ed., *Europe's Population in the 1990s*, Oxford: Oxford University Press, 1996, 49–53.

World War is that the fluctuation in birth rates is stronger than before, which can be attributed to the effects of recurrent changes in social and population policy, including forceful pronatalist measures. Thus, in Hungary from 1953, or in Romania from the mid-1960s, the birth rate rose greatly for a short period, as a consequence of the prohibition of induced abortions (Figure 2.2). However, in the communist countries, the ban on abortion was shortly replaced by complete liberalization (Hungary), unknown in Western Europe at that time, or the population adapted to the new circumstances by relying on other methods of birth control (Romania). Therefore, in a number of countries, the decline of fertility was substantial. In Hungary, crude birth rate reached the lowest levels in 1962–65 (12.9‰–13.1‰), a negative record in Europe and the world at the time, with the total fertility rate dropping to 1.8. The fluctuation of rates was also facilitated by positive incentives such as the introduction or the increasing of family and maternity support. The repeated cycles of decline and rise had significant effects on later population patterns, especially on the age structure. They have, namely, generated demographic waves that are repeated, albeit on shrinking scales, whenever the affected female cohort reaches childbearing age (i.e. in every 20–24 years ever since). This phenomenon is not unknown in Western Europe either, where a remarkably great demographic wave was generated by the baby boom.

3. When examining fertility, we find remarkable differences in the internal dynamics of the major regions throughout the twentieth century. The gaps between the fertility levels of Western European countries widened considerably in the interwar period, thus the swift convergence of the two decades after the Second

World War could only counterbalance this development. The 1960s and 1970s again saw increasing differences in fertility rates; then came the rapid tendency of unification in the 1980s regarding both the crude birth rate and the total fertility rate. In summary, despite the general fertility decline, as a result of successive periods of divergence and convergence, the gap between the countries with the highest and the lowest fertility did decrease in absolute numbers; however, there was little change proportionally between the beginning and the end of the century (Table 2.2).[27] As opposed to this, in the societies of East Central and South-Eastern Europe, fertility rates changed in a hectic fashion in the post-war decades, often from one year to the next, and therefore no internal unification of the region can be identified for any considerable period (Figure 2.2). A peculiar internal unity did emerge after the fall of communism, when fertility declined to such an extent that these countries, with a few exceptions, found themselves among the ones with the lowest family size in Europe.

Causes of changes

Changes in fertility are the results of the interplay of several demographic, socio-economic and cultural factors, which are often difficult to separate from each other.[28] Similarly to trends in fertility, which varied widely in different societies, the determinants or the combination of determinants underlying these developments may have also diverged significantly.

Conventional interpretations emphasize the role of structural factors associated with socioeconomic development. We already referred to the explanations centred on demographic factors according to which the decline of infant and child mortality reduced the need for having excess births to generate the desired number of surviving children. Among socioeconomic factors, population theories most often point out the effects of modernization (more specifically economic progress as well as urbanization) on the decline of fertility in Europe. However, even if industrialized and urbanized regions usually have lower birth rates,[29] and the characteristics of settlement itself may affect fertility, industrialization and urbanization still exerted their influence indirectly, through mediating factors, such as the improvement of education levels or the growth in female employment, which are inversely correlated with fertility in most cases.[30] True, there are important exceptions, such as Italy, where the lowest female employment was accompanied by the lowest fertility level at the end of the century.[31]

In addition, there is a similarly long tradition in research, which rather proposes more direct links between economic factors and fertility than assumes a correlation between birth rates and modernization in a wider sense. Economic theories of fertility maintain that family size is determined by a household's drive to maximize satisfaction by balancing the benefits against the costs of children. Benefits may include the intrinsic value of the child to the parents; the value of the child's labour to the household; the security provided by children in times of stress and in old age; as well as cash support from the state. The costs of childbearing might consist of the value of goods and services spent on the child; the time devoted to childrearing;

earnings forgone, especially by the mother; physiologic wear and tear of childbirth, health risks to the mother, etc.[32] Throughout the twentieth century, the costs of childrearing increased and the economic benefits of childrearing declined for several reasons, including the decline of agriculture and self-employment, legal restrictions on child labour, compulsory education, rising housing and educational standards and costs, and growing female employment increasing the opportunity cost of the time of women. Thus, couples were led to reduce the number of children to create a new balance between costs and benefits.

The economic approach to fertility can be challenged on several grounds: it is often static, decontextualized and relies on a narrow notion of rationality. A major result of the European Fertility Project was that fertility decline took place under a wide variety of economic and social conditions. In England, for example, sustained fertility decline began around 1890, when 15 per cent of the male labour force worked in agriculture and 72 per cent of the population already lived in urban areas. Bulgaria began its fertility transition only twenty years later, although at a lower level of economic development: 70 per cent of the male labour force in agriculture and 18 per cent urban.[33]

A more sophisticated and influential attempt at this type of interpretation was put forward by Richard A. Easterlin, who emphasized the relationship between aspirations (or, desires) regarding the living standard and the actual economic conditions in explaining fertility changes.[34] His model asserts that if the gap between lifestyle aspirations and living standard widens, couples react by lowering the number of births, but if they can realize their preconceived lifestyle, fertility does not need to be controlled to such an extent.

Although this interpretation can undoubtedly explain several short-term changes in fertility, its evidences are not necessarily exhaustive and do not apply to all the cases. It can, for example, account for the fertility decline in the 1930s in Europe, but it does not shed light on the reasons why in many countries (France, England and Wales, Sweden and Germany) fertility plummeted below the net reproduction level even before 1929, that is, before the Great Depression set in. Similarly, this theory can rationalize the higher number of children born to women reaching childbearing age in the 1950s, but it cannot give an appropriate explanation for the events in the 1970s, when, for example in the United Kingdom, fertility first declined then rose, although the relative wages of cohorts entering parenthood did not conform to this pattern.[35] Furthermore, it does not offer any rationale for the long-term trend of fertility decline, because this occurred despite a universal increase of welfare and fulfilment of the aspirations of wide social strata in the twentieth century. The shortcomings of the interpretation mostly originate from its view that regards childbearing as a rational decision in which the only aspect considered by the parents is estimation of costs and benefits.

In addition to socioeconomic processes, cultural factors also shaped reproduction.[36] Changes in the desired number of children can also be attributed to individualization and secularization in twentieth-century Europe. Individualization in this regard means that, in the course of the century, family and child centredness was continually pushed to the background by values that favour the self-realization of the individual. This 'silent revolution' of values progressed especially in the last decades of the century, first in Western Europe, then in other regions as well.[37] Philippe Ariès claims that parents from the 1960s on are less and less willing to organize their lives around their children and try to arrange their affairs so that it would happen the other way round, i.e. they organize childrearing around their lives. However, this is difficult to achieve, hence a decline in the number of children.[38] Or, as formulated by van de Kaa regarding Western Europe, the 'king-child-with-parents' of the 1930s was replaced by the end of the century with the 'king-pair-with-a-child'.[39]

A former, marked presence of religious values and norms in family and public life promoted establishing a family and the birth of higher numbers of children. Thus, the weakening of values related to religion (the process of secularization) opened up possibilities for a decline of fertility as well. Moreover, it was not only religiosity and affiliation to churches that weakened considerably from the 1960s in most (Western) European countries, but also the identification with other traditional institutions of society. Individualization (the emphasis on the importance of the individual vis-à-vis other social entities, such as the state, the church, or the local community) also gained a greater role in family life in this way.[40]

These explanations in the literature of fertility decline have been primarily proposed regarding Western and Southern Europe, but the causes they expose also apply to East Central Europe and the Balkans, as factors associated to modernization (most of all, industrialization and urbanization) obviously played a role here as well.

The structural shifts in society explain important East Central European phenomena such as the post-Second World War fertility decline that occurred in parallel to the Western European baby boom. In this period in East Central Europe, there was a marked decrease of the agricultural population, which had shown high fertility levels in the previous decades.

As elsewhere in Europe, economic cycles in East Central Europe may have also contributed to short-term fluctuations in fertility, at least in the first half of the century. For example, the low fertility level of the 1930s may be attributed to a large extent to the Great Depression. However, in the second half of the century, economic factors became predominantly important in another way, in the sense of a growing gap between economic aspirations and actual standards of living. A drop in fertility in the region from the 1960s may be largely traced back to a widening gap between suddenly rocketing desires regarding the standard of living and the reality.[41]

Still, as in Western Europe, socioeconomic factors can only partly explain fertility decline. Fertility had been declining continually in all social groups in the course of the century. The trend affected not only industrial and urban, but also agricultural, urban and rural populations, as well as highly qualified women in the labour force and women with poor education and no employment.[42]

It seems, then, that in the interpretation of the East Central European fertility decline, an emphatic role should be attributed to the related norms and values, to the change in the desired number of children that affected all strata of society.[43] Research on regional differences in fertility suggests that these are independent factors and cannot be originated from the above socioeconomic factors like the levels of urbanization, education, female employment, etc. Neither at the end of the nineteenth century, nor in the interwar period, nor in the 1960s did the latter explain much of the regional disparities in fertility.[44]

An East Central European characteristic is that most of the short-term fluctuations after the Second World War were caused by political factors. On the one hand, the significant effects of measures of population policy are obvious. Fertility was greatly affected by the zigzags of the regulation of abortion. The aforementioned 1953 Hungarian tightening in the abortion law significantly increased the number of births temporarily, and the shortly succeeding full liberalization obviously contributed to their rapid decrease. Moreover, the remarkably high East Central European ratio of induced abortions from the 1950s all through the period under examination (in a Western European comparison) facilitated long-term fertility decline as well. Pronatalist measures, especially maternity support, did have tangible effects in the other direction, at least in the short term.

Trends in mortality: from uncertain to certain lifetime

The second factor in natural increase is mortality, just like mortality transition constitutes an important aspect of the demographic transition. Twentieth-century Europe saw profound changes with regards to deaths as well, of which the following deserve special attention:

1. Mortality declined considerably and universally in the continent (disregarding war-related deaths), albeit with regionally diverging dynamics.
2. As a unique phenomenon in the peacetime population history of the industrialized world, from the 1960s in most communist countries mortality rates began to rise again, and this tendency diminished only after the regime change.
3. The variation of mortality indicators within Western Europe lessened; however, between the Eastern and Western half of the continent, a strong divergence unfolded in the last decades of the century. At the same time, stratum-specific mortality differentials persisted in all countries, and the gap between female and male mortality widened.

1. The decline of mortality is a universal process that affected the whole of Europe throughout the nineteenth and twentieth centuries – and especially from the late nineteenth century. Whereas in traditional societies death was a threat to people at any age, by the end of the twentieth century, deaths mostly concentrated in old age and a growing proportion of the population began to come close to what might be called the biological or physiological limit to human life span.[45] As a result, there emerged a security of life wholly unknown before, or, as Arthur E. Imhof put it, a transition from uncertain to certain lifetime took place.[46] Nevertheless,

mortality decline took different courses in different European regions in the twentieth century. All through this period, a West–East and a North–South gradient is present, although the latter had become considerably less pronounced by the end of the century.[47] Disregarding war-related deaths, mortality indicators in Western and Southern Europe declined continuously. Tables 2.3 and 2.4 show male and female life expectancy at birth at different points in the twentieth century. At the beginning of the century, in the countries with the most favourable indicators (the Scandinavian countries except for Finland), male life expectancy at birth was hardly 50 years; by the end of the 1980s, it surpassed 70 years in every Western European country, and was close to 75 in Norway and Sweden. For females, the increase was even faster, so that in 1990, Western European women could expect to live 6.5 years longer on the average than men. Nevertheless, the improvement of mortality did not occur at a steady pace in either respect. The rise in life expectancy was rapid in the first half of the century and was pronounced even in the 1950s and the early 1960s. Then it slowed down in the second half of the 1960s and the following decade, to quicken its pace from the late 1970s again.[48]

Infant mortality deserves special attention, partly because it was the most important contributor to mortality improvement, and partly because it is an excellent indicator of social progress. This is because it depends on several significant social and cultural factors, such as infant and child protection, attitudes towards children, availability and quality of health care, lifestyle of the population, or health-related knowledge of the parents. Infant mortality also improved all through the twentieth century. In 1900, this indicator was over 200‰ even in Germany and was hardly below 100‰ in Sweden and Norway. However, by the end of the 1980s, it dropped to a fraction of these figures, with less than 9‰ of children dying before their first birthday in each of the Western European countries (Table 2.5). The decline was especially rapid between 1950 and 1990, when an approximately 5% annual drop was observed in infant mortality in 15 Western and Southern European countries, and thus the level of this indicator fell to its one-fourth in the course of four decades.[49] Despite the major decline, East Central European and, especially, South-Eastern European infant mortality was unfavourable in a European context all through the period under examination.

2. East Central and South-Eastern European changes in mortality in the first two-thirds of the twentieth century more or less conformed to Western European tendencies, showing considerable advancement.[50] Life expectancy at birth rose remarkably for both sexes in the interwar decades. This was primarily caused by the significant decline of infant mortality. The immediate aftermath of the Second World War (poor nutrition and poor public health conditions) caused mortality to rise, but soon it began to improve again. The next approximately 15 years can be regarded as the most rapid period of change with respect to mortality in several countries. In this period, internal mortality differences in the region moderated, and countries like Czechoslovakia and Hungary caught up with several Western European countries. However, from the mid-1960s, mortality indicators

TABLE 2.3 Male life expectancy in various European countries, 1900–2000 (in years)

	1900	1910	1920	1930	1940	1950	1960	1970	1980	1990	2000
United Kingdom	44.1	51.5	55.6	58.7		66.4	67.9	68.7	70.2	72.9	75.4
France	45.3	48.5	52.2	54.3		62.9	66.9	68.4	70.2	72.7	75.3
Netherlands	46.2	51.0	55.1	61.9	65.7	70.6	71.5	70.7	72.6	73.6	75.5
Belgium	45.4			56.0		62.0	67.7	67.8	70.0	72.7	75.1
Ireland	49.3	53.6	57.4	58.2	59.0	64.5	68.1	68.8	70.1	72.3	73.9
Germany/FRG	40.6	47.4	56.0	59.9		64.6	66.9	67.4	69.6	72.9	75.0
Austria	39.1	40.7		54.5		61.9	65.6	66.5	69.0	72.4	75.1
Switzerland	45.7	50.7	54.5	59.3	62.7	66.4	68.7	70.3	72.4	74.2	76.9
Sweden	50.9	54.5	54.8	61.2	64.3	69.0	71.2	72.2	72.8	74.8	77.4
Denmark	50.2	54.9	55.8	60.9	63.5	67.8	70.4	70.7	71.1	72.0	74.5
Norway	50.4	54.8	55.6	61.0	64.1	69.3	71.6	71.2	72.3	74.9	76.0
Finland	42.9	45.3	43.4	50.7	54.3	58.6	65.5	66.5	69.2	70.9	74.2
Italy	42.6	44.2	49.3	53.8		63.7	67.2	69.0	70.6	73.5	76.6
Spain	33.9	40.9	40.3	48.4	47.1	59.8	67.4	69.6	72.5	73.4	75.8
Poland				48.2		55.6	64.8	66.8	66.9	66.5	69.7
Czechoslovakia		42.8	47.7	53.7	56.5	62.2	67.6	66.1	66.8	67.5	71.6/69.1
Hungary	36.6	39.1	41.0	48.7	55.0	59.9	65.9	66.3	65.5	65.1	67.4

Notes: United Kingdom 1891–1952: England and Wales; Czechoslovakia 2000: Czech Republic/Slovakia; Hungary: present territories; Different years: England and Wales 1891–1900, 1910–12, 1920–22, 1930–32, 1950–52; France 1898–1903, 1908–13, 1920–23, 1928–33; Netherlands 1890–99, 1900–09, 1910–20, 1921–30, 1931–40, 1950–52, 1980–81; Belgium 1891–1900, 1928–32; Ireland 1900–02, 1910–12, 1925–27, 1935–37, 1940–42, 1950–52, 1961, 1971, 1980–82; Germany 1891–1900, 1910–11, 1924–26, 1932–34, 1949–51, 1960–62, 1970–72; Austria 1901–05, 1906–10, 1930–33, 1949–51, 1959–64; Switzerland 1889–1900, 1910–11, 1920–21, 1929–32, 1939–44, 1948–53, 1958–63, 1968–73, 1978–83; Sweden 1891–1900, 1901–10, 1916–20, 1926–30, 1936–40, 1946–50, 1960–64, 1970–74; Denmark 1895–1900, 1906–10, 1916–20, 1926–30, 1936–40, 1946–50, 1961–62, 1970–71, 1980–81; Norway 1891–1901, 1901–11, 1911–21, 1921–31, 1931–41, 1946–50, 1979–80, 1994; Finland 1891–1900, 1901–10, 1911–20, 1921–30, 1936–40, 1946–50, 1960–64, 1970–74, 1981; Italy 1899–1902, 1901–10, 1921–22, 1930–32; Czechoslovakia 1909–12, 1920–22, 1929–32, 1937, 1949–51, 1960–61; Poland 1931–32, 1948, 1960–61, 1970–72, 1980–81; Hungary 1900–01, 1910–11, 1920–21, 1930–31, 1941.

Sources: United Nations, ed., *Demographic Yearbook, 1948,* New York: United Nations, 1949 (Western Europe 1900–40); Eurostat, ed., *Bevölkerungsstatistik: Daten, 1995–1998,* Luxembourg: Eurostat, 1999 (Western Europe 1960–70; United Kingdom 1980; Belgium 1980–1990; Germany 1980; Austria 1990; Finland 1981); Council of Europe, ed., *Recent Demographic Developments in Europe, 1996,* Strasbourg: Council of Europe, 1996, 55–57 (Western Europe 1980–1990); Oscar W. Gabriel and Frank Brettschneider, eds., *Die EU-Staaten im Vergleich,* Opladen: Westdeutscher Verlag, 1994, 502 (France 1950; Ireland 1950–52; Germany 1970–1972; Italy 1950); Peter Flora, ed., *State, Economy, and Society in Western Europe,* vol. II, Frankfurt/M.: Campus, 1987, 96 (Austria 1906–10, 1959–64), 97 (Belgium 1891–1900), 98 (Denmark 1895–1900, 1906–10, 1916–20, 1926–30, 1936–40, 1946–50), 99 (Finland 1891–1900, 1936–40, 1946–50), 101 (Germany 1891–1900, 1924–26, 1932–34), 102 (Ireland 1900–02, 1910–12), 103 (Italy 1899–1902, 1901–10), 104 (Netherlands 1890–99), 105 (Norway 1891–1901, 1931–41, 1946–50), 106 (Sweden 1891–1900, 1916–20, 1926–30, 1946–50), 107 (Switzerland 1899–1900, 1948–53, 1968–73), 108 (England and Wales 1891–1900, 1950–52); Franz Rothenbacher, *The European Population since 1945,* Houndmills: Palgrave, 2005, 174 (Czechoslovakia 1909–12–1997–98), 647 (Poland 1952/53–1998); Franz Rothenbacher, *The European Population since 1945,* Houndmills: Palgrave, 2005, CD-ROM Publication (Spain 1900–1990); William C. Cockerham, *Health and Social Change in Russia and Eastern Europe,* New York: Routledge, 1999, 148 (Poland 1931–32, 1948); *OECD Factbook 2007. Economic, Environmental and Social Statistics,* Paris: OECD, 2007, 214 (Europe 2000); *Time Series of Historical Statistics, 1867–1992,* Budapest: KSH, 1993, 107 (Hungary 1900–90).

TABLE 2.4 Female life expectancy in various European countries, 1900–2000 (in years)

	1900	1910	1920	1930	1940	1950	1960	1970	1980	1990	2000
United Kingdom	47.8	55.4	59.9	62.9		71.5	73.7	75.0	76.2	78.5	80.2
France	48.7	52.4	56.1	59.0		68.5	73.6	75.9	78.4	80.9	82.7
Netherlands	49.0	53.4	57.1	63.5	67.2	72.9	75.3	76.5	79.3	80.1	80.5
Belgium	48.8			59.8		67.3	73.5	74.2	76.8	79.4	81.4
Ireland	49.6	54.1	57.9	59.6	61.0	67.1	71.9	73.5	75.6	77.9	79.1
Germany/FRG	44.0	50.7	58.8	62.8		68.5	72.4	73.8	76.1	79.3	81.0
Austria	41.1	42.1		58.5		67.0	72.0	73.4	76.1	78.9	81.1
Switzerland	48.5	53.9	57.5	63.1	67.0	70.9	74.1	76.2	79.1	81.1	82.6
Sweden	53.6	57.0	57.6	63.3	66.9	71.6	74.9	77.1	78.8	80.4	82.0
Denmark	53.2	57.9	58.1	62.6	65.8	70.1	74.4	75.9	77.3	77.7	79.3
Norway	54.1	57.7	58.7	63.8	67.6	72.7	76.0	77.5	79.0	80.6	81.4
Finland	45.6	48.1	49.1	55.1	59.5	65.9	72.5	75.0	77.6	78.9	81.0
Italy	43.0	44.8	50.8	56.0	57.5	67.2	72.3	74.9	77.4	80.0	82.5
Spain	35.7	42.6	42.1	51.1	53.2	64.3	72.2	75.1	78.6	80.5	82.5
Poland				51.4		64.2	70.5	73.8	75.4	75.5	77.9
Czechoslovakia		45.9	50.8	57.5	60.5	67.0	73.4	73.0	73.9	76.0	78.4/77.4
Hungary	38.2	40.5	43.1	51.8	58.2	64.2	70.1	72.1	72.7	73.7	75.9

Notes: United Kingdom 1891–1952: England and Wales; Czechoslovakia 2000: Czech R./Slovakia; Hungary: present day territories; Different years: England and Wales 1891–1900, 1910–12, 1920–22, 1930–32, 1950–52; France 1898–1903, 1908–13, 1920–23, 1928–33; Netherlands 1890–99, 1900–09, 1910–20, 1921–30, 1931–40, 1950–52; Belgium 1891–1900, 1928–32; Ireland 1900–02, 1910–12, 1925–27, 1935–37, 1940–42, 1950–52, 1961, 1971, 1980–82; Germany 1891–1900, 1910–11, 1924–26, 1932–34, 1949–51, 1960–62, 1970–72; Austria 1901–05, 1906–10, 1930–33, 1949–51, 1959–64; Switzerland 1889–1900, 1910–11, 1920–21, 1929–32, 1939–44, 1948–53, 1958–63, 1968–73, 1978–83; Sweden 1891–1900, 1901–10, 1916–20, 1926–30, 1936–40, 1946–50, 1960–64, 1970–74; Denmark 1895–1900, 1906–10, 1916–20, 1926–30, 1936–40, 1946–50, 1961–62, 1970–71; Norway 1891–1901, 1901–11, 1911–21, 1921–31, 1931–41, 1946–50, 1979–80, 1994; Finland 1891–1900, 1901–10, 1911–20, 1921–30, 1936–40, 1946–50, 1960–64, 1970–74; Italy 1899–1902, 1901–10, 1921–22, 1930–32; Czechoslovakia 1909–12, 1920–22, 1929–32, 1937, 1949–51, 1960–61; Poland 1931–32, 1952–53, 1960–61, 1970–72, 1980–81; Hungary 1900–01, 1910–11, 1920–21, 1930–31, 1941.

Sources: United Nations, ed., *Demographic Yearbook, 1948,* New York: United Nations, 1949 (Western Europe 1900–40); Eurostat, ed., *Bevölkerungsstatistik: Daten, 1995–1998,* Luxembourg: Eurostat, 1999 (Western Europe 1960–70; Germany 1980; Belgium 1990; Finland 1981; Austria 1990); Council of Europe, ed., *Recent Demographic Developments in Europe, 1996,* Strasbourg: Council of Europe, 1996, 55–57 (Western Europe 1980–1990); Oscar W. Gabriel and Frank Brettschneider, eds., *Die EU-Staaten im Vergleich,* Opladen: Westdeutscher Verlag, 1994, 502 (Germany 1970–1972; France 1950; Ireland 1950–52; Italy 1950); Peter Flora, ed., *State, Economy, and Society in Western Europe,* vol. II, Frankfurt/M.: Campus, 1987, 96 (Austria 1906–10, 1959–64), 97 (Belgium 1891–1900), 98 (Denmark 1895–1900, 1906–10, 1916–20, 1926–30, 1936–40, 1946–50), 99 (Finland 1891–1900, 1936–40, 1946–50), 101 (Germany 1891–1900, 1924–26, 1932–34), 102 (Ireland 1900–02, 1910–12), 103 (Italy 1899–1902, 1901–10), 104 (Netherlands 1890–99), 105 (Norway 1891–1901, 1931–41, 1946–50), 106 (Sweden 1891–1900, 1916–20, 1926–30, 1946–50), 107 (Switzerland 1899–1900, 1948–53, 1968–73), 108 (England and Wales 1891–1900, 1950–52); Franz Rothenbacher, *The European Population since 1945,* Houndmills: Palgrave, 2005, 174 (Czechoslovakia 1909–98), 647 (Poland 1952–1998); Franz Rothenbacher, *The European Population since 1945,* Houndmills: Palgrave, 2005, CD-ROM Publication (Spain 1900–1990); William C. Cockerham, *Health and Social Change in Russia and Eastern Europe,* New York: Routledge, 1999, 148 (Poland 1931–32); *OECD Factbook 2007. Economic, Environmental and Social Statistics,* Paris: OECD, 2007, 215 (Europe 2000); *Time Series of Historical Statistics, 1867–1992,* Budapest: KSH, 1993, 108 (Hungary 1900–90).

TABLE 2.5 Infant mortality in various European countries, 1900–2000 (infant deaths per 1,000 live births)

	1900	1910	1920	1930	1940	1950	1960	1970	1980	1990	2000
United Kingdom	154	105	80	60	61.0	30.0	22.5	18.5	12.1	7.9	5.6
France	160	111	123	84	90.5	52.0	27.5	18.2	10.0	7.3	4.4
Netherlands	155	108	83	51	39.1	25.0	17.9	12.7	8.6	7.1	5.1
Belgium	172	135	110	100	93.2	53.0	31.2	21.1	12.1	7.9	4.8
Ireland	109	95	83	68	66.4	46.0	29.3	19.5	11.1	8.2	6.2
Germany/FRG	229	162	131	85	64.1	55.0	35.0	23.6	12.6	7.0	4.4
Austria	231	189	156	104	74.2	66.0	37.5	25.9	14.3	7.8	4.8
Switzerland	150	105	84	51	46.2	31.0	21.1	15.1	9.1	6.8	4.9
Sweden	99	75	63	55	39.2	21.0	16.6	11.1	6.9	6.0	3.4
Denmark	128	101	91	82	50.0	31.0	21.5	14.2	8.4	7.5	5.3
Finland	153	118	96	75	88.3	44.0	21.0	13.2	7.6	5.6	3.8
Norway	91	67	58	46	39.1	28.0	18.9	12.7	8.1	6.9	3.8
Italy	174	140	127	106	102.7	64.0	43.9	29.6	14.6	8.2	4.5
Spain	186	149	164	117	108.7	64.2	44.0	28.3	12.3	7.6	3.9
Poland				143	140.0	108.0	56.0	33.2	21.3	16.0	8.1
Czechoslovakia			139	135	98.8	77.7	23.5	22.1	18.4	11.3	4.1/ 8.6
Hungary	223	195	193	153	130.1	85.7	47.6	35.9	23.2	14.8	9.2

Notes: United Kingdom 1900–1930, 1950: England and Wales; Czechoslovakia 2000: Czech Republic/ Slovakia; Different years: Austria 1922; Spain 1901; Czechoslovakia 1919; Poland 1938.

Sources: Brian R. Mitchell, *European Historical Statistics, 1750–1975*, New York: Macmillan, 1981, 140–142 (Western Europe 1900–1930, 1950; Denmark 1940); United Nations, ed., *Demographic Yearbook, 1948*, New York: United Nations, 1949, 406 (Western Europe 1940); Eurostat, ed., *Bevölkerungsstatistik: Daten, 1995–1998*, Luxembourg: Eurostat, 1999, 182–183 (Western Europe 1960); Council of Europe, ed., *Recent Demographic Developments in Europe, 1996*, Strasbourg: Council of Europe, 1996, 54 (Western Europe 1970–1990); Franz Rothenbacher, *The European Population since 1945*, Houndmills: Palgrave, 2005, 26 (Spain 1950–90; Poland 1950–90; Czechoslovakia 1950–1990); Franz Rothenbacher, *The European Population since 1945*, Houndmills: Palgrave, 2005, CD-ROM Publication (Spain 1901–1940; Poland 1930–1938; Czechoslovakia 1919–1940); *OECD Factbook 2007: Economic, Environmental and Social Statistics*, Paris: OECD, 2007, 217 (Europe 2000); *Time Series of Historical Statistics, 1867–1992*, Budapest: KSH, 1993, 218 (Hungary 1920–1990).

in most of the communist countries began to stagnate or deteriorate, and thus the dynamics of their development differed significantly from that observed in Western Europe.[51] The change did not affect every country, age group, social class and gender in the same way. In Czechoslovakia and Bulgaria, it was less pronounced, but in Hungary it emerged in a dire form, so much so that it is sometimes referred to as an epidemiological crisis.[52] Women's mortality rates turned relatively favourably, because even in Hungary, their mortality improvement only slowed down. This also meant that the mortality gap between the sexes was wider in East Central Europe than in most of the countries of Western Europe: 9 years when considering life expectancies in Poland in 1990. Age and social differences also prevailed. In all communist countries, the deterioration of mortality affected middle-aged working-class males the most.[53]

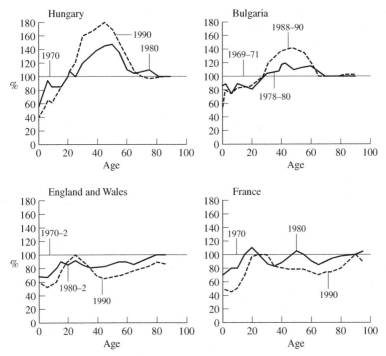

Notes: Mortality rates in or around 1970 are set at 100 in each case. Rates for other years are expressed as a ratio to the 1970 rates.

FIGURE 2.3 Trends in mortality by age in selected European countries, 1970–1990 (males) *Source*: France Meslé, 'Mortality in Eastern and Western Europe: A Widening Gap', in David Coleman, ed., *Europe's Population in the 1990s,* Oxford: Oxford University Press, 1996, 133. Data derived from the unpublished database of the INED (Institut National d'Études Démographiques), Paris.

Differences between communist and Western European countries can be best highlighted by trajectories of age-specific mortality. As Figure 2.3 shows, between 1970 and 1990, in England and France, mortality improved in all age groups, except for men around 20 years of age, where it stagnated. The improvement was not even. In England, it was the highest for infants, children and those between 40 and 60 years of age. In France, infants, children and those between 40 and 70 years of age enjoyed its benefits the most. In contrast to this, in two communist countries that can be considered symptomatic in this respect (Bulgaria and especially Hungary), all male age groups except for the ones under 20 had deteriorating mortality, sometimes in a dramatic fashion. In Hungary, the mortality risk of a 40-year-old man was about 60% higher in 1990 than 20 years before.[54] In other words, 40-year-old men in 1965 could expect to live 32.7 years more (here, the effects of the continuing mortality decline among the under-30s and especially infants and children no longer hold), whereas two decades on, they could expect to live only 29.5 more years. For women, the figure of 36 years of life yet to be expected did not change.

3. It can be established that in Western and Southern Europe, mortality differences among countries were unanimously and almost continuously lessening throughout the century.[55] Although this convergence did progress in the first half of the century, after the Second World War there were still relatively significant mortality differentials among Western European countries. In 1950, the gap between countries exhibiting the best figures (the Netherlands, Norway, Sweden and Denmark) and the poorest (Finland) was 12 years. The clear convergence of the succeeding decades is indicated by a rise of 3 years in male life expectancy at birth in the Netherlands between 1950 and 1990, while the corresponding figure is 12.3 years in Finland. Because of the rapidity with which Finland caught up, in 1990 Sweden (the country ranking first in this respect) had only 3.3 years of advantage on Finland, still ranking last.[56] Of all the major demographic phenomena, the greatest degree of convergence occurred undoubtedly with regard to mortality among Western European countries.[57]

East Central European mortality conditions did occasionally converge with Western Europe in the course of the twentieth century, but, on the whole, between the beginning and the end of the century, divergence prevailed.[58] From the mid-1960s, whereas Western Europe enjoyed a continuation of improving mortality conditions, in East Central Europe (as discussed above), male mortality began to deteriorate. This was the commencement of strong divergence in mortality between Eastern and Western European trends, which was further strengthened by the rapid unification within Western Europe in the 1980s, especially regarding infant mortality.[59]

In the course of the twentieth century, remarkable changes occurred in the mortality differentials between men and women as well. The longer life span of women is a modern phenomenon, which could be observed in certain parts of Europe (Switzerland, Sweden) already at the end of the eighteenth century. In the early twentieth century, the gap was about 2–3 years generally, but then it began to widen. By 1990, even the narrowest gap amounted to 5.5 years (Ireland). The female life expectancy gain is present in all age groups, that is, infant mortality is already higher among boys than girls. Nevertheless, from the 1980s on, the growth of the gap between male and female mortality slowed down, and in a few countries, a moderate process of levelling off began. The causes underlying the latter process are elaborated on later.[60]

The causes of mortality changes

The causes of mortality decline rank among the highly debated issues in population history. Regarding the twentieth century, first of all, views on the role of medical science and technology vary greatly. Yet, mainstream literature considers medicine to exert crucial influence in this respect only in the second half of the twentieth century even in the most advanced European countries.[61] Certain infectious diseases (such as smallpox or diphtheria), against which preventive vaccination had been used already in the nineteenth century, were an exception here. For most infectious diseases, mortality had begun to decline before medicine could have cured or prevented them through vaccination, which can be explained by better living conditions, and most importantly by improving nutrition, which vested the population with more resistance to epidemics. Tuberculosis (the most frequent cause of death among adults in the nineteenth century) belongs to this group of diseases. It was largely eradicated in Western Europe in the first half of the twentieth century, even though its treatment became available only after the Second World War.

Another area where developments had contributed from early on to the declining mortality was the growing body of knowledge on the prevention of diseases. Propaganda by volunteer and governmental organizations made information accessible to ever larger masses of people. The rising levels of education alone facilitated these processes, as attending school become universal. However, it was also considered an overt function of education to promote knowledge on health and hygiene. There was a change in attitudes to infants and children as well, as parents and society alike began to pay more attention to their health and welfare. Working conditions also changed for the better. Notable health effects can also be attributed to improving conditions in housing, which resulted in a disappearance of crowded living arrangements and in healthier, more hygienic living environments.[62] Moreover, sanitation measures of municipal and central governments (such as building sewage systems, the provision of clean drinking water and control over the sale of food products) had considerable effects as early as the first decades of the twentieth century.[63] In the second half of the century, because of strengthening state commitment to social policy, health care became accessible practically to the whole society and thus medical innovations made possible by technical advancement benefited the masses.

The combined effects of all these factors resulted in the so-called epidemiological transition.[64] This concept, which originated with Abdel Omran, refers to a historic shift in the characteristics of mortality and more specifically in the nature of fatal diseases. After the long-standing 'age of pestilence and famine', in the late eighteenth century Europe entered the 'age of receding pandemics', which remained predominant by the late nineteenth century. In this period, infectious diseases as well as maladies of the digestive and the respiratory organs (e.g. pneumonia) were the leading causes of death. Then, in the twentieth century, a third era called the 'age of degenerative and man-made diseases' began, during which former major causes of death were gradually replaced by cardiovascular and cancerous conditions and other types of degenerative health problems caused by human activity. The ratio of the latter grew from one-fifth to three-quarters of causes of deaths in the developed European countries in the course of a hundred years.[65]

The remarkable improvement of mortality was not simply the result of adults living longer. In the first decades of the century, the rise of life expectancy was primarily the consequence of the declining infant and child mortality. The greatest reduction occurred with regard to early childhood – especially with the eradication of epidemics, as a result of the aforementioned vaccination, improvement of hygiene, better nutrition for infants, etc. In older age groups, the prevention and subsequently the treatment of tuberculosis witnessed a spectacular advance. The mortality of those over 60 years of age did not improve in a similarly remarkable manner; however, from the 1970s, the life expectancy of this age group did also significantly rise.

The divergence observed between communist and Western European societies in the last third of the twentieth century can be plausibly explained by differences in the social conditions and the lifestyle people led, even though environmental problems and several other factors did also contribute to it. On the one hand, the shortcomings of the healthcare system, especially as regards prevention, obviously played a role in the deterioration of the Polish, Bulgarian or Czechoslovakian situation. Estimates are available about the so-called medically avoidable deaths, which refers to mortality that would not have occurred had medical attention been provided promptly and at an appropriate level. The proportion of deaths within this category in the mid-1980s was estimated to be 9% in Czechoslovakia and 15% in Poland,[66] indicating that avoidable deaths were significant but not the leading causes of premature mortality in the region.[67] There is enough evidence that the lifestyle of the population carried high health risks. Excessive smoking, consumption of animal fats and alcohol, as well as the lack of regular exercise, all belonged to the unhealthy lifestyle. The fact that middle-aged males with working-class background were at greatest risk for premature death suggest that the characteristics of working were also contributors to the unfavourable trend: poor working conditions, excessive overtime and the prevalence of second jobs in some countries, the stress resulting from poor organization, etc.[68] Social stress in the widest sense may also have contributed to health problems in communist Europe, including conflicts in people's everyday lives related to the authoritarian political system and the shortage economy, the persistent feeling of defencelessness along with the poverty of culturally coded abilities to cope with stressful situations.

All in all, the East Central and South-Eastern European deterioration of mortality can be considered system specific, that is, it can be attributed to the communist political and social system.[69] Important evidence comes from the comparative analysis of the demographic transition. For example, in Austria and Finland, the main tendencies were identical with those in Eastern Europe in the previous stages of the demographic transition,[70] and differences emerged only in the period of communist rule. Furthermore, after the collapse of communism, from the early and mid-1990s, mortality began to improve in the region, creating the possibility of convergence again.

The improvement of mortality in every society proceeded with significant class-specific and status-specific differences. The mortality of higher social strata had already been lower at the beginning of the twentieth century and they could keep most of this advantage all through the century, even if over time some narrowing took place in mortality differentials between classes in Britain and several other countries.[71] Blue-collar workers become the victims of accidents more often and they have a higher risk to die from cancer, cardiovascular diseases or liver damage at a younger age. This is not only because they are more often exposed to harmful effects in their work, but they are more inclined to neglect their illnesses and, especially, smoking and alcoholism is more widespread among them. As Michael Anderson demonstrated in the British case, the wives and children of many men in high-mortality occupations also had high death rates in 1950.[72] Studies on this issue show that, in all Europe, those with better education lived longer even if they had the same occupation. As for differences among European societies, a comparative study of 32 countries in the early 1980s revealed that gaps in mortality by social group did exist in the Scandinavian countries, the Netherlands, and East Germany, but that they were smaller there. West Germany, France and Italy showed differences in the middle range, whereas the differences between the life expectancy of different social groups were large in Spain, Romania, Hungary and the United States.[73]

The differences in the mortality of males and females present throughout the twentieth century in European societies are rooted in biological and social factors. Recent findings show that the genetic characteristics of women contribute to a more effective protection from diseases; first of all, their hormone system is more accommodating when the functioning of the immune system and the protection from cardiovascular illnesses are considered. Differences in lifestyle and everyday attitudes are even more important, however. In contrast to what traditional masculine social roles demand, feminine roles do allow an expression of emotions and an avoidance of conflicts, which both reduce the degree of everyday, health-affecting stress. Women have closer family and social relationships, which contributes to the maintenance of their psychological balance and is also beneficial for them in times of illness. Moreover, taking care of their children and other family members, they develop a more conscious attitude to health problems, which includes the propensity for seeking medical advice and practising prevention. Male work often involves greater physical strains and carries more risks of accidents. Moreover, men commit suicide and fall into addictive behaviour more often than women.

Women increased their advantage with regards to life expectancy over men in the course of the century, because the risk of perinatal death for women plummeted drastically in the twentieth century and thus female excess mortality vanished. Moreover, men's lifestyles changed for the worse more than women's: for instance, a major element was the spread of smoking. The growth in mortality differences specific to two sexes has halted or the difference has begun to shrink from the 1980s in several European societies, which was related to the levelling in men's and women's lifestyles in industrial societies.[74]

Migration in Europe: a turnaround of flows

The third factor in the changes in population size is migration, which may also have a significant impact on the structure of the population.[75] Because migrants tend to be young and are often more educated than the average, having a strong sense of initiative along with other distinctive features, the movement of people does affect the countries and regions of origin and destination, as regards demographic, and even cultural, ethnic and religious characteristics.

Migration might take different forms, such as one person or one family moving to town or masses fleeing their home in times of war. The definition comprises all these possibilities: migration means the change of a person's place of residence, more exactly, a permanent or semi-permanent change of residence that is at a large enough distance so that the migrants are no longer able to attend their former place of work. The determinants of migration are also manifold. From a historical perspective, it was the natural-ecological and socioeconomic factors that predominantly led to migration, but in the twentieth century, political causes have gained paramount significance. These and several other criteria might be used when distinguishing between types of migration:[76]

1. Geographical factors (the direction and distance of migration) are of primary importance. On this basis, we can differentiate between internal (local and regional) and international migration. The latter may take place within a continent or between continents ('overseas migration').
2. The temporal dimension of migration is also an important variable. This makes possible the differentiation between temporary migration (e.g. working or studying in another region or country) and permanent migration (e.g. moving to another country). The temporary or permanent nature of the migration is often unclear for the people involved; however, historians generally have the advantage of knowing the results of movements.
3. The analysis may also address the social aspects of population movement. The composition of migrant communities may differ with regard to sex, class origin, occupation, ethnicity and level of education. Furthermore, individual and mass migration can also be distinguished from each other, though the boundaries between them are often not clear-cut.
4. The motives of migration represent further important criteria. Generally, voluntary and forced migration can be distinguished, although again, the borderline between them may not always be sharp. Voluntary migration most often results from economic considerations, whereas forced migration most often results from environmental, political or war-related causes.

In the following sections, the above aspects provide the basis for a discussion of major population movements affecting Europe in the twentieth century. The focus is on international migration, while internal population movement is addressed in a later chapter dealing with urbanization.

Overseas migration

The migration of Europeans to other continents reached its climax between 1881 and 1910, when about 20% of the natural increase of the continent's population was lost. In the early twentieth century, this amounted to 1.3 million people annually. European emigration spread from west to east. In the mid-nineteenth century, emigrants were mostly natives of the British Isles, but later Germany and Scandinavia, then, by the turn of the century, Southern and East Central Europe became the main sending regions. In all, 27 million people left Europe between 1891 and 1920. The main target of emigration was the United States, with 58% of

European overseas emigrants arriving there between 1890 and 1910. Other important destinations in the late nineteenth and early twentieth century included Canada, Argentina, Brazil, Australia, New Zealand and South Africa. Many Europeans moved to the colonies as civil servants, soldiers or engineers.[77]

The First World War almost completely stopped the process of overseas migration, with the belligerent parties hindering both the emigration of their men of military age and the movement of citizens from enemy countries. Furthermore, the war made sea travel, and thus migration, difficult to manage and often even dangerous.

Nevertheless, the migration of Europeans did not return to pre-war levels even after hostilities ended. There were several reasons why emigration rates fell. The most immediate change was that the United States introduced restrictions on immigration from 1921, with the purpose to reduce the total number of immigrants and to control their ethnic composition. In the 1921 Emergency Quota Act, immigration was restricted annually to 3 per cent of the total number of each immigrant group already residing in the United States. The Immigration Act of 1924 further restricted immigration to 2 per cent, even though the number of new arrivals did not fall immediately because of delays in implementation.[78] These measures primarily aimed at the reduction of Asian immigration, but they also hindered Southern and Eastern European arrivals. The less developed regions, such as the Balkans, would have joined in the process of overseas migration at this point, but hardly had the opportunity, not having a considerable share in the flow before, which meant a rather low quota set for them. The Great Depression was another force hindering immigration, reducing the attractiveness of the unemployment-ridden United States. Thus, in the 1920s, on the average, 0.7 million people per annum left Europe for overseas destinations, and this figure dropped to 0.13 million in the 1930s. Despite the shifts in immigration policies, the United States remained by far the most important destination.[79]

After the Second World War, the number of those leaving Europe reached a climax, rising to about half a million annually between 1946 and 1960. However, the significance of overseas migration was gradually weakening, a phenomenon partly caused by the strict restrictions that communist countries placed on their citizens' movement. In fact, the migration balance of Europe has been positive since the mid-1960s, that is, more arrive to the continent than leave it. First, the independence of former colonies induced a notable flow of repatriation. Significant numbers of Frenchmen returned from Algeria, Britons from African and Asian colonies, Dutch from Indonesia and, in the 1970s, Portuguese from Africa. Even more importantly, the persistence of strong economic, cultural and political ties with the former colonies, as well as humanitarian considerations, contributed to the flow of great numbers of overseas immigrants into Western European countries from the 1960s.[80]

European immigration I: flows induced by political factors

Compared to the nineteenth and even earlier centuries, the proportion of migration flows caused by wars and political factors grew greatly in the twentieth century.[81] The

First World War not only caused masses of refugees to flee, but several of the peace treaties also included the resettlement of ethnic minorities. Thus, after the war, approximately 1 million Germans were forced to leave their homes in Poland or Alsace, and 0.9 million Poles moved from Russia to Poland. About 1 million people fled from the Soviet regime and the civil war, many of them settling in Western Europe. The greatest population movement took place in Turkey, where the massacres committed against Armenians induced a flow of refugees. The Lausanne peace treaty resulted in the expulsion of 1.35 million Greeks from the country, whereas 0.42 million Turks were forced to leave Greece. A similar population exchange occurred between Greece and Bulgaria. From the end of the war, a large number of Hungarians (0.5 million) also left their homes in territories annexed by the successor states and settled within the redrawn Hungarian boundaries. Finally, in the 1930s, 0.3 million people fled from Spain as a consequence of the civil war.

However, all these numbers are dwarfed when compared to the population flows induced by the Second World War. In this deluge, it was not only huge armies that roamed Europe, but also streams of civilians. Several million Jews were deported, the majority of whom were then killed. The number of Jewish victims during the war amounts to about 5.6–5.9 million. The migration flow was the largest in the Third Reich, the authorities of which systematically intended that the occupied territories contribute to satisfying the labour needs of the German war economy. From the Netherlands, Belgium or France, workers were usually attracted to Germany with higher wages, whereas from Eastern Europe, they were most often recruited by force. At the height of German war efforts, in August 1944, there were 7.8 million foreign workers, forced labourers and prisoners of war working in Germany, comprising almost one-third of the total work force.[82] In the last stage of the war, civilians fleeing East Prussia, Silesia, Pomerania and other Eastern German territories comprised a further mass of several million.

At the end of the Second World War, about 40 million refugees were registered in Europe. Although most of them eventually did return home, this was not yet the end of the exodus. Ethnic cleansings following the war affected, in the most direful manner, Eastern European Germans, whose relocation originated in agreements between the Allies and in initiatives of the governments of the countries where they had been living.[83] Altogether 7.5 million Germans were systematically relocated from Poland, Czechoslovakia, Romania and other countries in the region. According to estimates, about 12.3 million Germans had to leave their homes between 1945 and 1950 (including the refugees mentioned above) and a further 2 million were killed in persecutions.[84] Most Germans ended up in the Western zones: the 1950 West German census found that 19% of the population consisted of refugees, persecutees or emigrants. This ratio grew to 24% by 1960 with the East German emigrants.[85] A population exchange was also initiated at the Potsdam Conference between Czechoslovakia and Hungary; Yugoslavia and Hungary; and the Soviet Union and Romania. These were carried out asymmetrically, that is, the size of the affected populations differed in the respective countries. In addition, from the Eastern Polish territories annexed by the Soviet Union, 3 million Poles were deported to Poland.[86]

For communist regimes, an important element in controlling their population was making free movement impossible, thus getting rid of the option that people 'vote with their feet', as a phrase for emigration expresses rather vividly. In spite of this, 14.2 million people fled or emigrated from the communist countries between 1950 and 1992/1993. A large number among them were German, a fact that may be explained when two circumstances are considered. On the one hand, until the building of the Berlin Wall in 1961, many East Germans may have seized the opportunity that the Potsdam treaty offered by ensuring freedom of movement between the Eastern and Western sectors of Berlin. From West Berlin, then, there was practically nothing to stop anyone who wished to go to West Germany. Until 1961, about 3.58 million made this journey to flee from East Germany, whereas 0.5 million moved in the opposite direction.[87] On the other hand, 2.8 million Germans in Eastern Europe, who had not been displaced before, relocated to West Germany. The largest numbers came from Poland, the Soviet Union and Romania. One consideration why communist countries allowed this German emigration was that it promoted ethnic homogenization. However, the economic and foreign policy concessions given by West Germany constituted another reason. The most infamous example is the Romanian practice. Following the Schmidt–Ceaușescu agreement, Romania received a considerable sum of hard currency (DM 8000) from the FRG for each ethnic German citizen allowed to emigrate.[88]

Uprisings against the communist regimes resulted in a temporal abandonment or relaxation of border control several times, which the refugees acted on. Thus, in late 1956 and early 1957, roughly 194,000 people emigrated from Hungary, and similar events occurred in Czechoslovakia in 1968–69 (160,000 refugees) as well as in Poland in 1980–81 (250,000 refugees).[89]

At the time when regime changes took place in Eastern Europe, migration to the West again began to flourish. Again, it was East Germans who left in the highest numbers, and, in fact, emigration from the former GDR territories remained uninterrupted all through the 1990s. In this latter case, of course, the cause was not political, but better work opportunities and higher standards of living attracted people. However, politically and ethnically induced migration remained no unfamiliar phenomenon in the 1990s, either. The wars during and after the disintegration of Yugoslavia turned about 4 million people into refugees (even if for a part of them it was only temporary). Most of them remained in the region, but roughly half a million people left for Western Europe.

European immigration II: economically motivated flows

The migration of labour between regions and countries has a long history in Europe. It is well known that in the Middle Ages, the peregrination of students as well as the periods craftsmen spent working abroad served as instruments of knowledge transfer. In addition, industrial workers and agricultural seasonal labourers similarly roamed Europe in great numbers, in search of better work opportunities. At the time, less developed territories also often attracted migrants, where immigrant artisans and peasants received a number of privileges, but growing economic and wage differences made this practice obsolete by the nineteenth century.[90]

In the early twentieth century, only few restrictions hindered the movement of labour within Europe. This time, many foreigners worked in Germany (0.95 million), mostly Poles and Italians. Similarly, there were many foreign workers in France. The highest ratio of foreign labourers in proportion to the country's population lived in Switzerland where they amounted to 600,000 people (mostly Germans, Italians and Spaniards) in the years before the First World War. In the interwar years, the movement of labour slowed down within Europe. On the one hand, there were now bureaucratic rules that made crossing borders more difficult than before the First World War, even though these were minor obstacles compared with the restrictions after the Second World War. On the other hand, similarly to overseas migration, the enormous unemployment of the Great Depression constrained finding employment abroad. France was the only country to receive a significant flow within Europe, and, in fact, for some time, this country became the number-one migration target in the world, with almost 2 million foreign workers arriving there between 1920 and 1930.[91]

However, the fast economic development after the Second World War attracted foreign labourers to Western Europe in greater numbers than ever before. In the 1950s, mainly Italians went abroad to work, then from the 1960s, the stream of guest workers accelerated, with Spaniards, Portuguese, Greeks, Yugoslavians and Turks joining the movement. The climax occurred in 1973, when there were 7.5 million guest workers employed in the 9 countries of the European Economic Community (EEC) and the European Free Trade Association (EFTA) countries. The major host countries included Germany (2.5 million), France (2.3 million) and Switzerland (0.6 million). The economic recession induced by the oil crisis brought about a plunge in the number of guest workers. Whereas in the peak year, foreign labourers amounted to 12% of the labour force in Germany and 10% in France, a decade later this figure was around 7–8%.[92]

Meanwhile, it was not only the number of guest workers that changed but also their origin and internal composition. Among the sending countries, Italy, Spain and Greece lost ground, whereas Portugal, Yugoslavia, Morocco, Algeria and, most importantly, Turkey moved to the forefront. There was also a tangible shift from temporary or returning to permanent migration. In the 1960s, it was primarily young and single men who took employment in Western Europe this way, intending to stay only for a few years to collect capital with which to start a family and a small business back in their home country. Consequently, they integrated into the receiving society only to a minimal degree, and, actually, no need for their permanent integration emerged on either their side or the host country's.

However, from the 1980s, workers tended to arrive with their families, thinking of a longer stay, even intending to settle permanently. A chain migration began, with close family members and other relatives, even friends, joining the guest workers. Their children attended school. In fact, a number of these children were born in the host country, which did help their integration, yet it still lagged behind the parallel increase in the expectations of the communities of migrants and the natives. In many cases, this led to conflicts between both sides.[93]

A further circumstance that made the integration of the immigrants more difficult was that by the 1990s they were coming from an ever-growing number of countries and in ever-increasing numbers from regions outside Europe. This latter tendency was strengthened by Western European countries admitting refugees in large numbers from several war zones and authoritarian regimes of the world because of humanitarian considerations. Germany was among the countries most generous in this regard, giving asylum to 1.4 million people between 1983 and 1992 alone (Table 2.6). In the early 1990s, 36% of immigrants in France were European (mostly Portuguese), whereas 39% came from the Maghreb countries. In 1994 in Germany, 28% of foreigners were Turkish and only 22% came from the European Union (EU). All in all, 49% of immigrants living in the EU arrived from outside Europe.

TABLE 2.6 Foreign population in the FRG, 1961–1994

	1961	1971	1980	1989	1994
Foreign population (in thousands)	686	3439	4453	4846	6991
of these, women (%)	31.1	38.2	41.2	45.0	42.3
Foreign population as % of total population	1.2	5.6	7.2	7.7	8.6
Foreign labour force as % of total labour force	2.6	10.3	9.9	7.8	9.4
Continent of origin (%)					
Europe	76.9	72.4	56.2	51.4	54.6
Asia (including Turkey)	3.9	21.6	37.5	41.3	37.6
Africa	1.1	1.5	2.3	3.4	4.2
America	2.9	2.6	2.5	2.7	2.6
Australia	0.1	0.2	0.2	0.1	0.1
Unknown	15.1	1.7	1.2	1.1	1.0
Proportion of selected countries (%)					
United Kingdom	1.3	1.1	1.8	1.8	1.6
France	2.9	1.6	1.5	1.6	1.4
Netherlands	9.5	3.2	2.4	2.1	1.6
Austria	8.4	4.7	3.9	3.5	2.6
Italy	28.7	17.2	13.9	10.7	8.2
Greece	5.8	11.5	6.7	6.1	5.1
Spain	6.4	7.9	4.0	2.6	1.9
Portugal	0.1	2.2	2.5	1.5	1.7
Turkey	1.0	19.0	32.6	33.3	28.1
Yugoslavia	2.4	17.3	14.2	12.6	18.7
Poland		1.4	1.4	4.5	3.8

Notes: 1994: data for unified Germany.
Sources: François Höpflinger, *Bevölkerungssoziologie,* München: Juventa, 1997, 122.

TABLE 2.7 Proportion of foreign population in selected European countries, 1960–2004 (% of total population)

	1960	1970	1982	1990	1995	2000	2004
Great Britain		2.5	3.9	3.3	3.4	4.0	4.9
France	4.7	5.3	6.8	6.4		5.6	
Netherlands	1.0	2.0	3.9	4.6	4.7	4.2	4.3
Belgium	4.9	7.2	9.0	9.1	9.0	8.4	8.4
Germany/FRG	1.2	4.9	7.6	8.2	8.8	8.9	8.9
Austria	1.4	2.8	4.0	6.6	8.5	8.8	9.5
Switzerland	9.5	16.2	14.7	16.3	18.9	19.3	20.2
Sweden	2.6	5.1	5.0	5.6	5.2	5.4	5.1
Denmark					4.2	4.8	4.9
Norway					3.8	4.0	4.6
Finland					1.3	1.8	2.1
Italy		0.3	0.5	1.4	1.7	2.4	3.9
Spain					1.3	2.2	4.6
Poland						0.1	
Czech Republic					1.5	1.9	2.5
Hungary					1.4	1.1	1.4

Sources: François Höpflinger, *Bevölkerungssoziologie,* München: Juventa, 1997, 121 (Western Europe 1960–1990); *OECD Factbook 2007: Economic, Environmental and Social Statistics,* Paris: OECD, 2007, 253 (Europe 1995–2004).

The ratio of the foreign population had been rising significantly in every Western European country from the 1960s, by 1995 reaching 9.0% in Belgium, 8.8% in Germany, 3.4% in Great Britain, 4.7% in the Netherlands, 8.5% in Austria, 5.2% in Sweden and 18.9% in Switzerland (Table 2.7). However, data on the ratio of the foreign population may be misleading for two reasons. First, they include legal immigrants only, whereas the number of illegal immigrants was estimated around 2 million in Western Europe. Second, in certain countries, immigrants may obtain citizenship quickly, and thus their foreign status is terminated, whereas in other countries, naturalization is a more complicated process. The high ratio of the foreign population in Switzerland, for example, also originates from the frequent lack of Swiss citizenship even in the third-generation descendants of the immigrants.

As opposed to Western Europe, in the eastern part of the continent the guest worker movement was only on a very low scale, except for Yugoslavia, which sustained a special relationship with the West. In the other countries, the politics of allowing citizens to take Western European jobs did not surface at all, because it would have interfered with the assertion of control over citizens' movements and would have presented an obstacle to the maintenance of state monopolies on information and foreign currency. In addition, a shortage of resources emerged in the planned economies, including the shortage of labour, which excluded that economic policy could allow foreign employment for large numbers. Considering the reception of guest workers, there were other obstacles in addition to political ones, most of all the low level of wages and the lack of the convertibility of currencies. Suffering from extreme shortage of labour because of large-scale emigration, the country employing guest workers from other communist countries in the largest number was the GDR, doing so exclusively on the basis of bilateral agreements, organized centrally and with a strict rotation scheme of workers. However, this involved only a few tens of thousands at a time, arriving from Poland and Hungary and then, in the 1980s, mostly from Vietnam, Cuba and Mozambique.[94]

Causes and implications of migration

Decisions about migration are shaped by economic, social, political and cultural determinants. Several migration models and theories aim at identifying these factors and they also describe the effects of population movement at its origin and destination.[95] Research usually highlights the following major features having an impact on migration:

1. Push factors that urge the members of a community or society to leave. High unemployment, the lack of political democracy, limits to upwards social mobility and low income levels rank high among the push factors.
2. The pull factors discussed in the literature refer to the attractiveness of the target of migration: high standard of living, tolerance to immigrants, simple rules of settling down, and a favourable labour market situation being among the most important of these.
3. A third group includes intervening factors that may ease migration or make it difficult, such as geographical distance, access to transportation or the availability of information on the destination.
4. The individual characteristics of the potential emigrants also matter, because migration is a selective process. That is, a combined effect of different factors does induce some to migrate whereas it does not others. The most frequent selection is by age, gender, health status, occupation, education, and the sense of initiative.[96]
5. Social factors (such as bureaucratic regulations and restrictions, or even cultural and commercial exchange between the countries) also play a role, both in the sending and the host countries. Some researchers classify these among the push and pull factors. Others consider the push–pull approach reductionist and argue that factors may be interpreted only within the framework of 'migration systems theory', with an emphasis on the linkages and interplay between individual factors.[97]

Economic incentives (higher real wages or low level of unemployment) were and are key determinants of migration: in most cases where there is a net flow from one region or country to another, it is from the relatively poor to the rich one. The internal migration in Western European countries after the Second World War belongs to this type, as exemplified by the population movement from Southern to Northern Italy. Still, economic disparities alone cannot explain international migration, because however strong these may be, they can be counterbalanced by other political, social, linguistic, or geographic factors. This is why overseas migration decreased considerably during the World Wars. Similarly, in the 1950s and 1960s, political obstacles kept migration from communist countries to Western Europe at a low level, even though strong economic incentives obviously existed.

The various degrees to which different factors exert their influence may determine the structure of migration as well. If pull factors are dominating, then higher social strata are overrepresented among the migrants. Brain drain (the migration of highly qualified professionals) is a good example here. If push factors predominate, the social composition of the migrant population is usually more diverse. For instance, the post-Second World War ethnic cleansing in several East Central European and Balkan countries equally affected highly and less educated groups.

As for the demographic, economic and social consequences of migration, these greatly depend upon the conditions under which a movement occurs, and thus possible outcomes may vary. The most straightforward implications are the demographic ones: emigration causes population loss and vice versa. In the case of internal migration, we can find relevant examples in the second half of the twentieth century in Southern and East Central Europe, where the flow from rural to urban areas resulted in the depopulation of whole villages and even regions. In target countries of international migration, in contrast, the populations of major cities were further boosted by the flow. For example, in Great Britain in the 1980s, 73% of immigrants settled down in the seven largest cities.[98] As mentioned before, except for forced migration, the migrant population is mostly comprised of younger age groups, thus such movements contribute to a change in the age structure of host societies. At the same time, European experience in the late twentieth century shows that this effect does not necessarily prevent the ageing of the host society. The lack of rejuvenation was demonstrated by West Germany, the country affected most by immigration in the decades after the Second World War (Table 2.8).

As for economic impacts, migration might channel surplus labour, and the earnings of the guest workers transferred home improve the balance of payment of sending countries. This was the case for most Southern and South-Eastern European countries from the 1960s. In 1973, remittances amounted to 47% of Turkish, 37% of Portuguese and 24% of Greek exports, that is, guest workers employed in Western Europe represented the strongest branch of the export industry of these countries.[99] Undoubtedly, however, emigration might contribute to a loss of highly qualified workers and thus to a deterioration of human capital as well. Some estimates claim, for instance, that Sub-Saharan African countries lost 30% of their highly qualified labour force between 1960 and 1987, and that these people mostly found employment in Western Europe.[100] In the GDR, emigration or, rather, flight to the other Germany, resulted in such dire shortage in certain professions (most notably doctors and engineers) by the end of the 1950s that it endangered the functioning of the entire economy and public services. The more important

TABLE 2.8 Possible implications of international labour migration

a) Possible consequences for sending countries

Demographic consequences	Decreasing population pressure (+)
	Deformation of population structure (−)
	Decreasing population size (−)
	Increasing ageing of the population (−)
Economic consequences	Decreasing unemployment (+)
	Improving balance of payment because of earnings transferred home (+)
	Losing qualified labour (brain drain) (−)
Social consequences	Professional, language and other types of knowledge of those repatriating (+)
	Intensifying international relationships (+)
	Conserving traditional societal and political structures (−, +)
	Loosening family and other social relationships (−)
	Problems of integration for those repatriating (−)

b) Possible consequences for host countries

Demographic consequences	Accelerating population growth (+)
	Rejuvenating population (+)
	Changing ethnic composition (?)
Economic consequences	Easing or terminating labour shortage in specific sectors, easing the pressure on wages (+, −)
	Pressure on wage levels by growing supply of labour (−)
	Faster economic growth as a result of increasing production base and consumer demand (+)
	Excess demand on infrastructure (e.g. on the housing market) (−)
Social consequences	Savings on education costs (+)
	Mobility opportunities of the native population (+)
	Pluralization of culture and society (+)
	Problems in integrating migrants, ethnic separation with all its consequences, e.g. anomie (−)
	Political consequences, e.g. increasing xenophobia (−)

Note: Notes in parentheses indicate the favourable (+) or unfavourable (−) character of the possible consequences in the European context.

Source: Author's own interpretation based on François Höpflinger, *Bevölkerungssoziologie*, München: Juventa, 1997, 135–136.

human capital became among growth factors in the course of the century, the higher significance such losses had in sending countries. In cases when the majority of emigrants return to their home country, as did Italian and Spanish guest workers of the 1960s and 1970s in Western Europe, human capital may increase, because those returning home take with them their knowledge and attitudes absorbed in a more advanced economic environment.

If host countries have the means to influence the scale and structure of migration to comply with their own needs, then the negative effects of migration usually emerge only locally or in a few sectors – such as the greater supply of labour putting constraints on wage levels, or the development of the infrastructure lagging behind growing needs. In this case, positive effects dominate, which strengthen growth at the level of the national economy by satisfying the demand for labour in areas of shortage, creating a larger market, saving education costs to the host country, etc. However, if migration occurred in other ways, impossible for the host country to control and plan, then in the short term, it had several negative effects on both economy and society. The population flows after the two World Wars took place in such scenarios, leading to housing shortage, unemployment and other social maladies in the most affected countries.

Among the possible outcomes of migration, the impact on social and political structures and attitudes also deserves attention. Repressive political regimes often force dissidents (politicians and other citizens) to leave the country. If such a flow of emigration occurs on a mass scale, it may contribute to the consolidation of the regime, at least in the short term. Large-scale emigration also undoes family and social ties. As a counterbalance to these effects, we may consider the already mentioned advantages coming from the improved knowledge of those repatriating with regard to their profession/occupation, better skills in foreign languages, as well as the intensification of transnational relations of the population.

From the viewpoint of host countries (especially in the last decades of the twentieth century), negative social consequences emerged as well, including the migrants' segregation, which led to the slumming of urban areas, the deterioration of schools or an increase in xenophobia. These issues have undoubtedly become eminent in Western Europe, the region most affected by immigration, and even the idea of 'the irresistible rise of multiracial' societies appeared, as formulated in the case of Britain.[101] However, these problems are mostly conditioned by the host societies: negative attitudes toward immigrants may be stronger if a society at the same time must also face severe socioeconomic changes. The level of xenophobia also depends on how welcoming and inclusive the given society is, that is, different societies may react differently to the same situation.[102] The success in integration also varies greatly by immigrant group, as illustrated by post-Second World War British migration. By the 1990s, among Asian immigrants the Chinese (and especially those from Malaysia, Taiwan and Singapore) had become the group most successful in economic terms. Indians were also considered thriving, but this group was stratified. Pakistanis were seen as less prosperous, and the least successful was the Bangladeshi immigrant community – also based on per capita income.[103]

Another important fact to keep in mind is that immigrants significantly improve the chances of mobility for the native-born population. This is because immigrants usually take jobs with lower status and lower earnings than the native population, as a result of their poor language skills and lack of knowledge of the local culture. For instance, in the late 1980s in France, 69% of foreigners were blue-collar workers, whereas this ratio was only 30% in the host population.[104] This made it possible for a considerable portion of the host population to move up the social ladder.

The population of Europe today: a second transition?

The last two decades have witnessed significant changes in the demographic conditions of Europe, which affected fertility, mortality and migration alike. The current demographic changes are often interpreted in the framework of the so-called second demographic transition.[105]

Framing recent population changes

The concept of the second demographic transition was proposed by Dirk J. van de Kaa and Ron Lesthaeghe. They claim that the fundamental characteristic of this era is that fertility drops below the total fertility rate necessary for net reproduction (which is ca. 2.1 in Europe) and thus it cannot secure the endogenous replacement of population, that is, long-term balance of births and deaths.[106] The transition began roughly in the mid-1960s, when the baby boom ended and fertility showed radical changes in most of the Western European countries. All this, according to van de Kaa, corresponds to value changes in society, the most important of which are individualization discussed earlier and the transformation of traditional gender roles. Van de Kaa characterized the shifts in norms and values as a transition from 'altruistic' to 'individualistic' orientation. In this view, the declining fertility of the first half of the twentieth century was primarily the result of the growing responsibility for the family and offspring, whereas in contrast, the declining fertility of the second demographic transition occurring at the end of the century was brought about by an increasing emphasis on the self-realization of the individual. Marriage and, especially, childrearing demands an investment of material resources and time that hinders the realization of career, leisure and consumption objectives of the individual. Individualism, then, means that these objectives gain more importance in the life of the individual than before and consequently modifications emerge in nuptiality and family structure, as well as new family forms becoming widespread. Truly, as is discussed in the next chapter, from the 1960s, fewer people entered marriage and their average age at marriage was on the rise, which delayed the birth of the first child and shortened the length of the period that women spent in marriage while still at childbearing age. A further change was the pluralization of marriage and family forms, primarily seen in rising ratios of divorce, cohabitation without marriage, births outside marriage and single parenting. New methods of contraception, simpler and safer than ever before, made it possible to separate sexuality from childbearing. In addition, women entered the work force in growing proportions, whereas there emerged obvious conflicts and tensions between a full career and childbearing. All these had marked influences on fertility.

These phenomena characterized the population history of the whole of Europe in the late twentieth century, but the dynamics of changes varied by each society to a great extent. Fertility began to decline rapidly in Western Europe from the 1960s, with the pace of the decline slowing down in the 1980s. At the turn of the millennium, total fertility rates above 1.7 were observed in France, Ireland and the Netherlands, whereas the lowest figures of around 1.3 were found in Germany and Southern Europe. In former communist countries, the regime change was the turning point after which fertility dropped drastically, and today, with the exception of Albania, these countries belong among the ones with the lowest fertility, with total fertility rates between 1.2 and 1.3.

Nevertheless, the concept of the second demographic transition remains a contested one.[107] Now, no critical scholarly opinion seriously questions the significance of the mentioned changes in demography and family development. Moreover, it has not been systematically and thoroughly refuted either that the final decades of the twentieth century constitute a new demographic phase, primarily because the causes of changes, especially the ones behind fertility decline, are fundamentally different from determinants observed earlier. At the same time, it is doubtful whether this concept is the most appropriate one for describing these phenomena. As one of its critics, David Coleman, plausibly argued, the second demographic transition is not 'second', because it cannot be clearly distinguished from the first; it is not 'demographic', because it also entails several other changes (in culture, in family structure, in economy, etc.); and, most of all, it is no 'transition', because the end point of the process cannot be identified.[108]

Mortality

Changes in mortality do not belong to the key elements of the model of the second demographic transition, even though the improvement of mortality continued in Western and Southern Europe through the 1990s. The mortality indicators of former communist countries (having stagnated or deteriorated before) underwent differential changes. In some countries (Slovenia, Poland, the Czech Republic), there came a period of rapid progress. In Hungary, an improvement began from the mid-1990s, but the change was slow. In several South-Eastern European countries (and especially in the Soviet successor states not discussed here), the deterioration persisted even before the turn of the millennium, so that the gap between these countries and Western Europe was widening until recently. The main reason behind this is that in Western Europe the rapid improvement of health care (especially regarding the prevention and treatment of cardiovascular and cancerous diseases) was accompanied by a favourable mass scale change in the health lifestyle of the population. This did not occur in the given group of ex-communist countries.

Migration pressure

The migration pressure on Europe (particularly on Western and Southern Europe) has significantly increased in the past two decades.[109] This can be unanimously seen in the growth of the number of residents of foreign origin in 18 European countries under examination from 16.0 million to 20.4 million between 1990 and 2000.[110] Also, these figures greatly underestimate actual immigration, because they exclude illegal immigrants and also disregard immigrants who obtained citizenship in the meantime. The number of naturalizations was 5.8 million in the EU between 1992 and 2002. Numbers were especially high in France and Germany, with ethnic Germans arriving from East Central and Eastern Europe (*Aussiedler*), who constituted a considerable share of the migrant population in the latter.[111]

Turning to temporal changes, the number of immigrants dropped in the early 1980s, then the migration flow accelerated again in the few years after 1988. In the last years of the century, the pace of immigration slowed down again. The largest host countries are traditionally Germany and France, but the proportion of foreigners living in Switzerland, Austria and Belgium was high as well at the turn of the millennium (Table 2.7).

As regards the origin of migrants, one-third of the foreigners living in Western Europe are citizens of other Western European countries. About one-fifth are from Turkey and the territory of the former Yugoslavia, and another fifth are from Africa. Asians and East Central/Eastern Europeans amount to one-tenth each.[112] Since 1990, the ratio of those arriving from the former Yugoslavia and East Central and Eastern Europe has increased in the greatest degree. This also means that around the turn of the century, the intra-European East–West migration increased, which received further impetus from the countries of the region joining the EU, even though the flow did not reach the mass scale anticipated by many. Although the EU has declared the right of its citizens to settle and work in all other EU countries (a right that can be restricted only temporarily even for new members), it does not guarantee political and social rights (i.e. full citizenship to settlers).[113]

Another important structural change compared with earlier decades was that from the 1980s, the ratio of political refugees grew considerably. In 1991, the number of refugees in Western Europe was twice that of foreigners arriving with the primary objective to find better employment.[114] This situation emerged despite only less than 10% of those applying for asylum being granted it on the average. The origin of the refugees had changed over time, mostly in accordance with political changes and wars in the world and especially in the proximity of Europe.[115]

Changes in the age structure

The demographic transformations discussed above initiated changes in the age structure of the European population that have lately attracted growing attention both in the media and in politics. If fewer children are born, and, at the same time, people live longer, there is a twofold pressure on the age distribution of the population, which results in a move toward ageing. The Western European experiences of current decades show that immigration only lessened the dimensions of this process but did not fully counterbalance it.[116]

In the early twentieth century, the age profile of European societies resembled a pyramid, in which the majority of the population was comprised of younger generations and any deformation of the triangle shape was the result of missed births and surplus deaths brought about by wars. However, by the end of the century, in most societies, the image of the age distribution was more like a tree, or (as some put it and not without intending an allusion) an urn. The narrow base indicated smaller numbers in younger generations, whereas in the upper regions of the age profile, a peculiar peak emerged. Particularly the ratio of over-80-year-olds has grown in the last decades: for example, in 1950 in Germany they amounted to 1% of the population and to 3.8% in 1995.

The ageing process obviously has significant social consequences, similarly to the transformation of family structures, which are discussed in the next chapter. Suffice to mention here that the aged are the greatest receivers of social benefits (primarily pension and health care) and thus the growth of their ratio affects the demand for welfare services as well. In the last one or two decades, this process has often appeared in debates on European welfare states as a factor overburdening public finances and thus making the retrenchment of the welfare state inevitable. However, the impact of the shifts in the age structure on the European welfare states has not been as immediate and direct as often claimed and will not necessarily be as straightforward in the near future, either. Although the ratio of the aged grew within the population throughout Europe, the change of the age structure had no significant effects until the turn of the millennium. On the one hand, the ratio of young dependants decreased in the population, and thus at the end of the twentieth century, the ratio of all dependants in the population was smaller than a hundred years before in most countries. On the other hand, the nature of old age as a life-stage changed also. It is no longer the synonym of illness, and many elderly people stay active economically and socially; they are not only consumers of resources but contribute to the creation of wealth and welfare in a variety of ways: employment, volunteering, helping their families. True, when in the coming decades the Western European baby-boom generation reaches old age, and when in East Central Europe the small post-regime change generations will comprise those in working age, there may be an aggregation of the difficulties in financing the pension system. The decline of the proportion of the active population necessarily results in either a decrease in the relative value of the benefits (compared with earnings), or an increase in contributions and taxes, or some combination of the two. However, it must be emphasized that only a relative decrease will most probably occur, because the dividend of future economic growth must also be taken into account. In addition, even if the transformation of the age structure has unfavourable effects on the sustainability of welfare programs, it does not necessarily lead to the erosion of welfare benefits by itself. The future direction of welfare state transformation also depends on the economic and labour market situation and, most of all, political conditions that largely determine decisions on the size of redistribution.[117] These and other issues of the development of European welfare states are discussed in detail in chapter 5.

3

FAMILIES AND HOUSEHOLDS

The family is a social institution related to biological reproduction (birth, ageing and death) as well as to crucial social and economic processes (the socialization of children, the production of goods, services and welfare, etc.). It is also affected by demographic changes, social policies, cultural values and religious institutions. Several of these aspects surface in the definition of the family: it is a close domestic group consisting of people related to each other by bonds of descent, sexual mating and/or legal relationship.[1] The formation and functioning of the family is biologically determined (if nothing else, everyone has parents); however, these aptitudes are fundamentally influenced by the above-mentioned social and cultural factors. As a result, diverse family forms emerge from the same biological foundations, and family arrangements are greatly varied in time and space. Yet, some version of the family has been present in all societies throughout history, making family an institution equally characterized by a remarkable adaptability, that is, change, and resilience.[2]

It is important to differentiate the family, based on kinship, from the household, primarily defined by its functions. A household comprises a single person living alone or group of persons sharing a living accommodation, aggregating and distributing their individual incomes, most clearly indicated by the fact that they routinely have meals together. Consequently, a household may be identical with a family, but not necessarily. On the one hand, there are one-person or solitary households, which do not qualify as families and, on the other hand, non-family members, such as servants, may belong to a household, a situation especially frequent in earlier times.[3]

Although the diversity of family configurations is a fundamental fact of family history, in addition to examining differences and providing a perspective on their change over time, the identification of similar patterns is also among the major tasks of the discipline of family history, which has become one of the most frequented branches of social history since the 1960s. The systematic historical study of the family as we know it today originated from various approaches emerging from the 1950s. The first major source was population research. French demographers provided historians with the tool of family reconstitution that enabled them to establish the past patterns of fertility, nuptiality and mortality based on an extensive number of demographic events, and to follow these phenomena over several generations. British researchers, and most notably Peter Laslett, went further than the originators of the method, concentrating on demographic patterns. They established family as well as household patterns from mass demographic data and interpreted them in relation to economic and social institutions.[4] Another pioneer of the discipline was Philippe Ariès, whose book *Centuries of Childhood*, published in 1960, plausibly and imaginatively used cultural evidence while studying the family, and, in particular, the attitudes towards children within the family and society at large.[5] In the footprints of Ariès and following the Annales tradition, several family historians linked the study of demographic patterns to changes in family patterns and sexual behaviour, thus relating social and cultural phenomena to *mentalité*. A further major drive for the emergence of modern family history was the study of nineteenth century urban residential conditions in England and the United States, which integrated census data into the study of household and family patterns, and related them to several other types of sources.[6] Although these developments clearly gave impetus to the study of family in early modern and modern Europe, more recent family history has always integrated perspectives and methods from family sociology to a large extent. One strand of sociological research influencing historical approaches was the interaction between family and work. Because in recent decades there have been claims in industrial societies that the family is in decline and even the desirability of its survival has been questioned, family sociology and family history have also made efforts to analyse the dissolution of families and the emergence of new or atypical family arrangements.

In the following, the most important aspects of family development in twentieth-century Europe are discussed. First, the historical patterns of family formation are outlined; then, changes in European family and household structures are addressed; third, the interpersonal relationships between family members and the attitudes towards children are examined; fourth, a separate section is devoted to the process of the pluralization of family forms; and finally, recent European changes in family patterns are discussed.

Marriage patterns: on the two sides of the Hajnal line

In his influential study of 1965, Hungarian-born English demographer John Hajnal argued that historical marriage patterns had two main types in Europe, emerging from the late Middle Ages. West of the St Petersburg–Trieste line, there existed the 'European marriage pattern', whereas east of it, a different type of family formation can be observed, which basically conforms to nuptiality found in other parts of the world, and which therefore Hajnal considered the 'non-European marriage pattern'. The European or, rather, the Western European marriage pattern was characterized by a relatively late age at first marriage and by a high ratio of lifelong celibacy, that is, of those never marrying. In Western Europe, typical average ages of marriage in early modern rural communities were 27–28 for men and 25–26 for women, and between the seventeenth and mid-nineteenth century, there is no evidence of any significant change. After the mid-nineteenth century, an even further rise in average age of marriage is evident in many parts of Western Europe. As to lifelong celibacy, before 1800, the characteristic proportions of the never-married population were around 10%, but in some regions in the later nineteenth century, ratios climbed up to 20% and even above. As opposed to this pattern, in much of East Central Europe people entered marriage when relatively young and only a small proportion of the population stayed single.[7]

Hajnal's data ran roughly to the end of the nineteenth century, but the model arguably remained valid in Europe at least until the mid-twentieth century. Nevertheless, there also occurred significant and specific transformations in marriage patterns in twentieth-century European societies. The average age at which people entered their first marriage all over Western Europe around the turn of the twentieth century (circa 28 years for men and 26 for women) was high when compared with the societies of other continents or to other regions in East Central and South-Eastern Europe, and it essentially persisted even in the interwar period. However, after the Second World War, the average age at first marriage decreased significantly: by 2–3 years for men and by 3–4 years for women in most Western European countries between 1950 and 1970. This was another signal of the renaissance of marriage and family; the sudden rise of birth rates and their stabilization at this high level for more than a decade after 1950 was discussed in the previous chapter. Then, usually from the mid-1970s, the age at first marriage rapidly increased again, and by the late 1980s, the Western European mean was at the same level as in the early twentieth century. In the two periods, the same countries can be only partially found at the extreme ends of the scale. At the beginning of the century, Irish, French and German men and Irish, Austrian and German women were the oldest when entering marriage, whereas at the end of the century it was Danish, Swedish and Swiss women and men. At the turn of the twentieth century in Western Europe, the youngest at first marriage were Finnish women and men, but at the end of the century Belgian, British and Austrian women, and British, Belgian and Finnish men occupied this position (Tables 3.1 and 3.2).

Lifelong celibacy, which is captured in statistics by the ratio of those never married in the cohort of 45–54-year-olds, showed a similar tendency in Western Europe, although it must be noted that this indicator follows changes in nuptiality with a lag of several decades.[8] At the turn of the century, celibacy fluctuated between 8% and 28% for men and 10% and 24% for women, with the lowest levels found in Germany for both sexes and the highest ones in Ireland. In most Western European societies, the rate of lifelong singles declined among men in the first half of the twentieth century, whereas stagnation or a small-scale increase can be observed for women. From the 1950s, except for Denmark, a further decrease ensued among men, and there was an even more significant decline regarding celibacy among women in every country. The advancement of the process is clearly indicated by

TABLE 3.1 Average age of women at first marriage in European countries, 1900–1990 (year)

	1900	1910	1920	1930	1940	1950	1960	1970	1980	1990
United Kingdom	25.8	26.0	26	25.7	25	22.1	21.3	22.4	23.0	25.0
France	25			23		23	23.0	22.6	23.0	25.6
Netherlands	26	26	26	25.4	26	24.7	24.9	22.9	23.2	25.9
Belgium	25.4	24.8	25.3	23.6		23.4	21.9	22.4	22.3	24.3
Ireland			29			26.7	25.2	25.3	24.7	26.5
Germany/FRG	25.5	25.3	26.1	26.2	24.5	24.5	22.8	22.5	22.9	25.3
Austria	27			25		24.5	23.3	22.9	23.2	24.9
Switzerland				27.1	26.2	24.7	23.6	24.2	25.1	26.8
Sweden						22.0	22.5	23.9	26.0	27.5
Denmark						21.8	21.6	22.8	24.6	27.6
Norway	26	26	25	26.7	26	23.6	21.4	22.8	23.5	26.3
Finland	25		25	25	25	22.7	22.5	23.4	24.4	25.0
Italy	24	24	25	24	25	24.6	24.2	23.9	23.9	25.6
Spain	24.5	25.1	25.7	25.8	26.7	26.5	25.0	23.7	23.1	
Poland	23.6			24.9			21.9	22.6	22.8	
Czechoslovakia	25.4			24.8		23.0	21.1	21.4	21.7	
Hungary	22.5	22.3	23.6	23.8	23.0	22.8	21.9	21.0	21.3	21.5
Romania	20.3	21.7						20.2	21.1	
Serbia/Yugoslavia	20.1			21.7		22.3	22.1	21.3	22.2	
Bulgaria	20.8	20.9	21.5	21.6		20.9	20.7	20.8		

Notes: United Kingdom 1900–1960: England and Wales; Poland 1900: German, Russian and Austrian territories later becoming parts of Poland; Czechoslovakia 1900: Bohemia, Moravia and Silesia; Hungary: present territory; Different periods: United Kingdom: 1901, 1911, 1931; Belgium: 1947, 1957; Germany: 1925, 1933, 1939; Switzerland: 1941; Norway: 1946; Poland: 1931, 1978, 1984; Czechoslovakia: 1947; Hungary: 1941, 1948; Romania: 1899, 1912, 1966, 1977; Yugoslavia: 1931; Bulgaria: 1926, 1934, 1956, 1965, 1975.

Sources: Hartmut Kaelble, *A Social History of Western Europe, 1880–1980*, Dublin: Gill and Macmillan, 1989, 16 (Western Europe 1900–1940, unless indicated otherwise; France 1950); Eurostat, ed., *Bevölkerungsstatistik: Daten, 1995–1998*, Luxembourg: Eurostat, 1999 (Western Europe 1960–1990); Council of Europe, ed., *Recent Demographic Developments in Europe*, 1996, S. l., 1996, 35 (United Kingdom 1970–1990); *Patterns of First Marriage: Timing and Prevalence*, New York: United Nations, 1990, 9 (Czechoslovakia 1900, 1930, 1947; Bulgaria 1900–1934), 10 (United Kingdom 1901, 1910, 1931; Norway 1930, 1946; Poland 1900, 1931; Romania 1899–1912; Serbia 1900, Yugoslavia 1931–1948), 11 (Belgium 1900–1947; Germany 1900–1939; Netherlands 1930; Switzerland 1930–1941; Spain 1900–1940), 224 (England and Wales 1950–1960; Ireland 1950–1960; Sweden 1950–1960; Denmark 1950–1960; Norway 1950–1960; Finland 1950–1960; Italy 1950–1960; Spain 1950–1980; Poland 1960–1984; Czechoslovakia 1947–1980; Romania 1966–1977; Yugoslavia 1950–1980; Bulgaria 1956–1975); Józsefné Csernák, 'Házasság és válás Magyarországon', in *Magyarország történeti demográfiája (896–1995)*, Budapest: KSH, 1997, 352 (Hungary 1900–1930); *Time Series of Historical Statistics, 1867–1992*, Budapest: KSH, 1993, 130 (Hungary 1941–1990).

the fact that between 1950 and 1970 in Norway the number of unmarried females in the 45–54 age group fell from 20.7% to 9%, in Sweden from 19.1% to 8%, and in England and Wales from 15.1% to 8%. In other countries, the scale of the change was smaller, but it also started from lower initial levels. From the 1970s, the ratio of never-married women continued to decrease, because this was the

TABLE 3.2 Average age of men at first marriage in European countries, 1900–1990 (year)

	1900	1910	1920	1930	1940	1950	1960	1970	1980	1990
United Kingdom	27.2	27.5	28	27.0	27	26	25.1	24.0	25.2	27.2
France	31			27		26.3	26.4	24.7	25.1	27.5
Netherlands	28	28	28	27.3	28	27.5	25.9	25.0	25.5	28.2
Belgium	27.3	27.0	27.2	25.9	26.5	26.5	24.7	24.4	24.3	26.3
Ireland			35			31.3	29.5	27.4	27.1	28.3
Germany/FRG	27.8	27.9	27.5	28.3	28.2	27.7	26.2	24.9	25.7	27.9
Austria	30			28		27.7	26.4	25.6	25.9	27.4
Switzerland				28.7	29.2	28.1	27.0	26.5	27.4	29.2
Sweden						27.1	26.4	26.4	28.6	29.9
Denmark						26.5	25.6	25.3	27.2	30.0
Norway	28	28	28	29.7	28.8	27.9	26.2	25.5	26.2	28.7
Finland	27	27	28	28	28	26.0	26.1	25.3	26.5	27.0
Italy	28	27	29	27	28.3	28.7	28.5	27.4	27.1	28.6
Spain	27.4	27.8	27.9	27.2	29.4	29.0	28.3	27.5	26.0	
Poland	26.6			26.9			25.3	25.7	25.9	
Czechoslovakia	27.4			27.3		27.4	25.2	24.6	24.7	
Hungary	26.4	26.2	26.7	26.8	27.5	26.4	25.3	24.0	24.0	24.2
Romania	24.5							24.5	24.9	
Serbia/Yugoslavia	23.0			24.4		22.1		24.9	26.1	
Bulgaria	24.2			23.9		24.0	24.2	24.5		

Notes: United Kingdom 1900–1970: England and Wales; Hungary: present territory; Different years: United Kingdom: 1901, 1911, 1931; France: 1954, 1962; the Netherlands: 1947; Belgium: 1947; Germany: 1925, 1933, 1939; Switzerland: 1941; Norway: 1946; Italy: 1936; Czechoslovakia: 1947; Poland: 1931, 1978, 1984; Hungary: 1941, 1948; Romania: 1899, 1966, 1977; Yugoslavia: 1931, 1948; Bulgaria: 1934, 1956, 1965, 1975.

Sources: Hartmut Kaelble, *A Social History of Western Europe, 1880–1980,* Dublin: Gill and Macmillan, 1989, 16 (Western Europe 1900–1940, unless indicated otherwise); Eurostat, ed., *Bevölkerungsstatistik: Daten, 1995–1998,* Luxembourg: Eurostat, 1999 (Western Europe 1960–1990); *Patterns of First Marriage: Timing and Prevalence,* New York: United Nations, 1990, 9 (Czechoslovakia 1900–1947; Bulgaria 1900, 1934), 10 (United Kingdom 1901, 1911, 1931; Norway 1930, 1946; Poland 1900, 1931; Romania 1899; Serbia 1900, Yugoslavia 1931, 1948), 11 (Belgium 1900–1947, Germany 1900–1939; Netherlands 1930; Switzerland 1930–1941; Italy 1936; Spain 1900–1940), 223 (England and Wales 1950–1960; Ireland 1950–1960; France 1954–1962; Belgium 1947–1960; Netherlands 1947–1960; FRG 1950–1960; Austria 1950–60; Switzerland 1950–1960; Sweden 1950–1960; Denmark 1950–1960; Norway 1950–1960; Finland 1950–1960; Italy 1950–1960; Spain 1950–1980; Czechoslovakia 1947–1980; Poland 1960–1984; Romania 1966–1977; Yugoslavia 1970–1980; Bulgaria 1956–1975); Józsefné Csernák, 'Házasság és válás Magyarországon', in *Magyarország történeti demográfiája (896–1995),* Budapest: KSH, 1997, 352 (Hungary 1900–1930); *Time Series of Historical Statistics, 1867–1992,* Budapest: KSH, 1993, 130 (Hungary 1941–1990).

period when those in their twenties in the 1950s, the decade characterized by booming marriage rates, entered the cohort of 45–54-year-olds under examination here. However, this process did not affect men, because by this time, their indicators had been more or less stagnating. As a result, for the first time in the century, female celibacy dropped below male rates: in 1990, the average for men in Western European societies was 10.7% and for women 7.1% (Tables 3.3 and 3.4).

TABLE 3.3 Male celibacy in European countries, 1900–1990 (ratio of never-married men in the age group of 45–54, %)

	1900	1910	1920	1930	1940	1950	1960	1970	1980	1990
United Kingdom	11.0	12.1	12.0	10.8	9.5	9.3	9.2	9.2	8.9	9.0
France	10.6	10.7	9.1	9.1	8.7	8.9	10.7	10.2	10.8	8.9
Netherlands	12.8	12.7	12.0	10.8		8.7	7.6	6.7	8.2	7.8
Belgium	15.9	14.5	13.0	10.5		8.5	9.1	8.0	8.1	8.0
Ireland		28.6		31.4	33.5	31.0	29.7	28.1	22.5	15.8
Germany	8.5	8.2	6.5	6.0	6.1	6.1	4.9	4.5	7.3	9.3
Austria	11.1	16.8	14.7	11.4	10.0	9.3	7.9	6.7	7.3	9.7
Switzerland	15.9	15.2	14.6	13.8	13.4	13.0	11.8	9.8	8.7	9.8
Sweden	12.7	14.3	15.3	15.8	16.1	15.7	14.4	13.4	10.9	16.2
Denmark	8.3	9.1	9.5	9.1	9.2	9.3	9.5	9.4	9.2	10.6
Norway	10.9	11.9	12.2	13.9		15.1	13.3	12.5	10.9	9.8
Finland	13.6	15.8	19.1	25.5	26.9	11.8	10.1	11.1	13.6	13.9
Italy	11.3	10.7	10.6	9.5	9.2	8.7	8.9	10.9	8.8	10.4
Spain	6.4	6.6	7.5	7.6	8.2	9.0	8.4	8.2	9.4	
Poland	6.1		5.0	4.2			3.9	4.3	5.3	
Czechoslovakia		6.2	6.5	6.0		5.3	5.3	5.2	5.7	
Hungary	4.9	5.8	5.2	5.0	5.8	6.0	5.4	4.1	5.0	6.1
Romania	5.0							2.6	2.2	
Serbia/Yugoslavia	3.0			4.9		5.3		3.6	3.8	
Bulgaria	3.0			2.9			1.9	1.6	1.9	

Notes: Western Europe 1980–1990: 45–49-year-old cohort, 1900–1970: 45–54-year-old cohort; United Kingdom 1901–1971: England and Wales; Ireland 1911: the territory of the later republic; France 1921, Austria 1920: 50–59-year-old cohort; Austria 1910: the territory of the later republic; Austria 1939: 40–49-year-old cohort; Spain 1900–1940: 46–50-year-old cohort; Czechoslovakia 1910–1921: Bohemia, Moravia and Silesia, 40–49-year-old cohort; Czechoslovakia, Poland 1900–1931: 45–49-year-old cohort unless indicated otherwise; Poland 1900: German, Russian and Austrian territories later becoming parts of Poland, 40–49-year-old cohort; Yugoslavia 1931–1948: 50–54-year-old cohort; Spain, Romania, Yugoslavia, Bulgaria: 45–49-year-old cohort unless indicated otherwise; Belgium 1980, Austria 1980, Czechoslovakia 1947–1980, Poland 1960–1980, Romania 1966–1977, Yugoslavia 1970–1980, Bulgaria 1956–1975: ratio of those married by the age of 50; Hungary 1910–1920, 1980–1990: 45–49-year-old cohort; 1900, 1930–1970: 45–54-year-old cohort; Different years: England and Wales: 1901, 1911, 1921, 1931, 1939, 1951, 1961, 1971; United Kingdom: 1982; France: 1901, 1911, 1921, 1931, 1936, 1946, 1962, 1968; the Netherlands: 1899, 1909, 1947; Belgium: 1947, 1961, 1991; Ireland: 1911, 1926, 1936, 1951, 1961, 1971, 1981; Germany: 1925, 1933, 1939, 1961; Austria: 1934, 1939, 1951, 1961, 1971, 1991; Switzerland: 1941; Denmark: 1901, 1911, 1921, 1935; Finland: 1991; Italy: 1901, 1911, 1921, 1931, 1936, 1951, 1961, 1971, 1991; Czechoslovakia: 1921, 1947; Poland: 1921, 1931, 1978; Hungary: 1941, 1949; Yugoslavia: 1931, 1948; Romania: 1899, 1966, 1977; Bulgaria: 1934, 1956, 1965, 1975.

Sources: Peter Flora, ed., *State, Economy, and Society in Western Europe*, vol. II, Frankfurt: Campus, 1987, 214–215 (Austria 1900–1970), 216–217 (Belgium 1900–1970), 218–219 (Denmark 1901–1970), 220–221 (Finland 1900–1970), 222–223 (France 1901–1968), 224–225 (Germany 1900–1970), 226–227 (Ireland 1911–1971), 228–229 (Italy 1901–1971), 230–231 (the Netherlands 1899–1970), 232–233 (Norway 1900–1970), 234–235 (Sweden 1900–1970), 236–237 (Switzerland 1900–1970), 238–239 (England–Wales 1901–1971); United Nations, ed., *Demographic Yearbook. 1990*, New York: United Nations, 1992, 540–543 (Western Europe 1980); United Nations, ed., *Demographic Yearbook. 1995*, New York: United Nations, 1997, 569–572 (Western Europe 1990); Eurostat, ed., *Population, Households and Dwellings in Europe: Main Results of the 1990/1991 Censuses*, Brussels–Luxembourg: Eurostat, 1996, 20–24 (Italy 1991); *Patterns of First Marriage: Timing and Prevalence*, New York: United Nations, 1990, 9 (England and Wales 1939; Czechoslovakia 1910–1930; Bulgaria 1900, 1934), 10 (Poland 1900–1931; Romania 1899; Serbia 1900; Yugoslavia 1931–1948), 11 (Austria 1939, Spain 1900–1940), 235 (Belgium 1980, Austria 1980, Czechoslovakia 1947–1980, Poland 1960–1980, Romania 1966–1977, Yugoslavia 1970–1980, Bulgaria 1956–1975); *Time Series of Historical Statistics, 1867–1992*, Budapest: KSH, 1993, 6–7, 11, 13 (Hungary 1900–1990, author's calculations).

TABLE 3.4 Female celibacy in European countries, 1900–2000 (ratio of never-married women in the age group of 45–54, %)

	1900	1910	1920	1930	1940	1950	1960	1970	1980	1990	2000
United Kingdom	13.6	15.8	16.4	16.4	16.7	15.1	11.4	8.0	5.7	4.9	7.3
France	11.5	11.2	10.9	10.9	11.5	12.2	9.1	8.7	7.3	7.1	10.3
Netherlands	14.0	15.0	15.2	14.9		13.3	11.4	8.4	6.3	5.2	7.4
Belgium	16.8	16.4	15.4	13.3		10.6	9.2	7.8	6.0	5.1	6.3
Ireland		24.0		23.9	25.1	25.7	23.1	18.8	13.4	10.3	10.9
Germany	10.3	10.7	10.4	11.5	13.2	12.6	9.6	9.9	6.4	5.2	7.3
Austria	13.3	12.3	16.6	17.0	18.0	14.3	12.2	11.3	8.7	7.6	8.7
Switzerland	17.4	17.8	17.7	17.9	19.7	19.2	15.9	12.6	9.4	8.8	10.1
Sweden	18.9	20.7	22.2	22.5	22.2	19.1	12.3	8.0	5.8	9.7	16.4
Denmark	13.1	14.7	15.6	15.6	15.5	14.1	10.3	7.1	5.3	5.5	9.8
Norway	17.8	19.9	20.8	21.8		20.7	14.3	9.0	5.3	5.6	8.1
Finland	14.9	16.2	19.7	24.6	28.0	19.0	15.0	12.3	10.3	9.9	12.8
Italy	11.2	10.9	11.7	12.4	13.1	14.8	13.8	13.9	9.6	7.9	8.1
Spain	10.2	10.2	10.6	11.7	13.7	14.9	14.0	12.7	10.1		13.0
Poland	7.8		8.2	7.1			9.1	7.8	5.9	4.8	6.0
Czechoslovakia		8.5	8.9	6.0		9.2	6.5	5.1	3.7	3.5	3.3/6.7
Hungary	4.8	5.7	5.5	6.1	8.0	8.2	7.3	5.6	3.8	3.8	4.4
Romania	3.0							4.0	3.6		
Serbia/Yugoslavia	1.0			4.7		5.8	6.1	5.9	5.0		
Bulgaria	1.0			1.4			2.1	2.1	2.1		

Notes: Western Europe 1980–1990: 45–49-year-old cohort, 1900–1970: 45–54-year-old cohort; United Kingdom 1901–1971: England and Wales; United Kingdom 2000: England; France 1921, Austria 1920: 50–59-year-old cohort; Ireland 1911: the territory of the later republic; Germany 2000: the territory of former West Germany; Austria 1910: the territory of the later republic; Austria 1939: 40–49-year-old cohort; Czechoslovakia 1910–1921: Bohemia, Moravia and Silesia, 40–49-year-old cohort; Czechoslovakia, Poland 1900–1931: 45–49-year-old cohort unless indicated otherwise; Poland 1900: German, Russian and Austrian territories later becoming parts of Poland, 40–49-year-old cohort; Bulgaria, Yugoslavia, Romania, Spain: 45–49-year-old cohort unless indicated otherwise; Czechoslovakia 1947–1980, Poland 1960–1980, Romania 1966–1977, Bulgaria 1956–1975, Yugoslavia 1960–1980: ratio of those married by the age of 50; Czechoslovakia 2000: Czech Republic/Slovakia; Hungary 1910–1920, 1980–1990: 45–49-year-old cohort, 1900, 1930–1970: 45–54-year-old cohort; Yugoslavia 1931–1948: 50–54-year-old cohort; Different periods: England and Wales: 1901, 1911, 1921, 1931, 1951, 1961, 1971; United Kingdom: 1939, 1982; France: 1901, 1911, 1921, 1931, 1936, 1946, 1962, 1968; the Netherlands: 1899, 1909, 1947; Belgium: 1947, 1961, 1991; Ireland: 1911, 1926, 1936, 1951, 1961, 1971, 1981; Germany: 1925, 1933, 1939, 1961; Austria: 1934, 1939, 1951, 1961, 1971, 1991; Switzerland: 1941; Denmark: 1901, 1911, 1921, 1935; Finland: 1991; Italy: 1901, 1911, 1921, 1931, 1936, 1951, 1961, 1971, 1991; Czechoslovakia: 1921; Poland: 1921, 1931; Hungary: 1941, 1949; Yugoslavia: 1931, 1948; Romania: 1899, 1966, 1977; Bulgaria: 1934, 1956, 1965, 1975; the whole of Europe 2000: at the time of the nearest census.

Sources: Peter Flora, ed., *State, Economy, and Society in Western Europe*, vol. II, Frankfurt: Campus, 1987, 214–215 (Austria 1900–1970), 216–217 (Belgium 1900–1970), 218–219 (Denmark 1901–1970), 220–221 (Finland 1900–1970), 222–223 (France 1901–1968), 224–225 (Germany 1900–1970), 226–227 (Ireland 1911–1971), 228–229 (Italy 1901–1971), 230–231 (the Netherlands 1899–1970), 232–233 (Norway 1900–1970), 234–235 (Sweden 1900–1970), 236–237 (Switzerland 1900–1970), 238–239 (England–Wales 1901–1971); United Nations, ed., *Demographic Yearbook. 1990*, New York: United Nations, 1992, 540–543 (Western Europe 1980); United Nations, ed., *Demographic Yearbook. 1995*, New York: United Nations, 1997, 569–572 (Western Europe 1990); Eurostat, ed., *Population, Households and Dwellings in Europe: Main Results of the 1990/1991 Censuses*, Brussels–Luxembourg: Eurostat, 1996, 20–24 (Italy 1991); Franz Rothenbacher, *The European Population since 1945*, Houndmills: Palgrave, 2005, 33 (Belgium 1980, Austria 1980, Italy 1980, Spain 1950–1980, Czechoslovakia 1950–1990, Poland 1960–2000; the whole of Europe 2000); *Patterns of First Marriage: Timing and Prevalence*, New York: United Nations, 1990, 9 (Czechoslovakia 1910–1930, Bulgaria 1900, 1934), 10 (England and Wales 1939, Norway 1946, Poland 1900–1931, Romania 1899, Serbia 1900, Yugoslavia 1931–1948), 11 (Austria 1939, Spain 1900–1940), 235 (Czechoslovakia 1947–1980, Poland 1960–1980, Bulgaria 1956–1975, Romania 1966–1977, Yugoslavia 1960–1980); Eurostat, *European Social Statistics: Demography*, Luxembourg: Eurostat, 2000, Table F11 (Spain 2000, Czech Republic/Slovakia 2000); *Time Series of Historical Statistics, 1867–1992*, Budapest: KSH, 1993, 8–9, 12, 14 (Hungary 1900–1990, author's calculations).

The index of lifelong celibacy plausibly identifies long-term shifts in nuptiality, but, as noted before, it is less sensitive concerning short-term variations. Indicators reacting more directly, such as the total first marriage rate, show that in most Western European countries, rapid changes began in the marriage propensity of young people from the 1970s – similarly to what was seen for the average age at first marriage. Nuptiality considerably declined in every country in the 1970s; it plummeted the most in the Netherlands. This process continued in the 1980s in most countries, although the pace of decline slowed down. Furthermore, in the two Scandinavian countries with low willingness to marry (Denmark and Sweden), there was a slight rise in marriage figures at this time.[9]

The differences among Western European countries in the mean age at first marriage were at their lowest in the 1930s and 1940s, but then they increased again, so that by the 1980s, they were on the same scale as they had been at the turn of the century. As regards the ratio of those never marrying, the variation increased until the 1960s (men) and 1970s (women), and then a relatively large-scale unification followed. Despite the latter process, the differences were still greater in 1990 than they had been in 1950.[10]

Although deviating from a strict obedience to the St Petersburg–Trieste line, we can see that marriage patterns at the turn of the twentieth century conformed to Hajnal's 'non-European' type. However, they did so not only in Eastern and South-Eastern Europe, but also in East Central Europe, even if they constituted only a moderate version, rather than a full manifestation of the type.[11] In these regions, marriage was entered at a younger age and was almost universal. In 1900, the average age at marriage for women was 20.8 years in Bulgaria and 24 years in Poland; for men, it was 24.2 and 26.6, respectively. In the Balkans, only 1–3% of women and 5–6% of men did not marry in their lifetime, and the celibacy rate in East Central Europe was only slightly higher than these figures (Tables 3.1–3.4).

In the first decades of the twentieth century, Hajnal's 'non-European' or Eastern European marriage pattern faded in East Central Europe, although there was no marked change in the Balkans.[12] After the Second World War, conforming to West European and North American trends, the already high willingness to marry further heightened in these regions. The ratio of those entering marriage increased, especially among those widowed or divorced, and the average age of those entering their first marriage lowered. Furthermore, whereas in Western Europe there was a kind of turn in nuptiality from the late 1960s (as discussed earlier), east of the Hajnal line there was only a slight change in the popularity of marriage. In fact, in several countries the lowest levels ever were observed in the average ages at first marriage in the 1970s: for instance, in 1975 in Bulgaria brides were 20.8 and in Romania 21.1 years old. In parallel with this, the age difference between marriage partners shrank.[13]

From the mid-1970s, the willingness to join in matrimony decreased in East Central Europe, too. The average age at marriage slowly began to increase. Meanwhile, this process progressed even further in Western European societies; thus, in this regard, the two regions did not converge but they actually diverged from each other until the end of the century.[14] A faster change was found in the marriage rate in East Central Europe, which was reflected more clearly by marriage rates calculated by calendar year than by the celibacy ratio. For example, in Hungary, had age-specific nuptiality rates observed in 1987/1988 persisted, 82% of men and 92% of women born in the second half of the 1960s would have been married by the time they were 50, which is a significant decline compared with former times.[15] Similar developments were found in the Balkan countries as well. Despite the changes in the 1980s, the comparatively high ratio of married people and the young age at marriage unambiguously show that marriage had a monopoly in partnerships, as it were, in other parts of East Central Europe and the Balkans until the 1990s.

Interpretations of family formation patterns

Research has so far concentrated on the identification and description of marriage patterns in Europe as well as the divergences from these, and has paid less attention to the analysis and interpretation of how these patterns emerge. As a consequence, no explanation proposed so far can be considered comprehensive regarding historical changes in family formation or even more specifically, changes in the age at marriage and the level of lifelong celibacy. Nevertheless, the most influential propositions connect variations in nuptiality to Judeo-Christian religious and cultural roots or a lack thereof, to the scarcity of resources in traditional rural economy and to the strategies that can be used to exploit resources, or to inheritance practices.

The distinguished family historian Michael Mitterauer argued that one of the major prerequisites of the European marriage pattern can be attributed to Christianity. In contrast to the Jewish religion, which is considered its predecessor, Christianity was founded not on descent but on conversion. Because descent did not matter as far as salvation was considered, ritual practice did not rest on kinship, either. An indication of this is that descent was consciously disregarded in the succession of church offices. In this sense, Mitterauer suggests, the hostility of Christianity to the principle of descent decisively contributed to the weakening family ties, to the disintegration of kin groups. Even though this process of breaking lineage structures influenced European regions in various ways, it constituted a major determinant of family formation. The impact of this disposition on the transformation of family structures is also reflected in a significant ratio of children leaving the family household upon entering young adulthood, which, in turn, contributed to the delay in marriage age and to the increase in the ratio of celibacy.[16] Similar effects originated from the lack of attributing a significant role to propagation (*Fortpflanzung*) from a ritual aspect, and therefore there was no religious pressure for marriage.[17]

John Hajnal claimed that the European marriage pattern emerged in the sixteenth and seventeenth centuries, and before that period, early marriage had been widespread in Western Europe, too. In the early modern times, the region had a high population density and limited resources, most of all, considering food production, and thus the threat of disequilibrium was imminent. Entering marriage at an older age and the diffusion of celibacy functioned as kinds of natural birth control. This way, women spent fewer fertile years in marriage, which resulted in lower fertility, because there was a strong tendency in traditional Europe to restrict non–marital sexual relationships.

Another important line of argument connects the changes in marriage patterns to modes of property transmission. The claim is that despite the many local variations, most of traditional Western Europe followed the practice of impartible inheritance, with the eldest son inheriting all property, and therefore the other male children left the parental household when reaching adulthood to find employment elsewhere in order to accumulate property. This way, they tried to live up to the expectation that a male entering marriage should have his own household, and, in particular, the basic means of production. In areas with impartible inheritance, the land was passed to a single heir, the successor child, who took possession of the parental farm usually at an older age, but the children who left the household also needed a considerable time to accumulate enough property to start a family.[18] In the Eastern regions of Europe, inheritance typically followed different rules, that is, partibility, with not only one child inheriting. Thus, here there was no incentive to leave the parental household early and no obstacle to marrying at a younger age.[19] In these regions the prevalence of larger and more complex households made it possible for the relatives to exercise tighter control over the relationships of the young. In contrast, in Western Europe, such control was more difficult because many of the young left the parental household and took up neolocal residency, and because the separation of nuclear families had progressed further.[20]

However, the above findings and claims are unconvincing in several respects. The interpretations that ground late first marriage in relative overpopulation attribute to society such awareness, and such ability to control the reproductive behaviour of the individual, which is doubtful to have ever existed. Furthermore, current research has revealed significant regional variations in nuptiality within modern Western Europe, which do not properly conform to differences in inheritance patterns. For instance, regions affected by the Reformation were characterized by partible inheritance and older ages at marriage at the same time, which casts doubt on the idea that the mode of inheritance could shape marriage patterns. Rather, succession laws and customs may be considered as being only one set among several interrelated social and economic factors influencing family behaviour.[21] For similar reasons, interpretations based on Christian doctrines and traditions can hardly account for the variations in land transmission practices.

Moreover, the above explanations cannot have any validity for the twentieth century, when famine was no longer a threat and when the scarcity of land could not have been a decisive determinant of family behaviour, because it was no longer the most important resource. Even though we may assume that patterns and social norms related to marriage, institutionalized earlier, survived in the twentieth century, the inertia of norms can provide only a partial explanation.

The review of the interpretations of twentieth–century family formation trends cannot be complete without the discussion of two major phenomena. One is the youthful marriage pattern and the near universality of marriage in the 1950s and

1960s; the other is the successive rise in the age at marriage and the growing popularity of alternative forms of living arrangements in Western Europe, the latter of which are described in more detail later. It needs to be stressed that the transformation of marriage patterns was embedded in wider social and cultural changes. The willingness to marry was greater in Western Europe in the two decades after the Second World War than was known at any time in history before. However, the change in the marriage pattern was not the only significant demographic change of the period, because a marriage boom went hand in hand with the baby boom. The same parallelism applies to the decline in marriage frequency throughout the continent from the 1960s, which was in turn accompanied by declining fertility. Not only the parallelisms of several demographic changes, but also the striking similarities in the trends of family formation in most countries of the continent suggest that comprehensive societal changes led to the shifts in marriage patterns. We return to several of the underlying factors later, such as value changes (individualization and secularization), and the shifts in economic and employment structures (industrialization, urbanization, and the marked increase in female employment), when discussing the pluralization of living arrangements.

Beside cultural changes, other factors can also be identified that had an impact on nuptiality. The decline in the age at marriage had already begun in the 1930s in several parts of Western Europe, which is often explained by the emerging disequilibrium in the ratio of the sexes as a consequence of events in the preceding periods (migration, war losses and military recruitments before the Second World War). These factors did not surface in all countries in the same way, and their thorough examination is still a research task to be performed. However, the effects of these factors favourable to marriage persisted and even gained strength after the Second World War, nonetheless. It is also frequently assumed that the economic conditions after the Second World War exerted beneficial influences on nuptiality. Nevertheless, this argument is not as plausible as it seems at the first glance, because the economic hardship in the aftermath of the war and increased female employment are factors usually unfavourable to family formation. Of the few empirical studies on these relationships, one focusing on Great Britain found that economic conditions did not promote early marriage in that period. Thus, we rather claim that the rapid economic growth of the 1950s created an optimistic 'reconstruction sentiment', which improved the willingness to marry, rather than supposing a direct contribution of economic factors to family formation.[22]

A complex set of factors underlie the resuming decline in nuptiality beginning in the 1960s as well, even if we disregard the general normative shifts in society. Although the decrease in the willingness to marry may seem to be a return of early twentieth-century Western European patterns, in fact it occurred under profoundly different social conditions and in parallel with a marked internal transformation of marriage. The change in women's role in family and society is decisive in this regard, which was reflected in legal emancipation and especially in the diffusion of female employment and education. Among the many consequences, addressed in detail later, this had effects toward an equalization of gender roles, which did reduce the attractiveness of marriage, because the division of labour within the family is one of the advantages that marriage has over living on one's own. Furthermore, whereas earlier, moderate nuptiality indicators showed a refraining from partnerships in general, the similar tendencies of the last decades of the twentieth century can be observed in parallel with the popularity of unmarried cohabitation. Modern methods of birth control (the contraceptive pill and intrauterine devices) did not only lower fertility but also encouraged 'nubile' cohabitation and affected the timing of marriages. These facilitated the lengthening of the phase of pre-marital partnership and cohabitation, because fewer marriages were entered into with pregnancy being the immediate reason. In addition, extramarital pregnancies and births have become more acceptable in society, so these did not increase the number of marriages to the degree that they used to.

Similarly, the development observed in the Eastern half of the continent after the Second World War, which made marriage even more universal there than before, was the result of the interplay of several factors. On the one hand, it is obvious that marriage as an institution of partnership was traditionally dominant in the region. Its transformation in any way was fundamentally hindered by the isolation of communist regimes, which inhibited or delayed any economic and social diffusion processes, including the spread of other, alternative partnership forms from Western European societies as well, where they were prevalent in the post-war period. Furthermore, this marriage pattern was preserved by the social and cultural uniformity prevailing in the regime, which allowed little variability in individual life courses. On the other hand, a relatively high degree of social security made it possible to plan life's important events, such as marriage. An even more compelling explanation is that in communist countries, social policy prioritized married couples in the distribution of several services, most of all housing. Under the conditions of the shortage economy, then, this was an important incentive to marry. A similar effect arose from the conditions of dictatorial regimes, where the public sphere became dominated by indoctrination and hypocrisy, thus the attractiveness of collective activities had diminished, and citizens retreated to the private sphere, and most notably to the 'safe haven' of marriage and family.

Changes in family and household structure: contraction and nuclearization

In family research, and particularly in popular tradition, it was held evident for a long time that in pre-industrial Europe, families and households were large and complex in structure, primarily as a result of the high number of children and because more than two successive generations lived together, along with extra kin, including cousins, nieces and nephews, and uncles and aunts. The founders of family sociology, such as Frédéric Le Play and Wilhelm Heinrich Riehl, suggested that industrialization led to a decline in household and family size, because fertility decreased and the extended family household was replaced by the nuclear family, consisting only of the couple and their under-age children. However, from the mid-1960s, Peter Laslett and his colleagues at the Cambridge School of Historical Demography (the Cambridge Group for the History of Population and Social Structure) began to accumulate new evidence that contradicted this dynamic of change and questioned, at least regarding England, that large and complex households had ever been prevalent. Their research, considered by many as a breakthrough in family history, primarily relied on the systematic use of the method known as family reconstitution. Originally developed by the French demographer Louis Henry, this method entails the collection of data on the births, marriages and deaths in individual families from parish registers. On this basis, relevant information can be reconstructed on the number of children, level of infant mortality, average age at marriage, intervals between births, etc. When such data collection is performed on a mass scale (for whole communities and over a long period) and is complemented by other sources, an accurate image of the major characteristics of family structure in the past can be gained. The findings of Laslett and his colleagues show that in the period between the late sixteenth and the late nineteenth century, the average household size in England was relatively stable, about 4.75 persons.[23] Based on this and other evidence, Laslett rejected the view that in traditional Western European societies, the stem family would have been the dominant form of living arrangement. Instead, he rather suggested that the nuclear family was a major and prevailing feature of the Western family system. Primarily, there were demographic limits to the emergence of large and complex family households. High infant and child mortality as well as the prevalence of premature deaths in later stages of life did not make the formation of large households possible. Taking into account the relatively low average household size, it cannot be verified either that a high number of kin and servants, boarders and lodgers normally lived together in a single household.[24]

Consequently, it seems plausible that there was little change in family and household size and structure in Europe up to the end of the nineteenth century, although the research literature is not wholly consistent in this regard. However, the changes occurring in the course of the twentieth century were undoubtedly significant, with a decline in the average number of persons living together in a household and a simplification of family and household structure.

Even if concepts are often defined differently and the comparability of data poses some questions, the trends of the average change in household size are rather unanimous in the twentieth century. The average size of households already referred to, which is usually regarded as the simplest but most comprehensive indicator of household structure, significantly declined everywhere. As Peter Laslett's calculations for North-Western Europe suggest, in the early twentieth century, the average household size was around 4.5 members.[25] In 1901 in France, the occupied dwellings had an average of 3.5 persons living there; this is the lowest figure that we are aware of, although it must be noted that this pertains only to larger towns. In the same years in England and Wales, the averages were 4.5 habitants. As a result of the rapid decline in England in the interwar period, the difference between the two countries had diminished by 1950, with the average size of households being 3.1 persons in France in 1954 and 3.2 persons in England and Wales in 1951. These figures roughly correspond to the average household size in the Western half of Europe, which comprised 3.35 persons around 1950. This may be established with certainty because the quality and comparability of data had been improving from the 1930s, as a consequence of more and more representative methods applied in a growing number of societies to produce household statistics. French and English data moved in similar directions in the post-Second World War period as well, in 1990 reaching 2.6 persons living in a household on average in both countries. A persistent decline also took place in other parts of Western Europe, with average households amounting to 2.98 persons in 1970 and 2.55 in 1990 (Table 3.5). In parallel with this process, a moderate levelling off did also occur among Western European countries in this regard from the middle to the end of the century.

In the first decades of the twentieth century, the average size of households in several countries of East Central Europe did not differ significantly from that observed in the Western half of the continent. In 1930 in Czechoslovakia, Hungary and Poland, a typical household comprised 3.8, 3.9 and 4.4 members, respectively, declining further, to 3.3 in Czechoslovakia and 3.6 in Hungary, by the mid-century. The decline has been uninterrupted since 1950; thus from the 1960s the households in the latter countries resembled their Western European counterparts in that respect. The process of contraction was less remarkable in Poland, where the average household size remained considerably higher throughout the second half of the century (Table 3.5).[26]

Related to these processes, two further trends in the transformation of household structure are also obvious: the retreat of larger households on the one hand, and the rapid rise of the significance of one-person households on the other. The decline of the ratio of larger households with five or more members followed a course similar to that of the average household size. This is not unexpected, because it was one of the most important causes of the latter trend that fewer people lived in the larger households. As can be inferred from household and housing statistics, in the early twentieth century, households of five and more members dominated in every country in Western Europe (France and Belgium are exceptions, but in these countries data are available only from larger settlements), but their decline was rapid already in the first half of the century, with their ratio mostly below 20% in most societies around 1950. Because of further decline, in the 1980s, it was only in Ireland that households with five or more members represented a significantly higher ratio than 10% (Table 3.6). In Southern and East Central Europe, the decline in large households also proceeded. Around 1930, the share of households with five or more members was still at 38.4% in Italy, and even higher in Poland, with 45.8%, whereas it was 31.3% in Czechoslovakia and 33% in Hungary.[27] These ratios were considered high compared with levels in Western Europe, but the number of children per family declined rapidly in the next decades in several regions of Southern and East Central Europe as well. This process strongly affected the size of households, but it did not result in uniformity. By 1961, Czechoslovakia with her 16.7% ratio of large households and the 8.4% ratio of this household category in 1991 did not differ from the Western European

TABLE 3.5 Average size of households in European countries, 1900–2000 (persons)

	1900	1910	1920	1930	1940	1950	1960	1970	1980	1990	2000
United Kingdom		4.4	4.1	3.7		3.2	3.0	2.9	2.7	2.6	2.3
France	3.5	2.9			3.1	3.1	3.1	2.9	2.7	2.6	2.4
Netherlands	4.5	4.4	4.3	4.0	3.7	4.5	3.6	3.2	2.8	2.4	2.3
Belgium	4.3	4.1	3.8	3.4		3.0	3.0	2.9	2.7	2.7	2.4
Ireland	4.9	4.8	4.5	4.3	4.2	4.2	4.0	3.9	3.7	3.3	3.0
Germany/FRG	4.5	4.4	4.0	3.8	3.3	3.0	2.9	2.7	2.5	2.3	2.2
Austria		4.5		3.6		3.1	3.0	2.9	2.7	2.5	2.4
Switzerland			4.2	3.9			3.3	2.9	2.5	2.4	
Sweden	3.7	3.7	3.6	3.5	2.8	2.9	2.8	2.6	2.3	2.1	2.0
Denmark	4.3	4.1	4.0	3.7	3.2	3.1	3.0	2.7	2.4	2.3	2.2
Norway	4.5	4.2	4.1	4.5	4.2	3.2	3.1	2.9	2.7	2.4	
Finland	4.6	4.4		3.6		3.6	3.3	3.0	2.6	2.5	2.2
Italy	4.5	4.7	4.4	4.2	4.3	3.0	3.6	3.3	3.0	2.9	2.6
Poland		4.8	4.4				3.5	3.4	3.1	3.1	
Czechoslovakia				3.8		3.3	3.1	2.9	2.8	2.6	
Hungary		4.7	4.3	3.9	3.8	3.6	3.1	3.0	2.8	2.6	

Notes: Unless indicated otherwise, data for private households; different data: United Kingdom: 1911–1931 England and Wales; France 1911: towns over 5000 inhabitants, 1901–1946: occupied dwellings; the Netherlands 1947: dwellings; Belgium 1910–1930: towns over 10,000 inhabitants, 1910–1947: occupied dwellings; Germany 1927: towns over 5000 inhabitants, 1950: with West Berlin, 1999: the territory of former West Germany; Austria 1910: larger towns of the country, occupied dwellings; Denmark 1901–1930: occupied dwellings, Copenhagen; Finland 1900–1930: occupied dwellings, 1900–1910: Helsinki, Turku, Tampere, Uleaborg, 1930: Helsinki; Norway 1930: occupied dwellings in towns; Italy 1931: larger towns, occupied dwellings; Hungary 1910, 1920, 1930, 1941: average habitants per dwelling; different years: England and Wales: 1911, 1921, 1931; United Kingdom: 1951, 1961, 1971, 1981; France: 1901, 1911, 1946, 1962, 1975, 1982; the Netherlands: 1899, 1909, 1947, 1971; Belgium: 1947, 1961, 1981; Ireland: 1901, 1926, 1936, 1946, 1961, 1971, 1981, 1991, 1997; Germany: 1925, 1927, 1939, 1961, 1987; Austria: 1934, 1951, 1961, 1971, 1981, 1991; Sweden: 1945; Denmark: 1901, 1916, 1981, 1991; Norway: 1946; Italy: 1901, 1911, 1921, 1931, 1936, 1951, 1961, 1971, 1981; Czechoslovakia: 1961, 1991; Hungary: 1941, 1949; Poland: 1921, 1931, 1978, 1988.

Sources: Peter Flora, ed., *State, Economy, and Society in Western Europe*, vol. II, Frankfurt/M.: Campus, 1987, 285 (Austria 1910), 289 (Belgium 1910–1947), 295 (Denmark 1901–1930), 298 (Finland 1900–1930), 302 (France 1901–1911), 306 (Germany 1927), 308 (Ireland 1926–1946), 311 (Italy 1931), 313 (the Netherlands 1947), 316 (Norway 1930), 319 (Sweden 1930), 322 (Switzerland 1920–1930), 324 (England and Wales 1911–1931); Bernhard Schäfers, *Gesellschaftlicher Wandel in Deutschland,* Stuttgart: Enke, 1995, 294 (Germany, Great Britain, the Netherlands, Belgium, Italy 1990); United Nations, ed., *Demographic Yearbook. Special Issue: Population Ageing and the Situation of Elderly Persons,* New York: United Nations, 1993 (Western Europe 1950, 1960); Eurostat, ed., *Economic and Social Features of Households in the Member States of the European Community,* Luxembourg: Eurostat, 1982, 33 (Western Europe 1970); United Nations, ed., *Demographic Yearbook, 1995,* New York: United Nations, 1997, 596–604 (Western Europe 1990); Ray Hall, 'Family Structures', in Daniel Noin and Robert Woods, eds., *The Changing Population of Europe,* Oxford: Blackwell, 1993, 102 (the Netherlands 1980); Franz Rothenbacher, *The European Population since 1945,* Houndmills: Palgrave, 2005, 43 (the Netherlands 1980–1990, FRG 1980, Austria 1991, Italy 1951, Czechoslovakia 1950–1991, Poland 1960–1988); Franz Rothenbacher, *The European Population, 1850–1945,* Houndmills: Palgrave, 2002, 51 (France 1946, mortality 1899–1947; Belgium 1900–1930; Ireland 1901–1946; Germany 1900–1920, 1939; Austria 1910, 1934; Sweden 1900–1945; Denmark 1901–1940; Norway 1900–1946; Italy 1901–1936; Czechoslovakia 1930; Poland 1921–1931); Eurostat, *Eurostat Yearbook 2002,* Luxembourg: Eurostat, 2002, 33 (Western Europe 1997–2000); Tamás Faragó, *Nemek, nemzedékek, családok és rokonok a XVIII–XX. században* (Doctoral dissertation, MTA Kézirattár), Budapest, 1994, Melléklet 59 (Hungary 1910); József Kovacsics, ed., *Magyarország történeti demográfiája,* Budapest: KSH, 1963, 295 (Hungary 1930, 1949); *Time Series of Historical Statistics, 1867–1992,* Budapest: KSH, 1993, 82 (Hungary 1920, 1941, 1960–1990).

TABLE 3.6 Households with five or more members as related to the total number of households in European countries, 1900–1990 (%)

	1900	1910	1920	1930	1940	1950	1960	1970	1980	1990
United Kingdom		41.0	36.9	28.1		17.8	16.0	14.5	11.4	8.0
France	25.4	15.3			16.0	18.0	20.1	19.1	11.9	10.3
Netherlands		42.9			28.6	41.4	27.0	20.4	11.7	7.1
Belgium		26.9	19.3	16.7	14.9	14.6	16.0	16.1	11.4	8.2
Ireland		44.0			40.8	38.6	35.4	35.2	32.3	26.6
Germany/FRG	44.4	42.4	33.4	25.9	18.7		14.0	12.9	8.0	5.1
Austria		37.4				18.2	17.0	17.0	13.0	10.0
Switzerland	43.0		38.6	32.5			21.0	16.0	9.0	6.5
Sweden	33.4	32.8	30.1	27.2		17.5	13.1	10.0	6.0	5.3
Denmark	32.5		25.1	18.8		17.8	15.0	12.7	7.4	4.7
Norway		44.1		39.4		20.3	21.0	17.0	12.0	8.3
Finland	44.9	42.7		26.3		28.3	25.0	18.3	10.0	7.8
Italy	43.8	42.4	41.3	38.4	39.6	33.3	27.0	21.5	14.9	11.3
Poland			51.3	45.8			26.5	23.9	16.9	17.1
Czechoslovakia				31.3		20.8	16.7	13.2	10.1	8.4
Hungary				33.0			17.0	14.0	10.6	8.0

Notes: Unless indicated otherwise, data for private households; different data: United Kingdom 1911–1950: England and Wales; France 1911: towns over 50,000 inhabitants, 1901–1946 occupied dwellings; the Netherlands 1947: occupied dwellings; Belgium 1910–1930: towns over 10,000 inhabitants, 1910–1947: occupied dwellings; Austria 1910: occupied dwellings; Sweden 1930: dwellings, Stockholm; Denmark 1901–1930: occupied dwellings, Copenhagen; Norway 1930: urban occupied dwellings; Finland 1900–1930: occupied dwellings, 1900–1910: Helsinki, Turku, Tampere, Uleaborg, 1930: Helsinki; Italy 1911: five cities, occupied dwellings, 1931: 11 big cities, occupied dwellings; Hungary 1930: the distribution of dwellings in settlements over 10,000 inhabitants; different years: England and Wales: 1911, 1921, 1931; United Kingdom: 1961, 1981, 1991; France: 1901, 1911, 1946, 1962, 1975; the Netherlands: 1909, 1947, 1971, 1991; Belgium: 1947, 1961, 1991; Ireland: 1926, 1936, 1946, 1961, 1971, 1991; Germany: 1925, 1933, 1939, 1991; Austria: 1951, 1991; Denmark: 1901, 1916, 1981, 1991; Italy: 1901, 1911, 1921, 1931, 1936, 1951, 1961, 1971, 1991; Czechoslovakia: 1961, 1991; Poland: 1921, 1931, 1978, 1988.

Sources: Peter Flora, ed., *State, Economy, and Society in Western Europe,* vol. II, Frankfurt/M.: Campus, 1987, 285 (Austria 1910), 289 (Belgium 1910–1947), 295 (Denmark 1901–1930), 298 (Finland 1900–1930), 302 (France 1901–1911), 306 (Germany 1927), 308 (Ireland 1926–1946), 311 (Italy 1911, 1931), 313 (the Netherlands 1947), 316 (Norway 1930), 319 (Sweden 1930), 322 (Switzerland 1920–1930), 324 (England and Wales 1911–1931) – author's calculations; Eurostat, ed., *Economic and Social Features of Households in the Member States of the European Community,* Luxembourg: Eurostat, 1982, 30–39 (Western Europe 1960–1970); K. Schwarz, 'Household Trends in Europe after World War II', in Nico Keilman et al., ed., *Modelling Household Formation and Dissolution,* Oxford: Clarendon Press, 1988, 79–80 (England and Wales, Germany, Austria, Sweden, Denmark, Norway, Italy 1950); François Höpflinger, 'Haushalts- und Familienstrukturen im westeuropäischen Vergleich', in Stefan Hradil and Stefan Immerfall, eds., *Die westeuropäischen Gesellschaften im Vergleich,* Opladen: Leske und Budrich, 1997, 100 (Western Europe 1960–1980); Eurostat, ed., *Population, Households and Dwellings in Europe. Main Results of the 1990/1991 Censuses,* Brussels–Luxembourg: Eurostat, 1996, 120–121 (Western Europe 1990); Ray Hall, 'Family Structures', in Daniel Noin and Robert Woods, eds., *The Changing Population of Europe,* Oxford: Blackwell, 1993, 103 (United Kingdom 1971–1981, France 1968–1982, the Netherlands 1971–1981, Belgium 1970–1981, Germany 1970–1980, Denmark 1970–1981, Italy 1971–1981); Franz Rothenbacher, *The European Population, 1850–1945,* Houndmills: Palgrave, 2002, 52 (France 1946, the Netherlands 1909, 1947, Belgium 1947, Ireland 1926–1946, Germany 1900–1939, Switzerland 1900, Sweden 1900–1930; Norway 1920–1930, Italy 1901–1936, Czechoslovakia 1930, Poland 1921–1931); Franz Rothenbacher, *The European Population since 1945,* Houndmills: Palgrave, 2005, 45 (United Kingdom 1950, Austria 1951, Denmark 1950, Finland 1950, Italy 1951, Czechoslovakia 1950–1991, Poland 1960–1988); Tamás Faragó, *Nemek, nemzedékek, családok és rokonok a XVIII–XX. században* (Doctoral dissertation, MTA Kézirattár), Budapest: 1994, Melléklet 49 (Hungary 1930); *Time Series of Historical Statistics, 1867–1992,* Budapest: KSH, 1993, 76 (Hungary 1960–1990).

pattern. The Hungarian development was almost identical to this, whereas large households remained more prevalent in Poland and also in Italy (Table 3.6).

Wherever data are available for the whole country, one-person or solitary households counted for less than 10% of all households in Western Europe before the First World War, with the exception of Belgium. In the following decades, the rise of this type was moderate, but in the second half of the century, it became markedly rapid. In the late 1980s in Sweden, one-person households constituted 40% of all households; in the other Scandinavian countries, West Germany, Switzerland and Austria about 33%; and in the United Kingdom, France, the Netherlands and Belgium approximately 25%. The data for Southern Europe and Ireland show a more protracted transformation again (Table 3.8). The same holds for East Central Europe, where the presence of one-person households also grew, but starting from relatively low initial levels, with 7.3% in Czechoslovakia, 9% in Poland and 6% in Hungary in 1930, and remaining lower than the Western European mean in the following decades. In 1990, one-person households in both Hungary and Czechoslovakia amounted to almost 25%, and in Poland 20%, of all households. In Western Europe a ratio lower than this was observed only in Ireland (20%). In this regard, then, the difference between the societies of East Central and Western Europe remained significantly greater than was the case regarding both average household size and the ratio of large households (Table 3.7).

However, it was not only the size of households that declined; their structure also became less complex. The process known as the nuclearization of the family was of crucial importance in this respect. As shown above, the findings of family history research suggest that in North-Western and Central Europe the majority of people lived in nuclear, or as often referred to, conjugal family households even in preindustrial times, that is, in domestic units that included only the core of the family, the spouses and their dependent children. Complex households, including extended and multiple family households, such as stem families and joint families, were less widespread.[28] The available data, mostly obtained from the second half of the twentieth century, show that the nuclearization of family households continued in the twentieth century: the regularity of multigeneration cohabitation (parents and adult children or grandchildren living together) and the number of other kin living with the nuclear or core family (siblings, uncles, aunts, etc.) decreased in the period. For instance, in 1961 in West Germany, there were more than one million three-generation households, but merely half this figure was registered in 1982.[29] As early as in 1920 in Switzerland, there were relatively few households where relatives lived with the core family, but their share shrank to its third, to a mere 2% of all households by 1980. However, in Southern Europe, where the agricultural population remained more significant, this ratio was remarkably higher, amounting to 8% in Italy in 1971.[30]

Although, as shown above, in East Central Europe on the whole, there was a remarkable stability in marriage patterns, in other respects the social environment and the quality of family life changed considerably in the course of the twentieth century. The average household size of 4–4.5 persons in the early twentieth

TABLE 3.7 The ratio of one-person households to all households in European countries, 1900–1990 (%)

	1900	1910	1920	1930	1940	1950	1960	1970	1980	1990
United Kingdom		5.3	6.0	6.7		11.0	11.9	18.1	22.0	26.7
France	4.4					18.6	19.9	22.3	25.0	27.0
Netherlands		9.6	9.7	11.2		9.7	11.9	17.1	22.0	29.9
Belgium		14.2	15.0	11.3		15.8	16.8	18.8	23.0	28.4
Ireland				8.3	9.4	10.4	12.6	14.2	17.0	20.2
Germany/FRG	7.2	7.3	6.7	8.4	9.8	19.0	20.6	25.2	31.0	33.6
Austria		6.3				18.0	20.0	26.0	28.0	29.7
Switzerland	9.5		8.6	8.5			14.2	19.6	29.0	32.4
Sweden				12.2		21.0	20.2	25.3	33.0	39.6
Denmark	8.8	10.0	9.5	10.9	13.5	14.0	16.0	21.4	29.0	34.4
Norway			9.4	11.3		15.0	18.0	21.1	28.0	34.3
Finland	6.7	7.5		8.7		10.3	19.3	24.0	27.0	31.7
Italy	8.8	9.2	9.1	9.6	9.1	10.0	10.6	12.9	18.0	20.6
Poland			6.1	9.0			16.4	16.1	17.4	18.3
Czechoslovakia				7.3		10.8	14.2	17.1	22.9	25.3
Hungary				6.0		10.0	14.5	17.5	19.6	24.3

Notes: Unless indicated otherwise, data for private households; different data: United Kingdom 1911–1950: England and Wales; France 1901–1946: occupied dwellings; the Netherlands 1947: occupied dwellings; Belgium 1910–1930: towns over 10,000 inhabitants, 1910–1947: occupied dwellings; Austria 1910: occupied dwellings; Sweden 1930: dwellings, Stockholm; Denmark 1901–1930: occupied dwellings, Copenhagen; Norway 1930: urban occupied dwellings; Finland 1900–1930: occupied dwellings, 1900–1910: Helsinki, Turku, Tampere, Uleaborg, 1930: Helsinki; Italy 1911: five cities, occupied dwellings, 1931: 11 cities, occupied dwellings; Hungary 1949: estimate; different years: England and Wales: 1911, 1921, 1931; United Kingdom: 1961, 1981, 1991; France: 1901, 1946, 1962, 1975; the Netherlands: 1909, 1947, 1971, 1991; Belgium: 1947, 1961, 1991; Germany: 1925, 1933, 1939, 1991; Austria: 1991; Ireland: 1936, 1946, 1961, 1971, 1991; Denmark: 1901, 1911, 1921, 1981, 1991; Italy: 1901, 1911, 1931, 1936, 1961, 1971, 1991; Czechoslovakia: 1961, 1991; Poland: 1921, 1931, 1988.

Sources: Peter Flora, ed., *State, Economy, and Society in Western Europe,* vol. II, Frankfurt/M.: Campus, 1987, 285 (Austria 1910), 289 (Belgium 1910–1947), 295 (Denmark 1901–1930), 298 (Finland 1900–1930), 306 (Germany 1927), 308 (Ireland 1926–1946), 311 (Italy 1911, 1931), 313 (the Netherlands 1947), 316 (Norway 1930), 319 (Sweden 1930), 322 (Switzerland 1920–1930), 324 (England and Wales 1911–1931); Eurostat, ed., *Economic and Social Features of Households in the Member States of the European Community,* Luxembourg: Eurostat, 1982, 30–39 (Western Europe 1960–1970); K. Schwarz, 'Household Trends in Europe after World War II', in Nico Keilman et al., ed., *Modelling Household Formation and Dissolution,* Oxford: Clarendon Press, 1988, 79–80 (England and Wales, Germany, Austria, Sweden, Denmark, Norway, Italy 1950); François Höpflinger, 'Haushalts- und Familienstrukturen im westeuropäischen Vergleich', in Stefan Hradil and Stefan Immerfall, eds., *Die westeuropäischen Gesellschaften im Vergleich,* Opladen: Leske und Budrich, 1997, 102 (Western Europe 1960–1980); Eurostat, ed., *Population, Households and Dwellings in Europe: Main Results of the 1990/1991 Censuses,* Brussels–Luxembourg: Eurostat, 1996, 120–121 (Western Europe 1990); Franz Rothenbacher, *The European Population, 1850–1945,* Houndmills: Palgrave, 2002, 53 (France 1901; the Netherlands 1909–1947; Belgium 1947; Ireland 1926–1936; Germany 1900–1939; Switzerland 1900, 1920; Denmark 1901–1940; Norway 1920, 1946; Italy 1901, 1920–1936; Czechoslovakia 1930; Poland 1921–1931); Franz Rothenbacher, *The European Population since 1945,* Houndmills: Palgrave, 2005, 46 (Czechoslovakia 1950–1991, Poland 1960–1988); Tamás Faragó, *Nemek, nemzedékek, családok és rokonok a XVIII–XX. században* (Doctoral dissertation, MTA Kézirattár), Budapest: 1994, Melléklet 38, (Hungary 1949); *Time Series of Historical Statistics, 1867–1992,* Budapest: KSH, 1993, 76 (Hungary 1960–1990).

TABLE 3.8 Female employment in European countries, 1900–1990 (% of all employees)

	1900	1910	1920	1930	1940	1950	1960	1970	1980	1990
United Kingdom	29.2	29.6	29.5	29.8		32.6	32.7	36.3	39.2	42.9
France	30.8	28.8	37.5	31.2	30.9	32.2	33.3	36.0	39.8	43.4
Netherlands	24.3	24.9	25.0	25.6		23.4	21.5	26.3	30.3	39.2
Belgium	29.9	28.4	23.5	24.3	23.2	29.7	30.2	32.7	37.3	41.6
Ireland				30.5	31.9	26.7	25.6	26.7	28.7	31.6
Germany/FRG	30.2	29.1	30.0	33.0	30.3	35.8	37.3	36.6	37.8	40.8
Austria	34.2	34.7		34.0	33.4	33.8	39.4		40.8	41.0
Switzerland	36.6	35.7	36.9	35.6	32.8	33.7	34.1		36.1	38.1
Sweden	35.1	33.3	34.2	32.0	30.1	29.8	33.6		45.2	47.9
Denmark	37.4	37.4	36.4	37.6	32.1	33.7	30.9	39.4	44.1	46.1
Norway	35.2	37.1	34.5	32.5		27.4	28.2		41.3	44.9
Finland		37.2	39.3	39.5	39.9	36.7	43.7		46.1	47.1
Italy	29.1	32.5	28.1	25.2	25.3	26.4	30.7	28.3	33.3	36.8
Hungary	25.2	22.1	29.8	26.1	27.3	29.2	35.5	41.1	43.4	44.5

Notes: Western Europe 1900–1950: unless indicated otherwise, employees and workers (without those self-employed and the employed family members); United Kingdom 1901–1950, 1970: Great Britain; Western Europe 1950: ratio within civilian employees; different data: Germany 1907, 1925: including managers; Finland 1910–1940: workers only; Norway 1911: including servants; different periods: Great Britain: 1901, 1911, 1921, 1931; France: 1901, 1906, 1921, 1931, 1936, 1954; the Netherlands: 1899, 1909, 1947; Belgium: 1947; Ireland: 1926, 1936; Germany: 1895, 1907, 1925, 1933, 1939; Austria: 1934, 1939, 1951; Switzerland: 1941; Denmark: 1901, 1911, 1921; Italy: 1901, 1911, 1921, 1931, 1936, 1951; Hungary: 1941, 1949.

Sources: OECD, ed., *Historical Statistics, 1960–1994*, Paris: OECD, 1996 (Western Europe 1960, 1990); OECD, ed., *Historical Statistics, 1960–1984*, Paris: OECD, 1986, 33 (Western Europe 1980); Oscar W. Gabriel and Frank Brettschneider, eds., *Die EU-Staaten im Vergleich*, Opladen: Westdeutscher Verlag, 1994, 513 (Great Britain, Belgium, Ireland, Germany, Denmark 1950; Western Europe 1970); Peter Flora, ed., *State, Economy, and Society in Western Europe*, vol. II, Frankfurt/M.: Campus, 1987, 452–456 (Austria 1900–1951), 463–466 (Belgium 1900–1947), 474–479 (Denmark 1901–1940), 486–490 (Finland 1910–1950), 499–506 (France 1901–1954), 514–518 (Germany 1895–1939), 543–545 (Ireland 1926–1936), 553–558 (Italy 1901–1951), 563–567 (the Netherlands 1899–1947), 573–578 (Norway 1900–1950), 586–591 (Sweden 1900–1950), 599–604 (Switzerland 1900–1950); A. T. Mallier and M. J. Rosser, *Women and the Economy: A Comparative Study of Britain and the USA*, London: Macmillan, 1987, 20 (Great Britain 1901–1931); *Time Series of Historical Statistics, 1867–1992*, Budapest: KSH, 1993, 36–37 (Hungary).

century discussed above in itself seems to support the claim that the complex household was not dominant in East Central Europe either; nor, in particular, was the form known as the joint family, in which the couple shares a household with their married children, possibly grandchildren, and other kin as well as non-relatives of various kinds. In addition, a further simplification occurred in the family structures of East Central Europe in the twentieth century. Relatives other than the members of the nuclear family gradually disappeared from the household, and less complex (extended or multiple) family households were formed, for instance, by kin in the ascending line living together. Moreover, the functions of such living arrangements also changed. Therefore, the direction of change was similar to what characterized Western European societies. However, the transformation differed in its scale because shifts in East Central Europe occurred in a protracted manner.

Even if the nuclearization of family households did progress in East Central Europe in the first half of the century, in 1949 at least an estimated 22–24% of all households comprised more than one core family or included kin in addition to the nuclear family in Hungary.[31] The survival of the relatively high level of household complexity in Hungary is indicated by the fact that in 1990, 11.8% of households still belonged to this category and 19.1% of the population lived in such households. The most typical case was parents and married child/children or a widowed parent and the child's family living together. These are considerably higher ratios than those observed in the Western part of the continent. In 1970 in each of the seven Western European countries examined in a survey (England, the Netherlands, Belgium, Switzerland, Norway and Finland), the ratio of complex households was between 4% and 6% and it reached 7% or 9% only in Finland, depending on the definition applied.[32]

In East–West comparisons, the case of the Balkans is a particularly intriguing example, where complex family household structures were a long-standing tradition before the twentieth century.[33] It appears that the formation of extended or multiple family households had fewer social obstacles here than elsewhere in Western Europe. Even if there are few statistical data on South-Eastern European family structure in the nineteenth and early twentieth century, a convincing body of ethnographical and anthropological evidence suggests the presence of the peculiar joint family, large and highly complex, lineal-lateral multiple family household (*zadruga*) in the nineteenth-century peasant population of the Balkans. Furthermore, although the fully developed form of the joint family had almost completely disintegrated by the interwar period, in certain isolated rural communities, its remnants were still discernible in the mid-century, even in some regions of East Central Europe.[34] Here, the extended family or the households comprising several core families were established living arrangements. That is, where parents lived to see their children marry and start a family, they often formed a joint household with the families of their children. Thus, at a certain phase of the family cycle, such households may have been widely prevalent indeed, despite their low share observed for the whole population.

Naturally, we can hardly suppose a direct link between the nineteenth-century peasant joint family and the existing forms of complex households in twentieth-century East Central Europe, not even in the Balkans, because the functions of such cohabitations had changed significantly. The relatively high ratio of the urban population in complex households in the decades after the Second World War in itself is indicative that it was not, or not primarily, production processes that led to their formation, because urban conditions exclude this explanation in the first place.[35] In this period, decisively different causes led to the formation of extended families, most of all the housing shortage.[36] The same applies to rural areas, where, mostly as a consequence of the collectivization of agriculture, the functions of the family were subject to a profound transformation. At the same time, the relatively high ratio of extended and multiple family households may be, in a large part, the consequence of the survival of norms promoting them.

Furthermore, not only did the structure of households become less complex in the twentieth century throughout Europe, but, as an important direction of change, their separation from each other also progressed. In the late nineteenth century, even formally distinct households were often intertwined, a case in point being a worker employed by his landlord and often also paying for his lodging with labour. In Budapest, even in 1910, only 42.6% of households existed by themselves alone in one dwelling; the rest were lodgers, night lodgers or persons actually renting a part of the dwelling, but by 1930, already 60.8% of households occupied a dwelling alone.[37] Therefore, what we see is not simply a crystallization of nuclear family households, but also a separation of nuclear families from kin and others, as well as the formation of the spatial conditions of intimacy in the dwelling. This process further progressed in the second half of the century, with a decrease, especially, in the number of household members who were not actually related to the family.

Causes of changes in household structure

The fundamental factor underlying the decline in the size of households in twentieth-century Europe was a marked contraction of the average number of children of families, as a result of falling fertility, as discussed in the previous chapter. At the beginning of the twentieth century, families with four or more children were common throughout Europe. The reduction of the fourth and further births had already begun in the first half of the century in Western Europe. After the Second World War, even though fertility rose temporarily, this process accelerated and even expanded to third births. The ratio of the latter to all births was 15–20% in the 1950s, dropping to 9–15% by 1980 in Western European countries, except for Ireland.[38] This process spread to Southern Europe, then to East Central Europe and the Balkans. Although third births represented 15% of all births in Hungary in 1935, after a more or less continuous decline they amounted to only 9–10% in the 1970s, and only in the second half of the 1980s did this ratio increase slightly. An even greater decline was found regarding the ratio of fourth and further births to all births.[39] At the same time, in parallel with the decline in the number of families with three and more children, the ratio of childless families did not increase in Europe, rather, it declined between the early century and the 1980s. There were only a few exceptions to this, such as England and Germany/West Germany, where the ratio of permanently childless families rose from 10% and 12% before the war to 15% and 17%, respectively, by the 1970s. The reduction of childlessness undoubtedly rooted in the decline of infertility, especially as a result of the suppression of venereal diseases and medical advances in treating infertility resulting from other causes, such as inflammations. The single-child family, a common type in interwar France, also became rarer in the post-war decades, or at least, it did not become more frequent in Europe. As a consequence of these processes, especially in the two or three decades after the Second World War, there was a unanimous diffusion of the two-child family, in addition to the decline in the average number of children.[40]

Another factor that lowered the average household size and simplified its structure has already been discussed, namely the diminishing number of non-kin household members living with the family, including maids, servants and other employees in farms and small shops or workshops; even those who remained in employment typically did not live with the family anymore, and thus were not the members of their household any longer, either. A good example here is Germany, where in 1910, 17% of all households lodged non-relatives, whereas this group had virtually disappeared by the end of the century.[41] In addition, this process was related to the decrease of the number of small workshops and trade.

In most regions in East Central Europe and the Balkans, there were no traditions on family farms for employing non-relatives who would also integrate into the household, like in many parts of Western Europe. After the communist takeover, there were also political reasons against taking on such workers, which led to the rapid and complete disappearance of the group of domestic servants as well, who previously lived in, and thus increased the size of, more affluent households, and whose number was not insignificant even in the interwar period.

A further factor significantly contributing to the decline of average household size was the spread of one-person households. On the one hand, this was the result of the improvement in mortality and the subsequent rise in the number of the elderly who were either employed or, because of the expanding social welfare services, were less and less dependent on their relatives and were also intent on keeping their own dwelling and their independent lifestyle. Thus, a growing number of elderly people lived alone; women and widows were overrepresented among them. On the other hand, primarily in the 1960s, the number of young people, and especially young women, living alone rose, and they began to create a special urban lifestyle/culture for themselves in urban areas (singles).[42] However, it is true that the data indicate stagnation in the 1970s in several countries (the Netherlands, Norway and West Germany), and in the 1980s, there was a clear decline in the ratio of young adults not living with their parents.[43] In the decades after the Second World War, and especially from the 1970s, because of booming divorce numbers, the ratio of single-parent families also rose, and, in these, the parent often also lived alone and formed a one-person household after the child(ren) had grown up. As a consequence of these factors, by the 1980s, most adults in Western Europe lived in households without dependent children. Only in Ireland did more than half of the adults live in households with children.[44]

The rise in the share of one-person households in East Central Europe was primarily the result of the growth in the number of singles and elderly people living alone, but it partly followed from the improvement in life expectancy, and the increasing separation of families also contributed to the process. The rising number of divorces similarly created more one-person households, but the transformation of youth lifestyles contributed less than in Western Europe, because early marriage kept its dominance and thus the premarital independent households of the young did not have a considerable presence in East Central European societies, not even in the last third of the century.

Relationship between partners and attitudes towards children: growing symmetry and attention

Nevertheless, it is desirable not to restrict the examination of family changes to size and composition. In Europe, and, in general, in the Western World, as a result of a long-term process dating back at least to the early modern period, the family underwent complex changes involving not only nuclearization and the stabilization of the composition, but also the fundamental transformation of interpersonal relationships within the family. Families became more egalitarian, their rigid hierarchies (meaning, most of all, patriarchy) eased up and family members earned an increasing degree of autonomy. In addition, the intimacy of family life also grew as the emotional ties between the spouses gained a greater role and childrearing became the centre of family life. This development, also known as the emergence of the privatized family or the romantic revolution in family life, arguably first began in the middle classes and spread from there to the upper and lower classes. The process continued well into the twentieth century, and it was more or less complete by the mid-century in most European societies.[45]

Conjugal relationships

The emergence of a new, more egalitarian understanding of the role of the spouses (also called the 'symmetrical family'[46]) was essentially related to the change of women's position in society. The increase in female employment was, on the one hand, an indication of the altered social position of women. On the other hand, as several historians and sociologists claim, it was the most important individual factor of the transformation of family relationships; therefore, it can equally be regarded as both the consequence and the cause of changes. In this respect, not only the rise in the ratio of female employment is worthy of attention, but also the nature of female work and the improvement of women's relative wages, as compared with men's.[47]

In the early twentieth century, there were moderate differences in female employment among Western European countries. In 1900 in Austria, Switzerland and the Scandinavian countries, a little more than a third of all employees were women, and the corresponding ratio was around 30% in Germany, France, Belgium and Great Britain. Relatively few women worked in the Netherlands, where their share was below 25% of all employees. Although female employment increased considerably in all countries engaged in the First World War, it declined again (often dropping below 1900 levels) and usually did not digress from this level in the interwar period, mainly as a result of economic hardships and especially mass-scale unemployment (Table 3.8).[48]

In the decades after the Second World War, in Western Europe, the ratio of women among all employees usually increased, but this development was far from being equally paced and linear in all countries and in all periods. For example, in the Netherlands, first there was a decline, and only in the 1970s did female employment grow on a larger scale.[49] There was a partial rearrangement in the rank order of the countries of this region between 1945 and 1990: the Netherlands and Ireland were at the end of the list all through this period, whereas in the Scandinavian countries a rapid development resulted in the highest female employment (45–48%), even though they (with the exception of Finland) had belonged to the middle range after the Second World War.[50] The process accelerated in the 1970s and 1980s, when women already comprised one-third of all employees, even in those countries where they traditionally stayed away from the labour market, such as in the Netherlands, where the ratio of women among all employees grew by 8.9 percentage points between 1980 and 1990, thus reaching 39.2%. However, although the number of women entering the labour force, in fact, rose steeply in Denmark, Sweden and Norway, in several countries the rise in female employment was entirely, or almost entirely, the result of a decline in the male activity rate, such as in Austria, West Germany, Ireland and Switzerland.[51] In Southern Europe, female employment was always significantly below Western European levels.

In addition to the data presented so far, age-specific female employment levels are also good indicators of the persisting differences within Western Europe. Even though women in their early twenties took jobs in similar ratios (about 60–70% in all countries), marriage affected their participation in the labour market in varied patterns. Whereas in the 1970s in Great Britain, Sweden, France and Denmark, 50–70% of women between the ages of 30 and 50 returned to work after child-birth, in other countries (e.g. the Benelux or Ireland), only 20–35% of women between the ages of 40 and 50 were in employment.[52]

At the turn of the century and in the interwar period, female employment in East Central Europe fell in the middle range in a Western European comparison. Female employment rose rapidly even in an international comparison in the 1950s and 1960s. As a result of this development in the 1960s, the communist countries, and, most of all, Poland and East Germany, were in the lead in Europe, with the Scandinavian countries approaching, and only Finland reaching, their levels. The ratio qualifies as particularly high when we consider that in communist countries part-time jobs hardly existed, whereas this form of work was widespread in Western Europe, with part-timers amounting to 39% of female employees in Great Britain, 45% in Norway, and 32% in the Netherlands around 1980.[53] After the mid-1970s, the female employment gap closed somewhat between the countries of East Central and Western Europe, because levels had reached their peak by then in the communist countries, although the upward trend continued in all Western European societies.

The characteristics of female jobs also changed significantly. In the first half of the century, women's educational levels were greatly lagging behind men's, which considerably contributed to them taking jobs that required lower qualifications. Yet gender differences in education had already been gradually fading in that period, as indicated by the growing ratio of female students at universities: in 1930, Poland had the most remarkable figure, reaching 34%.[54] From the 1950s, women's education levels rocketed throughout Europe and became particularly high in East Central Europe. In 1960, of the Western European countries considered here, only Finland (46%), France (41%) and Sweden (33%) reached or surpassed the ratios found in

Poland (35%), Czechoslovakia (34%) and Hungary (30%), and the ratio of female students in these latter countries consistently remained among the highest in the following decades of the century. Consequently, in this region, the ratio of women in several professions requiring high qualifications, such as teachers, approached or reached that of men's starting from the 1960s. At the same time, women in communist countries also experienced the existence of the 'glass ceiling': the level of real wages and salaries was lower in the sectors primarily employing female labour than elsewhere. In the 1970s, Hungarian women, on the average, received three-quarters of men's wages for the same job, which was basically the same relative level as found in West Germany, Finland, Great Britain or the Netherlands, and it was significantly lower than the ratios observed in Italy (85%), Denmark (86%) or Sweden (92%).[55] Although the high ratios of women participating in education and the high female employment levels show the success of the emancipation policies of the communist countries, the persistence of significant discrepancies between men's and women's earnings shows the limits of these practices.

The fact that women joined the labour force on a mass scale was, in itself, an indication that women's goals and aspirations, as well as public attitudes towards the position of women in society, had undergone radical transformations. In the early 1980s, a survey of the European Commission showed that, in most of the Western European countries examined, the majority of the population, and not only women themselves, thought it desirable for women to seek gainful employment and for partners to share family-related tasks equally.[56] Another opinion poll conducted a few years later, around 1990, showed that 64–80% of those questioned preferred that both spouses contribute to the household income, except for the Netherlands, where only 32% responded this way.[57] Whereas a Gallup opinion poll found that in 1952 in Great Britain, the great majority considered an appropriate income and housing the most important to a happy marriage,[58] in the 1980s and 1990s, respondents in Great Britain, as well as in the other Western European countries, considered patience, mutual respect and sexual pleasure to be most crucial. Material aspects and class origin ranked at the end of the list in both recent studies cited.[59]

The actual practice of the division of labour in the family only partly reflects this value change, but a levelling-off process between the sexes has been taking place in this respect, at least from the 1960s. Although it is difficult to estimate what scale it reached, time budget studies show that in the mid-1960s in three Western European countries examined (Belgium, France and West Germany), in urban families with children, where both parents had a job, men spent only 8%, 14% and 7%, respectively, of the time that women did on housework. However, the amount of leisure time may be a more appropriate indicator, because it reflects the longer time men spend working outside the household. The study cited found that the differences in the amount of leisure time are smaller, but still considerable, with women in the aforementioned three countries commanding 69%, 64% and 66% of men's leisure time, respectively.[60] In the following decades, equalization between the sexes undoubtedly advanced. In the 1980s, as an average of seven Western European countries, men spent 20% of women's time on household chores and women's spare time already amounted to 95% of men's.[61] Compared with Western Europe, actual equality in the family emerged to a significantly smaller degree in East Central Europe, and less than what could have been expected on the basis of the stormy socioeconomic transformations after the Second World War, including the rise in female employment during communist times, which created a good basis here for abolishing patriarchy and enhancing women's emancipation. Neither normative relations, nor popular views on women's roles, nor the sharing of household tasks changed here so rapidly from the 1960s as in Western Europe.

In order to facilitate the understanding of this process, it is worth hereby referring to a 1965/1966 study that showed that in Hungary married urban women who had children and held jobs commanded only 52% of the spare time of men with a similar status, which was lower than the Belgian, French and West German figures cited above (69%, 64% and 66%) even then.[62] Another series of studies found that 15–69-year-old women's spare time declined compared with men's between 1963 and 1976, and despite recovering in the next decade, it reached only 73% by 1987.[63]

The transformation of expectations regarding marriage also signals the contradictory nature of East Central European family development. On the one hand, similar to Western Europe, personal choice and romantic love undoubtedly replaced instrumental criteria and parental influence as the main basis of spouse selection in all strata of East Central European societies by the last third of the century. On the other hand, there were signs of the perseverance of traditional considerations in spouse selection. International comparative value studies reveal that in East Central European societies in the 1990s, significantly more people considered the abundance of material goods (e.g. high income, good housing conditions) important for a happy marriage than in Western Europe, and fewer thought mutual understanding and tolerance crucial in that respect.[64]

The attitudes to children

Although seminal works on family history have illuminated the changes in the meaning of childhood and the situation of children in European societies in the seventeenth and eighteenth centuries,[65] still relatively little research and scarcely any comparative studies have been dedicated to this topic as regards the twentieth century. However, we may consider Lawrence Stone's verdict valid for the twentieth century as well, which claims that one of the most explicit developments of the past four centuries of Western family history was a virtually continuous growth of attention to children, even though specific attitudes toward children did alter in this period, at times being more permissive and at other times taking the opposite direction.[66] Here, we pursue two major lines of investigation, both of which indicate how public attention towards children, as well as social conceptions, values and norms related to them, have changed in the course of the century. Thus, the discussion first focuses on social policy measures targeting children, including the development of childcare facilities, then on the development of children's rights.

State support for families and children is mainly the outcome of the post-war decades; however, some measures had already been adopted in the interwar era or even earlier in several European countries. Concern about the health and well-being of children was a major motive behind the adoption of the first measures allowing mothers to take time off from work before and after childbirth.

Maternity benefits had been introduced by the end of the First World War in almost all Western and South European countries, but their level was moderate, usually amounting to 4–8 weeks of maternity leave with no or low cash benefits. After the Second World War, these programs expanded, but with great intra-European differences, especially as regards the cash payments during maternity leave. In 1975, the most generous maternity benefits were paid in Sweden, Italy and West Germany, and the lowest in Norway, the United Kingdom and Switzerland.[67] The communist countries were remarkable in this respect, where in the period after the Second World War, a sophisticated system of maternity support was established, consisting of maternity leave, cash benefits and labour protection. Considering the relative levels, these benefits, complemented by the protection of pregnant women and mothers with young children by labour law, far surpassed the average of European countries. For instance, in 1985 in Hungary, a new generation of 'child nursing allowance' was introduced, which reached the level of sickness benefit and was initially paid until the child was one year old, then extended to cover the first one and a half years, with an additional eighteen months of lower payment. This programme was more generous than the similar scheme in Sweden, which had been long considered as the most advanced system in Western Europe.

In fact, pronatalism has a long tradition in Hungary, which was the first country in Europe to introduce family allowance, called 'childrearing supplement', for state employees in 1912.[68] In the interwar period, some other countries also began to pay family allowance (Belgium, France), but it truly diffused during and after the years of the Second World War. The size of the benefit varied greatly. In 1961, in Italy, the family assistance for two children amounted to 21.5% of average earnings in the processing industry; in Belgium, to 16.5%; and in Norway, to 2.5%; whereas this benefit did not yet exist in Germany. Later, from the 1970s, differences became more moderate in this area, although in Italy, formerly providing the largest allowance, this program completely ceased to exist by 1990.[69]

Childcare facilities (crèche and kindergarten), appearing in the nineteenth century in Europe, were originally maintained by religious and other charity organizations. These provisions were intended to assist disadvantaged and single-parent families, that is, they originated in welfare considerations. They were also meant to provide children with a better living environment and to protect them from crime and other dangers of modern urban life. Publicly funded kindergartens were set up in Portugal and Finland in the 1880s, but state intervention in this area was usually minimal and limited to the control of adequate childcare standards. Although in most countries engaged in the World Wars, the number of kindergartens increased with the rise in female employment, their poor relief character persisted all through the period of wars, not in the least because minimal public resources were allocated to this end.[70] In the aftermath of the Second World War, there was little demand for public childcare, because the level of labour force participation by mothers with young children was still low. However, from the 1960s onwards, governments began to extend the support to all children of working parents. In addition to the well-being of children, several other motivations influenced this process. The Nordic governments pursued gender equality and the establishment of women's equal opportunities in work through the development of childcare facilities, whereas in France and Italy, pronatalist and educational considerations carried more weight. Different objectives in public policy sometimes resulted in similarly high levels of provisions of childcare; for instance, in 1988 in Belgium and France, 95%, in Italy, more than 85%, in Denmark, 85%, and in Sweden, 80% of children of the appropriate age were enrolled in kindergarten. In other cases, the result was more moderate: in West Germany, 65%, in the Netherlands, Finland and Norway, 50% each, and in the United Kingdom, only 35% of children attended pre-primary institutions in the late 1980s.[71] Thus, regarding the role of public institutions in child care, the considerable differences within Western Europe persisted all through the twentieth century. Correspondingly, families retained a greater role in care where the establishment of these facilities was not a priority of public policy.

In East Central Europe, the ratio of children attending kindergarten was close to the Western European average in the first half of the century, but then surpassed it considerably. Although allowances for children and maternity benefits were motivated primarily by welfare and pronatalist objectives, childcare institutions were intended to give the opportunity to mothers with young children to take jobs on the one hand, and were established in view of their educational significance on the other. In addition, in the period after the Second World War, communist indoctrination also increased public attention to children, treating the younger generations as prime targets of political education on the basis that ideological messages were supposed to be better received by them than by adults, and this also contributed to the large-scale development of state childcare facilities.

Family allowance and other child-related social policy measures undoubtedly signal a heightened public concern about children. However, in the twentieth century, societies did not simply pay more attention to children, but the nature of public attitudes to children also underwent significant changes. Considerations for children's welfare and optimal living environment did play a role in these policies, but the measures often were also governed by other sets of motives, in particular, pronatalism referred to above: they were regarded as instruments to increase population size. Therefore, other phenomena should also be examined as possible indicators of how the non-instrumental attention to children changed and how children were treated.

Although little comparative data is available on cultural values related to children from the early twentieth century in Europe, it appears that in the past century the main direction of change in attitudes to children was the increasing respect for children's personality and autonomy. Evidence for this claim includes isolated but revealing information from two French opinion polls from the first and the second half of the century. In 1938, 30% of the French parents surveyed expressed that it was the parents' task to choose a career for children, but only 4.4% shared this opinion in 1977.[72] Göran Therborn offers more systematic evidence on the transformations of attitudes to children based on the comparative, long-term analysis of children's rights. He argued that the laws and administrative forms of state intervention played a significant role in shaping the modern concept of childhood (for example, through regulating schooling and the conditions for work) and thus could enable us to draw conclusions regarding the changes in social attitudes to children.[73]

Therborn focuses on three main areas of change in children's rights in the twentieth century. The first is the replacement of the traditional patriarchal family with a newly emerging child-centred family, in which parents have equal obligations to the child, and in which the child's best interests enjoy priority over other considerations (e.g. custody decisions in divorce cases are not based on the guilt or the lack thereof of the parties). The second aspect concerns the realization of children's equal rights with regard to both inheritance and paternity irrespective of whether they were born in or out of wedlock. The third research area is how children's autonomy and personal integrity are realized, primarily with regard to the legal prohibition of corporal punishment by parents and guardians, or the legal possibilities of children to divorce their parents or guardians (a new right emerging at the end of the last century in several countries).[74]

Although numerous family historians regard the early modern period as an era when momentous changes in ideas about childhood (the so-called discovery of childhood) had occurred, yet it may appear surprising that children's rights in the sense referred to above did not prevail in any country by the beginning of the twentieth century.[75] Parents did not have equal rights concerning their children, and in divorce cases, the courts did not exclusively consider the children's best interests when deciding on custody. Children born outside marriage were discriminated against everywhere: a good example is the widespread use of expressions such as 'illegitimate' and 'illicit' child, and often not because of some obsolete legal tradition; the German civil code codified this usage as late as 1896, the Swiss code in 1907.[76]

Table 3.9 indicates the surprising temporal differences in changing this situation. Norway and Sweden were the first to introduce legal equality both between spouses and between children during the First World War, soon followed by the other Nordic countries. Only England and Scotland kept up with them to some extent, changing family law in the interwar period.

It seems that the golden age of marriage and family after the Second World War conserved family law, as it were, because then there were hardly any significant changes in children's rights in the Western European countries, with the exception of West Germany. However, legislation was conspicuously active in the 1970s and 1980s in Western Europe, when a number of countries guaranteed children's basic rights, a process largely furthered by the activities of the UN and other international organizations (see e.g. the UN recommendation of the equal rights of children born out of wedlock in 1959), and more recently, by the rulings of the European Court

TABLE 3.9   The development of children's rights in European countries before 1990

| | *Rights* | | |
	Child-centred family	*Equality*	*Integrity*
To 1918	Norway: 1915 Sweden: 1915, 1920	Norway: 1915 (Sweden: 1917)	
To 1945	Denmark: 1925, Finland: 1929 England: 1925, Scotland: 1925	Denmark: 1937 (Finland: 1922)	
To 1970	Hungary: 1952 Ireland: 1964 FRG: 1957–58	Hungary: 1952 Sweden: 1970 England: 1969 (FRG: 1969)	
To 1980	Austria: 1970s France: 1970 Italy: mid-1970s Netherlands: mid-1970s	Finland: 1975 (Austria: 1970s) (Switzerland: 1974) (France: 1972) Italy: 1975	(Norway: 1972) (Sweden: 1980)
To 1990		Ireland: 1987 Scotland: 1986 Belgium: 1987 Netherlands: 1986 Austria: 1990	Norway: 1981 (Finland: 1983) (Denmark: 1985) (Austria: 1989)

Notes: Child-centred family: positive legal formulation of parents having equal obligations to the child, and the child's best interests enjoy priority over other considerations (e.g. in custody litigation cases); equality: children's equal rights are legally guaranteed concerning both paternity and inheritance, regardless of whether they were born in or out of wedlock; integrity: children's autonomy and personal integrity is guaranteed by right with regard to both the legal prohibition of corporal punishment by parents and guardians, and the children's right to divorce their parents or guardians; parentheses indicate a partial realization of rights; countries examined include England, Austria, Belgium, Denmark, Finland, France, Ireland, Norway, West Germany, Italy, Scotland, Switzerland, Sweden and Hungary.

Sources: Göran Therborn, 'The Politics of Childhood: The Rights of Children in Modern Times', in Francis G. Castles, ed., *Families of Nations: Patterns of Public Policy in Western Democracies*, Aldershot: Dartmouth, 1993, 256 (Western Europe; complemented with dates from the text); Mezey Barna, ed., *Magyar jogtörténet*, Budapest: Osiris, 1996; Nizsalovszky Endre, *A család jogi rendjének alapjai*, Budapest: KJK, 1963, 254–262 (Hungary).

of Human Rights in Strasbourg.[77] Although Belgium and Switzerland had not codified the prioritizing of children's interests in divorce litigations by 1990, the differences regarding children's rights definitely decreased in (Western) Europe by the 1980s.[78]

This holds true even despite emerging differences in one specific area. In the 1970s and 1980s, a new generation of children's rights emerged: the recognition of children's autonomy and personal integrity, in the sense discussed above. It originated in the notion that the protection of children's rights must be supplemented by granting participatory rights to children.[79] However, Norway was the only country to guarantee these rights with consistency before 1990, not only prohibiting children's corporal punishment in the family, but also giving children a right to divorce their parents or guardians. Besides, the institution of an ombudsman for children was also created.[80] In the other Scandinavian countries and in Austria, only the prohibition of corporal punishment was legislated.[81]

Communist countries were clearly vanguards of children's rights. Here, there was a great turn in family law in the years after the Second World War. Women's equality in the family was declared, the necessity to protect children was emphasized, and the discrimination against those born out of wedlock was abolished. The third generation of children's rights (the rights to personal autonomy and personal integrity) did not emerge in the communist period, and was only partially guaranteed in East Central Europe in the 1990s.

Therborn argues that the significance of patriarchism in the legal system is clear among the factors explaining the development of children's rights. If this was weak, children's rights could be guaranteed early (Scandinavia). Similarly, the greater the presence of egalitarian principles in the legal system, the greater the chance they would be applied to children (West Germany). However, the Code Napoleon, as a judicial predecessor, and traditions of Roman law exerted negative influence in this regard (Southern Europe), whereas the centralized nature of legislation (Scandinavia), openness to international cultural influences and a sensitivity to international trends in legislation (Scandinavia), a strong constitutional court (West Germany), as well as strong liberal and left-wing parties (Denmark and Norway) all promoted the codification of children's rights.[82]

Nevertheless, care must be taken when interpreting legal developments, because the implementation of laws might have diverged in societies and popular behaviour did not necessarily follow regulation. This is the more so because other studies show smaller differences in attitudes to children than observable in family law. Although value surveys are available only from the end of the twentieth century, these reveal great similarities in expectations toward children throughout Western Europe. In the early 1980s, honesty ranked first everywhere among the values parents considered important in childrearing, followed by tolerance with, and respect for, other people, good manners (politeness and neatness in France and Belgium) and responsibility, usually in this order.[83] Ten years later practically the same results were found, with the difference that responsibility ranked first then.[84]

Besides (and, in a few cases, instead of) these personal qualities, certain characteristics received special emphasis in some countries. Among the most important of children's personality traits and parents' educational objectives were, for example, independence in Denmark; independence and diligence in West Germany; obedience, loyalty and self-control in Great Britain; self-control, obedience and religious belief in Ireland; obedience again in Northern Ireland; hard work in France and Belgium; and loyalty in Italy.[85]

Although there are no long-term comparative value studies available in this area either, the World Values Survey of the early 1990s, cited above, suggests that no distinct East Central European pattern of values related to parenting emerged after the Second World War, even though some commonalities are detectable in the

region. Patterns in Czechoslovakia showed independence the least important anywhere in Europe as a quality that children can be encouraged to learn at home,
whereas Hungarian parents thought of their roles and tasks similarly to what was
found in the majority of Western European countries, emphasizing the autonomy/
independence of children. In this regard, there appeared a dividing line within
Western Europe as well, between the aforementioned countries and Great Britain,
Ireland, France and Italy, where children's independence was less promoted
whereas parents' sacrifices gained more weight.[86] A common European trait was an
emphasis on good manners, but, in other respects, weaker parallelism prevailed
between European societies in educational objectives. In East Central European
countries, hard work and thrift were emphasized more than in Western European
countries, whereas tolerance was attributed smaller importance than anywhere
in Western Europe but Norway.[87]

Interpretations and debates

Characterized by separation from the broader kin group and community, respecting
the autonomy and integrity of family members, mutual affection and care, the concept
of the modern nuclear family has been shaped by the contribution of various directions
of family research. Michael Anderson distinguishes between three major traditions in
family history: the demographic, the household economics and the sentiments
approaches. These paradigms sometimes yield conflicting results and interpretations,
but more often they complement each other and equally advance the understanding
of the development of the family in modern and contemporary Europe.

The effect of demographic factors on family life is straightforward. With regard
to a few changes referred to above, the contraction of households and families, and
the transformation of their composition, resulted in households becoming domestic
units in which nuclear families normally lived. The disappearance of servants, lodgers
and kin from these households, along with the decline of the mortality rate and the
reduction of the phase of childbearing, also contributed to stabilizing the composition of families. Thereupon, the growing stability of the family structure created a
good basis for the emergence of attitudes characteristic of the nuclear family, such
as intimacy.[88]

For many researchers, the major cause of changes was the transformation of
the functions of the family, and especially the shifts in the household economy and
the nature and the location of work. The pre-industrial family, and, in particular,
the traditional peasant household community, represented a unit of subsistence,
providing the basic form of labour organization.

Although a greater economic differentiation had already changed the system of
family production in pre-industrial times, yet it was the process of industrialization
that relieved the family of most of its economic functions all over Europe. This
process began in the eighteenth century in Western Europe and, for a great part,
took place in the course of the twentieth century. Parallel with industrialization
and commercialization, wage labour gained ground. Family members able to

undertake paid work became independent of the household economy in growing numbers, which contributed to the decisive weakening of patriarchism. The father lost his role as head of the labour organization, and thus the institutional foundation of his authority over family members. Furthermore, the spread of contractual labour diminished the significance of the parental inheritance and, thus, was also an agent of the emancipation process in family. With the surrender of economic functions, greater freedom of choice was granted to family members to define their roles and to select their occupations, as well as the appropriate marriage partner. The detachment of the home from the place of work also gave more space to family members to develop their own lives. In a similar manner, as neolocality took over from patrilocality in the case of newly married couples, they gained greater freedom to lead their private life.

The loss of productive and other tasks made it possible for two functions to emerge as central: the socialization of children and the provision of emotional support for the family's adult members.[89] Similarly, the 'loss of functions', or (with some euphemism) the family's 'discharge from functions' enabled the family to become the place of privacy.[90] This process can be largely associated with social strata booming in the course of the twentieth century, namely salaried employees and the middle classes. This also explains why the modern nuclear family became virtually continent-wide by the second half of the twentieth century.

Other experts find it more plausible to interpret this process as a transformation of economic functions. Pierre Bourdieu argues that the modern family does not separate itself from economy, but the relationship of the two is transformed. Based on their economic power, the bourgeoisie are able to fully separate the place of work from the home and to save family life from the direct influence of economic factors. This behaviour becomes part of the bourgeois habitus that the families transmit from generation to generation. The habitus constitutes 'symbolic capital': it forms the basis of social differentiation and has a great role in marriage and other social relationships, that is, in the reproduction of social status and position.

However, one can reasonably question whether the demographic or the household economics approaches, which often resort to functionalist interpretations, could indeed offer a convincing explanation of the transformation of the European family over the past centuries. Philippe Ariès, Lawrence Stone and Edward Shorter, considered principal representatives of the sentiments or cultural approach, identify the essence of the changes not in the shifts in the economic environment or in the demographic structure of the family. They locate it in the strengthening of emotional ties between spouses and between family members in general and in the desire for recognition of personal freedom and autonomy within the family.[91] As Shorter put it, 'the nuclear family is a state of mind rather than a particular kind of structure or a set of household arrangements. ... What really distinguishes the nuclear family ... from other patterns of family life in Western society is a special sense of solidarity that separates the domestic unit from the surrounding community'.[92]

Shorter attributes the 'surge of sentiments' within the family to the emergence and spread of capitalism clearly predating industrialization. He considers increased participation of young, unmarried people, and in particular, women, in the free-market labour force, as well as increased living standards and the separation of the place of work and home, instrumental in what he calls the 'romantic revolution'; however, he finds the 'ethos of market transactions' to be the decisive factor, which in essence means individualism. The diffusion of new attitudes essential on the marketplace and 'learned egoism' induced the liberation of emotional and sexual relationships. The desire for freedom therefore was rooted in capitalist ideas, which was then transferred to sexual behaviour and family life.

Accordingly, Shorter believes that romantic love and sexual freedom appeared in non-agricultural lower classes, because they were exposed to market capitalism first. Romantic love as the basis of marriage and partnership diffused and by the second half of the twentieth century, it gradually triumphed almost everywhere in the continent. Not fully consistently, he also holds that maternal love and good mothering as well as domesticity emerged in the middle classes because these were made possible by their higher standards of living.[93]

In contrast, studying English social history, Stone argues that what he called 'affective individualism' was already firmly established around 1750 in the middle and upper classes, and the nineteenth and twentieth centuries witnessed the spread of this pattern to lower strata. The rise of affective individualism meant primarily that marriage was based on personal attraction, and family bound together by strong emotional ties. Stone traces the transformation of family-related attitudes mainly to a growing interest in the self and the recognition of the uniqueness of the individual, along with a pursuit of personal autonomy, which ultimately resulted from changes in religious and political thought. He finds the diffusion of Protestantism a decisive factor, which emphasizes the private nature of the connection between man and God, and, especially religious introspection originating from the Calvinist anxiety about salvation, but he also argues for a link between the fall of absolute monarchy and the demise of patriarchal authoritarianism in the family.[94]

The changing perceptions of childhood were first systematically addressed by Philippe Ariès, who argued that in the traditional society, the idea of childhood as a distinct phase of the life course did not exist. As soon as people could take care of themselves, they became members of the adult society and worked, dressed and behaved accordingly. However, attitudes to children began to alter and the modern concept of childhood emerged. This stage of life was more and more separated from adulthood and the specific needs of infants were acknowledged, which is indicated by new attitudes in education, literature and garments specifically produced for children. Infants became regarded as vulnerable human beings, who needed to be protected but also disciplined and systematically educated. In parallel, the modern concept of parenthood emerged, including responsibilities for children, and the elements of public responsibilities for children appeared as well. Ariès is not really specific about the timing of the process and how social differences shaped it. Still, it seems clear that he regards the seventeenth century as the beginning, and the

Western European aristocracy and the educated classes as the pioneers, of this development. Concerning the latter point, there is little disagreement among scholars, but numerous family historians think that the modern concept of child-hood is most probably a product of long-term development, stretching to the late nineteenth century and even beyond.[95]

Although proponents of the sentiments approach strongly argue for the significance of cultural factors in the emergence of the modern nuclear family, their reasoning is often more intuitive than resting on systematic evidence. There is as yet no comprehensive mechanism proposed in a coherent way for the transformation of beliefs and notions related to the family; moreover, the effect of these beliefs is not fully elaborated either as yet. Thus, several scholars following this tradition discuss the culture of the family as hardly linked to economic factors or to the change in work organization. Especially for Ariès and Stone, changes in family life are almost entirely induced by new religious ideas, philosophical thoughts and educational concepts. Shorter's analysis of change is more structured and includes the influence of market capitalism on interpersonal relationships in the family, but he also concludes by referring to capitalism primarily as the carrier of an ethos, thus underestimating the significance of other aspects of socioeconomic change.[96]

Even if the sentiments school tends to overstress the role of cultural factors and to play down other factors that arguably influence culture in any society, a major contribution of these authors has been their initiative to draw attention to aspects of family change mostly neglected by family history, such as new attitudes towards children, or the emerging desire for privacy in families. They vividly portrayed these phenomena and set the research agenda for modern European family history for a long time. The elaboration of convincing accounts of causal relationships obviously needs the effort of the whole range of family research.

Divorce and the pluralization of family forms: the silent revolution of values at work

The modern nuclear family discussed in the previous sections became dominant by the mid-twentieth century throughout Europe. However, the structural features, ideas and behaviours associated with it had not been fully developed everywhere in the continent yet by the time that many of these characteristics had already started to erode in some societies. The changes, also known as the pluralization of marriage and family forms, particularly progressed in Scandinavia from the 1960s onwards. Although this was a complex process, the transformation of the attitudes to marriage and family is well reflected in the great increase in divorce as well as cohabitation and extramarital births, and therefore these developments are discussed in detail.

Divorce

Large differences can be found in European family development in areas in which legal regulation plays a great role. A most obvious example here is the dissolution of unions.[97] Divorce law was varied across Europe in the early twentieth century and diversity survived until the last third of the century. For instance, in Finland, not only were spouses able to divorce before the Second World War but the courts also abandoned the fault principle as the only grounds for divorce as early as 1917. In Italy, there was no legal possibility for the dissolution of unions until 1970, whereas in Spain divorce was legalized only in 1982.[98] However, the 1960s and 1970s brought about considerable convergence in this respect, because countries applying the most restrictive regulations eased their rules for divorce significantly (with the obvious exception of Ireland, which held out until 1997).[99]

Thus, in addition to the differences in the levels of modernization, religious faith and demographic conditions, legal regulation also played a fundamental role in the fact that divorce rates varied to a great extent even in the years before the First World War in the Western half of the continent.[100] Regarding the number of divorces per 100 marriages, the difference between Switzerland and England/Wales was twenty fold in 1900. Wherever divorce was possible, the break-up of marriages multiplied manifold by the mid-century. The ranking of the countries regarding frequency also changed. Whereas in the interwar period the fewest people continued to separate in England/Wales, Austria moved to the first place (here divorce rates were high in the territory of the later republic even before the First World War), but by 1960, she was overtaken by Denmark and Sweden. The rise of divorces was especially large-scale from the mid-1960s, with long-time leader Scandinavia and latecomer Great Britain being at the top in this regard. In the mid-1970s in Sweden, there were half as many divorces as there were marriages, and this ratio improved only a little in the next decade. In Great Britain and Denmark, marital disruption climaxed in the mid-1980s, approaching half the number of marriages. At this time, divorce rates were around 30% in most Western European countries (Table 3.10).

As for the East Central European region, the divorce rates of the Czech territories (later Czechoslovakia) and especially Hungary were among the highest ones in Europe in the early century and between the Word Wars. After the Second World War, family dissolution rates rose rapidly in the region, where divorce laws were liberalized earlier than in most Western European countries. Data available for Poland in this period show that significantly more people were divorced here than in Southern European Catholic countries. At the end of the 1980s, beside the Nordic countries and Great Britain, the highest union disruption rates occurred in East Central European countries (East Germany, Czechoslovakia and Hungary), as shown by the number of divorces per 100 new marriages shown in Table 3.10. This index is sensitive to family formation nonetheless. Other indicators, such as the total divorce rate, that control the fluctuation of the number of marriages signalled an increase on a smaller scale in the 1970s and a moderate decline in the second half of the 1980s in several East Central European countries. After 1945, the social composition of those divorced also changed remarkably, because divorcees became younger (similarly to those getting married) and between 1950 and 1990, there was also a rise in the divorce ratio of families with children.[101]

TABLE 3.10 The number of divorces per 100 new marriages in European countries, 1900–1990

	1900	1910	1920	1930	1940	1950	1960	1970	1980	1990
United Kingdom	0.2	0.2	0.8	1.1	1.6	8.6	6.9	14.0	40.1	46.3
France	2.6	4.6	5.6	6.8	9.9	10.5	9.4	10.2	24.3	36.9
Netherlands	1.4	2.0	3.0	4.5	4.4	7.8	6.4	8.3	28.5	29.7
Belgium	1.2	1.9	2.1	3.5	5.1	7.1	7.0	8.7	21.8	31.5
Germany/FRG	1.7	3.0	4.1	7.2	8.0	15.8	9.4	17.2	26.6	29.6
Austria	0.7	1.3	6.2	12.5	12.6	16.3	13.7	19.6	28.7	36.0
Switzerland	4.0	5.6	6.4	8.8	9.5	13.1	12.5	16.0	30.5	28.3
Sweden	1.3	1.8	3.1	5.1	5.9	14.8	17.9	29.9	52.9	47.8
Denmark	2.1	3.7	4.4	7.9	9.8	17.7	18.6	26.2	51.4	43.6
Finland	0.7	1.0	2.2	4.5	4.3	10.8	11.1	14.8	32.2	52.5
Norway		2.8	3.6	4.9	3.4	8.5	10.1	11.7	29.8	46.4
Italy									3.7	8.1
Spain									4.7	9.3
Poland						4.1	6.1	12.3	13.0	16.6
Czechoslovakia						9.8	14.4	19.7	28.7	31.1
Hungary	3.7	4.7	6.6	7.1	7.8	10.6	18.7	23.6	34.6	37.5

Notes: Different data: United Kingdom 1900–1990: England and Wales; different years: France: 1937; Austria: 1937; Switzerland: 1941; Spain: 1981; Hungary: 1906–1910, 1911–1915, 1921.

Sources: Peter Flora, ed., *State, Economy, and Society in Western Europe*, vol. II, Frankfurt/M.: Campus, 1987, 162–164 (Austria 1900–1970), 167 (Belgium 1900–1970), 170–171 (Denmark 1900–1970), 174–175 (Finland 1900–1970), 178–179 (France 1900–1970), 182–183 (Germany 1900–1970), 190–191 (the Netherlands 1900–1970), 194–195 (Norway 1910–1970), 198–199 (Sweden 1900–1970), 202–203 (Switzerland 1900–1920), 205–206 (England and Wales 1900–1970); Jean Kellerhals, Jean-François Perrin and Laura Voneche, 'Switzerland', in Robert Chester, ed., *Divorce in Western Europe*, Leiden: Martinus Nijhoff, 1977, 200 (Switzerland 1930–1960); Franz Rothenbacher, *The European Population since 1945*, Houndmills: Palgrave, 2005, 165 (Czechoslovakia 1950–1990), 671 (Poland 1950–1990), 93 (Austria 1990), 327 (Germany 1990); Franz Rothenbacher, *The European Population since 1945*, CD-ROM Publication, Houndmills: Palgrave, 2005 (Western Europe 1980–1990, Spain 1990); *Történeti statisztikai idősorok, 1867–1992*, I. kötet, Budapest: KSH, 1992.

The high divorce rates emerging in the second half of the twentieth century thus indicate a characteristically contradictory attitude to marriage in the East Central European population. Whereas the traditional marriage pattern survived in the region to the 1990s, divorce figures continually increased throughout the century and were constantly above the Western European average.

The pluralization of family forms

After the Second World War, it was not only the number of divorces that rocketed in Europe, but there were other significant changes in family development. Of these, the rapid diffusion of cohabitations and extramarital births deserve special attention.[102]

The phenomenon of couples living together without entering marriage had been well known long before the twentieth century, especially in certain subgroups of the population. However, in the 1960s and early 1970s, cohabitation became more prevalent than earlier in two Scandinavian countries: Sweden and Denmark; in 1975, in Denmark 30% and in Sweden 29% of women aged 20–24 chose this form of partnership. At this time, the ratio of such relationships was still low in other societies, e.g. in 1975 in France 4% and in 1976 in Great Britain 2% in the same cohort. Then in the second half of the 1970s, and especially in the 1980s, cohabitation became increasingly popular in other Western European countries as well. In 1990, in the young female age group mentioned, 24% lived in such a relationship in Great Britain, 24% in France, 23% in the Netherlands, 18% in Germany and 18% in Belgium.[103] In the meantime, the ratio grew further and reached its climax in the early and mid-1980s in Denmark and Sweden with 45% and 32%, respectively, followed by a decline in the succeeding years.[104]

In the 1960s and 1970s, cohabitation prevailed primarily in the young age group referred to above and the proliferation of such relationships was considerably more limited even among those but a few years older. Even though traditions of such partnerships also existed in some countries (e.g. in France) in the working class, at that time this form of living arrangement was still associated with university or college students, because such couples first appeared around campuses.[105] This may be most probably explained by longer education, the progress of women's emancipation, the spread of modern contraceptive methods, and by the rejection of traditional values: all of which were characteristic of students (Table 3.11). However, in the 1980s, cohabitation diffused in various social classes and milieus, as well as age cohorts. It became the highest among 25–29-year-olds in 1990 in Denmark and Germany, with 41% and 21%, respectively.[106]

Of course, divergences can also be found here. Cohabitation without marriage did not spread in all European countries to the degree discussed so far, because the

TABLE 3.11 The ratio of women cohabiting before marriage in European countries, 1947–1977 (%)

	Marriage cohorts			
	1947–1965	*1966–1970*	*1971–1975*	*1975–1977*
United Kingdom		4.0	12.0	20.0
France		13.0	22.0	31.0
Sweden	39.0	53.0	81.0	89.0
Denmark			80.0	
Norway	11.0	15.0	26.0	47.0

Notes: United Kingdom: currently married women, without Northern Ireland; France, Denmark: currently married women; Sweden, Norway: women married at any point in time; different years: United Kingdom: 1966–1970, 1976–1977; France: 1966–1970, 1976–1977; Sweden: 1950–1965, 1970–1975, 1975–1981; Norway: 1970–1975.

Source: *Patterns of First Marriage: Timing and Prevalence,* New York: United Nations, 1990, 253.

ratio among 20–24-year-old women was merely 1% in Italy and 4% in Ireland even in 1990. Moreover, such cohabitation was usually transitory and short, characteristically preceding marriage elsewhere as well. Although this was not yet a trait in partnerships started between 1968 and 1970, later it was relatively rare for children to be living in these households. For example, in the early 1980s in West Germany, 10% of cohabiting couples had children and only a third of these children were born from the current relationship.[107] Two Scandinavian countries (Denmark and Sweden) were important exceptions, where long-term cohabitation was widespread and large numbers of children were born to such couples.[108]

As we have seen, in most Western European countries, the decline in the frequency of marriages from the 1960s took place parallel to a significant proliferation in cohabitation. A characteristic feature of East Central European family development is that here cohabitation did not boom even by the 1980s. It seems that in this region, a decline in nuptiality only made pre-marriage relationships longer and was not associated with a rise in cohabitation. In addition to its low ratio, the nature of existing cohabitations was also distinct in the region. In Western Europe, usually the trial marriage type of cohabitation of youngsters prevailed, which was rarely linked to social disadvantage (a situation found in French and English big cities).[109] In contrast, in East Central European societies, women who cohabitated characteristically had poor education, or were divorcees with children or were widows.[110] A good example indicating the divergence from Western Europe is that in the 1970s in several East Central European countries, the ratio of cohabitation was the lowest in the cohorts of the 20–24 and the 25–29-year-olds – in the same cohorts in which marriage was most frequent and where in Western Europe the ratio of cohabitations was the highest. In contrast, the ratio of cohabitations gradually increased in the over-30 age groups and reached its heights among those over 60; in this latter cohort, the majority of cohabiting partners had been widowed. The underrepresentation of the young was largely because of the housing shortage, because singles in their teens and twenties only rarely had their independent dwelling in East Central European countries.

Extramarital births, like cohabitation, had reached relatively high levels even before the twentieth century in certain social groups in Europe. However, the ratio was below 10% in all Western European countries in the early twentieth century, with the exception of Austria and Sweden, where they amounted to 13.5% and 11.4% of all births, respectively. In the interwar period, this magnitude was only temporarily surpassed by a few countries (Austria and Sweden remaining at the top), but it was declining from even this, mostly relatively low level up until the 1960s.

Real change in this regard was brought by the 1960s again. From this decade, the greatest rise in the ratio of extramarital births is found in Sweden and Denmark: from 15% to 40% in the former and from 10% to 33% in the latter country between 1965 and 1980. The rise continued in these Nordic countries, so that they ranked first in European statistics in 1990 with 47.0% and 46.4%, respectively, and in the meantime, they were joined by Norway (38.6%). In other countries, the rise in extramarital births began later but progressed at a fast pace, and subsequently showed considerable convergence at the end of the twentieth century. Nevertheless, in contrast to the high Scandinavian figures referred to, in Switzerland and in Italy, only 6.1% and 6.5% of all births were extramarital even as late as 1990 (Table 3.12).

TABLE 3.12 Extramarital births as a ratio of all births in European countries, 1900–2000 (%)

	1900	1910	1920	1930	1940	1950	1960	1970	1980	1990	2000
United Kingdom	4.0	4.1	1.6	4.6	4.4	5.0	5.2	8.0	11.5	27.9	39.5
France	8.8	9.5	9.9	8.3	6.3	7.1	6.1	6.8	11.4	30.1	42.6
Netherlands	2.6	2.1	2.1	1.8	1.4	1.5	1.4	2.1	4.1	11.4	24.9
Belgium	7.4	6.1	7.1	4.0	3.1	2.6	2.1	2.8	4.1	11.6	28.0
Ireland	2.7	2.8	2.7	3.2	3.2	2.6	1.6	2.7	5.0	14.6	31.5
Germany/FRG	8.6	9.0	11.2	12.0	7.6	9.7	7.6	5.5	7.6	10.5	23.4
Austria	13.5	12.1	23.0	27.1	22.8	18.3	13.0	12.8	17.8	23.6	31.3
Switzerland	4.5	4.5	4.4	4.4	3.8	3.8	3.8	3.8	4.7	6.1	10.7
Sweden	11.4	14.2	15.7	15.8	11.3	9.8	11.3	18.4	39.7	47.0	55.3
Denmark	9.6	11.1	11.7	10.7	8.8	6.5	7.8	11.0	33.2	46.4	44.6
Norway	7.3	6.6	7.6	7.1	6.4	4.1	3.7	6.9	14.5	38.6	49.6
Finland	6.3	7.4	8.6	8.3	9.3	5.2	4.0	5.8	13.1	25.2	39.2
Italy	5.9	4.9	4.7	5.0	3.8	3.4	2.4	2.2	4.3	6.5	9.7
Spain							2.3	1.4	3.9	9.6	17.7
Greece							1.2	1.1	1.5	2.2	4.0
Czechoslovakia			11.5	11.3	8.0	6.2	4.9	5.7	5.7	7.7	21.8/ 18.3
Hungary	9.6	9.6	8.0	8.9	8.4	8.5	5.7	5.2	6.6	13.1	29.0
Poland			5.8			5.1	5.7	5.0	4.8	5.8	12.1

Notes: United Kingdom: 1900–1950 England and Wales; different years: France: 1938; Ireland: 1925; Germany: 1938; Austria: 1937; Czechoslovakia 2000: Czech Republic and Slovakia; Hungary 1900–1910: contemporary territory.

Sources: Peter Flora, ed., *State, Economy, and Society in Western Europe*, vol. II, Frankfurt/M.: Campus, 1987, 162–164 (Austria 1900–1950), 166–167 (Belgium 1900–1950), 170–171 (Denmark 1900–1950), 174–175 (Finland 1900–1950), 178–179 (France 1900–1950), 182–183 (Germany 1900–1950), 185–186 (Ireland 1920–1950), 187–188 (Italy 1900–1950), 190–191 (the Netherlands 1900–1950), 194–195 (Norway 1900–1950), 198–199 (Sweden 1900–1950), 202–203 (Switzerland 1900–1950), 205–206 (England and Wales 1900–1950); Eurostat, ed., *Bevölkerungsstatistik, 1998*, Luxemburg: Eurostat, 1999 (Western Europe 1960); Council of Europe, ed., *Recent Demographic Developments in Europe*, S. l., 1996, 42 (Western Europe 1970–1990); Franz Rothenbacher, *The European Population, 1850–1945*, CD-ROM Publication, Houndmills: Palgrave, 2002 (Ireland 1900–1910); Franz Rothenbacher, *The European Population, 1850–1945*, Houndmills: Palgrave, 2002, 160 (Czechoslovakia 1920–1940, own computation), 566 (Poland 1927, own computation); Franz Rothenbacher, *The European Population since 1945*, Houndmills: Palgrave, 2005, 164 (Czechoslovakia 1950–1990, own computation), 670 (Poland 1955–1990, own computation); *Magyar Statisztikai Évkönyv, 1900*, Budapest: M. Kir. Statisztikai Hivatal, 1901, 23–24 (Hungary 1900); *Magyar Statisztikai Évkönyv, 1910*, Budapest: M. Kir. Statisztikai Hivatal, 1911, 24–25 (Hungary 1910); *Time Series of Historical Statistics, 1867–1992*, Budapest: KSH, 1993, 148 (Hungary 1920–1990); http:// epp.eurostat.ec.europa.eu/statistics_explained/index.php?title=File:Live_births_outside_marriage,_as_share_ of_total_live_births_(%25).png&filetimestamp=20110303071332 (Western Europe 2000; Spain, Greece 1960–2000; Czech Republic 2000; Poland 2000; Slovakia 2000).

The diffusions of extramarital births and of cohabitations in the last four decades of the century are signs of new attitudes to family and especially to marriage, which can be well shown with the case of the Scandinavian countries and in particular, Sweden and Denmark. The population's educational level and standard of living being high, contraception and birth control being readily available in these two countries, it is plausible that the rise in extramarital births originated in the transformation of family-related value orientations: a growing number of people separated marriage and cohabitation from childbearing. As opposed to socioeconomic factors, value changes have a particularly substantial influence in the transformation of the family and thus in the prevalence of extramarital births in the 1980s.[111] However, the determinants of attitudinal changes and the relationship between value change and socioeconomic factors have not been convincingly elaborated with regard to post-war Europe as well.

Compared with the levels prevailing in the Western half of the continent, the East Central European ratios of extramarital births can be considered medium (Poland), or medium to high (Czechoslovakia and Hungary) in the first two-thirds of the century. From the 1960s, the tide changed, and in most Western European countries, more extramarital births were registered than in East Central Europe societies, and by 1990, the gap widened considerably between these regions (Table 3.12). Another source of difference between European regions was that in East Central European countries, extramarital births were significantly more frequent among disadvantaged women than in Western Europe throughout the whole twentieth century and particularly from the 1960s, when in Western Europe, well-educated groups were increasingly represented, which was similar to that of the case of cohabitation.

Determinants of changes

The pluralization of family forms is a complex process originating from several factors. The most important elements include the changes in the employment structure, and urbanization, the growth of female employment, the alterations in value orientations and the activities of the welfare state. Several of these aspects have already been discussed in detail, and thereby are reviewed only briefly in the following.

Concerning economic changes, the family as an institution was strongly affected by the transformation of the employment structure. The decline of the agrarian population and the growth of the industrial and the service sectors promoted both urbanization and the diffusion of female employment, which clearly contributed to the diminishing of traditional family forms. Among the several mechanisms involved, it needs to be emphasized that the ratios of divorce, cohabitation and extramarital births are all higher in the urban population. This is related to the lower degree of community control in urban areas, as a result of which deviations from traditional family patterns could not be sanctioned.

A further outstanding factor was the growth in female employment, leading to the change of women's position in the family. The advance of female employment was also promoted by the rapid rise of women's education in the twentieth century, inducing women's aspirations to pursue their own career objectives. Having an independent income meant that women could redefine their role in the family and aim for a more equal share of responsibilities and rewards. This process proceeded with several contradictions, such as the emerging double workload of women, and undoubtedly increased the chance of marital conflicts, which women were less prepared to tolerate at their own expense than before, leading to a higher level of union dissolutions.

The dynamic change in value orientations after the Second World War was yet another important challenge to traditional family forms, and as we have seen in the previous chapter, this can plausibly be described as individualization and secularization. Broadly defined, individualization means the increasing emphasis on the realization of the individual's rights in relation to other entities, whereas in the context of family history, individualization means that individuals are less willing to take on the responsibilities and commitments that marriage and family entail. The other relevant process, secularization, reduced the influence of religious ideas and the control of the church on family life, and thus gradually diminished traditional dispositions.

The expansion of the welfare state, which is the subject of one of the next chapters, also considerably affected the family. Major functions of care, that had previously been assumed by the family, were taken over by public institutions. The benefits provided for old and sick people and also for single parents weakened the family as a safety net and made it possible for many to pursue their individual objectives and leave usual family commitments behind.[112] The combined effect of these factors explains to a considerable degree why the system of traditional family forms was increasingly replaced by alternative family arrangements in the last decades of the twentieth century in most of the European societies.

Families in the new millennium: the post-modern as a return to the pre-modern?

The turn of the millennium brought further significant changes in marriage patterns, family structure, interpersonal relations within the family, and other related phenomena discussed in the previous sections. The dynamics of transformation were the greatest regarding the diffusion of new types of family arrangements. The transformation was mostly gradual, although after the collapse of communism, changes accelerated in East Central and South-Eastern European countries so much that in these societies the post-1990 era can be considered a new phase of family development.

Characteristics of family formation

At the turn of the millennium, a tangible tendency in the formation of unions was the weakening willingness to marry and the continuing diffusion of cohabitation all over Europe.[113] Marriage rates continued to decline in Western Europe, which traditionally had the lowest nuptiality in the continent, and this process also affected Southern Europe, albeit not to a similar degree. Declining nuptiality also spread to former communist countries in the 1990s, where in this respect, relatively little change could be observed in the preceding decades. The economic hardships of the regime change, the growing openness of the region to foreign cultural and other influences, a desire to adopt Western values and lifestyles, the suddenly rocketing living standard aspirations of the population and the expansion of higher education are among the major causes. In the early 1990s, the transformation appeared primarily in the decline of the ratio of those entering marriage; however, the ones who did marry still did so at a relatively young age. By the millennium, the average age at marriage began to rise significantly in several East Central European societies as well.[114]

Parallel with the decline in nuptiality, the diffusion of cohabitation continued in the European societies of the new millennium. Even if the direction of changes has been broadly uniform in the continent, considerable differences between countries prevailed regarding both the current levels of cohabitations and the dynamics of changes. Of 25–34-year-old women involved in a union, 40% or more were parties in unmarried couples in the Scandinavian countries and in France, but this figure was well below 10% in Southern Europe in 2000. Although the greatest transformation affected the former communist countries in this respect in the 1990s, the divergence among them was considerable as regards the diffusion of cohabitation. In Slovakia and Poland, nubile cohabitation hardly took root by 2000, because only 3–4% of the given cohort of young women lived with their partners as unmarried couples. In other countries of the region (the Czech Republic, Slovenia and Hungary), the figures fell in the middle range of European national averages (Table 3.13).[115]

The scale of the changes is remarkable; still, some consider it a new myth that by the end of the century individualism had abolished traditional family constraints in Europe.[116] In line with this suggestion, it is not advisable to exaggerate the significance of the alternative forms of partnerships, even in those Western European countries where they are most frequent. On the one hand, the inertia of marriage norms has been considerable, with the huge majority of the population (75–90% of women in the 20–34 age group) in all Europe still considering marriage as the desirable form of partnership. In addition, with the exception of a few countries, the ratio of those married usually significantly surpassed that of those in unmarried couples even in the 25–34-year-old female cohort, in which non-married cohabitation was the most frequent.[117]

It is often debated whether the diffusion of cohabitation contributed to marriage losing its popularity and what effects it might have had on other characteristics of family life, such as the number of children, attitudes to children and child poverty. It is difficult to give answers with general validity to these questions because, in addition to the various degrees to which cohabitation prevailed, countries were diverse regarding the significance of different types of cohabitation as well. As shown above, in a number of Southern and East Central European countries, unmarried couples were rare. Elsewhere, such as in the United Kingdom, Austria and Germany, the cohabitation of young, unmarried and childless couples was the

TABLE 3.13 The ratio of married and unmarried persons among women aged 25–34 in European countries, 2000–2002

	Married (%)	Cohabiting without marriage (%)	Non-married cohabitation as % of all couples
United Kingdom	41.9	20.3	32.6
France	37.9	28.3	42.8
Netherlands	48.0	24.5	33.8
Belgium	45.7	18.3	28.6
Ireland	43.8	12.9	22.7
Germany	52.8	15.2	22.4
Austria	45.8	20.1	30.5
Denmark	39.9	30.3	43.1
Finland	40.4	26.7	39.8
Norway	38.2	27.2	41.5
Italy	49.8	4.2	7.8
Poland	60.2	2.1	3.4
Czech Republic	57.7	4.5	7.2
Slovakia	60.3	2.0	3.2
Hungary	56.9	11.5	16.8
Romania	68.6	7.1	9.4
Slovenia	45.2	12.1	21.1

Source: Zsolt Spéder, 'Változások az ezredfordulón', in Rudolf Andorka, *Bevezetés a szociológiába*, Budapest: Osiris, 2006, 417.

most frequent, and thus it featured as a kind of trial marriage. Some even go so far as to claim that in some countries (typically in France), cohabitation is becoming an alternative to marriage. In countries of Scandinavia (Iceland, Sweden, Denmark and Norway) this has already happened: cohabitation before marriage has virtually become the norm; what is more, couples typically live and bring up their one or two children while staying unmarried. Nonetheless, cohabiting partners who have children often do marry after some time.[118] The diversity of the size and form of cohabitation clearly suggests a similar variety in the social impacts of this kind of family union.

Several of the proponents of the 'second demographic transition' discussed in the previous chapter argue that the quality of partnerships has become a major concern in life by the late twentieth century – a process that began at least in early modern Europe. Paradoxically, the growing importance of an agreeable relationship further increased the vulnerability of unions, as reflected by the divorce rates, the rise of which has typically slowed down, but did not terminate at the end of the twentieth century. Divorce was still less characteristic in Southern Europe (Italy, Spain, Greece and Portugal), as opposed to the high frequencies observed in the United Kingdom, Scandinavia (Sweden, Denmark) and East Central Europe (the Czech Republic and Hungary). The total divorce rate (showing what ratio of marriages would end in dissolution if the divorce intensity were constant) was 10% or less in Southern Europe, whereas in the latter countries, it exceeded 40%. In countries with high divorce ratios, marriages broke up ever sooner and union disruption increasingly affected couples with young children. This had an impact on the family structure as well: the ratio of single parents becomes higher, the spatial separation of fathers and their children is more frequent and growing numbers of children live with step-parents.

The increasing pluralization of family forms and especially the diffusion of non-married cohabitation received great public attention all over Europe. This was heightened by the consideration that the new living arrangements can only partially be the functional equivalents of marriage, because their stability is considerably lower. Instability became an important issue, especially from the viewpoint of childrearing. On the one hand, it increases the ratio of single parents, which is one of the greatest risk factors of child poverty, and, on the other hand, it is often disadvantageous with respect to children's emotional stability and thus their development.

There is clear evidence that single parents (who are overwhelmingly women) and their children are more exposed to poverty than other family types in Western societies. The lack of appropriate income after the break-up of the partnership primarily originates from women's smaller earnings, which had been a characteristic of early female employment as well. Moreover, the position of single mothers on the labour market is even more unfavourable throughout Europe. In addition, keeping two households is more costly than maintaining the former common household. Sweden, with its extensive welfare state, has come closest to eradicating poverty among single mothers and their children, even if the income of this group lags behind two-parent Swedish families.[119]

In public debates on new family arrangements, there is no serious challenge anywhere in Europe regarding the right of the individual to decide on the form of their partnership. Instead, the debate focuses on whether society should protect the institution of marriage in indirect ways. One characteristic position claims that any kind of differentiation between marriage and cohabitation is unacceptable because it means interference with the private sphere. Thus, cohabitation should essentially enjoy the same legal status as marriage. Another stance claims that the abolition of legal differentiation would undermine the institution of marriage, which, in turn, would have negative consequences for children and possibly for other family members as well. A third line of argument focuses on legal emancipation being exactly against the will of unmarried couples, who intend to avoid a close relationship by choosing a looser form of union.[120] These standpoints are so closely intertwined with value choices that they cannot be evaluated on the basis of sociological considerations alone. However, it is clear that more and more European countries witnessed the emancipation of new family forms at the millennium.

The variability of life courses

The novelty of current, 'post-modern' family development is often illustrated by contrasting it to conditions prevailing a few decades ago. In the 1950s and 1960s, sociologists proposed the ideal type of the 'modern family cycle', in which the life of the modern family consists of distinct phases in a set order.[121] In the first phase, marriage is followed by the couple establishing a home to prepare for the birth of their first child. The next phase is the period of the primary socialization of children under school age, then follow the phases of the family involved in rearing pre-adolescent and adolescent (13–16-year-old) children. When the last child leaves the parental home, there commences the period of the shrinking family, often called the period of the 'empty nest', which lasts until one of the spouses dies. After this, the widowed spouse is usually in the phase of old age.[122] Although it is obvious that the model does not provide an accurate description of the realities of family life for the whole period, not even for the two or three post-war decades, one can still assume that the majority of the European population did yet progress through these phases in this era. Even compared with late nineteenth-century conditions, individual life courses and family life had become more foreseeable, and differences between families in this respect decreased, i.e. the life courses have homogenized and a kind of 'normal biography' (René Levy), or the 'standardisation of life courses' (Martin Kohli) has emerged.[123]

There were numerous demographic, social and economic preconditions to the emergence of the modern family cycle. The composition of families became more stable, because there were fewer premature deaths, and hence the occurrence of widowhood and remarriage declined. The diffusion of family planning not only decreased the number of children, it also made the timing of births more accurate. Child mortality decreased dramatically, and the age difference between siblings became small, thus families could progress through the adolescence and young adulthood of children more quickly and safely. Besides demographic transformations, other factors also facilitated the modern family cycle. Childrearing has become the focus of family life as well as a primary function of the emergence of the family cycle. The high level of employment and rising income levels made it possible for families to establish their own homes, which the parents would be able to maintain even when they were left on their own.[124]

Approaching the new millennium, this 'standard' family became an increasingly poor image of reality. The extended time spent in education and rising youth unemployment made it impossible for many to leave the parental household when reaching young adulthood, and even if this did occur, it was often not accompanied by a subsequent marriage and starting a family. If young adults lived with their partners as unmarried couples, the instability of these partnerships, discussed earlier, was a great obstacle to the realization of the modern family cycle. Marriages also became increasingly unstable in the second half of the century, and thus a great variety of life courses diverging from the 'normal biography' appeared.[125] Other phenomena, such as rising ratios of childless marriages, delayed childbirths and the boom in extramarital births, also eroded the modern family cycle.

These intertwined processes provide a basis for the remarkable claim that the family development of the post-modern age, from several aspects, constitutes a return to pre-modern times.[126] As described earlier in the chapter, before industrialization it was the frequent premature death of spouses, the subsequent remarriage of the surviving spouse and the high child mortality that produced a great variability in family composition. Once again, the post-modern family was highly characterized by instability that resulted from the high incidence of divorce, subsequent remarriage and extramarital sexual relationships as well as other phenomena addressed earlier. This interpretation rests on well-established evidence and might result in important conclusions, most notably that the development of the family as an institution is not linear and not irreversible, but family arrangements may return to earlier forms and types. Still, it certainly must be complemented with the understanding that, as regards the functions of the family and the characteristics of relationships within the family, we cannot assume a return to the pre-modern. It is exactly the transformation of these relations and functions of family arrangements that results in the revival of earlier forms in specific areas of family development.

4

SOCIAL STRATIFICATION
AND SOCIAL MOBILITY

Social stratification is a classic subject of sociology and social history, probably attracting the attention of most researchers and instigating the most intense debates in these disciplines. The term stratification refers to the fact that similarities and differences in the position of individuals in society, that is, social inequalities, are not distributed randomly but follow specific patterns: thus we can distinguish between relatively homogeneous groups, whose members share important characteristics. Nevertheless, there has been a long-running scholarly debate over how many dimensions of inequality can and should be taken into account by stratification research, and precisely which these should be.

Wealth and income are of unquestionable importance when describing and analysing social stratification. At the same time, stratification may also be defined by political (exercising power at work or in society) or cultural (high-status consumption practices, sophisticated manners and privileged lifestyle) phenomena as well. In addition, factors affecting stratification include social assets (access to high-status social networks, memberships in associations and unions), prestige (good reputation, fame and moral integrity), and also the possession of human capital (high qualifications, professional experience, skills and expertise).[1]

The diversity of assets and resources underlying stratification systems suggests that they are multidimensional and complex, as a result of which sociological and historical research has to examine them by considering all the above factors combined. However, researchers often argue that the system of stratification can be plausibly described and adequately understood with a more limited number of dimensions, because their complexity is only apparent, and the involved factors are not equally significant.

It is a long tradition in Western social sciences to claim that only one principle is really fundamental to the comprehension of the sources and structure of social stratification. Karl Marx and other influential social theorists maintained that social differences, at least since the nineteenth century, can be plausibly explained by economic factors, such as ownership of land, factories, liquid assets, and labour power. Marxists also thought that the great divide is primarily between the classes owning and not owning property, or, more precisely, between those individuals who own capital and means of production, and those who sell their labour. Others regarded differences in power to be the primary source of stratification and held all other factors secondary. For example, Ralf Dahrendorf found 'a clear line (...) between those who participate in the exercise of authority (...) and those who are subject to the authoritative commands of others', and that positions and authority in different organizations provide the ultimate reason for the emergence of class conflicts.[2]

However, such extreme forms of reductionism have long been criticized. For instance, already at the beginning of the twentieth century, Max Weber had claimed that income is not defined solely by the possession of capital or means of production because qualification and expertise have a decisive influence on income as well. In addition, in latter decades non-economic assets have arguably gained further importance in the stratification systems of highly developed industrial societies. Consequently, single-factor theories of stratification have lost their appeal.

When several factors are taken into account, methodological and practical difficulties of analysis inevitably multiply. Another major tradition in stratification research addresses this problem by focusing on a comprehensive social phenomenon, which affects a wide range of assets and resources, that is, several dimensions of inequality. The focal point is most often occupation, because the occupational structure has a decisive role in allocating income, authority, prestige, etc. among individuals. Furthermore, as a distinguished expert on social stratification argued, occupations are 'not only the main conduits through which valued goods are distributed but are also deeply institutionalised categories that are salient to workers, constitute meaningful social communities and reference groups, and provide enduring basis of collective action'.[3]

Regardless of whether scholars apply a reductionist or a more synthetizing approach in the analysis of inequalities and stratification, almost all of them resort to a final simplifying procedure by differentiating between a relatively small number of distinct groups, calling them classes, strata, status groups or others. Referring to some contemporary examples, Dahrendorf argued for a two-class scheme, and Frank Parkin for six occupational classes, with the principal cleavage falling between the manual and non-manual categories; Erik Wright elaborated a 12-category neo-Marxian scheme, and Robert Erikson and John Goldthorpe proposed an 11-category neo-Weberian classification.[4] New classification schemes continue to be regularly put forward, and there are controversies about, among others, the conditions under which classes or strata have emerged and whether the proposed categories were purely nominal entities or have also been meaningful to the individuals involved.[5] The ways through which individuals change their positions between social groups (i.e. the scale and characteristics of social mobility) have also been the subject of interest from very early on in the history of research into social stratification.

This volume devotes several chapters to various dimensions of social standing, so the main concerns of this chapter are the historical changes related to the structural positions that people occupy in the system of social stratification and the development of social groups based on these positions. Thus, first income inequalities, then sectoral characteristics of the workforce and changes in the employment structure in the course of the twentieth century are addressed. This is followed by separate discussions of the development of the main social strata and classes, as well as an outline of changes in social mobility. Finally, the main trends in the stratification of European societies in recent decades are studied.

Trends in income and wealth distribution: the inverted U-curve and 'the great U-turn'

The income and wealth of individuals in a society are apt to determine their social position, and may even condition their life expectancy. Therefore, even if the way income and property are allocated among the members of society is not an exclusive determinant, the distribution of wealth remains one of the most crucial and visible dimensions of social stratification.

There are several possibilities for describing the distribution of income in society and for comparing different societies in that respect. One is the examination of changes in personal income, which defines the income position of different groups in the population, independent of their class position. In historical research, long-term changes in the income differences of particular classes and strata as well as in the ratio of wages/salaries and returns on capital equally attracted attention. In recent decades, gender differences in income have also been intensively studied. The following discussion mostly concentrates on the long-term transformation of the disparities in personal income because international research has recently focused on this aspect, which also aroused the greatest controversies. Other aspects of income distribution and changes in the distribution of wealth are dealt with on the basis of their main trends.

The distribution of income

The changes in income distribution in modern history are often described by the Kuznets curve, named after the Nobel laureate economist Simon Kuznets, who studied the phenomenon and established its rules. The curve, shaped as an inverted U, shows that differences in income first increased and then began to decline in industrial societies in the course of roughly the past two centuries.[6] Although still relatively little related information is available on the nineteenth century, research has broadly confirmed that the curve was indeed turning upward during the industrial revolution, i.e. income differences were on the increase. This was tangible primarily in the changes in personal incomes, with those in the upper income levels commanding a growing share of the total income, whereas the share of the poorer strata declined. Class differences increased, especially at the expense of the strata playing less significant roles in the process of industrialization. Similarly, the income of female employees lagged considerably behind that of men. However, in the course of the twentieth century, a development of opposite trends followed, that is, income gaps gradually moderated in industrial societies: the standard deviation of personal incomes fell, the ratio of wages and salaries to returns on capital increased and the income differences between social classes faded. Women's income disadvantage to men also diminished.[7] Although the presence of the Kuznets curve, showing inequalities first rising then falling with economic development, has been verified in a number of industrial societies, these general trends did not prevail everywhere in every period or with equal intensity in Europe.[8] In particular, tendencies of levelling off have halted or even reversed in several European countries, beginning with the 1970s and 1980s.

As regards the concrete scale of changes in personal incomes, in the first decades of the twentieth century in Western European countries, the richest 10% of the population commanded 35–40% of the total income on the average. Norway and Austria had values below the mean, around 30%. Germany, Denmark and Sweden conformed to the average, whereas in Finland and in Great Britain, income concentration was higher. Until the middle of the century, the equalization process was rapid in almost all countries, and especially in Scandinavia, where the income share of the richest decile of society dropped from 34–36% to 27–29% between 1935 and 1950.[9] The relative income position of the upper strata also weakened drastically in Great Britain throughout this period. From the middle of the century, the process of relative loss for the richest continued on, but not at the previous rate. In West Germany, France, Italy and the Netherlands, the top decile still commanded about 30% of incomes in the early 1970s. A more moderate income concentration characterized Great Britain, whereas the lowest values were found in some Scandinavian countries and Austria.[10] The most substantial changes occurred in the top half of the upper decile, that is, in the top 5%. The lower half of the top tenth suffered only a minor decrease in their relative income position (Table 4.1).[11]

As regards the situation of the strata with the lowest income, reliable data are even scarcer. These show that in the first third of the twentieth century, their position changed for the worse, that is, in this period the middle strata may be regarded as the winners of the transformations. For example, in Denmark and Germany, the income share of the middle strata (those between the richest 10% and the poorest 60%) was between 26% and 32% in 1910. These figures equally showed an 8 percentage points growth by the late 1930s. During the First World War and the following decades, the tendency of the middle classes gaining ground continued, whereas, parallel to this, the relative position of the poorer strata either stagnated or improved to a small degree in Western European countries. After the late 1950s, for two or three decades, the income position of the poorest was generally improving, even though at this time differences between societies became greater. The situation of those belonging to the lower income groups remained the same or deteriorated in Great Britain, Norway and Denmark, whereas it improved in the other Western European countries (Table 4.1).[12] It must be emphasized, however,

TABLE 4.1 Distribution of income in European countries, 1910–1990

a) Share of the population with highest 10% (1910–1970) and 20% (1980–1990) income (as % of total personal income)

	1910	1920	1930	1940	1950	1960	1970	1980	1990
Great Britain				38.8	33.2	29.1	27.5	35.6	38.2
France					36.2	34.0	29.3	38.4	38.4
Netherlands					36.1	31.8	29.5	34.7	34.7
Belgium								35.1	35.6
Germany/FRG	40.5		36.5	36.0	36.0	39.4	33.7	_35.3_	_36.4_
Austria			28.4		_22.6_	24.9	24.7		
Switzerland					37.3	37.8	32.3		
Sweden		39.2	44.5	33.7	28.8	25.9	24.0	30.8	31.8
Denmark		38.9	39.9	36.8	28.6	27.3	_32.0_		
Norway	_29.8_		_38.2_		28.6	27.2	24.7	32.8	33.3
Finland		50.9	48.3	38.3	32.8	30.5	30.2	31.4	31.9
Hungary						20.2	15.9	18.6	20.9

b) Share of the population with lowest 20% of income (as % of total personal income)

	1910	1920	1930	1940	1950	1960	1970	1980	1990
Great Britain						9.7	5.6	3.5	2.5
France						2.8	3.8	3.1	3.0
Netherlands						2.2	2.4	4.4	4.1
Belgium								4.2	4.2
Germany/FRG						1.8	3.9	_10.5_	_9.6_
Austria					4.6	4.2	4.9		
Switzerland						2.4	9.5		
Sweden		1.7			3.2	4.6	6.3	8.4	4.0	3.3
Denmark		1.4			4.6	4.2	3.9		
Norway	_3.8_		_2.1_			2.0	4.8	4.1	3.9
Finland						3.5	2.1	4.5	4.3

Note: Underlining indicates limit regarding comparability.

Source: Hartmut Kaelble, *Sozialgeschichte Europas: 1945 bis zur Gegenwart,* München: C. H. Beck, 2007, 213–214.

that after the Second World War, in the period of rapid economic growth, even the stagnation of the relative income position implied a considerable improvement in the standard of living.

In communist countries, a tendency towards a fast levelling of incomes occurred after the Second World War. In 1962 in Czechoslovakia, the upper decile of the population accounted for only 14% of the total personal income, signalling the most egalitarian income distribution in Europe, and probably all over the world.[13] In addition, up to the early 1970s, the share of income taken by the poorest groups noticeably increased in these countries. Meanwhile, the position of the middle strata remained largely unchanged. However, from the 1970s in the East Central European region, income inequalities were on the rise again. It is important to note that, parallel to the levelling of incomes, distinct forms of inequalities emerged with regard to the access to consumer goods and services in the communist countries. Under the conditions of chronic shortage economy, many better-quality and sought-after goods and services were available only to groups that were privileged by the regime, such as party leaders, high-ranking members of the state administration and armed forces, eminent sportsmen or leading scientists, and in specialized chains of shops or through other channels of distribution, which are outlined in chapter 6. Consequently, real inequalities in material aspects were greater in communist societies than what was indicated by income distribution statistics.[14]

After the launch of the Luxembourg Income Study (1983), which harmonized and standardized the microdata of many national and other surveys in order to facilitate comparative research, there was a significant increase in data on the income distribution of European societies. Even though the methodology and conclusions of the analyses based on the surveys often differ regarding details, their findings agree in that in the 1980s, Scandinavian countries (and especially Finland) had the most egalitarian distribution of income in Western and Southern Europe, which can be attributed to extensive welfare programs, i.e. the great scale of redistribution by the state.[15] Relatively small income differences characterized Belgium and Luxembourg, followed by the Netherlands and West Germany. The middle range included Portugal, the United Kingdom, France and Italy. The highest inequalities were found in Spain, Switzerland and Ireland among the countries studied by Anthony B. Atkinson.[16]

Remarkably, at the end of the 1980s, it was not the communist countries any more that had the lowest income inequalities in Europe; it was the Scandinavian countries and notably Finland, referred to above. Moreover, even West Germany had greater equality than most communist countries regarding the distribution of net income in society (Table 4.2).

As discussed earlier, in the last decades of the twentieth century, the decline in income differentials halted, and even turned to increase again in several countries in Western Europe and overseas. This phenomenon is known as 'the great U-turn', implying that the trend identified by Kuznets has reversed.[17] The turn was indicated by the changes of both the position of highest-income groups and the income ratios of the poorest, and it also manifested in the changes of more comprehensive measures, such as the Gini coefficient. Nevertheless, the rise in inequalities was generally small in Europe, and affected only approximately half of the countries of the continent. In several countries, such as France, Finland and Italy, the levelling of incomes continued into the 1980s and 1990s.[18] In Europe, the most marked changes occurred in the United Kingdom, where the deterioration of the position of the poorest and the improvement of the relative situation of the richest were both significant. Here the Gini coefficient grew by 10 percentage points, first because of rising unemployment, then as a result of waning redistribution by the state. After 1990, a slight reduction of inequalities occurred, so it would be illogical to interpret the

TABLE 4.2 Gini coefficients in various countries, ca. 1985–2000

	Second half of the 1980s	Mid-1990s	2000
United Kingdom	30.4	31.2	32.6
France	29.6	27.8	27.3
Netherlands	26.8	25.5	25.1
Belgium	23.5		
FRG	24.5	28.3	27.7
Austria	23.6	23.8	25.2
Switzerland	33.6		26.7
Finland	20.7	22.8	26.1
Sweden	22.0	21.1	24.3
Denmark	22.8	21.3	22.5
Norway	23.4	25.6	26.1
Italy	30.6	34.8	34.7
Poland	26.8	38.9	36.7
Czechoslovakia	20.1	25.7	26.0
Hungary	24.4	29.4	29.3
Soviet Union	28.9		
United States	34.1	36.1	

Notes: Different years: Austria 1983, 1999; Switzerland 2001; Denmark 1983; Italy 1984; Czechoslovakia 2002.

Sources: Anthony B. Atkinson, Lee Rainwater and Timothy M. Smeeding, *Income Distribution in OECD Countries. Evidence from the Luxembourg Income Study,* Paris: OECD, 1995, 49 (Finland, Sweden, Norway, Belgium, Netherlands, France, United Kingdom, United States in second half of the 1980s); Göran Therborn, *European Modernity and Beyond: The Trajectory of European Societies, 1945–2000,* London: Sage, 1995, 153 (FRG, Switzerland, Czechoslovakia, Hungary, Poland, Soviet Union, in second half of the 1980s); *OECD Factbook 2007,* Paris: OECD, 2007, 231 (Austria 1983, Denmark 1983, Italy 1984, other countries of Europe, United States around 2000).

process as irreversible.[19] Even more spectacular was the erosion of income equality in the post-communist countries. Detailed data are available for three East Central European countries, showing that the situation of those in the upper-income groups improved, and of those in the lowest deteriorated considerably in Hungary and Poland, and, on a smaller scale, in the Czech Republic in the 1990s.[20]

With the few exceptions mentioned, the societies of Western Europe had a special position among other industrial nations, regarding both their levels and dynamics of income inequalities. The comparison with the United States is especially suggestive, where, starting from higher original levels, the decline in income inequalities stopped around 1970, earlier than in Western Europe, then from the 1970s and 1980s inequalities increased at a higher rate than in any European country. The Gini coefficients show that only two countries in Western Europe, namely Ireland and Switzerland had income inequalities equalling that of the United States by the new millennium. By European standards, the ratio of those living in poverty was also high in America, far surpassing even the Irish level.[21]

As opposed to abstract statistical categories applied so far, historians rather analyse the positions of occupational groups or social classes. This approach reveals how belonging to different social groups is associated with the distribution of income in the whole society. Still, relatively little is known about these aspects of nineteenth-century Western European inequalities, even if it is obvious that differences in income were higher between occupational groups and social classes at that time compared with the second half of the twentieth century. The most extensive and earliest figures describe the relative wages of occupational groups in Britain, revealing that income differences significantly decreased in the course of the twentieth century. In 1913–14, higher professionals earned 3.5 times more than the male average in this country, which dropped to 1.7 times by 1978. The wage differences between higher professionals and unskilled workers dropped from 5.2 times to 2.4 times in the same period. Between 1913 and 1978, not only did the wage differences between blue-collar workers and white-collar salaried employees decrease, but there was a process of levelling off within each of these two occupational categories as well. Whereas before the First World War, skilled workers earned 68% more, and craftsmen 98% more than unskilled workers, by the mid-1950s, these gaps narrowed to 43% and 80%, and by the late 1970s to 28% and 38%, respectively. The differences had originally been considerably higher among the subgroups of salaried employees, and the equalization process developed slowly.[22] The British case was not an isolated one. The European magnitude of the process and the often inherent conflicts are demonstrated by Jürgen Kocka's interpretation of the fall of the Weimar democracy in Germany. When analysing the reasons behind this event, he attributes great significance to the fact that the gap between white-collar salaried employees and workers closed before and during the First World War, which the former experienced as a threat to their social standing, and which increased their responsiveness to extreme ideologies.[23] Although during the Great Depression, the gap between incomes increased again, in the 1950s the levelling process resumed in Germany, and the available sources indicate that similar processes took place in other European democracies as well after the Second World War until the 1980s. Equalization between occupational groups usually halted by this time, that is, processes occurred largely similar to what has been seen above regarding the changes in personal incomes.

Although the dynamics of wages and salaries were not determined merely by market mechanisms in Western European countries either, in the communist countries income differences were shaped more directly by political intentions and decisions, which was largely facilitated by the government being the biggest employer. The income structure was completely transformed compared with the interwar period. The salaries of teachers, doctors and other white-collar employees were set so that they were significantly closer to the wages of workers. For example, in 1960 in Czechoslovakia, white-collar employees earned only 17% more than manual workers. However, differences in other countries were greater: 42% in Bulgaria, 57% in Hungary and in Poland. The differentiation within major occupational groups was also smaller than in Western Europe. Skilled workers could expect higher wages than the unqualified, but the difference was only between 5% and 20%, and in Poland there was no difference between them at all. Political priorities were well reflected in the low incomes of the agricultural population. On the one hand, they were intended to motivate the movement of labour to industry, and on the other, they reflected the anti-peasant attitude of communist doctrine and the correspondingly identical dispositions of the nomenclature. However, after collectivization, from the 1960s, the process of peasant incomes considerably approaching those of industrial workers was well under way in most East Central and South-Eastern European countries.[24]

Even in late twentieth-century Europe, gender loomed as a more important determinant of income than occupational group. Although non-manual employees earned more than manual workers, the income of female white-collar employees was lower than that of male manual workers in all European countries, with only a few exceptions. Moreover, women had less authority (responsibility and decision-making power) in the workplace. This may not be explained simply by differences in qualification. On the one hand, in several countries, for example, in West Germany, such differences had already vanished by 1980; on the other hand, women's wage disadvantage to men could also be observed when qualifications were the same. In this respect, there were no considerable regional divides in the continent. The exceptions by the end of the century include only the Scandinavian countries and the United Kingdom, where belonging to class (manual or non-manual occupational group) slightly overruled gender as a determinant of income.[25]

Changes in wealth distribution

It has long been known that wealth is more unequally distributed in society than current income.[26] For example, whereas in the 1980s, the Gini coefficient for income usually fell between 20 and 40 in Western Europe, regarding wealth distribution it was between 50 and 90.[27] Nevertheless, less systematic historical knowledge is accessible on wealth than on income. More detailed information is available only for a few countries that shows that inequalities of wealth distribution became considerably more moderate in the course of the twentieth century, albeit equalization advanced at a slower pace and less evenly than in the case of incomes (Table 4.3). Great Britain provides the most detailed sources again. Whereas in 1923 in England and Wales, the richest 1% owned 61% of all private economic property and the top 10% owned 89%, by 1972, they commanded only 32% and 70%, respectively, and in 1980, 18% and 49% of the total wealth. The moderation of wealth concentration in the interwar period was slow, gaining pace during the Second World War and in the 1950s and early 1970s, then basically stagnating from the 1980s. However, the process does not mean that the rich decreased in number. The figure for properties above 100,000 pounds rose from 300 to 540 in the interwar period, and the number of those worth over a million pounds rose from 9 in 1930 to 21 in 1972.[28] The value of wealth belonging to lower categories rose even faster not only in Britain but elsewhere in Western Europe as well. In France, inheritance

TABLE 4.3 Distribution of wealth in European countries, 1902–1979

a) Share of the richest 1% (as % of total personal wealth)

	1902– 1913	1920– 1929	1930– 1939	1950– 1959	1960– 1969	1970– 1979
England and Wales		61	54	45	31	32
France	50	45		31		26
Belgium					28	
Germany/FRG	31					28
Switzerland					43	30
Sweden		50	47	33	24	21
Denmark						25

b) Share of the richest 5% (as % of total personal wealth)

	1902– 1913	1920– 1929	1930– 1939	1950– 1959	1960– 1969	1970– 1979
England and Wales		82	77	71	56	56
France	80	65		53	45	
Belgium						47
Germany/FRG	51					
Switzerland					63	53
Sweden		77	70	60	48	44
Denmark						47

Note: Averages of the indicated periods.

Sources: Hartmut Kaelble, *Sozialgeschichte Europas: 1945 bis zur Gegenwart,* München: C. H. Beck, 2007, 223.

lists reveal an unambiguous tendency: whereas at the beginning of the century the richest 5% bequeathed 80% of wealth, a gradual decline led to the figure dropping to 39% by 1975.[29] Another sign of the fall in wealth differentials was that a growing ratio of citizens accrued some kind of savings. In West Germany in 1962, 60.1%, and in 1983, 90.3% of the population had a savings account. Ownership of real estates in the same country grew as well, although at a slower pace, from 38.8% in 1969 to 45.5% in 1983.[30] However, these figures do not refer to the value of assets, and in this respect other studies have yielded contradictory findings regarding post-Second World War West Germany.[31] Research has also revealed that financial wealth continued to be distributed more unevenly than other types of wealth in every country.

The causes of the changes

When explaining the shifts in twentieth-century income distribution, the research attributes the greatest role to political determinants and to changes in the labour market and the qualification levels of the labour force. In the following we first investigate those factors that were the causes of the decline of income inequalities in the first two-thirds of the twentieth century discussed above, and then the reasons for the reversing trend at the end of the century are presented.

As Gerhard Lenski formulated it in his classic work, among the political factors resulting in the reduction of income differences, a special significance must be attributed to the strengthening power of lower-income worker and employee groups asserting their political interests, which was primarily a consequence of the extension of franchise.[32] In the interwar period, strata in the lower-income categories were given franchise basically in all European countries, which shifted the political power relations between the economic elite and the labour force. In parliamentary systems, a consequence of this process was the decline of liberal parties that, in economic terms, represented the interests of upper-income groups and the rise of Social Democratic and Christian Democratic mass parties, finding their major constituencies among employees and other lower-income groups. The unionization of the labour force also advanced in the workplace, primarily during and after the First World War, and later after the Second World War. The growing organizational strength of workers and of trade unions in general facilitated the wage dispute, which contributed to fading income differences as well.

The significant role of political factors in shaping income distribution has been convincingly shown by Lenski and other scholars.[33] However, the interpretation that explains the distribution process as a result of the political representation of economic interests may not claim universal validity, because the political and associational rights did not prevail in authoritarian political systems and dictatorships, although the material interests of the workers were emphasized in these regimes as well. Moreover, the strength and influence of unions differed widely in Western European democracies, which is not reflected in the tendencies of income changes. In France, where trade unions were relatively weak and fragmented, until the 1960s, income differences decreased to a greater degree than in West Germany, where the union movement was both more centralized and stronger.[34]

A different emphasis appears in another line of explanation also based on political factors, attributing a major role to the emergence of the welfare state and especially its expansion after the Second World War. Institutions and measures of the expanding social policy, such as the minimum wage and the linking of the rise of pensions to the average increase in wages and salaries, or progressive income taxation, equally contributed to the shrinking of the income scale in post-war Western Europe. The income tax was used most vigorously as an instrument of levelling in Sweden, where in the early 1970s, there was a 76.5% marginal tax rate on the highest incomes.[35] Nevertheless, this latter line of argumentation supports rather than contradicts the former interpretation, because political factors, such as the extension of franchise and the growing organizational strength of the labour (the emergence of trade unionism) both contributed to the expansion of the welfare state.

Political determinants surfaced even more directly in the communist countries, where, as suggested earlier, governments had a distinguished role in defining income ratios. The party-state considered political merit, social preference, the demands of the planned economy and other factors when setting the income structure. In early communist regimes, property and market performance (in the context of the otherwise restricted and regulated marketplace) played only a minor role among factors affecting income, but later their weight increased, especially in countries initiating market reforms from the 1960s.[36]

Changes in the labour market and the qualification of the labour force also influenced the income structure significantly throughout Europe. In the course of the twentieth century, the qualification levels of the labour force improved considerably, as a result of which the polarization of society by education disappeared: a small group of university graduates vis-à-vis the overwhelming majority with only elementary education was no longer the case. The rise in the ratios of those completing tertiary and secondary education contributed to the moderation of income inequalities. As the Dutch economist Jan Tinbergen argued, in the twentieth century and especially in the immediate post-war decades, both the supply of highly qualified labour and the demand for skills increased rapidly. However, as Tinbergen maintained, the balance of supply and demand changed after a while, with education producing highly qualified professionals in higher numbers compared with the increase in demand for them: as he stated, in the first two-thirds of the twentieth century, 'the race between technological development and education (...) was won by education'.[37] As a consequence of the excess supply, the wage and salary advantage of those with secondary or tertiary education shrank compared with those unqualified or with only elementary education.[38]

Another important characteristic of the changes in the labour market in the twentieth century, to be discussed in detail later, was an increase in the ratio of employees, accompanied by a decline in the number and proportion of those self-employed. Of course, there were considerable income differentials within both groups, but traditionally these were on a larger scale among those who were self-employed. Thus, the marginalization of the latter group meant that global income differences became less pronounced.

Yet another factor was the supplantation of agricultural activities characterized by low wage levels in the course of sectoral transformations. Furthermore, the wage advantages of industry that resulted from its earlier modernization and consequently higher productivity and thus higher profitability became more moderate compared with agriculture and the service sector in the course of the twentieth century. In practice, this meant, for example, that the productivity and profitability of farms grew faster than that of industrial companies, and thus the former managed to lessen their disadvantage.[39]

Demographic changes also affected the labour market. With the deceleration of population growth in Europe, reserves of labour force became smaller. Fertility had declined in the more educated classes before, but in the course of the twentieth century, social groups with lower education levels gradually joined the low fertility pattern. Therefore, unqualified labour was also scarcer, which raised its price and facilitated the catching up of the lower incomes.

Having inventoried the most important causes underlying the dynamics of income in twentieth-century Europe, it can be established that there are further, country-specific factors as well. For example, in Great Britain, an important role is attributed to the periods of inflation in the century in closing income gaps between social groups, because such years saw the fastest advance of this process (during the First World War, in the late 1930s and during the Second World War, and in the early 1950s).[40]

Let us now turn to the explanation of the reversing trend occurring in several countries from the 1970s, that is, the stagnation or repeated increase of income differences. Most of all, it must be emphasized that the factors promoting equalization before have disappeared or lost their intensity. The strengthening of trade unions came to an end partly because unemployment was markedly on the rise in almost all Western European countries from the early 1970s. Although welfare programs were retrenched only in a few countries, the expansion of the welfare states slowed down and the restructuring of welfare schemes included cuts in some benefits. Similarly, by this time traditionally low-paying sectors had already become marginalized in Western Europe, as a result of which they could not lend significant impetus to equalization any more. Although in earlier times, a labour force with insufficient skills and thus commanding modest wages had been disappearing from Western Europe, the number of overseas immigrants with low qualifications multiplied manifold, and their moderate income levels significantly raised income inequalities. Of the former factors counteracting income inequalities, basically only one remained in place, namely, the continuing decrease in differences in the qualification levels of the non-immigrant labour force. However, this was offset by new forces strengthening income differences.

The rise of unemployment has to be listed first, occurring in the period of recession triggered by the 1973 oil crisis. With unemployment reaching a mass scale, unemployment benefits usually ceased to be as generous as before, thus those losing jobs were more exposed to the threat of poverty. The ratio of unemployed university graduates reached especially high levels by the 1990s, which led to a deterioration of the income position of young graduates of tertiary education compared with what had been the norm in the previous decades. Changes in family structure taking place since the 1960s also greatly contributed to increasing income differences in two respects. First, as a consequence of the diffusion of extramarital births and of divorce, the number of single-parent families considerably increased, and they were more threatened by poverty than two-parent families. Moreover, the parents bringing up a child or children alone were usually women, who earned less than men, and whose labour market position was weaker in other respects as well. Second, toward the end of the twentieth century, a new family model began to spread in several Western European countries, such as Germany, having double income and no children. Such families did not have to cover child-related expenses, and thus they had a higher probability to enter upper-income groups, which also contributed to growing income inequalities in late twentieth-century Europe.[41]

As regards wealth differences, the increasing state redistribution definitely facilitated their moderation in almost the whole century: for example, a rise in the progressiveness of income taxes drained many of the sources from which wealth could be accumulated. Property taxes were also widely introduced, typically but not exclusively during wars and economic austerity. In periods of depression and inflation, huge properties often vanished completely. After the Second World War in East Central Europe or in Great Britain, nationalization also greatly curbed wealth differences. Furthermore, as a result of the general rise in income levels, groups that earlier merely covered their daily living expenditures were now able to save up. The rising standard of living, as is shown later, made it possible for them, too, to buy property and consumer durables, such as apartments, valuable home furnishings and cars. This process was complemented by the diffusion of savings accounts, pension funds and other forms of monetary savings. The British social historian Richard H. Tawney termed these savings 'popular wealth' and claimed their growing visibility already in the interwar period, although they can be considered to be existent on a mass scale only from the 1950s in Western Europe and even later in Southern and East Central Europe. In this regard, the level of economic development directly affected the distribution of wealth.[42]

Sectoral distribution of the labour force: roads to post-industrialism

When studying social stratification, the study of income and wealth distribution needs to be complemented by further aspects of social divisions, first and foremost by the characteristics of employment structure. The starting point might be the analysis of the ratio of those working in major sectors of the economy, because the sectoral distribution of labour is of crucial importance regarding both economic development and social transformations. The close connection to economic development is shown, on the one hand, by economic growth and technological progress resulting in substantial shifts between economic branches. On the other hand, productivity varies by sector; therefore shifts in their relative positions (the advance of sectors with higher profitability) may promote economic growth in themselves.[43] In addition, the sectoral distribution of labour greatly determines the share of individual trades and occupations, and thus it also affects social stratification. As suggested earlier, occupation is closely related to income levels, and it has a considerable impact on living standard and lifestyle.[44]

Different economic activities are traditionally assigned to one of three main categories. The primary sector includes agriculture, forestry and fishing. The secondary sector comprises the different branches of industry (the processing industry, mining, energy production and construction), whereas the tertiary sector includes diverse types of services (education, health, research, commerce, transportation, telecommunications, banking and insurance, mass media, public administration, etc.).

There has emerged a relatively straightforward pattern in the change of the relative size of those employed in the individual sectors over the past two centuries of Europe, which was identified as early as the 1930s and 1940s by economists like Allen G. B. Fisher, Colin G. Clark and Jean Fourastié.[45] They argued that the ratio of the agrarian sector has continually decreased, whereas the ratio of the industrial sector first increased then began to decline. In contrast, the ratio of those employed in the service sector was continually on the rise in all national economies. Against this background, they also commenced the so-called three-sector hypothesis, implying the imperative of the transformation of agricultural society via industrial society to the service or post-industrial society. There are few theories in economics that have been verified empirically and convincingly to the extent that the model of sectoral transformations has been attested. At the same time, and in parallel with the general thrust of development, an international comparison reveals significant differences between societies regarding the relative size of the sectors as well as the timing and dynamics of structural change throughout the twentieth century.

The agrarian sector

The decline of the agrarian population had started well before the period under examination all over Europe, albeit at varying paces. However, at the turn of the nineteenth and twentieth centuries, the primary sector was still the largest branch everywhere, with the exception of Great Britain and Belgium, where those employed in industry dominated since 1821 and 1880, respectively. In fact, the majority of European countries, apart from Britain and a corridor from Switzerland to Sweden, were still considered agricultural countries on the eve of the Second World War, at least regarding the distribution of labour (even though agriculture was no longer the major source of gross national product). Nevertheless, the scale was wide. In Albania, more than 80% of the labour force earned their living in agriculture, in Bulgaria 80%, in Romania 79%, in Hungary 53% and in Spain 52%. There were countries where the primary sector still employed the most people, although less than half of the population, such as Portugal (49%), Ireland (48%), Italy (48%), France (36%) or Czechoslovakia (36%).[46] Finally, a third group included those (mostly North-Western and Central European) economies where agriculture represented the smallest ratio of the three sectors by the Second World War; examples include Denmark and Sweden (29–29%), as well as Germany (26%). On the eve of the Second World War, agrarian employment was especially low in Belgium, and in Great Britain it was already plainly marginal, with 6% (Table 4.4).

The rapid economic growth after the Second World War diminished the agrarian population in Western Europe to a fraction in the course of a few decades. As a result, in 1990, only 2% of the population worked in agriculture in Belgium and the United Kingdom, 3% in Sweden and West Germany, and only 4% in the Netherlands, an important exporter of agricultural produce. With 5%, France was in the middle range, and the ratio was 8% in Italy, Austria and Finland. The data for the latter two obviously also represent highly developed forestry. Southern Europe occupied a middle position (Spain 10% and Portugal 17%). The decrease was of a slower pace in East Central and South-Eastern Europe. Albania had the highest ratio in Europe, with 55%, but Romania (29%), Poland (28%), Bulgaria (18%) and Hungary (18%) were also among the countries with large agrarian populations by European standards.

TABLE 4.4 Sectoral distribution of the economically active population in European countries, 1910–1997

	1910			1930			1950			1960			1980			1997		
	Agriculture	Industry	Service	Agriculture	Industry	Service	Agriculture	Industry	Service	Agriculture	Industry	Service	Agriculture	Industry	Service	Agriculture	Industry	Service
United Kingdom	9	52	40	6	46	48	5	49	46	4	48	48	3	42	56	2	27	71
France	41	33	26	36	33	31	27	36	37	22	39	39	8	39	53	5	26	70
Netherlands	29	33	38	21	36	43	20	34	46	11	42	47	6	45	49	4	22	74
Belgium	23	45	32	17	48	35	13	50	37	8	48	45	3	41	56	2	26	71
Ireland	51	15	34	48	16	36	40	24	35	36	25	40	18	37	45	10	28	62
Germany/FRG	37	41	22	29	40	31	23	43	34	14	48	38	4	46	50	3	37	60
Austria	32	33	35	32	33	35	33	37	30	24	46	30	9	37	54	7	30	64
Switzerland	27	46	28	21	45	34	17	47	37	11	50	39	5	46	49	5	27	69
Sweden	49	32	19	39	36	25	21	41	38	14	45	41	5	34	61	3	26	71
Denmark	36	28	36	30	29	41	25	34	41	18	37	45	7	35	58	4	27	70
Norway	39	25	36	36	27	37	26	37	37	20	37	44	7	37	56	5	24	72
Finland	80	12	8	71	16	13	47	28	25	36	32	33	11	35	54	7	28	66
Italy	55	27	18	47	31	22	42	32	26	31	40	29	11	45	44	7	32	61
Spain	56	14	30				50	26	25	42	31	27	14	40	46	8	30	62
Poland	77	9	14	66	17	17	54	26	20	48	29	23	31	39	30	21	32	48
Czechoslovakia/ Czech Republic	40	37	23	37	37	26	39	36	25	26	46	28	11	48	41	6	42	53
Hungary	58	20	22	55	24	23	51	23	26	37	35	28	20	43	37	8	33	57

Note: Because of rounding off, the sum may not be equal to 100%. Czechoslovakia had ceased to exist by 1997 so data is for the Czech Republic.

Sources: Gerold Ambrosius and William Hubbard, *A Social and Economic History of Twentieth-Century Europe*, Cambridge, MA: Harvard University Press, 1989, 58–59 (Europe 1910–1980); OECD: *Labour Force Statistics, 1977–1997*, Paris: OECD, 1998 (Europe 1997).

Industry

Great Britain was not only the 'first industrial nation', but the dominance of industry had the lengthiest sway here as well, lasting from 1821 to 1959. Long industrial periods, in terms of the relative size of industrial employment, also took place in Belgium (1880–1965), Switzerland (1888–1970) and (West) Germany (1907–75). However, in some countries, industrial employment predominated only for a few years, such as France (1954–59) and Italy (1960–65), and there were countries where this phase was missing altogether. About two-thirds of the European countries had a period of relatively predominant industrial employment. It was a unique European phenomenon that industry became the major sector of employment for some time. Outside Europe, it occurred only in Taiwan, around 1980. It was characteristic neither in the United States, nor in Japan, Australia, Canada or South Korea, because in these countries the tertiary sector immediately replaced agriculture as the largest employer, that is, 'the industrial age' in this sense was missing.[47]

Industrial employment climaxed in the 1960s in Western Europe, usually covering 40–45% of all those employed. The largest branches within industry included classic heavy industries (mining, metallurgy, steel processing, engineering industry, energy production and the like), but some future industries had already emerged, such as pharmaceutics, electronics and car production. The latter had turned into mass production in this period.

In Southern Europe and in the communist countries, including some of the least-developed regions in Europe, the progress of industrialization was rapid after the Second World War. This progress brought the ratio of industrial employees in communist countries to among the highest in the world. For example, in East Germany in the early 1970s, 50.2% of the active population worked in the industry. This ratio was 49.4% in Czechoslovakia at its peak in 1980 and 45% in Hungary in 1970.[48] There were ideological reasons behind the prominence of the industrial sector in post-war East Central Europe. The new political elite had confidence that the Soviet model would make it possible to eliminate backwardness (and thus to increase military potential) through industrialization and especially the development of heavy industry. In addition, communist parties considered the working class as the major basis of the regime and thus they regarded its expansion to be a prime political interest, placing it into the centre of social and economic policy. However, forced industrialization not only entailed enormous social costs but also was realized at the expense of other economic branches, thus leading to huge economic imbalances and the erosion of foundations of future growth.

There was another path to the transformation of economic sectors in Europe as well, one leading directly from an agrarian to a service-oriented society. Greece, the Netherlands, Norway, Denmark, Finland, Ireland and Spain followed this type of development. In the first three countries, the high ratio of those employed in navigation was a decisive contributor. It was not an insignificant factor in the latter three countries either, but in these cases the main explanation was late industrialization, which could strongly rely on labour-saving technologies.

The high ratio of industrial employment had important social and political consequences already in the early twentieth-century in Europe, which are also related to the characteristics and the organization of industrial work. Whereas in agriculture and in services, workers usually perform their tasks independently and even in isolation, in industry, the labour force is mostly concentrated in factories, and the division of labour is highly regulated and hierarchical. These circumstances promoted the emergence of class identity among workers and enhanced their level of organization, which, in turn, initiated similar developments in other social groups, also strengthening their group or class identity. In the United States, the lack of social revolutions and antagonistic class conflicts can arguably be related to the direct transition from an agrarian to a service economy, and, in particular, to the relatively small social weight of the workers in large-scale industry melting diverse industrial occupations into classes, and forming particularistic interests and groups into a labour movement. In contrast, in Europe, the predominance of the industrial sector and, most notably, the distinct characteristics of the organization of industrial work contributed to 'class politics', i.e. the sharper opposition of social classes. The most obvious manifestations were the revolutions after the First World War, but industrialism had political consequences tangible all through the century, including the strength of parties representing workers' interests or the relatively high level of unionization. Furthermore, the concentration of workers deepened social problems and made them more visible, which contributed to the emergence of the modern welfare state, an intense involvement of the government in social matters, from the late nineteenth century. The high ratio of industrial employment decreased the possibilities of mobility for workers, and it also affected the urban structure; there were hardly any places similar to European industrial towns in other regions of the world.[49]

Sooner or later, industrial employment started to drop throughout Europe. In parallel to deindustrialization, a large-scale restructuring of industry also took place, affecting both heavy and light industry. The deterioration of coal mining had already begun in Western Europe in the 1950s. Later, shipbuilding and the textile industry, then the steel industry, followed. The process was not painless. The areas where the above branches had been concentrated often turned into crisis regions for decades. To give a few examples, the decline in coal mining had dire effects on Wallonia, the Newcastle region, Alsace-Lorraine, the Saar region, the Ruhr and even the Basque country. The oil crisis (1973) was of decisive influence in this regard, because it accelerated the structural transformation of the economy. Traditional factory-based, large-scale industries definitively gave way to more modern branches of industry and to service. To illustrate the momentum of the process, in the United Kingdom, industrial employment fell by 12.6 percentage points between 1974 and 1989; in Belgium by 11.7 percentage points, in Switzerland, by 9.2 percentage points, in France by 9.3 percentage points, and in Germany and Italy by 6.9 percentage points.

In East Central Europe and the Balkan communist countries, this process began later and took place at a slower pace, sluggishly until the regime change. When in the 1970s in Western Europe structural transformations were well under way, communist planned economies were still continuing development programmes in the old structure. This delay greatly contributed to the deterioration of their competitiveness in the 1980s and ultimately to the collapse of the regimes. As a further consequence, East Central European and South-East European countries had to perform economic restructuring all of a sudden, during the period of the regime change and at a time when other social and political problems also emerged, which, with the exception of Slovenia, led to great social distress everywhere.

The service sector

In the decades after the Second World War, the tertiary sector gained a dominant role in employment even in countries of Europe where the leading position had earlier been occupied by industry. The change first took place from the late 1950s in the United Kingdom, Sweden and France, then gradually in all other countries by the 1970s. Thus, by the 1980s, services employed the absolute majority of the workforce, with the exception of Ireland, the Mediterranean and the communist countries. However, intra-European divisions were still marked in that respect. In the late 1970s, the corresponding ratios of the communist countries ranged from 24% (Bulgaria) to 41% (Czechoslovakia and East Germany). As a further indicator of the different employment structure of European regions, in 1990, the ratio of workers employed in commerce, catering, finance and other business services in the total labour force was 20–30% in Western Europe, whereas in East Central Europe the same figure was only 7–12%.[50] However, by the millennium, the number of those employed in the service sector also grew rapidly in the latter countries, because services absorbed most of the labour that was becoming excessive in the declining industries and agriculture.

It had become one of the important European characteristics of services by the late twentieth century that a significant number of those employed in the service sector were public employees or civil servants. Considering all services provided by public institutions and companies (including the postal services, public transport, telecommunications and others), the share of state employees in the civilian sector in 1985 was 38.3% in Sweden, 37.4% in Denmark, 25.7% in France, and in Germany 18.9%. In contrast, also taken without the military, this figure was 14.8% in the United States.[51] From the 1980s, several Western European, and from the 1990s, East Central European countries have privatized some of the public service companies, such as railways, but similar moves generated heated debates and the practice failed to become a general phenomenon. Proponents of privatization pointed out the cost-effectiveness of private companies, whereas its adversaries maintained that it often led to deterioration in the quality of services and argued that the extensive public service sector had a positive effect on job security and offered higher wages than the private sector, especially for the poorly qualified and for women.

Having reviewed all three sectors, it must be mentioned that with time, structural changes occurred not only between them but also within the branches. These transformations present a challenge to research because the classification of some economic activities is fairly ambiguous, and detailed data are not always available. Uncertain cases have always been around, but their number grew considerably by the end of the twentieth century in the most developed societies. The examples include especially service-oriented occupations necessary for industrial production such as researchers or railway personnel employed at industrial companies. The sectoral classification of several activities is not clear-cut and thus the tertiary sector is a kind of 'residual category' (C. Clark), which in itself raises its share among the employed.

Since the service sector is heterogeneous, and some occupations included in it are often embedded in industrial production, whereas others are far from the primary and the secondary sector (e.g. health care), suggestions emerged for replacing the triadic sector classification with more sophisticated approaches. Probably the most popular one of these scholarly perspectives for the most part leaves the other two sectors as they are, but proposes four sub-categories within the tertiary sector, thus, ending up with a six-sector model. The division includes the branch of distributing activities (transportation, commerce and communication); of business services (finance, planning, accounting, legal services, etc.); of social and community services (education, health care, public administration, social services, etc.); and of personal services (catering, leisure, culture, body care, etc.).[52] Although data are available for only the four largest Western European countries, changes in sectoral distribution still yield useful information on how the internal structure of services was transformed in the course of the twentieth century. The ratio of those employed in the distribution/communication branch grew only slightly; actually, it basically stagnated in the past decades in Germany. The expansion of business services is striking, especially in the post-Second World War period, but their absolute size still lagged behind that of the other branches at the end of the century. The greatest rise occurred in the ratio of those employed in social and community services, making this sector the largest service branch, followed by distribution/communication. Finally, there are no unified developmental trends in the four countries regarding the ratio of those making their living from personal services. Their presence faded in two countries and grew in the two others between 1920 and 1990. Thus, we find that most of the growth of the tertiary sector in the twentieth century was partly the result of the rise in the number of those employed in social and community services in the countries examined, and partly that of the boom in business services, activities related to industrial and agricultural production.[53]

The causes of the changes

Explanation is required regarding the reason why the transformation of economic sectors occurred in the twentieth century following the above patterns all over Europe, even all over the world. As Colin Clark has already established, the peculiar dynamics of the changes largely originate from the differences in the demand for the goods and services provided by specific sectors. The demand for agricultural products and particularly for foodstuffs is inelastic, that is, physically limited: individuals consume basically the same amount of food today as they did a hundred years ago, under the conditions of considerably lower standards of economic development and purchasing power, even if the quality and the value of the consumed food increased. In contrast, the demand for the goods of the industrial sector and especially for services is elastic, and, consequently, essentially insatiable. Thus with the rising standard of living the internal structure of demand of private households shifts to products supplied by industry and services.[54]

A further explanation of the shifts between agriculture, industry and services lies in the growth of labour productivity, which is faster in the primary and secondary sectors than in services. Thus labour becomes excessive in the former two, which then moves to the tertiary sector because, as suggested above, the demand for services is practically insatiable. A supplementary factor is that the mechanization and centralization of industrial production increase demand for certain types of services (e.g. maintenance and transportation).[55]

National characteristics are plausibly explained by natural, environmental and geographical conditions, as well as positions occupied in the international division of labour. Low population density and high distance from international markets increases the ratio of those working in transportation and communication. A country specializing in supplying certain goods or services for the international market has high employment in the relevant branch, which accounts for the high employment ratio of the British textile industry in the nineteenth century, and Denmark's relatively big agrarian sector even in the second half of the twentieth century, or the considerable share of sea transportation in the employment structure of Norway, Greece and the Netherlands for a great part of the twentieth century. The smaller a country or region, the more prominent these factors may become, and the more the employment structure may diverge from that of other economies.

Social classes and strata: expanding centre and fading contours

As suggested above, many of the assets and rewards in society, including income, prestige and power, are assigned through the social roles and primarily through occupations that individuals possess, and thus it is plausible to determine the social standing of people by grouping them with regard to their social positions. In this setting, occupational structure has been widely considered as the major element of the entire social structure in modern Western society.[56] Accordingly, in the following discussion, the structural changes of different occupational groups and the characteristics of trades and jobs are used as the basis for examining the transformation of social structure in twentieth-century Europe.

The shifts between the economic sectors, discussed earlier, entailed significant but diverse consequences for the structure of labour, which can be considered from several perspectives. One of the possible approaches is the analysis of how the share of the self-employed and employees changed.

The self-employed

The number of self-employed substantially declined throughout Europe in the twentieth century. A major constituent of the process was the fall in agricultural employment, which resulted in the shrinking of the stratum of independent peasants, because those working in agriculture were decisively, or, at least, largely independent smallholders all over Europe (hereby disregarding the majority of communist countries, where collectivization took place from the early 1950s). The remaining agricultural sector underwent a structural change as well, which contributed to the diminishing of independent labour. The tendency was also facilitated by the vanishing of craftsmen's workshops and small stores, one of the consequences of industrial concentration and the transformation of commerce. As regards concrete development, at the beginning of the twentieth century, the number of self-employed workers was around 20% in most Western European countries, which then at least halved by the end of the century. The decrease was especially rapid in the decades after the Second World War. In 1907 in Germany, 20% of the economically active population belonged to this group, and only 9% in 1980. If France is regarded as traditionally being the country of small proprietors, then its 45% ratio of self-employed in 1926 was obviously higher than the European average. By 1980, the level dropped considerably, to 15%, which was still considered high in a European context. The share of the self-employed exceeded this only in Spain, Ireland, Greece and Italy.[57] Nevertheless, the pace of decline slowed down throughout the continent by the end of the century. Actually, in Italy and Spain, the percentage of self-employed stabilized at a relatively high level, and in Great Britain it even rose somewhat from a much lower point. The reversal of the trends was often the result of the tense labour market situation; many saw an alternative to seeking employment in becoming independent contractors and starting their own business, even if it implied a lower income.[58]

In communist countries, because of the almost complete nationalization of private businesses and the restrictions on private property, the stratum of the self-employed shrank radically in the 1950s and 1960s. The only countries where the collectivization of agriculture fractionally occurred were Yugoslavia and Poland, and therefore the number and ratio of the independent farmers remained relatively high there. In the other countries, independent farmers, craftsmen and tradesmen existed in small numbers, as outliers in society, with no perspective for growth at all. After the regime change in the post-communist countries, small business and the stratum of self-employed reappeared or expanded considerably, not only in agriculture but also in industry, commerce and other services.

Parallel to the decline of self-employment, unpaid family labour also shrank considerably. This group mostly included women assisting in the family farm, shop or workshop. In the interwar period, they accounted for 10–20% of the total labour force in Western Europe, and came close to one-third in East Central and Southern Europe. By the early 1960s, the proportion of family labour was cut in half in most parts of the continent and declined even more drastically in East

Central Europe. By the end of the century, this group represented only a small percentage of the economically active population, with the exception of a few countries, including Greece, Romania and Poland.[59]

Employees

In parallel with the falling ratios of the self-employed, employees (those working for other persons or businesses under contracts for wages or salary) comprised a widening group of the economically active. However, the stratum of blue-collar and white-collar employees not only grew but also underwent significant internal transformation. Whereas blue-collar workers had previously dominated among employees, from the late nineteenth century, the group of white-collar salaried employees emerged and continually expanded, including employees whose task does not entail regular manual work (such as managers, office workers, engineers and commercial employees). In numbers, this meant that in Great Britain, the ratio of white-collar employees within the total labour force was already 19% in 1910, and it increased to 40% by 1980. Elsewhere in Western Europe, it started from a lower level and reached similar or higher values, the highest in Sweden with 59%. The dynamics were usually faster in the second half of the century than in the first. The ratio of white-collars remained below 10% throughout East Central Europe between the World Wars, but climbed to 25–30% by 1980.[60]

The rise in the ratio of employees was related to the previously discussed restructuring of economic sectors, because white-collar jobs prevailed in services. A growing proportion of employees found work in public services (health care, education, public administration), but the private sector also received its share. The structural transformation and technological development of industry strengthened this tendency by shifting the former balance between manual and non-manual activities in this sector as well. In branches of industry leading technological development, such as the chemical industry and electrical engineering, white-collar salaried employees made up between one-quarter and one-third of the total work force by the 1980s in Western Europe.[61]

The changes in the shares of the self-employed and employees highlight important aspects of twentieth-century social development. At the same time, the heterogeneity of these categories is so high that this approach cannot rival the identification and characterization of the major classes and strata. In the course of the transformation of the social structure, whole classes have disappeared or changed in fundamental ways in the twentieth century. In the following discussion, the main trends of the twentieth-century transformation of the upper class or the social elite, the middle class(es), the working class and the peasantry are outlined.[62]

The upper class

The upper class was equally affected by twentieth-century social transformations regarding its size, internal composition, economic status and political influence.

The social position of the upper class did undergo significant changes, as a consequence of the logic of socioeconomic development, but it was exposed to even more striking moves in times of revolution and war. The most dramatic changes were concentrated on four periods in the twentieth century, including the revolutions and the formation of new nation states in the aftermath of the First World War (primarily in East Central Europe), the emergence of dictatorships in the interwar period (Italy, Germany, Spain, Portugal), the collapse of dictatorships and the rise of new communist dictatorships after the Second World War, and finally, the fall of the latter around 1990.[63]

After a relatively slow transformation in the nineteenth century, the first half of the twentieth century brought huge losses to the landed aristocracy and to the nobility in a wider sense. The First World War washed away the Central European monarchies and discredited the political role of aristocracy. For many families, the war and its aftermath also meant an economic catastrophe, because it wiped out their investments and financial wealth.[64] After the First World War, in several countries, their lands and other assets were partly or fully expropriated, their privileges were curtailed and they were even forced to emigrate. For example, in Austria, titles of nobility were abolished and in Germany, the libraries, castles, parks and other real properties were expropriated in return for compensation. In some countries of Western Europe, such as Great Britain, Belgium, the Netherlands and three Scandinavian countries, the monarchies survived – a sign that the transformation was not so radical. Here, the nobility proceeded to merge with other elements of the upper class, primarily with industrialists.

Although the great turning points in political history rarely coincide with milestones in social history, 1945 joined 1789 and 1918 in bringing important changes in the history of the aristocracy. During the Second World War and the decades following it, the supplantation of the aristocracy accelerated; some claim it even caused its disappearance as a class. Even if this does not apply for all countries, it is definitely true for Germany. Here, the stratum of *Junker* military officers was almost completely annihilated during the war, and by the end of the century, hardly any aristocrats could be found in leading diplomatic and military positions, which used to be traditional places of refuge for the nobility. Changes were more gradual or even ambiguous in Great Britain. Here, during the Second World War, not only did military and political leaders emerge from the lower strata, but the progressive taxes introduced had dire effects on old, land-based wealth as well. A growing proportion of accumulated wealth originated in industrial, financial and other companies in the post-war decades, but the ratio of large real properties remained significant in wealth, although not only as the possession of land, but also of urban buildings. The British aristocracy survived, which is illustrated by the fact that the richest person and the largest landowner in 2000 were dukes. In addition, most of the peers in the House of Lords assumed their position by birth. However, the dramatic weakening of the position of the aristocracy is shown by the change in the function of their castles. Whereas in the heyday of aristocracy, these buildings were the bastions of power and signs of wealth and high status all over the British

Isles, this was no longer the case at the millennium. Most of those who held on to the castles obviously decided to do so because of their respect for the past, and the maintenance of the buildings often caused a pressing problem for their families. Many could afford to cover maintenance costs only by opening their castles to the public, which also became the precondition for receiving support from public conservation programmes for historic buildings.[65] At the end of the century, the surviving aristocratic titles, such as earl and duke, were undoubtedly sources of prestige for their bearers, but beyond that, they offered little social and political influence.

The aristocracy traditionally had strong positions in the Eastern regions of Europe as well, but the land reforms carried out in several countries of East Central Europe and the Balkans in the interwar period had already diminished the concentration of landed properties. One of the objectives of the land reforms was the restructuring of land ownership by nationality, e.g. in Romania, where it resulted in the loss of holdings by Russian landowners in Bessarabia and of Hungarian landowners in Transylvania. In Hungary and Poland, land reform did not proceed to reach such scales after the First World War. In 1935 in Hungary, the 1500 landowners with property greater than 600 hectares commanded 24% of the cultivated land, and in Poland, landowners of over 300 hectares possessed more than 20%.[66] However, the few years after the Second World War brought about the end of the economic and political power of the aristocracy in the region, and partly even its physical annihilation. Beginning before the communist takeover, the parcelling out and nationalization of big estates completely expropriated the landed properties of the aristocrats. These steps were complemented with other restrictions, such as the prohibition of the use of titles of nobility and the disenfranchisement of political rights. In the end, after the communists assumed power, many aristocratic families avoided persecution only by emigration.

The aristocracy was able to preserve its power the longest in Spain and Portugal, based on the concentration of landed properties. In 1930 in Spain, landowners possessing property over 500 hectares commanded approximately two-thirds of the land, which greatly exceeded any East Central European ratio. It shows how slow these changes were in that regard: even in 1962, approximately half of all the Spanish lands belonged to 1.8% of agricultural estates.[67]

However, in the course of the twentieth century, aristocracy was not the only segment of the upper class that suffered changes in social positions; industrialists, bankers and other members of the business elite met serious challenges as well. Wars and revolutions often affected these groups equally badly, primarily in East Central Europe, but elsewhere too, as exemplified by the car maker Renault in France, who was ousted because of his collaboration with the Nazis.[68] The business elite was constrained by the increase in state taxation, but from the mid-century the scale of public ownership also widened considerably in Western Europe (most of all in France and Great Britain), taking place in direct opposition with the interests of big business.

Another noteworthy process concerning the upper classes was the rise of professional management and the split between the ownership and management of corporations, mainly as a result of growth in the size of business enterprises. Lacking the necessary expertise, major shareholders and other owners of companies would not necessarily be appropriate to fill such positions; therefore from the late nineteenth century, this role was increasingly assumed by the managerial class, possessing up-to-date economic, legal and technological knowledge. The great family firms of the nineteenth century usually disappeared or were transformed into joint stock companies, which also made it simpler to attract capital. In Germany, the professionalization of the management and the structural transformation of the biggest industrial companies began relatively early, and had progressed considerably already in the nineteenth century, whereas in Great Britain and France, family firms still played a great role in the interwar period, vanishing only after the Second World War. However, not only was the direct personal ownership of firms replaced by more indirect control, but the decline of family-organized capitalism also facilitated the emergence of dispersed, share-based ownership through joint-stock companies. In addition, owners of the joint-stock enterprises were often companies themselves, such as banks, insurance companies, pension funds and other investment funds. As a result, instead of the owners, managers filling the position of director and other company leaders increasingly disposed over the capital embodied in the company. The managerial class grew in number, with incomes showing greater dynamics than capital revenues, that is, the increase of the power of the managers took place at the expense of the capital owners to a significant extent. Leading managers became members of the upper class not only because of their administrative position and high income but also because their influence often brought them joint ownerships of the companies they directed. Against this background, the American sociologist James Burnham proposed the concept of the 'managerial revolution' in 1941, according to which managerial professionals pursuing their own interests formed a new class, superseding the old ruling class of capitalists. The thesis provoked serious criticisms later: critics pointed out that many big corporate firms continued to exist in which individuals or families exercised control based on their shareholdings, and in the late twentieth century, trends of shareholder fragmentation reversed in several respects.

The tendencies introduced undoubtedly opened up channels of mobility to the upper class and constrained big wealth in the most part of the twentieth century. The upper class became more open, as one could enter it by expertise as well. The members of the new managerial class were partly recruited from the middle class, which, to a certain extent, decreased the internal unity of the upper class. However, those newly arriving assimilated into the milieu they entered. Moreover, directors, board members and other leaders of business companies still came mostly from among the upper class, thus securing the continuance of their privileged position. The review of the changes in income and wealth distribution had also shown that a huge proportion of assets were still concentrated in the hands of the top few per cent of society. Many claim that the closure of the wealthiest strata constituted one of the main obstacles to social mobility in European societies.[69]

The changes were more significant in the political elite, because the members of the ruling elite were forced to a greater degree to share their power with other social groups. This gained momentum after the Second World War and was first and foremost the consequence of the enfranchisement, which is considered in chapter 7. When Social Democratic, Peasant and other newly established parties won seats in the parliament and became members of the government in Great Britain, Germany, Austria, Scandinavia and elsewhere from as early as the 1920s, the composition of the political class altered in fundamental ways. The opening up of the political elite was not restricted to democracies. In the Franco era in Spain, the army became an important channel of mobility for middle-class youth, raising them to leadership positions in state and military administration.

After the Second World War, the openness of the political elite declined even in most of the Western European democracies. Politics had increasingly become a profession, with all the positive effects this had on the stability of the political process. However, this also stabilized party elites, making it increasingly difficult to enter them from outside the party bureaucracy. This phenomenon also emerged in the new democracies of East Central Europe in the 1990s, after the regime change. In contrast, the scientific, church and cultural elites remained more open everywhere in post-war Europe.

As a further development in the upper class, the number of those in the 'functional elite' increased. In addition to economic and political leaders, this social layer included those in the leading positions of public administration, research, science and education, the churches, culture, the entertainment industry, the military and the judiciary. The rise of the functional elite increased the diversity of the upper class considerably, particularly in the post-war decades in Europe. Political, military, economic, scientific, religious and other elites varied greatly as regards the extent of their integration into the upper class; they had very strong subcultural differences, and they also differed in the degree of their openness.[70] The openness or closure of the upper class and especially of the functional elite was fundamentally related to the characteristics of education, which are dealt with in chapter 9.

The replacement of the upper class and the elite was radical in the communist countries after the Second World War, even almost complete. Here, not only were former political leaders removed, often persecuted or annihilated in their physical existence, but also the nationalization of the large companies and big agricultural estates led to the elimination of the entire economic elite. At the same time, the positions of the functional elite (university professors, engineers, managers, etc.) were also shaken. At the initial stages of the recruitment of the new elite, political considerations overruled all others, even professional criteria. According to this experience, in 1957, Milovan Djilas, a Yugoslav communist dissident, discussed the formation of a 'new class' enjoying special privileges. Later, the communist elite underwent a process of professionalization to some extent, but capability and achievements mattered only in a limited way, even in such soft dictatorships as in Hungary and Poland. Symptomatically, in the 1980s, the political and the economic elites were more closed in most communist countries than in the majority of Western

European societies (an issue that is addressed later in the chapter).[71] These characteristics of the elites greatly diminished the economic and social performance of the communist regimes.

After the collapse of communism, in most countries, the impeachment of the former political elite did not take place on a similar scale as after the Second World War in the region, or, for instance, after the fall of the military regime in Greece in the mid-1970s. The reason behind this was primarily that in the last years of communist rule there were relatively few victims of political oppression, because the organized political opposition was weak and thus could not be a target for severe repression. With the exception of Romania, the succession of power proceeded in a largely peaceful manner. Moreover, communist parties were huge organizations, sometimes with membership accounting for as much as 10% of the population, reaching many more when family and other social ties are taken into account. That is, a high proportion of the population (with an overrepresentation of those occupying higher status in society) felt compromised and disinterested in retribution. In addition, the first years of democracy brought dire social and economic difficulties, which gave birth to a widespread nostalgia for the previous regime and facilitated indifference to politics. This meant that support for the impeachment of the previous elite weakened, with the notable consequence that the change of elites was not comprehensive, either.[72] Moreover, there were significant differences in this regard in the region. In the Czech Republic, the former East Germany and Albania, almost everyone who was among the political elite or a public figure in the previous regime had to leave their position. Elsewhere this did not occur (Hungary and Poland), and the actual change in the composition of the elite was mostly voluntary and a result of negotiations – partly because the communist parties had a well-developed reform wing in these countries. The limits of the elite change were also the result of compromises in Romania, where some claim the revolution was the preventive action of the old elite with the objective of preserving their power. In Bulgaria and Slovakia, the change of the elites affected only the highest political level, and many of the old nomenclature were given important positions in the new political regime. As a result, in the latter group of the ex-communist countries, an abundance of the members of the former political elite were able to convert their political or social capital into economic capital.[73]

The middle class(es)

The definition of the middle class constitutes a serious challenge for research on social structure. Even though the working class also comprises several strata or groups, the middle class has been characterized by more limited internal solidarity, more diverse living conditions, more fragmented political and interest representations, and smaller inclination to collective action, all through the twentieth century. Therefore negative definitions often surface: according to one of them, the middle class is the social layer between manual industrial workers and peasants on the one hand, and the upper class/elite on the other. Others define the middle class as comprising those in non-manual, white-collar occupations. These definitions equally classify the self-employed and non-manual employees with no property (and, more generally, people occupying very dissimilar work and market positions) as belonging to the middle class, signalling that the middle class cannot be considered as a class in a strict Marxist or Weberian sense. When discussing the issue, some authors emphasize the complexity of this social layer by using the plural form, speaking about the middle classes.

However, there exist factors that provide internal cohesion for the middle class, including the relationship to other social groups and cultural similarities. As in the case of other social layers, middle-class identity taking shape in the eighteenth century was significantly related to distinguishing and demarcating itself from other strata in society. First, merchants, craftsmen, professors and lawyers distanced themselves from the privileged representatives of the *ancien régime*, then another cleavage emerged and gradually gained momentum by the middle of the nineteenth century, dividing the middle class from the lower strata, particularly the workers. It is not difficult to recognize that the differentiation in both cases was motivated by the threat that members of the middle class felt regarding their status and values by the actions and aspirations of other classes. *Mutatis mutandis*, this kind of differentiation was still an important element in the self-understanding and attitudes of the middle class in the early twentieth century, manifesting itself in political commitment and alliances, but even in cultural preferences as well. As to cultural cohesion, generalizations are difficult to make (also for regional differences), but middle-class culture arguably included a positive attitude towards thrift, rationality, emotional control, respect for knowledge and education, regular work, a desire for independence and family-centeredness. These characteristics also originated in earlier periods, but they were considered important elements of middle-class culture in the early twentieth century and even beyond, all around Europe.[74]

The size of the middle class grew considerably in the course of the twentieth century, especially in the Western half of Europe. In the mid- or late nineteenth century, it is estimated to include about 5% of the population in Western European countries, although there are authors who claim that by the end of the twentieth century, it comprised more than half of the population.[75] The dynamics of the growth of the middle class are indicated by the term 'middle-class societies' in discussions on Western Europe of the second half of the twentieth century. Political significance is also attributed to the size of the middle class, assuming that the existence of a broad middle class is beneficial for the functioning of parliamentary democracy, because the middle class plays a stabilizing and moderating role in society, preventing political polarization between the upper and the working classes.

Traditionally, the middle class included owners of small businesses (tradesmen and craftsmen, sometimes called petite bourgeoisie) and practitioners of independent occupations that can be called professionals (such as doctors, engineers and lawyers). This so-called old middle class was joined by the salaried employees from the late nineteenth century, which were categorized as the 'new middle class' by early industrial sociologists. Salaried employees qualified for middle-class status by their income, lifestyle and identity, although they did not own means of production, and they were not self-dependent. This stratum, dynamically growing in the twentieth century, has been partly employed by the government, but private firms also hired rising numbers of engineers, lawyers, accountants and other highly qualified professionals from the ranks of the middle class. Their income was significantly higher than that of workers and often even that of shopkeepers or craftsmen, members of the traditional or old middle class. Even the type of compensation (monthly salary) differentiated them from workers, who received wages based on daily or hourly rates, often directly tied to work performance. They also had markedly higher levels of education and better working conditions than workers, clearly occupying a position between the manual or blue-collar workers and the management, which lent them a sense of distinctiveness and identity. The sense of interdependence was even stronger between salaried employees working in public institutions and administration, because they often enjoyed special privileges with regard to remuneration, prospects for promotion or pension. The rise of the new middle class can be plausibly illustrated by the example of Great Britain, where clerks represented 0.8% of male employees in 1851, 5.7% in 1911, and 10.5% in 1951.[76] Several partly interrelated aspects of social and economic development discussed above contributed to the expansion. Factors include the process of bureaucratization, the distension of the activities of the state, and especially the welfare state, as well as the growth of company size and the development of the tertiary sector. These all created demand for both highly qualified experts and employees performing administrative activities.

It was not only the size, but also the complexity, of the new middle class that increased considerably in the course of the twentieth century. Because the expansion of the stratum of white-collar employees also brought about rapid internal differentiation, identifying these employees with the new middle class gradually lost its plausibility from the interwar period. The development of industry, commerce and other service branches proceeded toward larger unit size and concentration. Consequently, the division of labour became more advanced, and hierarchy more pronounced, within companies. This meant that the previously sharp dividing line between workers and those performing non-manual tasks faded with respect to both income and working conditions. However, new sharp divisions appeared at the same time between management, middle management and office workers. Clerical work became routinized, career prospects diminished, and the income of employees in these jobs often did not reach that of manual workers. Internal differentiation of the salaried employees had emerged markedly already in the first half of the century in Western Europe, that is, earlier than in the case of workers, for whom changes accelerated from the mid-century. In post-war Western Europe, the middle class took on even more heterogeneous forms. A number of occupations appeared that could not be classified as worker in the traditional sense, and the income and the working conditions of these occupations were often less advantageous than those found in blue-collar jobs. An example here is the cashier in large supermarkets, a position that requires practically no qualification, the worker is under strict control, the work itself is monotonous, and the income is relatively low. This is why some analyses of social structure do not consider people with such occupations as members of the middle class.

Thus, we see that several internal divisions within the middle class survived all through the twentieth century, and new ones also emerged. To conceptualize these developments in social structure, the terms upper middle class, lower middle class, and petite bourgeoisie are also used, especially with regard to the second half of the century. The upper middle class includes those in high income and professional positions, but the considerably larger lower middle class embraces those in office and administrative jobs, teachers, etc. Income differences are significant between the two strata, but their hierarchy is less clear-cut regarding working conditions and job security. On the one hand, members of the upper middle class often work longer hours than those in the lower middle class; on the other hand, the latter stratum is heterogeneous when working conditions are considered. For example, job security may be better for those employed in the public sector than in a job with higher income in the private sector, and working conditions may often also be more favourable in the former segment.[77]

Research literature also distinguishes the middle class and the petite bourgeoisie, the latter comprising small proprietors (owners of hotels, restaurants, shops, small factories), that is, a stratum that was an important component of the old middle class.[78] This distinction often relies on the argument that members of the petite bourgeoisie share a particular *Weltanschauung* and political behaviour. They are often willing to support the far right, as was the case in Germany in the 1920s with National Socialism, or, referring to less radical movements, in France in the 1950s with Poujadism, and in Italy in the 1990s with the *Lega Nord*. It is often argued that the new developments of capitalism in the twentieth century, particularly economic concentration, endangered the existence of the members of this stratum, which radicalized their political behaviour. Undoubtedly, this layer gradually diminished all through the century, being unable to compete either with large-scale industrial corporations or with hotel and commercial chains. At the same time, its supplantation was not as complete as foreseen by Karl Marx in the nineteenth century. In some countries and regions, such as in Central and North-Eastern Italy, not only did traditional catering and commerce remain strong, but also small industrial businesses successfully modernized their plants and became subcontractors to big industry.

In addition to the factors discussed above, contours of the middle class faded for other reasons as well. Social cleavages have not persisted, even though these social divides helped to define and separate the middle class from other groups in nineteenth-century and early twentieth-century Europe. Accordingly, the sense of identity based on middle-class culture also weakened. Former adversaries, the nobility and the aristocracy, basically disappeared in the twentieth century as rival social groups. At the same time, the tensions and demarcations between the working class and the middle class were still strong in the interwar decades, but the dividing line between them changed fundamentally by the end of the century. This process was promoted by the transformation of middle-class culture in the course of the twentieth century.

On the one hand, several of its components have diffused in society as a whole, such as the ideal of marriage based on romantic attachment, child-centeredness and respect for individual rights. At the same time, several distinctive cultural characteristics that were vivid at the beginning of the twentieth century did fade, or were lost, within the middle class itself. Examples of these include the primacy of work, the emphasis on thrift, orderliness, and the cohesion of family life. As a result, the former distinctiveness of middle-class culture disappeared, and culture ceased to be an important source of middle-class identity. This is why the middle class has been referred to as 'the class without consciousness', or, 'the classless class' from the mid-century. Nevertheless, there are factors that prevailed at the end of the twentieth century that maintained some coherence within the middle class, including individualism, performance orientation, as well as an inclination of parents from diverse segments of the middle class to send their children to good schools and the willingness to make great sacrifices for their children's education.[79]

Obviously, the study cannot offer a detailed analysis of the regional and national differences with regard to the middle class in Europe. However, it is clear that in East Central Europe as well as in the Balkans and in some societies of Scandinavia, the size of the middle class was traditionally small. Moreover, this layer differed from its counterpart found in Western European societies in several aspects, including composition and culture. In the economically more advanced Western Europe, in the course of the nineteenth century, the backbone of the middle class was constituted by tradesmen, bankers, artisans, industrial entrepreneurs and later managers, referred to by the German research literature as *Wirtschaftsbürgertum*.[80] The number and the significance of the *Bildungsbürgertum*, including lawyers, clergymen, public administrators, doctors, professors and other professionals, rose from the late nineteenth century, but they occupied a subordinate position until the mid-twentieth century.[81] As suggested earlier, in Western Europe, these two components of the middle class were related to each other. Their connection was gradually becoming stronger already in the nineteenth century, and it was based on shared identity, especially on their differentiation from the landed nobility and the lower classes. In contrast, in East Central Europe, not only did the size of the middle class remain limited but also the composition became distinct, and the integration of different elements of the middle strata was less complete.[82] The entrepreneurial bourgeoisie, the *Wirtschaftsbürgertum*, remained weak. Moreover, such positions were filled by industrialists or bankers of foreign or other ethnic origin (such as German, Jewish or Armenian) to a great degree. The development of the *Bildungsbürgertum* was not undisturbed either, because in the multiethnic empires prevailing in the region, the elites of the dominant ethnic groups played significant roles vis-à-vis the native population. All this, under the growing ethnic tensions in multiethnic empires, hindered such integration of the bourgeoisie as seen in Western Europe in the late nineteenth century. Moreover, the relationship between the middle class and the nobility also diverged from the Western European pattern. The culture and ethos of the aristocracy and nobility influenced the middle class more strongly than in Western Europe, and the political dominance of the nobility survived longer.[83]

Having said that, the social significance of the nobility faded, already in the second half of the nineteenth century, and the general European tendencies observed also prevailed in East Central Europe, i.e. the size of the middle class grew, especially because of the expansion of the new middle class, and, in relation to this, its internal differentiation progressed. The fragmentation of the middle class in East Central European societies in the interwar period can already be attributed not only to traditional ethnic divides but also to the emergence of 'modern' divisions, such as the ones in relation to self-employed or employee positions, working conditions, and income.

In communist regimes after the Second World War, nationalization affected small properties as well, almost completely wiping out the old middle class. In 1960 in Poland, the ratio of the economically active population involved in small-scale industry and commerce was 1.5%, a mere one-sixth of what it had been in 1931.[84] In communist East Central and South-Eastern Europe, engagement in traditional intellectual and white-collar occupations was essentially possible only by becoming a state employee. Thus, the middle strata were almost exclusively recruited from among white-collar employees, a group that expanded continually and remained more homogeneous than in Western Europe, until the regime change. At the same time, the group was characterized by a lack of identity or autonomy, and its income levels were close to those of blue-collar workers. Therefore the term middle class can be applied only in a strongly limited sense when describing societies of the region in this period. From the 1960s, groups of small proprietors and businesses saw a slow regeneration, although the differences in this respect were great in the region. This process was the most forward in Poland, Yugoslavia and Hungary. In Hungary, the number of artisans, retailers, dentists, lawyers and other self-employed as well as those employed by them amounted to about 5% of the active population in 1980.[85] However, the distinct, socialist version of the petite bourgeoisie was under strict political and economic control until the fall of communism, and ideological countercampaigns often focused on the 'mentality of the petite bourgeoisie', such as an alleged overemphasis on consumption, antagonistic to the official doctrine of the regime.

The working class

The concept of class is the least contested in social and historical research when referring to blue-collar workers. The working class appears, at least between the mid-nineteenth and the mid-twentieth centuries, as a *par excellence* class because of its considerable cohesion, which is based on the relatively homogeneous social position of the workers forged relatively early. As a result, a strong group identity emerged along with the massive labour organizations, making collective action effective.[86] In North-Western and Central Europe, in urban areas and in industry, paid work had already become the dominant form of work by the middle decades of the nineteenth century, and workers had already reached a common understanding in relation to the capitalist entrepreneurs exploiting them; in addition, there was a growing body of shared experience regarding collective action (in the forms of demonstration, strike or machine wrecking).[87] Nevertheless, this unity was relative, and could be called strong only when compared with other social strata, which is indicated by the heated theoretical and political debates starting from the mid-nineteenth century regarding the assessment of the internal changes of the working class.

The composition, the group consciousness and the social position of the working class transformed considerably with changes accelerating from the mid-twentieth century. As regards the proportion of blue-collar workers within the whole class, it continued to grow to a varying degree in individual countries for a while in the twentieth century, and then it started to decline, as a result of which the class lost its dominance everywhere among those employed. The magnitude of the change can be illuminated by the examples of two major Western European nations. Whereas in 1910 in Great Britain, 71% of all employees were blue-collar workers, by 1980, this level shrank to 38%; in a similar period (1921–75) in France, the ratio dropped from 49% to 39%. In a few countries of Western Europe, the proportion of workers climaxed in the first half of the century, but in most societies, the peak was reached some time in the 1950s and 1960s, and even later in Southern Europe.[88]

Among the causes for changes, sectoral shifts affecting the weight of industry must be emphasized. Still, industrial employees cannot be identified entirely with the group of blue-collar workers. On the one hand, industrial companies hire white-collar employees as well, and on the other hand, the tertiary sector also employs blue-collars. Moreover, the share of industrial employees not belonging to the working class had increased, that is, the structural transformations of industry are also responsible for the erosion of the working class.

As to the composition and other internal characteristics of the working class, before the First World War, reality verified Eduard Bernstein's 'revisionist' position, because significant income disparities within the working class emerged between skilled, semiskilled and unskilled workers. In this respect, the twentieth century brought about a reverse development. Corresponding to the general tendency of decline in income inequalities continuing into the 1980s in Western Europe, the differences between the incomes of these workers groups also decreased. Still, the integration of the working class did not proceed because other factors facilitated heterogeneity.

As a consequence of the rapid economic growth in the post-war era, the number of new entrants to the labour markets increased, and their social background became more diverse, contributing significantly to the internal differentiation of the working class. In this respect, the flow of the agricultural population into industry had a major effect. In countries where industrialization advanced most rapidly, the integration and assimilation of the migrants from rural areas to the traditional working class took place only superficially. People who had newly become industrial workers preserved much of their former culture, often also keeping their village homes, thus diverging in lifestyle and attitudes from the traditional segments of the working class. Moreover, the international migration of labour, discussed in detail in chapter 2, brought ethnic diversity, particularly to places where guest workers arrived in large numbers from the 1960s, such as Switzerland, France, Germany and Belgium.

In addition, women entered occupations formerly reserved for men in growing numbers, their different mentality and aspirations further increasing the heterogeneity of the working class.

All these developments could not prevent the occurrence of further important tendencies: the advancement of working-class emancipation and the transformation of the workers' relationship to other social strata. An important reason behind this was the significant rise in the average level of skills and qualifications of workers. On the one hand, the weight of the textile and other light industries employing the most unskilled and semiskilled workers declined. Moreover, technological progress reduced the demand from industry for such labour in the order of millions, a tendency also affecting agriculture. In addition, it was not only the qualification levels of the workers that improved, but their children's chances for education as well. As is shown in chapter 9, the children of blue-collar parents were entering university in low numbers even in the mid-century, but in the following decades the expansion of higher education increased opportunities for them in this regard. Equal opportunities still did not prevail, but the change in favour of the manual workers was tangible all over Europe.

The rising living standard also contributed decisively to the emancipation of the working class. The period of the World Wars was radically different from the second half of the century in this respect as well, although the changes in the standard of living for individual countries was significantly influenced by whether they belonged to the bellicose countries in the World Wars and whether they were among the occupied or the defeated ones. In addition, real incomes were also cut back by the Great Depression in the more fortunate societies. Even in the times of economic prosperity, the majority of the working class teetered on the border of poverty, and in times of massive long-term unemployment they often could not escape it. If they sank into poverty, with all its demoralizing and degrading effects, they were also subjected to moral attacks, with many blaming them for not being able to change the course of their life. In contrast, the economic boom taking shape in Western Europe in the 1950s and 1960s brought about an unprecedented continual and rapid rise of real income in all countries, and for the poorest, unskilled groups as well. The incomes and consumer habits of the Western European working class notably approximated those of the middle class. Workers began to buy the same types of goods and services as members of the middle class, and differences were visible mainly in the quality of cars, the length and location of holidays, or the brands of consumer durables. These changes were also reflected in the spending structure of households. In the mid-century, French unskilled workers spent about half of their household expenditures on food, and the remaining half was also dominated by basic necessities such as heating, electricity and clothing. This was twice the amount that professional households spent on basic items. In contrast, in 1980 in workers' households, the ratio dropped to one-fourth, which equalled only one and a half times the amount of the corresponding expenditure in the households of middle-class professionals.[89] Changes in consumption patterns are addressed in detail in chapter 6.

As the living standard of workers rose, closing the gap between strata, their social protection also improved greatly as a consequence of the achievements of the welfare state. As is shown in the next chapter, workers were the first to enjoy the services of social security in every country from the late nineteenth century. However, these early social benefits were modest. Pensions, for example, after a significant increase in the interwar period, amounted to about 15% of the average earnings in 1939, even in the most generous welfare systems in Western Europe.[90] In addition, insurance against unemployment was introduced only in some Western European countries during the Great Depression. The 1960s witnessed a breakthrough in the field of social security, when after decades of moderate growth following the introduction of the system, the level of social security benefits and the scope of services increased significantly.[91] In addition, during the economic prosperity starting with the 1950s, unemployment practically disappeared in several countries, which further enhanced the everyday security of workers.

As a result of these processes, the relation of the working class to other classes changed. In addition to those aspects of this transformation already referred to in the case of the middle class, a growing number of workers lived in mixed marriages, especially because workers' wives found it easier to find simple, non-manual work in the service sector. Nevertheless, as a consequence, status inconsistency grew in these classes: although workers with the highest wages possessed a similar position as members of the middle class regarding their material conditions, the status they occupied in society did not improve the same way, which consequently 'drew them back' to the working class.

In the context of the developments discussed, several observers stressed the weakening class consciousness of workers in the period after the Second World War, resulting in the waning intensity of class conflicts.[92] The decline of class struggle was undoubtedly promoted by the structural changes of the working class and the relatively higher living standard, also referred to as the embourgeoisement of workers. Another factor was the institutionalization of class conflicts, with the growing acceptance and influence of trade unions and parties representing workers' interests, and even their inclusion in political decision making. However, there were limits to the reconciliation of interests and 'taming' of conflicts, signalled, among others, by the recurring strikes and mass demonstrations throughout Western Europe in the last decades of the twentieth century. For example, the CGT (*Confédération générale du travail*), the otherwise highly influential French trade union, lost control, for a considerable time, over the events of May 1968.[93] Several empirical studies have also demonstrated that the distinction in society between manual and non-manual work remained sharp even at the end of the century in Europe, providing considerable support for arguments stressing the cohesion of the working class.

From the 1970s on, new and substantial social cleavages arose in Western and Southern Europe. A new social stratum emerged, the members of which were faced with growing unemployment, and unable to solidify their positions in the labour market. The backslide of members of this group was so marked that it became questionable whether they still belonged to the working class; thus, a new term, underclass, has been introduced to distinguish this stratum. According to Peter Saunders, the underclass has four major characteristics: its members face multiple social deprivations; they are socially marginalized; they almost fully depend on state welfare benefits; and their culture is characterized by resignation and fatalism.[94] Various groups are overrepresented in the underclass, including immigrants whose level of education is low, or who are entirely unqualified, and speak the language of the host nation poorly. The social integration of non-European immigrants has been made especially difficult by cultural differences, and thus high numbers of ethnic minorities, such as Algerians in France, Moroccans in the Netherlands and Bangladeshis in Great Britain, emerged in this class. At the same time, other marginalized groups, such as disabled people, drug addicts, long-term sick and unemployed people also belong to this category in significant numbers.

As to the social structure of East Central Europe, the tendencies discussed above also surfaced in this region during the interwar period, with the important difference that, except for Czechoslovakia, the proportion of industrial workers was considerably lower than in Western Europe, and the composition of the working class also diverged. As a distinct characteristic of the region, agricultural workers (or agrarian proletariat) were significantly represented in the working class. Despite its gradual shrinking, the proportion of the rural population making a living on paid work in Poland and Hungary exceeded the share of industrial workers in the interwar period.[95] The number of industrial workers had already grown significantly at that time, but in Poland and Hungary, skilled workers were pushed into the background for the time being, mainly because of the rapid expansion of the textile industry and the rise in the employment of unskilled women.

Regarding the history of the working class, the middle of the century can be regarded as a turning point in this region as well, but not in the same sense as in Western Europe. It was certainly a most crucial process that as a result of large-scale industrialization, the number of workers started to grow rapidly in the communist countries of East Central Europe and the Balkans. As suggested earlier in the chapter, by the 1970s and 1980s, especially in East Germany and in Czechoslovakia, the proportion of workers in the economically active population reached a high level in an international context; in this sense, the goal of creating a 'workers' state' was definitely realized. In addition, because of the dominance of heavy industry and big companies, workers employed in large-scale manufacturing were represented more significantly within the working class here than in Western Europe. This condition gave certain homogeneity to the working class. At the same time, because of rapid industrialization, the significance of workforce migrating from rural areas to cities was greater than in Western Europe. According to surveys carried out around the 1970s, the majority of the industrial workers in Hungary, Yugoslavia, Romania and Bulgaria had a rural background. Workers having urban roots retained their dominance only in Czechoslovakia, in East Germany, and to a smaller extent in Poland.[96] A marked change took place regarding the status of the working class compared with other social groups. The relative income position and social status of workers improved, especially compared with the interwar period, but also with contemporary Western European levels. In 1937, Polish non-manual employees earned three times as much as manual workers, whereas in 1960, the difference shrank to 9%.[97] Compared with Western Europe, job security was also significantly higher. However, all this did not mean that the living standard and the life chances of the workers developed according to the declarations made by communist regimes, or that raising the living standard would have been more successful than in Western Europe. Regarding consumption, workers in the communist countries increasingly lagged behind their Western European counterparts. Moreover, the relative equality of incomes was accompanied by other types of inequalities in these societies, putting the workers at a disadvantage as far as health or mortality conditions were concerned. Finally, the high ratio of workers among the employed in communist countries started to decline later but changes remained significantly slower than in Western Europe. After the regime change the process accelerated here as well.

Peasantry

Although in North-Western Europe the agricultural population was merely a relative majority at the beginning of the twentieth century, in some parts of Southern and East Central Europe as well as the Balkans their proportion fell between 70% and 90%. However, in this segment of society, there were other continuities with the past. Traditional peasantry still existed in the first decades of the twentieth century, not only in economically underdeveloped Southern Europe or the Balkans but in Western Europe as well. The latter social group not only relied on agriculture for their living but pursued rural activities within a distinct, collective social order as well, following its own traditions and rules. They were involved in subsistence farming that primarily aimed at satisfying their day-to-day necessities, instead of commodity production. Peasants spent most of their working time not directly on cultivating the land and breeding animals, but producing, constructing and maintaining tools and buildings required for such activities, as well as housing and clothing. The organization of work relied on the family as its foundation, and resulted in a division of labour based on strict roles defined by gender and age. In the interwar period, the dissolution of traditional peasantry advanced considerably. One of the most significant changes happened in the realm of politics. Although just a few decades before industrial workers, as well as the middle and the upper classes, had been in the focus of political struggles, and peasants had hardly had any political representation in the national parliaments of Europe, the World Wars fundamentally altered this situation. In East Central Europe, the Balkans and Scandinavia, peasant parties managed to organize themselves as well as to attract substantial political support from the peasantry and subsequently to develop into a major political force. This in itself signalled the opening up of the peasant society, which also proceeded in economic and cultural terms.

The transformation of European agriculture accelerated after the Second World War.[98] This process continued to be reflected primarily by the decreasing share of people making their living in agriculture, but the lifestyle of the remaining agrarian population altered as well, though many of the people belonging to this stratum remained religious, lived according to a more traditional family model, had a higher fertility rate, and could not allow themselves to go on vacation, especially on a summer holiday. However, the mechanization and modernization of the production process, growing incomes and a closer contact with the urban environment changed the frames of peasant life. Already by the 1960s, significant shifts had taken place in Western Europe in the value orientations as well as the lifestyle of the remaining members of the peasantry. Typical paraphernalia of consumerism, such as radio, television and subsequently the automobile were introduced to peasant households, approximating the peasant lifestyle to that of urban dwellers. Peasantry was not enclosed in its world like earlier: the production did not focus primarily on the local market, and the sons and daughters of peasants married outside their class.[99]

Traditional peasantry vanished in Western Europe by the end of the century, and persisted only sporadically in Southern Europe. Here, the decline of peasantry was so rapid that it could not have happened merely through the natural process of retiring. Large numbers of people working in the agrarian sector immigrated to industrial centres, or left their original livelihood for industrial employment established in villages. The integration of rural migrants to new branches most often involved tensions. After abandoning agriculture, these people integrated most frequently in two steps: first into the most insecure and modestly paying jobs in industry or services, and becoming a 'real' worker only after that, climbing the ladder of job hierarchy.[100] Because most of the immigrants were young people, the ageing of the agrarian population speeded up in these regions.

Transformation was not only rapid but turbulent after the Second World War in most of the East Central and South-Eastern European countries, where the partition of large estates secured the basis of peasant lifestyle for a certain period, but collectivization, which was launched in successive waves and usually completed by the early 1960s, put an end to it. Large state or cooperative farms were not pursuing subsistence farming any more, and most often they became specialized. The status of people working there approximated that of industrial workers: they carried out specific tasks of a larger production process during set working hours. At the same time, they usually complemented their primary job with small-scale 'household farming', and, after the most repressive Stalinist period ended, the cultivation of small plots of land was tolerated by the communist regimes, because political leaders were well aware of the low productivity of collective farms. However, this did not hinder the dissolution of traditional peasantry, but preserved traditional peasant work systems and mentality in many respects, primarily among older generations. In countries where collectivization did not happen or was only partial (Poland and Yugoslavia), the process was slower, but various forms of government intervention and indoctrination (such as price control, produce delivery, prosecution of Churches, ideologically biased education and conscript army) contributed to the erosion of traditional peasant culture. Nonetheless, the inclination of peasants towards remaining self-sufficient and their limited market-oriented attitude was still an important characteristic of Polish agriculture even in the 1970s.[101]

The traditional peasantry was dissolved in the communist countries by often relying on forceful and even violent measures, but nonetheless, the transformation of the lifestyle of the rural population was greatly hindered by communist policies. The emerging communist regimes openly discriminated against the peasantry, first, because of ideological reasons, and second, because they aimed at a redistribution of resources, such as capital and workforce, from agriculture into industry. The privileged position of the urban population was sustained in several respects throughout the communist era. In Hungary, for example, public housing construction programmes did not affect villages, and even the level of some welfare benefits, such as family allowance, was lower for members of cooperative farms. Most importantly, incomes were significantly smaller in rural than in urban areas, but the gap was even wider in other aspects of the quality of life (certainly regarding housing, education and health conditions). In the shortage economy, consumer supply was even worse in villages than in towns: in the 1980s in Romania, villagers frequently had to go to the nearest town to buy bread, and similar phenomena prevailed in other countries as well.

However, it is certain that after collectivization had finished, the hostile attitude of communist regimes towards the rural population abated. Members of cooperatives and those employed by state farms were given rights that were previously the privilege of industrial workers and state employees, and consequently they too were entitled to receive a pension and health insurance. Thus, despite all the disadvantages, peasantry and the rural population in general experienced the period starting with the 1960s as an era of emancipation in the communist countries, with the exceptions of Albania and Romania.[102]

The agricultural policy of the EU and its predecessors played a special role in shaping peasantry in Western Europe. Based on strategic, social and environmental considerations, the EU created a complex and extended system of agricultural subventions. Support given to producers contributed, on the one hand, to the modernization of agriculture, and thus to the erosion of peasantry, but on the other hand it prevented a further shrinking of the agricultural sector. From the mid-1960s French and Danish farmers profited from this support particularly, and later agricultural producers in Southern Europe benefited as well. The incomes of these farmers depended heavily on EU and government subsidies and market protection, which invigorated their political activities and interest representations: blocking roads with agricultural vehicles and other demonstrations of farmers were particularly frequent in France and in Brussels, the centre of the EU.

Social mobility: trendless fluctuation?

The overview of the historical changes in social stratification cannot be complete without casting at least a cursory glance at social mobility, which is defined as the movement of individuals and social groups within the social hierarchy. Historians and other scholars are interested in the history of social mobility for the obvious reason that it has a significant impact on the formation of classes and strata. Low social mobility strengthens class solidarity: most of the individuals remain in the class to which they are born, and thus common social experience accumulates throughout generations. In the wake of this process, distinct subcultures are formed, and members strongly identify with their social group, which facilitates the formation of classes and furthers collective action.[103] Therefore, high mobility is considered to be an important factor of cohesion in modern societies, because it opens up vistas for the talented and ambitious members of the lower strata to 'climb the social ladder'. Thus, high mobility works as a safety valve, but it also contributes to the effective functioning of social and economic institutions, because it enables the most capable people to occupy the key positions. In addition, equal opportunity expressed in high mobility is important for the prevalence and perception of social justice.[104] One of the founding fathers of mobility research, Pitirim Sorokin, argued for a strong relationship between democracy and social mobility, maintaining that in democratic societies the social positions of citizens cannot be determined by birth, because mobility chances are major elements of individual freedom.[105] However, swift changes in the social hierarchy may also have adverse psychological effects on individuals and can thus be socially destructive, depending on the way individuals and societies experience the phenomenon.[106]

Social historians and sociologists generally study social mobility through occupational change, more specifically by comparing the present position of individuals with those of their family of origin (intergenerational mobility). A significantly lesser interest is dedicated to intragenerational mobility, namely, to the changes in the social position experienced by the same individual during his or her career or lifetime. It is also common to differentiate between upward and downward mobility, that is, moving up or down the social hierarchy.

Thus, employment has a significant role not only in research focusing on social structure, but also on mobility, and for similar reasons: it has a decisive role in defining income, social status, and other important social determinants. At the same time, it is also obvious that examining mobility based on employment status has its own limits. On the one hand, a job does not precisely define the social position of an individual, because the latter is influenced by several other factors, such as educational level or the type of residence. In addition, attributing one job to one individual is not always possible even in a particular moment, and especially not throughout one's lifetime. For the farther we go backwards in history, and move away from industrial societies, the more tangible the problem becomes, because in agrarian societies, the differentiation of occupations was limited and the everyday activities of peasants were diverse.[107] In addition, mobility surveys focusing on occupational mobility disregard a significant part of the population. Members of the upper class cannot be plausibly identified on the basis of their occupations. Moreover, this criticism is also highly relevant in the case of women, who were usually not gainfully employed in the past. Consequently, their social status was primarily defined by their husband's position, making marriage the most important channel of social mobility for them.[108]

Although the rise in mobility rates is traditionally identified with enhancing equal opportunities, the increase in mobility does not always mean that society has become more open, because it can result simply from the change of the size of certain social groups. For example, if the demand for manual workers declines, and more middle-class jobs are created, and the number of children in middle-class families is not sufficient to meet this demand in the long run, then children of the lower classes will climb the social hierarchy even if otherwise no change (in education or in other social spheres) occurred supporting the equalization of opportunities in society. In this case, thus, the increase of upward mobility was simply triggered by shifts in social structure, and not by the growing openness of society. This type of mobility is termed absolute or structural mobility. As opposed to this, relative mobility or social fluidity takes place if the upward mobility of children in lower classes grows more rapidly than is required by changes in the employment structure and in the number of children born in the groups of origin and destination.[109]

Trends in absolute and relative mobility

According to the results of a number of historical and sociological studies, social mobility has significantly increased in European societies since the end of the nineteenth century.[110] Changes in the social structure and employment are of primary concern here, including the expansion of the middle class discussed earlier. The stratum of white-collar employees was remarkably enlarged, with the combined result of more opportunities for the social mobility of workers, members of the lower middle class and petite bourgeoisie as well as the peasantry.[111] The German example illustrates the restructuring of the middle class and the role of this process in growing mobility. Whereas before the First World War, only one-fifth of the members of the lower middle class had working-class or low-income family origin, in West Germany, their proportion was already one-third in the 1950s and 1960s. Even more, whereas in the interwar period, only 2% of children born in the lower middle class entered the upper middle class, in West Germany, the same ratio reached 12% in 1969.[112] However, downward mobility increased as well. Before the First World War, during the Weimar Republic, and even in West Germany in 1955, only 3% of the lower middle class dropped from the upper middle class, whereas in 1969, the figure grew to 20%. The proportion of members of the lower middle class descending to the working class or peasantry was significantly lower.[113]

In the early twentieth century, the position of unskilled workers was especially intricate because demarcation lines tended to be the most consolidated between them and skilled workers. In the interwar period, the social differences between unskilled and skilled labourers began to fade in Western Europe, which facilitated social ascent for the former and at the same time depreciated the value of this upward mobility because of the gradual disappearance of this cleavage.[114] However, research focusing mainly on urban areas also demonstrated marked variations between European countries with regard to the prospects of unskilled workers in the first half of the century. They had little chances for upward mobility in industrial cities, such as Bochum or Ludwigshafen. Mobility was stronger in cities with a well-developed service sector, such as in cities with a port (exemplified by Rotterdam), in administrative centres such as Berlin and Copenhagen, or traditional trade centres, such as Graz and Toulouse. The same logic is applied at the level of countries as well: in the Netherlands, where the service sector was extended by European standards, mobility channels were wider for the unskilled, whereas in Germany, characterized by a larger proportion of industrial employment, these channels were significantly more restricted.[115]

The transformation of the upper class discussed above, including the weakening of the aristocracy and the inclusion of managers into the business elite, also supplies arguments for the increase of social mobility. In the British social elite, despite the slowness and unevenness of the process, we can detect a move towards greater openness, which was most visible in the elite of public service and the military, because the introduction of open competitive examinations reduced the intake from the upper classes and the landed gentry. Whereas the end of the nineteenth and the first half of the twentieth century saw the shift from ascription to achievement, which primarily favoured the upper middle class regarding the civil service and armed forces, after the Second World War, the same positions were increasingly occupied by educated offspring of lower middle-class and working-class parents. In 1939, about one-tenth of higher civil servants came from state schools; by 1967, the proportion climbed to one-third. If social origin is regarded directly, at the latter date, one-third of higher civil servants had a working class or routine white-collar family background.[116] It is nevertheless true that other groups of the upper class were less permeable. British aristocracy and landed gentry were more exclusive than the group of civil servants and the military already in the nineteenth century, and these families, as well as the financial elite, remained closed in the second half of the twentieth century. The British economic elite were in intense contact only with the upper layer of the middle class. Between 1900 and 1919, in the largest 200 private corporations, 77.5% of the members of the board of directors came from the upper middle class, and this figure shrank only to 68.5% by the 1960s. Meanwhile, the proportion of members of the lower middle class climbed from 15.2% to 21.5%, but the percentage of those having a working-class origin remained below 10% throughout the whole period.[117]

Thus, studies on specific cities or social groups presented valuable empirical evidence for the increase in social mobility in twentieth-century Europe. At the same time, assessments questioning the rise in social mobility in industrial societies appeared relatively early. A well-known example is Pitirim Sorokin's interpretation from the 1920s. According to Sorokin, mobility grows in certain industrial societies in particular periods, whereas in other societies and at different times, mobility declines. In other words, instead of any definite linear or perpetual tendency, volatility, or 'trendless fluctuation' prevails in social mobility.[118] Notions of growing mobility were already refuted by empirical research regarding the first half of the century in the case of the most industrialized country, Great Britain. Considering the cohort born in the 1890s, intergenerational mobility was slightly higher than for cohorts born in the following three decades, after which mobility showed a slight growth again. It is remarkable that in the first half of the century,

TABLE 4.5 Mobility trends in Great Britain in the first half of the twentieth century

	Birth cohort				
	Pre-1890	1890–1899	1900–1909	1910–1919	1920–1929
Upwardly mobile (%)	16.5	23.3	23.2	21.2	20.9
Downwardly mobile (%)	33.0	25.9	24.6	24.6	25.3
Total % mobile	49.5	49.2	47.8	45.8	46.2
N	697	540	751	772	755

Note: The sample included men aged 20 and over; data were collected in 1949.

Source: Anthony Heath, *Social Mobility*, Glasgow: Fontana, 1981, 86.

downward mobility surpassed upward mobility. This period, thus, presents a mixed overall picture: the years of economic depression saw increasing social immobility, whereas in other times, greater mobility prevailed (Table 4.5).[119] Therefore, considering the fragmented results referring to other societies, research on social mobility in Europe in the first decades of the twentieth century can be interpreted as inconclusive in several respects.

The account we have about the mobility of European societies in the mid-twentieth century decades is more precise and comprehensive, primarily because of the research carried out by Robert Erikson and John H. Goldthorpe, which has generally been regarded as the most thorough analysis conducted in the field so far.[120] As for absolute mobility rates in European countries, they experienced strong fluctuations and no specific trends in the second third of the twentieth century. Absolute mobility increased in several countries, whereas in other cases it decreased with time, but turns in trends were detected as well (Figure 4.1). In other words, Erikson and Goldthorpe's results are similar to the assessment formulated by Sorokin. However, Erikson and Goldthorpe primarily concentrated on relative mobility (social fluidity) because this is what they considered to be the real indicator of social openness. In this regard, concerning European development as a whole, they did not see any convincing sign of long-term increase or decrease, but rather stability. As for characteristics of individual countries, they found that the mobility of France and England complied with the general or average development. Hungary's high, although decreasing, mobility rates may be explained first of all by forced collectivization. The reason behind growing mobility in Poland was that although the communist regime did not carry out collectivization, a forceful restructuring of society was pursued by other means. Such attempts had already been prepared by the Second World War, which caused in Poland the most severe social changes throughout Europe. Crossing the boundaries between blue-collar workers and white-collar employees was particularly difficult in Germany, because of the highly developed system of vocational training. Italy and Ireland stood out with the low mobility of their agricultural population, but in Italy significant regional differences applied in this regard as well: without the *mezzogiorno* this country would have shown similar mobility patterns to France or England.[121]

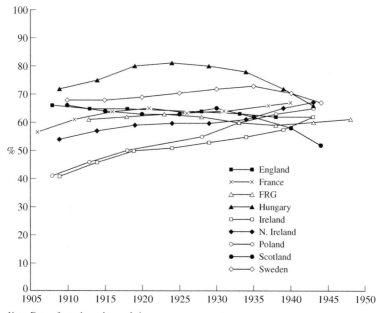

FIGURE 4.1 Trends of total mobility rates (absolute mobility) in European countries by birth year, 1905–1950
Source: Robert Erikson and John H. Goldthorpe, *The Constant Flux: A Study of Class Mobility in Industrial Societies*, Oxford: Clarendon Press, 1992, 74.

Although Erikson and Goldthorpe published overall indicators of social openness, or relative mobility as well, these types of comprehensive data are loaded with a series of methodological difficulties. The indicators refer to the 1980s, and show that relatively small differences regarding mobility patterns were found in most of the Western European countries. Disregarding the USA, which had higher mobility rates, two groups of European countries diverged from the majority of the continental countries. In the communist societies, mobility was high, although with considerable variations between societies. Furthermore, Sweden was equally characterized by significant social openness. This result, which was reinforced later by other surveys as well, suggests similar trends for the neighbouring Scandinavian countries (Table 4.6).[122]

In the last decades of the twentieth century, all evidence points toward changes in the international trends of social mobility. Richard Breen and his colleagues surveyed the mobility of ten European countries: their research period began in the 1970s and they adjusted their methods to the research conducted by Erikson and Goldthorpe to enable long-term comparisons. According to the results of Breen and his fellow researchers, absolute mobility stagnated or slightly increased in most of the examined countries from the 1970s on, with a marked growth in upward mobility and a decline in downward mobility. In a schema of eight classes suggested by Goldthorpe and referred to earlier in this chapter, an average of two-thirds of

TABLE 4.6 Relative mobility (social fluidity) in industrial countries in the 1980s

	Fluidity value
Scotland	0.19
Northern Ireland	0.18
Ireland	0.16
Netherlands	0.16
France	0.16
FRG	0.13
Italy	0.12
England	0.09
Hungary	0.02
Sweden	−0.17
Poland	−0.18
United States	−0.20
Czechoslovakia	−0.23

Note: The level of cross-national average has been set at 0. Positive figures reflect lower than average, whereas negative figures reflect higher than average fluidity.

Source: Robert Erikson and John H. Goldthorpe, *The Constant Flux: A Study of Class Mobility in Industrial Societies,* Oxford: Clarendon Press, 1992, 381.

men were mobile in this period: they belonged to another class than their family of origin. Among the countries examined, Hungary was the only exception, where mobility declined significantly during these three decades, still remaining above the European average. Sweden and Italy showed similarly high mobility to Hungary. Gradually but significantly, the differences in the mobility rates of individual countries also decreased in this period (Table 4.7).[123] Contrary to absolute mobility, relative mobility was characterized by a general upward tendency, with Great Britain as the sole exception, although in Germany, the trend is difficult to determine because of frequent fluctuations. In the case of France, Sweden and the Netherlands, evidence clearly points to an increase in social fluidity. Hungary, Poland and Ireland also exemplify the growth in social openness, but these results are based on a small body of data. At the same time in Hungary, the surge between 1970 and 2000 was concentrated entirely in the 1970s; the tendency was stagnation in the 1980s, and decline in the 1990s. Consequently, when interpreting social fluidity, differences between individual European countries should not be disregarded: the countries with the most openness were Sweden, Norway, Hungary, Poland, and in the 1990s, the Netherlands, whereas Germany, France, Italy and Ireland belong to the least open countries. As opposed to trends in absolute mobility, no convergence can be detected among countries in this respect.[124]

With regard to the East Central European region, we have already made some relevant observations. However, it is worth having a closer look at this region, because a primary concern of mobility research after the Second World War was to compare the social mobility of communist and capitalist countries. Researchers also regarded communist systems as 'social laboratories', or 'naturally occurring

TABLE 4.7 Rates of absolute mobility in European countries, 1970–2000 (% of the male population)

	Germany	France	Italy	Ireland	Great Britain	Sweden	Norway	Holland	Poland	Hungary	Average	Dispersion
Total mobility												
1970s	61.6	66.6		56.7	63.0	70.8		66.3	59.4	77.5	66.3	48.0
1980s	62.1	67.5	69.5	61.3	61.8	71.4	71.9	67.7	61.0	74.9	66.9	25.8
1990s	60.3	67.0	72.1	66.1	60.8	71.0	68.1	65.7	67.4	71.6	67.7	19.9
Upward mobility												
1970s	31.7	25.9		21.6	32.8	35.1		36.1	22.1	26.9	28.0	37.1
1980s	33.6	29.1	29.0	27.9	33.1	35.3	39.3	38.9	24.8	34.7	32.6	22.9
1990s	33.3	29.9	35.9	31.4	31.7	36.6	34.2	37.7	26.3	35.9	33.4	11.4
Downward mobility												
1970s	12.4	17.9		18.4	17.9	19.0		14.5	18.8	26.2	18.7	17.3
1980s	12.2	16.8	11.8	14.7	17.7	19.4	15.9	15.2	18.0	21.1	16.3	8.7
1990s	13.0	16.4	10.4	14.1	19.0	18.6	17.9	16.3	19.6	17.8	16.2	8.0

Notes: The table includes the sum of absolute mobility (total mobility) and two components of vertical mobility (upward mobility and downward mobility). Horizontal mobility is not included in the table; average and dispersion figures also include Israel.

Source: Richard Breen and Ruud Luijkx, 'Social Mobility in Europe between 1970 and 2000', in Richard Breen, ed., *Social Mobility in Europe*, Oxford: Oxford University Press, 2004, 48.

experiments', in which governments tried to influence mobility prospects consciously, comprehensively, and in the long run.[125] Hungary is the only country in the East Central European region where surveys are also available from the interwar period; these data are comprehensive even in a global context, revealing that absolute mobility in Hungarian society was low in the first decades of the century. According to the 1930 census, 37% of male earners and 48% of female earners belonged to a social group different from their family of origin.[126] Fragmented evidence suggest that Polish society was similar in this regard to the Hungarian, whereas the more industrialized Czechoslovakia and the poor, but relatively egalitarian, countries of the Balkans had a higher mobility.[127]

Between the 1950s and 1970s, absolute mobility grew to a level in European communist countries that was remarkable even in an international comparison, and exceeded the average of Western European societies. Still, mobility realized this way cannot be considered as unique, because in this respect, most of the communist countries were equalled or even surpassed by some capitalist countries, such as Finland. Another important circumstance is that in East Central Europe, mobility usually reached its peak in the 1970s, followed by a decline.[128]

A similar picture emerges in the case of relative mobility, also increasing in the 1950s and 1960s in communist countries compared with the period preceding the war, and reaching a high level in international comparison.[129] However, from the 1970s, social fluidity also ceased to increase further, and although it remained high, it was not exceptional in Europe. Some Nordic countries (Sweden, Finland) matched or exceeded the social fluidity levels of communist countries. Relative mobility figures in Czechoslovakia, for example, were similar to the respective Swedish ones.[130] Thus, views about the unique communist or socialist mobility system became obsolete, which was also suggested by the diversity of mobility patterns in the region. In Poland, for instance, there was significant fluidity between manual and white-collar jobs, which was not the case in Hungary.[131] Furthermore, several researchers interpreted the situation as a freezing, or even as a case of emerging rigidity, of the social structure in communist countries.[132] This assessment cannot be regarded as plausible as far as the whole society is concerned. However, the communist political and economic elite undoubtedly became exclusive with time, and began to recruit itself from its own circles. It is symptomatic that by the 1980s in Czechoslovakia, and even more characteristically in Hungary, the social openness of the elite dropped to a lower level than in neighbouring Austria (Table 4.8).[133]

In summary, thus, several historical studies have demonstrated the increase of social mobility in Europe regarding specific strata, cities, and even countries. At the same time, the results of the most comprehensive studies refuted, or at least contested, the idea according to which mobility increased throughout the twentieth century. Conflicting results can be partially reconciled because historians most frequently focused on absolute mobility, whereas recent sociological studies showed a growing interest in relative mobility. In the middle decades of the century, 'trendless fluctuation' seemed to prevail in Europe as a whole, especially regarding relative mobility. At the same time, regional variations were considerable. In

TABLE 4.8 Post-war mobility (self-recruitment) patterns of men in higher bureaucratic and managerial positions in Austria, the Czech lands, Slovakia and Hungary in the 1980s (%)

Age group (year)	Austria	Czech lands	Slovakia	Hungary
18–35	27	36	29	41
36–50	28	24	12	20
51–65	25	15	9	11

Note: % of sons in higher white-collar positions, whose fathers had the same positions; dates of data collection: Austria 1982; Czechoslovakia 1984; Hungary 1986.

Source: Max Haller, Tamás Kolosi and Péter Róbert, 'Social Mobility in Austria, Czechoslovakia, and Hungary: An Investigation of the Effects of Industrialization, Socialist Revolution, and National Uniqueness', in Max Haller, ed., *Class Structure in Europe: New Findings from East–West Comparisons of Social Structures and Mobility*, Armonk and London: M. E. Sharpe, 1990, 191.

Scandinavia and East Central Europe, social fluidity was higher in the examined period than in the Western or Southern parts of the continent. However, in the last third of the century, general tendencies have altered, and signs of a moderate increase in social openness surfaced in Europe, although this again does not apply to all societies.

Factors influencing social mobility

The increase in absolute mobility that prevailed in several European countries and periods of the twentieth century can primarily be explained by processes that had also been taking place in earlier periods as well, but stepped up during the twentieth century. Such a development was first of all the acceleration of the sectoral change in the economy. These shifts have been discussed above, thus we only evoke the fact here that the process was uneven in Europe, and the leading economic branches also varied to a great extent. The expansion of both the industrial and the service sector facilitated social mobility, although in diverging ways: industry played a preeminent role in restructuring the agricultural population, whereas labour from both the primary and the secondary sectors was attracted by the service sector.

Two influential theoretical approaches exist describing and interpreting trends of social fluidity. One of them is referred to as the 'liberal theory of industrialization', represented by the classic works of functionalist sociology, such as the contribution of Talcott Parsons.[134] According to this school, economic growth leads to high mobility even without any other favourable social circumstances, because industrialization facilitates the competition between companies and nations. Competition, as the argumentation of this approach goes, tends to encourage the acknowledgement of achievements, and the resulting meritocracy enhances mobility. However, research carried out in Europe in the past decades, which has already been partly discussed above, does not confirm such a claim. On the one hand, mobility did not increase steadily and in parallel with economic expansion, whereas on the other hand, the stage or level of economic development is not directly related to the extent of mobility. On the contrary, several examples show that economic advance leads to the moderation of the openness of society, as was the case in Hungary and Sweden in the last decades before the turn of the millennium.

According to the other line of argument, social fluidity reaches a similar (uniformly high) level in all industrial societies based on market economy and with the dominance of the nuclear family. It is supposed that mobility starts to increase beyond a certain threshold of the industrialization level. Structural changes related to industrialization offer similar opportunities for the members of society, which they try to utilize while being forced by the inner drive for mobility.[135] However, we may not find any threshold in economic history beyond which relative mobility rates would routinely rise or correspond in individual societies.[136] The interpretation is flatly contradicted by the social development of the end of the twentieth century, during which the relative mobility rates of European countries diverged rather than converged. Industrialization, or more broadly speaking, economic growth, thus may explain basic similarities between mobility patterns at most, but other factors also need to be considered, particularly to explain mobility differentials and dynamics.

Among the further determinants, political factors are to be considered as well. As we have seen, mobility increased significantly everywhere in the communist systems. The collectivization of agriculture that took place in the 1950s and early 1960s undoubtedly served as a major element in facilitating mobility and explains most of the unique characteristics of mobility patterns in relation to the rest of the continent. One of these is the outstanding mobility between manual workers in agriculture and industry. The role of collectivization in shaping mobility is supported by the fact that in the two communist countries where the transformation of agriculture did not take place, namely Yugoslavia and Poland, social fluidity showed no significant differences when compared with capitalist countries.[137] Moreover, the new regimes settling in after the communist takeover tried to favour individuals and social groups they considered reliable, primarily the working class, when allocating social positions, whereas individuals and groups that they considered hostile (kulaks, intellectuals, public servants of the previous regime, individuals and families deemed politically unreliable, etc.) were discriminated against. Methods used in order to reach these social goals were diverse and included physical repression (imprisonment, resettlement), dismissals from jobs, and the positive or negative discrimination of social groups at university entrance. The steps increased both intragenerational and intergenerational mobility, because white-collar employees or people with that social background were forced to accept blue-collar jobs, and their positions were in turn filled by manual workers. The realization of these measures varied in the region. In most countries, the early 1950s witnessed the greatest repression and social upheaval, but even in this period Hungary, for example, was more affected than Poland. However, from the 1960s on, discrimination became more moderate as a general tendency. Exceptions included Czechoslovakia, where children coming from politically unreliable families were prevented from going to universities after 1968. In sum, political practice and even political engineering had a significant effect on mobility figures in this region after the Second World War.

The historical experience of the East Central European countries calls attention to the possible negative social consequences of mobility usually underestimated in research. Collectivization was carried out forcefully, and thus the mobility it generated often led to a number of social problems, such as anomie, growing suicide rates, exodus of the rural population and spreading of alcoholism.

However, the impact of state activities on mobility was significant in another respect as well, namely in enhancing income equality. As research convincingly demonstrated, low income inequality increased the openness of class structures.[138] The existence of this relationship is obviously not confined to East Central Europe and the post-war period, because the first schemes of modern social policy emerged in Europe as early as the late nineteenth century. Still, the real expansion of the welfare state took place after the Second World War, and especially from the 1960s on in Western Europe. Welfare schemes, such as unemployment and health insurance programmes, shielded individuals from social risks, thus also helping them make use of mobility chances. Accordingly, high mobility rates in Scandinavian countries can be at least partly attributed to the extensive activities of the welfare state. As a further issue related to the role of the government, the impact of education on social mobility is often regarded as crucial, and is addressed in chapter 9.

However, further factors exist, which were not directly related to industrialization or government activities, but influenced mobility nonetheless. Wars, and especially the Second World War and the ensuing mass migration, figured highly among them. Refugees were usually unable to maintain their previous status, which resulted, in their case, in downward mobility. At the same time, they were strongly motivated to help at least their children reach their previous social position, which in turn triggered upward mobility. High relative mobility among members of the generation born in the 1920s in Germany can be mainly explained by the fact that members of this age group migrated to the West German state in large numbers from East Germany.[139]

Recent trends in social stratification: dissolving classes and new inequalities

Several analyses and theories have described and interpreted the social changes of the industrialized world in the late twentieth century. However, the two most influential conceptualizations are undoubtedly post-industrialism and post-modernism. The theory of post-industrialism concentrates on transformations within the structural characteristics of the system of production, whereas post-modernism stresses the importance of ideologies, social movements and culture in shaping social stratification.[140] In the following discussion, these two approaches are concisely introduced, then their validity is assessed in the light of the recent tendencies of social stratification in European societies.

Approaches to post-industrial and post-modern society ...

Although the notion of post-industrial society has been the subject of debate since as early as the 1890s, the term was coined and later expanded upon at length by the American Daniel Bell and the French Alain Touraine in the 1960s and 1970s.[141] In 1960, Bell predicted that the ideological opposition characterizing the Cold War would gradually disappear, and in its wake, new post-industrial structures would arise just to embrace the regions which were industrialized in his time. Later, in *The Coming of Post-Industrial Society* (1974), he elaborated on the economic and social changes in the late twentieth century and set out the key features of post-industrial society, in which technological progress shifted the economy away from manufacturing towards services. These changes, Bell argued, resulted in the transformation of the characteristics of work as well as social structure: industrial manual jobs would be replaced by white-collar professional and technician occupations, and the predominantly working-class society would shift to a system based on the middle class. The driving force of the new society would be innovation and thus, knowledge, particularly theoretical knowledge. The production of goods and provision of services would be largely reliant on research and development. This distinguishes the new era from the time of the first and the second industrial revolution, because the source of knowledge would no longer be experience but rather science, making the modern university the centre of knowledge, production and dissemination. The huge expansion of knowledge has a profound influence on the execution of power. A new class, the 'knowledge class', would be formed, which would compete with the political and the business class to a certain extent, but it would serve them at the same time, and none of the three classes would have dominance over the others. These changes should have an influence on the prevailing values and norms: society controls market forces and the seeking of profit, and economic and social management would be realized by forecasting, modelling and planning. Instead of the traditional class policy shaped by conflicts of distribution, problems of social security or the state of the environment would appear prominent.[142]

Similar or even more radical ideas have been formulated by other scholars regarding the determinants of social stratification in the late twentieth century. These studies also assumed that the role of employment and economic factors would be taken over by other factors, such as human capital or political power, and that social dominance would be attained either by intellectuals[143] or by the new class of managers.[144] Regarding post-communist East Central Europe, it was proposed that the system of 'capitalism without capitalists' emerged because no class of private proprietors existed before the establishment of the market economy. The coalition that governed post-communist societies was made up by former dissident intellectuals, who contributed to the fall of communism, and a new managerial class recruited from technocrats, and also from members of the former regime, holding senior positions during communism in economy, culture, public administration and politics.[145]

As for other major interpretations of recent social changes, post-modern social theory is fragmented. On the one hand, this fragmentation is related to the fact that post-modernism was originally an artistic movement and the term has come into wider use since the 1970s to specify a number of philosophical, critical and socio-logical positions, assuming a break with modernism or modernity. On the other hand, post-modernist writers reject establishing a systematic social theory or writing a com-prehensive social history; they refute the scientific method in general. Therefore, defining post-modernism as a coherent approach to the analysis of contemporary European societies seems to be implausible. If we search for the lowest common denominator of the post-modern writers dealing with social structure and stratifi-cation, including scholars, such as Jean Baudrillard or Jean-François Lyotard, then we can see that they intended to establish post-modernism as a novel perspective on late twentieth-century Western societies. They maintain that this type of society is funda-mentally different from the earlier ones, thus, the discourse of modernism and the notions used in analysis (such as community, state, class, etc.) are not applicable any more. Inherited material and cultural assets, that is, class, ceases to define the position of the individual in society. Identities and organizations based on class cease to exist, even though they used to dominate the political arena in the mid-twentieth century. As a result, 'status crystallization' diminishes, social classes dissolve, and thus, even the most advanced capitalist countries cannot be regarded as class societies any more. Zygmunt Bauman argues that the post-modern world appears for the individual as the market of infinite choices, the network of 'imagined communities', none of which can maintain our attention or our loyalty in the long run.[146] In the post-modern era, taste, choice and commitment define the social group to which one belongs, and consequently borderlines between groups are blurred and uncertain.[147] However, beyond proposing an understanding of the contemporary world, post-modern authors usually make too little effort in considering the underlying social and economic factors. They point out that wealth becomes more evenly distributed, small property is increasingly common, occupations become more professionalized, markets are more and more globalized, and consumption has a growing importance in defining status and lifestyle.[148] In fact, consumption is given a key role in their argumentation because they regularly expound the idea that even before the post-modern era, in the wealth-iest countries, social inequalities had already been determined by consumption rather than the production process. This is the social constellation that unfolds further in the post-modern age, when consumption is governed not by the use value of products but their potential of expressing and demonstrating lifestyle, taste and status.[149]

Indeed, by the turn of the millennium, European societies, and advanced industrial countries in general, underwent major changes, making social structure more complex and rendering its elements less recognizable as well as more intricate to be conceptualized. This situation provided a fertile ground for questioning the validity of the traditional approaches to social stratification. Describing the details of this social transformation exceeds the scope of the present volume, so we confine ourselves to discussing the most essential aspects when assessing the plausibility of the above interpretations.

Bell's understanding, or rather his prediction, of the future society certainly proved valid in the sense that in the last decades of the twentieth century, all European countries saw an intense restructuring of employment. The proportion of employees in the service sector boomed, the source of which was the decline in the number of earners in industry and agriculture. The dynamics of the process is signalled by the accelerated fall in industrial employment from the 1980s on: between 1979 and 1993, member states of the Organisation for Economic Co-operation and Development (OECD) lost an average 22% of industrial jobs. Some Western European countries, such as Belgium, France, Norway, Sweden, Spain and the United Kingdom, were particularly affected by this process, because in these economies, one-third to one-half of the jobs in the secondary sector ceased to exist in less than a decade and a half.[150] Parallel to this, the social group of white-collar employees enlarged, and the number of manual workers dropped. Within the category of white-collars the proportion of highly educated professionals or university graduates grew most significantly. Not independently of this change, scientific knowledge has played an increasing role in the social life and economic development of the past few decades. Producing, processing and disseminating information is considered today by many as the 'fourth' or 'quaternary sector', arguing that these services are crucial and distinct, and thus make an individual sector rather than being merely elements of the tertiary sector.

These processes have been accelerated by new technologies, such as the computer and the internet, both of which reached not only workplaces but also homes, and thus have a profound influence on production and forms of obtaining information, as well as on spending leisure time. Other knowledge-intensive technologies, such as biotechnology, also exist, with a similarly dynamic trajectory of advance.[151] Nevertheless, differences in internet penetration signal that European countries are capable of integrating these new technologies to varying levels. In 2009, Icelandic (93.2%), Norwegian (90.9%), Swedish (89.2%), Dutch (85.6%) and Danish (84.2%) households had the highest rates of internet access in Europe, whereas some countries, including France (63%) and Italy (53%) in Western Europe, clearly lagged behind.[152]

Post-modern social theories duly stress that in the late twentieth century, beside the vertical determinants of social stratification (such as employment and related factors of income, power, education and prestige), other, horizontal, ones also played an important role. Such constituents include gender, age, ethnicity, regional belonging, the type of settlement/residence and characteristics of family relations (marital status, number of children and number of earners in a family). These aspects are referred to as horizontal because such inequalities partially 'intersect' with vertical differences which are preeminently related to employment. Salaries of female employees, for example, are characteristically lower than their male counterparts' in the same occupation and even position. Consequently, social conflicts occur more and more between these groups and not between classes. The expansion of groups heavily dependent on state redistribution, including primarily the long-term unemployed and pensioners, is an illustrative example. The interests of these groups diverge from those of the active population as far as economic and social policy and redistribution in general are concerned. Therefore, no matter how diverse these groups are, their common interests are significant enough to establish common political commitments and voting patterns.[153]

In advanced Western European societies, traditional class and group-specific subcultures and milieus, which involved distinct mentalities and social behaviour, show symptoms of disintegration, or, at least, signs of decline along with social milieus and lifestyles undergoing individualization and pluralization. An important indicator of this process is the fact that class-specific conditions related to income and employment play a less important role in defining the social milieu and the lifestyle of the individual. In the 1930s and 1940s, British workers coming home from the factory or the dock wore the same type of clothes, which included the typical cap, and the muffler, distinguishing them from white-collar employees as well as from other social groups. Around the turn of the millennium and even earlier, clothing was no longer so strictly defined. Rather, clothing has been more and more turned into an expression of how one wished to present his or her own identity and belonging to the social group of choice. Membership of the same occupational group, thus, is frequently characterized by diverse clothing and life-styles. The same holds the other way round: for example, individuals coming from lower and higher classes may belong to the same alternative milieu of the youth, expressed among other factors by the related style of clothes worn. In post-industrial societies, employment or status are often not sufficient enough for defining identities. What seems to be decisive instead is the lifestyle or the value preferences of the individual. Thus, raising children and being family-oriented can be more important to someone regarding his or her identity than occupation. The pluralization of lifestyles is also shown by the growing number of milieus, groups sharing distinct attitudes and values. In the wake of the increasing complexity of the social structure, international research in the past few decades, from Germany to Great Britain, has distinguished at least eight or ten groups when examining social stratification and mobility, because this is considered the least that is necessary for the proper description of stratification. In addition, individuals frequently regard their 'subjective' belonging to a milieu and their lifestyle as more important in defining their own social position than their ascription to an 'objective' occupational group.

Factors underlying the pluralization process are primarily the increase of the living standard and the length of leisure time, which moderate material constraints, and loosen time restraints. Although the pluralization of milieus and lifestyles applies primarily to the middle classes, the improvement of the living standard and the homogenization of living conditions made goods available for the lower classes that were previously the privileges of middle or upper classes, such as comfortable flats, trips abroad, or tertiary education. The convergence of living conditions has several further aspects: new districts were built in cities, inhabited by classes of different income, and equally influenced by a number of risks characterizing modern urban life, such as environmental risks, accidents, crimes, etc.[154] As a consequence of the individualization process that also appeared in other segments of social life, such as in family development discussed in chapter 3, the expression of individual lifestyle choices became increasingly independent from former social and spatial limitations. Individualization was also aided by the population's growing level of education, because that requires, and allows for, increasing self-reflection.[155]

... and their criticisms

All in all, social theories of post-industrialism and post-modernism (mostly independently from but often reinforcing each other) convincingly unravelled the tendencies of late twentieth-century European societies in several respects. However, there are important points that raise questions about the plausibility of the interpretations that they offer.

First of all, large-scale changes in the employment structure are far from being a uniquely new, late twentieth-century phenomena. As discussed earlier, the increase in the share of the service sector has characterized European and other societies for a long time. It has certainly accelerated in the final decades of the century, but in itself it does not necessarily incur a fundamental transformation in the way societies function. More importantly, the growing employment in the tertiary sector at the end of the twentieth century did not result in a change of the nature of occupations as radical as it has been frequently supposed. On the one hand, most of the jobs in the service sector (according to some estimates about half of them) basically still contribute to industrial production.[156] Many of these positions were created in a way that activities that were carried out earlier at industrial companies (e.g. cleaning) were now delegated to other companies, in other words, were outsourced. Therefore the expansion of the services sector was, to a considerable extent, the result of simple redistribution of activities. Consequently, the character of work performed did not transform as much as suggested by the dynamism of the tertiary sector. On the other hand, jobs within the service sector remained heterogeneous. Although European societies are characterized by a growing educational level and the professionalization of occupations by the new millennium, positions requiring comprehensive knowledge and skills were not created as widely as assumed by representatives of the theory of post-industrialism. Rather, in the past two or three decades, opposite tendencies gained weight in the labour market, because certain types of employment required a lower level of skills than earlier ones (deskilling).

The widening gap between the incomes of higher and lower white-collar employees signals social polarization. Within services, the proportion of those activities grew most which required low qualification (including most eminently personal services) and thus they entailed low income as well. A significant social group is affected: in Western Europe, about 6–15% of the employed population, in which women are highly overrepresented.[157] In addition, technological development often led to an increased monotony of work and the deterioration of working conditions. Examples include the effect of computerization on trade and office work (e.g. data entry). These processes surfaced in the industrial sector as well. Traditionally well-paid positions requiring secondary education were decreasing rapidly: they became obsolete partly as a result of technological advance, and partly because a significant part of industrial jobs was exported to countries with low wages. Competition of the latter also greatly contributed to the erosion of the relative income position of unqualified workers, that is, the lower strata of the working class. An additional impetus came from the deterioration of working arrangements for some groups of workers. The last two decades of the century have been marked by a move away from lifelong employment towards less secure jobs and non-standard or atypical forms of work contract, especially in Southern and East Central Europe. These forms include temporary jobs, part-time jobs or 'forced' self-employment ('contract by assignment'), the process sometimes referred to as 'the increasing casualization of work' and thus employees are left with weaker countervailing rights against managerial authority.[158]

Regarding changes in social inequalities an even more striking development than the income polarization within certain occupational groups was the emergence of mass unemployment from the mid-1980s in almost all countries of Western and Southern Europe. Unemployment rates at the end of the millennium reached or approached 10% in Spain, Italy, Greece, France and Germany.[159] The long-term unemployed, the atypically employed and low-income workers created the core of the group that seems to be mostly affected by social exclusion.

These developments did not affect every country in the same manner. What was outstanding as a trend in the United States at the turn of the millennium was the low quality of a large number of new jobs created in the tertiary sector ('McJobs'), whereas in Europe, the high level of unemployment was most striking. But Europe was not homogenous either: problems in Great Britain were more similar to difficulties of the USA than to challenges of the labour market surfacing in continental Europe.[160] At the same time, no matter whether we consider low-paid positions in the service sector, or the impact of mass unemployment, we equally see the prevalence of traditional factors of stratification related to occupations and the labour market position.

The survival of traditional factors of stratification, along with other empirical evidence, suggests that horizontal factors remain secondary as bases of social inequality in Western Europe.[161] Traditional classes and strata continue to define life chances. Educational level, for example, is closely related to class position, and the correlation has changed little in the past two or three decades in most European societies. This assessment is even supported by anthropometric evidence. At the beginning of the twentieth century in Great Britain, working-class boys were shorter by an average of 2.5 inches (ca. 6.4 cm) compared with their middle-class peers, and the difference remained almost the same after a hundred years. Also, class-specific subcultures survived to a great extent and continued to define the political commitments and behaviour of classes.[162]

The outlined phenomena may provide ground for drawing more general conclusions regarding the stratification and overall social trends in Western Europe around the turn of the millennium. Applying a long-term perspective, Colin Crouch argues that as a result of what he calls 'mid-century social compromise', workers and other employees were granted important social rights from the 1950s and their relative social position significantly improved. However, by the end of the millennium, 'purer forms' of capitalism returned, the significance of which theories of post-industrialism or post-modernism failed to recognize. Although the fragmentation in structures of authority and loyalty, the 'new structurelessness', undermined major traditional institutions, such as the family, the church, and even the influence of political parties on the individual, yet capitalist and managerial authority prevailed and by the end of the century, it was actually strengthened. New information technologies, in fact, facilitated the reshaping of the work process in a hierarchical, Fordist fashion in many services (for instance, in banks and insurance companies), even though one or two decades ago, it seemed that the old principles of work organization would give way to less strictly regulated, post-Fordist forms, putting a greater emphasis on employees' interests, and relying more on their participation and cooperation. In addition, efforts surfaced in several countries towards restructuring public services along the line of similar standards, imported from the private economy, and to give a greater role to managerial control in the public sector as well. No dramatic changes have happened so far, but these tendencies are clearly unfavourable for the bulk of the employees, and are difficult to reconcile with the original, optimist predictions of theories on post-industrial societies.[163]

Challenges affecting the relative positions of workers and employees are arguably best explained by the structural changes described in European societies. The decline of manual work also implied the weakening of the social weight and political strength of the traditional working class. The social groups replacing it did not possess the same cohesion and did not display the same level of organizational strength. A process similar to the disintegration of the group of manual workers did not take place within the capitalist-managerial class. This class is not homogenous either, but its interests are accommodated by a well-structured body of consultant firms, professional journals, newspapers and other institutions, being unavailable to the same extent to other groups. Thus, in the field of strategic decision-making in economy, actors can be clearly identified. As Crouch concludes, 'capital with its associated management therefore becomes the class which retains the clearest definition in what at first sight seems to be a classless society'.[164] The balance of class power was also challenged by other forces, including the growth of individualism and the advance of globalization, which also surface in other chapters of the volume. Crouch, with good reason, puts emphasis on globalization, which emerged primarily as a result of the liberalization of the international capital markets and the increase in global organization of production. It gradually released capital from its dependence on national labour markets and thus on nation states as well, which tended to protect the interests of workers. Nevertheless, we should add that there remained significant variations in Europe regarding the social rights of workers and other employees at the turn of the millennium. Their position was strongly determined by the extent and ways in which institutions of the welfare state encountered market forces and modified their impact. To understand these changes, the development of the welfare state in Europe is the subject of the next chapter.

5

THE WELFARE STATE

The term 'welfare state' was introduced in the early 1940s by the British Archbishop William Temple as a reaction to what he called the Nazi and the Stalinist 'warfare state'.[1] It has become a key concept in contemporary political discourse and academic debates, referring to a form of society in which the state provides its citizens with a certain level of well-being by means of income transfers and social services.[2] This definition is not exclusive and undoubtedly broad enough to leave room for various interpretations of the welfare state. In fact, there exist diverging approaches emphasizing various aspects of how a state intervenes in welfare matters and how we can grasp these efforts.[3]

One way to give a more complete description is classifying and assessing the specific policies and schemes that constitute the welfare state, which is ironically called the 'accounting approach'.[4] In this respect, it is worth considering what is regarded by major international organizations as social welfare activities. The International Labour Organization (ILO) includes nine branches in social security, distinguishing between, on the one hand, social insurance programmes (occupational injuries insurance, as well as health, pension and unemployment insurance), which are provided in return for the contribution of the insured, and, on the other hand, schemes of social assistance when this individual contribution is missing (public health, means-tested assistance, special benefits for public employees, benefits for war victims and family/maternity allowances).[5] The OECD applies a broader definition, because it publishes data for member states that cover public social expenditure on health care, various pensions, unemployment benefits, education, social assistance, maternity and family benefits, disability assistance and minimum income support schemes. Recently, the OECD has not been considering expenditures on education, but includes the costs of labour market policies and housing support in addition to the above.[6] Broadly in line with the OECD, the statistics of the EU classifies under social protection expenditures those costs that are related to health care and sickness benefits, invalidity, disability and occupational injury benefits, old-age and survivors' pensions, maternity and family allowances, unemployment compensation as well as public employment services (vocational guidance and resettlement), and, finally, housing support.[7]

In recent literature on welfare state development, there has been a shift from an emphasis on social policy measures and the assessment of welfare efforts to a focus on welfare outcomes, such as the mitigation of poverty and inequality, educational opportunities or the quality of employment.[8] Some scholars even contend that the whole 'welfare mix' should be studied, that is, all the institutions contributing to welfare, or at least the households, the market and the state.[9] This idea is undoubtedly attractive, because it rests on a comprehensive account of welfare production. At the same time, the inclusion of every type of welfare activity, and especially private ones, overburden the concept of the welfare state. Unemployment, for instance, can be relieved through social insurance benefits or social assistance, but also through the creation of new jobs. However, if public expenditures on job creation are included, consistency requires the inclusion of similar private expenditures, such as investments. Thus, the application of the functional approach would broaden the scope of analysis to an extent difficult to handle in a historical study; therefore, we have to renounce the use of this approach.

The welfare activities of the state have become diversified in twentieth-century Europe, calling for the adoption of a broad perspective on social welfare. At the same time, the various definitions and approaches presented above underline the central role of social security programmes, such as health, pension and unemployment insurance. The emergence of social security was seminal to the evolution of the welfare state; moreover, these schemes remain the pillars of social protection even today, and therefore, most of the welfare efforts go towards their maintenance. In addition to practical considerations, such as the availability of historical information on welfare programs, this is the reason why we focus on social security in the following discussion. Further important aspects of the social welfare activity of the state, such as the labour market and education, are covered in other chapters.

The beginnings of the welfare state in Europe: the first social security programs

In Europe, there had already existed some institutions of collective welfare provision before the nineteenth century. Churches, families along with the broader kinship, and local communities provided support for the needy who could not maintain themselves because of illness or other exceptional circumstances. However, this support was low profile and access was mostly accidental and even arbitrary. Moreover, receiving support stigmatized the beneficiaries, who ceased to be regarded as full members of the local community or the family. The state traditionally played hardly any role in establishing social security except for the usually meagre state pension provided for disabled veterans, high-ranking public servants, or the workers of state-owned manufactures and mines. However, the rapid social and political changes of the nineteenth century presented challenges that traditional welfare institutions could not meet. On the one hand, industrialization and urbanization concentrated poverty in urban centres, thus making it more conspicuous and tangible. On the other hand, societies increasingly embraced the idea that poverty and the lack of social security were not an inescapable condition or exclusively the responsibility of individuals but rather a social problem to be solved.[10]

In the middle of the nineteenth century, it seemed that the key to this problem lay in voluntary, mutual insurance associations devoid of state intervention, which had had a long tradition in mining and in some other branches by then.[11] The voluntary insurance associations had, nonetheless, several shortcomings. They were fragmented and small and therefore could not share risks appropriately; furthermore, they provided cover only against a limited number of risks (they did not allocate any old-age pensions, for example); their services were highly inadequate and were offered only to the workers' elite, prosperous enough to accumulate some savings anyway. Consequently, the real breakthrough in the development of social welfare institutions was marked by the emergence and spreading of social insurance, in which the state played a central role either directly or indirectly.

The history of modern social policy goes back to the German legislation of the 1880s. The first mandatory state sickness insurance for industrial workers, favoured by Chancellor Bismarck, was introduced in 1883 and was followed by a separate accident insurance (1884) as well as an old-age pension insurance (1889).[12] Without actually emulating the German model in every detail, social insurance schemes usually labelled as workers' insurance at the time were catching on fast in Europe. East Central European countries were also quick to adopt these early social welfare institutions. Austria, including the Czech lands, had been the second and Hungary the third country in the world to introduce workers' sickness insurance in 1892.

A good indicator of how fast social insurance spread is that by 1901, all Western European societies had at least one type of accident, sickness or old-age pension insurance regulated by the state, and by the First World War, the majority of the countries ran some kind of insurance scheme against all three risks.[13] Nevertheless, it took decades until the first social insurance acts were passed in all these three areas in all Western European countries. Switzerland, as the latecomer in this respect, introduced pension insurance in addition to the two other existing basic schemes only by 1946 (Table 5.1).

These social insurance schemes differed markedly from poor relief, charity and the other welfare institutions of the preceding decades and centuries. The new programs were limited and even meagre but had the potential for dynamic growth from the beginning. It was all the more so because the main intention of social insurance was not simply to provide assistance for the needy, but to prevent emergency situations through routine measures. Therefore it involved and supported not only the most destitute social strata but wide segments of society. In addition, the prevailing feature of the new schemes was their reliance on state legislation and they required the mandatory membership of certain social groups. The new programs obliged potential beneficiaries to pay contributions, but it was

TABLE 5.1 Date of introduction of social security schemes in selected European countries

	Accident insurance		Health insurance		Old-age pension insurance		Unemployment insurance		Family allowance
	Vol.	*Comp.*	*Vol.*	*Comp.*	*Vol.*	*Comp.*	*Vol.*	*Comp.*	
United Kingdom	1897	1946		1911	1908	1925		1911	1945
France	1898	1946	1898	1930	1895	1910	1905	1967	1932
Netherlands		1901		1929		1913	1916	1949	1940
Belgium	1903	1971	1894	1944	1900	1924	1920	1944	1930
Ireland	1897	1966		1911	1908	1960		1911	1944
Germany/FRG	1871	1884		1883		1889		1927	1954
Austria		1887		1888		1927		1920	1921
Switzerland	1881	1911	1911			1946	1924	1976	1952
Sweden	1901	1916	1891	1953		1913	1934		1947
Denmark	1898	1916	1892	1933	1891	1922	1907		1952
Norway		1894		1909		1936	1906	1938	1946
Finland		1895		1963		1937	1917		1948
Italy		1898	1886	1928	1898	1919		1919	1936
Czechoslovakia		1887		1888		1889	1921		1945
Poland		1883		1889		1889	1924		1947
Hungary		1907		1891		1928		1957	1912

Abbreviations: Vol.: voluntary insurance supported by the state and mandatory insurance with partial provision. Comp.: compulsory insurance.

Notes: Poland: health insurance 1889: West and Upper Silesia only; Czechoslovakia: health insurance 1888: Bohemia, Moravia, Silesia only; old age pension 1889: miner's scheme; Hungary: family allowance was partially introduced in 1912; the nominally existent unemployment benefit was completely terminated in 1986.

Sources: Jens Alber, *Vom Armenhaus zum Wohlfahrtsstaat. Analysen zur Entwicklung der Sozialversicherung in Westeuropa,* Frankfurt/M.: Campus, 1987, 28 (accident, sickness, pension and unemployment insurance in Western Europe); Christopher Pierson, *Beyond the Welfare State,* Cambridge: Polity Press, 1991, 108 (family allowance in Western Europe); Gábor Gyáni, *A szociálpolitika múltja Magyarországon,* Budapest: MTA Történettudományi Intézet, 1994, 11–13 (Hungary); Stein Kuhnle and Anne Sander, 'The Emergence of the Western Welfare State', in Francis G. Castles, Stephan Leibfried, Jane Lewis and Herbert Obinger, eds., *The Oxford Handbook of the Welfare State,* Oxford: Oxford University Press, 2010, 71 (Czechoslovakia), 73 (Poland).

not only these revenues that were redistributed; rather, they were complemented by either the employer, or the state, or sometimes both. By virtue of past contributions, members earned rights to benefits, which could not be overridden by a relatively high income status or any other, similar considerations. As opposed to the traditional forms of relief, the new social insurance schemes were more differentiated in their functions and wider in their scope. The schemes provided cover against predefined major risks (such as occupational accidents, sickness, old age, death of a family member and unemployment), and they were not limited to narrow social groups but had a wider scope, usually based on occupational and income criteria. A further special feature of social insurance was that (at least at the early stage) it centred on male breadwinners instead of women and children, the main beneficiaries of traditional poor relief.[14]

Although there was no uniform sequence in the introduction of the individual insurance schemes in various countries, generally it was industrial accident insurance (or workmen's compensation) that was given the green light first, followed by sickness, and then, in turn, by old-age pension insurance.[15] Unemployment insurance usually came fourth: there were European countries mandating it only well after the First World War or not at all. Still, by 1920, in 10 out of 13 major Western European countries, the unemployed were already supported by the state in one form or another (Table 5.1).

The major reason for this particular sequence of introduction rose from accident insurance being the most congruous, with liberal economic views prevailing at the end of the nineteenth century, stressing individual liability and advocating the idea of self-reliance. Even though accidents were often considered as a natural consequence of industrial production, accident insurance could be justified by redefining the traditional notion of taking personal responsibility for damages caused. Thus, expenses incurred by the new insurance were often covered exclusively by the employers. Health and old-age pension insurance represented a more obvious break with liberalism, because they provided security against risks not related to employment, and thus could not be considered as damages caused by the individual. In addition, sickness and old age were the major factors of poverty, the alleviation of which demanded more resources than were needed for workmen's compensation; this also delayed their introduction. The relative belatedness of unemployment insurance can also be explained when it is considered that this scheme constituted the most radical refusal of the liberal economic doctrine, including the liability principle and its legal implications.[16]

Nevertheless, the timing of the introduction in itself reveals little about the coverage and the quality of a particular program. Early social insurance had a limited social reach, constrained to industrial labourers, and, particularly, workers in heavy industry, and provided only moderate benefits. Pensions in those days amounted to some 10% of average wages, or even less. As is discussed later, early schemes progressed through a so-called maturing process, expanding with time and covering larger and larger sections of the population as well as granting generous benefits. At the same time, there are examples, especially in Scandinavia, of schemes launched relatively late, yet offering extensive benefits for a wider circle of citizens or employees straightaway.

As pointed out earlier, the intervention of the state in social welfare unfolded at a different pace in each country, and marked divergences can be detected in the organizational forms of the early social security systems. One of the major types was compulsory insurance, in which the state mandated membership in a specific insurance, without prescribing the actual company with which the client was to take out the insurance. Thus, in this type, the state played a central role in setting and enforcing the rules of operation and it was also involved in the running of the scheme, but had a modest role in financing the system. Beside Germany, this arrangement characterized both the early Austrian and the Norwegian social security programs; moreover, it was also present in the British social security system from 1908 onwards. Both the German and the British systems integrated an abundant number of voluntary insurance companies in the system, leaving their independent status intact.[17]

The other main type (state-subsidized voluntary insurance) had been adopted by Belgium, France, Italy, Sweden, Denmark and Switzerland in the beginning. In these countries, the state played a less dominant role, limited to setting the operational framework of the social security system, along with controlling and subsidizing its operation. Setting the standards of benefits and other conditions of services as well as the amount of contributions was left to the individual insurance funds. In most of the cases, benefits were commensurate with contributions, and vertical redistribution among social strata was modest. However, unlike private insurance, contributions were not calculated on the basis of individual risk, and thus, in this regard, solidarity prevailed.[18]

The expansion of the welfare states: institutionalized solidarity

After the modest beginnings of social policies in the nineteenth century, the twentieth century saw the dynamic growth of the welfare state in Europe. The expansion was particularly fast in the decades following the Second World War up to the mid-1970s, which was followed by an era of slower growth in the history of most Western European welfare states, whereas in some of the other countries there was even a slight decline in the engagement of the state in welfare services.

The dynamics of welfare states are well illustrated by the trends in social expenditures. However, expenditures alone cannot properly reflect the specific structural characteristics of welfare systems; therefore we also seek to map out the changing features of welfare institutions and the major aspects of social rights, including coverage and the standards of services.[19]

Trends in welfare expenditures

At the turn of the century, Germany undoubtedly paid out the most on social insurance expenditures and social expenditures in general among European countries. In 1900, about 1% of the gross domestic product was spent on these programmes, whereas they totalled 2.6% before the First World War.[20] However, exact comparison is hindered because the relatively extensive body of comparable data regarding West European social insurance expenditures is available only from as late as 1930.[21] At this point, it was still Germany where the most resources (5.2% of the gross domestic product (GDP)) was allocated for these purposes.[22] Great Britain was second on the list with 4.6%, with Austria closely following with 4.4%. Ireland and Denmark came in the middle of the list (2.8% and 2.6%), whereas other Scandinavian countries spent a markedly lower percentage of their domestic product on social insurance: 0.7% (Finland) and 1.1% (Sweden) (Table 5.2).

TABLE 5.2 Social insurance and social security expenditures in selected European countries, 1900–1990 (as a percentage of the GDP and net material product)

	Social insurance expenditures						Social security expenditures				
	1900	1910	1920	1930	1940	1950	1950	1960	1970	1980	1990
United Kingdom				4.6		7.1	10.0	11.0	13.8	17.7	17.3
France						4.8	12.6	13.4	15.3	26.8	27.1
Netherlands				1.5		3.7	7.1	11.1	20.0	28.6	28.5
Belgium						6.1	12.5	15.3	18.1	25.9	25.6
Ireland				2.8		5.5	8.9	9.6	11.6	21.7	18.9
Germany/FRG	1.0	2.6		5.2	4.3	7.3	14.8	15.0	17.0	23.8	22.7
Austria				4.4		6.5	12.4	13.8	18.8	22.4	24.8
Switzerland				1.4		4.0	6.0	7.5	10.1	13.8	14.4
Sweden				1.1		5.2	8.3	11.0	18.8	32.0	35.9
Denmark				2.6		5.9	8.4	11.1	16.6	26.9	28.4
Norway				1.0		3.6	5.7	9.4	15.5	20.3	
Finland				0.7		1.9	6.7	8.7	13.1	18.6	21.4
Italy						3.3	8.5	11.7	16.3	18.2	23.4
Czechoslovakia							10.8	15.8	18.0	18.9	
Hungary				5.2		3.2	3.8	5.8	8.9	14.2	18.4
Poland								8.9	10.7	15.7	

Notes:

Social insurance expenditures:

In Western Europe between 1950 and 1970 including public health expenditures but excluding the special benefits for public servants, provisions for war victims and social assistance; Western Europe 1980–1989: excluding public health care expenditures; Germany from 1950 onwards: West Germany; Germany 1913: including poor relief; Germany 1930–1940: author's own calculation based on Statistisches Bundesamt, ed., *Bevölkerung und Wirtschaft, 1872–1972*, Stuttgart: Statistisches Bundesamt, 1972, 219–224, 260; for Denmark, Ireland and the United Kingdom figures referring to the fiscal year between 1 April and 30 March are presented as a percentage of previous year's GDP; Western Europe 1989: author's own calculation based on ILO, *The cost of social security: Fourteenth international inquiry, 1987–1989*, Geneva: ILO, 1996, 109, 165

(United Kingdom), 107, 164 (France), 108, 165 (Ireland), 108, 164 (Germany), 107, 163 (Austria), 109, 164 (Switzerland), 109, 164 (Sweden), 107, 163 (Denmark), 108, 165 (Norway), 107, 164 (Finland), 108, 165 (Italy); Hungary: including pension expenditures of public employees; spending on the four major social insurance schemes (accident, health, pension and unemployment insurance); Hungary 1950–1990: a total of current health expenditures including public health care but excluding health care investments; different years: United Kingdom 1980: 1979–80; France 1950: 1952, 1970: 1972; Germany 1910: 1913, 1940: 1938; Switzerland 1950: 1951; Ireland 1930: 1929, 1950: 1953; Western Europe 1990: 1989; Czechoslovakia 1950: 1952; Hungary 1940: 1939, 1990: 1989.

Social security expenditures:
Social security expenditures as per the ILO definition (see in text); figures for Denmark, Ireland and the United Kingdom referring to the fiscal year between 1 April and 30 March are presented as a percentage of previous year's GDP; different years: United Kingdom: 1974/1975, 1979/1980, 1989; France: 1952, 1989; The Netherlands: 1989; Ireland: 1953, 1989; Germany: 1989; Austria: 1989; Switzerland: 1951, 1989; Sweden: 1989; Denmark: 1974/1975, 1989; Finland: 1989; Italy: 1989; Czechoslovakia and Poland: as percentages of net material product.

Sources:

Social insurance expenditures:
Peter Flora, 'Solution or source of crises?', in W. J. Mommsen, ed., *The Emergence of the Welfare State in Britain and Germany, 1850–1950*, London: Croom Helm, 1981, 359 (Germany 1913); Statistisches Bundesamt, *Bevölkerung und Wirtschaft, 1872–1972*, Stuttgart: Statistisches Bundesamt, 1972, 219–224, 260 (Germany 1930–1938); Jens Alber, *Vom Armenhaus zum Wohlfahrtsstaat*, Frankfurt/M.: Campus, 1987, 60 (Germany 1900, Western Europe 1930); Peter Flora, ed., *State, Economy and Society in Western Europe, 1815–1975*, vol. I, Frankfurt/M.: Campus, 1983, 456 (Western Europe 1950–1970); Wolfram Fischer, ed., *Handbuch der europäischen Wirtschafts- und Sozialgeschichte*, Bd. 6, Stuttgart: Klett-Cotta, 1987, 217 (Western Europe 1980); ILO, *The Cost of Social Security: Fourteenth International Inquiry, 1987–1989*, Geneva: ILO, 1996, 109, 165 (United Kingdom 1989), 107, 164 (France 1989), 108, 165 (The Netherlands 1989), 108, 165 (Ireland 1989), 108, 164 (Germany 1989), 107, 163 (Austria 1989), 109, 164 (Switzerland 1989), 109, 164 (Sweden 1989), 108, 165 (Norway 1989), 107, 163 (Denmark 1989), 107, 164 (Finland 1989), 108, 165 (Italy 1989); Béla Tomka, *Welfare in East and West*, Berlin: Akademie Verlag, 2004, 119–122 (Hungary 1930–1990).

Social security expenditures:
Peter Flora, ed., *State, Economy, and Society in Western Europe, 1815–1975*, vol. I, Frankfurt/M.: Campus, 1983, 456 (Western Europe 1950–1970); ILO, *The Cost of Social Security: Eleventh International Inquiry, 1978–1980*, Geneva: ILO, 1985, 57–58 (Western Europe 1980); ILO, *The Cost of Social Security: Fourteenth International Inquiry, 1987–1989*, Geneva: ILO, 1996, 74–75 (Western Europe 1989); ILO, *World Labour Report 2000: Income Security and Social Protection in a Changing World*, Geneva: ILO, 2000, 313 (Belgium 1990); Béla Tomka, *Welfare in East and West*, Berlin: Akademie Verlag, 2004, 124–125 (Hungary 1950–1990); ILO, *The Cost of Social Security: Eleventh International Inquiry, 1978–1980*, Geneva: ILO, 1985, 59 (Czechoslovakia 1960–1980, Poland 1960–1980); Wolfram Fischer, ed., *Handbuch der europäischen Wirtschafts- und Sozialgeschichte*, Bd. 6, Stuttgart: Klett-Cotta, 1987, 221 (Czechoslovakia 1952).

From the post-Second World War period, more complete as well as more consistent time series are available regarding welfare expenditures, including the ILO data collection of the costs of social security (Table 5.2).[23] Social security expenditures relative to the GDP show a slower rise in Western Europe immediately after the Second World War and at the end of the century, and a rapid increase in the 1960s and 1970s. In 1950, West Germany had the highest ratio of expenditures. France, Belgium, and Austria were also spending a high percentage of the GDP on social security, whereas countries with a relatively low budget included the Scandinavian countries, the Netherlands and Switzerland. The latter countries turn out to be the ones with the highest rate of growth in the following two decades, with the exception of Switzerland, which kept its position at the end of the list in Western Europe from the 1950s till the end of the century. Countries that had been traditionally big spenders (West Germany, Belgium and Austria) were overtaken by the Netherlands at the end of the 1960s, which was in turn superseded by Sweden one decade later. Regarding the period between 1950 and 1990, Sweden had the highest rate of growth, with the Netherlands and Denmark following close behind; France also exhibited a rapid expansion in this period; West Germany, from its leading position at the mid-century, experienced a moderate rise; while in the UK social security spending increased to the smallest extent. By the end of the 1980s, Sweden's expenditure rate of 35.9% was the highest, leaving the Netherlands (28.5%) and Denmark (28.4%) in the following positions well behind.

Social security schemes play a special role among social welfare programs and their development is also primarily addressed in the present chapter. Since they cover only a part of all social welfare expenditures, it is worth having a look at the OECD data collection based on a broader definition outlined above (see Table 5.3 for the second half of the century).[24] Using this broader approach, then the ratio of social expenditures to the GDP increases considerably as early as the beginning of the twentieth century; however, the emerging trends are rather similar to the one seen in the case of social security.[25]

The sporadic data available on interwar East Central Europe suggest that the countries of the region were not lagging far behind Western European countries in terms of the ratio of welfare spending. For instance, Hungary's social security expenditures in relation to the country's GDP in 1930 proved to be fairly high even by Western European standards, although these figures include the pension paid to state employees, too (Table 5.2). The legacy of the highly developed German social security system that certain regions of Poland inherited was further improved upon in 1927 and 1933 in several respects.[26] The same applies to Czechoslovakia, where the adoption of Austrian social insurance in the Czech lands paved the way for further development. However, what may be striking is how moderate the communist regimes' welfare efforts proved compared with that of Western countries in many respects. The ratio of funds allocated for social security purposes in Czechoslovakia practically stagnated between 1965 and 1980.[27] In the period between the middle of the century and 1970, Poland and Hungary were increasingly left behind by Western European societies both in terms of social

TABLE 5.3 Social expenditures in selected European countries, 1950–1990 (as a percentage of the GDP)

	1950	1960	1970	1980	1990
United Kingdom	14.8	15.1	20.0	24.5	24.6
France		13.4	16.7	28.3	31.4
Netherlands	13.3	18.9	28.7	40.2	35.1
Belgium		18.3	23.4	36.0	31.6
Ireland	14.7	14.0	19.8	29.0	24.3
FRG	19.2	21.7	24.7	31.0	27.4
Austria		20.4	24.8	32.6	29.2
Switzerland	7.4	8.8	12.5	19.7	22.5
Sweden	11.3	15.2	25.9	37.9	40.1
Denmark	10.4	14.4	22.6	32.8	35.3
Norway	9.2	13.7	21.1	26.1	34.0
Finland	10.5	12.7	17.2	24.8	31.4
Italy		16.5	21.3	27.0	26.2
Hungary		11.3	13.9	19.6	27.8

Notes: OECD definition of social expenditures including income maintenance programs (sickness benefit, old-age pension, etc.) as well as public spending on education, health and housing; Western Europe 1950–1990: excluding services provided for public servants; Hungary 1960–1989: including social expenditures for public servants; Hungary 1960: without public spending on housing; different periods: Denmark: 1951/1952, 1960/1961, 1970/1971; Hungary: 1989; Hungary 1970, 1980, 1989: author's own calculations.

Sources: Jens Alber, 'Germany', in Peter Flora, ed., *Growth to Limits: The Western European Welfare States Since World War II*, vol. 4, Berlin and New York: De Gruyter, 1987, 325 (Germany 1950–1980); OECD, *Social Expenditures, 1960–1990*, Paris: OECD, 1985, 80 (France, 1960–1990); Richard Parry, 'United Kingdom', in Flora, ed., *Growth to Limits*, vol. 4, 393 (United Kingdom 1950–1980); Joop Roenbroek and Theo Berben, 'Netherlands', in Flora, ed., *Growth to Limits*, vol. 4, 720 (The Netherlands 1950–1980); Jos Berghman, Jan Peeters and Jan Vranken, 'Belgium', in Flora, ed., *Growth to Limits*, vol. 4, 815 (Belgium 1950–1980); Wolfgang Weigel and Anton Amann, 'Austria', in Flora, ed., *Growth to Limits*, vol. 4, 584 (Austria 1950–1980); Peter Gross and Helmut Puttner, 'Switzerland', in Flora, ed., *Growth to Limits*, vol. 4, 648 (Switzerland 1950–1980); Maria Maguire, 'Ireland', in Flora, ed., *Growth to Limits*, vol. 4, 464 (Ireland 1950–1980); Sven Olsson, 'Sweden', in Flora, ed., *Growth to Limits*, vol. 4, 42 (Sweden 1950–1980); Lars Norby Johansen, 'Denmark', in Flora, ed., *Growth to Limits*, vol. 4, 234 (Denmark 1950–1980); Matti Alestalo and Hannu Uusitalo, 'Finland', in Flora, ed., *Growth to Limits*, vol. 4, 167 (Finland 1950–1980); Stein Kuhnle, 'Norway', in Flora, ed., *Growth to Limits*, vol. 4, 110 (Norway 1950–1980); Maurizio Ferrera, 'Italy', in Flora, ed., *Growth to Limits*, vol. 4, 517 (Italy 1950–1980); OECD, *Social Expenditure Statistics of OECD Member Countries*, Labour Market and Social Policy Occasional Papers, No. 17, Paris: OECD, 1996, 19 (social expenditures, Western Europe 1990); UNESCO, *Statistical Yearbook*, 1993, Paris: UNESCO, 1993, 416–418 (educational public expenditures, Western Europe, 1990); OECD, *National Accounts. Main Aggregates, 1960–1997*, vol. I, Paris: OECD, 1999 (GDP, Western Europe, 1990); Endre Gács, 'Szociális kiadásaink nemzetközi összehasonlitásban', *Statisztikai Szemle*, vol. 63 (1985), no. 12, 1228 (Hungary 1960); *Magyarország nemzeti számlái. Főbb mutatók. 1991*, Budapest: KSH, 1993, 85 (social benefits in Hungary, 1970); *Beruházási Évkönyv, 1980*, Budapest: KSH, 1981, 18 (social investments in Hungary, 1970); *Népgazdasági mérlegek, 1949–1987*, Budapest: KSH, 1989, 66 (amortization of social investments in Hungary 1970); *A lakosság jövedelme és fogyasztása, 1960–1980*, Budapest: KSH, 1984, 21 (fringe benefits in Hungary, 1970); 'A Világbank szociálpolitikai jelentése Magyarországról', *Szociálpolitikai Értesítő*, 1992, no. 2, 54 (Hungary 1980–1989).

security and social expenditures.[28] However, this trend began to turn around from the 1970s. On the one hand, this was caused by the decreasing rate of the growth in expenditures in Western Europe. On the other hand, paradoxically, the aggravating political and economic difficulties resulted in the increase of the percentage of social expenditures in relation to the GDP in several East Central European countries; economic growth regressed, but the expansion of welfare programs was continued. Nevertheless, an evaluation of these programs also reveals that the welfare arrangements of communist countries were distinct, generating expenditures that did not exist in Western Europe, most importantly the ones related to full employment and that are not included in either the ILO or the OECD statistics analysed above. The discrepancies between the welfare systems are discussed later in more detail.

The most striking feature of the changes in welfare expenditures in the twentieth century is their precipitous increase, especially in Western Europe. The increasing differentiation of welfare programs and their more generous eligibility rules brought about the dynamic growth of expenditures. Moreover, the standard of welfare benefits also improved at a pace exceeding the rate of economic growth. The following discussion thus presents these trends and addresses the mechanisms and institutions of welfare states in twentieth-century Europe.

The differentiation of welfare programs

Occupational accident, sickness, old-age pension, unemployment insurance and family benefits kept their major role in welfare services throughout the twentieth century, because they started to expand soon after they were introduced, providing an increasingly effective protection against side or collateral risks in addition to core ones included earlier. Moreover, brand new types of benefits appeared as well. Differentiation had already taken place in the interwar era, and it gained further momentum after the Second World War. This diverse process can be illustrated by examples taken from major areas of social security.

Initially, health insurance covered the costs of shorter illnesses. The early types of health insurances concentrated on cash allowances; for instance, in Germany, the access to hospital care was still limited for workers in the interwar period, and in Great Britain, the Health Insurance Act of 1911 provided no cover for hospitalization or the services of specialists. With the exception of a few countries like Denmark, in-kind benefits were catching on only after the Second World War. Despite the increase in the level of cash benefits, in-kind provisions (such as hospital care and medicine costs) were gradually superseding them among expenditures because the growth of accessibility and costs was more dynamic in the latter.[29] Health insurance progressively included conditions as well that cannot be classified as illnesses (pregnancy, post-natal care and birth control).[30]

In the area of pension insurance, a gradual extension of the schemes took place to include a number of risks, such as old age, disability, and the death of the breadwinner of the family. By the Second World War, old-age pension insurance had been established in all the Western European countries with the exception of Switzerland, and social security included disability pension and the death of the breadwinner only in 11 and 8 countries, respectively.[31] The post-Second World War decades saw the extension of pension insurance in all respects, and the development included the linking as well as the convergence of the various types of pension, which is discussed below in greater detail.

As regards unemployment insurance, attempts were made to adjust services to the financial status of the families everywhere in Western Europe except France by the Second World War, through benefits tied to the number of dependants. Furthermore, from the late 1960s onwards, it was a characteristic trend to consider the causes of unemployment in calculating benefits. In the case of mass layouts resulting from economic recession or technological modernization, the benefits could have almost equalled the amount of former wages.[32]

In addition to the ones mentioned above, examples of emerging new benefits assimilated with social security included the entitlement of elderly people for care, introduced in 1968 in the Netherlands; or wages paid to employees of bankrupt companies in Germany.[33] Furthermore, there was a growth in welfare services falling outside the scope of social security, such as housing support and education grants.[34] Nevertheless, the quick expansion of welfare programs ended in the 1970s (a development that we return to later in this chapter).

The process of expansion and functional differentiation, visible in all major areas of social security and all countries in post-war Western Europe, did not imply that the individual schemes entailed the same significance or showed the same dynamics of growth. As demonstrated above, pension insurance was usually not the first one to be introduced among social security programs; yet pension expenditures took little time to exceed those of other programs. The ratio of pensions was already the highest among all items everywhere except France as early as 1960, amounting to about half of all social insurance expenditures on the average followed by health care. The ratio of expenditures on education were on the increase after the Second World War, but, with the exception of Finland, the trend reversed in the 1970s, whereas the ratio of pension and healthcare spending showed a steady increase in the given period, even though with significant fluctuations and at the expense of family benefits as well. The inertia of pension expenditures is shown by their increasing ratios even under the conditions of slowing economic and welfare growth from the mid-1970s.[35] Mass unemployment emerging in the 1970s and 1980s also brought about considerable changes in the construction of welfare states. Although a high ratio of unemployment had already surfaced in the industrial countries between the two World Wars, the commitment of the state for income maintenance used to be weaker at that time than in the post-war period. As a result of this commitment, unemployment benefits left their impact on the structure of welfare budgets in a number of countries, yet the unemployment benefits still accounted for a relatively low percentage of the total social security costs in Western Europe.

Up until the Second World War, major trends in the development of welfare institutions in the East Central European region coincided with those of Western

Europe. Striking similarities are found in social security becoming the main element of the welfare system, and both in the way the programs became differentiated and in their internal structure, such as the growing importance of pension expenditures. However, from the middle of the century, the functions of social security changed in a contradictory way in communist countries. On the one hand, the almost complete termination of social assistance increased the importance of social security. On the other hand, considerations of social policy prevailed in areas that were relatively autonomous in Western European societies (e.g., the pricing of goods and services, or the labour market), thus the weight of social security decreased within the overall welfare system. The differentiation of social security programs continued in East Central Europe as well, but with special emphasis on supporting industrial production and the mobilization of labour in particular. Programs focused mainly on risks associated with the ability to work, as indicated by the low level of pension spending and the relatively high ratio of health expenditures in the first two decades after the Second World War. However, in the following period, the ratio of pension spending grew, whereas health expenditures were decreasing at the point when the falling trend in Western Europe turned around. Further remarkable structural features of welfare efforts in East Central Europe were the relatively high level of family benefits and the complete lack of unemployment benefits.[36]

Major trends in coverage

The first social security schemes covered only a small proportion of the population or those employed. The only exceptions were Germany and, in a certain respect, England and Denmark. In Germany, the majority of the labour force had occupational injuries and pension insurance already at the turn of the century, and the same applies to England concerning occupational injuries insurance and to Denmark with regard to health insurance in 1910 (Tables 5.4 and 5.5).[37]

One of the major twentieth-century trends in social rights was the growth in the ratio of those covered by social security. This process had already gained momentum in the Scandinavian countries between the two World Wars but elsewhere in Western Europe the development towards universality (the inclusion of the whole population in insurance schemes) also accelerated after the Second World War. Although universal coverage had not been established everywhere even by the end of the twentieth century, the levels reached were so high by 1980 that, as Peter Flora formulated it, Western European social security systems could be regarded as mature in this respect.[38]

Whereas political rights diffused principally from the top down through the social hierarchy, social rights were mostly extended vice versa.[39] Typically, first workers with high-risk jobs were covered by social security programs, which were then extended to other industrial, then to agricultural workers, and later to dependants or survivors of insured persons. These groups were followed by high earners, and the self-employed were the last to be included. The inclusion of the self-employed,

TABLE 5.4 Coverage of health insurance in European countries, 1900–1990 (members as a percentage of the economically active population)

	1900	1910	1920	1930	1940	1950	1960	1970	1980	1990
United Kingdom			73	82	90	(100)	(100)	(100)	(100)	(100)
France	9	18	17	32	48	60	69	96		
Netherlands				(42)	(42)	54	60	74	85	(100)
Belgium	6	12	21	33	31	57	57	92		
Ireland				34	44	53	58	67	78	89
Germany/FRG	39	44	53	57	56	57	67	67	84	(100)
Austria	18	24	39	59		56	71	85	87	86
Switzerland			43	69	86	89	(100)	(100)	(100)	99
Sweden	13	27	28	35	49	97	(100)	(100)	(100)	(100)
Denmark	27	54	97	(100)	(100)	(100)	(100	(100)	(100)	(100)
Norway			55	56	86	(100)	(100)	(100)	(100)	(100)
Finland								(100)	(100)	(100)
Italy	(6)	(6)	(6)	7	47	44	76	92		
Hungary			25	27	27	46	85	97	100	100
Poland							54			

Notes: Figures in brackets are estimates based on legal regulations; figures for Western Europe for 1980 were interpolated from 1975 and 1987 figures; Ireland: data of those eligible for sick leave; The Netherlands 1930–1940: only sick leave benefits applied; The Netherlands 1970: data of those eligible for sick leave benefit; Switzerland: dates before 1945 refer to both health insurance and sick leave benefit, whereas later only include health insurance; Hungary 1924–1980: author's calculations based on the sources given below; Hungary 1940: estimate for 1939 on the current territory, see sources below; Hungary: persons eligible for cash sick leave benefits as a percentage of active population (1920–1950) and health insurance with or without sick leave benefit as a percentage of the total population (1960–1990); different years: The Netherlands 1989, Ireland 1989; Germany 1989, Austria 1989; Switzerland 1989; Sweden 1989; Denmark 1989; Norway 1989; Finland 1989; Hungary 1924, 1939.

Sources: Peter Flora, ed., State, Economy, and Society in Western Europe, 1815–1975, vol. I, Frankfurt/M.: Campus, 1983, 460 (Western Europe 1900–1975); ILO, The Cost of Social Security: Fourteenth International Inquiry, 1987–1989, Geneva: ILO, 1996 201 (Austria 1987), 203 (Austria 1989, Denmark 1987, 1989), 204 (Finland 1987, 1989), 205 (Germany 1987), 206 (Ireland 1987, Germany 1989), 207 (Ireland 1989), 211 (The Netherlands 1987), 212 (The Netherlands 1989), 213 (Norway 1987), 214 (Switzerland 1987, 1989, Norway 1989), 216 (Sweden 1987, 1989); ILO, Yearbook of Labour Statistics, 1995, Geneva: ILO, 1996, 164 (Austria 1987, 1989), 165 (Germany 1987, 1989), 166 (Ireland 1987, 1989), 167 (The Netherlands 1987, 1989, Norway 1987, 1989), 168 (Switzerland 1987, 1989), 169 (Sweden 1987, 1989); ILO, International Survey of Social Services. Studies and Reports, Series M., No. 11, Geneva: ILO, 1933 363–370 (Hungary 1924, 1930; author's own calculation); Statisztikai Negyedévi Közlemények, XLIII (1940), 204 (Hungary 1939; author's own calculations); Statisztikai Évkönyv. 1990, Budapest: KSH, 1991, 17 (Hungary 1950–1980, insured persons as a percentage of total population); Egészségügyi helyzet. 1972, Budapest: KSH, 1973, 90, 108, 114, 164, 167, 191 (Hungary 1950–1980, insured persons as a percentage of the population); A társadalombiztosítás fejlődése számokban, 1950–1985, Budapest: Kossuth, 1987, 52–55 (Hungary 1950–1980, ratio of people eligible for sick leave); Time Series of Historical Statistics, 1867–1992, vol. I, Budapest: KSH, 1993, 36 (Hungary, active wage earners; author's own calculations); Statisztikai Évkönyv, 1990, Budapest: KSH, 1991, 17 (Hungary 1990).

TABLE 5.5 Coverage of pension insurance in selected European countries, 1900–1990 (as a percentage of the economically active population)

	1900	1910	1920	1930	1940	1950	1960	1970	1980	1990
United Kingdom				82	90	94	86	83		
France	(8)	13	14	(36)	48	69	92	93		
Netherlands			52	58	65	64	(100)	(100)	(100)	(100)
Belgium	9	29	(29)	51	(44)	57	89	100		
Ireland					44	55	64	71	86	(100)
Germany/FRG	53	53	57	69	72	70	82	81	91	(100)
Austria		2	(5)	43		51	75	78	82	85
Switzerland						(100)	(100)	(100)	100	(100)
Sweden			(100)	(100)	(100)	(100)	(100)	(100)	(100)	(100)
Denmark				95	(100)	(100)	(100)	(100)	(100)	(100)
Norway						(100)	(100)	(100)	(100)	(100)
Finland						(100)	(100)	(100)	(100)	(100)
Italy	0	(2)	(38)	38	38	(39)	89	99		
Hungary				16	30	47	85	97	100	100

Notes: Figures in brackets are estimates based on legal regulations; Denmark 1930: only disability pension; Ireland: only widow's and orphan's pensions up until 1960; United Kingdom 1930–1940: estimate based on health insurance figures; Hungary 1950–1990: as a percentage of the population; Hungary 1940: estimate for 1939 based on present territory from sources given below; different years: Ireland 1989; Germany 1989; Austria 1925, 1989; Switzerland 1989; Sweden 1989; Denmark 1989; Norway 1989; Finland 1989; figures for Western Europe for 1980 had been interpolated from figures of 1975 and 1987; Hungary 1939.

Sources: Peter Flora, ed., *State, Economy, and Society in Western Europe, 1815–1975,* vol. I, Frankfurt/M.: Campus, 1983, 460 (Western Europe 1900–1975); ILO, *The Cost of Social Security: Fourteenth International Inquiry, 1987–1989,* Geneva: ILO, 1996, 201 (Austria 1987), 202 (Austria 1989), 203 (Denmark 1987, 1989), 204 (Finland 1987, 1989), 205 (Germany 1987, 1989), 206 (Ireland 1987), 207 (Ireland 1989), 211–212 (The Netherlands 1987, 1989), 213 (Norway 1987, 1989), 215 (Switzerland 1987, 1989), 216 (Sweden 1987, 1989); ILO, *Yearbook of Labour Statistics, 1995,* Geneva: ILO, 1996, 164 (Austria 1987, 1989), 165 (Germany 1987, 1989), 166 (Ireland 1987, 1989), 167 (The Netherlands 1987, 1989), 168 (Switzerland 1987, 1989); ILO, *Compulsory Pension Insurance: Studies and Reports,* Series M, No. 10, Geneva: ILO, 1933, 106–107 (Hungary 1930); *Magyar Statisztikai Évkönyv, 1940,* Budapest: KSH, 1941, 47, 56–57 (Hungary 1940); *A társadalombiztosítás fejlődése számokban, 1950–1985,* Budapest: Kossuth, 1987, 59 (Hungary 1950–1980); *Statisztikai Évkönyv, 1990,* Budapest: KSH, 1991, 17 (Hungary 1990); *Time series of historical statistics, 1867–1992,* vol. I, Budapest: KSH, 1993, 36 (Hungary, active earners; author's own calculations).

especially farmers, was a complicated process, because they often resisted the idea of regularly paying contributions that social security involved. In the last stage, non-employed social groups, such as students, became insured in their own right in several countries.[40]

When examining approaches to eligibility, two basic types can be distinguished before the First World War: the first determined by the type of work and depending on the payment of a contribution, the second based on means testing. Examples of the former, Bismarckian type of social insurance include the old-age pension in Germany, which, at the beginning, only workers were eligible for and which was commensurate with their contributions. The first means-tested state pension was introduced in Denmark in the 1890s, and a similarly means-tested pension scheme, not tied to previous history of contributions for eligibility, was adopted by Great Britain in 1908.[41] Later on, this double pattern of eligibility began to change with the principle of means test gradually losing ground already in the interwar period and becoming further marginalized in the second half of the century.[42]

Moreover, the principle of citizenship as a criterion for eligibility emerged at an early stage. Sweden adopted a contribution-based pension scheme with universal coverage for all citizens in 1913, which provided low-level services.[43] However, citizenship gained a considerable role in the assertion of social rights between the two World Wars and especially after the Second World War. In this respect, the major international milestone was the Beveridge Report released in Great Britain in 1942 and the subsequent reforms for which it served as a basis. Sir William Beveridge and the government committee under his leadership elaborated the program for the post-war restructuring of the British welfare system. The Report set out to grant extensive social rights to all citizens. Although it had not been realized completely, the post-Second World War restructuring of the health insurance system (the establishment of the National Health Service) applied the citizenship principle when defining qualifying conditions for welfare benefits. The impact of the Beveridge Report and the British health-care reform proved to be long-term. In the two post-war decades, welfare systems still developed along the principles of eligibility that had prevailed before, and citizenship became a significant criterion for eligibility only from the 1960s and 1970s, especially in Scandinavia.[44]

At the same time, the various approaches to eligibility showed signs of convergence in post-war Western Europe as well. In countries where universal and unified social security existed, benefits became more differentiated and thus better reflected the differences in incomes and in the contributions paid. This trend prevailed in the United Kingdom as well as in Scandinavian countries between 1959 and 1966, where an earnings-related supplementary pension was introduced in addition to the flat-rate state pension. However, in countries where an earnings-related pension system was in operation, flat-rate elements were introduced, like in the Netherlands, Italy and Germany in 1956, 1965 and 1972, respectively.[45]

As far as East Central Europe is concerned, in Czechoslovakia, social security coverage expanded dynamically already after the First World War. In Hungary and Poland, the ratio of people covered by social security increased but still stayed at a relatively low level in the interwar years. However, after the Second World War, the ratio of citizens eligible for social security services increased at a fast rate in East Central Europe, which brought about a convergence regarding coverage, East Central European ratios approaching those of the leading Western European countries. At the same time, the politically driven discrimination of certain social groups, first of all peasants, in the 1950s is striking. The most blatant manifestations of discrimination disappeared soon, and in the 1960s and 1970s, the unifying tendencies of eligibility rules along with the rapid extension of coverage can be regarded as a move towards universality, which was a trend similar to the one prevailing in Western Europe. Furthermore, in East Central Europe, social insurance coverage was extended to include the whole population usually by the 1970s, earlier than in several Western European countries.

The level of welfare benefits

Early social insurance programs were of low standards and static because the level of benefits was not tied to changes in prices, wages or economic growth. For example, in the case of pensions, up until nearly the mid-twentieth century, it was not supposed that the start of the payment of pensions would coincide with retirement and therefore the pension would enable the insured to live off it alone.[46] However, particularly in the period after the Second World War, the value of benefits was approaching earnings levels.[47] Benefits were no longer designed only to relieve the most severe social emergencies but were also aimed at maintaining the former standard of living and relative social status of the insured. Seminal in this process, the German pension reform of 1957 introduced the idea of 'dynamization', which implied that pensions were linked to the income level of the economically active population, enabling the inactive segment of the society to have their share in the dividend of economic growth as well. The underlying principle was solidarity between the younger and the elderly cohorts; it was also referred to as 'the contract between generations' (*Generationsvertrag*). In accordance with this symbolic contract, it was not the pool of accumulated pension contributions that covered the costs of pension benefits but the amounts paid by the active population and, when retiring, older generations could rely on the solidarity of younger generations in a similar manner. Although the main importance of the German reform lies in its long-term impact, it also brought about an immediate and radical increase in the level of pensions: a 65.3% increase for manual workers and 71.9% for white-collar employees.[48] This principle had been implemented in Germany in the area of other benefits as well, such as sick pay, and other countries followed suit, although with a variety of approaches.[49]

The development of pension and sick pay, the two most important cash benefits, reflect changes in the relative level of welfare services. In 1939, the mean level of pensions in twelve Western European countries amounted to 12% of workers' average wage, the replacement level being the highest in Germany and Italy at that time.[50] In 1950, pensions already corresponded to approximately 20–30% of the average wages in Western Europe, with the exception of a few countries, such as Austria and France, where it exceeded 50%. In 1985, the Western European average of replacement levels was well above 50% and in a number of countries, such as Austria, Belgium, Italy, Finland, Norway and Sweden, the typical pension exceeded two-thirds of average wages. At the other end of the scale was Ireland, with an average value slightly below 50%.[51] A similar dynamic upward trend prevailed in the relative level of sick pay, which nearly tripled between 1930 and 1985. By the 1980s,

90–100% of the wages were paid as sick pay in a number of countries, such as Austria, Finland, Germany, Norway and Sweden, whereas the lowest percentage was paid in Belgium, Great Britain and France.[52]

Although in terms of coverage, countries in East Central Europe were lagging behind in the interwar period, the level of benefits relative to income converged markedly to those in Western Europe. Early communist regimes in East Central Europe were characterized by the levelling of various benefits, which was accompanied by the withdrawal of some of the former entitlements (another way of discriminating against certain social groups, e.g. former public servants). The standards of benefits continued to fall behind those in Western Europe, which is clearly shown by the low level of pensions in both absolute and relative terms. In 1982, the replacement rate was only 30% in East Germany and 45% in Czechoslovakia, and in Hungary it stood out at 57%.[53]

Despite trends of levelling off, work and the income derived from employment had always played a crucial role when calculating social security benefits, and in due course, the governments put increasingly less emphasis on closing the benefit gaps in East Central Europe. The level of pensions was closely linked to incomes to motivate employees to stay in the labour market when labour was in short supply.

Social welfare systems: the three-plus-one worlds of welfare

When studying the history of the welfare state, the analysis of welfare expenditures, social security coverage and the level of benefits is essential. However, scholars have also attempted to explore the various features of the welfare state relative to each other and discern complex welfare systems. The resulting typologies of welfare states, which classify individual welfare systems by considering both their quantitative and qualitative features, have attracted wide critical acclaim in scholarship.

The three worlds of welfare capitalism

There had been several attempts in research to develop comprehensive frameworks for comparative welfare analysis, but the most influential typology has undoubtedly been proposed by Gøsta Esping-Andersen in 1990, who distinguished three 'worlds' of welfare capitalism: the liberal, the conservative/corporatist and the social democratic welfare regimes. The regimes differ according to the role of major institutions (the state, the market and the family) in producing and allocating social welfare; the degree of decommodification (i.e. the degree to which social services are available as a matter of right, and a person can maintain a socially acceptable standard of living without relying on the market); the dominant mode and locus of solidarity; as well as the kind of stratification system promoted by social policy. The concept of decommodification is central to Esping-Andersen's argumentation. In this respect, there are three major factors, which have already been put in a historical perspective: the qualifying conditions for benefits; the standard or level of income maintenance benefits; and the coverage of welfare schemes. Decommodification is

TABLE 5.6 Main characteristics of welfare regimes

	Social democratic	Conservative	Liberal
Basis of social rights	Citizenship, universality	Work performance, social status	Means test
Organizing principle	Citizenship guarantees and social security	Social security	Social assistance and private insurance
Administration	State	Corporative self-governance	Central and local public, market
Role of market in the welfare sector	Minor	Limited	Significant
Role of private insurances	Minor	Limited	Significant
Role of means-tested benefits	Minor	Limited	Significant
Role of services in the welfare sector	Significant	Limited	Limited
Role of policies towards full employment	Significant	Limited	Minor
Degree of income redistribution	Significant	Medium	Low
Role of welfare institutions	Levelling off, egalitarian	Status protection	Market correction
Social character	Middle class	Middle class	Dual society
Degree of poverty	Low	Moderate	High
Examples	Sweden, Denmark, Norway, Finland	Continental Western Europe (such as Germany, France, Austria, Italy)	United States, United Kingdom (with limitations)

Source: Based on the works of Gøsta Esping-Andersen and their interpretation by István György Tóth with minor additions and alterations, including Gøsta Esping-Andersen, *The Three Worlds of Welfare Capitalism*, Cambridge: Polity Press, 1990.

high when many citizens are eligible for generous benefits with few restrictions. Based on an in-depth empirical survey of the factors referred to above, Esping-Andersen suggested that welfare states can be clustered into three categories (Table 5.6).[54]

Social democratic welfare systems are mainly characterized by strong state intervention, universal social rights, commitment to full employment, as well as a high degree of decommodification. Not only are the most deprived strata of society eligible for welfare services but wide segments of the middle classes are as well. The inclusion of the more affluent citizens also serves the interests of the less prosperous because it is possible only if the standards of welfare benefits are raised to a level satisfying the needs of the middle classes as well. Where universalism is the main guiding principle, the most destitute citizens receive the same quality services, whereas in liberal systems, as is discussed below, separate welfare programs of different standards are established for the poor and the middle classes. In social democratic welfare systems, there is a single social security system serving all social strata. At the same time, cash benefits, such as pensions and sickness benefits, often do reflect income differences. This model crowds out the private welfare programs: on the one hand, no demand for them emerges, as state programs provide services of high standards; on the other, the middle classes have to join state welfare schemes, and therefore, their members are mostly not in the position to afford supplementary private insurance policies. Thus all major strata of the society become supporters of the welfare state, or, to put it differently, 'all benefit; all are dependent; and all will presumably feel obliged to pay'.[55]

This is the system out of the three in which the degree of vertical redistribution is the highest. The social democratic welfare regimes strive to establish the individual's independence of both the market and the family. The responsibility of childcare and caring for the elderly is, to a large extent, shifted from the family to the state. This is possible only by establishing an extensive system of social services. This strategy aims for enabling parents, mothers in particular, to find a work–life balance so that they do not have to give up their jobs if they have a child. As suggested above, social democratic welfare systems are committed to full or high-rate employment. First, this is because a high rate of employment decreases the severity of potential social problems. Second, a high-quality, universal social welfare system is costly to operate and requires a great number of taxpayers and contribution payers. Sweden, Denmark and Norway are examples of social democratic welfare regimes.

The desirability of extensive social rights had never been questioned in the conservative or corporatist welfare states, but they are closely tied to work and employment, which perpetuates class and status differences in the area of social benefits and beyond. The state takes an active role in the welfare system; therefore the private sector remains weak in this regard. The degree of vertical redistribution is relatively low; that is, benefits reflect incomes and the amount of contributions paid. Corporative regimes are usually sympathetic towards the Church, and thus they show a tendency to support traditional familyhood. The underlying idea of subsidiarity suggests that families can provide a higher standard of nursing and care than either the state or for-profit institutions; hence the state is expected to intervene with the life of the family only if the latter fails to fulfil its caretaking role. The conservative welfare regime dominates most of continental Europe, including France, West Germany, Italy, Switzerland, Austria, Belgium, the Netherlands and Finland.[56]

The liberal welfare state is markedly different from the first two types because it relies on the market when providing welfare services. With their minimum involvement, governments encourage private initiatives, such as private pension and private health insurance schemes; and often there also exists direct support for these solutions in the form of tax reductions and subsidies. When allocating benefits, the principle of means test is used; therefore, the clientele of public welfare schemes mostly consists of low-income working-class groups and benefits are often associated with a stigma. At the same time, substantial vertical redistribution is hindered by the low standard of social provisions and the strict rules set to eligibility. As a result, limited social rights and a low degree of decommodification follow, along with an urge to fill in even the most poorly paid jobs. In fact, the lack of social security is regarded as a drive to economic growth. Thus, liberal regimes present the highest level of inequality among the systems considered here. Society is split into two groups: the poor, who are the clients of the welfare state, and the majority of citizens, who are the beneficiaries of various private insurance schemes. There is a basic conflict of interest between the two factions. Whereas the first group depends on state welfare programs for their livelihood, the more affluent and politically more influential majority gets barely anything or nothing from these programs, and is thus not interested in the maintenance of these programs that freeze the quality of welfare services at a low level. The epitome of the liberal welfare regime is the United States. Out of the European countries investigated in the present study, Ireland and the United Kingdom fall into this category. However, it has to be noted that in both countries all citizens are eligible for public health care, which clashes with the basic tenets of the liberal regime, and therefore these two countries deviate from the classic liberal type.

Typologies are of use for comparative welfare research for a variety of reasons: they enhance the analytical depth of the investigation and contribute to a better understanding of causality, and they can also serve as tools for hypotheses formulation and testing.[57] Nonetheless, criticism formulated against them cannot be neglected. One critical view argues that Esping-Andersen failed to correctly specify some of the countries. Maurizio Ferrera maintains that countries of the Mediterranean should constitute a type in their own right, a 'Southern' or 'Latin Rim' model of social policy, because these do not guarantee a social minimum and a right to welfare; moreover, they are characterized by their strong focus on the family ('familialism').[58] A further line of criticism argues that the typology is characterized by Swedo-centrism, i.e. it has a bias for the social democratic model and implies its supremacy.[59] However, Esping-Andersen insisted that the Mediterranean countries form subgroups of the conservative models. Although appreciating the unique features of all the systems, he maintained that there was no need to add more categories to the typology.[60] In an attempt to refine the regime approach, it has also been claimed that the focus on class analysis led to the neglect of other dimensions of inequality, such as status, ethnicity, and especially gender. Esping-Andersen regarded this last piece of criticism as the most justified one, and therefore in a later book, he systematically discussed the role of the family in the production of welfare and acknowledged the household economy as the foundation of post-industrial welfare states.[61]

Esping-Andersen's typology became a major point of reference in the literature of social welfare by the millennium. However, it is also important to point out that his typology reflects the prevailing conditions of the last decades of the twentieth century. Even if the inertia or path dependency of various welfare models is taken into consideration (because established class alliances, vested interests and ideologies retard their transformation), the validity of the typology cannot go back earlier than the beginning of the 1960s. Typologies are by definition static and are incapable of accommodating change, and thus welfare may have had three worlds in the 1980s and two or four at some other points in time. As long as the major variables introduced by Esping-Andersen are considered when examining welfare systems (i.e. rules of eligibility, the degree to which benefits substitute incomes and the coverage of programs), all countries fall into either the conservative or the liberal category in the first third of the twentieth century in Western Europe, even if there are considerable differences between the individual systems. The system labelled as social-democratic emerged only later in Scandinavia. Moreover, communist welfare systems, discussed below, fall completely outside the scope of this typology.

The concept of the European social model

Alongside the differences presented above, there is no gainsaying that Western European welfare systems have always had several features in common, especially in the period after the Second World War. Some analysts regard these common characteristics as so significant that they claim the existence of a uniform Western European social model, often referred to as 'the European social model'. It is a relatively recent term and has been widely used since the mid-1980s, when Jacques Delors, then president of the European Commission, placed it at the centre of his agenda of deepening European integration. According to the most established view, the emergence of the model is the result of the success of Western European states in combining rapid economic growth and social progress. Analysts put the main emphasis on the Western European welfare state being particularly developed, but they often accentuate the existence of highly institutionalized and politicized labour relations as well.[62]

Several important arguments have been formulated for the plausibility of the European social model. On the one hand, the responsibility of the state for the welfare of its citizens has a long tradition on the continent even though the individual countries took diverse paths in this regard. In the first half of the twentieth century, there were considerable differences between the welfare systems of Western European countries, many of which disappeared by the 1950s, and their systems continued to converge in the following decades. As a result, by 1990, variation between Western European countries decreased in such important areas as the ratio of welfare expenditures, the structure of welfare spending and the coverage of social security.[63] This conclusion is also supported by Esping-Andersen's typology, according to which all countries of continental Western Europe belonged to the conservative-corporate type by the last third of the twentieth century. Three Scandinavian countries pertained to the social-democratic, and two Anglo-Saxon ones fall under the liberal category, with only one-fourth of the citizens in Europe living in these latter ones.[64]

Moreover, the greatest convergence from the 1980s took place between the Scandinavian and a number of continental countries, adhering to the social-democratic and the conservative models, respectively.[65] In the language of the convergence theory, these societies formed a 'convergence club'. It seems the amalgamation process meant that the emerging systems included elements of both the social democratic and the conservative regimes, such as universal coverage and benefits based on work performance.

Similarities within Western Europe stand out even more if peculiarities here are contrasted with the welfare systems of other industrialized countries and regions, e.g. the United States, Japan, Australia and parts of South-East Asia, where, with some minor exceptions, schemes of public welfare were established at a later stage and remained more constrained. A number of researchers argued that at the end of the twentieth century an extensive welfare state and the consequent high level of social rights became major distinctive features of Western European societies in an international context.

Finally, despite the dominant role of nation states at its cradle and in its infancy, the European social model assumed a supranational quality with the foundation of the EEC and its successors. Social policy in the EU is still the competence of the member states, but in certain areas related to employment (for instance, employment in other member states and women's equal opportunities), some common regulations had been introduced as early as the Treaty of Rome. From the 1990s onwards, the standardization of social legislation has been gaining new momentum and has been extended into new areas.

The development and the sustainability of the European social model have become one of the important themes of contemporary European political discourse. The concept has also received serious criticisms. One of the critical approaches maintains that the European social model does not have a clear-cut, widely accepted definition. Moreover, many observers argue that social diversity is so significant in Western Europe that the concept of a common 'model' can hardly be justified. Consequently, it is more plausible to assume the coexistence of a variety of models, or 'families of nations'.[66]

Scholarly debates on the European social model have been fairly inconclusive so far. There are strong arguments for adopting the concept of the European social model, because Western European societies, or, at least their majority, have had important shared features for the last decades, particularly in the area of welfare discussed above, which support the existence of such a model. However, even if we accept this argumentation, important questions still remain open, such as geographical validity and the timescale of the plausibility of the model: whether it existed until the 1980s and then started to disintegrate, or whether it can be applied to present-day Western Europe as well. It is also unclear how countries and regions outside Western Europe fit the model.

An additional model: the communist welfare system

Terms like welfare state, welfare policy and welfare society are usually applied in the context of market economies based on private property or plural democracies and hardly in the case of communist states.[67] At the same time, the concepts of collective responsibility for the well-being of the citizens and the institutions serving this end were existent in communist countries. Moreover, although the state was not the only actor providing for the welfare of the citizens here either, it undoubtedly had a leading role in this field. These circumstances justify the use of the term 'welfare state' in the context of communist countries as well.[68]

However, it has to be emphasized that social rights in communist countries emerged in a peculiar structure. Compared with Western Europe, the most striking difference was full employment as the basis of social welfare, even if it did not prevail in all countries and regions at all times and even if it was coupled with low wages. The right to employment was so much of an overriding principle in most of the communist countries that it was also given constitutional guarantee. For the purpose of realizing full employment, a wide array of social and economic policies were deployed, ranging from the allocation of labour to the establishment of a dense network of childcare facilities to encourage female employment. However, the major source of the high activity rate was the drive of individuals towards employment, because social benefits were closely linked to jobs in the public sector. Alternative social schemes (such as social assistance) were virtually non-existent, which already implied citizens being compelled to go out and work. In addition, those without a job were often criminalized. It is also worthy of note that in the so-called shortage economy all resources (labour among them) were scarce and the insatiable demand for labour made finding a job easier and put employees in a better position when negotiating with employers. Moreover, labour law ensured that dismissing an employee was not simple. The East German labour code of 1977 declared that the contract of employment could be terminated only by another contract, that is, with mutual agreement.[69] This arrangement obviously cost dearly because it hindered the efficient employment of labour: it was difficult to reallocate labour between efficient and less efficient branches and factories on the one hand, and to correct poor-quality work on the other. This system could be sustained in the long run only by protecting companies from competition and the consequences of underperformance through the system of a planned economy.

Although full employment was always a major consideration of communist countries in their economic policies, it was implemented in various ways at various times in different countries. After collectivization took place in some of the agricultural regions, labour surplus was the result. Also there existed a so-called latent or hidden unemployment, which meant that, in order to keep up economic indices and conform to administrative rules and regulations, companies also employed workers whom they could not actually supply with sufficient tasks at work.[70]

Social security was the next pillar of the communist welfare system. Considerable structural differences to Western European countries persisted until the fall of the communist regimes. In most Western countries, the state was playing an ever-greater role in the operation of the social security system after the Second World War. However, the complete nationalization of the welfare system in East Central Europe gave communist states a stronger influence in this field than any of the states of the West would have. Although there were organizational differences between the countries of the East Central European region, these left the inherent logic of the operation of the systems practically intact.

The main concern of the social welfare system was equality, although some of its institutions created new inequalities. Political merits were rewarded by premium pensions, access to higher-than-average quality health care services or holiday resorts. Occasionally, special rules applied to exceptionally straining or hazardous occupations. At the end of the 1980s, 4% of the East German population had access to special provisions. These benefits were available to top officials of the state apparatus, employees of the intelligence service (*Stasi*), and later, to policemen, firemen, prison guards and servicemen. Those in a few select white-collar occupations (engineers, doctors, veterinarians and scientists) had been given pension supplements from the 1950s onwards in the hope of preventing their emigration. Supplementary pensions were also granted to those who had been persecuted by the Nazis as well as to members of workers' voluntary paramilitary troops (*Kampfgruppen der Arbeiterklasse*), and writers, artists and directors of cooperatives were included in the scheme after 1986.[71] Even though other communist countries did not have such a sophisticated system of privileges, advantaged statuses in the welfare area existed in all of the states of the region.

Another major, although not invariably important, welfare institution was the subsidizing of some basic consumer goods and services, the declared objective of which seems to coincide with that of other tools of welfare policy: to keep up and even increase the purchasing power of wages and to level them off. However, the function of subsidizing was different from that of other welfare benefits, because not only was it designed for the implementation of some welfare policies, it also helped to sustain inefficient economic production. A number of research findings suggest that subsidies had little actual impact as far as social policy is concerned, primarily because they were more available for more affluent segments of the society than for those with an average income. Moreover, in some areas (e.g. health care), they resulted in the squandering of resources.[72] Nevertheless, subsidies put great strain on the budgets of communist countries, especially in East Germany, where funds spent on subsidies exceeded social security expenditures in the 1980s.[73]

Another distinct characteristic was the major role of workplaces and thus, the so-called fringe benefits in social policy. In Western European countries, welfare services provided by companies were not unknown, but in East Central European communist regimes, these benefits became more diverse and significant. In addition, there emerged a unique combination of classical factory-based social policy and of state social schemes implemented through companies. Depending on their size, factories and various other employers ran an assortment of kindergartens, surgeries, sports clubs, recreational centres and holiday resorts. Products in short supply were often distributed through the workplace as well; housing was a case in point, but the allocation range included the occasional potato and apple sale as well.

Determinants of welfare development: the logic of industrialism versus class alliances

As discussed above, in the nineteenth and twentieth centuries, some type of the welfare state did emerge in all the countries of Europe and later a robust expansion of welfare services occurred everywhere. Several explanations have been proposed in historical and social research as to why the welfare state caught on so universally. Others focused on the differences between the various types of the welfare state, that is, why the industrialized countries introduced public welfare schemes at different times and in various manners, and why they took deviating paths. The next section examines the major factors shaping welfare development.

The functionalist approach

The long-established functionalist approach attributes the emergence of the welfare state to socioeconomic changes, the 'logic of industrialism'.[74] The representatives of this school argue that the living conditions that industrialization resulted in called for the introduction of public welfare programs from the end of the nineteenth century onwards, and, in turn, the resources created by robust economic growth did enable their introduction. Social change in this respect refers primarily to the emergence of a working class with no properties and concentrated in large urban areas, but relevant changes included the separation of individual and family incomes, the loosening up of family and kinship ties; there occurred a growth in the ratio of the elderly population as well. Governments aimed for meeting the needs of those segments of society that became exposed to various risks because of these changes by launching welfare programs. Later in the course of the twentieth century, social deprivation became more moderate. Then, however, a demand for a well-trained, reliable and mobile labour force arose, which could be more easily met with the help of welfare measures. Opportunities presented by industrialization include, first of all, resources generated by economic growth as well as the centralization and professionalization of state bureaucracy, and hence its increasing efficiency. In addition, improving communication channels could be used by both state bureaucracy and by emerging social classes/groups organizing themselves politically.[75]

Some authors claim that effects of economic development are primarily mediated to welfare systems by demographic factors, because industrialization results in a decrease in mortality and fertility rates, whereas for an ageing population, welfare services are more in demand. It has also been proposed that program duration is positively correlated with coverage, because once created, welfare schemes tend to be inert and therefore are bound to become increasingly extensive.[76]

Obviously, there is a link between socioeconomic development and the welfare activities of governments. In the course of modernization, social problems emerged that public systems could provide remedies for and industrialized countries had more resources at their disposal to be allocated for these purposes. At the same time, we can plausibly refute arguments that directly attribute the emergence and development of the welfare state to social and economic transformations. There is no evidence that once modernization reaches a certain level, welfare programs inevitably do emerge and keep on expanding if the economy is prospering, and, in contrast, in times of economic recession, a need for the retrenchment of the welfare state necessarily presents itself.[77]

Empirical studies show that although between 1880 and 1914, social security acts had been passed in almost all the countries of Western Europe, these societies were at different levels of socioeconomic development at the time of legislation. Moreover, as Jens Alber and other scholars rightly point out, the first social security systems in the 1880s were not actually introduced in England (the most industrialized and urbanized country of the time), but in Austria and Germany, which were lagging behind it at the time.[78] The same applies to the expansion of social policy. The most dynamic growth in terms of welfare development in the interwar period took place in Scandinavia, a region that cannot be regarded as particularly developed at the time. Moreover, countries that were at the same developmental stage after the Second World War in economic terms allocated different percentages of their GDP for welfare purposes, and their welfare institutions also showed considerable differences.[79]

Finally, economic determination is also not plausible in the sense that mature and generous welfare systems would become a burden for economy in time, which would invariably create a need for restrictions and downsizing. It was not Scandinavia where the need for government-run welfare institutions was questioned most strongly in the 1980s after one hundred years of welfare expansion, but Great Britain, where social spending was already relatively low by that time.[80]

The conflict theory approach

Another characteristic line of interpretation, the conflict theory approach emphasizes the seminal role of political factors, arguing that collective political actors (labour movement, political parties and interest groups) played a decisive role in both the launch and the development of welfare schemes, because only political struggle can raise people's awareness of social problems, such as poverty or social insecurity. Moreover, social problems are resolved only if it is in the interest of a social group that effectively represents its interests vis-à-vis other groups. However, it is obvious that the outcome of this political struggle depends heavily on the prevailing balance of power, which was strongly altered during the late nineteenth and the twentieth centuries by the diffusion of the parliamentary system and the progress of enfranchisement. According to the (neo-)Marxist version of the same approach, workers' political and trade union activities enlivened, and it was exactly the organizations of the strengthened and more articulate working class and the social democratic movement in particular that managed to induce welfare development.[81]

Representatives of the pluralist wing of this approach argue that it is not only the working class that stands up for gaining social rights or defending existing ones but other classes too, as well as social groups that cannot even be labelled as classes, e.g. pensioners. Consequently, it was not only workers', but also conservative parties that greatly contributed to the expansion of the welfare state in the late nineteenth century and in the course of the twentieth, which is well illustrated by the momentous German pension reform implemented during Konrad Adenauer's chancellorship.

There is indeed plenty of evidence suggesting the importance of political factors in the emergence and development of the welfare state, and these factors cannot be constrained to the social democratic movement. The circumstances under which social security programs were introduced in various countries seem to rebut the existence of a direct cause-and-effect relationship between the demands of the labour movement and social legislation. On the one hand, it is a plausible argument again that such schemes were taking shape in countries at different levels of development regarding social democratic parties, workers' organizations and trade unions.[82] Moreover, the introduction of social security programs did not usually take place in response to the demands of the socialist workers' movement but often against a backdrop of their outright refusal.[83] For example, German social democrats opposed the enactment of Bismarckian social security laws, claiming that they were meant to arrest revolutionary tendencies (which they actually were).

Nevertheless, the link between the type of governance and early social security legislation is obvious. Autocratic, or, rather, semi-parliamentary systems (such as Germany, Austria, Denmark up until 1901, Finland and Sweden) introduced these schemes earlier than full-blown parliamentary democracies (such as France, Belgium, the Netherlands, Norway and Great Britain). The former group of countries set up about seven times as many compulsory insurance schemes in Western Europe by 1900 as the latter.[84] The political elites of these semi-parliamentary regimes aimed at strengthening their legitimacy by gaining stronger legitimacy through the introduction of welfare measures, which becomes explicit if we consider the fact that a high ratio of social security schemes had been established in these countries right before not entirely democratic and legitimate parliamentary elections.[85]

Subsequent developments do not supply more evidence for the leading role of any political movement in the evolvement of the welfare state either. Between the turn of the century and the First World War, it was democratic systems under a liberal rule that underwent the most dynamic growth in this respect. Between the two World Wars, the situation had changed again, with development being the most rapid when and where social democratic parties performed well at national elections.

Following the shifting conservative–liberal–social democratic leadership, in the post-war decades (up to the middle of the 1970s at least), no dominance of one political faction can be detected over the others in Western Europe.[86] In this period, social policy ceased to be a heavily disputed political-ideological issue and the extension of welfare services was supported by not only ruling social democratic parties but also conservative ones, as was the case, for example, in the Netherlands or France.[87] Furthermore, there are signs suggesting that the lasting rule of leftist parties thwarted the increase of welfare expenditures. On the other hand, the expansion of welfare programs was given a boost where left-oriented parties ruled in a most competitive political environment, taking turns at government with the Christian democrats.[88]

The emergence and the dynamics of social policy can be understood in full if the scope of study is not restricted to the role of working class and social democracy in this process, but the focus is broadened to include all the political forces and the interrelationships between them as well. According to Gøsta Esping-Andersen, a generous welfare state could emerge and persist only where, in addition to the working class, the middle classes (and the new middle class in particular) were also involved in the welfare system and thus became both its beneficiaries and supporters. The Scandinavian social democratic welfare regime is an epitome of this. The social security schemes designed separately for the middle classes in the conservative welfare systems of Germany, France or Austria were to earn the loyalty of the middle classes as well. In some cases, even the position of the rural classes influenced the development of the welfare state significantly. In Sweden, peasants turned into long-term advocates of the welfare state, because they were included in the welfare system at an unusually early stage, in the first decades of the twentieth century. In contrast, where the often delicate conditions of class coalition formation were lacking and only the segments with the lowest income were eligible for most of the benefits, like in Great Britain, the welfare system had weaker social support, and in the last decades of the twentieth century, the sustainability of the welfare state was fiercely questioned.[89]

Consequently, the weakness or strength of neither the social democratic nor the conservative political movement by itself is relevant to the emergence and development of the welfare state. However, different political movements had obviously different preferences how to structure the system. Whereas social democrats excelled in the extension of coverage towards universality, which often resulted in a lower standard of some benefits, conservative parties regarded employment as a basis for social rights and accordingly pressed for more differentiated welfare benefits.

Convincing as they may sound, interpretations focusing on political factors are still unable to give a full account of all major phenomena related to welfare development. One major criticism against them is that in most cases, there are economic and social transformations underlying political processes. For example, the fact that the layer of employees was on the rise throughout the twentieth century decisively contributed to the increase of the number of voters who had a vested interest in generous benefits provided by the welfare state. Moreover, there are welfare schemes that originate in decisions of political nature but, once they were established, their path of development was determined by social and economic factors. If, indeed, as a result of political decisions, a pension scheme fully covered the population, then, as the population grew older, pension spending was bound to expand.[90] Similarly, the introduction of unemployment benefits can be seen as the spin-off of political struggle, but once the scheme is introduced, rising unemployment generates increasing expenditures.[91]

Other factors

There are several further interpretations of the development of the welfare state, which do not rely on such consistent theoretical framework as the ones presented above, and thus, do not become real alternatives to them. The 'institutionalist' approach highlights the role of 'path dependency', the nation states and political elites as well as the rivalry between states. The concept of path dependency considers why already established systems persist and claims that social policy is highly determined by the existing institutional structure, or, in other words, consequences of decisions made in the past are difficult to evade. Others argue that the main prerequisite for the introduction of comprehensive welfare measures was that state organization became more centralized and bureaucratic with the rise of the nation state. Strong government bureaucracies could fulfil major organizational tasks that the introduction and operation of welfare systems involved with higher efficiency. For reasons of power politics, philanthropic or other considerations, the elite of such nation states could become the advocate of social reforms, which is a top-down approach to reforms. Rivalry between nation states also had a considerable impact on the development of welfare regimes and became the starting point of a diffusion process on an international scale.[92] It is striking how fast the Bismarckian welfare system caught on in other countries before the First World War; and the closer a country was situated to Germany, the more advanced welfare system she adopted, irrespective of how economically advanced the country in question was.[93]

Historical research has also been conducted on the importance of political ideologies and, in particular, of religious and moral commitments. It was observed a long time ago that the welfare systems of Catholic and Protestant countries showed marked dissimilarities.[94] Although systematic research is scarce in this field, some evidence shows that cultural values such as honesty as well as trust contributed to the establishment of the modern welfare state. The development and the wide social acceptance of the welfare state in Scandinavia, for example, have been linked to piety and the population's high level of trust in, and loyalty to, the state.[95]

In conclusion, there is no single theory providing a full explanation for the emergence and development of the welfare state; all the interpretations presented above add various aspects to the overall picture. The functionalist school focusing on socioeconomic development offers the most convincing explanation for the universality of the emergence and the expansion of the welfare state in Europe, whereas the variations in the welfare development of the individual countries are best accounted for by approaches focusing on political, institutional and cultural factors.[96] Which of these approaches is the most valuable depends on which aspects of the welfare state we intend to study; in particular, which historical period and which individual society is under investigation.

Trends in social welfare at the end of the century: crisis and retrenchment or marginal adjustment?

Criticism and performance

From the middle of the 1970s onwards, the welfare state received an increasing amount of criticism in Europe, and even its crisis was now a subject widely discussed. Criticism dwelt on basically four main areas.[97]

1. Proponents of (neo)liberal (or, in a somewhat different context, neoconservative) economic and social philosophy argued that the intervention of the state in the economy invariably results in a system greatly restricting the freedom of the individual. Compulsory insurance clashes with the right to freedom of choice of the individual, and high and progressive taxes infringe on property rights. Friedrich Hayek, a main representative of this approach, claims that the concept of social justice that the welfare state strives to achieve subverts the justice of the market, because it takes away the properties of the successful and wealthy as well as prolongs the dependency of the needy. Hayek also concludes that welfare benefits may be granted to the most disadvantaged people at most, but citizenship may not form the basis of any social right.[98]

This view questions a basic value choice underlying the welfare state, namely, that the alleviation of poverty and social inequalities can be justified even if it costs some degree of limitation on property rights. After the Second World War, several generations of both social and Christian democrats stood for a compromise between the principles of the market economy and social solidarity. Neoliberal ideals also conflict with the idea promoted by Thomas H. Marshall, according to which civil, political and social rights are all merely different generations of rights. Neither of them has priority over the others but rather each is reinforced by the other. In other words, social rights foster the exercise of both civil and political rights.[99] The fundamental differences in the above standpoints provide little opportunity for drawing closer to a consensus regarding the welfare state. This may at most take place through the understanding of all the social implications of the specific positions.

2. The discourse on the squandering and inefficient operation of the welfare state as well as on the so-called welfare crimes was in its prime in the 1970s and 1980s in Western Europe. It was also argued that in welfare systems of universal eligibility, citizens with no obvious need of benefits also acquired them. Neo-Marxists criticized the welfare state because, despite using up massive resources, it cannot either eliminate poverty or help people escape their underprivileged status. Moreover, according to criticism formulated by neoconservatives, the welfare state is responsible for the decline of traditional welfare institutions based on local communities and the family, making citizens heavily dependent upon the state.

The proliferation of welfare bureaucracy after the Second World War and the advantages taken of welfare systems are irrefutable facts. Cheating of the unemployment benefit system was shown in several countries, as well as contribution frauds by employers and trickery by health-care institutions when reporting their expenses.[100] However, public health insurance and pension funds insisted that their administrative and other operational costs are markedly lower than those of their private counterparts, often suggested as alternatives. An argument against the replacement of universalism with means test was that the running of systems based on means test incurs higher expenses, and they stigmatize people and discourage them from trying to find jobs because employment generally puts an end to eligibility. Moreover, they do not aim at preventing poverty from emerging but try to alleviate it retroactively, which costs more and might not even bring sufficient results. Finally, in systems based on means test, benefits often fail to reach those who are most in need, mostly because they do not have access to the necessary information. However, proponents of welfare programmes can primarily rely on some hard facts related to social stratification when searching for arguments: in countries with an extensive welfare system, the levels of poverty and social inequality are considerably lower than in countries where the welfare state is less robust.[101]

3. The most important criticisms in contemporary debates on social policy are the ones claiming that welfare measures have a negative impact on economic performance. After the decline of Keynesianism, these ideas advanced to mainstream status and discourse in economics became dominated by the neoclassical approach by the last decades of the twentieth century. Two of the potential burdens of welfare programs were especially accentuated. First, welfare benefits provide disincentives for labour. Secondly, taxes and contributions levied in order to cover the costs of social programs have negative impacts on savings, and thus, on the level of investments.

It seems to be obvious that in the case of generous unemployment benefits, it takes longer for unemployed people to find new jobs than they would in systems providing lower allowances. In addition, in countries where eligibility rules of sick benefits are more relaxed, absenteeism is more common, or early retirement decreases the activity rate.[102]

Furthermore, the taxes financing welfare benefits have repercussions on the economy: social security costs encourage the export of capital; public investments crowd out private investment; state pension funds decrease the savings of private individuals; high taxes decrease the supply of labour, and minimum wages and the protection of employees in general make the recruitment and employment of work force cumbersome; redistribution damages the self-regulatory mechanism of prices, etc.

In contrast, there are a similar number of arguments for the positive growth effect of welfare transfers. Welfare programs create considerable extra demand and thus have a macroeconomic stabilizing effect. High standard social benefits and the security of the workplace provide incentives for the workforce to take further training, which, in turn, increases productivity. Countries where public welfare is weak have higher social inequality and a higher crime rate. Or, for instance, not only has criminality a negative impact on investments, but it also generates high additional social costs.[103]

In order to weigh the individual factors, to map out how they are interrelated and to explore their impact on the broader political, social, and cultural environment, models loaded with theoretical preconditions and set perspectives are obviously not expedient. Instead, we argue that one could arrive at a more plausible evaluation if one carries out the comparative analysis of real-life systems. Although this task cannot be performed here, economic history still offers some lessons, nonetheless.

It is well shown in research that in the post-1950 decades, the most impressive economic growth in Western Europe took place in countries where welfare spending also grew at the highest rate (Austria, Finland, and Norway).[104] In contrast, the countries with the lowest rate of GDP growth were Great Britain and Switzerland, whose welfare expenditures increased in the smallest degree in the given period, and from the 1960s onwards, their public social spending accounted for a lower ratio than in the countries of robust economic growth.[105] Peter Lindert's most sophisticated empirical research on the experience of industrial countries in the last decades of the twentieth century could not present any evidence for the negative impact of the government's welfare involvement on economic growth either and suggests that social spending did not have any negative influence on the domestic product of OECD countries. On the contrary, between 1962 and 1981, expanding welfare transfers resulted in a higher rate of economic growth when controlling for other variables. It was only the last period examined, between 1978 and 1996, when any negative impact of welfare expenditures on economic growth can be pinpointed, but this proved to be insignificant.[106]

4. Finally, there are also external factors not related to the efficiency of the welfare state that may pose risks to financing social policy. The ones recurring in debates most frequently are demographic change and globalization.

As discussed in a previous chapter, birth rates reached a historical low in all of the European welfare states by the millennium. In 2000, the total fertility rate everywhere was below the replacement level, that is, the level necessary for the long-term reproduction of the population. At the same time, the life expectancy of the population has been and still is on the increase, and, as a consequence, the ratio of elderly citizens has increased. The ageing population obviously puts strain on the welfare systems, because pensions make up the biggest item on the list of expenditures, and the major part of healthcare budgets will also be allocated for providing for the elderly. Because most of the projections do not calculate any increase in fertility in the forthcoming decades, the process of ageing is unlikely to halt. This is regarded by many as the greatest single threat to the future sustainability of the European welfare states. Therefore, those who favoured the retrenchment of welfare schemes relied on the latter as a major argument.

However, the ageing process of the population in European countries has been less dynamic than it was often assumed in these debates. The trend is not unprecedented, either: there have already been periods in European history when the rate of the population's ageing equalled or even exceeded today's. If the whole of Europe is considered, the number of elderly people (above 65 years) grew continuously from 1960 onwards; however, the rate of growth was twice as high between 1960 and 1980 as between 1980 and 2000.[107] If the most advanced industrial countries are considered only, the difference between the ratio of elderly people within the total population in 1960 and at the millennium is even less significant.[108] On the basis of his estimates, Francis G. Castles refuted the argument that in industrialized societies the sustainability of extensive welfare schemes has been or will be thwarted in the near future by the ageing of the population, and he subsequently labelled this as a 'crisis myth'.[109]

Globalization and the unrelenting worldwide economic competition emerging in its wake have been regarded as the major threats to the European welfare system since the 1990s. At the economic level, globalization means the expansion of trading, financial and capital investment activities beyond national borders, which results in the welfare states being increasingly exposed to competition with countries with lower wages and lower social security costs. In the 1990s not only did South-East Asia become a competitor for Western European countries, so did the former communist countries. Employees' associations were concerned that governments would increase their competitiveness by sizing down social expenditures, and so the 'race to the bottom' would start, that is, governments would cut back welfare programmes in competition with each other in order to create a more accommodating environment for business. Although this scenario has not been realized, globalization had an undeniably serious effect on the operation of the European welfare states, as is shown below.

Retrenchment versus marginal adjustment

Alterations have been made to the welfare system in Western European countries since the 1970s, and some downsizing has also taken place in certain branches of welfare. One of the areas undergoing significant changes was the protection of the unemployed. Welfare states traditionally preferred 'passive' support to provide income maintenance in times of distress, which meant that cash benefits, such as unemployment benefits, were unconditional and were not accompanied by any other measures. However, from the 1990s, measures were increasingly taken in order to make people return to work as soon as possible by 'active' labour market policy. The new policy, often labelled as 'workfare' instead of welfare, strived to eliminate long-term unemployment by retraining, job counselling, placement in jobs, support given to employers providing the unemployed with job opportunities and an assortment of similar other tools. Active labour market policy and the creation of new jobs was the underlying idea of the 'Third Way' policy implemented by Labour in Britain in the 1990s and adopted by a number of other Western European social democratic parties. In addition to positive incentives, several countries introduced negative ones as well: strict conditions were set to eligibility for the unemployment benefit and there were instances of reducing its amount. Qualities of the labour market policy mostly depended on the type of the welfare system: coercive measures have been preferred by liberal systems (Great Britain and the USA), whereas Scandinavian countries put the emphasis on positive incentives.[110]

Furthermore, a slow increase in the share of the private financing and delivery of social welfare can be seen at the expense of the public sector. Services bought by citizens directly from the market (e.g. private pension schemes) as well as services sourced out by the state for private enterprises (such as old people's nursing and medical care) also come under this category. In countries like the Netherlands, Norway, Denmark, Sweden, Germany and the United Kingdom, insured individuals have had the opportunity to pay pension contributions into private alongside with public pension funds since the 1980s. However, this generally implied only a minor supplement to the state pension, like in the case of Sweden from 1998: those choosing this option could pay 2.5% out of their 18.5% contribution into private pension funds. The share of publicly financed services provided by the private sector rose more rapidly than that of privately financed services, but they were mostly restricted to minor programs. At the turn of the century, more than half of the homes for the rehabilitation of alcoholics in Sweden, children's homes in Norway and old people's nurseries in Germany were in private ownership.[111] However, privatization was not typical of all the countries and even changes in the most affected countries listed above were not profound. The private share of social expenditure in several countries is expected to grow as the private retirement schemes mature; however, by the middle of the 1990s, the private share of social expenditures was only 4.1% in Denmark and 6.9% in Sweden. In Western Europe, it was the Netherlands and the United Kingdom where the private share of services was the highest, at 16% and 16.8%, respectively.[112]

If we consider the whole of Western and Southern Europe, the ratio of means-tested social benefits also increased to some extent compared with those provided on the basis of citizenship. However, the moderate nature of this change is signalled by figures showing that the share of targeted benefits in total social expenditures increased from 9.2% to 9.8% between 1990 and 1997 in 14 Western and Southern European countries. Moreover, the trend toward selectivity was primarily typical of Great Britain and Ireland, both belonging to the liberal welfare regime, but in none of the other countries.

Therefore, these changes altogether can be regarded as marginal in relation to the totality of welfare programmes. Even the most basic inquiry can serve as a rebuttal of the views maintaining that reforms brought about the decline of the welfare state in Western and Southern Europe. Data for the last two decades of the twentieth century suggest that it was only Ireland's and the Netherlands' social expenditures (excluding education) that decreased in relation to the GDP of the respective counties, which was primarily caused by a fall in unemployment rather than the downsizing of the welfare state.[113] The 15 member states of the EU spent 3.4 percentage points more on public social programmes in the same period (Table 5.7). At the same time, national differences observed earlier still persisted, with Scandinavian countries spending most generously on social welfare and Southern European countries having a considerable increase in related expenditures.[114]

TABLE 5.7 Social expenditures in the OECD and EU countries, 1980–2001 (as a percentage of the GDP)

	1980	1985	1990	1995	2001
OECD–21	17.7	19.6	20.5	22.5	21.9
EU–15	20.6	22.9	23.4	25.6	24.0

Source: OECD, *Social Expenditure Database* (SOCX, www.oecd.org/els/social/expenditure, retrieved on 10 August 2008).

Looking beyond expenditures, we find that major welfare schemes remained intact in Western Europe and continued to operate with relatively small alterations in the 1990s and beyond. Moreover, new programs had been introduced and already existing ones were extended. In this period, for example, family benefits were substantially expanded in Germany as well as tax credits on dependent children. Popular and media response to the extensions of the welfare system was obviously weaker than to welfare downsizing; although the cutbacks of benefits triggered street protests, people were less likely to take the issue to the streets when benefits became more generous. A closer examination of the functioning of welfare systems reveals no radical changes either. Nonetheless, the liberal regimes on the one hand, and the social democratic-conservative models on the other, became even more detached from each other. This trend was triggered by neoliberal reforms being implemented primarily in countries where the liberal approach to welfare prevailed anyway.

The United Kingdom is a symptomatic case in this regard, where under the government of Margaret Thatcher (1979–90) anti-welfare sentiments were articulated by the government in a way unique in Europe. Requirements for eligibility for some welfare benefits became stricter and other reforms were implemented to this end. However, despite the radical rhetoric of the government, these changes did not bring about profound changes in the welfare system: the basic principles governing the National Health Service (NHS), and the institution of public health care prevailed, that is, comprehensive health care providing services for all citizens and financed by taxes remained intact. Furthermore, social expenditures increased from 24.1% to 27% of the GDP between 1978 and 1992.[115]

On the whole, amidst the public discourse on the 'crisis' and the retrenchment of the welfare state and despite the discontinuation of certain welfare benefits and the more restricted eligibility rules for others, in the last decades the welfare state has been institutionalized and consolidated in Western and Southern Europe and, with the exception of a few countries, welfare expenditures have continued to increase or have remained steady at a high level.

However, there have been changes in European societies in the last two or three decades that affected the welfare state in a negative way. First of all, the global economic environment underwent a radical transformation. Western European national economies became increasingly embedded in the world economy, where the other players usually have lower labour costs and all of them spend less on public welfare services. The challenge to remain competitive never ceases and Western European governments have to be adaptive, which affects welfare programmes as well. Moreover, major social and cultural changes have also taken place in Western Europe. The political basis of the welfare state weakened, as the previously almost unanimous social consensus about its legitimacy and necessity began to corrode from the 1970s. The welfare state, a method of taming capitalism, has been and is under attack primarily because of the erosion of those segments of the society that had a vested interest in maintaining welfare programs. The most important aspect here is the diminishing of the working class, but, at the same time, social structures also became more complex, and the pressure potential as well as the political influence of employees weakened because of the already indicated processes of globalization. Further social challenges originate from changing demographic and family patterns as well as lifestyles (which are discussed in other parts of the volume), which necessitate a better recognition of the contribution of households and families to welfare production. Finally, changes resulting from the shift of value orientations that demanded a new balance between individual and collective responsibilities also affect the welfare state.[116]

East Central Europe after the regime change

In the early 1990s, at the beginning of the 'triple' transformation in East Central Europe, observers formulated diverse scenarios regarding the possible future of the welfare systems of the region. Bob Deacon, a prominent expert on the social policy of the region, envisioned heterogeneous, divergent paths of development, implying that Hungary would opt for a liberal-capitalist, Poland for a post-communist-conservative-corporatist and Czechoslovakia for a social democratic welfare system.[117] However, most scholars, including G. Esping-Andersen, predicted the dominance of the liberal welfare regime in East Central Europe in the near future, taking two major factors into account.[118] On the one hand, they argued that international financial institutions (mainly the International Monetary Fund [IMF] and the World Bank) prefer a liberal welfare policy, which might have a strong impact on the course the transformation would take, particularly in countries with large foreign debts (Poland and Hungary). On the other hand, there was a line of political reasoning among experts, namely, that the 'most articulate and politically best-organized social forces' give preference to the liberal model.[119]

Inarguably, neoliberal approaches to transformation did surface during this period: Hungary between 1995 and 1998 as well as 2006 and 2009 is a good example here, when social expenditures decreased along with measures implemented replacing the universal schemes by means-tested ones and the complete or partial privatization of public programmes took place. The relative weakness of organized labour in the region facilitated the liberal transformation. However, opinion polls suggested that the majority of East Central Europeans had a preference for the fully-fledged European social model, which suggested that neoliberal reforms of the welfare system in the region would clash with the voters' will.[120] No wonder then that in the 1990s, eligibility for most of the social benefits remained and new programmes were even introduced, such as unemployment benefit and social assistance. Universal coverage continued to be the main principle underlying the East Central European welfare systems. Moreover, not even the partial neoliberal reforms turned out to be irreversible: from 1998 in Hungary and from 2005 onwards in Slovakia, the new governments restored universality in the schemes in which these had been abandoned.

This is not to say that individual East Central European countries did not show any difference in their social policies during the political and economic transformation

process. Poland combined an economic shock therapy with the incremental transformation of its welfare system, but the pension reform involving some major
changes to the system received relatively broad backing from the political elite
(unlike in Hungary).[121] In the Czech Republic, the liberal discourse on economic
issues prevailing in the first half of the 1990s went alongside a solid financial
support for social security. Here, the most radical reforms were made in the area of
health care: a system of several competing insurance companies had been set up,
preserving citizenship as the requirement for eligibility along with universal
coverage.[122] For most of the 1990s, Slovakia stood out, with an even slower speed
of changes, though after the millennium, this country implemented the most
radical liberal measures in the welfare system, which were partly revoked a few
years later.

However, external political players and analysts had to realize, either with
disillusionment (IMF, World Bank) or with contentment (EU), depending on their
ideals, that despite all the changes and differences, the rapid transformation of the
welfare system into a liberal one modelled upon the USA failed to take place in the
region. Although East Central European systems did not fulfil the liberal scenario,
they do not fit into any other models of the Esping-Andersen typology either.
Rather, they follow a hybrid welfare state model dominated by features of social
democratic and conservative welfare regimes.

6

WORK, LEISURE AND CONSUMPTION

Work is undoubtedly central to the human existence, but the meaning and the practice of work vary greatly among different cultures and epochs. Referring to some of the major directions of development, in early modern Europe the activity of work began to be associated with the human endeavour of intervening in nature with the aim of eventually conquering it. This tradition lived on into the second half of the twentieth century. In his classic work, Max Weber argued that the reformation facilitated the revaluation of work in European culture, even if this process had started to unfold in earlier centuries. This increasing appreciation of work gained a further impulse when seventeenth-century classical political economy explicitly connected the idea of work to the idea of value. Thus, work was more and more associated with those activities that were either salaried jobs or professions, or yielded some kind of income. Consequently, the status of work improved to a great extent in the modern age: work (more exactly paid work) became the basis of social recognition and political activities. However, the representatives of classic political economy, including Adam Smith, already emphasized the potentially negative effects of the division of labour, and Karl Marx elaborated on the alienation that the new capitalist production system created. The ambivalence of approaches to and attitudes towards work have persisted in the twentieth century as well.[1]

Not only work but consumption and leisure have, naturally, also existed in all societies throughout history. However, the identification and conceptualization of specific activities of consumption is a relatively new phenomenon. For a long time, the interest centred around production and exchange, and consumption was regarded 'unproblematic'. It was assumed that it is innate for people to consume and desire more and better goods. It was in the twentieth century that consumption began to be widely studied as a distinct aspect of human activity, first by the classics of sociology. This emerging interest was deeply rooted in changes taking place in the world of consumption. It is a relatively novel, twentieth-century development that consumption has evolved into a mass phenomenon, and acquired a major significance in the way societies function. Whereas the nineteenth century is generally interpreted as the period of the emerging society of work, the twentieth century is increasingly regarded by many as the period when consumption became the central pillar of economic, political and social life. The proliferation of material goods is merely one aspect of this process, because the changes in the structure of consumption and its quality (such as commercialization as well as homogenization on an international scale) and the growing influence of consumption on identity formation also represent substantial differences. In connection with these processes, the significance and meaning of free time available for people fundamentally transformed in the twentieth century, and new leisure habits appeared. This change is frequently described as the emergence of consumer society and mass culture.[2]

In the following, we outline the major trends of the twentieth-century history of work and consumption in Europe. First, we consider the transformations of the nature and social significance of work as well as the social relations involved in the production process, including industrial relations. Then, we outline changes in the material standard of living, which has long been a major theme of history, and especially of economic history. Discussing the standard of living allows us to study the evolution of the level and the structure of consumption, with special regard to such crucial aspects as the consumption of food and consumer durables, as well as housing conditions. Next, we discuss the qualitative aspects of consumption, which necessarily involves reviewing the development of mass consumption, including such processes as the expansion of mass production, the commercialization of consumption, and its convergences in Europe. Other topics to be addressed within this context are the changes in the size and role of leisure time in the life of individuals and society, the commercialization of leisure, and related to these phenomena, the expansion of mass culture (the latter also being highly relevant because it is often assessed as a detrimental tendency of the consumer society). Major recent controversies and critical positions concerning consumption and consumerism are also presented. Last, we deal with the evolution of the quality of life at the end of the twentieth century, which enables us to address not only the dividends but also the social costs of economic growth and consumption in contemporary Europe and attempts to establish novel concepts of well-being.

The world of work: Fordism and post-Fordism

Several aspects of the twentieth-century changes in the world of work have already been discussed in previous chapters. We studied sectoral changes, including the fall in the share of agricultural and industrial employment as well as self-employment, and the rise of services and gainful employment, which fundamentally transformed working conditions. The expansion of female employment and its structural changes also had profound effects, which were touched upon when we discussed family patterns. The dynamics of wages are examined later in the next chapter along with living standard. In this section, we focus on further changes affecting work and workers in Europe in the twentieth century, particularly wage labour, which became the most important form of work in the century. The major concerns are the changes in the nature and social significance of work, more specifically how people worked (labour conditions), how much time they allocated for work (working time, unemployment) and how employees and employers bargained collectively in the labour market (industrial relations, unionization).

Changes in the organization and nature of work

Advancing industrialization in the nineteenth century had a significant impact on working practices. It facilitated the diffusion of new values and patterns of behaviour related to work, which, for example, included regular and more disciplined work, the separation of work time and home time, the reduction of personal initiative on the job, as well as the acceptance of a permanent supervision over working activities. It also altered the forms of work organization, leading to the decline in work organized in or by the household economy, and the diffusion of wage labour. However, the new organizational forms of work had been still characteristic of only a smaller segment of labour in the early twentieth century, that is, the traditional family economy and larger enterprises based on wage labour existed in parallel even in the most industrialized countries.[3] Except for Great Britain and Belgium, agricultural employment dominated in Europe at the beginning of the twentieth century. The predominance of rural work yielded greater significance to the family economy, but family business played a fundamental role in small-scale industry and trade as well. The collective work of family members considerably increased the cohesion of the family, but also preserved hierarchical relations. Because family members did not enter the labour market, they provided their work without a wage or a salary. This type of work organization often predetermined the life perspectives of the young people, because it motivated them to continue on with the family business, which usually did not require formal training, the practice gained during work proving to be sufficient.

Nevertheless, the direction of development was straightforward in the first half of the century. Wage labour expanded further, whereas the weight of family work and the number of self-employed workers diminished. This can be specifically attributed to the falling share of agricultural workers among employees, but large numbers of small-scale industrial and commercial family businesses were also crowded out by big corporate companies.

From the middle of the century, the decline of the family economy and proportion of the self-employed accelerated in all Europe. On average, only 15% of the active population belonged to this group in the 1960s in Western Europe, and 25% in Southern Europe, the concrete ratio mostly depending on the relative weight of agriculture in the given national economy. The labour market was characterized by paid employment at the end of the century: around 85–95% of the economically active population in the most advanced countries belonged to the group of dependently employed. Still, in the last decades of the century the related changes were diffuse, because in most of the countries the number of self-employed continued to decrease, but in some cases there was a moderate return to this form. The reasons are studied later.

In due course of the regress of family businesses in the second half of the century, unpaid family labour practically disappeared. Whereas in the 1930s, 12% of the active population in England, and 16.4% of that in Germany, belonged to this group, by the end of the century the ratio declined to 0.4% and 1%, respectively. Similar processes went on in other societies of Western and, starting from a higher level, of Southern Europe.[4]

From a gender perspective, the advance of paid labour was an ambivalent process. On the one hand, it resulted in the emergence of the 'separate spheres' of husband and wife, in which paid labour was the domain of the male, whereas domesticity and care of the children were interpreted as being appropriate to the female character. The resulting 'male breadwinner model' took shape in the nineteenth century and advanced in most of the twentieth century in Europe. However, the advance of paid labour also swept women into the labour market. The share of women employed gainfully, as considered in chapter 3, began to rise considerably in the communist countries from the 1950s and a decade later in Western Europe, which began to erode this arrangement.

The diminution of unpaid family work enhanced the growth of productivity. Nonetheless, it also had several negative economic and social consequences. Family businesses lived in a symbiosis with larger organizations, and functioned as a kind of labour force buffer. During times of economic boom, many family members left the family business and started to work gainfully to take advantage of the higher incomes in the prospering corporate sector. And vice versa, during recession dismissed employees found refuge in the family economy, where the income level was lower, but provided a status more favourable than being unemployed. With the decline of the number of family businesses from the last decades of the twentieth century, this latter possibility had mostly ceased to exist, which, in turn, increased the pressure on state welfare programmes financing unemployment benefits.[5]

Nevertheless, the expansion of gainful employment in the twentieth century cannot overwrite the fact that other forms of labour still persisted. Among these the most important is domestic work, which is a labour-intensive and socially indispensable activity, having a strong gender dimension as well, because this work is mostly done by women. This type of work is rarely recognized equal to wage labour in the European, or generally, in industrial societies, which is shown by the fact that GDP calculations disregard those goods and services that were produced by domestic work, whereas they count into the GDP the ones that are purchased on the market.

Throughout the century, there have been major transformations in the nature of work and in working conditions. The dominance of agriculture at the turn of the nineteenth to twentieth century implied that work usually meant hard manual activity. In manufacturing, machinery and equipment had already appeared in many production processes; however, they were not applied everywhere and the operating of machinery had often been exhausting. Still, workshop administration and supervision in industry were mostly performed by foremen and skilled workers who carried out manual work themselves but also determined how the labour at the shop-floor level was to be organized, from which manual workers clearly benefitted. Because the owners and managers of the factories pursued productivity increase not only by installing more effective machinery but also by accelerating the pace of work, the so-called scientific management movement of the early twentieth century sought to rearrange the work and administration at the shop-floor level.

The emblematic figure of scientific management was the American Frederick W. Taylor, whose ideas and methods were quickly received all across Europe. Taylor published his first study in 1890. One of his main goals was a greater division of labour in the workplace, so as to break down the production process to simple tasks. The meticulous analysis and fragmentation of the individual tasks of workers were expected to allow the harmonization of movements in time and space (time-and-motion study), so that the productivity of work could considerably improve. This productivity level then became a standard for other workers as well. The organizing functions were to be removed from foremen and senior workers, and at the same time, full managerial authority of the workplace was to be achieved. The managerial control was to be based on the greater specialization of labour and the scientific analysis of the working process, providing managers with information necessary for decisions, such as hiring. Besides a more effective utilization of the working time, the greater division of labour required fewer skills from the employees and allowed managers to employ workers with lower wages. Taylor also believed that the new model would result in a more equal distribution of profits than the earlier system. As suggested, Taylor's influence was significant, although he also had several radical ideas that had never been implemented.

The scientific management movement reached its high peak with the introduction of the assembly line. It was first applied in the Chicago meat industry in the USA during the 1890s, but also relying on Taylor's ideas, Henry Ford created the first major assembly line system in the Detroit car factory in 1913. Ford's invention was quickly adopted by European manufacturers as well, by which managers tried to further accelerate the labour process. Just like their American counterparts, they organized the working process in a way that the workers did not need to make decisions, thus avoiding a loss of time during production. The movement of the conveyor belt itself dictated the pace of work, and the workers carried out a couple of repetitive motions.

Taylorism was fiercely criticized and resisted by workers, trade unions and even managers by the time it emerged. Critics maintained that it attempted to systematically erase skilled industrial work and the solidarity among employees and classified workers as quasimachines, disregarding the needs of employees and the social context of work. Later debate also revolved around the issue of whether Taylorism can be regarded as a historically specific movement, or, as Harry Braverman argued, whether it could be considered the essence and manifestation of the capitalist organization of work.[6] All in all, even if Taylor's ideas had not been wholly put into practice, Taylorism spread well beyond America and became a foundation of the Fordist model, which realized standardized mass production, and became the dominant mode of work organization in the twentieth century. Because scientific management intended to reorganize factories by giving full control over the working process to managers, it also facilitated the rise of managerial class, which was addressed in chapter 4.

After the Second World War, the accelerating sectoral shifts had considerable impact on the nature of work. The quick eclipse of agriculture, which equally took place in the Western as well as in the Southern and Eastern regions of the continent, and the expansion of services moderated the prevalence of hard physical labour to a great extent. Industry also underwent fast changes, contributing to the recess of manual work. However, within industrial work, the rigid division of labour was progressing further, including assembly line production, which became universal in the 1950s and 1960s. The advance of Fordism raised problems from multiple aspects. Not only did it generate the resistance of employees, but it also had economic limitations with regard to consumer demand. This system was suitable for mass production, as demonstrated early on by the increase of productivity in the case of the Model T, which was manufactured in a single colour and single type at the Ford factory. Notwithstanding, generating specific needs became an important means for creating additional consumer demand in the second half of the twentieth century, which could not be sufficiently met by the assembly line production. The proposed solution was 'flexible specialization', which required decentralization at the level of the workplace, and with respect to labour force, it demanded the deletion of the assembly line practice, the increase of flexibility in the labour force and thus its qualification, and often the introduction of team work. The resulting new system of production is often called post-Fordism.[7]

Post-Fordism appeared from the late 1960s, when in parallel to traditional, hierarchical workplaces, those forms of work organization also began to expand that put greater emphasis on the initiative of employees. The representatives of the work reform movement, which spread mostly in Sweden and Germany, claimed that it would serve both the humanization of work and the efficiency of production, if labour was organized so as to give autonomy to groups of workers in planning and performing tasks. Therefore, in companies adhering to the principles of flexible specialization the conveyor belt was dismissed. The demarcation lines between managers and workers were lessened and replaced by more flexible structures of management and production to enable short-term customized production and to guarantee job satisfaction. The Swedish Volvo factories in Kalmar and Uddevalla, opened in 1974 and 1989, respectively, merited the highest attention with their specific system designed to accommodate human-centred production based on work groups building whole cars. In these factories, the management tended to lengthen work cycles (which often took only a few moments in the car industry); thus, cycles could even amount to two hours. Therefore, it was symptomatic that these Volvo plants, often seen as a European alternative to Toyotism and lean production, operated only until the early 1990s.[8] Post-Fordist structures have stayed marginal in industry, because the acclaimed economic benefits have probably been exaggerated. Instead, post-Fordism remained one of the several new strategies in managing labour and satisfying consumer demands. Its elements were mostly adopted by service companies and such high-profile international giants as BMW, Nike and Adidas. As George Ritzer rightly noted, it was the explicitly Fordist practices of the fast-food chains that really characterized late twentieth-century advanced industrial (or post-industrial, for that matter) societies, rather than those of post-Fordism.[9]

Trade unions and industrial conflicts

The transformation of working practices, which brought about worsening conditions for many workers, was one of the several reasons why unionization gained momentum in most countries in Europe at the end of the nineteenth century and beginning of the twentieth century. This process had historical antecedents, because skilled workers, such as the representatives of professions like printers, cigar-makers and carpenters, organized trade unions in the very early phase of industrialization. During the nineteenth century, many unskilled workers joined the unions. In certain industrial branches (railways, mining, steel industry, engineering industry) peculiarly strong organizational power was achieved by the end of the century. However, trade unions still functioned under uncertain legal conditions in almost every country at that time. In classic liberal political doctrine, their activity was unacceptable, because they tended to limit market competition, forming a kind of labour force cartel by a joint operation of their members in order to improve their income status and conditions of work. Therefore, in many cases, they were treated as illegal, and were opposed by the state. Even if they could evade persecution, the lack of recognition hindered their operations, because they could not negotiate and enter into agreements.

Trade unions had already been usually linked to some political ideology or party in the nineteenth century, and this practice persisted later on. There were social democratic, Christian, liberal and communist trade unions, the influence of which was far from being equal. In Great Britain, the liberal trade unions founded on guild traditions were pushed to the background at the beginning of the twentieth century. However, just as in other European countries, they became marginal later on. After the *Rerum Novarum* (1891), Christian trade unions were established in several countries, and there were often Protestant and Catholic branches as well. From the turn of the century, the social democratic trade unions increasingly gained ground and began to overshadow other organizations. By 1910, every European country (except for Great Britain and Ireland) had fostered social democratic or socialist trade union movements. After 1917, the communist ideology also appeared in the trade union movement, but these types of movements lost their significance or were liquidated by force before the Second World War.

One can distinguish between four main phases or thresholds in the institutionalization of trade unions, which mainly took place during the twentieth century: (1) legitimization: the granting of the workers' right to establish trade unions by the employers and the state; (2) legalization: the recognition of the right to strike and other lawful collective actions; (3) representation: accepting the right of trade unions to enter collective bargaining, negotiate and make contracts on behalf of the members; and (4) integration: the involvement of trade unions into the formation of economic and social policy. These stages more or less followed each other but the development was not linear: rights that had been granted were often challenged and occasionally even withdrawn.[10]

In some countries (such as in Switzerland and the Netherlands), the establishment of trade unions had already been fully legalized after 1848. In others, legal recognition had only been partially realized, or agreements and laws regulated, which practically legalized the activity of trade unions as exemplified by the deal between the employers' association and the trade unions in Denmark (1899) or the British acts concerning liability in case of strikes or other collective action (1906, 1913). Thus, full legal recognition of trade unions usually took place in the late nineteenth and early twentieth century.[11]

The right to strike was of primary importance in supporting trade union pursuits, because without this legalized form of action, collective bargaining could not be continued efficiently, only in a form of 'collective begging'.[12] The road to recognize the right to strike proved to be winding and long, stretching into the twentieth century. Although industrial action belonged to the tactics of worker protest well before the establishment of trade unions, the 'organizational revolution' at the end of the nineteenth century clearly contributed to the massive strike waves sweeping through Europe. Around 1890 (that is, in the years of the turn of the century), industrial actions multiplied, which were often associated with political goals as well.

The First World War brought about a fundamental change in the status of trade unions in Europe. During the war, trade unions, similarly to social democratic parties, entered into agreements with governments. The trade unions supported war efforts with their own instruments (for example, renouncing strikes) and in exchange, they became the recognized partners of employers and governments, and they also acquired the right to bargain for wages and other working conditions on behalf of their membership in practically all belligerent countries, with the exception of Great Britain.

In the post-war revolutionary wave, the representatives of workers were included in some countries (Austria, Germany, and Czechoslovakia) in the monitoring of the implementation of collective agreements. In Germany, special courts were established to settle labour disputes, which had considerable worker representation as well. A further significant development in labour affairs was the establishment of the ILO in Geneva in 1919, affiliated to the League of Nations. The ILO made recommendations and advised governments to enhance working conditions with an emphasis on the harmonization of labour law and practice in the member states, and also defined trade unions as the legitimate representatives of employee interests.

The First World War and the following couple of years witnessed the rapid expansion of the trade union membership all over Europe. In many countries, the organizational level was unprecedented and in several cases has remained unmatched ever since (Table 6.1). The intense activity of the trade unions was also

TABLE 6.1 Trade union membership in European countries, 1913–1995 (% of gainfully employed)

	1913	1920	1925	1930	1935	1940	1946	1950	1955	1960	1965	1970	1975	1980	1985	1990	1995
United Kingdom	23.1	45.2	30.1	25.4	24.9	33.1	43.0	44.1	44.5	44.3	44.2	48.6	51.7	52.8	43.9	40.1	32.2
France							43.8	30.2	23.5	19.2	19.1	21.0	21.1	17.1	12.2	9.2	8.6
Netherlands	16.9	35.8	24.8	30.1	31.0	29.4	40.4	42.0	38.9	41.0	38.4	36.0	35.5	32.4	24.5	22.3	22.9
Belgium							25.1	40.2	45.6	40.7	40.0	42.3	53.3	51.2	51.5	53.9	55.7
Ireland							26.9	38.9	42.7	45.8	50.7	54.2	55.4	57.4	48.8	48.2	44.2
Germany/FRG	21.5	52.5	28.2	32.7			22.9	33.9	34.2	34.2	32.7	31.8	33.0	33.6	31.2	29.9	26.5
Austria		51.0	41.9	37.6			47.8	57.9	58.8	57.8	56.9	55.4	51.5	50.8	49.4	45.2	38.9
Switzerland		26.3	18.7	23.6	27.0	26.3	38.6	37.5	35.8	35.0	32.3	29.9	32.3	30.7	27.2	26.3	22.7
Sweden	9.4	27.7	28.7	36.1	40.9	54.0	63.1	67.3	69.2	70.7	65.4	66.6	73.2	78.2	81.5	82.4	87.5
Denmark	23.1	48.3	35.5	36.9	41.9	46.2		53.2	58.3	60.2	61.1	62.1	68.3	77.5	78.6	74.5	78.1
Norway	7.6	20.3	13.5	19.0	27.7	36.7	43.8	50.2	52.7	51.6	51.1	50.0	50.8	54.1	54.3	53.1	52.5
Finland							34.7	29.9	28.7	29.3	32.7	51.4	65.6	70.0	69.0	72.5	78.8
Italy								40.3	33.1	22.4	23.4	34.0	44.1	44.4	36.5	33.6	32.4
Spain													(31)	5.7	7.0	8.9	13.5

Notes: If not indicated otherwise, the table contains the net rate numbers, that is, the membership without the retired or unemployed members, at the per cent rate of earners; gross rate numbers, that is, the total number of members at the per cent rate of earners in the following countries: United Kingdom 1913–1940; Germany 1913–1940; Austria 1920–1930; Denmark 1913–1940; Norway 1920–1940; different years: France 1921, 1926, 1931, 1936; Germany 1947; Norway 1910; Spain 1977, 1981.

Sources: Bernhard Ebbinghaus and Jelle Visser, *Trade Unions in Western Europe since 1945*, London: Macmillan, 2000, 63 (Western Europe 1946–1995); Jelle Visser, *European Trade Unions in Figures*, Deventer and Boston: Kluwer, 1989, 21 (Austria 1920–1935), 41 (Denmark 1913–1940), 70 (France 1913–1940), 95 (Germany 1913–1930), 151 (Netherlands 1913–1940), 174 (Norway 1920–1955), 193 (Sweden 1913–1940), 219–220 (Switzerland 1920–1965); George Sayers Bain and Robert Price, *Profiles of Union Growth*, Oxford: Blackwell, 1980, 134 (Germany 1946), 158 (Norway 1910).

TABLE 6.2 Unemployment rate in European countries, 1920–2004 (%)

	1920–1928	1929–1938	1950–1959	1960–1972	1973–1979	1980–1987	1988–1999	2000–2004
United Kingdom	11.1	11.1	1.6	2.9	4.8	10.5	7.9	5.0
France				1.9	4.3	8.9	11.2	9.1
Netherlands	8.3	8.0	2.0	1.3	4.7	10.0	6.0	3.2
Belgium	3.4	8.0	6.9	2.3	5.8	11.2	8.8	7.3
Ireland			8.2	5.2	7.3	13.8	11.8	4.3
Germany/FRG	8.1	8.5	6.1	0.8	2.9	6.1	6.4	8.3
Austria		12.0	6.1	1.5	1.4	3.1	4.0	4.1
Switzerland	2.7	2.8	1.3	0.1	0.8	1.8	3.3	3.4
Sweden	11.5	5.3	2.2	1.4	1.6	2.3	6.9	5.5
Denmark	16.1	10.6	9.5	2.0	4.1	7.0	6.7	4.9
Norway	15.3	7.8	8.4	2.0	1.8	2.4	4.6	4.0
Finland		3.9		1.9	4.1	5.1	11.1	9.2
Italy				3.9	4.5	6.7	9.0	8.8
Spain				2.6	4.9	17.6	19.5	11.1
Poland	6.2						12.6	18.5
Czechoslovakia/Czech Republic							−/5.2	−/7.9
Slovakia							13.2	18.6
Hungary							7.0	5.8

Notes: The average of the given years; United Kingdom 1920–1928: Great Britain; because of the alterations of definitions, the comparability of data that pertain to the period before the Second World War is limited; different years: Belgium 1921–1928; Sweden 1925–1928; Switzerland 1950–1951; Poland 1927–1928, 1993–1999, 2000–2003; Czech Republic 1993–1999, 2000–2003; Slovakia 1994–1999, 2000–2003; Hungary 1989–1999, 2000–2003.

Sources: Nicholas Crafts, 'The Great Boom: 1950–73', in Max–Stephan Schulze, ed., *Western Europe: Economic and Social Change since 1945*, London: Longman, 1999, 49 (Germany, United Kingdom, Netherlands, Belgium, Austria, Switzerland, Sweden, Denmark, Finland, Norway 1929–1938); Barry Eichengreen, *The European Economy since 1945*, Princeton: Princeton University Press, 2004, 264 (Western Europe and Southern Europe 1960–2004); Brian R. Mitchell, *European Historical Statistics, 1750–1975*, London: Macmillan, 1980, 174 (Belgium 1921–1928, Denmark 1920–1928), 175 (Germany 1920–1928, Netherlands 1920–1928), 196 (Norway 1920–1928, Poland 1927–1928, Sweden 1925–1928, Switzerland 1926–1928, Great Britain 1920–1928), 177 (Austria 1950–1959, Belgium 1950–1959, Denmark 1950–1959), 178 (Germany 1950–1959, Ireland 1950–1959, Italy 1950–1959, Netherlands 1950–1959, Norway 1950–1959), 179 (Sweden 1950–1959, Switzerland 1950–1951, Great Britain 1950–1959); László Csaba, *A fölemelkedő Európa*, Budapest: Akadémiai Kiadó, 2006, 92 (East Central Europe 1989–2003).

signalled by frequent strikes (Table 6.3). However, these actions were often unsuccessful, which was preeminently exemplified by the greatest industrial action of the era, the General Strike of 1926 in Great Britain. The moderate successes of the trade unions then had an impact on the number of members as well, which considerably fell in the 1920s in most European countries.[13]

The political climate in the 1920s proved to be more and more unfavourable for the trade unions, which was reflected in the loss of some of their recently acquired rights. Again, many employers did not regard trade unions as legitimate negotiating partners in Western Europe, whereas in East Central Europe and Southern Europe even the very right of existence was often questioned. Thus, from the mid-1920s, trade unions were banned altogether in Italy and Portugal.

After the onset of the Great Depression, the high level of unemployment all across Europe further hindered the realization of the interests of employees. In those two countries where trade unions were the strongest after the war (Germany and Austria), autonomous trade unionism was eliminated in 1933 and in 1934, respectively. After Franco's succession to power, trade unions were also proscribed in Spain. In these countries (as well as in Italy and Portugal, as mentioned above), successor organizations were established on the basis of corporatist principles: besides the manual workers and the white-collar employees, the self-employed and the managers also became members of the same organizations, which emphasized their distance from former practice even by their names. For example, in Germany, the German Labour Front (DAF, *Deutsche Arbeitsfront*) did not deal with the representation of interests in the paradigmatic sense, because Nazi ideology denied the existence of distinct interests of social groups. Instead, it organized leisure activities, and sought to educate and mobilize its membership, swollen to 25 million people by 1942, to support the ambitions of the regime.

The trade union movement was more successful (at least temporarily) in France, where they managed to make the system of collective agreements recognized, and the compulsory arbitration of labour conflicts was introduced in 1936. This was enabled by the coordinated action of communist and other trade unions, striking and seizing factories, as well as the support of the newly elected socialist Prime Minister Léon Blum. However, the achievements evaporated after the fall of the Popular Front government headed by Blum, because the ensuing right-wing government led by Édouard Daladier repealed them, and the subsequently organized general strike protesting against this act failed as well.

The situation of trade unions was most favourable in Scandinavia in the 1930s. Heated labour disputes also surfaced in the early 1930s in Norway and Sweden, but after the electoral victories of the social democratic parties, the organization of employers and employees reached an agreement in 1935 and 1939, respectively, which regulated their relationship in the long run.[14]

After the Second World War, the trade unions regained their formerly lost rights in European democracies; moreover, they acquired new ones. The employers and their organizations were more prone to cooperation and agreements with the trade unions, and employee representatives were also inclined to compromise, even if there were significant differences in this respect among the various states.

Cooperation within the sphere of industrial relations was enhanced by the memory of the economic depression and mass unemployment of the 1930s, but the formidable tasks of post-war reconstruction were also motivating factors in many countries. At the same time, the economic prosperity of the 1950s and 1960s enabled the employers and employees to achieve significant improvement in both wages and profit, even in the short run. The governments often supported this cooperation as well because the relative stability of industrial relations and the calculable development of wages yielded benefits with respect to the whole national economy. The related governmental policies included the establishment of the legal framework of cooperation and the protection of sectoral collective agreements, as well as the provision of different services for social partners, such as statistics and mediation.

The wide-ranging recognition of trade union rights was also facilitated by full employment, which considerably improved the bargaining position of employees. The political representation of employees also became more effective: social democratic parties advanced to being fully recognized actors in the political arena, and in addition the other parties also counted on employees' votes. As shown in chapter 5, the principles of the welfare state became widely accepted, which further facilitated the assertion of trade union rights within the companies and at the national level. The concentration process in economy along with the growth in company size resulted in a decision-making mechanism of firms, which offered a more accommodating platform for the negotiations with the trade unions. The cooperative attitude of employees and unions was enhanced by the fact that the traditional industrial sectors with strong unionization and a history of class struggle were continually losing ground, and were replaced by service branches with lower organizational strength of employees.

Although the peak that was reached after the First World War could not be exceeded everywhere, in the immediate post-war years, the membership of trade unions increased over the pre-war level in Western Europe. Between 1950 and 1975, unionization was usually extended further, except for Switzerland and France. From the mid-1970s, the recruitment efforts of unions were less successful. The ratio of membership increased only in Denmark, Finland and Sweden; in other countries, it remained the same or declined (Table 6.1). In the 1990s, the organizational level of employees was highest in Sweden and Belgium within Western and Southern Europe, and lowest in France, Spain and Portugal.[15] As a characteristic of the membership structure, the ratio of the younger generation (between 25 and 30 years) fell considerably short of their proportion within the total employment; moreover, it showed a decreasing tendency in the last decades of the century. Similarly to immigrants and white-collar workers, women were under-represented as well, even if their proportion within the membership significantly increased in the twentieth century.

Trade union activity was relatively low in the services dominated by private companies (most of all, commerce and telecommunications), which advanced to an eminent position within the tertiary sector. In contrast, the level of organization was high among public services, traditional industrial sectors and transportation (Table 6.1).

The division within the labour movement (especially the polarization between the reformist and radical factions) did not cease to exist, even though it moderated in most of the countries after the Second World War. With respect to Western and Southern Europe, the social democratic unions had the highest membership. Exceptions included Austria and Germany, where the social democratic and Christian democratic organizations were united early, as well as the Netherlands, where the merger took place later on, while in Finland the communist and social democratic unions did the same. Peculiar conditions emerged in Italy and France as well, where the communist trade unions merged, and in Spain and Portugal, where the communist trade unions exercised considerable influence after the democratization. On the basis of membership, the Christian unions counted as the strongest in Belgium.[16]

Finally, an important post-war trend in Western and Southern Europe was the inclusion of bodies of employees into the decision-making processes of the companies and into the national socioeconomic policy making. The consultations with representatives of unions had old traditions in the workplaces of countries such as Great Britain, Ireland and Denmark, which in turn became the model for employee consultation and information rights in Scandinavia, Belgium and Italy. However, this form of industrial democracy was based on the voluntary agreement of trade unions and employers, and they did not provide participation for the trade unions in the decision-making process of companies. In this respect, it represented a considerable advance that in a few countries, the employees acquired stronger licences when state regulation prescribed the compulsory involvement of works councils (representing both unionized and non-unionized employees) into the decision-making of larger companies. The origin of this system can be traced back to post-First World War Austria and Germany, but in many countries, it was introduced only after the Second World War: the Netherlands, Switzerland, Austria, the Scandinavian countries, Belgium and much later Spain belonged to this group.[17] The system of worker codetermination (*Mitbestimmung*), granting the most extensive participation rights to employees, was established in Germany. Under the terms of the law passed in 1951 in the 'montan' industry (primarily coal mining and metallurgy), the employees had the right to send the same number of delegates into the supervisory boards of companies as the management and owners. In 1976, this regulation was extended to all industrial enterprises with more than 2000 employees. The rights of management were secured by the fact that the president of the supervisory board could not be elected against the will of the owners. The system became a model for industrial democracy in other European countries, but schemes with similar scope were only established in Scandinavia and in the case of publicly owned companies.

The representatives of employees not only acquired consultation rights in the workplaces, or participated in company decision-making, but in the post-war era, they also conducted collective bargaining at the industry level, and trade unions were involved in shaping economic and social policy. The types and depths of participation diverged in Europe, but some forms of democratic corporatism emerged in all Western European countries until the end of the 1960s, and in Spain and Portugal, only after democratization in later decades.

The expansion of rights had significant, however contradictory, impact on the operation of trade unions. Union leaders acquired insider information, enjoyed higher salaries, and gained political influence. On the one hand, this development yielded professionalization, which enhanced safeguarding the employees' interest.

On the other hand, from the grass-roots level, it appeared as bureaucratization and increased the gap between the leaders and the ordinary members, and thus, contributed to the dropout of members, which, in turn, hindered the successful activity of the organization.

The general trends outlined here had specific variations in individual societies. Therefore, the forms and intensity of labour disputes also differed, mainly depending on to what extent trade union movements were unified and had a propensity for radicalism, what kind of participation rights existed, and what role the state played in regulating industrial relations. With a view to labour conflicts and industrial relations in general, three main patterns can be distinguished in post-war Western and Southern Europe.[18]

First, the so-called conflict-oriented type was peculiarly characteristic of France, Italy, and after the democratic turn, Spain, Portugal and Greece. The relation of employees and capital owners was polarized in this type, and (especially at the level of companies) was the least regulated. The opposing sides (the traditionally anti-unionist and paternalistic employers and the often uncompromising trade unions) recognized each other only to a limited extent, and often questioned each other's legitimacy. Agreements were mostly arrived at as the results of conflicts, rather than of negotiations, and for solving conflicts the state often resorted to *ad hoc* interventions. Polarization was strengthened by the fact that in the Southern European countries as well as in France, trade unionism was fragmented and unions strongly competed with each other, especially trade unions with either communist or reformist affiliation. The competition urged the individual unions to appear as the real representative of workers' interests and to be prepared for industrial action. In the meantime, this behaviour reinforced the anti-unionist sentiments of the employers.

In the pluralist type, found in Great Britain and Ireland, the relationship of capital and labour was characterized by conflicts rather than partnership. The two sides were aware of their diverging interests, but nevertheless, during handling conflicts, they also respected certain rules, and they refrained from questioning the rights of the other. In the competition based on these principles, the sides were willing to accept even failure, at least for the time being. However, the trade unions and the representatives of employers were fragmented, which had the effect that every group tried to safeguard its interest, which in turn reduced the already moderate chance of crafting or maintaining comprehensive, sectoral or national compromises. This was further strengthened by the fact that the state usually stayed away from negotiations, and left the regulation of labour relations to market forces. Furthermore, deindustrialization started in Britain early, and declining branches including shipbuilding, coal mining and textile industry were eminently represented, which accommodated industrial conflicts.

In the corporatist type prevailing in Scandinavia, Belgium, the Netherlands, and Switzerland, the well-organized and united trade union movement faced employer representations of similar character. Both sides showed willingness to cooperate and the ability to find consensus. The realization of this was enhanced by the institutionalization of collective bargaining. During the negotiations of employer and employee organizations, the wider economic interests were also taken into consideration. Therefore, the state readily supported the consultations taking the form of tripartism. A kind of corporatist subtype was the system of social partnership characteristic of Germany and especially of Austria, where the cooperation between employer and employee organizations on the level of companies and economic sectors were complemented by a systematic and highly effective state participation.[19]

After the Second World War, a couple of strike waves could be discerned, which practically swept all over Western Europe. Such periods are the years directly after the war, the late 1960s and the early 1970s. All in all, the intensity of the strikes was considerably higher within the conflict-oriented and pluralist types than within the corporatist type. The differences among days lost because of labour disputes were high, as can clearly be seen from the comparison of one group of countries, including the United Kingdom, Ireland, France, and Italy, with another one, involving the Netherlands, Germany, Austria, and Switzerland. Moreover, from the late 1960s in Switzerland, and from the mid-1970s in Austria, employees had practically stopped relying on strikes as a method of enforcing interests (Table 6.3).

Soon after the communist takeover, the trade unions lost their independence in East Central Europe. In conformity with the vision of Vladimir I. Lenin, they played the role of the 'transmission belt', that is, they were expected to transmit the decisions of the communist party towards the workers. Unions literally became mass organizations, with membership density reaching 90% or even more. However, they could not claim autonomy and the right to represent the interests of the employees because, according to the official ideology, the accession of communist parties to power automatically brought about the realization of the interests of the working class in all aspects of social life. Accordingly, industrial actions were rare, because they would be interpreted as attempts to overthrow the political power of the working class. If labour disputes still emerged, usually because of conflicts at the shop-floor level, then they were generally suppressed by police forces. Thus, the trade unions (notwithstanding often harsh working conditions) did not stand for the representation of labour interest; rather, they became part of the power structure of the party state. Union leaders assumed their positions almost exclusively from opportunism, with a view to personal advantages: higher income, favourable working schedules, and, on higher political echelons, the same privileges that the party elite enjoyed. In some countries, the management of social security was also transferred to the trade unions, and their activity in the workplaces rarely went beyond the organization of political programmes and celebrations, or the distribution of holiday vouchers.

The tight political control of unions was loosened in Hungary and Poland from the late 1960s, but still, East Central European trade unions remained discredited among employees during the whole period of communism. The sole exception was the Polish Solidarity (*Solidarność*), which emerged in Gdańsk during the strikes initiated by the increase of food prices in September 1980. Leader of Solidarity Lech Wałęsa, a charismatic person, was originally an electrician in the

TABLE 6.3 Industrial conflicts in European countries, 1906–1988 (number of lost days annually per 1,000 employees)

	1906–1910	1921–1925	1926–1930	1931–1935	1936–1940	1951–1955	1956–1960	1961–1965	1966–1970	1971–1975	1976–1980	1981–1985	1986–1988
United Kingdom	352	1372	145	166	84	105	185	132	220	519	559	407	110
France	223	969	201	64		202	101	143	50	184	148	66	30
Netherlands	134	564	141	202	23	17	35	8	13	35	25	19	5
Belgium			378	255	96	194	372	66	150	205	207	40	47
Ireland	345	462	59	152	360	229	85	328	592	274	593	319	181
Germany/FRG		657	225	32		54	26	18	6	47	42	44	1
Austria		482	135	21		30	22	58	15	20	2	2	1
Switzerland			64	36	18	10	1	96	1	1	2	1	0
Sweden	1335	1154	597	741	189	89	7	4	36	75	232	39	114
Denmark	86	696	43	54	312	4	113	249	20	382	69	243	39
Norway	253	1564	752	1502	609	60	157	105	13	50	33	48	184
Finland	281	106	292	45		91	764	150	106	604	493	296	400
Italy	147				54	254	286	657	919	1054	904	492	166
Spain		246	158	894									441
Poland		315	111	149	195								
Czechoslovakia		465	152	83	95							366	16
Hungary			37	29	54								

Note: United Kingdom: Great Britain.

Source: Adapted from Hartmut Kaelble, 'Eine europäische Geschichte des Streiks?', in Jürgen Kocka, Hans-Jürgen Puhle and Klaus Tenfelde, eds., *Von der Arbeiterbewegung zum modernen Sozialstaat. Festschrift für Gerhard A. Ritter zum 65. Geburtstag*, München: KG Saur, 1994, 66.

Lenin shipyard. Under pressure from protests spreading across the country, the Polish government hesitantly acknowledged the trade union as a legal organization, whose membership rapidly rose to approximately 80% of the active population. Because of the specific conditions (especially the power monopoly of the communist party), not only did Solidarity safeguard labour interests on the shop floor, it was also transformed into a political organization. Although the government unwillingly made several concessions, still it finally resorted to violence. On 13 December 1981 martial law was imposed, banning Solidarity; many of its leaders were imprisoned. From this point on, the movement continued, illegally, for years, which increasingly strengthened its political character and turned it into a reservoir for the political opposition. Finally, Solidarity regained legality again in 1988. The movement was a key factor in the Polish regime change, but with the establishment of political pluralism, its cohesion faded, and its political significance started to erode.

Representations of workers' interest played a special role in Yugoslavia, where the League of Communists of Yugoslavia announced the realization of the so-called worker's self-management in 1950, while the country was seeking its own way of socialism. This meant that the employees formed labour representations in every company, elected their own leaders, and participated in the decision-making process of the company. The advocates of self-management (well beyond the borders of Yugoslavia as well) hoped that the workers would freely and actively utilize their rights, the alienation of work would cease to exist, and contrary to the Soviet-type development, social ownership could be realized. Although the introduction of self-management initially boosted the growth of the Yugoslav economy, the inherent weaknesses of the model soon became transparent. The concept relied on the vague idea of social property, which differed from both private and state property. Even though workers were officially declared as owners of the companies, the assets were possessed both by the workers and by the society as a whole. Thus, the workers enjoyed only severely restricted property rights, excluding the free disposal over the assets of the companies. Central economic planning and management provided limited space for the independence of companies. In the absence of market signals, the firms could not allocate resources effectively. With the elimination of central economic planning in the mid-1960s, the lack of these signals as an obstacle disappeared; however, the Communist Party retained its monopoly in decision-making concerning every important personnel matter, which impeded the workers' participation in the decision-making process.[20]

Changes in working time

The traditional objective of trade unions, apart from achieving higher wages, was the improvement of working conditions and the preservation of the workplaces. However, the last two proved to be difficult to attain, even though the rights of trade unions became widely institutionalized, as observed in the case of several post-war Western European countries. Not only did the owners and managers refuse to give up their authority in determining the process of production, the diverging interests of the trade union members were also difficult to harmonize in this respect. In addition, the unremitting technological change and the evolution of market demands also hindered the realization of trade union demands with regard to working conditions and the stability of jobs. Therefore, already by the beginning of the examined period, both trade unions and employees developed an instrumental approach towards work, and they primarily focused on wage demands and aimed at limiting working hours.

At the end of the nineteenth century, the majority of European blue-collar employees worked 10–12 hours a day, six days a week, and paid leave did not exist yet. The growth of productivity made it possible to reduce working time, but these two processes did not evolve in a parallel manner at all, because employers and the government generally resisted the curtailment of working hours. It was typically argued that less working time would decrease the competitiveness of the given company or country against other companies or national economies that applied longer hours, eventually resulting in bankruptcy; that is, in the end it would be detrimental for the workers as well. The demand for the eight-hour working day appeared in the mid-1880s in Western Europe.[21] The 'three eights' (that is, the equal share of work, recreation and rest within the day) were echoed as a major slogan in May Day marches of social democrats from 1890, and these demands were usually bolstered by strikes as well. In 1870, the working week was the shortest in Great Britain, but by the turn of the century, several European states caught up. Before the First World War, the average weekly working time in Western Europe decreased to less than 60 hours, except for a few countries.[22]

With respect to the eight-hour working day, the breakthrough took place only in the period after the First World War. It was first declared during the Russian revolution in October 1917. This example was then followed by Finland, Norway, Germany, Poland, Czechoslovakia and Austria. In France, the law universally guaranteeing the eight-hour working day and the six-day workweek was passed in April 1919, and within the same year, other Southern and Western European states introduced similar regulations. Already at its founding conference in 1919, the ILO, an organization already referred to in this chapter, also urged its member states to standardize the maximum length of the working day. Subsequently, the unification of the length of the working day and of working conditions in general remained one of the key activities of the ILO, so that worries about decreased competitiveness vis-à-vis other countries could not hinder the improvement of working conditions.[23]

Efforts in that direction were not fruitless. By 1929, the weekly working time was considerably lower than one and a half decades earlier, and a general process of standardization could also be observed in this decade. According to the available data, the weekly working time in manufacturing was between 46 and 48 hours everywhere in the Western and Southern European states. During the Second World War and in the post-war period, the length of the working day increased again temporarily, but with the end of the reconstruction phase the descending tendencies continued.

Apart from the reduction of the daily working time, the increase in the number of days off also contributed to the reduction of weekly working time. The demand for half of the day off on Saturdays first appeared in England at the end of the nineteenth century, then other countries followed suit. Among the arguments listed in its favour, the most significant was that with its introduction, mothers and housewives could accomplish the preparations for Sunday. As a result, the argument continued, the sanctity of Sunday could be preserved, and family members could also dedicate their free time wholly to each other, thus increasing the cohesion of working-class families. Half-free Saturdays appeared in practice after the First World War, and were widely extended in the 1930s. Its expansion occurred parallel to that of claims for two weekly days off (free Saturdays and Sundays), which was soon put into practice in France, where the government led by the Popular Front introduced the 40-hour working week in 1936. However, two years later the law was revoked; the next government argued that it would hinder the efforts of the armament programme. The five-day working week was realized in most Western European countries only decades later, from the 1960s. Therefore, it can be argued on the whole that in Western Europe, the characteristic length of the working week (naturally, with significant regional and sectoral variations) was six days during the period before the First World War and five and a half days until approximately the mid-century, whereas after 1960, the five-day working week became common.[24]

Before the First World War, paid holidays and paid days off were rare. Paid holiday existed only in public administration and in some white-collar professions, and was hardly available for blue-collar workers. After the war, the introduction and extension of paid days off became important issues for the employees and labour organizations as well. Paid vacations were implemented in the Soviet Union and several East Central European countries in the 1920s. The pressure of trade unions and the initiative of the ILO led to the gradual introduction of paid vacations and public holidays in Western European countries as well. For example, in 1936, issuing a yearly week of paid holiday was made obligatory in multiple industrial branches in Great Britain.[25] Although the lengthening of paid holidays remained gradual after the Second World War as well, as a result of its uninterrupted increase, the amount of time that could be spent outside the workplace grew considerably by the new millennium. This was also complemented by extending the number of public holidays. In the late nineteenth century, public holidays (apart from Sundays) were usually linked to traditional religious festivities. Many of these (primarily in Catholic countries) evolved into lay holidays as well, thus adding to the number of paid days off. At the end of the twentieth century, the average aggregate amount of paid days off and public holidays was 36 days per year in Western Europe.[26]

The decline of the daily and weekly working time, the multiplication of public holidays, as well as the extension of the length of paid leave, all combined, reduced yearly working time dramatically. At the end of the nineteenth century, employees in Western European countries realized an average of 2600–3100 working hours per year. The number was the lowest in Great Britain; however, in the first decade after the First World War, most of the countries also reached this level. This was the period when the decrease in yearly working hours was the most intensive across all Europe. Although at a more moderate pace, the trend continued after the war and the reconstruction period as well. Consequently, by the 1990s, the average yearly working hours amounted to approximately 1600 in Western and Southern Europe. The Netherlands had the lowest level, with employees spending 1352 hours at the workplace, whereas Spain represented the highest value, with an average of 1815 hours annually (Table 6.4). In this respect, Western Europe excels among the industrialized regions of the world.

The decline of the amount and significance of time spent working is even more perceptible if we consider that the total number of years devoted to work decreased as well during the twentieth century. As time spent in school was extended, employees entered the labour market significantly later, and with the diffusion of old-age pensions, employees retired earlier from work. At the same time, the average life expectancy increased considerably (see chapter 2). Therefore, at the end of the twentieth century, people spent a significantly smaller proportion of their lifetime at work than a hundred years before, as illustrated by the case of Great Britain. According to estimates, in the mid-nineteenth century, the average British male worker spent a total of 124,000 hours at work in his life; by 1981, this declined to 69,000 hours. This meant that, deducting sleep and other physiological necessities, only 20% of the disposable lifetime was spent at work, as opposed to the previous 50%.[27] All these shifts implied that the role of leisure and consumption vis-à-vis work as a social activity increased profoundly over the twentieth century, which is addressed later in this chapter.

Unemployment and atypical employment

After the First World War, as a consequence of demobilization, conversion to a peace economy, and economic disorganization, the rate of unemployment rose everywhere in Europe. The removal of the direct consequences of the war did not substantially ease the tension of the labour market either; it often did not even do so in the non-belligerent countries. Thus, unemployment remained a major problem in the whole interwar period in Europe (Table 6.2). The level of unemployment was also relatively high even during the boom years of the 1920s (1924–29). It amounted to 10–12% in Great Britain, Germany and Sweden, and to 16–17% in Denmark and Norway. Moreover, the absolute number of people without a job increased compared with the first half of the decade: based on estimates for all European countries, the number of unemployed rose from 3.5–4 million between 1921 and 1925 to 4.5–5 million between 1926 and 1929.[28] However, it must be added that contemporary unemployment statistics are not always reliable: even if there are data available, they contain information about only the unemployment of workers and employees who were unionized or insured. Nevertheless, it seems certain that the level of unemployment in the 1920s had already considerably

TABLE 6.4 The length of working time in certain European countries, 1870–2000 (average number of annual working hours)

	1870	1880	1890	1900	1913	1929	1938	1950	1960	1970	1980	1990	2000
United Kingdom	2755	2740	2669	2656	2656	2257	2200	2112	2134	1967	1758	1698	1653
France	3168	3165	3119	3115	2933	2198	1760	2045	2025	1906	1696	1558	1443
Netherlands	3274	3194	3105	3037	2942	2233	2281	2156	2002	1774	1569	1414	1352
Belgium	3483	3344	3177	3064	2841	2229	2196	2404	2289	1916	1736	1699	1547
Ireland	3108	3017	2869	2795	2690	2182	2171	2437	2320	2149	1954	1922	1686
Germany/FRG	3284	3223	3108	3056	2723	2128	2187	2372	2144	1887	1696	1566	1465
Austria								2100	2073	1930	1755	1683	1527
Switzerland	3195	3083	2925	2834	2704	2281	2085	2011	1937	1868	1707	1608	1568
Sweden	3436	3187	2937	2745	2745	2152	2131	2009	1878	1710	1503	1546	1623
Denmark	3434	3172	2933	2742	2731	2301	2203	2071	1929	1960	1693	1492	1473
Norway						2283		2040	1939	1784	1512	1432	1379
Finland						2123		2035	1994	1917	1756	1677	1637
Italy	3000	3008	3006	3014	2953	2153	2162	1951	2012	1891	1724	1674	1612
Spain	2968	2876	2787	2710	2601	2342	2030	2052	2042	2124	1968	1832	1815
Hungary											1930	1710	1795

Notes: The data of those employed in full working time; Belgium, Ireland, Netherlands, Switzerland, Italy, Spain 1913: extrapolation based on the data between 1870 and 1900; different years: Ireland 1913; FRG 1913; Norway 1930; Finland 1930; Spain 1973.

Sources: *Groningen Growth and Development Centre* (GGDC) and The Conference Board, Total Economy Database, August 2004, http://www.ggdc.net (Western Europe 1950–2000; Hungary 1980–2000); Michael Huberman and Chris Minns, "The times they are not changin': Days and hours of work in Old and New Worlds, 1870–2000', *Explorations in Economic History*, 44 (2007), 548 (Western Europe and Southern Europe 1870–1913, United Kingdom, France, Netherlands, Belgium, Ireland, Germany, Austria, Switzerland, Sweden, Denmark, Italy, Spain 1929); Angus Maddison, *Dynamic Forces in Capitalist Development: A Long–Run Comparative View*, Oxford: Oxford University Press, 1991, 270–271 (Norway 1930, Finland 1930).

exceeded that of the pre-war period.[29] The rate of unemployment was particularly high in the traditional branches of industry, such as the textile, leather, iron and steel industries, as well as shipbuilding and coal mining, where market opportunities were diminishing because of the increase in the capacities of countries where the process of industrialization had started later. The problem was aggravated by the fact that European agriculture was struggling with similar problems. The increase of productivity, and especially, transatlantic competition, meant that a growing pool of labour force became redundant in the agrarian sector, seeking employment in other sectors of the economy. In the Southern and Eastern regions of Europe, the rapid demographic growth resulted in similar pressures for the labour market.[30]

However, all these negative tendencies were dwarfed by the impact of the Great Depression. After 1929, the rate of unemployment showed an unprecedented growth year by year. In most of the countries, the nadir of the recession arrived in 1932. Contemporary statistics accounted for 15 million unemployed in Europe in that year. The situation was especially severe in Germany, where there were 1.4 million unemployed before the crisis. By 1931, this number reached 4.5 million, and, according to certain estimates, grew to 7–8 million by the winter of 1932–33. This figure by itself amounted to one-third of the total German workforce, but the number of those only partially employed was the same. The crisis had lesser effects on the British labour market, where the peak of unemployment was reached in 1932, when 17% of the total number of the workforce could not find work.[31] In the case of these two countries, the aftermath of the crisis and the tendencies of unemployment in the rest of the decade showed marked differences. In Germany, after the national socialist takeover, the number of unemployed decreased rapidly as a result of a successful anticyclical economic policy, and in 1938, it amounted to only 2%. Great Britain practised an economic orthodoxy without state intervention even at the height of recession, which undoubtedly contributed to the prolongation of the crisis and thereby to the slower decrease of unemployment. However, the British example was not exceptional. Belgium and the Netherlands had a similar protracted moderation in unemployment: in the last peace year, the unemployment rate in these countries was still 18.4% and 25%, respectively.[32]

With respect to unemployment, the period between 1950 and 1973 was unique in a historical perspective, because the number of people in search of a job was never so low in Europe either before or after these decades. Moreover, this achievement was outstanding in the international context as well, because the unemployment rate in the United States was significantly higher in the 1950s and 1960s, and among the industrialized countries, only Japan had similarly low levels. In some of the Western European countries, the rate of unemployment was low already during the early 1950s, whereas in other cases (for example, in the Federal Republic of Germany, which received and had to integrate a massive influx of refugees), this level appeared later, by the end of the 1950s. The most spectacular unemployment rates of the Western and Southern European region can be dated to the early 1960s, when unemployment was generally below 2%, and many countries practically reached full employment. Ireland, Italy and the United Kingdom were exceptions to this trend, with a slightly higher unemployment rate of 2–3% (Table 6.2).

In the aftermath of the 1973 oil crisis, the labour market situation changed fundamentally in Western Europe. The system of stable, decades-long employment and of secure career perspectives that characterized the previous period suddenly began to dissolve. Structural change in the economy accelerated, which required more frequent job changes, further education, and occasionally, changes of occupation. However, in this context, it was the growth of unemployment that became especially remarkable: between the early 1970s and 1979, the average rate increased from 2.5% to 5% in Western and Southern Europe, and remained at that level for some years. By 1985, the ratio of job seekers nearly doubled again, and it also maintained a rate of 8–10% in the remaining years of the century. The level of unemployment was particularly high in Spain and Finland in the 1990s. The latter country had an average 12.2% rate between 1996 and 1999, primarily caused by the collapse of the market in the Soviet Union, its main trade partner.[33] A relatively minor proportion of the population was unemployed in Austria, Switzerland, Belgium and Portugal. However, even the employees of these countries could not evade the deteriorating situation in the labour market in the late twentieth century. For example, even though unemployment in Austria was low in the mid-1980s, 16.4% of men, and 14.6% of women, experienced it for some time over the previous five years, and joblessness concentrated among unskilled and semiskilled workers.[34]

The structure of unemployment underwent considerable changes as well. The number of the unemployed no longer rose exclusively during the phases of economic stagnation or contraction, and it was consolidated at a permanently high level. As a result, the number of people permanently jobless, often for several years, also increased. In addition, the rate of entrant unemployment among young people grew as well. The structure of unemployment also showed gender and regional characteristics. Female unemployment usually increased faster than male in the final decades of the century, even though the gender gap was not dramatic, and in the United Kingdom, Finland and Ireland in 1995 relatively more men were jobless than women. Young women were highly overrepresented in Southern Europe and France; in Germany, besides women, unskilled workers and immigrant workers had the same problems, although the labour market perspectives for the rest of the population improved, resulting in the segmentation of the labour market.[35]

At the same time, by the end of the twentieth century, an unprecedented proportion of the European population was employed. This phenomenon persisted despite the fact that younger people stayed in school for longer, subsequently entered the labour market later, and in turn elder people left it earlier. The high participation rate can be explained by the marked increase in the activity rate of women, a process that compensated for the decrease of the same rate amongst men.

Besides the growth of unemployment, other characteristics of employment also changed significantly from the mid-1970s. One of the transformations is often described as the expansion of 'flexible employment'. In its most extended use, the term means that employers have more autonomy in determining when and what kind of work the employees should carry out, and that employment is terminated faster and with fewer costs for the employer. This is largely facilitated if employees are contracted for short and limited terms, which allow the management to dismiss the employees if they do not fulfil their expectations, instead of, for example, further training, or if a change in the volume of market orders for the company makes the dismissals necessary. The same goal is attained if tasks are outsourced to self-employed people. In this case, employers do not hire workers in the traditional way, based on individual contract; they rather sign a 'contract by assignment', which is less binding for the employer, because it is based on the civil code instead of the labour code. Thereby employers can legally avoid paying social security contributions, and the self-employed are not entitled to a series of rights and social benefits. Temporary or limited-contract jobs, outsourcing to self-employed coworkers and some similar types of work are difficult to categorize within the traditional framework or concepts of labour, and thus, are also called 'atypical employment'. These tendencies represent an increase of the rights of the employer contrary to those of the employees.

Atypical employment diffused from the 1970s, but, nonetheless, it has remained within relatively narrow bounds until the present day. In the early 1990s, the ratio of this category of employees generally remained under 10% in Western and Southern Europe. Therefore, the traditional forms of employment, providing more extensive rights to employees, still dominated the labour market at the turn of the millennium. However, Greece, Portugal and especially Spain proved to be exceptions to this tendency. In Spain, one-third of the employees belonged to the category of atypically employed in 1991.[36]

In the communist countries, as discussed in chapter 5, full employment was a cornerstone of economic and social policy. The programmes of communist parties included the promise of full employment even before their accession to power, and later on, the right to work was even incorporated in the constitutions of these countries. However, it was not the ideological claims that led to the achievement of full employment within a relatively short period in the East Central and South-Eastern European communist countries, but rather the characteristics of the economic system: central economic planning (except for Yugoslavia) created an insatiable demand for every type of resource, including the labour force. As a result of the 'shortage economy' (a term coined by János Kornai) it was not simply full employment that evolved but rather a chronic shortage of labour force.[37]

Low wages and often harsh working conditions prevailed, but full employment and central economic planning in general had a favourable impact on the bargaining position of workers: the security of jobs was high, and employees were made redundant only in the most exceptional cases. Nevertheless, the fall of communism and the transition to market economy evoked dramatic changes in the labour market, including a rapid formation of mass unemployment, practically from one year to another. The rate of unemployment increased to more than 10% in Poland,

Slovakia, Bulgaria and Romania. In several successor states of Yugoslavia, including Serbia, Bosnia-Herzegovina, and Macedonia, unemployment rates reached 20% or, in some cases, even more than 40%. The percentage of those without a job remained single-digit in Hungary, and especially in Czechoslovakia and Slovenia. The problem of unemployment was also aggravated by the fact that it persisted on a relatively high level in most of the post-communist countries in the 1990s, and even in the years after the turn of the millennium.

The 1990s witnessed a profound change in the patterns of employment in East Central Europe, a move from long-term (often even lifelong) employment patterns towards less secure jobs and atypical forms of work contracts. One major form of the evasion of labour law became self-employment in this region as well. At the millennium, the proportion of self-employed people had increased well above the EU15 average (11.3% in 2000) in Poland, with 33.5% in 2001, but it was also higher in Hungary, with 17.4% in 2001, and the Czech Republic, with 14.5% in 2000. In the EU comparable figures can be found only in Greece (32.4%) and Spain (18.2%).[38] Even though this category included not only persons in atypical employment, a significant share fell within the category of 'forced' self-employment, because the status is not voluntarily chosen, they do not possess the same rights as regular employees.[39] All in all, compared with social welfare, working conditions (security at work, conditions of labour contracts, health and safety, and those other conditions at work that improve the working environment) showed more pronounced differences between the practice of East Central European countries and Western European standards at the turn of the millennium.

The evolution of the standard of living: quantitative and structural changes

There are multiple ways to define the standard of living; nevertheless, the conceptualization necessarily includes material well-being, measuring the consumption of goods and services by individuals or social groups.[40] In the following discussion, first the living standard based on this narrow definition is considered (also referred to as 'material standard of living'),[41] focusing on two aspects of the concept: the level and the structure of consumption.

The level of consumption

Until recently, the primary indicator of the material standard of living has been the real wage.[42] In the nineteenth century, national statistical offices began to collect data on wage trends, and before long, on changes in the costs of living as well. By deflating wages with the costs of living, it was also possible to characterize the trends in the standard of living. Between 1908 and 1912, the British Board of Trade collected data on wages, prices and expenditures of worker households in several European countries, with the aim of comparing real wages. In the interwar period, the ILO conducted an even more comprehensive data collection project in the same field. Economic historians have more recently analysed wage trends as well to determine the past trajectories of the standard of living.[43] The most significant deficiency of these projects was that they included only a part of the national populations and were not comprehensive even within the segment of employees. Because the samples were not representative, they were hardly suitable for comparisons.

Thus, in the related studies, the most frequently used measure of the standard of living is the per capita level of one of the economic output indicators (usually of the GDP or the gross national product [GNP]). These indicators are primarily used for practical reasons. On the one hand, compared with other assessments of the standard of living, a more general consensus exists about GDP/GNP calculations. On the other hand, not independent from the previous fact, they can be regarded as one of the most available and internationally comparable macroeconomic indicators (Table 6.5).

If we wish to rely on GDP (or any other output measure) for examining the material standard of living, it is advisable to consider some factors that may lead to the distortion of the actual level of material well-being.

Economic output also includes capital formation or accumulation (investment and inventory/stock), which evidently decreases the share of output consumed. Although investments may have a positive impact on well-being in the future, it does not necessarily have one in the present. Even in the long run, the impact of investments on the living standard is not inevitably proportionate to their size, because of, for instance, the varying productivity of investments.

The change in the ratio of capital formation and consumption in some European countries between 1920 and 1980 is illustrated in Table 6.6. It seems apparent that capital formation rates in the interwar period hardly exceeded the level before the First World War; however, they grew significantly later on, especially in the 1950s and 1960s. Massive investments became the fundamental factor of modern industrial growth in particular and of economic growth in general.[44] The increase of capital accumulation rates entailed a parallel decline of consumption rates; as a long-term result, consumption grew more slowly than national product. Austria and Germany were exceptions to this trend in the interwar period, as well as, although to a lesser extent, Great Britain.[45]

The crowding-out effect of capital formation over consumption after the Second World War was particularly significant in the communist countries. Whereas in the first half of the twentieth century, capital formation in East Central and South-Eastern Europe was low in an international comparison, and reached approximately the same level as in Southern Europe, later on it developed a powerful impact on consumption trends because of its intensity and highly cyclical nature. The high level of accumulation was related to the priorities of macroeconomic policy, as well as to the low efficiency of the economic system. Decision makers of the first half of the 1950s subordinated consumption to economic growth everywhere in the region. Capital formation reached 20% of the national income or more during the first half of the 1950s, by which time several countries exceeded

TABLE 6.5 GDP per capita in European countries, 1890–2000 (1990 Geary-Khamis international dollar)

	1890	1900	1910	1913	1920	1929	1930	1939	1950	1960	1970	1973	1980	1989	1990	2000
United Kingdom	4009	4492	4611	4921	4548	5503	5441	6262	6939	8645	10767	12025	12931	16414	16430	19817
France	2376	2876	2965	3485	3227	4710	4532	4793	5271	7546	11664	13114	15106	17730	18093	20808
Netherlands	3323	3424	3789	4049	4220	5689	5603	5544	5996	8287	11967	13081	14705	16695	17262	21591
Belgium	3428	3731	4064	4220	3962	5054	4979	5150	5462	6952	10611	12170	14467	16744	17197	20742
Ireland	2225	2495	2736	2736	2533	2824	2897	3052	3453	4282	6199	6867	8541	10880	11818	22015
Germany/FRG	2539	3134	3527	3833	2986	4335	4049	5549	4281	8463	11933	13152	15370	18015	18685	
Austria	2443	2882	3290	3465	2412	3699	3586	4096	3706	6519	9747	11235	13759	16369	16905	20097
Switzerland	3182	3833	4331	4266	4314	6332	6246	6360	9064	12457	16904	18204	18779	20931	21482	22025
Sweden	2086	2561	2980	3096	2802	3869	3937	5029	6739	8688	12716	13494	14937	17593	17695	20321
Denmark	2523	3017	3705	3912	3992	5075	5341	5993	6943	8812	12686	13945	15227	18261	18452	23010
Norway	1777	1937	2256	2501	2780	3472	3712	4516	5463	7208	10033	11247	15129	18177	18466	24364
Finland	1381	1668	1906	2111	1846	2717	2666	3408	4253	6230	9577	11085	12949	16946	16866	20235
Italy	1667	1785	2332	2564	2587	3093	2918	3521	3502	5916	9719	10634	13149	15969	16313	18740
Spain	1624	1786	1895	2056	2177	2739	2620	1915	2189	3072	6319	7661	9203	11582	12055	15269
Poland	1284	1536	1690	1739		2117	1994	2182	2447	3215	4428	5340	5740	5684	5113	7215
Czechoslovakia	1505	1729	1991	2096	1933	3042	2926	2882	3501	5108	6466	7041	7982	8768	8513	8630
Hungary	1473	1682	2000	2098	1709	2476	2404	2838	2480	3649	5028	5596	6306	6903	6459	7138

Notes: Czechoslovakia 2000: Czech Republic and Slovakia together; different years: Ireland 1910, 1913, 1921; Czechoslovakia 1937; Poland 1938.

Sources: Angus Maddison, *Monitoring the World Economy, 1820–1992*, Paris: OECD, 1995, 194–195 (Germany 1890–1990), 198 (Ireland 1890–1900); Angus Maddison, *The World Economy: Historical Statistics*, Paris: OECD, 2003, 60–61 (United Kingdom, France, Netherlands, Belgium, Austria, Switzerland, Sweden, Denmark, Norway, Finland, Italy, 1890–1913), 62–63 (United Kingdom, France, Netherlands, Belgium, Austria, Switzerland, Sweden, Denmark, Norway, Finland, Italy 1920–1960), 64–65 (United Kingdom, France, Netherlands, Belgium, Austria, Switzerland, Sweden, Denmark, Norway, Finland, Italy 1970–2000), 67–69 (Ireland 1913–2000, Spain 1890–2000), 100–101 (Poland, Hungary 1890–2000, Czechoslovakia 1890–1990, Czech Republic and Slovakia together 2000).

TABLE 6.6 Utilization of national product in European countries, 1921–1980 (%)

	1921–1930	1931–1940	1951–1960	1961–1970	1971–1980
United Kingdom					
Private consumption	82.0	79.7	66.9	60.9	61
Public/government consumption	8.9	11.4	16.9	18.9	20
Capital formation	9.1	8.9	16.2	20.2	19
Netherlands					
Private consumption				59.6	59.1
Public/government consumption				14.1	17.2
Capital formation				25.1	21.2
Germany					
Private consumption	72.6	67.45	58.7	55.9	56.1
Public/government consumption	11.2	17.30	14.4	15.4	19.6
Capital formation	17.0	14.75	26.8	28.7	21.4
Austria					
Private consumption	76.1	81.9	63.0	58.6	55
Public/government consumption	9.5	12.9	13.2	13.9	17
Capital formation	14.4	5.2	23.8	27.6	29
Sweden					
Private consumption	76.7	73.3	61.9	57.5	53
Public/government consumption	8.0	9.2	16.8	18.9	26
Capital formation	15.3	17.6	21.4	23.5	21
Denmark					
Private consumption	80	79	68.6	62.9	56
Public/government consumption	9	9	12.5	16.7	24
Capital formation	12.2	15.0	18.9	20.4	22
Norway					
Private consumption	72	72.7	60.0	54.6	53
Public/government consumption	8	8.4	12.5	16.5	18
Capital formation	20	18.8	27.5	28.9	32
Italy					
Private consumption	78.5	73.5	68.2	64.0	64
Public/government consumption	5.6	9.4	12.0	13.3	15
Capital formation	15.9	17.1	19.8	22.7	22

Notes: Different years: United Kingdom 1921–1929, 1930–1939, 1950–1958; Germany 1925–1930, 1931–1938, 1950–1959, 1973–1980; Austria 1924–1930, 1931–1937; Sweden 1950–1959; Denmark 1920–1930, 1950–1959; Norway 1930–1939, 1950–1959; Italy 1950–1959.

Sources: A. S. Deaton, 'The Structure of Demand, 1920–1970', in Carlo M. Cipolla, ed., *The Fontana Economic History of Europe,* vol. 5, Glasgow: Fontana, 1976, 93–94 (United Kingdom, Germany 1950–1970, Austria, Sweden, Denmark, Norway, Italy 1920–1970); Peter Flora, ed., *State, Economy, and Society in Western Europe, 1815–1975,* vol. II, Frankfurt/M.: Campus, 1987, 415–416 (Germany 1925–1938); OECD, *Historical Statistics, 1960–1984,* Paris: OECD, 1986, 62 (Netherlands, Germany 1973–1980, Netherlands 1960–1980), 65 (Netherlands capital formation 1973–1980); Gerold Ambrosius and William G. Hubbard, *A Social and Economic History of Twentieth-Century Europe,* Cambridge, MA.: Harvard University Press, 1989, 244–245 (United Kingdom, Austria, Sweden, Denmark, Norway, Italy 1971–1980).

the Western European average. Rates in Poland, Hungary, Romania and Bulgaria were unusually high, provided the level of economic development of these countries is also taken into consideration. Later on, meeting consumer demand was also gradually integrated into the goals of economic policy; however, because of the low effectiveness of investments, it was possible to reach an acceptable growth rate only with high investment rates, in other words, at the expense of consumption. For the period between 1971 and 1978, in Hungary, accumulation represented 35.2% of the GDP, while in Poland it amounted to 34.7% of the national income, which was significantly higher than the average 25% in Western Europe.[46] Accumulation also materialized in the growth of stock. The latter tendency can be explained by the unreliability of supplier links, the subsequent build-up of inventory, and the increase in the stock of goods that were hard to sell.

Sharp fluctuations in investment levels had a similarly considerable effect on the ratio of consumption. In Poland, for example, investment grew by more than 20% in 1953, whereas in 1954, it fell substantially.[47] The level of consumption, therefore, was heavily biased by the decisions of the central economic management responsible for determining the size of investments: the relation being one of the most important characteristics of the history of consumption in communist countries.

Furthermore, after the Second World War, the structure of investment in the region also differed perceptibly from the pattern of the market economies. For example, the average share of residential investments for the period between 1976 and 1980 was 30.2% in the Netherlands and 29% in West Germany, whereas in Hungary, it amounted to a mere 16.8%.[48] The neglect of housing and other sectors of infrastructure, such as health and education, which were considered unproductive by the socialist economic doctrine, led to considerable and hardly compensable negative effects on the quality of life and growth prospects in the long run.

It would be no use to get involved in the details of national accounts, because we do not have detailed historical evidence to elaborate on the elements of the accounts in twentieth-century European societies. Thus, we only suggest that the level of consumption might also be influenced by foreign trade, or, more exactly, the balance of payment, which is the difference between the export and the import of goods and services (balance of trade). In case a national economy presents a negative balance of trade, the deficit usually has to be financed by resorting to foreign sources, so that the level of consumption may benefit from loans. Obviously, the opposite scenario is also possible, namely that because of export surplus, a specific share of goods produced will not be consumed domestically. Regarding the average of Western European countries included in our investigation, foreign trade produced a substantial deficit only in the decade after the First World War (2.3% of the GDP), whereas in the following decades, it was moderate, with an average 0.5% annual deficit, which did not have a considerable effect on consumption. Germany and Ireland represented the two extremes of the scale: the former stood out with a relatively significant positive balance of trade, whereas the latter was characterized by a continuous foreign trade deficit from the 1960s.

In East Central European countries, consumption and capital formation exceeded the GDP in several cases. In Poland and Hungary, in the 1950s and 1960s, the difference was small but increasing, whereas in the following decade, it soared. In Hungary, domestic consumption exceeded GDP to the highest degree in 1978: at current price, it was 9.1% higher than the GDP. The situation was similar in Poland. This also meant that these countries could maintain the desired level of consumption and accumulation only with increasing foreign indebtedness.[49] However, the higher price of loans and the increased level of indebtedness entirely disabled them to resort to further external sources from the beginning of the 1980s. Afterwards, paying off debts required a positive foreign trade balance, the effect of which on the standard of living was the direct opposite of the previous years, that is, it decreased domestic consumption and accumulation. Other countries in the region were less externally indebted, but Romania still introduced a particularly strict payment policy in the 1980s, paying off almost all foreign debts, which resulted in a dramatic decline in the standard of living.

If we go beyond the narrow definition of the material standard of living, a number of further factors can be considered, perhaps more importantly, the number of working hours required for a certain level of consumption at an individual and at a national level. It is obvious that the more hours the active population spends at work, the shorter the free time will be, although for many, the latter is regarded as equally significant, or even more attractive, as the additional consumption of goods. Because we examined the twentieth-century evolution of working hours earlier (Table 6.4), we merely emphasize here that even at the end of the twentieth century, substantial differences can be noted with regard to the length of the average working day in different European countries. Research on the quality of life analyses several further determinants. This broader concept is dealt with later in the chapter.

Table 6.5 shows how economic output multiplied in Europe during the twentieth century. In Western Europe, GDP per capita increased on average five-fold between 1913 and 1990, and growth was fastest during the two decades after 1950. Growth differentials were also substantial among European regions and national economies. Regarding the whole period, the economic output advanced fastest in Southern Europe, followed by Western Europe, whereas East Central Europe and the Balkans were left behind.

As a combined result of the factors considered above, the dynamics of the level of consumption are different from the evolution of economic growth in twentieth-century Europe. The increasing ratio of investment, particularly after the Second World War in the communist countries, resulted in a slower increase of consumption compared with the growth of economic output. Both the balance of trade and the balance of payment had a considerably lesser impact on the standard of living. At the same time, the number of actual working hours decreased significantly throughout the century. It is difficult to assess to what extent this development counterbalanced the increasing ratio of capital formation as far as the living standard is concerned, but it arguably amply compensated for it.

The structure of consumption

Not only did the level of consumption show a dynamic growth in the examined period, its structure also underwent transformation. One of the most significant changes affected the share of private and public consumption, and the latter also included the consumption of central and local governments. Private consumption in European countries amounted to approximately 75–80% of the GDP in the 1920s. Five decades later, it declined to 55–65% of the GDP in Western European countries. At the same time, public consumption of goods and services increased considerably, the average share amounting to 12.9% in the 1930s, 13% in the 1950s, 14.2% in the 1970s, and reaching 18.4% in the 1980s (Table 6.6).[50] The change was clearly connected to the broadening functions of the state, and especially, to the expansion of the welfare state, which is addressed in detail in chapter 5. During the twentieth century, a range of activities previously organized within the frames of private economy, such as education or health care, were relocated to the state sector, because they were expected to be managed more effectively by public institutions. Besides these reasons, the advance of public consumption can also be attributed to the increase in the demand for welfare services.

Despite the growing size of public consumption, private consumption dominated throughout the twentieth century, the structural changes of which plausibly reflect the improvement of the standard of living. In the long run, the most significant tendency was the decline of the proportion of expenditures on food, clothing and household appliances/furniture.[51] This also meant that the population's burden of basic necessities lessened, and thereby an opportunity arose for meeting more differentiated demands. The increase in the proportion of expenditures of transport and communication, as well as of leisure, education and culture are adequate indicators of this change. However, it is true that the costs of maintaining a home were constituting an increasing part of family budgets, and provided transport costs are also added, the resulting sum largely used up savings on food and clothing expenses (Tables 6.7 and 6.8).[52] If pensions and other welfare transfers are also taken into consideration after the Second World War, and especially, with the expansion of the welfare state from the 1960s, then the East Central European level of public consumption was not higher than the corresponding average in Western Europe. Considering in-kind social benefits, such as health care, recreation, or nursery schools, their ratio within consumption was nevertheless comparatively high in the East Central European region.

Food

With the exception of Norway, more than 40% of the average European household expenditure was spent on food, drinks and tobacco in the first half of the century. In Italy, the costs of these items even amounted to two-thirds of the household budgets in the first half of the 1920s. Although the relative proportion of food had already set about declining in the interwar period, the war curbed this tendency. In

TABLE 6.7 Structure of private consumption in European countries in the interwar period (% of total household expenditures)

United Kingdom	Food	Clothing	Housing	Non-durable goods	Durables	Services	
1921–1925	32.1	11.2	8.3	22.8	6.1	19.5	
1926–1930	30.6	10.9	9.1	22.4	6.6	20.4	
1931–1935	27.6	10.0	10.5	23.0	7.0	21.9	
1936–1938	26.5	9.9	10.4	23.7	7.6	21.9	

Netherlands	Food	Drink and tobacco	Clothing	Durables	Other
1922–1925	32.5	9.3	14.6	9.0	34.6
1926–1930	30.8	9.4	14.4	9.1	36.3
1931–1935	28.0	8.9	13.0	8.5	41.6
1936–1939	28.9	8.7	12.9	8.1	41.4

Sweden	Food	Clothing	Housing	Other
1926	32.1	10.6	13.1	43.2
1928	26.5	11.1	12.3	50.1

Norway	Food	Drink and tobacco	Clothing	Rent and fuel	Household goods	Other
1930	32.0	6.8	13.7	16.8	5.4	25.3
1935	32.5	6.4	13.2	17.5	6.0	24.4
1939	32.1	6.6	13.6	15.6	7.7	24.4

Italy	Food, drink and tobacco	Other non-durable goods	Durables	Services
1921–1925	65.9	16.9	1.4	15.8
1926–1930	63.2	16.4	1.7	18.7
1931–1935	58.9	14.0	1.8	25.3
1936–1940	55.6	16.9	2.3	25.2

Source: A. S. Deaton, 'The Structure of Demand, 1920–1970', in Carlo M. Cipolla, ed., *The Fontana Economic History of Europe*, vol. 5, Glasgow: Fontana, 1976, 104.

TABLE 6.8 Consumption structure in European countries, 1960–1990 (% of total private household expenditures)

	1960	1970	1980	1990
France				
Food	41	27	22	19
Housing, h. energy	11	9	17	20
Household app.	11	10	9	8
Transport and comm.	8	12	14	16
Health	9	10	13	10
Leisure	7	6	6	8
Germany				
Food	36	30	25	16
Housing, h. energy	15	18	22	19
Household app.	10	8	7	6
Transport and comm.	8	14	15	17
Health	4	3	3	14
Leisure	7	9	10	10
Austria				
Food	42	32	24	20
Housing, h. energy	9	11	16	18
Household app.	11	9	7	8
Transport and comm.	10	13	17	17
Health	4	3	4	5
Leisure	8	6	6	7
Sweden				
Food	37	30	25	21
Housing, h. energy	14	22	26	29
Household app.	10	7	7	6
Transport and comm.	14	14	14	17
Health	4	2	2	3
Leisure	7	9	10	9
Italy				
Food	50	38	31	20
Housing, h. energy	10	13	13	15
Household app.	7	6	8	10
Transport and comm.	10	11	13	12
Health	5	4	4	7
Leisure	7	7	7	9
Hungary				
Food	51	49	45	37
Housing, h. energy	7	7	8	9
Clothing	15	12	9	6
Household app.	7	8	8	7
Transport and comm.	4	6	8	11
Health	5	6	6	8
Leisure	8	10	12	16

Notes: Abbreviations: comm.: communication; household app.: household appliances; h. energy: household energy; Hungary: personal consumption, which includes both individual consumption and in-kind social benefits; Western Europe: consumption of private households; different years: 1963, 1971, 1981, 1991; United Kingdom: Great Britain; food: food, drink and tobacco; leisure, Hungary: education, culture, sport and recreation.

Sources: Sabine Haustein, 'Westeuropäische Annäherungen durch Konsum seit 1945', in Hartmut Kaelble and Jürgen Schriewer, ed., *Gesellschaften im Vergleich*, Frankfurt/M.: Peter Lang, 1999, 375–380 (Western Europe); *A lakosság jövedelme és fogyasztása, 1960–1979*, Budapest: KSH, 1981, 64–65 (Hungary 1960–1970); *A lakosság jövedelme és fogyasztása, 1970–1986*, Budapest: KSH, 1987, 72–73 (Hungary 1980); *A lakosság fogyasztása, 1970–1990*, Budapest: KSH, 1993, 24–25 (Hungary 1990).

the first years of peace, the share of the income spent on food, drink and tobacco remained high, and the Western European average still reached almost 40% at the beginning of the 1960s. However, this trend was followed by a rapid decline throughout the whole region, and by the end of the 1980s, the expenditure ratio of food, drink and tobacco was usually reduced to approximately 20%, whereas at the turn of the millennium, the average of the fifteen EU member states was 16.5%.[53]

Therefore, in the decades after the Second World War, the effects of Engel's Law (the higher the household income becomes, the less is spent on food in relative terms) became increasingly manifest in Western Europe. Still, the weight of food expenses was also influenced by consumer habits. In Ireland, for example, a large ratio of the family budget was traditionally spent on alcoholic beverages: in 1970, this figure was 12%, which was twice as high as the same figure for the countries that were next on the list (Finland and the United Kingdom).[54]

Furthermore, the relative reduction of food prices (originating from the increase of agricultural productivity and the fall of import prices) also contributed to this general downward trend to a great extent. The price of food products came to include a growing proportion of costs derived from non-agricultural activities. Urbanization meant that the distance between consumers and producers grew, which led to bigger trade and transportation costs. The increased level of food processing and packaging entailed added values produced by the industry. But for these tendencies, food products would have represented an even lower ratio in household expenditures.

With regard to the interwar period, the ratio of household expenditures on foodstuffs was greater in East Central Europe than the Western European average. However, it is also evident that the significance of food consumption, regarding the household budget, also diminished in this region. Similarly, clothing expenses declined, whereas the share of consumer durables and housing grew.

After the Second World War, incomes and price ratios were subject to a complete and centralized restructuring in the centrally planned economies, which also influenced the distribution of household expenditures to a great extent.[55] In the emerging new consumption structure, the high proportion of expenses on food and excise goods (such as tobacco, coffee and alcohol) is particularly conspicuous. Per capita food consumption started to grow significantly in the mid-1950s, and in the case of basic food products, such as flour, meat, eggs, and other essential victuals, it soon reached the Western European average. After the years of scarcity during post-war austerity and the forced industrialization of the early 1950s, the population undoubtedly regarded these achievements as significant. However, East Central European households still spent more than half of their budget on food in 1960, as opposed to the Western European average, which was 40% at that time. Even more importantly, although in the West, the share of food and excise goods among expenditures decreased substantially, the ratio generally did not lessen in East Central Europe during the next twenty years, as illustrated by Hungary, where it amounted to 44.9% even as late as 1980.[56]

Regarding food consumption in Europe, the most important change in the twentieth century was the disappearance of malnutrition.[57] Insufficient calorie intake was not uncommon even at the *fin-de-siècle*. Anthropometric studies indicate that during the First World War, only 36% of the soldiers drafted in Great Britain reached 167 cm in height and 59 kg in weight, which can principally be explained by malnutrition. During the interwar period, nutrition improved still, despite occasional mass unemployment. The average daily energy intake in Great Britain had reached 2500 kcal (10.5 MJ) by the 1930s; at this level, most vitamin and mineral substance deficiencies disappeared.[58] The Second World War had a negative impact on food supply, but contrary to the practice during the First World War, Great Britain, as well as Germany and most of the belligerent Western European countries, were largely successful in maintaining the level of consumption, at least regarding calorie intake. Although the range of available food products diminished, and meat or milk became scarce, the energy intake of British urban working class families during the first war years was only reduced to 2300 kcal, and, in 1944, supply improved significantly. This was realized by the introduction of rationing, which persisted in the aftermath of the war, and in the case of sugar and some other food products, it was not abolished until 1953–54.[59]

The second half of the century saw the continuation of structural transformations in food consumption: the proportion of bread and potato declined, whereas that of meat, milk and sugar increased. In addition, the range of food products significantly widened, and a notable rise in the share of processed and branded food took place as well. The ratio of packaged supermarket goods (the origin of which was often impossible to track down) gradually grew. Workplace canteens, school cafeterias and other restaurants also gained an increasing importance in food consumption. At the same time, at least in Western Europe, households gradually switched over to ready-made or pre-cooked lunches and dinners.

Thus, it can be plausibly argued that sometime in the post-Second World War decades, the principal public health problem was no longer malnutrition, but rather the excess intake of calories, sugar and animal fat. In Western Europe, the first reports about the negative effects of this type of a diet, such as obesity and caries in the case of children, and coronary artery diseases amongst adults, had already been released in the 1950s. The situation was worsened by the increased consumption of tobacco and alcohol. Whereas smoking caused public health problems everywhere, excess drinking affected primarily the societies of Northern and East Central Europe.

Nutrition improved primarily as a consequence of the increased productivity of agriculture, which, in turn, mainly originated from mechanization and the use of chemicals (fertilizers, herbicides and pesticides) as well as veterinary medicine. Apart from the environmental hazards (soil pollution, nitrification of the ground water, and pollution of natural waters), the extended use of chemicals also caused further problems, because chemical residues ended up in products consumed by the population. The methods of preservation and marketing used by food industry, aiming at long shelf life and an appealing appearance, frequently led to a decrease in the quality of products. At the end of the twentieth century, the genetic engineering of industrial plants appeared as another potential threat. As a result of these problems, by the end of the century, nutrition once more became a centre of public attention. A whole range of scientific projects dealt with the detection of substances that are harmful or, on the contrary, beneficial to health. Food scandals, as well as often conflicting reports about the optimal diet, became recurring media issues.

Clothing

The share of household income spent on clothing had already set about decreasing in the interwar period, and this tendency continued after the Second World War, particularly in the wealthiest European states. Nevertheless, the variation in the ratio of expenditure spent on clothing was significantly higher than in the case of food. After the Second World War, the difference of its percentage between countries at the lowest (8%) and the highest (18%) end of the continuum was more than double. This was partly because of climate conditions. Norway and Sweden, for example, belonged to the group with high expenditure. In post-war East Central Europe, the share of expenditures on clothing was also high, which was not the result of some peculiar East Central European consumer preference, but rather the consequence of the high price level of clothes. It is also remarkable that although the expenditure on clothing was declining in Western Europe, the extent of the decrease was not as substantial as the reduction of food expenditures, and even this shrinkage was caused mainly by the moderation of prices, enabled by the use of synthetic materials.[60] At the beginning of the 1990s, households in EU member states spent on average about 7% of their income on clothing.[61]

The function of clothing is not simply to protect our bodies; it also has a traditionally crucial role of expressing social position and even identity. Fashion augustly represents these differences. Georg Simmel argued that fashion and its changes are often attributed to the efforts of lower classes in imitating the upper classes. Simmel claims that when the style of the wealthy becomes widespread, the upper classes abandon it and begin to follow another trend, in order to perpetuate their distinctiveness. Fashion, thus, connects the groups and individuals that follow the trends of fashion, and excludes the ones that do not. In this manner, fashion engenders similarity and a sense of a loose solidarity within a group, without demanding major efforts from its members.

The messages signified by clothing, as well as the way it is conveyed, went through important modifications in the past centuries, and this evolution also continued in the twentieth century. In eighteenth-century Paris or London, the social status, and more specifically, the profession of people could be alluded to easily from the garments they were wearing, because dress codes followed strict rules. However, bourgeois culture and the spreading of individualism introduced new trends into clothing as well, which came to express not so much affiliation to a social group, but rather the uniqueness of the individual. During the twentieth century, individualism in clothing began to prevail more directly than earlier.

Although conventions did not disappear, they clearly weakened, and individual style was given an increasing role in the selection of clothes and accessories.[62] This transformation had already been perceivable in the first decades of the century. Social hierarchy still had a role in clothing because the style of clothes worn in public spaces, particularly their quality, showed the social status of the wearer; perhaps not their specific occupation any more, but certainly their social class or rank. However, by the end of the century, this process resulted in a situation in which most often it was no longer possible to identify social class based on clothes as definitely as some decades ago. The same is true not only for clothes but for other products and symbolic goods as well: because of their rapid diffusion, it was difficult to link them to specific social groups, especially in the case of young people.

Showing social status and affiliation does not simply mean showing off one's affluence. As a British sociologist argued, clothing gives hints about its wearer, on his or her position, on continuums between such binary oppositions as masculine–feminine, elitist–democrat, wealthy–poor, sexy–chaste, young–old. It also reveals information about the image one wishes to project. Clothing, as consumption in general, may help the identity formation of its wearer, which can be well illustrated by the diffusion of blue jeans. In the Western Europe of the 1960s, blue jeans denoted the wearer's relative poverty, because wealthy people did not buy them. Wearing jeans was also a political message, because it propagated egalitarianism as opposed to elitist behaviour.[63] Furthermore, jeans also had a different message in the communist countries, where they were not easily tolerated by politics in the 1960s. Obtaining a pair of jeans was difficult in that period, and thereby their price was high as well. In sum, their initial connotations were thus wealth, as well as a certain opposition to the official ideology.

Housing

The share of housing expenses in family budgets grew steadily in Western Europe in the course of the twentieth century. The main reason for this was that real-estate prices increased faster than the average price level. This can chiefly be attributed to the housing shortage, which was a permanent problem throughout Western Europe during the entire twentieth century, especially in economically prosperous regions. The limited supply in the housing market dates back to the industrial revolution, when, as a result of the acceleration of urbanization, the demand for flats in urban zones grew to such an extent that they were impossible to meet. In the twentieth century, most countries attempted to improve the housing situation with public involvement. Governments offered diverse financial incentives for housing construction projects. In the United Kingdom, for example, two-thirds of the 1.5 million dwellings constructed in the 1920s were built with public assistance. Governments also functioned as immediate commissioners, as in the case of the United Kingdom after the Second World War. Furthermore, other forms of public intervention were implemented in order to compensate for the failures of the housing market: rent fees were maximized, and a legal framework was devised for the establishment of construction cooperatives.[64]

In the 1920s, construction activity had already been substantially enhanced in several countries. In the Netherlands, the yearly ratio of newly built flats per one thousand inhabitants was 6.3 in the second half of the decade; in Finland, this figure amounted to 6.6, whereas in Italy, it represented only 0.7. In most countries, the Great Depression did not cause a decline in this respect either. After the Second World War, the home building initiative continued to grow. The amounts spent on housing construction often represented 6–7% of the GDP, and the yearly ratio of newly built flats per one thousand inhabitants reached 10 in several countries. The construction of flats showed a marked boost in the 1970s and 1980s as well.

Notwithstanding, these efforts only slowed down the increase in housing costs, even less so because the new homes were increasingly spacious. The growth of the expense ratio spent on housing or rent was particularly remarkable in the three decades after 1960, when it doubled in Austria, France, Finland and Sweden, and almost tripled in Denmark. Not only did dwellings become roomier, but because of the change in family structures, a growing number of people lived single as well. For this reason alone, the costs of housing and energy per household increased, and energy prices grew well above their average in the 1970s.

In contrast, in the communist countries, the prices of housing and household energy were set at a low level, even though a considerable shortage of dwellings prevailed. In addition to the growing housing stock during the century, the quality and the equipment of homes improved as well. Some aspects of quality, such as aesthetic features, are difficult to assess, whereas others are more concrete, such as changes in floor space, the availability of electricity, running water and a separate bathroom (Table 6.9). In the interwar period, the installation of electricity was a priority all over Europe, and in some countries, practically all buildings had electricity by the 1950s. In Sweden, 94% of all homes had electricity installed by the mid-century, 95% in Belgium, and 98% in Germany. At the same time, only 15% of homes had electricity in Greece; moreover, in Portugal and in the Balkan countries, only approximately 50% of the households had access to electricity even as late as the 1960s.

Houses and flats also became less crowded. Between 1939 and 1970, the number of occupants per room dropped from 1.9 to 0.9 in Austria, and Greece experienced a similarly positive tendency, which indicates that major improvement in housing conditions also took place in countries that were economically less advanced. The change was brought about not only by rising incomes but by the growing desire for intimacy and personal space by couples and other family members.

The increasing availability of running water and a separate bathroom also reflects the growing comfort level of homes. Plumbing construction had already intensified in the Netherlands and the United Kingdom in the first half of the twentieth century, and by the mid-century, the availability of running water reached a level of 80–90%. However, even in these societies, bathrooms became a standard feature in homes only in the post-war decades (Table 6.9).

TABLE 6.9 Housing standards in European countries, 1950–1990 (items available in % of total households)

	1950		1990	
	Running water	*Bathroom*	*Running water*	*Bathroom*
United Kingdom	81.4	62.4		99.5
France	58.4	10.4	99.7	92.4
Netherlands	89.6	26.8	100.0	94.4
Belgium	48.5	8.4	99.6	87.7
Austria	34.2	10.6	98.7	90.4
Sweden	90.0	61.0	100.0	
Denmark	63.7	39.6	97.5	90.0
Finland	25.2	24.8	95.3	87.7
Norway	65.3	16.2		95.8
Italy	35.9	10.7		
Hungary	23.5	16.0	83.6	74.7

Notes: Different years: United Kingdom 1951 (running water), France 1954, Netherlands 1956, 1989, Belgium 1947, 1991, Austria 1951, Sweden 1960, 1993, Denmark 1955, 1991, Italy 1951, Hungary 1960; United Kingdom 1951: Great Britain; Netherlands 1956 and Norway 1950: running water in house or outside; Denmark 1955: rural data regarding running water; Finland 1950: running water in house or outside, with saunas in separate buildings, urban data; Norway 1950: rural homes.

Sources: United Nations: *Annual Bulletin of Housing and Building Statistics for Europe. 1961,* Geneva: Economic Commission for Europe, 1962, 8–11 (Western Europe 1950, Hungary 1960); United Nations: *Annual Bulletin of Housing and Building Statistics for Europe and North America. 1996,* New York and Geneva: Economic Commission for Europe, 1997, 28–29 (Western Europe 1990); *Lakásstatisztikai Évkönyv,* Budapest: KSH, 1991, 158 (Hungary 1990).

At the beginning of the twentieth century, tenement flats provided by employers were an important type of housing, particularly in countries where industrial and agricultural wage work was dominant. This housing form was maintained throughout the twentieth century, but its significance diminished considerably already in the interwar period. The other types of private tenements also lost their importance, whereas state or communal tenement flats became increasingly widespread, and after the Second World War, in most countries, the number of homeowners grew substantially as well.[65] At the turn of the new millennium, an average of two-thirds of households owned their own homes in Western Europe, and only in the case of Germany did rented flats outnumber privately owned ones.[66] Throughout Western Europe, the housing security of tenants improved as well, because after the Second World War, a series of laws protecting tenants were passed, and contract termination conditions became more favourable for tenants. In the East Central European communist countries, a significant part of the urban housing stock was nationalized in the post-war period. However, as is discussed in relation to urbanization, after the fall of the communist regimes, tenants could buy the flats they lived in at a favourable, or even at a merely nominal, price.

Consumer durables

The category of consumer durables is heterogeneous, because it includes, for example, both radio sets and passenger cars, although the latter may cost several hundred times more than the former. Considering the consumption structure of Western European countries, the share of durables was continuously growing in the examined period, and considerable changes took place within this category. Furniture, carpets, heating and cooking units have always represented major expenditure items, although in more advanced designs, they are still purchased by contemporary households. However, the range of available consumer durables expanded to a great extent, and significant structural shifts can be observed as well. For instance, at the beginning of the examined period, automobiles rarely appeared on the expenditure list, whereas at the end of the same period, they became the most important single cost element. Other consumer durables, such as radio and television sets, refrigerators, washing machines and personal computers also appeared in this era. These products often diffused in societies following a specific pattern. Their introduction to the market was slow, but the expansion accelerated as people became acquainted with them, and as the relative price dropped as a result of mass production, until they approached the point of market saturation, when further expansion slowed down again. The length of this cycle varied depending on several factors, but it was mainly determined by the price of the particular item. It can be observed as well that with every new product, the time span between the beginning of the market introduction and the point of market saturation became shorter. In the case of telephone sets, this cycle lasted about seven decades, and in the case of radio sets, four to five decades, whereas television diffused in only two to three decades (Tables 6.10–6.12). Personal computers reached most European households in about ten to twenty years. Even less time was required for the spreading of DVD players and mobile phones.

The automobile and the television are frequently regarded as the two most important consumer durables introduced in the twentieth century, mainly because both had a substantial role in reshaping lifestyles and in raising demand for further goods and services. As previously indicated, the costs of purchasing and operating cars became a major item of the consumption structure by the end of the twentieth century, and television and products related to it had a fundamental influence on the flow of information as well as on leisure. Because reliable data are available regarding their diffusion since their appearance, we can observe how these two types of goods spread in European societies (Tables 6.12 and 6.13). The automobile had already appeared in Europe before the First World War, but in 1914, its ownership ratio to a thousand inhabitants was only 3 in France and Great Britain. In the 1920s, the car fleet multiplied by four or even five and the economic crisis merely slowed down its expansion, but did not stop it. France and Great Britain were the leaders in introducing automobiles in Europe, and they retained their position in the entire interwar period, but Germany and Scandinavian countries also caught up with the lead. The mass expansion of the passenger car came after

TABLE 6.10 Number of telephone sets in European countries, 1910–1990 (number of sets/1000 inhabitants)

	1910	1920	1930	1940	1950	1960	1970	1980	1990
United Kingdom	16	22	41	67	102	149	251	477	434
France	7	12	26	39	56	91	172	459	482
Netherlands	4	22	36	52	69	132	260	581	462
Belgium	9	8	32	51	76	119	211	369	546
Ireland				15	25	52	104	187	297
Germany/FRG	20	29	50	53	43	104	225	464	671
Austria	6	19	22	42	56	93	193	401	589
Switzerland	17	36	68	110	184	298	482	727	905
Sweden	24	65	83	134	215	339	557	796	681
Denmark	4	80	98	117	154	224	342	641	972
Norway	20	49	68	83	135	195	294	460	502
Finland	13	7	34	50	78	137	257	496	530
Italy	3	3	10	15	24	68	174	337	555
Poland	1	3	6		9	30	57	95	
Czechoslovakia		6	11		31	74	138	206	
Hungary	4	6	12	19	13	48	80	118	178
Bulgaria	1	1	3	4	8		56	141	

Notes: United Kingdom, France, Netherlands, Sweden, Finland, Norway 1990: main lines; different years: Western Europe and Hungary 1929, 1969, 1949; Poland, Czechoslovakia, Bulgaria 1921.

Sources: Wolfram Fischer, ed., *Handbuch der europäischen Wirtschafts– und Sozialgeschichte*, Stuttgart: Klett–Cotta, 1987, Bd. 6, 150 (1920–1970); United Nations: *Statistical Yearbook 1990/1991*, New York: United Nations, 1993, 721 (1980–1990); Hartmut Kaelble, 'Europäische Besonderheiten des Massenkonsums', in Hannes Siegrist, Hartmut Kaelble and Jürgen Kocka, eds., *Europäische Konsumgeschichte*, Frankfurt/M.: Campus, 1996, 199 (Western Europe and Hungary 1914).

the Second World War, when real wages grew significantly, and the relative price of cars decreased as a result of mass production. By the 1970s, several countries already had one car per household, and by the 1980s, except for Ireland, all Western European countries reached this level. From this moment on, the pace of the expansion moderated, but it has never ceased.

The spread of television, and previously, of radio, was unique in the sense that the operation of the device largely depended on the development of broadcasting. The first television programmes, as discussed later, had already been broadcast before the Second World War in Great Britain and Germany, but the war interrupted the diffusion. Soon after the war, programmes were relaunched in Great Britain, and by 1950, the number of television sets to one hundred British inhabitants was one, reaching 10 by 1955. In several Western European countries, regular broadcast was launched in the early 1950, and in the second half of the decade televiewing spread rapidly. In Sweden, for example, the ratio of available television sets to one thousand inhabitants was one in 1955; however, in 1960, this figure increased to 156. A few years later, other countries also followed suit, and by the mid-1970s almost all households had a television set in Western Europe (Tables 6.12 and 6.13).

TABLE 6.11 Number of radio sets in European countries, 1930–1970 (sets/1,000 inhabitants)

	1930	1940	1950	1960	1970
United Kingdom	81	182	244	289	338
France	33	114	165	241	313
Netherlands	54	129	195	272	247
Belgium	74	135	179	289	352
Germany/FRG	50	172	180	287	324
Austria	76	101	190	279	290
Switzerland	26	131	221	270	295
Ireland	9	51	100	174	200
Sweden	78	196	307	367	366
Denmark	96	178	283	332	307
Norway	30	125	241	285	307
Finland	31	81	180	276	388
Italy	5	23	68	162	219
Hungary	35	46	66	222	245

Notes: Italy 1940: number of licenses: one license may apply to several sets; different years: United Kingdom 1931; France 1933, 1968; Netherlands 1968; Belgium 1934; Ireland 1971; Austria 1933, 1971; Sweden 1969; Italy 1931, 1971; Hungary 1938, 1979.

Sources: Göran Therborn, *European Modernity and Beyond,* London: Sage, 1996, 141 (Western Europe 1938–1960); own calculations based on Brian R. Mitchell, *European Historical Statistics, 1750–1975,* London: Macmillan, 1980, 700 (France 1933, 1968; Belgium 1934, 1970; Austria 1933, 1971; Denmark 1930, 1970; Finland 1930, 1970), 701 (Ireland 1930, 1970; Germany 1930, 1970; Italy 1931, 1971), 702 (Netherlands 1930, 1968; Norway 1930, 1970), 703 (United Kingdom 1931, 1970; Sweden 1930, 1969; Switzerland 1930, 1970); Rudolf Andorka and István Harcsa, *Modernization in Hungary in the Long and Short Run Measured by Social Indicators,* Budapest: University of Economics, 1988, 265 (Hungary 1925–1975).

The age of mass consumption: the democratization of luxury?

Qualitative aspects of consumption

The increase in the material standard of living and its structural changes were crucial elements of the evolution of consumption in the twentieth century. However, in addition to these aspects, we need to consider qualitative factors as well, which are connected primarily to the availability of adequate choices for consumers.[67] John Brewer considers the availability of a wide range of consumer choices as one of the crucial factors in the formation of consumer societies, not only in the case of goods that are of vital importance but also regarding goods that fulfil 'desires' instead of rational 'needs'.[68] Consumer choice is guaranteed if goods produced in the diverse parts of the world are easily available, and if consumers can make their own choices among these goods. Because people also shop abroad (principally, buying services as tourists), free travel and currency convertibility are also required for complete consumer autonomy.

In Western European countries, quality requirements of consumption were met at a high level already in the interwar period. Nevertheless, the First World War and the following years saw the introduction of passports, and travel became more

TABLE 6.12 Number of television sets in European countries, 1950–1990 (sets/1000 inhabitants)

	1950	1960	1970	1980	1990
United Kingdom	11	211	293	404	434
France		41	201	279	402
Netherlands		69	223	296	485
Belgium		68	216	298	447
Ireland		17	172	241	271
FRG		83	272	337	506
Austria		27	192	296	328
Switzerland		24	203	361	406
Sweden		156	312	381	471
Denmark		119	266	362	528
Norway		13	220	292	423
Finland		21	221	322	488
Italy		43	181	234	423
Hungary		10	171	258	409

Notes: 1980: number of licenses (number of sets in Western European countries may be significantly higher), except for the United Kingdom and Switzerland (here: number of sets); different years: Western Europe 1989; France 1969; Netherlands 1969; Ireland 1982.

Sources: A. S. Deaton, 'The Structure of Demand in Europe, 1920–1970', in Carlo M. Cipolla, ed., *The Fontana Economic History of Europe: The Twentieth Century*, Part One, Glasgow: Fontana, 1976, 125 (Western Europe 1950–1970); Eurostat: *Basic Statistics of the Community*, Luxembourg: Eurostat, 1992, 295 (Western Europe 1989); Rudolf Andorka and István Harcsa, *Modernization in Hungary in the Long and Short Run Measured by Social Indicators*, Budapest: University of Economics, 1988, 265 (Hungary 1960–1980).

complicated. Furthermore, currency restrictions were implemented in several countries in the wake of the economic depression, which decreased the range of consumer choices to a certain extent. Rationing, primarily of basic foodstuffs, was implemented and maintained in belligerent countries not only during the war but also in the years after its end. These economic restrictions were gradually phased out by the beginning of the 1950s in Western Europe, and thus no similar obstacles hindered the prevalence of consumer autonomy. Without doubt, accompanying the massive increase in purchasing power and the expansion of trade, the range of goods and services grew significantly from the 1960s in Western Europe. However, in this aspect, it seems plausible to stress continuity throughout the whole century (disregarding, of course, the periods of war).

Mass production and commercialization

It was a characteristic element of qualitative changes in consumption during the twentieth century that mass-produced goods gained currency. This consumption affluence was facilitated by the advance of the manufacturing industry, which started earlier, and gradually replaced small firms using handicraft technologies.[69] Dishes created by a potter, or furniture crafted by a carpenter, were more or less

TABLE 6.13 Number of passenger cars, 1910–1990 (number of cars/1000 inhabitants)

	1910	1920	1930	1940	1950	1960	1970	1980	1990
United Kingdom	3	7	21	43	42	105	209	268	353
France	3	5	23	46	37	121	252	345	416
Netherlands		3	8	11	11	45	192	292	368
Belgium		4	11	18	26	82	213	312	393
Ireland			10	18	24	62	134	203	235
Germany/FRG	1	1	7	20	7	81	227	369	436
Austria	0.4	1	3	5	6	57	162	285	394
Switzerland	1	2	14	19	27	95	221	340	457
Sweden		4	16	29	28	160	285	346	419
Denmark	1	5	20	31	26	89	218	278	320
Norway	0.4	1	7	19	18	63	193	292	354
Finland		1	7	8	6	41	152	246	380
Italy	1	1	4	7	6	40	192	309	456
Spain					3	9	50	190	317
Poland		0.2	1	1	2	3	45	60	160
Czechoslovakia		0.4	1	6	10	12	49	130	212
Hungary		0.1	1	2	1	3	23	87	187

Notes: Different years: Western Europe and Hungary 1914, 1922, 1929, 1939, 1949, 1979, around 1990; Spain, Poland, Czechoslovakia 1919, 1929, 1939, 949, 1959, 1969, 1979, around 1990.

Sources: Wolfram Fischer, ed., *Handbuch der europäischen Wirtschafts– und Sozialgeschichte*, Stuttgart: Klett–Cotta, 1987, Bd. 6, 143 (Western Europe and Southern Europe, Hungary 1914, 1929, 1939, 1949, Western Europe 1979, Poland, Czechoslovakia 1919–1979, Austria, Switzerland, Norway, Finland 1919); Wolfram Fischer, ed., *Lebensstandard und Wirtschaftssysteme*, Frankfurt/M.: Fritz Knapp Verlag, 1995, 224 (around 1990); A. S. Deaton, 'The Structure of Demand in Europe, 1920–1970', in Carlo M. Cipolla, ed., *The Fontana Economic History of Europe: The Twentieth Century*, Part One, Glasgow: Collins/Fontana Books, 1976, 124 (Western Europe 1922, 1960, 1970); Rudolf Andorka and István Harcsa, *Modernization in Hungary in the Long and Short Run Measured by Social Indicators*, Budapest: University of Economics, 1988 (Hungary 1960–1980).

unique items, because they were often custom-made and bore the characteristics of local industrial and artistic heritage. However, ceramics or furniture factories delivered mass products that lacked such individual characteristics. Production became standardized, sometimes even specified at a national level, and thus the potential for differences became restricted. Standardization had already started in the nineteenth century, and it expanded not only in industry, but also in trade and services: for instance, merchants, banks and hairdressers set opening hours, whereas previously they often followed the individual wishes of their customers in this regard.

Commercialization also advanced, which primarily included the integration of small farmers and other agricultural producers into a market economy with a shift from subsistence production to cash crop production – a gradual process with its origins in sixteenth-century European agricultural practices. In a broader sense, it also entailed the transformation of trade. Traditionally, trade was dominated by small, family-run businesses, covering the daily needs of people living in the vicinity. The introduction of department stores in the mid-nineteenth century was an important milestone in the transformation of trade and consumer culture, although these and the market attitude they represented gained ground to a larger extent only in the twentieth century.

The rise of department stores is usually attributed to changes in production: large-scale industry enabled the production of an increasing volume of goods, which, consequently, required a more efficient marketing system. Nevertheless, the change was not only quantitative in this case either. Department stores turned shopping into an entirely new kind of activity. Whereas businesses were highly specialized in the traditional system of trade, department stores, becoming prevalent from the mid-nineteenth century, offered a wide range of products. Prices were set, bargaining was not possible (which made the course of business more foreseeable), and purchases easier to plan. At the same time, certain products were discounted regularly, which was also a strategy in the price competition fought with other similar stores. Clients entering the store had no obligations to purchase goods; merely looking around was allowed. This activity was specifically encouraged with an aesthetically pleasing display of the goods. Similarly to the example of Bon Marché (a large and luxurious store opened in Paris in 1852), these commercial establishments paid close attention not only to the appearance of goods but also to the interior design of the stores.[70] Buildings of several storeys with large spaces were frequently constructed specifically for this purpose, with the aim of providing a spectacle with the architecture itself. Giant stairs, columns and galleries; the latest electronic appliances of the era; furniture exuding the air of upper middle-class homes: all were designed to fascinate visitors. The shiny exterior was indeed necessary, because department stores were mostly selling mass-produced industrial goods, which would not have been sufficiently appealing for the patrons by themselves. These stores had storage space for a large amount of products. To increase their mass appeal, they were also generally situated in central urban locations with good accessibility. The existence of public transport networks, established at the end of the nineteenth century, meant that department stores could be easily reached from more distant parts of the cities as well. A crucial element of the image projected by these stores was the good-mannered, dedicated salesman, who helps turn shopping into an elegant activity. The introduction of the exchange or return of goods also inspired customers to break away from their daily needs and indulge in some impulsive spending. Department stores advertised themselves as commercial entities that make quality consumption available for all, and 'democratize luxury'. However, in reality, until about the second half of the twentieth century, these stores were middle-class oriented. The elite continued to rely on their own exclusive sources, and did not belong to the group of typical department store customers. The members of the working class did occasionally visit department stores, but they had no means to purchase goods there on a regular basis. Thus, the middle class, and especially, middle-class women, became the principal target audience, for whom department stores had a special appeal, because these women were mostly tied to their homes. For them, therefore, department stores offered a new and important public space (Figure 6.1).

	14th century	15th century	16th century	17th century	18th century	19th century	20th century	21st century
International trade		spices	colonial goods/ sugar/alcohol/tobacco	cotton/ china			consumer durables	franchising chains
Modes of production		rationalized colonial plantations		entrepreneurial spirit/ wordly ascetism			Fordist production line	post-Fordist flexible production
Financial system	monetary economy		credit				consumer credit	
Nation-states		military provisioning				public education	welfare state	
Luxuries		nobility			urban financial bourgeoisie		petit bourgeois	lower middle class
Worldly ethics		materialism			romanticism		therapeutic ethic of self-realization	
Fashion		courts		cities			celebrities	youth subcultures
Commercialization system			promotional culture			department stores/ world exhibitions	marketing/design/ advertising/ professionalization	malls
Leisure industry					newspapers, books	women's magazines	cinema/-TV radio	mass tourism
Public discourse			luxury/ the wealth of nations		bourgeois household	citizen as consumer	consumer protection	critical consumption

FIGURE 6.1 Factors and characteristics of consumer society in Europe from the beginning of modern times until the present
Source: Roberta Sassatelli, *Consumer Culture: History, Theory and Politics*, London: Sage, 2007, 44.

Several historians even maintain that department stores also enhanced the cultural identity formation of the middle class: anyone could gain membership to this class, as long as they bought certain products in certain department stores. Moreover, Michael B. Miller suggests that department stores helped non-bourgeois classes to integrate into consumer culture.[71] However, this view seems to be controversial: when lower classes became regular customers of department stores, which happened in Western Europe around the mid-twentieth century, the stores themselves were already relatively stratified and did not represent the ideal of the middle class.

As indicated by the expansion of department stores, concentration and the disappearance of small family-type businesses from the market were important trends in the transformation of trade in the twentieth century. An additional major stage of this process was the diffusion of self-service shopping, which began in Europe after the Second World War. The spread of supermarkets or hypermarkets gained new impetus from the 1970s. These stores were usually larger than department stores, and they were often built next to residential areas, in the outskirts, where plots were less expensive, which helped keep operational costs down. Compared with department stores located at central and congested areas, these stores held a more favourable position regarding easy accessibility for transport of goods. Shopping centres aimed at providing an outstanding range of products in specific groups of goods (e.g., foodstuffs, furniture) or at making a wide array of different products available in one place.

The British Sainsburys and the French Carrefour were among the first large supermarket chains, selling principally food. By the turn of the millennium, in Great Britain, more than half of the food products purchased were distributed in supermarkets, and in France, the ratio was 75%. Besides the extensive variety of products, customers were also attracted by moderate pricing, because with bulk purchase and an effective distribution of products, large chains were able to set prices lower than traditional small shops. Concentration reached other sectors as well in the 1980s, such as furniture and interior decoration, DIY (do-it-yourself) products and construction material, electronic appliances, and stationery. Still, not all product groups were equally covered by supermarkets. For example, concentration did not take place to the same extent in clothing retail, where the individual taste of the customer is more pronounced.

From the mid-1970s, shopping centres, planned in detail, also started to appear in the outskirts of Western European cities. In these non-integrated centres, shops retained their individual commercial profile, but the establishment had a central organization, which set the opening hours, the types of businesses, and coordinated joint advertisement campaigns. Typically, these shopping centres also offered other services related to free-time activities, such as cinemas, restaurants, and fitness centres. A good example is Shopping City Süd, established south of Vienna in 1976, which advertised itself as the largest shopping centre in Europe.[72]

Motorization played a crucial role in the concentration of trade, because shopping centres that were far from housing districts could be reached most conveniently by car. At the turn of the millennium, the concentration of trade was further advanced by the expansion of information technology, which made it possible to design new logistics systems, contributing significantly to minimizing the costs of storage and transport. The introduction of these systems required considerable investment. Consequently, they were not within the reach of small companies. Small businesses that survived the concentration process often belonged to highly capitalized chains as well.

Concentration led to the progressive internationalization of businesses as well. An emblematic representative of this process is the Swedish company IKEA, the stores of which cover virtually the entire continent. At the end of the century, the largest companies with a strong presence abroad included the French Carrefour mentioned above as well as the Auchan group, the German Metro group, Aldi and Tengelmann. In clothing retail, for example, the British Marks and Spencer, the Italian Benetton, the Swedish Hennes und Mauritz and the Spanish Zara belonged to the same category.

Concentration of business was not uniform in Western and Southern European countries. In Great Britain, France and Germany, small businesses were suppressed, mostly in the food sector. In Southern European countries, such as Spain, Portugal and Italy, small businesses survived in larger numbers than in North-Western Europe, because customers were reluctant to give up small shops close to their neighbourhoods. In addition, the less concentrated structure of cities and extended historical districts favoured the survival of small businesses.

Nonetheless, the concentration of retail trade was nowhere as overwhelming in Europe as it was in the United States. Small, specialized shops, which are trafficking principally in clothing and products to meet special consumer demands, were still present in city centres at the beginning of the new millennium. However, an important tendency in the restructuring of city-centre business life has been the opening of plazas and malls, hosting several smaller shop units, often underground or near pedestrian zones.

In any case, the expansion of large businesses entailed several controversial consequences. Opponents of this phenomenon were worried that shops in city centres and housing districts would lose customers, and their disappearance could contribute to the deterioration of certain districts. They were also against the traffic load caused by shopping centres, which inflicted considerable environmental damage nonetheless. This is why in Belgium, for instance, government intervention aimed at blocking the concentration process. Other governments and local authorities introduced restrictions as well. In France, for example, a law was passed in 1996 to protect small groceries. In other countries, authorities gave building permits for shopping centres only for certain peripheral urban districts, which could evidently solve only a part of the problems. In Norway, the issuing of building permits was completely suspended while studies were carried out to survey the wider social and environmental impact of shopping centres.[73]

Homogenization tendencies

Although the expansion of international trade in the nineteenth century made a wide range of products available for consumers practically everywhere in the

European continent, purchasing imported goods was a real possibility only for the upper and the middle classes, whereas the majority of the population relied on locally produced goods. Therefore, significant regional differences characterized European consumption patterns at the turn of the nineteenth century.[74] However, throughout the twentieth century, and especially in the second half of the century, the homogenization of consumer habits gradually progressed in Europe. This change was also reflected by the principal indicators of the consumption structure. The differences in the amounts spent by the households of individual societies on food products, clothing, housing and other important items were considerably smaller in the 1980s than half a decade earlier, as shown by studies covering several countries.[75]

In addition, the consumption of various types of foodstuffs and drinks can illustrate the point. The consumption patterns of alcoholic beverages in Europe changed little in the first six decades of the twentieth century, apart from the fact that in most regions, alcohol consumption declined. During this time, Europe was divided into three different zones based on the consumption of different alcohol varieties: hard liquor, mostly vodka, was preferred in Scandinavia; people in the middle of the continent (the British Isles, the Netherlands, Germany, and the northern parts of East Central Europe) drank primarily beer; and wine was the most popular drink in Southern Europe. Beginning in the 1960s, alcohol consumption changed significantly in most societies, that is, the dominance of traditional drinks faded. Nations with a history of beer drinking consumed increasing amounts of wine, which was in Great Britain an exclusively imported commodity, whereas beer gained ground among Southerners traditionally excelling in wine drinking. A similar process took place in relation with the dominant type of fats used for cooking. Whereas at the beginning of the century, Mediterranean regions used almost exclusively olive oil, in the rest of Europe, people preferred butter and lard, or, in the North, fish oil. This north–south division was loosened partly because an increasing amount of oil was produced from sunflower and rape. These plants spread both in Southern and Northern Europe; however, they did not compete seriously with the traditional types of cooking fat until the 1970s. Another factor contributing to the homogenization was that the regular household consumption of olive oil grew in central and northern parts of Europe.[76]

Growing similarities also surfaced in the case of consumer durables, which were taking up an increasing share of household expenditures in the twentieth century. Differences, which were significant in the 1950s between Western and Southern European societies with regard to important consumer goods, diminished by the end of the century, not only within consumption structure, but also in the appearance and the characteristics of products. The brands of automobiles, computers, washing machines, television sets and mobile phones distributed became mostly identical in all countries. Remaining differences rather depend on the amount of purchasing power than on individual choices or national varieties of taste.

The homogenization of consumption patterns was the result of several factors. Obviously, among the most important reasons was the post-war convergence in the level of economic output in Western and Southern Europe, and in turn its consequence, the growing similarity of personal income. The increase in productivity and export capacity in agriculture was another factor, as well as the improvement of transport, the processing of perishable goods, and the rise in the amount of food imported from outside Europe. The convergence in industrial structure, and in general, the overall economic structure also advanced, which resulted in more similar conditions regarding supply and demand. The development of the international division of labour and trade, as well as the harmonization of economic policies (for example, within the framework of the EEC or EFTA) also promoted the levelling of prices, which, in turn, homogenized supply and demand to a further extent. In the last decades of the century, the EEC and its successor organizations also contributed significantly to the convergence of consumption, by creating favourable conditions for the flow of goods. In addition, within the EEC, common standards were introduced in several fields of industry and trade, which further enhanced the convergence of products. We also have to consider that the diffusion of values reinforced the unification of consumer preferences and habits. This phenomenon could be attributed to the widening geographical horizon of the average Western European citizen, primarily as a result of the growing volume of tourist and business travel to other European countries. H. Kaelble pointed out that several of these factors contributing to the homogenization process were most marked during the post-war boom in Western Europe (1950–73). This is essentially the period when the commonalities in the economic and urban as well as family and household structure increased, economic integration gathered impetus, and all of these factors advanced the convergence of consumer patterns, thus also explaining the timing and the dynamics of homogenization.[77]

Naturally, homogenization had its limits as well. National or even regional traditions in dietary habits, construction, interior decoration and other areas have remained perceivable up until the present day. The increase in immigration originating from outside Europe also worked against homogenization, because migrants brought diverse dietary and other consumption patterns. We also have to point out that the convergences within Western Europe fitted within the evolution of global consumption trends, which means that the phenomenon was not exclusively European. According to F. Gardes, the approximation to a common model was not peculiar to Europe, but rather meant a simultaneous move towards the consumption patterns of the United States.[78] Thus, some researchers describe the emergence of common consumption patterns as a process of Americanization.

'Shortage economy' in the communist countries

The qualitative features of consumption are particularly essential to study in the East Central European and South-Eastern European regions because divergence between communist and Western European countries was the most spectacular in these aspects. Similarly, the most important attributes of the post-war economic system in the region can be realized only by taking into account these characteristics as well.

Regarding product range and the availability of quality products, these regions were similar to Western Europe in the interwar period. Differences were caused mainly by lower living standards as long as it determined the range of sold products. A substantially larger contrast can be seen in the decades after the Second World War. Rationing and food shortage in the immediate post-war years were more or less inevitable consequences of the war destruction and the disorganization of economy, of inflation, and, in several cases, of foreign occupation and reparation deliveries. In this period, several countries of Western Europe also experienced serious difficulties; however, whereas in this region, supply was normalized within a few years, in East Central and South-Eastern Europe the economic system after the communist takeover evolved into what has been termed the 'shortage economy' by János Kornai. As it was elaborated in Kornai's classic study, shortages did not appear sporadically, but were universal, equally affecting consumer goods and services, foreign currencies, imported products and other resources. In addition, shortages were permanent, and thus had a pronounced impact on the behaviour of consumers, as well as other actors in the economy.[79] Because of chronic shortage, consumers had access to important goods and services through bureaucratic distribution mechanisms, such as advanced booking or allocation; they had to queue for them, or turn to the black market as an alternative.

The central management of the economy and political decision makers had an ambiguous attitude towards consumer demand in the communist countries. Symptomatically, instead of facilitating consumer choice, the idea of a scientific organization of consumption prevailed in the early phase of the centrally planned economies. According to this approach, imported from the Soviet Union, there is an ideal, scientific model of consumption, which can provide general guidelines for setting product supply in central economic planning. This centrally determined 'consumption plan', naturally, could calculate consumption only through the most important natural indicators, such as square meter, pair, kilogram, litre, piece, and other similar natural units, so quality characteristics or range of choice were not considered. The full practical implementation of this concept soon turned out to be a failure; nonetheless, in the centrally planned economies, some versions of the 'consumption plan' persisted until the regime change.[80]

Being increasingly successful in meeting consumer demand became a recurring goal of economy planners, because it was obviously a necessary condition of political stability. In the communist countries a large amount of popular dissatisfaction was caused by low-level provisions and shortages regarding everyday necessities. However, improving product supply appeared as a compromise made in favour of consumers at the expense of 'real' economic goals, such as the increase of investments, and thus the acceleration of economic development. As a result, official propaganda made consumption appear as something that can be reconciled with the goals of socialism only within certain restrictions. Politics labelled consumer desires imported from the West particularly in the 1950s and 1960s as dangerous, fearing that such attitudes of 'the petite bourgeoisie' could spread to the working class as well.[81]

The 'classic' system of shortage economy universally characteristic of East Central and South-Eastern Europe at the beginning of the 1950s went through a considerable change in several countries in the later decades. Reforms of economy management introduced in the 1960s, most comprehensively in Czechoslovakia and Hungary, aimed partly at meeting consumer demands. Political leadership in these countries also realized that Western patterns of consumption served as the model, and they wanted to enable the population to adopt or to imitate at least some elements of this model. Later, these reforms were withdrawn either partially, like in Hungary, or completely, like in Czechoslovakia.

Differences in the level of economic development and in the implementation of reforms are also attributed to substantial discrepancies between consumer experiences in the societies of East Central Europe and the Balkans. Moreover, rather than diminishing with time, these only increased after the period of High Stalinism. The German Democratic Republic and Czechoslovakia had the highest levels of consumption of basic products. Yet, Hungary was that country where consumer autonomy could be practiced most freely from the 1970s, because Hungary had the most reliable product supply and the widest range of goods. This was frequently described by the term 'Goulash Communism', first used by the Western media, which implied that there was a specifically Hungarian way of expanding consumption, which still conformed to the principles of socialism. Although the overall quantity and quality of basic foodstuffs available was adequate in Hungary in the 1970s and 1980s, unlike in several other communist countries, supply problems, even of these products, still occurred, especially in rural areas, and were even more severe in the case of consumer durables and services. In other words, the East Central European tendencies presented here applied to Hungary as well, and thus it is unfounded to regard 'consumer socialism' as a version of consumer society.

Therefore, despite reform attempts, shortage remained a basic characteristic of all the economies in the region until the regime change and its implications, such as searching for goods, postponing purchases, forced substitution, queuing, and quality problems. The housing and the automobile market, as well as the density of the telephone network, illustrate the situation well. In the 1980s, the average waiting time for the allocation of flats was 5–20 years in Bulgaria, 6–8 years in Czechoslovakia, and 15–30 years in Poland, depending on occupational, income and family status, the place of residence and similar factors. The waiting period in 1989 for the allocation of a Lada automobile (a type based on a Fiat model of the early 1960s and made in the Soviet Union) was 10–12 years in Bulgaria, 17 years in the German Democratic Republic, and 5–6 years in Poland and Hungary. Less popular models, such as the Soviet Moskvitch or the Romanian Dacia, were more easily accessible. It often took several decades to have a telephone installed. In the early 1980s, the number of households on the waiting list for telephones amounted to 57% of the subscribers in Poland and 11.3% in Czechoslovakia, whereas the figure was 0.7% in Belgium, 0.9% in France, and in several Western countries, all telephone demands could be satisfied practically immediately. In the German

Democratic Republic, even some types of washing machines were available only through advance booking, and after several years of patient waiting.[82]

Privileged groups had special channels for acquiring goods that were not available elsewhere. Members of the political and military elite, outstanding sportsmen, artists and scientists enjoyed privileges in the allocation of flats, cars, or getting a telephone installed. In several countries, there were special shops for this exclusive circle, selling products not available elsewhere. For those privileged with convertible currency, Western products or domestic ones in short supply were also available in specifically designated stores selling in American dollars or German marks, for example, the Pewex chain in Poland, Intershop in the German Democratic Republic, and IKKA in Hungary.

As pointed out earlier, shortage had a profound influence on the behaviour of actors in the economy. The same applies to consumption, because the shortage led to phenomena in the region that were non-existent in Western Europe, such as the emergence of the black market. Corruption was also widespread in the market of goods and services, although its extent and nature depended on the period and the country. Although bribery was not uncommon even in the case of foodstuffs in the 1980s in Romania, in Hungary it prevailed in relation to durable goods, such as quality furniture items. It can also be attributed to the deterioration of ethical standards that (with the exception of East Germany) corruption and graft became almost universal in health care: patients tried to obtain more favourable hospital accommodation, or simply, to receive better treatment by bribing doctors and hospital personnel.[83]

After the fall of the communist regimes, fundamental transformations took place in the trade sector of East Central Europe as well. Previously, shops, rather than carrying out traditional business activities, served the distribution of goods. This was reflected not only by the range of products but by the location, the external and the internal design of the shops, as well as by the display of products and the quality of service. All this changed with the introduction of the market economy. Trade became probably the most dynamically transformed economic sector. Furthermore, its privatization was also carried out among the first of similar projects, and many small businesses emerged, because the operation of these required moderate capital and skill. Thus, whereas in Western Europe, the centralization of commerce was the dominant trend, in the first years of market economy, decentralization prevailed in the East Central European region. Later, however, trends analogous to the ones discussed above regarding Western Europe emerged here as well. Shopping centres and supermarket chains appeared, usually operated by foreign companies, which sold the same products as similar types of stores in the rest of Europe.

Spare time, leisure and mass culture: *jeux sans frontières*

Mainstream historical research dates the emergence of leisure in the modern sense to the beginning of the eighteenth century in Western Europe.[84] Before that time, masses of labourers participated regularly in playful activities during holidays, and they sang, chatted, drank and even danced regularly on average workdays as well. However, the demarcation between working time and free time, set aside for leisure, which lies at the heart of the modern concept of leisure, did not exist. Even if this separation had already appeared in the early modern period, it took until the twentieth century to be fully established in European societies.

Earlier in this chapter we discussed major elements of this process, including the gradual decrease of working hours in various European countries and the prevalence of wage work, which also implied set working hours (Table 6.4). Shorter working hours and a fixed work schedule led to a fundamental change in the significance and meaning of leisure as an activity in European societies and considerably facilitated the separation of work time and leisure time. This process was accompanied by other transformations, such as the commercialization and diffusion of radically new forms of leisure.

Dancing and cinema

Industrialization also multiplied the forms of leisure and advanced their commercialization. Already in early modern European societies, several sorts of paid entertainment existed. One-man sideshows, for example, collected fees, and naturally, people had to pay in pubs as well. Still, the most favourite amusements, such as dancing, singing and chatting, were free, because participants created the opportunity for themselves. In the rapidly expanding cities of the eighteenth and nineteenth century, new types of entertainment appeared and signalled the increasing commercialization of entertainment. Theatres, operas, concert and dance halls, wax figure museums, as well as other venues of social life and leisure, emerged and prospered. Smaller villages were visited by strolling companies and travelling circuses. At the end of the nineteenth century, pubs, cafés and restaurants were still the most popular venues of entertainment, and most of these also offered music or some kind of a programme. Cafés were particularly numerous in Paris, where their ratio to one hundred inhabitants was one, whereas in London, one thousand people had to make do with just one similar institution. There were many dance halls, which were visited by a socially rather diverse audience. The English music hall, and its French counterpart, the café-concert, presented a unique mixture between theatres and cafés, featuring singers and diverse smaller productions, during which the audience could chat and drink, and they frequently sang along with the performers.[85]

Besides these entertainment options, other forms of leisure also appeared at the end of the nineteenth century, such as the phonograph, cheap illustrated magazines and periodicals, and particularly, the motion picture. The modern version of the motion picture, invented by the Lumière brothers in 1895 in Lyon, unlike its more simple predecessors, allowed not only one person to view the show by peeping into a box through a hole but made it available for a large audience through the use of a screen. Part of the invention was that the images composing the film were not produced individually, but were reproduced by photographic method on an industrial scale. In the first few years after the invention, short movies served as an entertainment primarily at fairs and other popular programmes. However, after the turn of the century, independent cinema buildings were constructed, the movies became longer, and their quality also improved. This way, they also became attractive for the middle class. Already before the First World War, cinema had begun to gain advantage over other forms of entertainment, such as the café–concerts or music halls referred to above.[86]

The number of cinema-goers grew dynamically in all social classes after the war. Cinemas, already screening sound movies from 1927, primarily entertained, but they also distributed information on less known countries and continents or new inventions. In addition, films were conveying and thus propagating new norms of social interaction, changes of fashion and lifestyle. It is particularly noteworthy in this respect that already in the 1920s, films represented and frequently idealized new female roles, in which women not only had a more liberal attitude towards sexuality, but were also smoking, drinking and driving cars, just like men. Cinemas brought changes in gender relations in other respects as well. Couples frequently watched movies together; thus the appearance of women at public entertainment venues became more accepted. Movies usually offered light entertainment; they did not deal with social problems, or if they did, they tried to diminish their significance. Nevertheless, by representing the consumption level and the habits of high society, they drew viewers' attention to social differences. Cinema also triggered the formation of mass culture as well as its internationalization. However, the latter process primarily meant the worldwide predominance of Hollywood productions already in the aftermath of the First World War.

Radio and television

It was the development of electronic media that had the most decisive impact on leisure activities and the expansion of mass culture over the long term. After being initially applied for military and navigational purposes, and a short experimental phase, radio broadcasts were launched in Europe in the mid-1920s. Broadcasting spread rapidly after its introduction: many stations were established, which were mostly public, and this remained unchanged for several decades. One of the biggest stations setting the international standard was the British Broadcasting Corporation (BBC), which was granted broadcast monopoly in Great Britain in 1922. The BBC was under government control, but it still retained a considerable autonomy. Receiver sets, which represented initially the bottleneck of the expansion of radio culture, spread rapidly in households throughout Western Europe in the 1930s: at the end of the decade, their number reached 182 sets per one thousand inhabitants in Great Britain, and Germany was not far behind, with 172 sets per one thousand inhabitants (Table 6.11).[87]

The first experimental television transmissions were launched as early as 1936 in Berlin and London. In Europe, television, like the radio some decades earlier, reached the masses first in Britain, where regular broadcasting was introduced in 1946. In the early 1950s, other countries of Western Europe started regular programmes as well, including Switzerland, Denmark, the Netherlands and West Germany, as well as East Germany and Poland (initially with modest time schedules for programmes and limited infrastructure everywhere).[88]

For several decades, in most countries, just one or two public-service broadcasting stations provided the programming, pursuing high cultural standards and aiming to maintain the diversity of the programmes, as well as not submitting programme policy to commercial interests. Apart from regular news programmes, airtime consisted mostly of theatre plays, concerts, children's programmes, films and sports broadcasts. Advertisements were highly restricted. In the Federal Republic of Germany, for instance, no advertisements were aired in prime time, or during weekends, and the combined length of advertisements on weekdays was maximized to 20 minutes in the 1980s.

The first commercial television channel in Great Britain was established back in 1955. However, the limited radio spectrum available for terrestrial broadcast remained an obstacle to the expansion of television for a long time. From the 1980s, satellite and cable television considerably increased the number of channels available in the average household (sometimes from just a few to several dozens or even hundreds) and gave an impetus to commercial televising. In France, Germany, Norway and other countries, the first private stations were established in the 1980s. They focused primarily on light entertainment, and in order to boost the number of viewers, they did not refrain from airing low-quality programmes: diverse talk-shows, soap operas, crime and other series made up most of the airtime, and in their news programmes, sensational events were more frequently covered than serious ones.[89]

In many respects, the effect that the appearance of television had on households was similar to the introduction of the radio a few decades earlier. As opposed to the communitarian quality of traditional leisure, requiring active participation and reinforcing group solidarity, television encouraged individual entertainment and a large measure of passivity. However, beyond these similarities, the impact of the television screen proved to be more intensive than that of the radio. The daily average time spent watching television was 2–3 hours by the end of the century in European societies, and in certain countries, it even reached 4–5 hours. The number of hours spent on watching TV was particularly high in low-income families; television sets were already available at affordable prices at that time. Television also highly affected the lifestyles of children and elderly people, because these age groups spent more time watching television than the average. Data on viewing hours reflected the tendency that television supplanted not only radio and cinema but also reading, playing family board games, and even conversation. Besides all these consequences, time spent on watching television was mainly at the expense of socializing and meeting other people.

It is certain that news programmes made it possible for the viewers to obtain information about remote events more quickly, and a small segment of the rest of the programmes also addressed social problems. At the same time, televiewing was increasingly criticized in the public, because television (particularly commercial channels) evidently promoted consumerism. The airtime of advertisements on commercial stations frequently amounted to up to one-third of the total programme length. In addition, other programmes conveyed commercial content, albeit often implicitly. Consumption, beauty, and fame were presented in most of the programmes as the primary goals of life and the major sources of happiness.

Several experts found the impact of television on children particularly worrying, because children are more prone to perceive the world represented in the programmes as reality. Furthermore, the fact that American films dominated television in Western Europe practically from the early days caused increasing public concerns as well. The television series reaching top viewership were *Kojak* in the 1970s, *Dallas* in the 1980s, and *Baywatch* in the 1990s. Productions made on the other side of the Atlantic were considered potentially harmful, because it was claimed that the spread of supposedly low-quality American mass culture threatened the integrity of national cultures in Europe. As a reaction, several countries (most eminently France) attempted to balance domestic and European, as well as American, productions by means of central media regulation.

Tourism

Mass tourism appeared in Europe at the end of the nineteenth century, in which Great Britain pioneered. Its principal destinations were places that offered recreational amenities for the wide array of urban residents. Seaside resorts were of particular importance, and they became easily accessible from the large industrial centres with the advance of railway and navigation. In the second half of the nineteenth century, holiday resorts on the coasts of the Channel developed rapidly, and the number of working class visitors grew as well. Apart from the beach, the appeal of these places was increased by hotels, pubs, restaurants, shops and other entertainment venues. On the Channel coast, Brighton became the best known destination spot, whereas in the North, Blackpool attracted the population of the Midlands. Similar fashionable resorts were Trouville in France, Ostende in Belgium, and Scheveningen in Holland (the fame of the latter two was also increased by the frequent visits of royal families).[90]

From its rise at the end of the nineteenth century to the second half of the twentieth century, mass tourism primarily meant domestic tourism. However, beginning with the 1960s, mass tourism became international: in Europe, it expanded primarily to the Mediterranean, and later, also to the Alps. The primary condition of the growing frequency of tourism was the rapid increase in personal incomes, intensified by the expansion of leisure time, and, especially, by the extending length of paid holidays. Another important factor was the development of air traffic, which made mass transportation convenient and affordable. Important changes were also introduced in the organization of trips. Travel agencies offered 'packages,' which included travel, accommodation, meals, guided tours, and other services. Because packages were bought in large numbers, offices could obtain services at lower prices, and therefore could offer more favourable travel options. This development had particular consequences mainly in the Mediterranean resorts. Complying with the demand set by travel agencies, large investments were carried out in tourism, which frequently resulted in an overcrowded environment. Hotels, restaurants and shops serving the needs of tourists were opened one after the other, and places started to lose their unique characteristics. In other words, tourism partly destroyed its major initial catalyst, that is, the attractive singularity of the spot. This process started in Spain (Costa del Sol, Costa Blanca, Costa Brava, Mallorca, Ibiza, Canary Islands), along the Mediterranean coast in France, and in Italy (Rimini). In Greece and in Yugoslavia, mass tourism took off later. Finally, Turkey, Cyprus and Portugal (Algarve), as well as Tunisia, also followed suit. In the 1990s, about 140 million tourists visited the European coasts of the Mediterranean every year. Similar tendencies appeared in tourist resorts in the Alps. Although the number of guests here was significantly lower than in seaside destinations, we can still talk about a case of mass tourism, particularly in the skiing season.[91]

The first phase of tourism in East Central Europe in the nineteenth century was primarily connected to bathing spa resorts, some of which had a large international clientele, such as Karlsbad (Karlovy Vary), although most of them were merely of local significance. Although with distinctive regional characteristics, the countries of the region also experienced the expansion of mass tourism after the Second World War. Early communist governments paid special attention to making holidays available for workers and other employees, who previously had rarely taken part in similar programmes. Such vacations were widely publicized in the propaganda of communist countries as an important achievement of socialism. Another distinctive feature was the collectivist, group-organized nature of tourism, which, on the one hand, was supposed to promote the idea of solidarity among workers, whereas, on the other hand, it served as a tool for political control, primarily in the case of trips abroad. Holiday homes owned by the state or by trade unions were the typical domestic summer destinations, which generally offered full pension at a low price, although with modest qualities. Rooms in these establishments were assigned either as rewards for work performance and other merits, or based on a waiting list. Foreign tourism was less extensive. Travelling, even to other countries of the Eastern bloc, was regarded as a privilege for the citizens of communist countries in the 1950s. From the 1960s, restrictions were gradually loosened, but certain countries, including the German Democratic Republic, Czechoslovakia, Romania and Bulgaria, maintained strict limits for travel, especially to the West. Citizens of the German Democratic Republic, for example, were allowed to travel exclusively to countries of the Eastern bloc, and only within strictly regulated intervals and conditions. Hungary and Poland were more permissive regarding travel, and from the 1970s, their citizens were allowed to travel to the West in set frequency, and even a small amount of Western currency was made available for travellers. Yugoslavs were practically free to move.

The fall of the communist regimes transformed the characteristics of tourism in the region to a great extent. The significance of domestic tourism dwindled because its traditional system of group trips and vacations subsidized by the state or companies practically terminated, and real wages did not enable many people to pay market prices for trips. In addition, citizens were eager to enjoy their newly acquired freedom of travel, and those who could afford it often opted for destinations in Southern Europe, or even further.

The emergence of mass tourism was significantly facilitated by the increase of spare time in Europe. The dramatic decrease of working hours during the twentieth century in itself made the amount of available free time greater, and technological advances that made domestic work easier had a similar effect. Also crucial in the formation of mass tourism was that the length of paid leaves and the number of paid holidays grew significantly.

This way, by the end of the twentieth century, tourism became one of the most important forms of spending free time in Europe. Holidays abroad also served as markers in defining and showing individual social status. Europe was converted into the biggest tourism market of the world, and at the turn of the millennium, 58% of all global tourist destinations were European, and 64% of foreign travellers were Europeans. At the same time, countries of the EU-15 group derived 14% of their combined GDP from tourism, a sector with a direct employment of 19 million people. France was considered the most important destination worldwide, with 70 million visitors, but Spain (42 million) and Italy (29 million) were also among the most popular countries among tourists. Regarding tourism within Europe, trends were mainly following a north–south direction, with Spain being the most popular country, particularly among German and British tourists.[92]

In the last two decades of the twentieth century, new branches of tourism also appeared and gained appeal, not displacing, but rather complementing traditional sea-side and skiing tourism. Rural tourism was one of these trends, specializing primarily in domestic guests.[93] The other branch of tourism evolving rapidly was city tourism. Large European cities have always been important tourist destinations, but in the last decade of the century, their popularity increased even further. An important factor facilitating this change was the restructuring of European commercial aviation in the 1990s. A new type of 'discount' or 'budget' airline (such as the Irish Ryanair or the British EasyJet) was formed in the wake of this change, selling tickets at considerably lower prices, although also offering lower-quality service. As a result, air travel also became available for short city visits. The main attractions of these two-night or three-night trips were primarily architectural, gastronomic and cultural sights, but certain events, such as sports games, fairs or festivals were also regarded as appealing enough for such short visits.

The consumer society and its critics: *de gustibus est disputandum*

In the previous sections, we outlined the remarkable increase in consumption and its associated structural shifts in Europe during the twentieth century, particularly in the Western part of the continent. In the societies of Western Europe as well as of North America and other advanced regions, this development created the basis for the emergence of the formation that has been labelled as consumer society (the term consumer culture is also used, more or less as a synonym). In the everyday usage of the term, consumer society is frequently identified with a high standard of living, which is clearly inseparable from it, but its scholarly meaning is more complex. It designates a social formation that is organized not around the production of goods and services but rather around their consumption. This means that the transition from the nineteenth-century and early twentieth-century 'producer' (or, rather, industrial) society to the consumer society of the late twentieth century did not only entail the spreading of sophisticated goods on a large scale but a range of other, eminently cultural changes as well. In other words, consumption and the system of attitudes and values attached to it became the central elements in the functioning of modern societies. However, despite its apparent unambiguity, the concept is full of contradictions. Since the moment of its appearance, it has not been used so much with an analytical aim but more with critical intentions to argue against the views and dispositions prevalent in advanced industrial societies that identify high-level consumption with social progress, and regard it as the most important measure of individual and collective success. The following section first addresses the debate around the concept and the advance of consumer society; then it investigates the controversies generated by consumer culture.[94]

The genesis of consumer society

Attempts to describe the formation of consumer culture, as well as to define its most important attributes, led to intensive debates in the field of history and sociology. Initially, researchers stressed the importance of industrialization in the transformation of consumption. This approach interpreted consumer society as a phenomenon that was brought about by the accelerated economic growth as well as mass production, and the beginning of the twentieth century was identified as the early stage of consumer society and culture in Europe. Recently, however, several authors have used a different argument and asserted that changes in consumption were the major cause of the formation of capitalism, even of the industrial revolution. This interpretation may be argued for by examining not only the expansion of supply within the historical path of consumption but including the trends of demand as well. Jan de Vries, Colin Campbell, Neil McKendrick and other researchers found novel and significant developments in seventeenth-century Holland and eighteenth-century England, which had been previously dated to much later periods. Among these are advertisements, refined marketing techniques, the diversification of trade, or hedonistic attitudes towards consumption.[95] Several recent works regard absolutist royal courts as crucial in the formation of eighteenth-century consumer culture, which competed with each other in fashion, and showed the lead for other classes as well. Consumption patterns of the elite in general trickled down to the lower social strata.[96] This approach, in a certain sense, is a return to the ideas of Werner Sombart's classic study, which examined the consumption of luxury goods from the late Middle Ages, and argued that luxury and colonial products, together with the formation of new social values and relations, significantly contributed to the change of lifestyle in early modern Europe. Figure 6.1 provides a review of several of these elements.

Research focusing on the nineteenth and the early twentieth century regard the establishment of department stores, and in general, the transformation of trade as crucial factors in shaping consumption. In the Europe of the interwar period, following primarily American examples, jobs in trade and marketing became highly professionalized: marketing experts, salesmen, stock keepers, fashion designers and fashion writers all belonged to this category. The transformation of the role of advertisements is also a good example of the way that discourse on consumption changed from the beginning of the twentieth century. New types of media proliferated: first picture magazines, then film and cinema, and later radio followed by television, and finally, the Internet, have all expanded the target audience of advertising. Although earlier advertisements were segmented by well-defined gender and social groups, with the introduction of new forms of media aiming at masses, the former specialization of advertisement decreased. This change was also supported by the fading of the boundaries between gender roles, and by the fact that in the age of mass consumption most products could rely on a wide range of potential customers. Trade and media were not merely promoting the purchase of specific goods, but also tried to create a continuous urge for the acquisition of products.

Research dealing with the second half of the twentieth century stresses primarily the significance of the introduction of technological innovations to everyday life: these, as we have noted above, mainly came from the group of consumer durables, such as telephone, refrigerator, television, and other items. The period of the Great Boom is given a particular significance because of the unprecedented pace with which the level of consumption started to increase in Western Europe.

Independent of the complexity of the precedents, the advanced form of consumer society in Western Europe took shape at the end of the twentieth century. Diverse elements of this formation have already been addressed in the present chapter. Consumer society evidently implies the high level of consumption and the abundance of free time that enable citizens to spend most of their time with consumption instead of work. The source of social changes and social identity in consumer society is not primarily work, or one's individual position in the production process and the resulting income, but rather the lifestyle and the way of living chosen by people in order to show their standard of living, or, in other cases, their opposition to consumerism. On the basis of the fundamental structural transformation of consumption, which includes the declining ratio of incomes spent on basic necessities, the purchase of goods is not regulated by need, but by desire, mostly inculcated by the media. Goods are frequently assigned a symbolic value, and become attributes of social position.[97] The existence of a wide range of consumer choices is also a precondition for the formation of consumer society. It has also been argued in research that in consumer society the potential power of customers increases against that of producers and service providers. Finally, in consumer societies, an increasing number of the aspects of everyday life become commodified, and as a result, are intensively permeated by market relations.[98]

Consumption as an object of criticism

Already in its early phase, the growth of consumption sparked much debate, which appeared in various forms.[99] Criticism of consumption and early forms of consumerism at the end of the eighteenth and the beginning of the nineteenth century usually targeted greed and the adoration of false idols, in line with traditional Christian language and morals. During the late nineteenth and the first decades of the twentieth century, such criticisms did not disappear, but new elements were introduced. Low-income citizens, who were spending at the expense of their savings, or beyond their social class, were frequent targets of public censure. Women also became targets of criticism: the French novelist Émile Zola wrote a novel on department stores already in 1883, presenting their adverse effect on frivolous women. The complexity of motives behind criticisms is well reflected by the fact that Jewish owners of large department stores were also often castigated not only for luring people into expenses, but also for driving smaller businesses bankrupt. In other words, a morally induced criticism of consumerism was intertwined with specific economic and social motivations. In the 1920s, the programme of the Nazi party included the goal of driving back department stores in order to protect small businesses. Once this party gained power, it aimed at a more direct anti-consumption policy as well, because consumer goals were difficult to reconcile with the ideology of the system, which demanded total loyalty, or with the preparations for war. Equally, attacks against French fashion or American jazz had easily identifiable nationalist roots in Nazi Germany.

At the end of the nineteenth century and the beginning of the twentieth century, the social democratic labour movement also attacked the early manifestations of consumer culture throughout Europe. According to criticism of the political left, the diffusion of consumerism was menacing worker's class consciousness by encouraging the pursuit of personal comfort and pleasure, thus influencing workers to assume bourgeois values. Still, numerous labour movement leaders hoped that instead of pursuing consumption, workers would choose the superior goals of the movement. In time, however, they experienced that the primary worries of the majority of the workers were low wages and long working hours, and not the prospect of becoming consumers. This is why in the interwar period, criticism from the Western social democratic and communist movement targeted the undoubtedly large social gaps regarding the level of consumption, and contrary to the previous periods, concentrated less on the wasteful spending habits of women workers or the aping of fashion.[100]

The first signs of the appearance of mass leisure and mass consumption revealed that the intellectual elite clearly feared the consequences of their impact on social stability, and the adverse effects of mass culture on high culture. This fact is illustrated by the opinion of two major thinkers of the late nineteenth and early twentieth century. The French Émile Durkheim claimed that common people are unable to control their desires once they are faced with an abundance of goods in shops and department stores, and this can lead to their moral confusion. As a solution, he suggested consumption be organized by dividing people into groups based on occupation and religion. Meanwhile, in his well-known work titled *The Revolt of the Masses* (1930), the Spanish José Ortega y Gasset foresaw the decline of high culture and of quality education. He argued that the growing purchasing power of the masses creates an opportunity for the realization of their less refined tastes in culture and in social life in general.

During and after the Second World War, austerity and scarcity initiated a temporary political and social consensus in Europe about granting priority to increasing the standard of living. Nevertheless, the unprecedented expansion of consumption in the boom decades further polarized the interpretations concerning consumption. Excessive consumption was frequently criticized as an activity induced exclusively by the advertising industry, and which represents a range of negative traits of the era: materialism, hedonism, bad taste, and emptiness. According to critics, consumption has a negative effect on individual identity, reducing it to that of a mere consumer who finds superficial pleasure in owning objects. Individual ambitions are aimed at fulfilling consumer desires, which destroys culture and refinement, and according to such fears, it loosens or completely dissolves communal ties. In this context (as argued earlier), the prevalence of American consumption patterns, which was also termed, with an obvious irony, as 'Coca-colonization', received attention.[101] Primarily, critics regarded the advance of American products of mass culture as undesirable because they considered that this would contribute to the weakening of national culture, and subsequently, to the decline of social cohesion.

Already, the first sociological analyses of consumption at the end of the nineteenth and the beginning of the twentieth century examined the phenomenon in its social and cultural context, and stressed the importance of consumption, and particularly of fashion, in signalling and maintaining social differences. This focus shifted after the Second World War: the topics of the manipulation of consumers by the media and the role of mass culture gradually came to the foreground.

The intellectuals of the Frankfurt School devised one of the most systematic critiques of consumer culture. Max Horkheimer and Theodor Adorno tried to show that 'consumer sovereignty', the wide freedom of choice of consumers, was merely apparent. They considered the market in late capitalist society not as the tool of meeting demands, but of maintaining power relations. The consumer, whose purchases do not serve needs, but are nevertheless encouraged in thousands of ways, is not sovereign, but rather a slave of goods. As a result of these processes, consumers become passive, superficial beings governed from above, whose civic and social traits are lost in the quest for material comfort. Adorno was particularly interested in the process of how art and culture became commodities, because he thought it led to their standardization and pseudoindividualization, that is, to the deterioration of culture.[102]

Other scholars have drawn attention to the fact that with the growth of commercial companies, customers are losing the remaining options of choice. The marketing of goods is growing in significance and it increasingly reflects the interests of the seller. As John Kenneth Galbraith argued, advertisement and marketing also become highly successful in influencing customers because customers are gradually drawing away from fulfilling their natural, physiological needs, and do not always even know for sure what they would like to buy.[103]

In several aspects, there seems to be a connection between the cultural pessimism of the Frankfurt School and the first postmodern theories of the 1980s, which also rejected modern consumer culture. These postmodern authors, up to a certain point, have a similar opinion of the issue: the difference between the practical value and the symbolic value of goods had been blurred in developed industrial societies by the end of the twentieth century to the extent that consumers find it difficult to interpret and understand the system. Consumption does not serve the improvement of the essential conditions of life any more. On the contrary, according to the French critical thinker, Jean Baudrillard, consumer choices are not based on the material or real value of goods, but rather on the 'image' of the goods, which have become completely detached from the objects themselves because of media manipulation and especially advertisements. Several representatives of post-modern theory surpass the critique of the Frankfurt School at this point, because they argue that goods do not even have a real symbolic value, and instead are merely colourful images, which are separated not only from practical value, but from social reality as well.[104]

The most important trend in the criticism of consumer society after the Second World War, therefore, questions whether consumers are capable of providing creative or at least active responses to the influences they receive, which are often manipulative. Juxtaposed to this interpretation, another strong opinion also appeared, backed up by the marketing industry as well, celebrating the increasing perfection of products and their growing consumption as the widening of opportunities, a way of self-realization that, in the end, makes people happy, because this is why they purchase them. Supporters of this latter stance qualify the criticism of consumer society as some sort of an elitist grumbling, pointing out that the masses are happy to keep on buying goods.[105]

Other observers acknowledge that consumers are vulnerable to manipulation, but still regard the growth of consumption with optimism, because the power relation between the seller and the buyer is not predetermined. There is a continuous interaction between producers and consumers: products take customers' needs into consideration, although they evidently influence them at the same time. Nonetheless, it is the consumer who has the last word, who is thus able to make independent decisions. There are also scholars who emphasize that not all individuals behave the same way in the process of consumption: some are prepared to make selections and even repulse manipulative intentions, whereas others are more vulnerable, and are less able to resist.[106]

Despite the influence of post-modern criticism and the opposing party stressing consumer sovereignty, both the optimistic and the pessimistic perspectives began to gradually lose their relevance from the 1980s. Aggravating environmental problems, the growing knowledge about manipulative marketing strategies, and increasing social inequalities all made previous tendencies of optimism untenable. At the same time, although the comprehensive, philosophical criticism of consumer society did not disappear, critical observers at the end of the century have no longer focused on consumption as such, but rather on the specific goods and services themselves. Certain production methods and products became the new focal points of the more diffuse discourse, and the extent to which they sustain the environment and serve the health of consumers developed into the key criteria in establishing their use value.

Americanization

As we have seen, Americanization was one of the central concepts of debates on the consumer society. Literature distinguished two major waves of Americanization (the one in the 1920s, and the other in the 1940s and 1950s), which were significantly dissimilar as far as the public perception of the growing American cultural and economic influence is concerned. The American cultural and economic transfer strengthened and assumed new forms after the First World War: on the one hand, as we have seen, it was represented especially intensively within film-making and music, and with such genres that could not be inserted into the European high culture – popular culture duality (as, for instance, jazz). As regards the simultaneously strengthening economic bearings of Americanization, these included the rationalized mass production and the transfer of new methods of services and marketing, as a previous chapter has already touched upon.

Europeans were fascinated by the achievements of American technological progress, including modern architecture, fast cars and aviation. Anti-Americanism was not unknown, but in that period the USA dominantly appeared as the ultimate paradigm of modern industrial society, which the less advanced Europe had to emulate. Consequently, Europeans accepted positively not only economic innovations but also the products of American mass culture, whereas the latter did not appear as competition to European culture but rather as 'exotic' supplements.[107]

As a consequence of the US's role and victory in the Second World War, as well as Europe's economic and cultural convulsion, the American economic–political–cultural transfer was highly intensified in Europe from the 1940s, especially in Western and Southern Europe. It was during this period that the influence of the USA became more complex than before and involved repercussions on popular culture, customs, diet, fashion, technology, business and political practices. The movie and television industry of the USA began to dominate the European media markets. It also became the major medium by which people perceived American customs, fashion and other products and way of life in general. Older and newer American consumer brands conquered the European market, such as Coca-Cola, Hoover, Disney, Lucky Strike and Levi's. Particularly visible was the spread of the fast-food chains from the 1970s including McDonald's, Burger King, KFC, Pizza Hut, Domino's

Pizza and later Starbucks. But other American innovations affecting the lifestyle also advanced, such as chain stores, supermarkets, laundromats or self-service car washes.[108] The European discourse on Americanization also reached a new stage: the judgement of Europeans of Americanization also became more multilayered than in previous periods, showing more elements of resentment. As we have seen, it was particularly intellectuals who strongly criticized this process. Although Americanization itself paved the road to globalization, nevertheless, according to some experts, it lost its momentum in Europe after the Cold War ended and globalization began to accelerate because the world-wide uniformities of the consumer society overshadowed American characteristics as well.

Even though the concept of Americanization continues to enjoy considerable popularity in scholarly and public discourse, its usage is not without problems, because it suggests that cultural and other transfers were unidirectional in the periods referred to above: they were transplanted from the active America towards a passive and recipient Europe. However, in reality transatlantic relations were complex in this period and, even if it is not plausible to talk about symmetry, are better interpreted as a two-way exchange or as a process of circulation. The consumption of European cars, clothes and cheese for that matter became part of the lives of many Americans. An additional and even more important characteristic was that Americanization was a highly selective process in which economic institutions and cultural products were transferred, involving active choice, adaptation and even rejection by Europeans. Consequently, European consumption patterns and especially distinctive cultural characteristics survived to a great extent. Although Europeans did not resist the advance of American consumer habits, goods and consumption patterns retained much of their distinctiveness in post-war Western Europe. A growing number of furniture items, automobiles, and television sets distributed in the region were produced in other Western European countries, displaying a characteristically European product design and style.[109]

Quality of life at the end of the twentieth century: the environmental and social consequences of economic growth

Western Europe experienced spectacular growth during the twentieth century, even if it did not affect all countries and all social classes to the same extent. However, already at the peak of economic prosperity, it became apparent that economic growth does not necessarily imply an improvement of economic and social performance in a broader sense. In this context, the plausibility of methods applied for measuring the level of economic activities after the Second World War (primarily such indicators as the GDP and the GNP) were also questioned. These indices were initially intended to assess the magnitude of economic activity, or more precisely of economic output, but with time, they became normative yardsticks for economic and social performance, that is, welfare in a wider sense.

The shifts in the interpretation of economic growth had several sources. On the one hand, the anti-materialist 'counterculture' of the 1960s, and the anti-growth environmentalist movements of the 1970s, represented important starting points.[110] On the other hand, the scholarly community also made its voice heard. Several researchers pointed out that economic growth may have severe negative effects. One hundred leading experts from all over the world established a group called the Club of Rome in 1968. In its widely acclaimed report *The Limits of Growth*, published in 1972, the group described, among others, the negative environmental effects and threats of economic growth. In the next decades, European societies directly experienced these problems, ranging from acid rains to global warming. The potential adverse impacts of growth on society are not so straightforward or obvious, because their consideration is closely related to value dispositions, and they are more socially and historically contingent, that is, different countries and classes can be affected in distinct ways. But social costs of growth arguably exist, and they include, for example, the loss of workplace security and the stress induced by rapidly changing technologies. Behind the evolution of the interpretations of economic growth we may also detect a transformation of cultural values and attitudes, which are outlined in chapter 9. Approaching the end of the twentieth century, the population of European countries placed greater emphasis on factors that are commonly conceptualized as quality of life or well-being, occasionally subjective well-being. All these changes in attitudes have been connected to the level of material standard of living as well. According to comprehensive international inquiries, such as the World Values Survey, well-being is more affected by alternative factors than by a further increase in consumption beyond a certain threshold of per capita income.[111] Public attention to the qualitative aspects of growth further increased from the 1980s, and already governments began to acknowledge that besides economic growth, its environmental and social impacts have to be considered as well.[112]

This is how the idea has gained ground that in the most advanced countries the increased supply of goods is not the highest priority, but rather that the quality of life is to be considered vital.[113] The concept of quality of life does include economic aspects (even consumption), but it is a more complex term. It also applies to civil and political rights, the state of the environment, the level of crime, social security, income inequalities, autonomy at work and several other factors that affect to what degree people feel content. It also implies the idea that not only the short-term effects of policy alternatives but also their long-term economic, environmental and social impact should be considered. Amartya Sen, an acknowledged expert in this scholarly field, regards the availability of free social choices for individuals as major elements of well-being, whereas 'social capabilities' are in Sen's vocabulary the real opportunities available to people. If choices are numerous, individuals can select the life goals most adequate to their circumstances and convictions. According to Sen, economic activity widens the range of choices available, but does not directly serve the realization of life goals. The result is less important than the possibility for people to be able to choose their own goals in life.[114]

However, that it is difficult to come to a widely accepted definition of quality of life is signalled by the debate on alternative approaches to the measurement of welfare. Most importantly, value orientations largely determine our ideas about quality of life, that is, individuals and social groups have distinct preferences about what they regard as the crucial factors of welfare. Evaluations, defining what we consider good and bad, important and unimportant, are prerequisites for determining human needs. Social inequality might illustrate the point: a certain degree of social inequality can be regarded as necessary, because it reflects the different preferences of individuals and groups, and motivates the members of the society to perform, whereas excessive inequality might harm social cohesion. However, it is difficult to draw an objective and scientifically definable line between the inequality that is socially beneficial and the one that is unacceptable or dysfunctional.[115] Assessing certain components of quality of life is also problematic. Subjective factors, such as satisfaction with life, are especially difficult to survey and compare.

Despite the difficulties, several attempts have been made to work out an adequate indicator of quality of life, often coined with similar denominations.[116] The alternative measurements follow three major approaches:[117]

1. *Extended accounts.* The first approach makes use of the accounts of economic output (GDP or GNP) and carries out adjustments on them to perfect their descriptive potential. GDP and other measures of economic output are based on the assessment of the monetary value of goods and services. Prices are basically determined by the amount that the consumers are willing to pay for them at the market, although costs and gains that are not subject to market transaction are not considered in these calculations. Therefore, the new indicators include those goods and services that do not enter the market but are beneficial for welfare, for instance, time spent on raising children or on domestic work, as well as the value of free time, and of informal education (e.g. time spent on visiting libraries and museums). In contrast, the components that are regarded as detrimental are excluded from the GDP, such as activities belonging to the category of 'regrettable necessities', which do not entail direct gain by themselves, but are required for other activities (expenditures related to the police, prisons, military and intelligence, maintenance of roads, commuting, etc.); investments necessary for future growth; as well as 'civilizational damages' (pollution of the environment, waste, traffic congestion and noise damage).

2. *Social indicators.* Another approach identifies desirable goals of society and estimates the success in the realization of these goals by virtue of complex social indicators. Typically the elements include income distribution and poverty, mortality, education, crime, housing and sometimes also political and civic rights. The idea of sustainable economic growth and consumption also influences the way quality of life is interpreted. Because this aspect is not reflected at all in GDP calculations, most indicators in question also emphatically take into consideration the quality of the environment and even the exhaustion of natural resources.[118]

3. *Indicators of subjective well-being.* The third direction of research interviews individuals directly about how they judge diverse aspects of their quality of life; in

other words, it measures a subjective sense of well-being.[119] A combination of these approaches, primarily of the first and the second method, also appears in practice.

The most widespread comprehensive indices include the Genuine Progress Indicator (GPI), the Index of Sustainable Economic Welfare (ISEW), and the Human Development Index (HDI). The GPI is a monetary indicator, which, in addition to economic output measured in a traditional way, considers the economic performance of households and deducts the value of activities not increasing welfare, as well as the value of environmental damage.[120] The ISEW is a composite index, which, similarly to the GPI, deducts the value of environmental damage, costs of commuting to the workplace, etc., and adds the value of non-paid domestic work. Furthermore, it also takes into consideration the level of income inequalities and the costs of traffic accidents.[121] The HDI, calculated by the UN, measures the performance of countries in three areas, namely life expectancy, access to knowledge, and economic development. This, in practice, means the combination of only four indicators: life expectancy at birth; school enrolment at the primary, secondary and tertiary levels; literacy; and the purchasing power value of GNP. Consequently, this indicator may be regarded as the least comprehensive, with an overrepresentation of education.[122]

Irrespective of which indicator is considered, the trends of the quality of life in industrial societies have been linked to economic growth over the long term. Notwithstanding, in the last decades of the twentieth century, this straightforward relationship disappeared. The improvement of the quality of life started lagging behind economic performance, that is, in the most advanced industrial countries, the principle of diminishing returns applied to economic growth: each percentage in the growth of economic output delivered a smaller increase, if any, in the quality of life.

Calculations suggest that the level of the ISEW dropped significantly in Great Britain between 1975 and 1990, although the GDP grew constantly in the same period. Analogous, although probably not so radical, differences can be detected in the case of some other countries that were included in similar surveys (the Netherlands and Sweden), whereas in the case of Austria and Germany, the ISEW stagnated, and it increased in Italy, although not to the same extent as the GDP. In similar periods, the GPI of the United States also declined (Figure 6.2).[123]

Therefore, in the most advanced countries, economic growth has not resulted in an improvement of the quality of life since the mid-1970s; on the contrary, in several cases, it even resulted in its deterioration. The most important reasons for the unfavourable development of the quality of life were ecological damage, the growing share of the socially underprivileged, and the increase of income inequalities.

The most compelling implication of these estimates is that welfare, or quality of life, is determined more by non-market activities than by those traditionally related to the market, even if this result is largely dependent on the method of

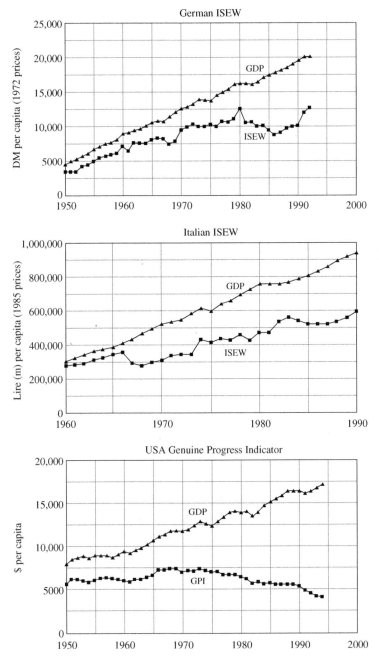

Note: ISEW: *Index of Sustainable Economic Welfare*; GPI: *Genuine Progress Indicator.*
See definition in text.

FIGURE 6.2 Indicators of quality of life (ISEW and GPI) at the end of the twentieth century
Source: Friends of the Earth website: www.foe.org.uk/campaigns/sustainable_development/progress.
2008.07.10

alternative calculations. Domestic work, such as cooking, cleaning up, and raising children, usually amounts to 25–45% of the GDP. In the late twentieth century, the value of leisure time was even higher than that figure in Europe. On balance, about two-thirds of the adjusted output originates from outside the market, and the actual GDP amounts to merely about one-third. Still, goods and services included in the GDP have not lost their relevance to welfare. Industrial societies seem to be conditioned to an overall continuous growth, which, however, could lead to considerable discontent if economic output begins to stagnate or fall. Furthermore, many societies in Europe and even more outside the continent have not yet reached that specific threshold of affluence and can still expect massive welfare returns to growth.[124]

The ISEW and other indicators related to quality of life, introduced as a critical reaction to the primacy and shortcomings of the GDP/GNP, also triggered countercritiques, which questioned the predominant reliance on value choices in the case of these indicators. However, in a less manifest form, value choices are present in GDP or GNP figures as well, and indicators like the ISEW only make value preferences more explicit. Research about quality of life, with all the difficulties, has drawn attention to the deficiencies of the indicators of economic output, and stressed the necessity of considering, in addition to economic growth, its environmental and social impact as well.

7

POLITICS AND SOCIETY

Politics is the activity of taking and implementing collective decisions that are related to the functioning of society, especially reconciling the conflicts over the distribution of resources and rewards. Thus, political events and structures can be conceptualized as particular social phenomena. However, the intersection of politics and society is complex and, subsequently, is interpreted in diverging ways. It is a long-standing tradition of social history to attribute a significant or even decisive role to social factors in shaping political relations. For instance, religious divides or changes in the employment structure substantially affect the support for political parties. In fact, this view prevalent in social history largely coincides with a classic approach of political sociology, proposed by Stein Rokkan and Seymour M. Lipset, who interpreted political phenomena by virtue of their social correlates, and, in particular, analysed and understood political systems in terms of how they are related to the structures of social cleavages.[1] However, representatives of modern political science promoted the scholarly perspective that politics as a distinctive phenomenon is worth studying in its own right. Moreover, classics of sociology (including Talcott Parsons and Niklas Luhmann) stood for the idea that politics forms a distinct subsystem of modern societies, which is separate from other subsystems, and, similarly to those, enjoys a high level of autonomy.[2] This is manifest in political institutions with distinct operational logics, as also elaborated by the representatives of political institutionalism. This latter approach shows how political organizations perpetuate their existence in the long run, and endeavour to increase their influence. Instead of stressing historical and social factors, others called for the analysis of the political behaviour of individuals and groups or their informal relationships, or claimed that in order to understand the sphere of the state and politics, one should examine political attitudes and culture.[3] From the 1960s, the idea that political behaviour should be primarily attributed to social (and economic) factors had been challenged, and numerous social historians also acknowledged that social development is significantly influenced by state activity and politics. Hence, the intersection of politics and society has become a major subject of social and historical research.

Thus, in the following, we also survey some major interrelated fields of twentieth-century European political and social life, among which social policy has already been discussed. In accordance with the main goals of this book, we focus on the direct social aspects of the functioning of political systems, and thereby the chapter does not touch upon the constitutional systems. Therefore, in-depth discussion of parliaments, governments and political decision-making processes are also dismissed. Arranging the study in this way necessarily posits a selective approach from the viewpoint of political science. Nonetheless, we readily acknowledge that the institutionalist and other approaches referred to above are essential for understanding the world of politics. Thus, we make use of several of these perspectives as well when studying the relations of politics and society.

In accordance with these aims, we first investigate social cleavages in twentieth-century Europe, in line with the Rokkanian tradition, which are not only vital for understanding how modern mass politics works but are also crucial to the historical understanding of how modern political systems in Europe evolved. Because franchise continuously expanded during the twentieth century, cleavages acquired an increasing significance, which points to the main theme of the next section. Parties have a decisive role in mapping (occasionally even deepening) cleavages, and thereby in representing the preferences of voters as well as in the political mobilization of the electorate. The twentieth-century development of European party systems is subsequently studied as well, wherein a separate part is dedicated to the political changes that ensued at the end of the century. Politics is formed not only by parties but by other social and political actors as well, and thus the history of civil society and social movements is addressed next. After discussing political culture and the development of media, which exercised a growing influence on political processes during the twentieth century, we examine the arguably most substantial political development in late twentieth-century Europe, that is, the regime changes in East Central and South-Eastern European communist countries.

Foundations of political behaviour: social cleavages

Members of societies always entertain diverse ideas about which principles should regulate the life of the community. Rephrased in the language of political science and economics, individuals and social organizations have infinite demands, whereas resources are relatively scarce, and therefore the members of society compete with each other for satisfying these demands. Both needs and resources can be either material (such as income) or non-material (including reputation, prestige, or justice). Articulating preferences and transferring them to governmental politics, as well as regulating the conflicts originating from the competition for meeting demands, all constitute tasks within the political system. Because this volume primarily focuses on social history, the social foundations of political conflicts arising in twentieth-century European societies are examined first.

Political science applies the concept 'cleavage' to describe and analyse those significant and persistent divides that exist among the members of the society with regard to their political views and forms of behaviour. Cleavages do not necessarily lead to conflicts, at least not on a regular basis, and the intensity of conflicts originating from them also varies. Therefore, they are not unequivocally important with respect to political processes. Political institutions or actors, such as parties and interest groups, attempt to represent voters' preferences, and thus to secure their support, mainly on the basis of cleavages. As it appeared in the above definition, a cleavage has to be deep and permanent for it to yield a clear and unflagging worldview that gives a worthwhile reason to establish and maintain a political organization. It is also important to stress that (as Giovanni Sartori pointed out) parties do not merely reflect cleavages but are also able to shape them to a certain extent: they give visibility to a particular set of social divisions and can politically exacerbate or downplay the importance of a cleavage depending on their organizational interests. The same holds for other political actors, such as special-interest groups, or lobbies, which also vigorously participate in the political process.[4]

Numerous conflicts of interest and lines of cleavages existed in the twentieth century and can still be found in contemporary European societies. The following are considered to be the most substantial by the research with regard to political development:[5]

- religious cleavages, based on attitudes towards religion and church, and on the relationship between different denominations and churches towards each other;
- ethnic cleavages, which are constituted by the conflicts between nations and ethnic minorities coexisting in a given political entity;
- class-based cleavages, resulting from diverging interests of employers and employees;
- regional cleavages, originating from the conflict of interests caused by the rural–urban, as well as interregional divides;[6] and
- cleavages emerging from the diverging attitudes towards the previous political system and the status quo.

Obviously, this systematization of cleavages does not apply to twentieth-century dictatorships, in which several modern political institutions, such as parties in the traditional sense, did not exist either.

Religious cleavages

As has been shown by the influential works of Stein Rokkan, the roots of the twentieth-century European political setting as well as the antecedents of party structures can be traced back to the age of the Reformation.[7] The religious-cultural difference between Catholics and Protestants was formed in the wake of the Reformation, which led to conflicts in the following centuries both between and within European societies. During the twentieth century, as is shown in chapter 9, all European countries went through a secularization process that lessened religious adherence and the influence of the church on people's everyday lives, which was expressed, for example, in the diminishing frequency of attendance at religious services. Notwithstanding, religion remained a substantial social cleavage in European societies, which had an impact on political processes. Furthermore, secularization itself created a new split between religious and non-religious, or even anti-religious social groups.

At the same time, the intensity of religion-related conflicts within individual societies varied significantly, and not in the least was determined by whether a particular society was Catholic, Protestant or of mixed religion. In homogeneous Catholic countries, such as Italy, Spain, Portugal and Austria, the Catholic versus secular conflict was regularly prominent. In these countries, the Catholic Church could establish strong social institutions with religious commitments: schools, trade unions, cultural organizations and press. These institutions yielded support for political mobilization as well. The Catholic Church safeguarded its positions particularly in the field of education: in the nineteenth century, primarily against liberals with often strong anti-church sentiments, then in the twentieth century, rather against left-wing political movements.

In Belgium, for example, the tension between the Catholic Church and parents preferring religious education, and political forces advocating secular education, persisted until the 1950s. Finally, the conflict was resolved by a compromise. In societies with mixed religious affiliations, such as the Netherlands, Germany or Switzerland, religious belonging led to deep political fissures. In these countries, party formation did not only depend on the religious versus non-religious dimension but also on which denominations the population belonged to. The most representative example in this respect is the Netherlands, where from the end of the nineteenth century, three large denominations (two Protestant and one Roman Catholic) established three independent cultural and political institutional structures. This phenomenon is referred to as *verzuiling* or pillarization in the literature. The pillars, the outwardly enclosed institutional systems, were acknowledged by the state, and thereby these long-persevered organizational forms began to weaken only from the 1960s. Consequently, during most of the twentieth century, three large denominational parties existed that merged only in 1979–80. In Protestant countries (Great Britain and Scandinavia), the role of religion was significantly lesser in shaping the political landscape, because in these states practically the entire population belonged to the state church, and therefore the church could not evolve into an autonomous political factor. Moreover, Protestantism was considerably less resistant to secular tendencies than Catholicism.

Ethnic and linguistic cleavages

The significance of ethnic cleavages is primarily linked to the historical patterns of nation formation. In certain European regions (particularly in East Central and South-Eastern Europe), the national and state frames did not coincide, and thus multiethnic entities evolved instead of more or less homogeneous nation states. Consequently, at the beginning of the twentieth century and in the interwar period, such political conflicts were more often significant in these regions than in the ethnically considerably more homogeneous Western Europe. Moreover, the nation state became the framework of democratic polity in Western Europe, which could not take place in the eastern parts of the continent. The history of the East Central and the South-Eastern European region in the interwar period provides ample examples for ethnic political conflicts, from the Serbian–Croatian tension to the Sudeten German–Czech opposition.

In the decades after the Second World War, many observers assumed that, with time, the ethnic-linguistic cleavages would altogether fade or even vanish. Seymour Martin Lipset and Stein Rokkan both argued that with the modernization of societies, ethnic splits would lose their significance compared with antagonisms based on class and economic structures.[8] However, developments in Western and Southern Europe in the 1970s and in South-Eastern Europe in the 1990s contradicted the scenario of lessening ethnic cleavages. Ethnic conflicts in Northern Ireland, the Basque country and in the Flemish region of Belgium, and later in the Balkans, showed the persistence, and at some places even increasing significance, of the ethnic dimension in politics, including the formation of parties.

Ethnic conflicts can be remarkably intense, even to the extent that such tensions occasionally lead to civil wars. However, similarly to religious divisions, the ethnic heterogeneity of a society does not necessarily result in severe conflicts. These collisions emerge only if the ethnic character is so strong that it suppresses identification with the political nation. Divergences in this regard are well represented by the three countries that were ethnically the most diverse in post-war Western Europe: Switzerland, Belgium and Spain. As to Switzerland, data available from the 1970s suggest that despite the ethnic complexity, the majority of the population, and the German-speaking citizens in particular, identified more with the Swiss nation than with their own canton or their own linguistic community.[9] The ethnic-linguistic composition of Belgium was more complex, where only the minority of the population (42%) confessed a Belgian national identity in the 1970s, suggesting that ethnic particularity was coupled with a crisis of national identity. In Spain, the ethnic setting was altogether distinct as well, because in some regions, such as Asturias, León and Castilla, the majority of the citizens identified with the Spanish nation, whereas such a link was loose elsewhere (Catalonia), and in some provinces (Galicia, País Vasco [the Basque autonomous community] and Navarra), the majority of the population were loyal rather to their region than to the country as a whole.[10]

Class-based cleavages

The basis of class conflicts is the opposing economic interests of capital and labour, or the division between the groups dominating the economy (including managers) and the employees. At the end of the nineteenth and in the first half of the twentieth century, this structural division clearly manifested in the substantial differences in the wealth and incomes of European countries, which undoubtedly encouraged the establishment of new types of political organizations. Social democratic parties formed at the end of the nineteenth century were established as class-based parties in the first place and aimed at representing the interest of the workers by primarily claiming franchise for them. With the extension of voting rights as discussed below, their electorate grew as well, gradually including wider strata of white-collar employees. Post-war trends in social stratification and the changes in the activity of the welfare state as discussed in chapters 4 and 5 (most of all, the moderation of income differences) inspired several social theorists from the 1950s (including Ralf Dahrendorf and Gerhard Lenski) to propose the decline of class conflicts in industrial societies.[11] However, this view was not universally endorsed among scholars, at least in its strongest form, and even less so, because the recurring increase of income differences throughout Europe from the 1970s weakened the plausibility of this position. J. Goldthorpe, for example, showed that traditional class ruptures were still conditioning political allegiances and voting behaviour at the end of the twentieth century.[12] Thus, on the basis of the results of empirical research, class cleavage did not lose its significance, but its relative importance decreased in European democracies after the Second World War.[13] Major evidence supporting the fading of class cleavage is that class affiliation played an increasingly lesser role in shaping voting patterns after the Second World War. The Alford index shows that between the 1950s and 1980s, except for France and Italy, the number of people whose party choice was based on class affiliation declined everywhere (Table 7.4). At the same time, differences between countries remained significant. Despite the decrease, in Scandinavia, Great Britain and Italy, class remained an important factor in party preference, whereas in Germany, Switzerland and Ireland, the role played by class affiliation in voting was minor. In the latter three countries, the significance of other factors in electoral choices increased, such as the dependence on state redistribution, occupation or lifestyle.[14]

Regional cleavages

If there are significant disparities between regions or types of settlements (for example, in the level of economic development, the dynamics of growth, or living standard), these may evolve into political conflicts as well. A characteristic type of this cleavage is the rural–urban divide, which traditionally emerged in the form of friction between the agrarian and the industrial sectors. Because governments can substantially alter the incomes of particular economic branches to a great extent with taxation, tariffs, investment policy and in other ways, these sectors often mobilize for their political representation. Rokkan also suggested that the rural–urban divide developed into a major cleavage when the state preferred urban interests to that of rural ones. However, the urban–rural schism is most often cultural as well. Urbanization, which accelerated in the wake of the industrial revolution, produced a distinct culture, which was primarily characterized by the advance of individualization, whereas in rural areas, traditional community prevailed to a greater extent. This process had significant political consequences, for instance, the urban population became more prone to political radicalism than the rural one. Division of this kind clearly manifested in Central Europe during the revolutionary period after the First World War, when, as opposed to urban mass mobilization and leftist radicalism, the rural population remained passive politically. Nonetheless, political conflicts not only surfaced between urban and rural areas but also between entire regions. During the twentieth century, such cleavages remained salient in Italy, with its strong provincial discrepancies.[15] Obviously, ethnic, religious and other divergencies may reinforce regional segmentation, as emerged in post-war Catholic Bavaria. However, it is plausible to conceptualize a cleavage as regional only if territorial demarcation coincides with religious or other splits, and it becomes a source of major political disagreement.

Attitudes towards the ancien régime *as cleavages*

At the beginning of the twentieth century, liberal and conservative parties had the longest history among European parties. However, during that period, it was difficult to interpret them in accordance with the four cleavages referred to above because these political parties were originally established on the basis of their different attitudes towards the eighteenth-century *ancien régime*. When the significance of this conflict practically disappeared, and the introduction of universal suffrage rearranged the constitution of the electorate completely, liberal parties traditionally representing business interests started to be marginalized. The decline happened all over Europe, but it was particularly rapid in Scandinavia and Great Britain. In the latter country, the Liberal Party was altogether pushed to the background within a short period during the 1920s. Conservative parties also faced a challenge with the emergence and consolidation of Christian democratic/Christian socialist parties, which ideologically resembled the conservatives, but more definitely represented the principles of social solidarity. Christian democratic parties usually crowded out and often even fully replaced their conservative counterparts from power, but did not succeed everywhere in this respect, which is also exemplified by Great Britain, where there existed no Christian democratic party at all.

The relationship with the previous regime became a distinctly important cleavage from the 1990s in post-communist countries, especially in those where dictatorship did not cease to exist as a result of revolutions or mass movements, but rather dissipated through peaceful negotiations. Here, the communist elite escaped impeachment and managed to transform its power and influence in many fields (for instance, in economy or in the media) in the new democratic system. Not only did this process raise moral questions, but the retained economic and other privileges distorted political competition as well, yielding advantages to the members of the ex-communist elite and their political partners. This development gave rise to a new political cleavage in the recently established democracies in the 1990s, which was based on the relation to the communist dictatorship and its beneficiaries.

With regard to the emergence and significance of cleavages as well as the functioning of political systems, the extension of franchise and subsequently the realization of universal suffrage were major developments of the twentieth century. Thus, the next section outlines the historical formation of suffrage.

Participation in political decision making: the development of suffrage

In most European countries suffrage, as well as a democratic government responsible to the parliament, had only been partially introduced by the turn of the nineteenth to the twentieth century.[16] Although some institutions of popular representation did exist in almost all European countries by that time, these cannot be regarded as democratic institutions in a contemporary century sense. Using the expression of Richard Rose, it is more precise to talk about constitutional oligarchies, because even though the governments obeyed the rule of law, the legislation and implementation of law was exercised by a small minority.[17]

The reason behind this was primarily the fact that franchise was limited everywhere on the basis of various, contestable considerations and in distinct ways. In certain countries, men had already been granted full franchise, such as in France (1848 and 1875), Switzerland (1848), Germany (1867), Greece (1877) and Norway (1898) (Table 7.1). However, women could not vote even in these countries at the turn of the century. In the rest of the European countries, only a minority of all men could exercise their voting right, which in turn was based on census suffrage: qualification was based on income, property or the level of education. In addition, the ballot was frequently not secret, thus regularly enabling the manipulation of the electorate, for instance, by putting pressure on employees by employers. Results were potentially garbled by the varying size of constituencies, and in some countries separate lists, such as curias, were devised for certain electoral groups, which again obtained disproportionate representation.[18]

Furthermore, parliamentarism was restricted almost everywhere before the First World War. Even assemblies that were formed through free elections based on relatively extensive franchise could not completely control governments, because the government, the ruler or some other non-elected body had broad political privileges.[19]

At the end of the nineteenth century, France's political institutions were the closest to the ideal of democratic elections and parliamentarism. After the 1852 restrictions, all men had had the right to vote since 1875, and the government was responsible to the *Chambre des députés*. Before the First World War in Great Britain, franchise was extended to two-thirds of all adult men, and they elected the members of the House of Commons by secret ballot. Nevertheless, the House of Lords, comprised of hereditary peers, retained significant authorities in legislation until 1911, when the constitutional crisis originating from conflicting competences was settled in favour of the House of Commons. In Germany, the lower house of the federal parliament (the *Reichstag*) was freely elected by adult men with

TABLE 7.1 Extension of franchise and the introduction of universal suffrage in European countries

	Proportion of voters before the extension (year: %)	First extension (House of Commons)	Later extensions	Type of inequality	End of inequality	Male franchise	Universal suffrage
England	1830: 2.3	1832	1867 1884	Businessmen, university votes	1948	1918	1929
France	1815: 0.25		1830			1793, 1848 1875	1945
Netherlands	1851: 2.4	1887	1896				1917
Belgium	1831: 1	1848	1893	Multiple vote franchise	1919	1919	1949
Ireland	1830: 0.2	1832	1867 1884	Businessmen, university votes	1923	1918	1923
Prussia/Germany				Tripartite franchise/-	1919	1849/1867	1919/1919
Austria	1873:6	1882	1897 Fifth curia	Clear differences between curias	1907	1907	1919
Switzerland						1848	1971
Sweden	1865: 4.8	1909		Rating of voters according to tax categories	1920		1920
Denmark	1849: 14–15	1866				1849 (30 years)	1915
Norway	1814: 10	1885				1898	1915
Finland							1906
Italy	1871: 2.3	1882: 7%	1912			1919	1945

Source: Stein Rokkan, *Staat, Nation und Demokratie in Europa*. Aus seinen gesammelten Werken rekonstruiert und eingeleitet von Peter Flora, Frankfurt/M.: Suhrkamp, 2000, 306–307.

franchise; however, it could exercise negligible influence on foreign policy and military matters, dominated by the *Kaiser*, and the Reichstag was also constrained in endorsing the budget. Prussia (the state with the largest population in the German Empire) had a census suffrage. In addition, representation was not proportionate: the electorate was arranged into three groups that were different in size, and each of these groups delegated one-third of the members of the Prussian parliament.

The First World War destabilized the position of the elite throughout Europe, and it politically mobilized wide segments of the societies, including those who did not possess political rights, and thereby contributed to parliamentarization and the extension of suffrage. Regarding the form of state, the new countries that came to life after the war, with the exception of Yugoslavia, all decided on the republican constitution. Even Austria and Germany followed suit. Consequently, the rights and responsibilities of the parliaments considerably grew in these countries. In turn, after the First World War, all men, or at least the majority of them, in those countries that had failed to catch up with this development earlier were granted the right to vote. As for women, in some countries, they had already acquired voting rights before and during the war. First among these countries was Finland (1906), followed by Norway (1913), Denmark, and Iceland (1915). After the First World War, women were granted suffrage in several other countries as well, although with the exception of the following states: Italy, Greece, Spain, Belgium, France and Switzerland. Although franchise restrictions still existed, nevertheless these were considerably less strict than earlier ones (Table 7.1).[20] There were some examples of regress as well: in smaller Hungarian settlements, open election replaced secret ballot in 1922, which seriously impeded the practice of democratically exercised voting rights. In addition, educational qualification in voting and other conditions were tightened, which led to a substantial decrease in the proportion of citizens with franchise. In the 1930s, the secret ballot was restored in every constituency.[21]

The extension of franchise did not necessarily lead to the formation or consolidation of the democratic political system after the First World War, which reflects the importance of other factors besides suffrage in this process. The consequences of the war (such as inflation and revolutions), the reactionary political repercussion represented by the establishment of the Soviet Union, the impact of the Great Depression and such long-term factors as the belated and disturbed nation formation, all contributed to the failure of democratization in most of the Central and East Central European countries. Beyond franchise, we cannot examine the complete range of factors determining parliamentary representation; however, among them several aspects of the political culture are addressed later.

The claim that comprehensive suffrage in itself does not guarantee the stability of a democratic political system was clearly shown by the fate of the Weimar Republic, where the combined figures of the extreme right and extreme left parties amounted to an absolute majority of votes in 1932. Although this election did not yet result in the seizure of power by extremists, nevertheless it eventually significantly contributed to the 'self-liquidation' of the Weimar democracy. Moreover, the extension of franchise enhanced political mobilization to a great extent, which in turn created one of the preconditions for the formation of political regimes regarded as totalitarian. Apart from the Soviet Union, such systems appeared only in Italy and Germany in the interwar period, but several countries witnessed the emergence of regimes in which parliamentarism was restricted, or which can be regarded as authoritarian. In the interwar years, Czechoslovakia was the only example among the newly formed or re-established East Central and South-Eastern European states that did not belong to this group.

Still, in North-Western Europe and Scandinavia, the extension of franchise in the interwar period contributed to the formation of democratic systems to a great extent. In these countries, former restrictions were gradually, or at once, waived, and thus by 1939, nine European countries had introduced universal suffrage for both men and women. The countries in question included Norway, Sweden, Denmark, Finland, Ireland, the United Kingdom, Luxembourg, the Netherlands and Czechoslovakia.

In these states the extension of suffrage also meant that blue-collar workers and white-collar employees comprising the majority or relative majority of the citizens acquired a decisive role in politics. Because the political ascension of the frequently radical labour parties seemed to be an alarming perspective for other political forces, electoral systems based on individual constituencies following the principle of first-past-the-post had been usually rearranged into proportionate representations in the interwar period. By this method, seats in the parliament were divided among political parties in proportion to their votes. In other words, the electoral minority also gained seats in the parliament, and a relative majority achieved in elections was hardly enough to form a government, except by entering into a coalition with other parties.[22]

In the post-war years, women were granted suffrage in Belgium and France. This event practically signalled the end point of the process of the extension of franchise, because Switzerland remained the only country where women had to wait until 1971 to participate in elections. Consequently, beside civil rights (freedom of speech, freedom of the press and freedom of association), political rights were also generally extended throughout Western Europe. As Thomas H. Marshall argued, citizens could enjoy their civil and political rights only if these were complemented with social rights, including health care, guaranteed minimum income and free education.[23] Post-war development of social welfare throughout Europe, as discussed in chapter 5, pointed to the direction that citizenship should entail social rights as well, which was seriously challenged only at the end of the century.

Political parties: systems and families

Political parties can be regarded as the most important intermediary institutions in democratic societies, linking electoral interests and preferences based on the above discussed social cleavages to the formal structures of political decision making. Parties are voluntary but formal organizations that aim to gain political power. Their functions include setting goals, grouping and expressing interests, and mobilizing the electorate, as well as recruiting members. This means that in democratic systems, parties have direct contact with voters and diverse interest groups, and they not only perceive the conflicting and contradictory needs and interests of the electorate, but also transform them into coherent and feasible goals and programmes that they subsequently represent. Parties compete in gaining the support of citizens, run for election, and upon winning, their delegates occupy governmental or other public positions. As suggested earlier, parties and their decision makers often also realize their own social and political goals, which is particularly possible if they constitute or participate in the government. All these features apply to pluralist democracies. Parties may exist in authoritarian or dictatorial regimes as well, but the political competition between them is seriously restricted or is lacking entirely.

Obviously, besides the parliamentary system relying on political parties, modern democracies have other important political institutions as well. In theory, some of them even represent alternatives to parliamentary democracy, such as the direct involvement of people in political decision making through referenda and plebiscites, when citizens decide on particular issues without the intervening of parties or the parliament. Nevertheless, if citizens were to reach decisions via referenda in all cases, then the costs of the decision-making process (informing voters about the alternatives, and organizing the vote) would be enormous, particularly in terms of time. Thus, no matter how essential direct democracy is for counteracting the oligarchic tendencies of modern democratic system, no democracy can dispense with parties, or for that matter, with parliaments and governments.[24]

Theoretically, separate parties may be formed along any social cleavage, and even on all of their particular combinations. Notwithstanding, the significance of the five traditional cleavages varies in different societies and historical periods. Therefore, cleavages do not necessarily lead to the formation of parties, because such organizations are established only if there is a substantial support by the electorate. When new clashes of interests are emerging in a society, they will most probably appear in the programmes of parties as well. This can manifest itself in that the existing parties assume the role of representing the marginalized (or newly emerging) interests; however, based on the cleavage, a new party may be subsequently formed. Obviously, popular support for parties is contingent on several other factors, such as the astuteness of their leaders, or available resources, including media representation.

There are several prerequisites for a party to survive over the long run. Most importantly, the party has to build up its programme on significant social conflicts. Furthermore, there has to be a social stratum (or several strata) with a relatively consistent and distinct system of values and beliefs, or even worldview, which provide the basis for the party. It is also required that the party establish an effective organizational structure.

After the Second World War, it was one of the essential trends of the development of parties that in Western Europe already well-established parties endeavoured to increase their appeal to even wider social layers. Their goal was to be able to form a government on their own and not engage in coalition, or to become a major faction in government. This goal could be realized only by reforming their original programme, which fitted the needs and the ideology of a more defined social group. Provided that this transformation towards a more popular political representation took place, their messages became increasingly blurred, and more difficult to distinguish from the platforms of other parties, or they sometimes even contained contradictory elements. These parties are also called 'catch-all' parties. All these changes were particularly characteristic of Christian democratic and social democratic parties. During this process, the former put gradually less emphasis on their religious attachments, whereas the latter discarded the idea of class conflict and class struggle. In contrast, minor parties could more efficiently retain their character, and could allow themselves to specialize in emphatically representing the interests of distinct social groups.[25]

Political parties and organizations show unique features, but could also be categorized according to the patterns of interests that they express, and to their political values as well as practical policy. Four ideological orientations or traditions played a particularly significant role in the formation of parties in twentieth-century Europe, which also led to the formation of distinct party families: socialism/social democracy, Christian democracy, conservatism and liberalism. In the following sections, we discuss the major twentieth-century trends of these party families, supplemented with some other party types that cannot be unequivocally grouped with any of these larger political platforms, but are important with regard to the cleavages discussed.[26]

Social democratic parties

The first social democratic parties were established in the last decades of the nineteenth century, in order to represent the interests of workers, who increasingly defined themselves as a distinct and cohesive class. The initial phase of their development was characterized by a radical programme, that is, by the goal of implementing socialism. With regard to their political representation, the First World War brought about a breakthrough when social democrats were involved in the government in most Western European countries. Their wartime role generated heated debates even within their ranks and deepened already existing conflicts between reformists and radical groups, which later even led to the split of the movement: social democrats wished to transform society within the framework of parliamentarism, whereas communists opted for seizing power in a forceful way, including violent actions or revolution. The secession of the communists further weakened the radicalism of the social democratic movement and facilitated their integration into the parliamentary system. The presence of social democrats in European parliaments and governments became common from the 1920s: in Germany, for instance, they formed an important part of the Weimar coalition.

In the second half of the century, social democratic parties went through further ideological changes, as shown by the German Social Democratic Party (*Sozialde-mokratische Partei Deutschlands* [SPD]), which in the early post-war years represented a Marxist stance regarding the ownership of property (that is, the party stood for the nationalization of large companies), and at the same time, rejected the North Atlantic Treaty Organization (NATO) and the initiatives for European integration. At the 1959 congress in Bad Godesberg, the SPD profoundly revised its programme, whereon it assumed a reformist position. This move was not unique, because after the Second World War, several other European social democratic parties were also reorganized, for instance, the Austrian SPÖ (*Sozialistische Partei Österreichs*), the Belgian PSB (*Belgische Socialistische Partij/Parti Socialiste Belge*), or the Dutch PvdA (*Partij van de Arbeid*). The transformation of French and Italian socialist/social democratic parties ensued at the end of the 1960s. These changes in turn enabled the extension of the electoral base and increased the governmental capabilities of these parties. Thus, social democratic parties began to resemble the 'catch-all' parties, that is, they opened towards the middle classes by integrating a broad range of interests into a centrist political platform. Nevertheless, this change required that they renounce the goal of realizing socialism. Social and economic changes of the post-war era contributed to this change as well. For instance, the growing economic activity of the governments, the achievements of the welfare state, and the decline of income inequalities all moderated the radicalism of the social democratic base. In several post-war Western European countries, such as Norway, Sweden and Austria, social democrats were vital and indispensable members of the governments. They became part of the political establishment in other countries as well. Nonetheless, the ideological transformation referred to above weakened the coherence of programmes and goals, which was coupled with the fact that social democratic parties were unable to provide convincing and distinguishable answers to the economic difficulties of the 1970s. They particularly could not come up with solutions suited to their traditional values and to the expectations of their core electoral base. Consequently, during the 1970s and 1980s, the popularity of social democratic parties declined in numerous countries, and they were also gradually losing their positions in the governments as well. The step that the British Labour Party and the German Social Democratic Party took in the 1990s was another ideological turn, referred to by slogans such as the 'Third Way' and the 'New Centre' (*Die Neue Mitte*). The programme of these parties became less characteristic vis-à-vis parties of the centre right, but the reorientation gave a new potential to attract new electoral groups nonetheless.

Christian democratic parties

Contemporary Christian democratic parties or their predecessors mostly emerged at the end of the nineteenth and the beginning of the twentieth century. Their foundation was a reaction to the individualist doctrine of liberalism, and to the socialist call for class struggle, as well as to the anti-church attitude of both. The cleavage originating from the process of secularization played a crucial role in their formation. One of the major conflicting issues between the churches (particularly the Catholic Church, and the social groups they represented) and the state was the status of church schools and religious education. Christian democratic parties also responded to cleavages arising from social inequalities. The idea of social justice was propounded on the basis of Christian social thought and backed by the ideological munitions provided by Papal Encyclicals (*Rerum Novarum* [1891] and *Quadragesimo*

Anno [1931]). Parties with Christian democratic orientation stood up for the interests of those social groups that were neglected by liberals representing urban business interests, and by social democrats representing the working class. Thus, they fought for the franchise of the agrarian population. Moreover, they acknowledged the right to property but also supported restriction on property rights for the public interest. In the late nineteenth and early twentieth century, Christian socialist parties were also active participants of political life favouring the social engagement of the state, though the extension of democratic rights was less central to their programme. These parties were marginalized by Christian democratic parties later in the twentieth century. After the First World War, particularly strong members of this group of parties were the Centre Party (*Zentrum*) in Germany, the Italian Peoples' Party (*Partito Popolare Italiano* [PPI]), the Austrian Christian Social Party (*Christlichsoziale Partei*), and already at that time Belgian and Dutch Catholic parties were also highly influential.

In general, the popularity of Christian democratic parties further increased in the first post-war decades. Their religious character became moderated, and their policy was not anchored in those ideas that churches propounded with regard to social questions but rather in the general set of Christian values. This shift may be interpreted as similar to the one that took place in the case of social democratic parties after the Second World War, and its repercussions were analogous as well: Christian democratic parties could develop into large people's parties, despite the continuing process of secularization. Electoral support of the following parties subsequently grew significantly: the Norwegian Christian People's Party (*Kristeligt Folkeparti* [KrF]), the Finnish Christian League (*Suomen Kristillinen Liitto* [SKL]), the Dutch Calvinist Party (*Staatkundig Gereformeerde Partij* [SGP]), and the Swiss Evangelical People's Party (*Evangelische Volkspartei* [EVP]). The advance of the Christian Democratic Union of Germany (*Christlich Demokratische Union Deutschlands* [CDU])/ Christian Social Union of Bavaria (*Christlich-Soziale Union in Bayern* [CSU]), successfully managing the German economic miracle in the 1950s and early 1960s, and the rise of the Italian Christian Democratic Party (*Democrazia Cristiana* [DC]) should be emphasized here as well. The Swiss Christian Democratic People's Party (*Christlichdemokratische Volkspartei* [CVP]) participated in all governments between the end of the Second World War and the 1980s. Several of these people's parties suffered a moderate loss of popularity from the 1980s on, as shown by the examples of Austria, Belgium or Italy. At the same time, the Dutch Christian Democratic Party (*Christen-Democratisch Appèl* [CDA]), the Irish *Fine Gael* or the German CDU/CSU kept their positions as well.

Christian democratic parties were also frequently called centre parties, because they occupied a position between the traditional left and the right in several respects. Their social doctrine maintained that traditional social institutions, such as family, churches and local communities, should be protected. In addition, according to the principle of subsidiarity, these parties attributed a significant role to not only the state but also to communities in solving social problems. These perspectives approximated them to conservative parties, which explains the rare coexistence of a strong conservative and a Christian democratic party in European societies. At the same time, they were markedly different from conservative political factions in their strong social commitment, and in the emphasis on public interests as opposed to individual rights.[27] Another element that related them more to the social democratic parties than to conservative ones was the dedication to supranationalism in Europe. The founding fathers of the institutions of European integration, Robert Schuman, Paul-Henri Spaak, Alcide De Gasperi and Konrad Adenauer were all Christian democratic politicians.

Liberal parties

Liberalism as the movement and ideology of the bourgeoisie emerged in the eighteenth century, and its political influence grew steadily in the following century. Thus, several twenty-first-century liberal parties obviously have a long history: the Belgian Liberal Party (*Partij voor Vrijheid en Vooruitgang* [PVV]), for example, dates back to 1846. The most important goals of nineteenth-century liberalism were the realization of civil rights and the abolition of social privileges; in these respects, the liberals were highly successful throughout Europe. However, considering partisan politics, liberalism was declining from the end of the nineteenth century, because, on the one hand, several of its claims had been realized, or were included in the programme of other parties as well, whereas, on the other hand, liberal parties mainly representing urban business interests were greatly and negatively affected by the extension of franchise, which is addressed earlier in this chapter. The parties gaining most profit from this process were the Christian democrats and the social democrats, whereas liberal parties, which constituted the majority or had a considerable share of seats in most of the parliaments just a few decades earlier, were thrust into the background in the interwar period.

All in all, electoral support for the liberal parties continued to erode after the Second World War. In most of the European countries, liberal parties stabilized their support at a relatively low level, usually below 10%. The major reason for this decline was that core aspects of liberal tenets, such as the protection of property rights, and the opposition to state intervention, were perceived by the majority of the electorate as favouring the interests of the wealthy class. However, there were exceptions as well: liberal parties in Belgium and the Netherlands strengthened in the 1970s and 1980s. Liberals also had strongholds in Ireland, Greece, Great Britain and Switzerland. Nonetheless, preserving this position was possible only by extending their programme beyond traditional liberal ideas. In some countries, such as Denmark, Sweden and the Netherlands, liberal parties were less characterized by the perpetuation of nineteenth-century market fundamentalism, or its late twentieth-century revival, and their programmes emphasized social justice.

However, a relatively narrow electoral base did not mean that liberal parties lost their political influence entirely in the second half of the twentieth century. Most of them participated in government coalitions for shorter or longer periods after the Second World War: the German FDP (*Freie Demokratische Partei*) for example, on the side of CDU/CSU or SPD gained a role in most of the West German governments of the post-war era. At the same time, the largest member of the family of European liberal parties at the end of the century, the British Social and Liberal Democrats, did not gain a role in the government until recently because of the non-proportional British electoral system.

Conservative parties

Political conservatism was born at the beginning of the nineteenth century as a countermovement to liberalism and radical social reform programmes based on abstract social theories. Contrary to liberalism and socialism, it was not conceived with the ambition of providing a comprehensive worldview. Its supporters claimed that radical, revolutionary changes would necessarily lead to social failures. Instead, they regarded society as a slowly evolving organic entity, based on traditions. In the early nineteenth century, conservatism had a significant social agenda, because as opposed to liberalism it wished to participate actively in mitigating social tensions caused by capitalism. Conservative parties entered government relatively early, often around the time of their foundation, and could generally maintain their influence in the first decades of the twentieth century. This is reflected by the fact that in the interwar era, all such parties remained in governmental positions for at least two years in Western Europe, and even in Southern Europe, except for the Spanish conservatives. In Scandinavia, they held governmental positions for a shorter period, and in the rest of the continent for a longer time.

Most of the post-war Western European conservative parties were established in the nineteenth century, and have gone through relatively little change since then. France is a significant counterexample, where the Gaullist movement, incorporating several parties, developed after the Second World War. After the war, the electoral support for conservatives declined throughout Europe because of the crowding-out effect of the expanding Christian democratic parties, with the exception of the British Conservative Party and the Danish Conservative People's Party (*Konservative Folkeparti* [KF]). From the 1970s, conservative parties also profited from the growing influence of the neoliberal ideology, advocating the rolling back of the state in economic and social affairs. Conservative parties formed cabinets in several countries, but later on, with the exception of Greece and Great Britain, they had a declining overall popularity again in the 1980s.

Communist parties

The establishment of the first communist parties dates back to the immediate aftermath of the Bolshevik revolution. These organizations, as noted above, were usually formed during a process of secession of radical groups from social democratic parties. In the first few months after the First World War, a few communist parties were involved in governments in Central and East Central Europe, but their popularity rapidly waned with political stabilization, and they were soon forced into opposition. Communist parties contested the parliamentary system, and wished to replace it even with violent means, and associated themselves with the Comintern (1919–43), and later the Cominform (1947–56), serving the foreign policy aims of the Soviet Union. Therefore their operation was frequently restricted or banned entirely in the interwar era and even beyond.

Although in the years of the Great Depression, communists regained a significant popularity in Germany, after the immediate aftermath of the First World War, only the Spanish PCE (*Partido Comunista de España*) ascended to power as member of the Spanish People's Front coalition government (1936–39). After the Second World War, communist parties gained a solid electoral foothold in some Western European and Southern European countries, whereas in other states, they considerably lagged behind the others, if they existed at all. Communist parties remained continuously successful at elections in Italy (*Partido Comunista Italiano* [PCI]), France (*Parti Communiste Français* (PCF)), Finland (*Suomen Kansan Demokraattinen Liitto* [SKDL]) and from the 1970s in Portugal, Greece and Spain. These parties made efforts from the 1960s to loosen their dependence on Moscow, and thus distanced themselves from the 1968 occupation of Czechoslovakia, although they had previously almost unanimously approved of putting down the 1956 revolution in Hungary.

From the 1960s, the communist parties in Western and Southern Europe articulated their commitment to parliamentary and democratic institutions more clearly than earlier and made efforts to broaden their appeal by embracing white-collar workers and new social movements, such as feminism. Moreover, they even questioned the politics of the Soviet Union, although in a covert way, without giving up the ultimate goal of realizing the communist society. This unique, 'Western' type of communist current was called 'Eurocommunism'. In the 1970s, the Italian Communist Party gained about one-third of the total votes cast; however, the largest members of this party family started to decline from the 1980s. Disregarding the few years directly after the Second World War, the only communist parties entering government in Western and Southern Europe were the Finnish Communist Party (*Suomen Kommunistinen Puolue* [SKP]/SKDL (several times after 1966)) and the French PCF (between 1981 and 1984).

Ethnic parties

Parties based on the ethnic–linguistic cleavage had already began to organize themselves at the end of the nineteenth century in Europe, and some of them are still active today, including the Basque Nationalist Party (*Partido Nacionalista Vasco* [PNV]) or the Swedish People's Party in Finland (*Svenska Folkpartiet* [SFP]). In the interwar period, several ethnic parties emerged and gained smaller or larger roles in the political life of East Central Europe and the Balkans, for instance, the Sudeten German Party (*Sudetendeutsche Partei* [SdP]) in Czechoslovakia. After the Second World War, their influence usually declined, which was exemplified by the fact that in Western Europe, only the Swedish People's Party could remain part of the government in the long run. By the end of the twentieth century, ethnic parties were able to preserve their electoral base mostly in Belgium, Spain and the United Kingdom, besides Finland. Belgium had a peculiar political landscape, because here all parties, including the Greens, counted on the support of either Flemish or Walloon voters. Nevertheless, it is only the Flemish People's Union that can be regarded as an ethnic party in the sense that it is organized to represent the interests of a given ethnicity. After the regime change in East Central Europe, a few ethnic parties were successfully established and participated in politics, and occasionally were even included in governments, for instance, the parties of Hungarians living in Romania and Slovakia.

Agrarian parties

The electoral support of agrarian or rural parties reflected primarily, but not exclusively, the size of the agrarian sector throughout the twentieth century. Parties with such orientation were established and played significant roles for a longer period in Scandinavia, in East Central and South-Eastern Europe, as well as in France, Switzerland and the Bavarian parts of Germany. The one with the longest history is the *Venstre* in Denmark, which was established in 1870. It entered the government in 1901 for the first time, and was considered to be the largest Danish party before the First World War. In the interwar period, agrarian parties were regular members of coalition governments, and in East Central Europe and the Balkans they occasionally even played a leading role. The Danish *Venstre* and its counterparts lost their electoral base after the Second World War, as a result of the often dramatic decline of the agrarian sector. Only a few sister parties were able to maintain their position in Switzerland and Scandinavia. The Swiss People's Party (*Schweizerische Volkspartei* [SVP]) was represented in all governments in the post-war decades, and frequently provided the Prime Minister as well.

This result was approximated by the Finnish Centre Party KESK (*Keskustapuolue*), already significant in the interwar period, which slightly improved its electoral performance in the 1980s. These examples show that some originally agrarian parties could accommodate the demands of the new political landscape after the marginalization of the agrarian sector. In addition, they incorporated novel aims into their programme that also concerned the non-urban population, such as the protection of the environment or the diminution of regional differences.

Parties in communist dictatorships

Regarding the development of parties and party systems after the Second World War, countries in East Central Europe and the Balkans followed a completely different path compared with those referred to above. Democratic parties along with parliamentarism revived everywhere after the Second World War, but the subsequent communist takeover put an end to their independent existence. In Hungary, Romania, Albania and Yugoslavia, the communist parties were the only ones to continue functioning, whereas in Bulgaria, Poland, Czechoslovakia and East Germany, a few other parties were formally allowed to exist but had to accept the power monopoly, or, in contemporary terminology, the 'leading role' of the communist party. The ruthless eradication of political rivals was not confined to the party system but affected all segments of social life. Institutions of civil society were terminated or strictly controlled, paying particular attention to the control of churches, which had the largest organizational and institutional strength, and of the media.

Although dictatorships in the interwar period did not bother with applying democratic formalities, communist regimes referred to themselves as 'people's democracies' and ritually conducted elections. Citizens could either vote for candidates of just one party (the communist party) or they could choose between several other candidates, all of which, however, were included in the ballot with the approval of the communist party. Participation at the elections was high, usually above 99%, and candidates of the communist party gained the same or similarly high support.

Thus, the elections were used as a mechanism for the mobilization and control of the population and as propaganda for the system. They were supposed to show that the overwhelming majority of the population accepted the system and were afraid of questioning even its most obvious deceits. Through these ceremonial elections and many other political events, the sceptics could experience the futility of any resistance. The discrepancy between democratic principles and anti-democratic practice resulted in an overall political apathy and cynicism in the society, which was far from contradicting the intentions of the political elite, because it enhanced the smooth exercise of power. Distortions of the political system left a grave legacy on the political culture of post-communist societies, which is addressed later.

Changes in the party systems: freezing and thawing out?

Seymour M. Lipset and Stein Rokkan hold that the major types of Western European parties were established in the period when universal suffrage was extended, that is, at the beginning of the twentieth century, and they remained stable in the following decades, or, in their words, the party systems were 'frozen'. It is a fact that the European party structure remained unchanged until the 1970s in several aspects. It was a sign of the stability that between the early 1920s and late 1960s, the only social democratic parties that could significantly improve their results at the elections were the Norwegian, the Swedish and the British. Electoral performance of the Christian democratic and Conservative parties was relatively stable as well: they lost ground in the political arena only in Norway and Sweden in the 1940s. Notwithstanding, the thesis of 'freezing' has to be handled with sufficient caution. On the one hand, several authoritarian regimes and dictatorships had already been established in interwar Europe. Besides the Italian fascist and the German national socialist systems, democratic rights and institutions were considerably curtailed in Portugal and Spain, and in major parts of East Central Europe and the Balkans as well. This authoritarian political landscape included the eradication of the multiple-party system or the restriction of competition among parties. On the other hand, power relations among parties or groups of parties in the democracies did not remain utterly unaltered with time. As we have seen, liberal and conservative parties had been formed the earliest, and already participated in parliamentary politics in the nineteenth century in Europe, and they had frequently comprised a bipolar party system. Parties belonging to the social democratic and Christian democratic families emerged at the end of the nineteenth century, and parliaments of Western European countries became tripolar with their development, because Christian democratic parties usually crowded out the conservative parties or belonged to the same bloc. In the interwar period, the rapid advance of social democratic parties and the decline of the liberals brought back the bipolar political setup.[28] The thesis on the stability of the party system is also undermined by the fact that most of the old parties went through substantial restructurings throughout the century. In other words, large parties active in the second half of the twentieth century regularly had a predecessor with a different name. Furthermore, parties frequently split, or groups dissatisfied with the functioning of the party broke off.

Consequently, we can talk about the freezing of the party structures between the 1920s and 1950s only with limitations, even with regard to Western Europe. Yet, it is a fact that electoral behaviour and political structures went through changes from the 1960s that were more significant than earlier. One of the manifestations of this change was the absolute majority that the Austrian social democratic party gained at the elections in 1971. However, in several Scandinavian countries (Norway, Denmark, and Sweden), social democratic parties fell out of the government for the first time in decades. Another example is the Dutch Catholic Party, which had staunchly retained about one-third of the total share of its votes since the First World War but lost about half of its supporters between 1963 and 1972.

Not only did power relations shift between existing parties, but factions with brand new programmes appeared as well. Green parties, which were established in all Western European countries in the 1970s, were probably the most important ones among these newly emerging organizations. These are usually regarded as representatives of 'new politics' (Table 7.2). Such parties evolved from environmentalist movements, and thereby the most important element in their programme was the protection of the environment, even at the expense of economic growth, based on the consideration that the costs of economic growth are damage to the biosphere: among other policies, they prioritized public transport as well as opposed any use of nuclear energy, which later in Germany and Sweden led to programmes of phasing out of all nuclear plants. Soon, their programme included broader social and economic aspects of ecological conservation: based on the idea that the profit produced by environmentally detrimental activities is primarily gained by the private sector, although the costs of these practices have to be met by the public, they considered governmental intervention in economy as necessary. They also wished to regulate the political interference of large corporations. Green

TABLE 7.2 Goals and ideals of 'old politics' and 'new politics' in Western Europe in the 1970s and 1980s

Materialist/'old politics'	*Postmaterialist/'new politics'*
Economic growth	'Sustainable economy' (economic expansion with no adverse effects on environment, even at the expense of growth)
Market economy, mass consumption	Social-needs economy, subdued consumption
Representational democracy	Civilian initiatives, non-governmental organizations ('grassroots democracy')
Strong military defence	Nuclear disarmament
Social order	Personal freedom
Traditional gender roles in family and society	Gender equality

Sources: Own compilation based on Jan Erik Lane and Svante O. Ersson, *European Politics,* London: Sage, 1996, 115–132; Russell J. Dalton, *Politics in Germany,* New York: Harper Collins, 1993, 135.

parties emerged at the local level, progressively gaining popular support and advancing to regional politics, only arriving at the national level of politics when they established strong local networks and had local support. Therefore, from the outset, green politics has accentuated grassroots-level political activity and decision making, enhancing the role of direct democracy, based on citizen involvement and consensual decision making. Besides ecological issues and democracy, green politics has also been concerned with civil liberties and social justice, including women's emancipation and non-violence. Green parties had already achieved local successes in the 1970s, and in the 1980s they were also represented at a national level in several countries: their members participated in the parliaments of Denmark, Belgium, Germany and Austria (Table 7.3).[29]

The transformation of loosely organized environmentalist movements into established parties, apart from such advantages as larger publicity or more effective organization, involved political costs as well, particularly when their members became members of the local or national parliaments. From that moment on, they were faced with the practical difficulties of realizing their ambitious ecological programme: the policies they pursued, such as the decrease of energy consumption by increasing energy prices, lessened their popularity. Moreover, they had to take stances on issues that did not belong to their original profile, and that divided their membership and electoral base.

Confronting these problems, in Germany, two factions were formed within the Green party (*Die Grünen*) in the 1980s: the 'realists' (*Realos*) and the 'fundamentalists' (*Fundis*). The members of the first group advocated slower realization of the programme and centralized organization, in order to maintain their popular support, and take governmental responsibility if such option arises. On the contrary, the *Fundis*, who were finally marginalized, wished to preserve the original character

TABLE 7.3 Foundation of green parties and first-time representation in European countries in the 1970s and 1980s

	Party	Year of foundation	Entering the parliament	Entering the government	Best results in parliamentary elections (%)	
			Date		1970s	1980s
United Kingdom	Ecology Party	1979				0.3
France	Les Verts	1978			2.2	0.9
Netherlands	Federatieve Groenen	1986	1989		–	2.1
Belgium	Agalev (Flemish)	1981	1985		0.1	4.1
	Ecolo (Walloon)	1978	1981		0.6	3.2
Ireland	Green Alliance	1987	1989		–	0.4
Germany/FRG	Die Grünen	1980	1983	1998	–	5.6
Austria	VGÖ (Vereinigte Grüne Österreichs [Unified Greens of Austria])	1982			–	2.2
	ALÖ (Alternative Liste Österreich [Alternative List Austria])	1982			–	1.9
	GA (Die Grüne Alternative [Alternative Greens])	1986	1986		–	4.8
Switzerland	Grünen	1982	1983		–	5.4
Sweden	MP (Miljöpartiet de Gröna [Environmental Party the Greens])	1981	1988		–	2.9
Denmark	Groene	1985			–	1.4
Norway	Miljoe	1989			–	0.8
Finland	Vihreä liitto (The Green League)	1982	1983		–	2.7
Italy	Verde	1987			–	2.4
Spain	Verdes	1989	1989		–	1.4
Greece	Oikologiki Kinisi (Ecological Movement)	1988	1989		–	0.6

Sources: Jan–Erik Lane and Svante O. Ersson, *Politics and Society in Western Europe*, London: Sage, 1991, 138–139, 143; György Fábián and László Imre Kovács, *Parlamenti választások az Európai Unió országaiban (1945–2002)*, Budapest: Osiris, 2004, 37.

of the movement by not seeking political power, despite its potentially adverse electoral repercussions. Fears were not entirely unfounded: the German greens, the most successful ecological party in Europe in terms of governmental participation, suffered major losses in popularity in the wake of the compromises they made as junior coalition partners of the social democrats in the federal government for seven years starting in 1998.

Besides the greens, other parties were established in Western Europe from the 1970s. In certain countries, for example, in the Netherlands and Luxembourg, a pensioners' party was formed, which was based on the electoral potential of the growing number of old-age citizens in elections. However, because this social group was systematically addressed by traditional parties as well, pensioners' parties in the end achieved moderate results. Constituting another type, the so-called protest parties were established in larger numbers, some of them also referred to as 'flash' parties by the literature, implying that they were often formed within a short period and disappeared just as quickly. The reason for their formation was usually a serious malfunction of larger parties, for instance, a corruption scandal, which diverted significant groups of voters. Another reason for organizing such parties was the failure of larger parties to adequately respond to crucial social problems. Migration was such an issue with which major segments of the Western European population were concerned from the 1970s. In those countries where the number of immigrants rose quickly, or there was a considerable migration pressure or the social integration of immigrants went slowly, new parties were formed with the goal of curbing migration. By the end of the century, the most prominent among these political groupings were the National Front (*Front National* [FN]) in France and the Austrian Freedom Party (*Freiheitliche Partei Österreichs* [FPÖ]). Another type of protest party was the Party of Democratic Socialism (PDS, *Partei des Demokratischen Sozialismus* [PDS]), which was established after the German unification and gained popularity in the eastern federal provinces of the country. Because officials of the former East German communist party were not allowed to take offices in the democratic system in Germany, the PDS could not be regarded as a communist successor party in a strict sense. It was rather a regional protest party, which, besides opposing the way German unification was realized, was built on the GDR nostalgia lingering in relatively large segments of the population.

It is also manifest that new generations identified to a lesser degree with the old parties. Unstable party preferences boosted the significance of short-term electoral choices, which could lead to an even more rapid expansion as well as decline of parties. Citizens tended to be less loyal to one party or another in the long run. However, the decrease in long-term preference was not drastic: taking the average of 12 Western and South European countries, the share of those who preferred the values of a particular party in the long run dropped from 75% to 62% between 1962 and 1992.[30]

The social position had in turn a lessening impact on electoral behaviour. As shown in Table 7.4, the role of class adherence and of religious affiliation had been crucial in defining party preferences in all Western European countries in the 1960s. In the following decades, the importance of these factors did not alter or declined, except in Italy.[31]

Nonetheless, the transformation of the social structure, cultural changes, as well as the appearance of new social conflicts all contributed to the shift in electoral

TABLE 7.4 Estimates of class voting (Alford index) in Western European countries, 1950s–1980s

	1950s and 1960s		1970s and 1980s	
	Year	Index	Year	Index
United Kingdom	1959	37	1983	30
France	1956	15	1978	18
Netherlands	1956	26	1986	26
Belgium	1956	25	1974	25
Ireland	1969	19	1987	6
FRG	1959	27	1987	14
Austria	1967	31	1986	25
Switzerland	1963	26	1975	15
Sweden	1955	53	1985	34
Denmark	1963	44	1987	29
Norway	1957	46	1985	29
Finland	1958	59	1987	39
Italy	1959	19	1976	31
Spain			1979	20
Greece			1981	18
Portugal			1983	26

Note: The index refers to the proportion of voters' preference complying with class position in percentage of the electoral group.

Source: Jan–Erik Lane and Svante O. Ersson, *Politics and Society in Western Europe,* London: Sage, 1991, 94.

preferences. Shifts in the employment structure, and particularly the decrease of industrial employment that previous chapters have already covered, had a decisive impact on the potential electoral base of parties. The internal homogeneity and cohesion of those working in the booming service sector was significantly lower than that of the working class, and especially than that of the workers in heavy industry, who had earlier made up a significant group. In addition, high level of social security considerably decreased the antagonism of capital and work, but generous welfare services created new conflicts as well, for example, between those workers who were paying regular contributions and those permanently unemployed, who were regularly receiving benefits.

The pool of voters of social democratic parties, which traditionally represented workers' interests, was highly affected by these structural shifts. Moreover, value changes threatened to wear away the electoral base of the Christian democratic parties, because one of the most important aspects of these transformations was the marginalization of religious values, that is, secularization. However, attitudinal changes were of a larger scope, including the loss of the appeal of material political goals and ideals; thus, social democratic parties were affected by the advancement of 'post-materialism' as well (Table 7.2).

Notwithstanding these changes, the new parties emerging from the 1960s did not fundamentally rearrange the party structure of European democracies, because,

TABLE 7.5 Representatives of party families in European countries at the beginning of the 1990s

	Communists	Social Democrats	Centre (Christian Democrats)	Conservatives	Liberals
United Kingdom		Labour (35)		Cons. (42)	LD (18)
France	PCF (11)	PS (38)		RPR (19)	UDF (19)
Netherlands		PvdA (32)	CDA (35)		VVD (15)
Germany/FRG		SPD (36)	CDU/CSU (42)		FDP (7)
Austria		SPÖ (35)	ÖVP (28)		LF (6)
Switzerland		SP (19)	CVP (20) SVP? (12)		FDP (21)
Sweden	VP (6)	SAP (45)	KdS (4) CP? (9)	MS (22)	FP (7)
Italy	PDS+RC (22)	PSI (14)	DC (30)		PRI (5)

Abbreviations:

United Kingdom:	Cons.	Conservative Party
	Labour	Labour Party
	LD	Liberal Democrats
France	RPR	*Rassemblement pour la République* (Gaulists)
	UDF	*Union pour la Démocratie Française* (Liberal Giscardists)
	PS	*Parti Socialiste*
	PCF	*Parti Communiste Français*
Netherlands	CDA	*Christen-Democratisch Appèl* (Christian-Democratic Party)
	VVD	*Volkspartij voor Vrijheid en Democratie* (Freedom and Democracy People's Party)
	PvdA	*Partij van de Arbeid* (Party of Work)
Germany	CDU	*Christlich-Demokratische Union Deutschlands*
	CSU	*Christlich-Soziale Union in Bayern*
	FDP	*Freie Demokratische Partei*
	SPD	*Sozialdemokratische Partei Deutschlands*
Austria	ÖVP	*Österreichische Volkspartei*
	LF	*Liberales Forum*
	SPÖ	*Sozialdemokratische Partei Österreichs*
Switzerland	CVP	*Christlichdemokratische Volkspartei*
	FDP	*Freisinnig-Demokratische Partei*
	SP	*Sozialdemokratische Partei*
	SVP	*Schweizerische Volkspartei*
Sweden	MS	*Moderata Samlingspartiet* (Conservatives)
	KdS	*Kristen Demokratisk Samling* (Christian Democratic Party)
	FP	*Folkpartiet* (Liberal People's Party)
	SAP	*Sveriges Socialdemokratiska Arbetareparti* (Swedish Social Democratic Party)
	CP	*Centerpartiet* (Center Party)
	VP	*Vänsterpartiet* (Leftist Party, formerly Communist)
Italy	DC (PPI)	*Democrazia Christiana* (Christian Democratic Party)
	PPI (DC)	*Partito Populare Italiano* (after 26.07.1993)
	PRI	*Partito Repubblicano Italiano* (Republican Party)
	PSI	*Partito Socialista*
	PDS	*Partito Democratico della Sinistra* (Democratic Party of the Left)
	RC	*Rifondazione Comunista* (Reform Communists, former *Partito Comunista Italiano* [PCI])

Notes: state of 1994; the results of the closest parliamentary elections in percentage in brackets; question mark after the name of the party refers to the uncertainty of categorization.

Sources: own compilation mainly based on Stefan Immerfall, *Einführung in den europäischen Gesellschaftsvergleich*, Passau: Wissenschaftsverlag Rothe, 1995, 112–113.

even if added together, they usually won only approximately 5–10% of the total votes. They reached a maximum of 20% only in exceptional cases in certain countries and periods. Therefore, traditional parties retained most of their positions, although they achieved this by relying on their traditional electoral base to a lessening extent (Table 7.5).[32]

Social movements: waves of contention

Beside established political parties and interest groups, social movements operate as intermediaries between citizens and formal political institutions. Social movements can be described most simply as organized efforts to promote or resist political and cultural change in society. A more exact definition underlines that in this type of collective challenge, individuals and groups, based on a shared identity, form dense informal networks, and they engage in collective actions vis-à-vis clearly identified antagonists.[33]

Even without being able to address the historical precedents of twentieth-century social movements, it is obvious that social protest and social movements were practically always present in European history and took different forms: food riots, land seizures, anti-tax rebellions, mutinies and general turbulence. These early movements were occasionally extensive and could even develop into peasants' insurrections or revolutions. Nevertheless, until the eighteenth century, they remained mostly isolated phenomena. Moreover, movements regularly aimed to restore some kind of 'natural social relations' or 'divine order', which was infringed by the elite according to the participants. However, enlightenment brought about a considerable change when not only the notion of natural rights appeared but also the idea that human beings are capable of altering social arrangements and creating a new social order. Afterwards, movements could aim not at correcting digression from the order but, on the contrary, at changing the very order itself. Nonetheless, the emergence of modern social movements had other preconditions as well, among which Charles Tilly highlights the significance of the emergence of an industrial economy and the formation of the modern nation state.[34] The new industrial capitalism advanced wage labour and concentrated wealth, which led to the emergence of new types of conflicts and antagonisms in society, particularly between capital and labour. State formation included the differentiation and centralization of governmental agencies as well as the strengthening of the regulatory capacity of governments and their organizations, which exercise a monopoly of legitimate violence over a specific territory. As a result of the concentration of power, the governments and other institutions representing the state turned into the major target of social protest. The diffusion of literacy, the rise of the popular press and several other factors related to the emergence of industrial capitalism also facilitated the expansion of these social movements.

Consequently, it is hardly surprising that several scholars identify the first modern social movements during the French Revolution.[35] Although the Girondists,

Jacobines and other political groups showed great heterogeneity and thus could not be welded together into an effective political body over the years, still they represented a new sociopolitical phenomenon with regard to setting aims, mobilization and forms of political activity. The revolutionary movements were characterized by differentiated, although partly utopian, political programme-making, mass mobilization by diverse political organizations and institutions, transregional communication between these institutions, as well as the combination of direct and indirect collective actions to achieve desired changes. In addition, the French Revolution changed the political language and vocabulary, and thus shifted the meaning of the word 'movement'. Although the concept previously carried the connotations of unrest, upheaval and in-betweenness, and although from that point on, the usage of the term was not vested with an unambiguous new meaning, its semantics absorbed the sense of being a continuous, purposeful, and socially embedded phenomenon. The word 'movement' went through further differentiation and alteration during the nineteenth century. In the early decades of the century, it mostly designated democratic, liberal and national endeavours. From the 1840s, the term 'social movement' was first used for naming the labour movement. At that time, the two concepts were closely intertwined, and it was only later that people also began to describe other forms of social protest with the term 'social movement'.

Several periodizations identify the dividing line somewhere in the second half of the nineteenth century, suggesting that in that era, the social movements of the age of industrialization appeared. Then the next period comes in the 1960s, with the arrival of the movements of the post-industrial period.[36] Other scholars differentiate between old and new social movements under the same periodization paradigm.[37] Nevertheless, these conceptualizations of periodizations have a major weakness in for the most part disregarding the radical transformation of social movements in the years after the First World War. Consequently, in the following discussion, we apply a different periodization when we discuss the three major waves of modern social movements and protest: the movements at the end of the nineteenth and at the beginning of the twentieth century, changes during the period after the First World War, and the characteristics of the movements in the decades after the 1960s.

Social movements in the era of industrialization

Polarization, the increasing role of organizational issues, differentiation and the growing interaction with adversaries and authorities were all substantial developments of social movements in the second half of the nineteenth century which also had profound long-term impacts on the character of movements. The political polarization was primarily a consequence of the increase of class cleavage, and itself had further repercussions: most of all, it strengthened the mobilization efforts and capacity of social movements. The labour movement intensified mobilization in order to counterbalance the political and economic advantage of the opponents. Not only did it organize political associations but it also had influence on the cultural life. Labour associations engaged in various cultural activities, such as running reading circles, debating evenings, festivals and gymnastic clubs. However, polarization increased again when distinctive Catholic workers' organizations emerged throughout Europe from the end of the nineteenth century, as already referred to in the discussion of the history of party families.[38] The arrangement of the new social issues into blocs was also a further manifestation of polarization. The dominant cleavage tended to increasingly determine the social experiences and themes. Therefore, the new movements often split, as could be seen in the feminist movement, for instance, which divided into a socialist and a liberal wing. Movements were usually linked to political ideologies and tendencies in the public discourse, which in turn restricted their potential for expansion. For example, this was precisely the case with the lifestyle and the youth movement that the public associated with the conservative political family at the end of the nineteenth and the beginning of the twentieth century.[39]

Another important feature of the social movement network that emerged around the turn of the century was the prevalence of a bureaucratic organizational framework. It was the labour movement, which advanced to a mass movement in Europe at the end of the nineteenth century, that first developed a massive organizational basis. However, the bureaucratic organizational form was not only characteristic of the working class movement but of other, similar currents as well that also cherished power aspirations. Nevertheless, this trend ensued in no small measure because the development towards bureaucratic organizational frameworks could meet broader social tendencies: one could easily pinpoint the same process in the economy or in parties.

The protest episode evolves into a social movement, as Sidney Tarrow emphasized, if it is able to sustain collective action against opponents. Although shared goals and identities definitely promote this process, modern movements could also exist for a long time because they were in constant interaction with the better-equipped adversaries as well as with the elites and authorities.[40]

In the industrial phase of social movements, the distribution of material wealth and the location of political power in society gradually developed into those fields of conflict around which social movements centred. However, beside the major movements dealing with these issues, movements with a clear programme of social transformation, but still, with less comprehensive claims, also emerged in Europe. The latter included the women's movement, and the youth movement, the peace movement, the lifestyle movement and numerous other groups. This process of differentiation became even more pronounced later in the twentieth century. Among these currents, the limits of this chapter confine us to deal with only those two movements that had the largest constituencies: the labour and feminist movements (both in a selective way).

The labour movement was strongly linked to trade unions and parties, as already discussed in this and a previous chapter. Here, we dwell on only two aspects of their development: on the one hand, the labour movement developed as the most transnational of all movements from the second half of the nineteenth century, and on the other, serious cleavages appeared within the social democratic movement at the time of the First World War, both of which had significant repercussions on its twentieth-century development. The First International (formally the International Working Men's Association) was founded in 1864 in London eminently by the most powerful British and French trade-union leaders of the time. At its peak, the International had several million members, among whom Karl Marx, Friedrich Engels and Mikhail Bakunin were the most prominent. The organization was considerably weakened by disagreements between the different wings of the association that centred on the ideology and strategy of the organization. Splits between the trade unionists and party politicians, as well as the socialists and anarchists, led to the dissolution of the organization in 1876. The failure of the First International did not prevent socialists from cooperating internationally in Europe, and finally, the Second International was established in Paris in 1889. Its demands included the eight-hour working day, universal suffrage and the right to unionize, but its final objective was the overthrow of capitalism. Before the First World War, significant splits re-emerged with regard to the desirable organizational forms within the social democratic labour movement in Europe. The syndicalist wing claimed that political activity should be centred on trade unions, which, accordingly, have to control labour parties. Another wing maintained that trade unions should focus on the workers' rights at the shop-floor level, whereas social democratic parties should concentrate on parliamentary elections. Several other divides surfaced as well: anarchosyndicalists, being most popular in France, Italy and Spain, supported spontaneous direct actions beyond strikes (such as the seizure of factories) and questioned the usefulness of partisan and parliamentary politics. Diverging from mainstream political strategy of the social democratic movement in Western Europe and also from the beliefs of the anarchosyndicalists, the Leninist doctrine emphasized the role of the communist party as the vanguard of the working class, which enables effective collective political actions, and did not restrict the activity of labour organization to the struggle for economic demands.

The First World War was a turning point in the political activity of the socialist labour movement. Before the war, despite ideological differences, proletarian internationalism and antimilitarism were major elements of the ideology of the movement. However, the majority of social democrats in Germany and elsewhere in the belligerent countries supported the war efforts of their respective national governments, whereas the left wing opposed this stance. Thus, the idea of internationalism was dismissed, and there emerged strong ruptures within the labour movement. The schism was internationally exacerbated and institutionalized when the far-left factions split from mainstream social democracy and entered the Communist International, which was established in 1919 and dominated by the Russian Bolshevik party. In 1923 a more moderate umbrella organization (the Labour and Socialist International, a forerunner of the present-day Socialist International) was also established on the basis of the Second International and other organizations, which represented most of the social democratic parties in Europe and beyond. The division of the labour movement and the antagonism of a radical,

Soviet-oriented communist faction and a social democratic wing largely contributed to political radicalization in interwar Europe.[41]

Even though the term feminism became commonly used from the 1880s, conscious and organized activities by women on behalf of women originate from earlier periods. By the mid-nineteenth century, issues related to what contemporaries labelled 'the woman question' were widely debated by the public in Britain and elsewhere on the continent. Liberal, mostly middle-class feminists mobilized for various causes, including the improvement of legal status of women, and against the exclusion of women from higher education and major segments of employment. The activity of the feminists further intensified from the late nineteenth century. On the one hand, the movements were strengthened by the emerging socialist organizations; on the other, they were reinforced and also challenged by the intensifying public discourse about the new roles of women, and the opposition to their political activism. The demand for the changes in property laws and marriage laws, and the right to work remained on the agenda, but at the heart of the campaign were the demands of suffrage.

The struggle for suffrage considerably relied on those methods that other social movements (particularly trade unions) applied in the period and that included organizing, lobbying and publishing pamphlets. However, the suffrage movement, especially in Britain, clearly underwent a radicalization in the early twentieth century. Activists increasingly appeared in public spaces: they organized mass demonstrations, and chained themselves to objects. By the eve of the war, British feminists also resorted to more aggressive means, especially after their non-violent contentious activity failed to produce tangible results. Militant suffragettes harassed politicians and destroyed properties by smashing windows or damaging mailboxes. In continental Europe, the feminist movement emulated some of these methods, but all in all, it was less radical, even though the realization of suffrage often was more difficult here, as shown earlier in the chapter. In France, for example, the Radical Party, the axis of parliament in the early twentieth century, considered the enfranchisement of women as a threat to the secular state, because it was expected that they would support the clerical political camp.

The period after the First World War brought about a relative decline of feminist movements, which can be partially explained by the fact that a breakthrough took place in Europe concerning women's voting rights. The aims and demands of feminists obviously differed in each European society to a considerable extent, but all in all, the focus shifted from civil and political rights to social and reproductive rights: the improvement of employment conditions and the possibility of birth control were increasingly emphasized.[42]

Mass mobilization and radicalization after the First World War

In the final phase of the First World War and in the immediate post-war years, European social movements greatly mobilized, as we have seen in relation to the trade union movement and strikes in an earlier chapter. However, it was not simply that the number of participants and the intensity of the movements increased, but also in many cases, the movements underwent overt radicalization, and extremist or totalitarian tendencies gained ground on the left, but especially on the right. Mobilization affected democratic movements as well; nevertheless, because of their impact on the political climate of the interwar era and the breakdown of democratic systems, we concentrate on these extremist currents in the following discussion.

Numerous factors that in each case appeared in different combinations and with various importance played a role in the success of the extremist or totalitarian movements. The subject generated an overwhelming range of hypotheses and approaches. Only a few scholars consider their approach monocausal but most of them emphasize a particular determinant or a set of causal relations. These partly overlapping elements include the manifold consequences of the First World War; the failure of goal realization by movements of origin; the political crises coming from the rapid transition towards a democratic nation-state in several countries in Europe; specific social and economic settings, such as inflation and unemployment; distinct social structural constellations, such as the weakness of the bourgeoisie; particular cultural traditions, such as the retardation of democratic political culture; features of the political structures, most notably the fragmentation of the party system; adverse effects of particular economic and policy measures, such as deflationary policy during the Great Depression; the possibilities of political organization enabled by liberal democratic systems; a wide perception of civilizational decay; and external factors, including the demonstration effects of other movements and the radicalizing effect of the 'red menace'.[43] Determinants can be discussed here only briefly, and thus we have selected some of the most significant factors and interpretations related to the war, specific social structures, the internal dynamics of movements and external factors.

The mobilizing and radicalizing effect of the First World War enhanced the emergence of extremist movements to a great extent. Social mobilization was literally realized, because the majority of young adult male cohorts went to war, and most of the women participated in war efforts by working in the economy or taking up civil service. The structure of the working class altered, because new, often unskilled workers took over the role of those conscripted. Society militarized in many respects: masses of people experienced and exercised violence during the war, which obviously increased their inclination to the similar resolution to conflicts. At the same time, positive perceptions of military experience, such as bravery, willingness to sacrifice and leadership became constituents of a new sense of community, especially in the far-right movements. This was also facilitated by the fact that at the end of the war, arms were drawn unnoticed out of military surveillance in many warmonger countries (especially among those defeated). Furthermore, the war caused considerable material loss and poverty in all belligerent countries and (again mostly among the defeated countries) endangered the social status of wide segments of society, and in particular, the middle classes, sometimes referred to as uprooting. The repercussions of the war obviously varied to a great extent according to whether the country was a victor, or a defeated one, and which conditions the peace treaties contained. Fascism emerged first and made its greatest advance in countries that suffered territorial losses or had been frustrated by peace settlements or in their territorial ambitions.

Another widely held explanation for the diffusion of extremist movements in interwar Europe is the absence of democratic traditions and social classes associated with these attitudes. The most influential version of this argument is the *Sonderweg* theory, referring to Germany's distinct historical path of socioeconomic development.[44] Even though the concept is highly controversial because it assumes the existence of a normal path of development, it emphasizes that Germany was characterized by belated industrialization, the late and distorted formation of the nation state, and the failure of the bourgeois revolution. These features distinguished Germany from other countries like England or France. Pre-industrial and authoritarian–bureaucratic elites, institutions and attitudes continued to exist even in the twentieth century, which also contributed to the retardation of parliamentarism, to the success of *völkisch*-nationalist-imperialist ideologies and to the survival of aggressive–militarist political culture, which is discussed separately elsewhere in this chapter. These long-term determinants provided the basis of the success of the Nazi movement besides short-term factors, including unjust peace dictates, inflation, or the economic crisis. The investigation of these long-term factors is all the more important because similar short-term problems occurred in other countries as well, although they did not lead to the development of a Nazi-like movement there.

The extremist movements emerged through the radicalization of more traditional movements. In Germany, for example, national socialism developed during the differentiation of *völkisch*-nationalist movements, whereas the communist one, as we have seen, originated from the radical left wing of the social democratic movement. The failure of the realization of political aims by the preceding factions was also among the factors of radicalization. Failures were not interpreted as a need for the moderation of aims, but as a necessity for more radical actions. Thus, the defeat suffered in the war, or in revolution, promoted the idea that more mobilization and activism were needed.[45]

These ambitions were facilitated by a transnational learning process. The success of related political factions or adversaries both in the particular country and abroad clearly resonated in the social movements. Obviously, for communists, the Soviet Union provided a role model throughout Europe in the 1920s. The diffusion of the Leninist and subsequently the Stalinist political practices was institutionalized by the establishment of the Comintern. Italian fascists served as a role model for the extreme right movements in the early 1920s, but from the late 1920s, the Nazis increasingly influenced their ideology, organization and political practice.

As suggested, the interwar extremist movements could be distinguished from earlier movements by their pre-eminent feature to intensify mobilization and action in an extraordinary manner so as to reach a final or absolute goal. These ultimate aims were conceived on an ideological basis, and pragmatic considerations had hardly any influence on them, that is, their correction was almost impossible. Moreover, their ideology was exclusive both in its perceived validity and in power relations. Their organizational form was characterized by a strong hierarchy and they eradicated internal democracy in favour of organizational efficiency. Obviously, these movements had significant peculiarities as well, more frequently in their ideologies, and only to a lesser extent in their organization and political practice. Whereas violence attains a positive value in fascist, and particularly in National Socialist ideology, it has been rather instrumental for communism.[46] Variations were also characteristic of extreme right movements. Some of them were authoritarian-traditionalist, supporting the preservation of traditional values, and maintained connections to the Church and to the conservative elites. On the contrary, fascist and Nazi parties sought the support of the lower middle class, the peasantry and the working class, and they were usually yet to a different degree characterized by nationalism, the cult of a leader, anti-Semitism, racial mysticism and anticapitalism.

New social movements

From the 1960s, several social movements appeared that had not existed before, or had been represented as mostly subaltern tendencies in European societies. These groups included, among others, the student movement, the peace movement and the environmental movement, as well as the gay and lesbian liberation movements. They generated significant public and scholarly attention, and theorists soon termed these as new social movements.[47] The new social movements are usually regarded as reactions to the perceived inadequacies of the political and social structures of advanced capitalist societies and differed from the old movements by their social base, values, organizational structure and strategies.

As to the social base of the movements, they attracted supporters by transcending traditional class cleavages. It is one of the most specific characteristics of these movements that they performed identity politics that did not rely on class divides but on self-identification of the supporters by other criteria, such as gender or sexual orientation. Identity politics enabled them to recruit supporters from a diverse social base and bond groups that were previously alienated by class divisions or political affiliation.

Thus, the rise of what is often called post-industrial society was central to the emergence of the new movements. This process was associated with generational changes and involved the formation of a new set of values, which was interpreted by R. Inglehart as the transition from materialist to post-materialist or self-expression values. This process of value change is addressed in chapter 9. In other words, new social movements spring up when modernity and modernization are not perceived as unilinear processes any more but rather as conditions full of contradictions, most of which are unintended results of modernity itself.[48] The new social movements are often interpreted as single-issue movements that mobilize against the adverse outcomes of modernity, such as the destruction of environment or the threat to peace by nuclear armament. The goals along which the new movements operated were usually radical, yet at the same time self-limiting as well, in a sense that they did not have the revolutionary aims and rhetoric that were characteristic of the traditional left-wing movements. Proponents of the new movements sought to transform society in a way that prevailing institutions would function more effectively and democratically. Accordingly, they preferred non-hierarchical organizational structures. Furthermore, these movements are often distinguished by their non-conventional strategies and activities, such as direct actions and civil disobedience. In addition, these new social groups deliberately exploited various forms of media representation, and thus could command a considerable part of society's attention, even if their actions involved a relatively low number of participants.

However heuristic the differentiation of new social movements is, it was plausibly suggested that they represent strong continuities with earlier or traditional forms of social protest and activism. A huge part of their agenda had already surfaced in earlier periods, which is most obvious in the case of the 'new' feminist movement or the peace movement. Craig Calhoun even identified several of their ambitions in the early nineteenth century.[49] Similarly, significant linkages exist to predecessors in terms of tactics and organizational forms as well. Thus, cultural issues, such as identity and self-expression, cannot be fully separated from more conventional agendas of social movements, including more equal income distribution or legal emancipation of specific social groups.[50]

In other chapters, we have already investigated a couple of these new movements enlivened from the 1960s and that also had older antecedents. Those older antecedents touched upon thus far include regional movements, embracing primarily regions in France, Britain, Belgium and Spain, and later and in distinct forms in Yugoslavia. The issues addressed by these currents are covered in chapter 9. Several of the concerns and intellectual sources of the environmentalist movements are examined in the final section of chapter 6, dealing with the quality of life. Moreover, green ideas were effectively translated into partisan politics, which is discussed earlier in this chapter. Therefore, in the following discussion, we study the student movements, the peace movement and the East Central European dissident movements within the rich plethora of late twentieth-century social movements.

A major wave of student movements ensued in the mid-1960s in Europe, with its peak in 1968. Although these social activities were not centrally coordinated, they reacted to one another keenly on the continent and beyond. Most prevalently, they appeared in France, but they managed to mobilize relevant social groups to a great extent in Italy and West Germany as well, and succeeded in linking their claims to more comprehensive political demands. Moreover, they also surfaced in other European democracies, and even in dictatorial regimes, such as in Spain, Greece, Poland and Yugoslavia. In Czechoslovakia, student unrest was without doubt one of the direct precedents of the Prague Spring. Ambitions of students varied, but the demands of these movements most often included the end of the Vietnam War, the non-hierarchical transformation of higher education, and more extensive political participation rights. In the communist countries, the democratization of the political system was a priority among the goals even if it could not always be formulated explicitly. The movements also called for such cultural and social transformations as sexual liberation and female emancipation. These movements climaxed in May 1968 in Paris, where workers' trade unions also gave uniquely significant support to them among the new social movements, but later on they began to quickly decline. This sharp ending played a role in that the critical assessment of the 1968 movements has generated strong debates up until recently. Their concrete repercussion is undoubtedly moderate, especially if it is compared with the aims of the movements, because besides more relaxed entrance requirements to universities and some other educational reforms, which were partly withdrawn later, they had little direct results. Nevertheless, the long-run consequences are more controversial. According to sympathizers, these movements contributed to the development of civil society and in turn to the democratization of European societies. On the other hand, critics of the process think that they resulted in the erosion of traditional norms, and they even damaged democracy by promoting left-wing intellectuals from that time on into a position from which they could appear as know-alls speaking in the name of the whole society. In any case, they certainly contributed to the acceleration of value and attitudinal changes in Europe, and provided lessons and stimulation not only for subsequent student movements, but also for other social movements. It is also worth noting that in its wake, several student activists played a considerable role in other political movements as well.[51]

As referred to above, late twentieth-century peace movements had significant antecedents. Europeans had organized numerous peace congresses already in the 1840s, and they convened in the Hague at the first peace conference in 1899. Direct precedents included similar movements in the 1950s–1960s, which were coined as anti-war because they were usually organized as forms of protests against armed conflicts and military intervention, as opposed to the peace movements springing up from the 1970s, which set in turn more preventive aims. Mobilization for the latter movements was mostly facilitated by the so-called Dual Track policy of NATO, that is the deployment of new nuclear weapons in Europe at the end of the 1970s and at the beginning of the 1980s, but also by the 1978 government proposition in West Germany for the conscription of women and the Falkland Islands War in 1982. The peace movement grew considerably from 1979 and it preeminently presented itself in the Federal Republic of Germany (FRG), which was primarily targeted by the missile installation plans of NATO. 300,000 sympathizers attended its Bonn demonstration in 1981, and similar protests sprang up in numerous Western and Southern European cities, such as Helsinki, Brussels, London and Madrid. Later on, the Persian Gulf War and the Iraq War generated more notable peace movements. The effect of peace movements is difficult to assess: even if they did not directly stop military operations or achieve actual reductions in specific armament programmes, they might have prevented or slowed down escalatory policies.

Social movements had peculiar manifestations in European communist countries. Occasionally, they grew to dramatic measures, like in 1953 in the GDR, or in Poland and Hungary in 1956, or in Czechoslovakia in 1968. However, except for these years, the communist period was dominated by the prevalence of massive official movements serving political mobilization and by the total lack of independent initiatives.

With regard to independent movements, the late 1960s witnessed slow changes, because independent movements became more regular, even if within exclusive bounds. Because of the repression exercised on civil society, these independent initiatives were usually intertwined with the critique of the system. For example, environmentalist activities easily associated with the protest against bureaucratic economic planning disregarding nature and environment, and thus with the revolt against the political system. In the 1980s, a Bulgarian green group carried the name *Ecoglasnosti*: an obvious reference to the political reforms initiated by Mikhail Gorbachev in the Soviet Union. In Poland, the ecological movement became active in 1980 and large-scale, highly politicized demonstrations opposed a planned Danube dam in Hungary in the late 1980s.[52]

At the same time, there also emerged explicitly anti-system movements in the East Central European countries from the 1970s. Although the concerns of these movements were occasionally similar to the movements gaining parallel ground in democratic European countries (mainly with respect to human rights), and the social background of their activists showed certain similarities, beyond these, they shared hardly any features. Most importantly, anti-system movements in the communist systems had restricted publicity: in most cases, the activists could communicate only with one another, or respectively, could transmit information pertaining to them through Western radio broadcasts, such as Radio Free Europe, to their fellow citizens. The communication space called 'second publicity' meant underground publications (the Samizdat) and meetings, wherein they communicated with the 'real existing' power by campaigning for signatures and giving declarations.[53] Writers, scholars, scientists, artists, students and ecclesiastical persons constituted their main social basis. They could establish a link towards a wider social publicity in Poland only through the Workers' Defence Committee (*Komitet Obrony Robotników* [KOR]) founded in 1976. The Solidarity movement, which was the direct continuation of the KOR when it was established in 1980, had a strong intellectual background already from the beginning, which proved to be one of the key factors in its success. Early protests also involved the Charta 77 dissident declaration in Czechoslovakia, which was signed by 242 people when it was made public in January 1977. The Hungarian opposition movements had a hardly greater core basis and they were more widely received only from the mid-1980s with the intensification of economic hardships. Nevertheless, with all their limitations, these dissident and protest movements played a crucial role as 'moral viruses' (referring to Václav Havel's famous metaphor) in resuscitating independent thinking and preserving civic traditions, and thus last but not least in initiating regime change.[54]

Political culture and political communication: civil society – the mass media

The extension of franchise and parliamentarism based on the competition of parties were essential for the formation of modern democracies in Europe. Nevertheless, historical experience testifies that the existence of these institutions is not sufficient for the emergence of a democratic polity. The way political institutions function is fundamentally dependent on ideas, values and attitudes: in other words, on the culture of the citizens participating in the political process.

Political culture

The notion of political culture denotes those attitudes that citizens embrace in relation to politics in a broad sense along with symbols and doctrines that together shape political behaviour and structure the political process.[55] According to the classic argument of political science, there are homogeneous as well as fragmented political cultures. Homogeneous political cultures are characterized by a consensus regarding major political goals and procedures among the actors of the political system. In opposition to this, hardly reconcilable political subcultures coexist in a fragmented political culture. The emergence of both types of political culture is strongly influenced by the characteristics of the given society: the first type usually appears in societies where political divisions are largely conditioned by class differences, whereas the other is likely to be formed in societies with numerous cultural-ideological divides.[56]

Nonetheless, political culture is not exclusively defined by social structure, or the cleavages discussed earlier; rather it has several other determinants. Although the concept is not contingent on a particular political agenda, research on political culture, which was greatly facilitated by Gabriel Almond and Sidney Verba's classic study on civic culture published in 1963, originated from an interest in the relation of political attitudes and democracy.[57] Research findings suggest that the active participation of citizens in public affairs, a well-developed civil society, the rejection of extremist ideologies, popular knowledge of how the democratic political system functions, and trust in political institutions are all constituents of democratic political culture and are instrumental for the operation of democratic political systems.

The consequences of deficiencies in democratic political culture are clearly shown by the example of Germany in the interwar period. The constitution of the Weimar Republic was well known for its extensive guarantees of political and human rights to citizens, and for its exemplary regulation of parliamentarism, despite certain legal inadequacies, which primarily concerned the regulation of the constitutional rights possessed by the *Reichspräsident*. Nevertheless, deadlocks in the functioning of democratic institutions had been substantial: coalitions operated with frictions and adherents of extremist movements (communists and the Nazis) fought battles against each other on the streets from the late 1920s.

As referred to earlier, short-term factors contributing to the political polarization and confrontation included the Bolshevik revolutions and the upheavals that broke out in their wake in Germany, the activity of the Comintern, and the economic and social maladies after the First World War, such as inflation and later the Great Depression. Although these factors were manifest in several other European societies as well, they had dissimilar repercussions on the political life of various countries. In the German case, the dysfunctions of the Weimar system are also attributed to the extreme ideologies and authoritarian attitudes prevailing in German society, most eminently in the elite and the middle class. The shifting balance of power between the extremist movements and political factions loyal to the Weimar democracy was a result of a complexity of factors, including the short-term ones referred to above. However, the constellation carried considerable weaknesses for democratic political culture: as the well-known adage goes, the Weimar system was 'a democracy without democrats'.

The change of political culture facilitated the stabilization of the democratic systems in Western Europe in the post-war decades. In order to demonstrate the transformation process, we turn again to the example of Germany, because the break between the interwar and post-war period was most pronounced in that country. In the early post-war years most observers reported the indifference or even hostile attitudes of the majority of the population towards the new democratic political institutions. The view that the disposition of German citizens was not favourable for democratic change was supported by public opinion polls conducted by the American army, known as the OMGUS (Office of Military Government, US) polls.[58] The results showed that sympathy with Nazi ideology strongly persisted even after the war, and half of the population thought that National Socialism was a good concept that was inadequately realized. The number of people who had a positive judgment of the Nazis was almost equal to those who had a negative assessment. Thus, reshaping political culture became the primary goal for the allies and the new West German political elite, and even the idea of re-educating the population appeared a preeminent task. The process also aimed at the creation of a new national identity, which included not only the traditionally strong cultural identity, but the identification with a democratic political community as well. Whereas the traditional image of the state in German political thought was of an autonomous power that individuals have to serve, the new political culture was built on the conceived balance between the rights and the obligations of the citizens and the state.

Popular acceptance of the democratic political regime improved quickly in West Germany. Whereas at the beginning of the 1950s only barely more than half of the population considered democracy the best form of government, by the mid-1960s, this opinion was held by the large majority of the population. An increasing number of citizens understood and endorsed principles of democratic policy, such as majority government, minority rights, individual civil rights, and the necessity of political disagreements and conflicts (Table 7.6). As a consequence of these changes, by the 1970s, national symbols, such as the German flag or the German

TABLE 7.6 Support for democratic principles and rejection of antidemocratic attitudes in the FRG, 1968–1990

	1968	1979	1982	1988	1990
Democratic values	Agreeing with the statement (%)				
'Every citizen has the right to demonstrate'	74	86	87	91	90
'Everybody should have the right to express an opinion'	93	95	94	94	92
Conflict versus order	Disagreeing with the statement (%)				
'The political opposition should support the government'	28	31	34	46	39
'Conflicts between interests are adverse to the public interest'	27	26	21	48	47

Source: Russell J. Dalton, *Politics in Germany,* New York: Harper Collins, 1993, 128–129.

anthem, aroused positive feelings from the majority of the participants in polls. Notwithstanding such poll results, the formation of a new national identity and patriotism was a less successful endeavour, because the memories of the extreme nationalism of the Nazi regime were too strong, which rendered any positive attitude towards the nation suspicious for many years. Even at the beginning of the 1980s Chancellor Helmut Kohl induced fierce public debates by using terms such as homeland (*Vaterland*) and even patriotism (*Patriotismus*).[59]

The mechanisms of change in political culture are not clarified theoretically in the scholarly literature, but it can be claimed that its fundamental rearrangement in the FRG was enhanced by several circumstances.[60] People who had been officials in the Nazi system, or who compromised themselves otherwise, were not allowed to take positions in the reestablished parties, in the media, or in state organizations. This permitted, on the one hand, that these institutions could indeed represent and convey democratic principles in an authentic way, whereas, on the other hand, the lack of politicians with an extremist political career did not mobilize extremists on the other side. Another factor was the unprecedented economic prosperity in the FRG in the 1950s and 1960s. Moreover, the emergence of democratic political culture was a self-enforcing process: the West German public experienced prosperity as a consequence of democracy after having lived under its sway for decades. Similar to the value changes, the transformation of the political culture was closely tied to generation shifts. Change is largely realized through these shifts, during which new generations with different social values and attitudes rise, and less by individuals altering their dispositions during their lifetime.

Although regarding earlier periods of the century we had little to rely on considering the characteristics of political culture, research was given a new thrust with large-scale opinion polls, enabling the compilation of databases about the political values and beliefs of citizens. Such systematic pieces of information about European societies are available from the 1970s, which show various aspects of loyalty to democratic systems, and of political activity.[61]

The way citizens' interest in politics is reflected has a crucial significance regarding the functioning of democratic political institutions. The success of the democratic political process is reduced by the citizens' indifference towards public affairs, whereas active participation in public affairs leads to a more effective control of politicians and political parties, which in turn gains more reliable information about electoral preferences, and at the same time lends more legitimacy to elected bodies. There were several signs of the decline in political interest and the involvement of the public at the end of the twentieth century in European democracies, including growing distrust in the political elites, decreasing loyalty towards parties, and diminishing participation in elections.[62] At the beginning of the 1990s, considerably less than half (on average approximately one-third) of the citizens participating in polls in Western and South European countries found politics important to their lives. The share was particularly low (less than 10%) in Spain, Italy, Portugal, Belgium, France and Ireland. It was only in the Netherlands and Norway that more than half of the people declared politics to be important to their lives. At this time, interest toward politics was higher in new democracies than in Western Europe; however, this advantage quickly wore away in the following years, because it was a direct consequence of regime change.[63]

It is also worth looking at which political values were fostered and which political ideologies were preferred by the European electorate. The rejection of extreme ideologies was characteristic all over Europe around 1990. According to public opinion polls, the average European voter was located at the centre of the left-right scale, and there were no significant differences among European countries with respect to the regions examined.

The active participation of citizens in public life is also indispensable to the functioning of democratic systems, or in other words, the existence of a well-developed civil society. The term civil society denotes that sphere of the society that is not directly related to the activity of state, private life and production. This sphere promotes the formation of a political culture in which citizens trust each other and the political institutions.[64] Organizations of the civil society include various voluntary formations, such as cultural, charity, political and similar associations, but involve trade unions as well. The development of civil society is most often measured by two indicators: the size of the membership in voluntary associations and of the level of trust. Regarding both of these aspects, communist successor states considerably lagged behind Western Europe, and were particularly below the level of Scandinavian countries in the period from which data are available.[65]

Obviously, it is a major determinant of the political process if citizens appreciate and are committed to particular political institutions. The level of satisfaction with democracy varied greatly in different European regions in the 1990s: it was significantly lower already at the beginning of the decade in East Central and South-Eastern European societies than in the Western European region. Later, the gap regarding popular satisfaction widened further, revealing serious legitimacy problems of the new political regimes.[66] This deficiency (which has detrimental effects on the functioning of democracy) can be explained by the fact that democratic institutions worked indeed in a less satisfactory manner in this region than in Western Europe. A further reason is that citizens of post-communist countries had a rather instrumental approach towards democracy, that is, they primarily expected their material living standards to improve after the regime change.[67] This argument is supported by the fact that the proportion of the population feeling nostalgia for the communist past was surprisingly high in the first half of the 1990s in most East Central European countries. Because consumption did not increase or even fell considerably in the first years after the collapse of communism, a major part of the population felt disappointed in the entire system of newly established democratic institutions.

Political communication

The functioning of modern political systems is fundamentally conditioned by mass communication. Citizens require information for their political decisions, and, obviously, only partial pieces of information can be gathered through direct experience; thus the citizens depend on the media as a source of information, whereby mass media largely influence the political process. If electors are not informed properly because of the bias of the media, then they are not able to properly assess competing political alternatives, nor can they properly evaluate the performance of parliamentary parties and politicians. Therefore, the freedom of the press and the balanced dissemination of information has been one of the oldest demands of democratic politics, the realization of which remained on the agenda even in the twentieth century.

Communication became one of the most rapidly developing branches of economy during the twentieth century. The immense economic-technological and socio-cultural transformation enabled the media to reach increasingly wider masses, and it changed the structure of media as well. As the twentieth century development of cinema, radio and television is addressed in chapter 6, the issues to be studied here are limited to the intersection of communication and political processes.

At the beginning of the twentieth century, the media basically meant the printed press. As a consequence of the diffusion of literacy, the political mobilization during the First World War and in the subsequent years, as well as the falling relative price and the improving physical and aesthetic quality of printed materials, newspapers started to grow rapidly both in number and volume after the war. Besides meeting the specific demands of certain social groups, it was in the interwar period that the mass press emerged, particularly in Great Britain and France. At the beginning of the 1930s, the number of daily papers exceeding one million copies in Great Britain was five, and in France it was three. Moreover, in Great Britain two tabloids (the *Daily Mail* and the *Daily Express*) were printed in more than two million copies a day. The daily paper with the highest print run in Germany was the *Berliner Morgenpost*, with 0.6 million copies sold.[68]

After the Second World War, the expansion of the printed press continued for a while. The circulation of both British tabloids had exceeded four million copies per day by the beginning of the 1960s, and the German *Bild-Zeitung* reached 2.5 million copies at the same time. From the 1960s, concentration progressed in the media market in Western Europe. This process was accelerated by the fact that television was an increasingly versatile competitor with growing influence, particularly challenging the illustrated papers. Thus, the number of daily papers started to decline. Copy numbers usually continued to grow but began to stagnate from the 1970s in the case of several large media-consuming nations, for instance, in West Germany, or even declined, as in the case of the United Kingdom. At the same time, a few media entrepreneurs had acquired a growing share of the market. The greatest media market actors of the 1980s included Rupert Murdoch in Great Britain, Robert Hersant and his family in France, West German publishers such as Springer, Bertelsmann, Gruner und Jahr, and Silvio Berlusconi in Italy.[69] Still, the market for newspapers recovered by the 1980s (the number of dailies even grew considerably) until the Internet challenged the printed press again around the turn of the millennium.

In communist countries, the printed press counted among the major tools of political indoctrination, and thus received exceptionally high subsidies, but at the same time the requirement of political loyalty was strictly applied to journalists. The communist party usually published its own national daily (such as the *Trybuna Ludu* in Poland, and the *Népszabadság* in Hungary) and regional units of the party were responsible for editing and distributing regional papers as well. In addition, trade unions or other communist satellite organizations also circulated papers, often reaching high copy numbers even by Western European standards. A good example is offered by the GDR, where the total number of copies of about three dozen dailies was nearly 10 million in the 1980s, whereas in West Germany, where the population was about fourfold, 375 daily papers sold 25 million copies. The German Socialist Unity Party (*Sozialistische Einheitspartei Deutschlands* [SED]) published two central newspapers: *Neues Deutschland* was the official organ of the government, and the most popular daily was the *Berliner Zeitung*, with 6 million sold copies. At the same time, the *Frankfurter Allgemeine Zeitung*, the largest quality daily newspaper in West Germany, did not sell even 0.5 million copies. The youth organization of the party, the FDJ (*Freie Deutsche Jugend*) had its own daily, similar to trade unions and fellow-traveller parties.[70]

Regarding its political influence, electronic media had an even more successful career during the century than the printed press. At the beginning, moving images were primarily meant to entertain, but interwar cinemas attracting large audiences projected newsreels before the prime-time programme, informing the audience about current political events. Audience numbers grew to such an extent that by the 1930s and particularly by the Second World War, the newsreel had become a significant source of political information for the European public. This process was facilitated by the governments (supporting the production and distribution of newsreels and regulating screening), because it offered them an opportunity to shape popular political views.

German National Socialists were ground-breaking in exploiting new technologies of mass communication for political purposes. On the one hand, they realized early that information represented by film and radio, even when manipulated, seemed perceptibly more credible to the audience than news delivered by the printed press. On the other hand, radio created yet another possibility in propaganda to influence public opinion because as a result of its technical requirements, it was centralized, and thereby it was essentially easier to control than supervising several hundreds or even thousands of editorial offices or presses. In addition, contrary to privately owned film studios and film distributors, radio stations were owned by the state from the onset, or were under governmental control. Possibilities offered by film and radio were utilized by governments in other countries as well, but not necessarily according to the paradigm of the Third Reich. The international newscast of the BBC, which was aired in several languages during the Second World War, merited fame precisely by its relative objectivity. It became more influential than the forthright propagandistic and less reliable programmes of other belligerent countries.

The radio undoubtedly transformed political communication from the 1930s, but the real change in this respect was brought about by television, which evolved to be the most important source of information. The reason for this was that television merged the visual authenticity of the cinema and the movies with the live time characteristic of radio programmes. News reached the audience more quickly, and could be disseminated to even those social groups that had previously had no access to printed media. At the same time, however, the broadcast information did not necessarily become authentic, because there was still enough room for political manipulation in thematization, that is, through suppressing some information and highlighting other. In addition, news broadcasted on television, perhaps because of generic characteristics, was usually far from in-depth coverage. Television influenced political processes in other ways as well, because watching television became a factor that played a crucial part in determining lifestyle in the last decades of the twentieth century. Television programmes and particularly advertisements had a substantial role in shaping tastes, and contributed to spreading the consumer attitude (a theme that is also explored in chapter 6).

Although in the previous decades of the century, private televisions had a subaltern role in Western Europe, the quick expansion of commercial channels began in the 1980s. From this time on, dual systems dominated television culture in Western Europe. The system consisted, on the one hand, of public TV stations operating on taxes financed by a combination of licence fees, state subsidy and advertising revenues, and on the other hand, of private channels running exclusively on commercials. These systems developed in a barely regulated manner in some countries (Italy), whereas they were established under systematic state regulation in other countries (Germany, Great Britain and France).[71]

The growing social impact of telecasting, which was further strengthened by the expansion of commercial channels, induced the critique of several political actors throughout the continent. Mass media were criticized particularly by green parties and Christian democrats. Doubts regarding television were also enhanced by the formation of large media companies in Western Europe at the end of the century. It was thereby accepted relatively early that state intervention into the media market was inevitable in order to prevent the establishment of monopolies and oligopolies. Because experience showed that the profit-oriented approach of commercial channels led to the neglect of certain programme types, such as children's programmes, or cultural programmes, therefore the idea of regulating programmes in some form was brought to the agenda as well. Moreover, with the expansion of commercial televisions, public channels assumed a completely new role. Although they were earlier frequently criticized for their political biases, and thus even the grounds of their existence were questioned, precisely for this reason, a growing number of observers pointed out in the 1990s that their broadcasting was preeminently necessary for balancing the programmes of the commercial media.

The impact of television on political processes was particularly obvious in the period during the regime changes in East Central and South-Eastern Europe. In the critical months of the fall of communism, the population of East Germany gained information from West German television about events in their own country or other countries of the Soviet bloc that affected them, and thereby these pieces of information had a crucial impact on the actions of East German citizens, and subsequently on the dynamics of events in the GDR. The influence of the screen was perhaps even more dramatic during the Romanian regime change, when television had a live broadcast of revolutionaries occupying the building of the television itself and using it for their own purposes. Therefore, television was not only a catalyst of the events but it also provided a site where the revolution was literally broadcast, and the majority of political actors complied with the power relations seen on television.

New developments of the 1990s: regime changes in Eastern Europe

The most important political current in Europe at the end of the century was arguably the fall of the communist regimes, and the subsequent establishment of new political systems. All in all, this change meant a convergence to Western European democratic systems: besides adopting numerous democratic institutions from constitutional courts to ombudsman offices, the representatives of the major Western European party families were formed in post-communist countries as well. However, similar party labels frequently concealed different political practice, which in itself showed that the new democratic systems had noteworthy peculiarities in a European comparison.

The communist regimes had gross long-term impacts on political life, probably more significant one than assumed by most observers around 1990. On the one hand, communist regimes had existed for a longer period than most twentieth-century dictatorships, for example, the Nazi regime. Furthermore, other authoritarian systems that persisted for similarly long periods, such as the Franco regime in Spain, did not nationalize the economy and eradicate the autonomy of several social institutions (such as churches) to the same extent. Therefore, in post-communist countries, the continuity in cleavages analysed earlier in this chapter as well as in party systems and parties with the era preceding dictatorship was significantly smaller than in Germany or Spain.

As for social cleavages, an important difference compared with Western Europe was the fact that several of the traditional social and political conflicts surfaced as less prominent ones in the post-communist countries in the 1990s. This is well exemplified by the relative insignificance of the religious cleavage, which contributed to the weak performance of Christian democratic parties in the region after regime change: even in Poland, which was uniformly Catholic, and had a higher level of religious affiliation compared with the other countries of the region, no large and unified Catholic party was formed.

The capital–labour conflict also surfaced and influenced the emergence of cleavages and the formation of parties in post-communist countries in a peculiar way. On the one hand, income differences significantly grew within a short period during the 1990s, which aggravated the importance of this conflict as well. On the other hand, social democratic parties, which regularly represented a major political faction in Western Europe, gained an important role only in countries, such as Czechoslovakia and some territories of former East Germany, where there was no communist successor party, which, in other societies, clearly marginalized the former within the electoral base. The situation was similar in the case of the communist parties: the existence of successor parties, even if they adhered to the principles of market economy, prevented the establishment of significant communist parties. At the same time, once communist successor parties gained power, they represented a contradictory attitude towards labour interests, because a significant part of their apparatus and their influential supporters were members of the nomenclature-bourgeoisie, capitalizing on the large-scale privatization carried out in the final months of the communist era or in the early post-communist years.

Not only did regional and rural–urban differences exist in post-communist countries but they usually also deepened in the initial period of the regime change. Based on these divisions and nostalgias for the peasant parties of the pre-communist era, agrarian parties were formed in most East Central European countries, and their voting share in the 1990s approximated the level of their counterparts in the Scandinavian countries. This result can still be regarded as moderate because the percentage of people earning their living from agriculture was substantially higher there than in Scandinavia. Moreover, these parties could not stabilize their position, which was also a result of the marginalization of agriculture in the region from the late 1990s.

During the political transformation, ethnic parties also emerged in most of the East Central European countries. Notwithstanding, their electoral basis was largely reduced by the fact that losses in the Second World War, border changes, ethnic cleansing, as well as deportations and the assimilation that ensued in the post-war decades lessened the share of ethnic minorities in the region. Czechoslovakia and Yugoslavia were unique cases because they remained multiethnic states. In the former, national conflicts strongly manifested in the Czech and Slovak opposition in the first two years after the regime change, eventually culminating in the split of the country into two separate states. Albeit less abruptly but also less peacefully, a similar disintegration process unfolded in Yugoslavia, which, except for Bosnia-Herzegovina, resulted in the establishment of nation states dominated by one nation, and thereby imposed serious limits on ethnic parties. In the rest of East Central and South-Eastern European countries, the formation and success of political organizations based on ethnicity were also moderate because of the relatively low percentage of national minorities. As noted earlier, the most successful ethnic parties were established by Hungarians living in Slovakia and Romania, who entered the successive governments as junior coalition partners several times.

Liberal parties, which represented a long-standing political philosophical doctrine and a significant party family in elder European democracies, emerged in almost all post-communist countries. These parties usually started their activities in alignment with the 'Washington Consensus', that is, following the preferences of the American government, the International Monetary Fund and the World Bank in economic policy, and were the supporters of 'shock therapy' in the region. However, after the ambiguous economic results and the grave social costs of this policy became apparent, the electoral support for liberal parties declined as well. In several cases, similar to the international organizations referred to above, these parties themselves conducted a thorough revision of their ideas about the desirable economic policy during the economic transformation process. Green parties performed moderately at the first democratic elections throughout the region and were not represented in any of the first parliaments.

As has been suggested before, the attitude towards the communist dictatorship and its representatives was an important cleavage in several ex-communist countries, primarily in those where successor organizations and politicians of the former communist parties remained active. Activists and groups of the democratic opposition of the communist era were frequently successful at the first free elections, but they regularly failed to consolidate themselves into parties or to stabilize their results. The example of Poland illustrates this trend: Lech Wałęsa, the charismatic candidate of the Solidarity movement, at that time already a party (having several million members in the late 1980s), gained about 40% of all votes in the first round of the 1990 elections and won only in the second round. Five years later, he did not make it to the second round, and his party had already fallen out of power earlier, in 1993, when it collected only 5% of the votes at the parliamentary elections.

In several countries, reformed communist parties were politically more successful than the democratic movements that catalysed the regime change. In some states, such as Czechoslovakia and in the unified Germany, individuals who compromised themselves in the previous system were excluded from public life. In other countries, however, this did not happen. Continuities with the past were disadvantageous for these parties at the first elections, but later they enjoyed the benefits of being successor parties. The assets included the well-established, effective apparatus and organization inherited from the previous era, the high membership figures, as well as the resources, such as offices and buildings, that exceeded the possessions of other parties. Their personal network in the economy and the media proved to be even more instrumental. During the often inadequately implemented, and non-transparent process of privatization (with the obvious exception of the former East Germany), earlier party leaders, as well as heads of companies and other institutions appointed by the party, exploiting their personal network, acquired substantial wealth, thus forming a distinct social group, which is referred to as nomenclature-bourgeoisie in the literature. Because mass communication, especially electronic media, had been among the most strictly controlled areas up until the collapse of the old regime, successor parties could rely on the sympathy of most of the media as well. Thus taking advantage of the fall in the standard of living caused by the economic transformation, and the political mistakes of new parties, at the second free elections, communist successor parties gained power in Bulgaria, Hungary, and Poland. In Romania, both the opposition and the government were dominated by notable politicians of the previous regime. This turn did not mean that citizens voted for the restoration of communism, and there was no danger of such a political twist, all the more so because leaders and bureaucrats of the former communist parties (being sober opportunists) more or less accommodated to the rules of the new democratic system. Furthermore, according to the argument of Richard Rose, 'ex-communists now have a personal interest in defending political freedoms, for they are obvious targets for the restriction of rights under an illiberal regime'[72] – because of either the troublesome privatizations or the obvious responsibility they hold for the wrongdoings of the communist regimes.

The relative weakness of traditional cleavages in the region resulted in the volatility of the new post-communist party systems, and even the political systems: neither the parties that brought about the political transformation nor the returned ex-communists ever held on to power for very long. The results of the first elections and party systems were unstable not only compared with the Western European political context of the same period but also in relation to elections and party systems of other countries experiencing democratic transformation, such as post-war Germany, Austria, Italy, or Greece, Portugal and Spain of the 1970s.[73] Nevertheless, the stability of the party structure increased by the turn of the millennium, and it became less disintegrated, even if it still remained fragmented in most East Central and South-Eastern European countries compared with Western European states.

8

URBANIZATION

Cities have occupied an important role in the political, cultural and economic life of European societies for thousands of years and urbanization (often defined as the relative concentration of the population in towns and cities) has underpinned European history for several centuries. However, it is a relatively recent development that in certain countries and regions the majority of the population lives in cities and other densely populated areas. Although none of the mid-nineteenth century societies could be described as predominantly urbanized, all of the industrialized countries, as well as a significant proportion of the less advanced ones, belonged to this category one and a half centuries later. Furthermore, in several aspects, the process of urbanization continues even currently; nevertheless, many regional variations are manifest in Europe. Although the existence, as well as the significance, of this rapid transformation is widely recognized, many of its fundamental concepts, such as the city itself, or urbanization, have remained controversial to the present day. The meaning of these concepts varies in different eras and societies; moreover, it may also differ according to the specific fields of research. Towns and cities can be defined by emphasizing their administrative borders, by relying on functional criteria (such as a central role in the region's cultural and economic life, or in administrative affairs), or by focusing on demographic and ecological aspects, including size and density of the population. Urbanization, likewise, has numerous conceptualizations. The cultural or behavioural approach regards urbanization as the proliferation of a particular quality of social relations, of distinct urban mentalities as well as behavioural patterns (*urbanitas*).[1] The structural approach primarily considers urbanization on the basis of the structural changes in society caused by industrialization, such as shifts in the production and the occupational structure. Finally, the demographic approach, which is the most common, understands urbanization as the spatial concentration of the population, and it often implies that the population and the social and economic functions are distributed within the urban space in a specific way.[2]

These diverse but not necessarily incompatible approaches provide similarly valuable tools for urban history and sociology.[3] Still, studies on urban history generally set on examining the changes in the spatial distribution of population, which is the starting point in this study as well. We can reasonably assume that the urban concentration of the population is connected to other phenomena, such as social values and way of life, as well as the physical characteristics of the settlement. Therefore, it might even serve as an indicator for them. Nonetheless, we also address the above-mentioned aspects of urbanization in the following pages.

The phase of European urban development from the First World War to the 1970s–1980s is usually regarded as the modern era of urbanization. The previous period is called the age of industrial cities, and the urban development of the final decades of the twentieth century is often described as post-industrial, at least in Western Europe. In this chapter, we outline the major characteristics of the modern and post-industrial phases of European urbanization. First, the trends of urban growth and the change of urban population are examined. Although on the whole, a large-scale urbanization took place throughout the twentieth century, urban development still cannot be interpreted as a linear process. Especially in the second half of the twentieth century, other significant, sometimes contradictory tendencies (with diverse intensity in different societies) can also be observed. It can even be argued that in many parts of Europe, urbanization, in the classic sense of the phenomenon, came to a halt, or, in some cases, was even reversed. These processes are described by urban historians and sociologists with such diverse and often overlapping and debated concepts as suburbanization, counterurbanization or disurbanization, which are addressed in this chapter as well. In addition, we also focus on the practices of urban planning and development, which had a decisive role in shaping the quality of urban life in contemporary Europe. Cities and other types of settlements do not exist separately, but they constitute larger, complex networks, which, in turn, may influence the functioning of each city. First, we address the historical characteristics of urban structure, then outline the major problems European cities faced in the late twentieth century and beyond.

Cities and towns in the twentieth century: the modern era of urbanization

The agrarian sector was dominant in European societies until the twentieth century, which had a decisive impact on the settlement structure as well. Around 1600, except for Northern and Central Italy and the Netherlands, only a minor part of the population lived in cities. At this time, 1.6% of the total population inhabited cities or towns, and by the beginning of the nineteenth century, the proportion of urban dwellers was still only 2.2%. However, urbanization advanced rapidly afterwards. It was closely connected to industrialization and economic change in general, which also implied that the dynamics of urbanization showed marked regional differences. For example, in England during the nineteenth century, the ratio of urban population quadrupled, whereas the same rate was lower in the Northern or Eastern regions of Europe. Furthermore, the later industrialization started, the more rapid was the pace of urban development.

Nineteenth-century urban growth produced ambivalent results: during the initial phase of industrialization, cities had unsanitary housing conditions and a high level of mortality. Birth rates were also lower than in the case of villages. Therefore, urban growth was mostly induced by the massive influx of rural population. Because the standard of the urban living environment was in many aspects below the rural one, it was primarily employment opportunities and higher available incomes that attracted workforce.

Nonetheless, it is difficult to assess the dynamics of European urbanization, because the definition of urban settlement has varied and is still different throughout diverse societies. In the nineteenth century, cities and towns were differentiated on the basis of their legal status, which generally included a certain degree of autonomy. However, divergences in the legal status usually originated from the distant past, so they often did not reflect either the size of the settlement, or the level of urban development, or its function in the urban structure. There were settlements that had gained urban status in the Middle Ages, but which nevertheless had gradually lost their importance since then, and there were in turn settlements with an opposite evolution. The repercussions of this inconsistency, although in a decreasingly marked way, can be observed even in the twentieth century. Measuring urbanization proves to be a difficult task, even if a seemingly unambiguous criterion (the concentration of population) is taken into consideration. Whereas from 1910, Danish settlements with 250 inhabitants were already considered urban, the population threshold for a settlement to be defined as an urban commune was 2000 inhabitants in France, and 20,000 in Italy.[4] The definition of cities is complex for other reasons as well. Along with the formation of large cities, settlements belonging to the agglomeration also developed, which usually became a part of the extended urban area after a certain delay. However, when this did occur, statistics might have indicated a sudden increase in the population of the city, whereas actual changes in the distribution of the population could scarcely be registered. A further problem originates from the formation of urban clusters. With the improvement of transport and communication, the connections among cities located relatively close to each other are often intensified to the extent that a conurbation emerges, although towns, cities and even villages remain legally separate entities. As a result, the demarcation of the settlements within these agglomerations cannot be performed on the basis of the number of the inhabitants. Therefore, the investigation and application of other criteria, such as the intensity of interurban relations, might prove to be expedient.[5] These problems render the comparison of different periods and societies with respect to urbanization difficult and should be mindfully considered when interpreting related data.

The growth of urban population in the interwar period

In the first six or seven decades of the twentieth century, European urban development (similarly to the tendencies of the previous century) was characterized by the rapid expansion of the urban population. Applying the UN criterion of a minimum of 20,000 inhabitants as the population threshold for the urban status,[6] at the beginning of the twentieth century, only Great Britain could be described as an urbanized country, where more than half of the population (altogether 64%) lived in urban areas in 1920. The urbanization ratio of several other countries, such as Germany, the Netherlands and Belgium, came close to 50%, especially if the agglomerations are also taken into account. In another group of countries, one-third of the population could be considered urban. This category included France, Italy, Denmark, Austria and Hungary, although the latter two provided a particular case of population concentration, because the majority of the urban dwellers lived in a single city. As for the rest of the societies, the urbanization rate was even lower, and reached 25% only in some cases. The proportion of urban population was particularly of a moderate level in the Balkan states: 12% in Romania, 9% in Bulgaria and 7% in Yugoslavia (Table 8.1).[7]

Starting from that level, the process of urbanization was not linear at all during the first half of the century. The First World War and the economic depression of the interwar period significantly hindered urban development. In addition, the Second World War also had a considerable detrimental effect on the process, with subsequent losses of life and physical infrastructure, as well as the frequent evacuation of the urban population, especially in Germany and Great Britain.

Interwar urbanization unfolded in a rapid way primarily in the countries with a medium level of urbanization, such as Sweden, Spain, Norway and Greece. However, the proportion of the population living in settlements with more than

TABLE 8.1 Urbanization level in European countries, 1920–1980 (urban population as a percentage of the total population)

	20,000 or more inhabitants			*100,000 or more inhabitants*		
	1920	*1950*	*1980*	*1920*	*1950*	*1980*
United Kingdom	64	71	79	50	52	71
France	37	45	58	23	17	44
Netherlands	45	56	57	24	31	45
Belgium	33	32	49	12	10	13
Ireland	21	28	38	14	18	31
Germany/FRG	41	41	60	33	27	34
Austria	36	40	37	31	33	29
Switzerland	25	29	28	15	21	34
Sweden	23	33	45	14	21	21
Denmark	32	45	52	23	34	38
Norway	23	33	40	18	20	23
Finland	17	22	38	6	14	24
Italy	32	41	53	14	20	28
Poland	18	26	45	9	16	28
Czechoslovakia	17	22	34	10	14	17
Hungary	31	34	49	15	20	29

Source: Wolfram Fischer, 'Wirtschaft, Gesellschaft und Staat in Europa 1914–1980', in Wolfram Fischer, ed., *Handbuch der europäischen Wirtschafts– und Sozialgeschichte*, Bd. 6, Stuttgart: Klett–Cotta, 1987, 54.

20,000 inhabitants also doubled in Bulgaria and Yugoslavia between 1920 and 1950, an increase that was achieved from a low starting ratio. Cities above medium size, with inhabitants surpassing 100,000 but less than 1 million, improved their relative position within the hierarchy of urban settlements. For instance, in Germany, already between 1910 and 1930, the share of the population living in this type of city increased from 21% to 37% of the total urban population. Although European urbanization advanced considerably in the first half of the twentieth century, in most of the European societies, only a lesser part of the population lived in towns and cities in the mid-twentieth century, and significant discrepancies also persisted among the levels of urbanization. The majority of the British and Dutch population was urban, whereas in other countries, the proportion of the urban and the rural population was approximately equal. France, Norway, Austria, Denmark, Italy and Spain belonged to this category. In the rest of the European countries, including East Central and South-Eastern European states, smaller settlements remained dominant in this period.

Urbanization after the Second World War

In the first post-war decades, urbanization was particularly rapid in the less advanced Eastern and Southern regions of Europe. Among the relatively moderately urbanized communist countries of the Balkan region, the proportion of urban population increased almost exponentially in Bulgaria, Romania and Yugoslavia.[8] The growth of the population of capital cities, with a privileged position with respect to the allocation of investment funds, was especially spectacular: between 1950 and 1980, the number of inhabitants in Belgrade increased from 0.4 to 1.7 million; in Sofia, from 0.6 to 1.2 million, and in Bucharest, from 1.1 to 2 million. Besides these capitals, urban development was considerable in 'socialist industrial cities' as well, which in many cases were developed from villages or no settlement precedent, associated with investments in heavy industry. This category includes Eisenhüttenstadt and Halle-Neustadt in East Germany, Sztálinváros (later renamed Dunaújváros) in Hungary, as well as Nowa Huta in Poland, originally established as a suburb of Cracow. A fast urban growth can also be observed in certain regions of Portugal, Spain, Greece and Southern Italy. For instance, the population of Lisbon quadrupled, and that of Porto quintupled in the second half of the twentieth century.

The rapid growth of cities was not exclusively limited to the European periphery, because the dynamics of development in the Western regions of France or in the surroundings of the Finnish capital were exceptionally high as well. Even cities such as Paris, Lyon, Munich and Stockholm (which were considered substantial in size already at the mid-century) had doubled their population in these decades. However, in most of the regions of Western Europe, urbanization generally remained moderate, which was manifested in the slow growth, or, occasionally, in the stagnation or the decline of large cities. The population of London, Berlin, Hamburg, and the bigger cities of the Ruhr, such as Essen and Dortmund, as well as of other urban centres like Amsterdam, Milan, and Vienna only scarcely increased, or was stagnating. In the same period, in many British, Belgian, and German industrial centres, the population was evidently shrinking.

As a result, at the end of the century, in many European countries, at least half of the population lived in cities with more than 20,000 inhabitants, and this figure remained below 30% only in a few countries. In 1980, the urbanization ratio of Albania (22%), Portugal (23%), Yugoslavia (26%) and Czechoslovakia (34%) stayed below the European average to the greatest extent (Table 8.1).

Nevertheless, it has to be stressed that these trends only reflect the population number in determining whether a settlement can be qualified as urban or not, because settlements with significantly smaller populations were and are still defined as urban in certain countries. In the second half of the twentieth century, these minor communities often had a highly developed infrastructure and numerous kinds of services, such as schools, banks, shops, leisure establishments, hotels, health centres, or a modern sewer system, which had not been available in earlier periods and were not necessarily characteristic in larger cities of other countries either. If these smaller settlements recognized as urban in certain countries are also taken into consideration, then 45% of the total population lived in cities in mid-twentieth-century Europe (as elsewhere in this volume, this calculation does not include the Soviet Union). In the case of Belgium, for example, the same ratio had already reached 92%. The European average exceeded 50% in 1960, and it climbed to 69% at the millennium. In the meantime, the number of countries with a dominantly rural population decreased rapidly, and in 1980, only Albania and Portugal belonged to this category, with urbanization ratios of 34% and 29%, respectively. However, as a result of the accelerated social transformations and a more permissive legal approach to granting urban status, by the new millennium, 65% of the Portuguese population became dwellers of urban communes.[9]

Consequently, no matter which definition is applied, an increasing segment of the population lived in densely populated urban areas in the post-war era. Nevertheless, this tendency is valid only for post-war Western Europe taken as a unit and for the second half of the twentieth century as a single analytical time frame. At this level, steady growth appears prevalent, but when investigated in more detail, significant divergences can be ascertained in the dynamics of urban development with respect to certain subperiods and regions.

In the most urbanized societies, the concentration of population slowed down, or, occasionally, even stopped around the 1960s. As opposed to this process, in the least urbanized countries, that is, in the Southern European region and in Ireland, a considerable part of the labour force had left agriculture for industry by the 1980s, and the share of the urban population had been increasing roughly until this decade. Similar tendencies prevailed in the communist countries. This phase of urbanization, characterized by its deceleration and by qualitative changes, is studied in the next section.

The causes of urbanization

The major determinant of urban growth in the twentieth century, and after the Second World War in particular, was the decline of agriculture, and the parallel expansion of the industrial and service sectors (analysed in chapter 4). Whereas the dominant economic activities of traditional societies, including agriculture, forestry, fishing and mining, demand that the population live in the proximity of natural resources, the work organization of industry and services requires the spatial concentration of the population. This concentration was realized by the relocation of labour force from rural to urban areas. In a series of European societies, the rural exodus reached a historical zenith in the 1950s–1960s. In the communist countries, one of the aims of collectivization was precisely to mobilize workforce for industrialization. Moreover, in the Southern and Eastern regions of Europe, fertility was generally high, and the growth of the population in this period was accelerated even in those Western European countries where it had scarcely increased during the previous decades. Furthermore, overseas emigration no longer functioned as a safety valve for the surplus of rural overpopulation to the same extent as it had done earlier, mainly at the turn of the nineteenth and twentieth century, because in Western and Southern Europe, it was capped by economic prosperity, and communist governments introduced travel restrictions to curb emigration. There were numerous factors involved in this: the flow of population from rural areas to urban centres, which included the increase of agricultural productivity, and the consequent formation of surplus workforce in agrarian regions; the improved transport system; the labour demand of industry; as well as the development of urban infrastructure. The interconnected development of industrialization and urbanization that characterized Western Europe in the nineteenth century protected the region from long-term developmental imbalances that affected other parts of the world and that were manifested in phenomena like excessive urban unemployment or uncontrolled urban development.

The growth dynamics of specific cities were usually related to whether the dominating economic activity of the settlement or the surrounding region belonged to an expanding or to a declining sector within the national and the global economy. Consequently, the development of industrial, port and capital centres was preeminent in the first two-thirds of the twentieth century. This group included industrial cities, such as Birmingham, Manchester and Katowice (Kattowitz), and port cities, such as Rotterdam, Antwerp, Marseilles and Naples. Nevertheless, by the 1950s, several traditional branches of industry, for example shipbuilding or the textile industry, had already begun to decline in Western Europe. In the cities where these branches were highly represented, the impact of structural reconstruction could usually only stabilize the number of the population, as, for instance, in Bordeaux, Hamburg, and Liverpool. However, from the 1970s, the necessity of structural change extended to wider sectors of the industry, which brought the development of further, previously flourishing industrial cities to a halt. In many cases, industrial branches that used the most advanced technology did not settle in the traditional industrial centres but selected other locations. As a result of this process, for example, Munich and Stuttgart evolved into significant industrial cities. Nonetheless, the fate of cities primarily depended on their potential and capability to attract the companies of the service sector.

In this respect, at the turn of the millennium, London and Paris were particularly successful and could be considered prominent European centres even in a global context, because both were chosen by a great number of companies, important in a global economic scale, for the location of their headquarters or affiliates.[10]

Suburbanization, counterurbanization and reurbanization: long-term trends, developmental anomalies and transitional phases

Although urbanization continued for a long time in several parts of Europe after the Second World War, during the post-war decades, transformations also took place that were difficult to reconcile with the concept of the growing spatial concentration of the population. Experts devised numerous models to grasp and explain novel tendencies focusing primarily on the recurrent cycles of the decentralization of the population within many societies and periods, and on their subsequent polarization reversals, thus suggesting the possibility of a cyclical or at least periodical urban development.[11] The models elaborated by L. H. Klaassen, L. van den Berg and other scholars evaluate the 1950s and the preceding decades in Western Europe as an era dominated by the tendencies of urbanization. During this period, the centralization of population prevailed in all aspects: there was a marked rural exodus towards cities, the population of large urban centres increased more rapidly than in smaller cities, and central areas within each city attracted new dwellers to a greater extent than suburbs. Contrary to this, the 1960s are usually described as the golden age of suburbanization in the most advanced industrial countries: this decade witnessed an intensive development of the external, suburban parts of the city, as opposed to the urban cores. The next decade, the 1970s, is often interpreted as the initial period of the so-called counterurbanization process, because the development of the largest cities was bridled in many countries, whereas the boundaries of suburban regions were gradually expanding: they incorporated previously separate cities or villages, which were not connected to the city centre in such a direct and intensive manner as typical suburban districts. Finally, in the 1980s, various large Western European cities showed signs of a certain urban revitalization process, as their capacity for attracting population strengthened: this phenomenon is also described by the term reurbanization.[12] Nevertheless, it has to be emphasized as well that this periodization is only of an approximate validity, not only because the demarcation lines of certain periods of social history rarely coincide with calendar decades, but also because even within Western Europe, these processes did not occur with the same intensity. They varied to such an extent that several of the terms referred to above generated heated debates among scholars, questioning their applicability and utility, and also raising the issue of whether in some cases, these concepts merely mask short, transitional phases, or particular developmental anomalies of certain regions or countries.

Suburbanization

The antecedents of suburbanization can be traced back to the nineteenth century, because already at that time successful entrepreneurs and financiers preferred their stately homes to be built on the outskirts of industrial and commercial cities. The improvement of transport rendered it possible to increase the distance between the home and the place of work, so this type of urban habitat acquired an increasing popularity among wealthier citizens in the time to come.[13]

In the interwar period, suburbanization gained further impetus in some Western European countries: new, more loosely built districts appeared in the territories around cities, which primarily provided housing and lacked important urban functions. Consequently, these were closely connected to the urban core.

In the interwar period, it was the development of garden suburbs that particularly advanced in England. These suburbs usually consisted of detached or row houses with small gardens, and were often constructed in order to provide homes for the not so well-off as well; the houses had a simple design and finish to make them more affordable. In addition, these projects also conformed to the *Home Fit for Heroes* campaign of David Lloyd George, which aimed at offering better houses for the soldiers returning from the First World War. Similar projects were implemented in several other European regions, where reasonably priced and simply built houses with gardens were offered to workers in the suburbs. The construction of these was often financed by large industrial companies with considerable capital strength, as well as a commitment for the welfare of employees, as, for example, by big industrial firms in the Ruhr area in the 1920s. Although it is evident that suburbanization in this period became extensive in only a few countries, the long-term significance of the phenomenon was considerable, because it offered models for similar developments in the second half of the twentieth century, when it appeared, with varying intensity, in most of the Western European countries.

Suburbanization in the interwar period was enhanced by numerous factors, including the demands of the broadening middle class, and especially the need of white-collar employees for a suburban habitat. During the economic depression, workforce became relatively cheap, compensating for other additional costs, because not only did the construction of these quarters require larger investments but also the loose arrangement of living space increased demands for communal infrastructure. Greater distances between suburban and urban parts demanded additional roads and railways, which were often developed in public works projects. The technological development of transport and transportation also aided the improvement of infrastructure: the growing demands were met by the introduction of suburban rail systems, followed by coaches and car transport. In addition, the process of suburbanization was stimulated by the new approach of planners who claimed that social problems of urban centres could be precisely alleviated with the creation of suburban areas. In his work titled the *Garden Cities of Tomorrow*, published in 1902, the British expert Ebenezer Howard argued that the difficulties caused by urban growth, principally congestion, could be solved by the construction of suburban districts with detached houses and gardens. Although the ideas of Howard had a more significant impact after the Second World War, his theses were already dispersed during the interwar period.

The real breakthrough in the process of suburbanization came about after the Second World War. Although, as it is widely known, the process had the greatest intensity in the United States, a considerable suburban expansion can also be observed in numerous Western European countries in the era.[14] British urban development since the 1950s showed the consistent tendency of a more rapid increase in the population of suburban districts than in the case of the urban cores (Table 8.2). Suburban areas developed particularly dynamically in the 1960s, but the process remained steady in the following decades as well. It is also evident that the focal point of suburban expansion shifted from inner to outer suburbs from the 1970s. Nonetheless, British suburbanization could be considered exceptional in Europe in several aspects: most of all, in terms of the early timing and of the high intensity of the process. In Scandinavia, the surge in suburban population growth can also be dated to the 1960s, and in other Western European countries, especially in France, Italy, Belgium, the Netherlands and Spain, the growth rates of suburbs began to exceed those of the inner-city districts only from the early 1970s, with a ratio difference less marked than in the case of Great Britain.[15] In the communist countries, this shift in urban growth rates occurred even later and with moderate intensity.

In the post-war period, the factors stimulating suburbanization remained relatively similar to those defining the trends of the interwar period, with certain elements gaining additional importance. First of all, public transport developed further, and the rapid improvement of living standards also enabled wider social groups to move to significantly more expensive suburban homes. This process was also induced by the negative elements of city life, such as the more and more obvious presence of crime or dilapidated public spaces. Originally, suburbanization closely followed the demands of families with children, who pursued optimal conditions for raising their offspring. Suburban areas offered a feasible solution, because the advantages of the proximity to urban centres did not have to be renounced either.

TABLE 8.2 Population change by functional zones in Great Britain, 1951–1991

| | Growth per decade (%) | | | |
	1951–1961	*1961–1971*	*1971–1981*	*1981–1991*
Great Britain (total)	4.97	5.25	0.55	2.50
Urban core	3.98	0.66	−4.2	−0.09
Ring	10.47	17.83	9.11	5.89
Outer area	1.74	11.25	10.11	8.85
Rural area	−0.60	5.35	8.84	7.82

Source: Tony Champion, 'Urbanization, Suburbanization, Counterurbanization and Reurbanization', in Ronan Paddison, ed., *Handbook of Urban Studies*, London: Sage, 2001, 149.

Although suburbanization gradually became one of the most prominent processes of post-war European urban development, beyond its expansion, its patterns were also transformed. As has been suggested in the case of Britain, at the beginning of the process suburbanization principally took place in the immediate urban outskirts, but later on it also involved external regions not directly connected to the cities, or even previously independent settlements. A further phenomenon called the 'urbanization of suburbs' was of even greater importance. Originally, suburbs were predominantly residential areas, and possessed only the most vital urban functions. However, later on, new centres were formed in suburbs as well, where a wide variety of services were offered to the residents. The expansion of the service sector created numerous workplaces, and attracted many companies as well that catered to the needs of a wider range of consumers, not only local inhabitants. These developments gradually blurred the difference between the functions of the inner-city districts and the suburbs.[16]

Counterurbanization

From the 1970s, several urban sociologists recorded even more radical changes in the population structure, a trend generally referred to as counterurbanization, or, in some cases, disurbanization. During this process, the spatial concentration of population not only comes to a halt but it also starts to decline.[17] To put it differently, the population of the most densely populated settlements or districts grows with less intensity than in the other areas, or may even drop.

Counterurbanization can take many forms. The most radical type of the urban polarization reversal occurs if an increasing number of inhabitants choose to live in rural settlements or small towns, where the way of life is different from both urban and suburban conditions. Nonetheless, other researchers argue that the phenomenon described as counterurbanization is nothing more than an alternative form of suburbanization, because it is almost impossible to precisely demarcate the different settlements in densely populated regions. In some cases, a smaller independent settlement could be located closer to the centre of the city than a suburban area of the same city. Therefore, counterurbanization can also be caused by a mere 'overflow' of the population beyond the administrative boundaries of the city, which might yield a lower representation of the urban population in statistics, yet still represents the spatial expansion of the city.

Notwithstanding the fundamental type of counterurbanization is the case when the population of smaller settlements, located either in the vicinity of large cities or in a greater distance from them, grows faster than that of big cities. The motives for moving to such smaller settlements usually lay in the social and environmental problems of cities, such as social deprivation, alienation, the poor residential community life, air pollution and the difficulties of transport. Thus, governments have made successful efforts to improve the social, educational and other conditions of smaller settlements, which in turn contributed to their increasing appeal. On the one hand, with advances in the development of motorization and of infrastructure (mainly of telecommunication), these smaller, occasionally even rural settlements could meet demands that once could only have been fulfilled by cities; and on the other hand, access to urban centres often became more rapid and convenient. Consequently, cities lost their previous monopoly on mass culture, as radio, movies and television culture penetrated rural regions as well.[18] Besides social and cultural factors, economic reasons may have also played an important role in enhancing counter-urbanization, because, for example, increasing urban real-estate prices could have motivated not only residents but also companies to move to smaller settlements, thus creating new jobs there as well. Furthermore, companies also made use of the comparatively cheap workforce reserves of these settlements.[19] From the 1960s, the increase in the number of pensioners, the unemployed and students contributed to the formation of a distinct social group, which was not dependent on daily urban commuting but in turn was sensitive to the changes of real-estate prices. Moreover, through inheritance or purchase, a growing proportion of families managed to acquire more than one real-estate property, which enabled breadwinners to reside in cities only on workdays, and they could spend their increasing numbers of days off in their rural home with their family.[20]

It seems that in the 1970s and in the first half of the 1980s, a faster population growth of smaller settlements ensued in the majority of the advanced industrial countries. Investigations carried out on the urban trends in Belgium, Denmark, France, the Netherlands, Sweden, Switzerland, Germany and Great Britain confirmed this tendency.[21] However, other studies indicated that counter-urbanization processes were significant in fewer countries, and were entirely absent in Southern Europe and in Ireland as well as in East Central and South-Eastern Europe.[22] Even experts who claim the existence of counterurbanization agree that before it could really expand, the process of counterurbanization slowed down, or, in some cases, even came to a halt by the beginning of the 1980s.[23] All in all, we can conclude that, although counterurbanization did take place in Europe in the 1970s, it remained within narrow boundaries both in geographic terms and regarding intensity.

Reurbanization

In the 1980s, there were signs of urban revival in several societies of Western Europe. Accordingly, the process of a renewed appeal of greater cities and especially their central districts from the 1980s was coined 'reurbanization'. Reurbanization could be identified on the basis of the number and distribution of urban dwellers. According to an estimate, in Western European cities, the share of urban cores within the total urban population growth increased to 47% between 1981 and 1991, although the same ratio was a mere 22% in the period between 1975 and 1981.[24] In some cases, the process led to population increase, but more often it resulted in the moderation or termination of the loss of inner-city populations (Table 8.3). It is also worth noting that cities with a historical city centre or a major university were particularly successful in stabilizing the population of their inner

TABLE 8.3 Reurbanization of cities in Western Europe, 1981–1991

| | Population growth (%) | | | |
	City total	Core (A)	Outer area (B)	(B)–(A)
United Kingdom				
Glasgow	−9.83	−4.83	−17.20	−12.37
Canterbury	3.39	8.24	2.84	−5.40
Oxford	7.21	10.64	6.35	−4.29
Cambridge	9.87	11.68	9.34	−2.34
Benelux countries				
Maastricht	2.79	16.57	−2.90	−19.47
Bruges	−6.80	−1.10	−9.45	−8.35
Zwolle	8.36	14.17	7.01	−7.16
Groningen	0.08	3.53	−1.89	−5.42
Apeldoorn	3.54	4.90	2.35	−2.55
Germany				
Ulm	8.37	12.67	7.60	−5.07
Krefeld	7.38	10.34	6.10	−4.24
Freiburg	8.89	11.29	8.41	−2.88
Denmark				
Odense	2.72	6.09	0.52	−5.57
Århus	6.60	9.08	4.18	−4.90
Ålborg	0.61	1.44	0.20	−1.24

Source: P. C. Cheshire, 'A New Phase of Urban Development in Western Europe? The Evidence for the 1980s', Urban Studies, vol. 32 (1995), no. 7, 1045–1064.

districts. As for the evolution of the population of larger cities as whole entities, hereby there were also signs of a reversal of the previous trends. The case of London supports this argument, because its population, after a marked decrease in the 1970s, started to grow again from the 1980s. Notwithstanding, urban deconcentration continued throughout the rest of Great Britain, although at a more moderate pace.[25]

There is no consensus in urban studies on whether reurbanization (that is, the repopulation of inner cities) can be regarded as a permanent tendency, or rather should be considered a disjunctive phase of development. The critical assessment of this question is also hindered by the fact that in many cases, reurbanization did not result in the revitalization of entire city centres. Instead, it led to the formation of dual urban cores, with the coexistence of run-down and exclusive areas. Moreover, diverging developmental paths of regions can be observed. Southern England, south-eastern France, south-western Germany, and north-central Italy were leading regions in economic growth in the final decades of the twentieth century. Therefore, cities in these areas had a greater appeal for potential residents than other parts of the respective countries.[26]

In any case, the reversal of counterurbanization trends is apparent, and requires further explanation. First of all, demographic changes have been major catalysts of the process. By the end of the twentieth century, the proportion of single and childless persons, primarily young adults, divorcees and widow(er)s, has increased significantly in Western European societies. Consequently, the proportion of households with children shrank. This demographic shift hampered the exodus from urban cores, because the ideals of 'a detached house with a garden' and 'living in green' were particularly attractive for families with children. On the other hand, the financial status of the social groups referred to above often impeded them in leading a more expensive suburban lifestyle. In addition, the population of Western European cities was considerably enlarged by immigrant groups, who were arriving in increasing numbers from the 1980s, and because they experienced difficulties in adapting in smaller, more closed communities, they also preferred larger settlements. Among the causes of reurbanization, evolution in the labour market has to be addressed as well. In the 1980s, the majority of new jobs were created in the financial and other business service sectors, concentrated mostly in larger urban centres because advanced transport facilities and a large reserve of highly qualified workforce were available there. Besides these, other branches of the service sector, for instance, catering and entertainment, became significant employers, thus further concentrating employment opportunities in the central districts of cities.[27] In historic city centres with privileged settings, like in the case of Florence, the tourism industry could also offer a substantial amount of workplaces and income possibilities. Finally, in several countries, for instance, in the Netherlands, further residential construction in green urban spaces was restricted by environmental considerations. Instead, urban designers focused on revitalizing dilapidated urban spaces, which were desolated in the process of deindustrialization, such as warehouses, docks, and factory grounds, from which primarily larger cities benefitted.[28] The latter tendency also indicates how the revitalization of the inner cities gradually became a conscious and crucial element of urban planning in the final decades of the twentieth century, for the purpose of which governments and cities mobilized vast resources. This process is addressed in detail in the following section.

Urban life and the use of urban space: visions and European peculiarities

Nineteenth-century urban transformations also affected the use of urban space to a great extent. The most significant changes took place in the case of the centres of cities and towns. On the one hand, financial services, such as banks, stock exchange, shops and offices, and venues of cultural life and leisure, such as theatres, museums, and restaurants, proliferated at the expense of industrial activities, and, in some cases, also constrained residential space. On the other hand, modern public transport, including railways and railway stations, required considerable space as well. The expansion of the functions of the state meant that in addition to public buildings with traditional functions, such as town halls and cathedrals, structures accommodating more recent public institutions, for instance, schools and hospitals, also appeared in the urban landscape. During the nineteenth century, the foundations of modern cities were laid down also in the form of conscious and systematic urban planning and management. Besides the boom in construction, the social consequences of industrialization, such as worries about the conflicts caused by the concentration of industrial workers, or the then recent importance of public health considerations, all justified the necessity of systematic urban planning. The most compelling example of systematic urban planning in the nineteenth century was the rebuilding of the centre of Paris, conducted by Georges-Eugène Haussmann, with a mandate from Napoleon III. Although the ideas of Haussmann had substantial repercussions all across Europe, he had considerably fewer contemporary followers in applied urban planning. Nevertheless, in the late nineteenth and early twentieth century the thorough reconstruction of urban infrastructure appeared on the agenda of every European city.[29]

Facets of modernity in interwar Europe

In the interwar period, numerous new approaches appeared both in urban planning and architecture that aimed at breaking with traditions in these areas. One of the most innovative and influential architectural currents was linked to the German Bauhaus circle, led by Walter Gropius. Architects following the Gropius school incorporated new and simplified forms as well as modern material, such as concrete, steel and glass, in the designs of buildings. Another contemporary architect, the French-Swiss Le Corbusier, proposed to solve urban congestion with the construction of gigantic, tower-like residential buildings that allow for ample space to be inserted between them, used for recreational purposes. These concepts as well as other similarly novel ideas were realized by the erection of only a few edifices or building clusters in this period, but they had a significant impact on urban architecture in the long run.

After the rapid development of cities in the decades the before the First World War, the principal aim of interwar urban policy in many Western European cities was to contain and manage growth. This was particularly important in London, because the spatial expansion of the city was enormous: as a result of the proliferation of areas with a lower building density, urban space tripled between 1921 and 1939, which in itself called for planning. Although the Great Depression and later the Second World War disrupted the realization of large-scale urban reconstruction, ambitious plans for the reorganization of London and the metropolitan area were elaborated during the 1930s. The planning concluded in the publication of the so-called Barlow Report (1937–40), which emphasized the disadvantages caused by the disproportionate population distribution in the country, especially in South-Eastern England. Impressed by the findings of the report, in 1938 the development of the London suburbia was restricted in order to preserve a preferable yet relatively intact segment of the city outskirts. The war experiences, especially the vulnerability of cities, also gave further impetus to the endeavours of urban decentralization. In 1943, the design concept of Patrick Abercrombie was accepted, which proposed the establishment of green belts around London, of a total width of nearly

9 kilometres, with further extensions that would separate London from newly founded cities, which were intended to absorb 1 million inhabitants.[30]

The interwar growth of Paris took off among less regulated circumstances. Whereas in London, new urban districts were built along electrical railway lines, and road constructions also followed the pace of urban development, the development of Paris suburbia often lacked the configuration and construction of adequate public transport networks and of good-quality roads. Although in 1928, Parisian authorities were ordered to devise a comprehensive plan for the development of the whole metropolitan area, until the end of the Second World War, scarcely any progress was realized.

It was Amsterdam that presented the most outstanding progress in the practical implementation of comprehensive and innovative plans of urban design as a response to the contemporary challenges of urban development. The projects for the reconstruction of Amsterdam were elaborated between 1928 and 1934, under the leadership of Cornelis van Eesteren, and were the first to break with the Haussmannian concept in practice and on a large scale. The Dutch urban designers thought that the creation of harmony and a connection between the inner city that developed organically over the centuries, following the arching structure of canals, and the relatively recent outer rings, which were built according to more functional principles, could not be achieved by homogenizing mechanically the two parts because that would have implied the Haussmannization of older urban districts. Instead of this solution, Dutch designers proposed to preserve the old city centre in its original form, and to simultaneously separate and unite historical and new urban areas by inserting extensive green zones between them. Except for an obligate pause during the Second World War, in the following three decades, this plan was thoroughly and systematically executed in Amsterdam.[31]

Italian Fascism as well as German Nazism fostered specific and large-scale objectives in relation to urban design. Urban architecture projects in interwar Italy placed particular emphasis on showing the alleged historical continuity with the Roman Empire. A series of cities was established copying the original structure of the Roman cities, where the main intersection of principal roads in the north–south and east–west directions was framed by a central square. Most of the newly constructed buildings also bore the stylistic features of classical Roman architecture, for example, the emphatic representation of columns, statues and arches. The Nazis had similarly definite concepts about urban planning, but the main aim of public construction in the Third Reich, similar to the communist regimes, was to 'erase the past'. The plans included the reconstruction of several cities, and particularly of Berlin, Nuremberg and Munich, as the emblematic places of the Nazi movement; however, the majority of these projects were not put in practice because of the war. Both fascist and Nazi urban design projects had to fulfil multiple goals. On the one hand, the spectacular buildings and fascinating squares were destined to emphasize the creative power and the mobilization capacity of the regime. In addition, the vast avenues and public squares were expected to provide a location for diverse mass events, which were also meant to show the power of the regime and to isolate the occasional sceptics. In both the Italian fascist and the Nazi regime, large-scale construction projects were carried out by means of public work programs, which were also designed to alleviate unemployment in the period of interwar economic depression.

Cities and urban design after the Second World War

The Second World War caused vast damage in most of the European cities. German urban areas were particularly affected by military operations: 60% of the inner cities of Berlin and Cologne were destroyed and the centres of many other cities, including Hamburg, Würzburg and Dresden, also required complete rebuilding. However, reconstruction projects of similar scale were also necessary in the British cities of Coventry, Exeter, Hull, Plymouth and Southampton, as well as in the Netherlands, in Rotterdam, in the French port city of Le Havre, and in the Polish capital, Warsaw. At the beginning, clearing away the ruins and undergoing the most essential reconstruction in housing had priority over all other considerations. Consequently, the architectural quality of the buildings erected during this phase was often low.

Nonetheless, later on, the necessity of urban planning was increasingly articulated, and its possibilities were also enhanced. On the one hand, similarly to the tendencies after the First World War, with regard to social infrastructure, urban planning provided means to meet the demands of the population that made great sacrifices during the war. Moreover, the rapid post-war industrialization and housing shortage outlined below also called for systematic urban development. On the other hand, state involvement in the economy was strengthened, which enabled the realization of costly urban designs, especially in the context of rapid economic growth.

The period after the post-war reconstruction phase in Western Europe is also referred to as the age of technocratic planning.[32] The architectural ideal of Le Corbusier permeated post-war European housing programs, principally because of its economic efficiency, because the shortage of housing still remained one of the most vital urban issues. This problem persisted even in non-belligerent countries and for a considerable period after the Second World War, which can be explained by the post-war growth of the population, the increase in the proportion of urban population, the transformations in household structure, and most of all, by the dynamically increasing needs regarding housing standards. Besides the physical damages caused by the war, the shortage in housing was also exacerbated by the massive influx of refugees to the cities in belligerent countries and by the suspension of housing constructions during the armed conflicts. Obviously, Germany was the country most affected by these problems: in addition to the damages to the living space, millions of East European German refugees and deportees arrived. To meet these needs, most of the Western European countries launched extensive housing construction programs in the 1950s: for instance, 500,000 new homes were completed in the Federal Republic of Germany every year during this decade.

Mainly based on economic considerations, politicians and urban planners often favoured the creation of residential districts consisting of large, multistorey blocks of flats. These new residential areas, springing up all over the continent, from Sheffield to Madrid, were characterized by a uniform and monotonous architectural concept, as well as by scarce public services. Nevertheless, with respect to this tendency, there were vast differences between European countries and cities. Whereas, for example, in the suburban parts of Paris, similar housing projects were built extensively, covering large areas, they were less prevalent in West Berlin, where building blocks usually consisted of fewer storeys, and urban planners also regulated the adequate proportion and condition of green zones.

Motorization, which was expedited in the 1960s, was generally regarded as increasing the freedom of movement of residents. Consequently, development projects were also aligned with this aspect of urban life. New roads, overpasses, underpasses and junctions were in turn built with the purpose of enabling quick access to the inner city. However, these expensive investments soon showed ambivalent results: although they did ease the flow of the traffic, they often led to the dereliction of the areas around principal motorways as well.

The period of technocratic urban development vision and practice lasted until around the end of the 1960s in Western Europe, which was succeeded by a period also called the age of the 'flight from modernism'. In this respect, the transformation of urban decision-making mechanisms is notable. Post-war urban planners tended to regard themselves as the ultimate representatives of common good, who are able to equilibrate diverging interests, and thus are not obliged to provide consultation mechanisms for the direct participation of the population in decisions. Nevertheless, the participation of citizens in decision making was in no small measure increasingly valued from the late 1960s. The growth of ecological awareness, the increasing activity of civil society in general, and of environmental and urban conservation movements in particular, encouraged the democratization of urban planning. In addition, the formal representation of conservationists and green movements at municipal assemblies, and later on, from the 1970s to 1980s, at regional and national levels of politics enlarged dynamically. Whereas previously, urban development was interpreted primarily as an engineering and construction task, from the 1970s decision making gradually drew in experts in social sciences as well. Furthermore, scepticism concerning extensive plans of urban reconstruction also became more marked, because these projects often resulted in new problems, and failed to produce an adequate increase in the quality of life of the urban population. The new needs and attitudes of the urban population were already apparent in the process of counterurbanization, described above, because it entailed the revaluation of the less crowded and more humane smaller settlements over larger cities.

Thus, as urban development slowed down from the 1970s, urban planners were challenged to formulate new priorities. The concepts of the preservation of historical heritage and the conservation of the natural environment were not altogether novel; however, their influence was substantially higher than previously. Instead of erecting new buildings, the new current of urban design rather focused on renovating older ones. In addition, urban rehabilitation was gradually expanded to the scale of entire districts, usually in the urban centre ('gentrification').[33]

In Mediterranean countries, the rapidity of metropolitan population growth, the shortcomings of planning and, to an even greater extent, of the enforcement of regulations, and the consequent spontaneity of development led to urban problems. For instance, the population of Rome grew very dynamically in the 1960s to 1970s, with successive waves of influx from other parts of the country. The lodging situation of newly arrived inhabitants was poor, with overcrowded rents or make-shift housing buildings multiplying despite the regulations of an urban development plan issued in 1962. The population of the area of the so-called *borgate* amounted to 800,000 and its inhabitants found it increasingly hard to put up with the lack of such elementary features of urban lifestyle as proper sanitation or running water. Subsequent constructions of paved roads, pavements, the introduction of public transport, as well as the building of schools and other public institutions required vast funds. Similarly, the *barracas* sprawling around large Spanish cities, such as Madrid and Barcelona, provided very poor living conditions for their residents. After the mid-1950s, Lisbon and Porto faced difficulties of the same nature. Illegal constructions also spread significantly on the peripheries of these cities. Furthermore, housing problems were further aggravated by the arrival of hundreds of thousands of repatriated Portuguese citizens after Angola and Mozambique gained their independence. In Athens, the massive population growth was also accompanied with anarchic urban development: during the 1970s, one in every five buildings was erected without building permits, with the result that these buildings were not connected to the sewer system.[34] Thus, it can be plausibly argued that in the Mediterranean region urban planning was usually unable to catch up with development broadly until the 1980s.

The peculiarities of European urban development

As described above, the evolution of European cities, determined by their particular historical traditions and by different developmental conditions, showed a great deal of diversity in the twentieth century. Nonetheless, there were a number of significant common characteristics of European urban areas, which become even more perceptible if we compare cities in Europe with their counterparts outside the continent.

The peculiarities of European urban life were most plausibly elaborated by Hartmut Kaelble in the historical literature.[35] As he argues, the most important feature of the European urbanization pattern is the peculiar physical appearance of the cities in the continent, preserved with conscious development and conservation efforts throughout the twentieth century. Most of the European cities possess a medieval or early modern urban centre and the inner city is usually dominated by edifices built in these periods, such as churches and cathedrals, city halls, marketplaces, town houses of the bourgeoisie, city walls and turrets. The urban structure of the centre itself, with its commonly narrow and winding streets and marketplaces, preserves the old structural patterns of the settlement despite later reconfigurations, during which, for instance, boulevards were often built at the sites of earlier city walls. Occasionally, these urban cores survived intact until the present day, like in Bruges, Venice or Bamberg. However, even if they perished partially or entirely, with their origins in the distant past, these buildings constitute one of the major sources of the identity of the citizens.[36] The evidences of nineteenth-century reconstruction projects are almost always visible in the city centres or in some of their parts, mostly in the form of buildings housing important public functions, such as, for example, schools, courts and railway stations, and, in the case of larger cities, theatres and museums. Avenues, often lined with nineteenth-century buildings similar in architectural style, tend to connect the centre with the outer urban districts.

The architectural traits of a long history unequivocally distinguish European cities from the American ones, where urban centres of the colonial times survived in only a few cases and sporadically. Moreover, as Kaelble suggests, compared with similar areas of the United States, Asia and other parts of the world, the urbanized regions of Europe also show several other particularities, such as the more extended preservation of the residential function of inner cities, the manifestation of nineteenth-century and twentieth-century social segregation in the appearance of urban districts, as well as the structural and architectural outcomes of systematic urban planning. A dominant part of these features can be interpreted as the result of the relatively moderate pace of growth of European cities in a global perspective. We have previously described the advance of European urbanization, reaching a considerable level by the second half of the twentieth century. However, whereas European societies reached this high ratio of urbanization over a long period, occasionally extending over centuries, Asian or American societies often achieved a similar level in a couple of decades. Furthermore, the proportion of the population living in metropolises with several million inhabitants remained relatively low in Europe. At the end of the twentieth century, Paris or London, with their respective 9.8 million and 9.2 million inhabitants, qualify as metropolises, but in a global context other European cities do not reach this rank (Table 8.4). Although the average urbanization ratio of Europe is similar to that of the United States or Japan, the European continent in particular is characterized by the high number of cities and their relative proximity. Metropolises with more than 2 million inhabitants are relatively rare: the combined number of the population of the thirty largest cities is considerably bigger in the United States than in Europe. In relation to this, another important feature of European and principally, Western European urbanization is the high proportion of small- and middle-sized cities within the total population and thus a consolidated position in the urban hierarchy.[37]

The particularities in the use of public space also contributed to the special quality of European urban life. Inner cities are of primary importance in this respect. As opposed to the cities of the United States and other continents, European urban centres managed to maintain their functional diversity throughout the twentieth century. Not only did they accommodate businesses, civic administration

TABLE 8.4 Leading cities in the European urban hierarchy, 1850–2000 (population in thousands)

1850		1900		1950		2000	
City	Population	City	Population	City	Population	City	Population
London	2320	London	6586	London	8860	Paris	9850
Paris	1314	Paris	2714	Paris	5900	London	9160
Berlin	446	Berlin	1889	Essen (Ruhr area)	4900	Essen (Ruhr area)	6533
Vienna	426	Vienna	1675	Berlin	3707	Madrid	4070
Liverpool	422	Glasgow	776	Manchester	2382	Barcelona	3988
Naples	416	Budapest	732	Birmingham	2196	Manchester	3976
Manchester	412	Hamburg	706	Vienna	1755	Milan	3890
Glasgow	346	Liverpool	704	Rome	1665	Berlin	3755
Birmingham	294	Manchester	645	Hamburg	1580	Katowice	3475
Dublin	263	Warsaw	638	Madrid	1527	Athens	3350
Madrid	263	Brussels	599	Budapest	1500	Naples	2973
Lisbon	257	Naples	564	Barcelona	1425	Rome	2898
Lyon	254	Madrid	540	Milan	1400	Birmingham	2456
Amsterdam	225	Barcelona	533	Glasgow	1320	Lisbon	2344
Brussels	208	Birmingham	523	Liverpool	1260	Hamburg	2196
Edinburgh	194	Amsterdam	511	Naples	1210	Bucharest	2054
Hamburg	193	Munich	500	Leeds	1164	Vienna	1928
Marseille	193	Milan	493	Copenhagen	1150	Budapest	1836
Milan	193	Marseille	491	Athens	1140	Lille	1697
Leeds	184	Rome	463	Bucharest	1100	Leeds	1660
Palermo	182	Lyon	459	Katowice	977	Zagreb	1650
Rome	170	Leipzig	456	Brussels	964	Warsaw	1644
Barcelona	167	Leeds	429	Amsterdam	940	Munich	1576
Warsaw	163	Wroclaw (Breslau)	423	Prague	938	Belgrade	1482

TABLE 8.4 (continued)

1850		1900		1950		2000	
City	*Population*	*City*	*Population*	*City*	*Population*	*City*	*Population*
Budapest	156	Sheffield	409	Stockholm	889	Frankfurt/M.	1440
Bristol	150	Copenhagen	401	Lisbon	885	Lyon	1416
Sheffield	143	Dresden	396	Munich	870	Torino	1400
Bordeaux	142	Edinburgh	394	Newcastle	830	Copenhagen	1397
Venice	141	Cologne	373	Rotterdam	803	Marseille	1355
Torino	138	Dublin	373	Warsaw	803	Stockholm	1346
Copenhagen	135	Lisbon	356	Sheffield	730	Valencia	1332
Munich	125	Belfast	349	Torino	725	Glasgow	1317
Bucharest	120	Bristol	339	Cologne	692	Porto	*1258*
Genova	120	Torino	336	Frankfurt/M.	680	Prague	1225
Prague	117	Rotterdam	319	Genoa	676	Stuttgart	1210
Wroclaw (Breslau)	114	Lodz	315	Lodz	675	Sofia	1192
Wolverhampton	112	Palermo	310	Marseille	661	Newcastle	1179
Newcastle	111	Stockholm	301	Antwerp	584	Amsterdam	1158
Valencia	110	Wuppertal	299	Dublin	522	Brussels	1121
Gent	108	Frankfurt/M.	289	Palermo	491	Seville	1050

Note: The methods of calculations concerning the population of the conurbations may vary considerably. Data in *italics* take extended conurbations into account; different date: Essen, Madrid, Katowice, Belgrade, Budapest, Bucharest, Prague 1999.

Source: Paul M. Hohenberg and Lynn Hollen Lees, *The Making of Urban Europe, 1000–1950*, Cambridge, MA: Harvard University Press, 1985, 227 (Europe 1850, 1950, if not indicated otherwise); Brian R. Mitchell, *European Historical Statistics, 1750–1975*, London: Macmilllan, 1980, 86–88 (Bucharest, Genoa 1850; Europe 1900; Marseille, Antwerp, Dublin, Frankfurt/M. 1950); Patrick Le Galès, *European Cities*, Oxford: Oxford University Press, 2002, 60 (Western Europe 2000, if not indicated otherwise); United Nations, *World Urbanization Prospects: The 1999 Revision*, New York: United Nations, 2000 (Essen, Madrid, Katowice, Belgrade, Budapest, Bucharest, Prague 1999).

and other public institutions, they also provided valuable residential space. At the beginning of the century, beside the middle and upper classes, the less wealthy social groups also occupied certain areas of the inner cities. This pattern of residence undoubtedly changed in the following decades, because during the processes of suburbanization and counterurbanization referred to above, a substantial share of the better-off population moved out of the inner cities. However, these tendencies never became as prevalent in Europe as in the United States, and by the end of the twentieth century, the urban exodus slowed down, or, in several cases, was even reversed. These tendencies are investigated in detail below.

It is without doubt that the argumentation of Kaelble is supported mainly by Western European empirical evidence, and even within this region, divergences from the features examined above and considered as prevailing or common occurred. Moreover, at the end of the twentieth century, the central districts of European cities also faced numerous challenges, which are addressed in the following discussion as well. However, the preservation of the functional diversity as well as the presence of relatively affluent residents in the inner cities chiefly contributed to the fact that the quality of European urban centres (with good housing conditions, acceptable public security and an ample offer of diverse leisure activities) remained unique even in a global perspective. These achievements are related to the historical heritage indicated above, but also to the systematic efforts of urban administration, urban planning and the welfare state during the twentieth century.[38]

Cities in the communist countries

Cities and urban life gained a particular importance in communist ideology, because they were closely associated with industrialization and they were attributed a key role in the formation of collective identity in the working class. Even though communist governments concentrated vast resources on urban development, these countries were characterized by underurbanization, that is, they achieved a certain level of industrialization at a lower urbanization level than other countries (especially developing countries, where overurbanization prevailed). A principal reason for this pattern was the collectivization of agriculture, resulting in a low efficiency of production: agriculture could supply the urban population with food only with a high level of people employed, yielding a considerably increased ratio of rural population.[39] During the four decades of their existence, communist systems also had a considerable impact on the spatial pattern of cities and the development of urban hierarchy.[40] The most important characteristics of the structural transformation of cities prevailing especially in the initial one or two decades, were the following:

- The real-estate market was abolished; the communist governments introduced set land prices. The location within the city had almost no economic significance from the point of view of the users (shops, offices or apartments) and the potential investors, because it affected real-estate prices only to a minimal degree.

- The majority of the available residential buildings and apartments in cities were nationalized and redistributed. Larger, upper-middle-class homes were divided into two or more separate dwellings. Local authorities supervised housing, including swap transactions, rents, and the distribution of new houses, by various legal norms and administrative mechanisms. Villages were less affected by these restrictive regulations and usually fell outside the scope of housing legislation.
- Retail trade and services were also nationalized, which resulted in the fusion and the concentration of smaller businesses.
- Public interests were prioritized over individual or local ones. Their enforcement was carried out through planning and by central authorities with a wide range of action.[41]

Nonetheless, these general features did not result in a total uniformity amongst communist countries or cities. Divergences appeared not only in the level of urbanization, but also in the physical patterns of the cities. The principal reason was the different urban historical heritage that urban planners had to take into consideration: medieval urban structures and buildings, monuments and sites vital for the national identity, and industrial establishments and wartime damages were all set constants for urban planning.

The restoration of destroyed historical districts became a priority in Poland after the Second World War, especially in the case of Warsaw (Stare Miasto, Krakowskie Przedmieście and Nowy Świat) and Gdańsk (Główne Miasto). Yet in smaller towns, for instance, in Elblag, Nysa, and Kołobrzeg, urban planners often opted for less demanding solutions: old buildings or their damaged structures were demolished, and new buildings were constructed. In Prague the entire historical inner city survived the Second World War, and was ready for conservation: this city possessed 1431 architectural and cultural heritage buildings on a total extension of 881 hectares. Contrary to the Czech example, Sofia had only a limited number of buildings that could be regarded as apt for preservation. Obviously, the more valuable and voluminous the historical heritage was, the more difficulties were faced in the reconstruction of cities according to socialist principles and practice of urban design.[42]

Because the inherited physical patterns often constituted limits for urban transformations, urban architecture and planning could unfold more freely in the design of new settlements and districts. Being relatively densely populated, East Central Europe could not provide such an amount of free space for new cities as the Soviet Union, which was a generic model in this aspect as well. Nevertheless, approximately forty new cities were founded in the region in the post-war decades. The new urban areas showed traits of considerable uniformity in all of the communist countries except Yugoslavia, because similar aims, ideals and means were implemented in their construction. They were built in the style of socialist realism of the 1950s, so they hardly differed in the case of Nowa Huta, Havířov or Eisenhüttenstadt. Forms and structures were almost identical, and it was only in the quality or the materials of the external finish that differences could be perceived. The same tendency towards uniformity prevailed in the large housing estate projects that were launched in the 1960s and 1970s to ease the severe housing shortage.

Housing estates were usually located in outer urban rings, but occasionally in urban centres as well.[43] The extensive application of prefabricated panel block technology resulted in a monotonous environment and buildings of poor quality. The dull aspect of these estates was heightened by their enormous size, because they often provided residence for several tens of thousands of residents. The density of buildings was also high. Moreover, additional infrastructural investments, such as traffic lines, parks and shops, were often implemented with a considerable delay or were not realized at all. In the context of the planned economy, the installation of industries and the improvement of housing and the urban environment mostly depended on the decisions made by numerous central authorities and sectoral bureaucracy, the principal focus of which, obviously, was not to satisfy the local interests of urban development.[44] Consequently, the architectural features of these areas also impeded the formation of functional local communities, which came through as an actual cultural shock for many residents who moved in from a rural environment.

The spatial structure of new cities and districts also reflected similar principles in the communist countries. Whereas in capitalist countries, new industrial inversions were concentrated in districts with more favourable plot prices and better transport capabilities, in post-war East Central Europe, planners were less bound by these considerations. Furthermore, in communist cities, different urban functions, such as production and housing, were separated in a more characteristic manner.[45] At the same time, the agglomeration tendencies of Western European urban development, described previously, were almost entirely absent in the region.

The post-war socialist transformation of cities materialized in some external, visually highly identifiable features. Because buildings in the urban centres were not regarded as particularly valuable, and were mostly transferred to communal property, the improvement of the inner city and the conservation of its buildings were generally neglected. Monuments of historical figures belonging to the periods that the communist ideology wished to erase were pulled down and later replaced by statues honouring the new heroes of the era. Ideological considerations also yielded changes in the names of streets, and occasionally, even of settlements. Shop boards were also modified: the names of previous owners disappeared, and were substituted with bleak inscriptions simply stating the profile of the shop. In general, cities became more drab and homogeneous, and lost a considerable amount of their previous diversity.[46]

Spatial segregation within the cities, that is, the separation of social groups of different social status and income, was regarded as an issue of preeminent importance by contemporary decision makers. The official ideology denied the existence of any segregation, showing the superiority of socialism over capitalism in this area as well.

It is remarkable that the spatial separation of lower and wealthier social classes in the region was less marked than in Western Europe already at the turn of the nineteenth–twentieth century.[47] The segregation of the population decreased further in the post-war years, as was clearly shown in the case of Warsaw.[48] Indeed, in socialist countries, almost all urban citizens were supposed to be able to live in the best districts of the city, because especially in the early stage, rents were low (almost nominal) and were only linked to the size of the house or apartment. The homogenization of income distribution was another crucial factor in decreasing spatial differentiation. However, there were counteracting factors as well. The most important mechanism facilitating the spatial segregation of social groups was the central distribution of scantly available housing. The conditions that made a certain real estate preferable varied in every city, but generally stately houses and apartments built in the pre-war period, or newly constructed ones, were preferred. According to the research of György Konrád and Iván Szelényi, conducted in Hungary in the 1960s, citizens in a higher social position and white-collar workers received flats with a nominal rent or apartments in new housing estates in a significantly higher proportion. Contrary to their situation, other social groups with lower incomes as well as the vast majority of the rural population had to acquire residences without state subsidies, which were subsequently more expensive.[49] From the 1980s at the very latest, growing income inequalities and the introduction of some elements of the market economy in the allocation of housing enhanced the spatial segregation of the population, as was pointed out in the case of Prague, Warsaw, and other cities.[50] Thus, although urban studies have not reached a consensus on this issue, most scholars agree that urban social segregation was indeed less intensive in the communist than in most of the capitalist countries with similar levels of development, though significant forms of segregation still existed.

Urban structure and spatial planning: hydrocephalous cities and vanguards of development

Urban hierarchies

In the study of European urban structure, the comparison of the size of the largest European cities in different time periods serves as a vantage point. Conspicuous shifts and remarkable continuity equally characterized the historical patterns of urban hierarchy. Whereas in 1850, the threshold for ranking among the forty largest European settlements was broadly 100,000 inhabitants, in 1950, this minimum limit increased to 500,000 inhabitants. Notwithstanding this growth, the hierarchy of the largest European cities remained largely the same between the mid-nineteenth and mid-twentieth centuries. London, Paris and Berlin preserved their leading positions. With slight differences, the same tendency can be observed in the case of several followers, such as Manchester, Birmingham, Vienna, Glasgow and Naples. Only a few cities, including Barcelona, Rome, Budapest, Copenhagen, Athens, and Bucharest, rose to rank within the twenty biggest cities in this period. At the same time, the further ranking showed greater volatility (Table 8.4).

Although the developmental dynamics of each city was the result of the combined effect of many factors, a few regularities can still be identified. Although at the beginning of the nineteenth century, the group of the largest cities included principally capitals and port cities, and fewer industrial centres, by the mid-twentieth century, the cities of industrial zones caught up. Traditional Mediterranean trade centres, like Venice, Palermo and Marseille, counted among the losers of the transformation of European urban hierarchy in the hundred years before 1950, and rising metropolises were principally industrial centres, such as, for instance, the cities of the Ruhr area, Katowice, and Manchester. It can be also observed that East Central European cities, which were industrialized with a relative delay, were also increasingly represented on the list of the large cities.[51] The functions of large metropolitan centres were fundamentally transformed without exception, as happened in the case of the traditional leading triad of London, Paris and Berlin, which reflected the tendency that the accumulation of diverse urban functions was of primary importance with respect to urban growth. Still, the most spectacular relative growth was not produced by the settlements ranking among the twenty or forty largest cities, but by the representatives of smaller categories. This tendency seems natural, because in a reduced urban population, even an increase of a few thousand or tens of thousands induced by the growth of one or few industrial companies might generate a significant dynamism.

In the second half of the twentieth century, as a result of the development outlined previously (most eminently of suburbanization) it became increasingly difficult to demarcate cities in several European regions. Still, it can be plausibly argued that the hierarchy of the largest European cities remained relatively stable in the second half of the twentieth century as well. At the turn of the millennium, it was still Paris and London that led the European urban hierarchy, and had the largest concentration of population, although in the meantime, the two cities switched places at the top of the list. As a continuation of the tendencies that started in the first half of the century, perhaps the most striking decline can be observed in the case of Liverpool and Glasgow, but the significance of Budapest, Vienna, and Copenhagen also lessened in a European perspective. Nonetheless, many East Central and South-Eastern European capitals and industrial centres, such as Belgrade, Zagreb, Sofia, Warsaw, and Katowice, as well as numerous Southern European cities, such as Milan, Madrid, Barcelona, Lisbon, and Porto, ascended in the hierarchy. The increase in the size of the population in the latter group principally resulted from the growth of agglomerations.

If the largest conurbations are compared, the leading positions of the ranking barely change. Paris and London are followed by several other capitals, such as Madrid, Lisbon, Berlin, Athens, Rome, and Warsaw. However, extensive economic conurbations are also represented, such as the Ruhr area, usually divided into several parts in population estimates, although if it was treated as a single unit, it would rank as the largest population concentration in Europe during the entire twentieth century. The list of big conurbations also includes Milan and its area, the Rhine-Main region (with Frankfurt am Main, Mannheim and other cities), as well as Naples, Barcelona, Hamburg, Stuttgart, Birmingham and Manchester (Table 8.5).

TABLE 8.5 The population of the largest European conurbations, 1950–2000

	Million inhabitants		
	1950	1975	2000
Paris	5.9	8.9	9.8
London	8.9	8.2	9.2
Rhine–Ruhr–North	5.3	6.5	6.5
Milan	3.6	5.5	4.3
Madrid	1.6	3.8	4.1
Barcelona	1.6	2.8	4.0
Manchester	2.5	2.4	4.0
Lisbon	0.8	1.2	3.9
Berlin	3.7	3.2	3.8
Rhine-Main (Frankfurt/M.)	2.3	3.2	3.7
Katowice	1.7	3.0	3.5
Athens	1.8	2.7	3.4
Rhine–Ruhr–Central	2.0	2.6	3.2
Naples	2.8	3.6	3.0
Rome	1.7	3.0	2.9
Hamburg	2.1	2.5	2.7
Rhine–Ruhr–South	1.8	2.3	2.7
Stuttgart	1.5	2.3	2.7
Birmingham	2.3	2.4	2.5
Munich	1.3	2.0	2.3
Warsaw	1.0	1.9	2.3
Vienna	1.8	2.0	2.1
Bucharest	1.1		2.1

Note: According to the definition of the UN, the denomination Rhine–Ruhr–North designates the Ruhr area (Essen, Dortmund, Bochum etc.); Rhine–Ruhr–Central stands for the region of Düsseldorf, Remscheid, Mönchengladbach, Solingen and Wuppertal; Rhine–Ruhr–South includes the areas of Cologne, Leverkusen and Bonn.

Source: United Nations, *World Urbanization Prospects. The 2001 revision,* New York: United Nations, 2001, 133, 256 (1950–2000, if not indicated otherwise); Patrick Le Galès, *European Cities,* Oxford: Oxford University Press, 2002, 60 (Paris, London, Berlin, Rome 1950; Paris, London, Madrid, Berlin, Athens, Barcelona, Rome, Birmingham, Manchester 2000).

One can also gain useful insights concerning the process of urbanization if the hierarchy of settlements is examined at a national level. In this respect, one of the most significant features is to what extent a specific primate city (usually the capital) occupies a dominant position in the political, economic and cultural life of the particular society.[52] Interwar European societies already showed a substantial divergence regarding the hierarchy of their cities. Capitals were the most dominant in the case of Austria, Denmark, Hungary and the United Kingdom. In 1930, the population of Vienna was twelve times bigger than that of the second largest city, Graz. The residents of Copenhagen outnumbered those of Århus by nine times, the population of Szeged was one-eighth of that of Budapest, whereas London's

TABLE 8.6 Primate cities in relation to the second and third cities of their countries in interwar Europe

Country	Year	Proportion of the population	Population of cities (in thousands)
1. Austria	1934	100:8:6	Vienna 1874, Graz 153, Linz 109
2. Denmark	1935	100:11:9	Copenhagen 834, Århus 91, Odense 76
3. Hungary	1936	100:13:12	Budapest 1052, Szeged 140, Debrecen 125
4. United Kingdom	1931	100:14:13	London 8204, Liverpool 1178, Glasgow 1089
5. Romania	1937	100:18:17	Bucharest 643, Chişinău/Kishinev 114, Cernăuţi/Chernivtsi 110
6. Finland	1936	100:26:25	Helsinki 284, Viipuri 73, Turku 71
7. Belgium	1936	100:30:18	Brussels 905, Antwerp 273, Gent 164
8. Czechoslovakia	1930	100:31:15	Prague 849, Brno 265, Ostrava 125
9. Germany	1933	100:32:15	Berlin 4242, Hamburg–Altona 1372, Cologne 757
10. France	1936	100:32:20	Paris 2830, Marseille 914, Lyon 571
11. Bulgaria	1934	100:35:24	Sofia 287, Plovdiv 100, Varna 70
12. Norway	1930	100:39:21	Oslo 253, Bergen 98, Trondheim 54
13. Greece	1928	100:40:10	Athens–Piraeus 592, Thessaloniki 237, Patras 61
14. Portugal	1930	100:40:4	Lisbon 594, Porto 232, Coimbra 27
15. Sweden	1937	100:48:26	Stockholm 544, Gothenburg 263, Malmö 144
16. Poland	1937	100:53:26	Warsaw 1233, Lodz 653, Lvov 317
17. Switzerland	1936	100:59:50	Zurich 250, Basel 148, Geneva 124
18. Yugoslavia	1937	100:70:36	Belgrade 267, Zagreb 186, Subotica/Szabadka 100
19. Netherlands	1937	100:76:62	Amsterdam 783, Rotterdam 599, Hague 487
20. Spain	1934	100:91:31	Barcelona 1148, Madrid 1048, Valencia 352
21. Italy	1936	100:96:75	Rome 1156, Milan 1116, Naples 866

Source: Mark Jefferson, 'The Law of the Primate City', *Geographical Review*, vol. 29 (1939), 229–230.

population was seven times larger than the total number of Liverpool's inhabitants (Table 8.6).[53]

In the second half of the twentieth century, the number of countries with a dominant capital still remained significant. Göran Therborn's typology regards a capital dominant if its population is at least three times larger than that of the second city, and if it retains all the major urban functions: Austria, Denmark, Hungary and France, for example, belong to this category (Table 8.7). Another type includes countries with one major urban centre. In this case the capital possesses the most significant urban functions, but it does not concentrate the country's population to such an extent as in the former type. Therefore, it is less dominant and permits a more balanced urban structure to be applied, for instance, in Poland, Sweden or Portugal. A third category of 'contested monocephalous' is

TABLE 8.7 States and capitals in Europe at the end of the twentieth century

Dominant capital	Country with one centre	Country with one centre in a contested position	Country with multiple centres
Austria	Bulgaria	Belgium	FRG
Denmark	Czech Republic	Spain	Italy
France	Finland		Netherlands
Hungary	(GDR)		Switzerland
Ireland	Norway		
Romania	Poland		
Serbia	Portugal		
United Kingdom	Slovakia		
	Sweden		

Notes: Dominant capital: the population of the capital is at least three times larger than that of the second largest city and does not share any major function with other cities; country with one centre: the capital does not share any major function with other cities, but its population is less than three times bigger than that of the second largest; country with one centre in a contested position: the second largest city possesses or claims certain special rights by being the capital of a territorial unit with a certain degree of autonomy; multiple centres: the major urban functions are shared among different cities.

Source: Göran Therborn, *European Modernity and Beyond,* London: Sage, 1995, 186.

established for the description of a competing relationship between a larger and a smaller urban centre and represents countries where the second largest city has special rights, generally as a result of regional autonomy, as in the case of Belgium and Spain. Finally, the fourth category includes countries with multiple centres, which are usually found in the countries of the medieval city belt including the Federal Republic of Germany, Italy, the Netherlands and Switzerland. In these countries, the principal functions are divided between larger cities. Data included in the table reflect the patterns of the 1980s. Albeit with slight modification, it can also be considered essentially valid for the whole second half of the century nonetheless, which indicates the significant spatial stability of economic and political power structures on the national level in Europe. Notwithstanding, some qualitatively different cases appear even within the specific categories. For example, in Austria, which can be classified as a country with a dominant capital, a considerable amount of authority is assigned to the provincial level as well. Similarly, systematic decentralization efforts in post-war France, or the process of devolution in the United Kingdom at the millennium, yielded some similar results. In contrast, in Hungary, which belongs to the same category of dominant capital, none of the factors referred to above challenged the dominance of the capital city in the last decades.

There also exist various other methods of measuring urban concentration. One of these is the contrastive analysis of the ratio of the population of cities with more than one million inhabitants to the total urban population in a given society. The residents of cities belonging to this urban category comprised more than one-quarter of the total population in most of the European countries in the second

TABLE 8.8 Urban concentration in European countries, 1965–1990 (%)

	1965	*1990*	*Change*
United Kingdom	33	26	−7
France	30	26	−4
Netherlands	18	16	−2
Austria	51	47	−4
Sweden	17	23	+6
Denmark	38	31	−7
Finland	27	34	+7
Italy	42	37	−5
Greece	59	55	−4
Portugal	44	46	+2
Poland	32	28	−4
Czechoslovakia	15	11	−4
Hungary	43	33	−10
Romania	21	18	−3
Bulgaria	21	19	−2

Note: Numbers indicate the share of the population that lived in cities with at least 1 million inhabitants in relation to the total urban population in 1990.

Source: Tony Champion, 'Urbanization, Suburbanization, Counterurbanization and Reurbanization', in Ronan Paddison, ed., *Handbook of Urban Studies*, London: Sage, 2001, 145.

half of the twentieth century, whereas in several societies this ratio even reached one-third of the total population (Table 8.8). However, in this respect the uni-linear tendency that characterized the increasing ratio of the urban population in the twentieth century did not prevail. The related table indicates a universal although moderate declining tendency between 1965 and 1990 with respect to urban concentration as defined above in more than a dozen European countries. The redistribution of urban population in favour of the cities that stand lower in the urban hierarchy can be considered a result of the more rapid growth of smaller cities, and of the fall in the population in larger cities.[54] The moderation of the growth in the population of the largest cities and the simultaneous acceleration of the growth of smaller ones is called 'polarization reversal'. Along with other phenomena, such as the population growth of rural areas, this development contributed to the conceptualization of counterurbanization, described in detail previously.[55]

The dominance of cities at the regional or national level often generated critical repercussions. Observers pointed out that the centralization of resources was detrimental to the citizens living in other areas and that the relative costs of providing services in large cities is regularly higher than that of middle-sized or smaller cities. Furthermore, the quality of life of residents in middle-sized settlements is arguably higher, both measured by objective indicators and by perceptions of the inhabitants themselves. Table 8.9 shows data from a Eurobarometer survey comprising the member states of the EEC, carried out in the mid-1970s, which indicates that in

TABLE 8.9 Satisfaction of the urban population with different aspects of life according to the size of settlement, 1976

Factor	The share of 'fully satisfied' population in settlements of different size (%)			
	Below 20,000 residents	20,000–99,999 residents	100,000–499,999 residents	More than 500,000 residents
Housing conditions	24.6	22.1	25.6	16.3
Residential area	31.8	26.9	30.1	19.6
Household income	11.4	11.1	12.5	4.7
Consumption	15.2	14.3	14.8	6.3
Job	22.0	18.6	20.0	10.2
Recreational facilities	20.4	16.6	18.6	10.2
Social benefits	17.4	14.9	12.2	3.8
Traffic	24.7	21.2	19.7	14.2
Health	31.3	24.0	28.1	20.9
Amount of free time	20.2	16.4	21.9	10.1
Society in general	9.1	6.0	6.3	4.3
Individual rights	22.2	21.2	25.3	18.7

Note: Calculations based on the data of the Eurobarometer (1976) survey in EEC countries.

Source: Paul L. Knox, *The Geography of Western Europe: A Socio–Economic Survey*, London: Croom Helm, 1984, 167.

almost all aspects, there was a negative correlation between the subjective well-being of the citizens and the size of the urban community they lived in.[56]

Urban and regional planning

As has been pointed out previously in this study, the problems of urban growth had raised the necessity of larger reconstructions and long-term urban planning relatively early, already in the second half of the nineteenth century. In the first half of the twentieth century, planners worked out sophisticated physical plans in great detail; however, few initiatives were implemented, and even fewer plans extending beyond the immediate metropolitan area were realized. The tide clearly changed from the middle of the century: planning became more practical and more extensive. Urban development schemes, created after the Second World War, and principally, during the 1960s, constituted three broad types in Europe. In the first type, planners designated preferential axes, which could divert urban growth from the urban cores towards the outskirts, in a radial pattern. The second version can be described as polycentric, aiming at establishing new growth nodes in order to counterbalance and thereby relieve the excessively dominant and thus overloaded urban centre. In the third case, planners gave priority to preserving unutilized, free urban spaces, subordinating other aims of urban development to this approach. These are not mutually exclusive patterns, and some schemes, which were realized, had features of all three types. In the following discussion, the main characteristics of some representative examples of these approaches are outlined.[57]

As has been previously discussed in this chapter, interwar and wartime urban planning in London aimed at curbing urban growth by establishing a green belt. This ambition prevailed in the post-war period, but by the 1960s, plans already accentuated the necessity of creating preferential axes of development. These axes or corridors were spread out in a relatively regular radial form from the centre of London. Urban planners did not intend to encourage the full urbanization of the axes, but rather to channel urban growth in an outwards direction. The axes generally led to a larger, rapidly developing city (for example, Ipswich closed the north-eastern corridor) and also had an excellent road and public transport infrastructure.

Post-war concepts of deconcentration of industries and population from contiguously built-up areas of the metropolis also led to the establishment of eight new towns beyond the green belt, which were designed in a way so that they would not occupy valuable arable land, with a smaller, already existing settlement as their centre and with good traffic connections with London. The project successfully contributed to accommodate metropolitan spillover: for instance, they reduced the number of daily commuters in the metropolitan area by 200,000. From the 1960s, similar urban developments were carried out in the south-eastern region of the country, on an even more extensive scale; Milton Keynes, Peterborough and Northampton all belonged to this group of newly created cities. Milton Keynes had 40,000 inhabitants in 1967, and this figure quadrupled by the 1980s. Cities of comparable functions were established in other parts of the United Kingdom as well, for example, East Kilbride and Cumbernauld in the vicinity of Glasgow.[58]

Similar plans were proposed in Copenhagen, where developmental axes, 'fingers' in the Danish terminology, were already constructed in 1947. In this case, urban planning aimed at preserving the areas between the axes in their entirety for agricultural activity. Still, the implementation was only partially successful, because construction in the axes encompassed areas significantly wider than in the original design.

To counterbalance the overpopulated Copenhagen region, the Danish Regional Developmental Act (issued in 1958) and other subsequent regulations also designated three major development centres in ulterior territories of Denmark, including Århus, Ålborg and Odense, which were later expanded into larger priority regions. Deconcentration schemes based on preferential axes were carried out in Hamburg, where a plan for these had already been accepted in 1921. The same general principles were applied by urban planners in smaller cities, such as Bremen, Freiburg, Trier and Saint-Étienne as well.

The advantage of constructing axes of development is that they can be flexibly adapted to future needs, which are difficult to estimate accurately in advance: they can be implemented gradually, and the width or the length of the axes can also be altered. Furthermore, the areas that they enclose can be accessed conveniently, and provide an ideal location for leisure activities. Nevertheless, because of the pressure of investors and occasionally, even of local residents, it is difficult to maintain the areas between the axes free of construction. Thus, the effective enforcement of this urban design approach requires an efficient local and central administration. An additional disadvantage is that in the areas in the vicinity of urban centres, the convergent axes might cause increased traffic congestion. Consequently, this solution is often regarded as more feasible in the case of cities of relatively moderate size, as we have referred to in the case of Copenhagen.

Plans of polycentric urban development suggested the construction of new employment growth nodes in the suburban areas that could relieve the over-concentration of urban functions in the city centre. Plans of this type with the most ambitious scale were executed in Paris and its metropolitan area after the Second World War. After the rapid interwar and post-war urban growth of the city, often lacking even the minimal prerequisites of structural integrity in many of the sub-urban areas, French urban planners came to the conclusion that the policy of restriction on the expansion of the city was no longer plausible; rather, it was more feasible to open up new directions for growth. In the case of Paris, the concept of developmental axes was also included in the projects launched in the mid-1960s. Nonetheless, the French model was different from the previous examples, because the main axes were not arching outward from the urban centre; instead, two axes were set to run in an approximately parallel position in the north and in the south, bypassing central urban areas (Figure 8.1). Vast urban and infrastructural developments were carried out along these axes, which in turn led to the formation of a

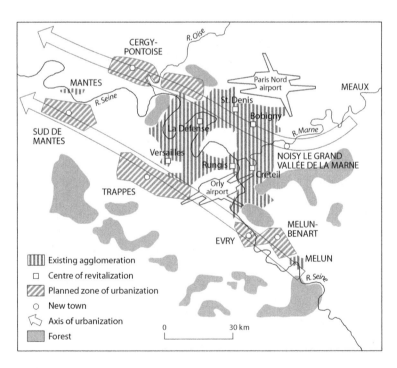

FIGURE 8.1 Regional development plan for Paris and its metropolitan area with the dual axes (1960s)

Source: Arnold J. Heidenheimer, Hugh Heclo and Carolyn Teich Adams, *Comparative Public Policy: the Politics of Social Choice in America, Europe, and Japan,* New York: St. Martin's Press, 1990, 272.

polycentric urban layout, that is, the coexistence of various urban centres. Besides this particular application of polycentric planning, Parisian suburbs were not characterized by such a strong urban hierarchy as could be seen, for instance, in the case of London.[59]

In France, an extensive regional policy was also implemented to curb the growth of Paris and to disperse the growth potential more evenly within the country. In 1964, regional planners designated eight counterpole urban centres (*métropoles d'équilibre*). The major aim of the plan was to create new jobs, especially in the tertiary sector, in these new centres, which consisted either of a city (for example, Marseilles) or of an urban cluster (such as Lyon–Saint-Étienne–Grenoble, and Nancy–Metz–Thionville). Later on, with a view to practical experiences, urban planners modified the developmental priorities. Instead of larger cities, they stimulated the growth of middle-sized cities (*villes moyennes*), with a population ranging between 50,000 and 200,000 inhabitants. On the basis of the consideration that the quality of life in these cities is higher, urban designers supposed that these settlements would retain the population of non-central regions with more success. However, from the 1980s a different development idea also emerged that proposed the lift of the restrictions on the growth of Paris, so that the capital could compete more efficiently among rivalling global centres. Still, decentralization remained an essential part of public policy and contributed to the dynamic expansion of cities like Grenoble or Strasbourg.

Similar programs of decentralization were launched in Belgium, but with considerable and particular obstacles, because Brussels lay north of the Flemish–Walloon ethnic division line, and had been officially recognized as a bilingual city since 1932 (see chapter 9). In the post-war period, immigration and the settlement of international organizations and corporations in the area led to the proliferation of French at the expense of Flemish. The increasingly French-speaking capital could spread only in the territory of the Flemish province of Brabant, which in turn triggered the resistance of Flemish politicians, who vigilantly guarded the linguistic and political status quo. This debate perpetuated tensions and hampered efficient regional and urban planning in the Brussels area, but it affected the growth of other Belgian cities as well: for instance, the latter turn in urban planning encouraged the development of Namur, intended to be the future capital of Wallonia.

Certain features of polycentric urban planning often appeared in other European urban areas as well. This type of development was carried out in the suburban areas of Frankfurt am Main, Kiel, Lyon and Newcastle-upon-Tyne, often involving the creation of entirely new settlements in the proximity of cities.

In certain regions (for example, in the western part of the Netherlands and in the Ruhr area), numerous cities in close distance to each other have existed for a long time. Here, the synchronization of multicentred development of conurbations and the conservation of less densely populated space were the principal challenges for urban planning. In the western regions of the Netherlands, cities shared the functions of a primate city and none of them reached a dominant position within the urban hierarchy. The geographical extension of these settlements comprised an almost continuous, horseshoe-like zone that is open towards the continent, starting with Utrecht on its eastern end, arching north through Amsterdam and IJmond, and descending through Leiden, The Hague and Rotterdam to the south end, marked by Dordrecht (Figure 8.2). Although initiatives for the realization of the concept of the *Randstad* ('ring city' in Dutch) had already appeared in the interwar period, it emerged as a fully coherent urban policy after the Second World War. The aim of the Dutch *Randstad* planning concept was that the existing towns and cities within the *Randstad* area did not fully coalesce, and green buffers were conserved between them; thus, the individual character and separate functions of the urban communes could be maintained. Furthermore, the horseshoe-shaped *Randstad* did not grow inward, and a green heart should preserve its agricultural functions, and even its particular tourism appeal. Finally, new industries should be encouraged to move to less developed regions.[60] The concept of *Randstad* could not be implemented in its entirety. Its potential realization was complicated by the mere fact that the area surrounded by the ring of cities also included smaller, although historically significant settlements, such as Gouda or Alphen. Nevertheless, the efforts of maintaining a multicentred urban area resulted in an improved quality of life in all of the cities within the region, which could have hardly been provided by other, unicentred European conurbations of the same size.[61]

Despite the fact that state intervention had far-reaching traditions in Italy, the relative weakness of the administrative structures within Italian regional development impeded the design and, in particular, the implementation of long-term plans. Consequently, the measures taken in relation to the development of the urban structure often served as the solution of pressing problems rather than the prevention of future ones. Moreover, marked differences between the north and the south placed further obstacles to the elaboration of a unified national plan of regional development. The challenges, which more advanced northern cities, such as Torino or Milan, were faced with in many respects resembled more the urban problems of Stuttgart or Munich than those of Naples or Bari.

Until the end of the Second World War, attempts at transcending national borders in regional development projects hardly existed in Europe. With the foundation of the institutions of European integration, prospects for transnational regional development plans were clearly improved. The first of the plans were devised in relation to the Maastricht–Liège–Aachen triangle, including areas of Belgium, the Netherlands, Luxembourg, Germany and western France, where a dense urban network meant that large clusters of a total of 43 settlements were located in the immediate vicinity of each other. Within the organizational framework of the EEC and its successor institutions, numerous authorities tried to coordinate and stimulate common urban planning, but these attempts were hardly translated into an effective policy.[62] After a series of new, less advanced countries joined the EEC from the 1970s, the importance of the European Regional Development Fund set up in 1975 increased, and later on, funds directed to the aims of regional development also appeared in the budget of the EU. Notwithstanding, the supranational tendencies of regional development have remained relatively moderate in Europe so far.

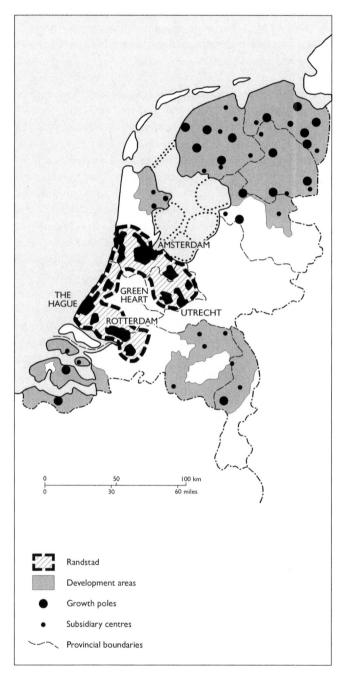

FIGURE 8.2 The *Randstad* and development areas in the Netherlands (late 1950s)
Source: Adapation from different sources including Andreas Aludi and Arnold van der Valk, *Rule and Order: Dutch Planning Doctrine in the Twentieth Century,* Dordrecht etc.: Kluwer, 1994, 114; H. Voogd, 'Issues and Tendencies in Dutch Regional Planning', in R. Hudson and J. R. Lewis, eds., *Regional Planning in Europe,* London: Pion, 1982, 112–126.

As for the East Central European communist countries, urban development strategies across the region facilitated a highly hierarchical urban network. Except for Bohemia and East Germany, there existed no well-developed urban network in pre-war East Central Europe, and the formation of the modern urban system in the post-war decades took place in a hierarchical manner in two respects. Urban development was directed by the central government relying on a high-degree resource redistribution, and, even more importantly, urban policy prioritized the top levels of the urban system. As far as the allocation of resources was concerned, the hierarchy was presided over by the capital, and below it, a few large cities, which were also the focal points of modernization efforts. Middle-sized and small-sized cities were located on the next level. Their access to financial resources, projected to a per capita figure, was considerably more moderate, except for the settlements that provided the site of some prioritized industrial developmental program. The term 'centralized decentralization' provides an apt description of the efforts of socialist regional planning to promote industrial development in the most backward regions by simultaneously developing only a few selected urban centres in these regions. Villages were located at the bottom of the hierarchy because communist governments were clearly biased against rural life and the countryside. Not only did classic theoreticians of the Marxist ideology identify rural settlements with backwardness and reaction (the same interpretations were often echoed in post-war communist parties) but the new regimes were in fact urban-based in their political support as well. There was a shift in this policy from the 1960s, because regional planning aimed at integrating the largest villages in the urban hierarchy. In turn, the smallest settlements were often declared to be 'non-viable', and thereby were marked to be gradually dissolved without any regard to the will of the affected local residents. An extreme example of this policy was represented by a campaign in Romania as late as in the 1980s, where numerous villages were demolished, widely referred to as the campaign of 'village destruction' already by contemporaries.[63]

Characteristics of the post-industrial era: technopolis and segregation

The preconditions of urban development had considerably changed in Europe by the 1970s. Whereas earlier, the management of metropolitan expansion ranked highest among the problems of urbanization, from this period, other issues, generated by the gradual shrinking of cities and the loss of industries and employment, as well as by the subsequent reurbanization phase, posed new challenges. Moreover, urban management evolved to be more complex and also gave rise to more conflicts. Urban societies were characterized by a more marked heterogeneity resulting from the growing ratio of residents living in poverty, as well as ethnic and cultural dif-ferentiation of the population. These changes appeared first and in the most marked way in Western and Southern European cities, but later on they also became perceptible in other parts of the continent, because they also occurred in the East Central European region after the democratic transition.[64]

Deindustrialization

European cities were largely affected by the profound structural transformation of the economy that unfolded in Europe after the 1973 oil crisis, and was increasingly linked to the process of globalization. In a broader sense, globalization means the intensification of transnational economic, political and cultural relations, whereas from the economic point of view, it involves the formation of a complex system, in which companies conduct business transactions and choose the locations of their production and services in worldwide dimensions. This process is primarily the result of the liberalization of global financial, commodity and labour markets that took place with the parallel decrease of regulative functions of the nation state and with technological developments in transportation and telecommunication. Although many worries concerning the repercussions of globalization on European societies have proved to be unfounded so far, the significance of the location of resources (including labour) diminished dramatically in determining the place of production, and European economies have been seriously affected by this transformation in the last three or four decades.[65] Although it was not the single cause, globalization largely facilitated deindustrialization: secondary sector employment was cut down drastically, with a particularly detrimental impact on larger cities that were traditionally industrial centres. Moreover, a part of the remaining productive capacity was also relocated from cities to smaller settlements. The extent of deindustrialization is reflected by the fact that 800,000 workplaces disappeared in the processing industry in Paris and its metropolitan area during the 1980s, which is equivalent to a 46% decrease.[66] Similarly, between 1960 and 1990, the ratio of industrial employees decreased from 40% to 13% in Helsinki, whereas in Stockholm it dropped from 38% to 14%.[67] Nonetheless, at the same time, numerous other jobs were created, especially in the financial sector, in trade and in other branches of the service sector. Cities were no longer principally the sites of manufacturing; instead they evolved into centres of service and management.

These new central functions of cities, crucial in the functioning of the emerging global economy, are emphasized in several recent theories on urbanization. The 'informational city' of Manuel Castells, or the 'global city' of Saskia Sassen, are distinct social systems that organize the new global order.[68] Out of all European cities, these analyses almost exclusively consider London as a centre significant from a global perspective. The diminished importance of European cities in a global demographic context undoubtedly originates from the population development of urban areas in the world. On the list of the world's largest conurbations, European cities continually moved down during the twentieth century. Even Paris and London were not among the twenty largest urban concentrations in 2000, and other European cities ranked even lower on the same list.

However, the above theories are lacking in that although they focus on the novel forms of global division of power, they neglect to take into account other significant analytical perspectives of urban development, and especially what quality of life a city provides for the residents. The descent of European cities in the global urban hierarchy can be primarily attributed to demographic trends, that is, to the low level of fertility in the continent. Furthermore, the distinct European characteristics of urban development, such as effective urban planning preventing excess growth of metropolitan areas, or a greater role of middle-size cities, also contributed to the low ranking. Considering the grave environmental and social problems of the world's largest conurbations, a decline in the global significance of European cities seems to be a reasonable price to pay in exchange for the controlled, moderate pace of development and the relatively high quality of life it entails (Table 8.10).

TABLE 8.10 The largest conurbations of the world in 2000

Order	Conurbation	Population of the city (in thousands)	Population of the conurbation (in thousands)	Population of the city in 1900 (in thousands)
1.	Tokyo	7769	29896	1496
2.	New York	7459	24719	3437
3.	Seoul	9831	20674	150
4.	Mexico	8591	19081	419
5.	São Paulo	10286	17396	240
6.	Manila	1711	16740	209
7.	Los Angeles	3642	15807	123
9.	Bombay	11536	15769	822
10.	Jakarta	9966	15086	170
11.	Osaka	2851	15039	852
12.	Delhi	9426	13592	238
13.	Calcutta	4630	12619	1481
14.	Buenos Aires	2957	12297	833
15.	Shanghai	9755	11960	840
16.	Cairo	7078	11633	570
17.	Rio de Janeiro	5625	10628	692
18.	Moscow	8272	10046	1096
19.	Istanbul	8793	9981	900
21.	Paris	2122	9850	2678
22.	Dhaka	9801	9801	127
23.	Karachi	9661	9661	132
24.	London	7263	9166	4505
48.	Madrid	2903	4669	540
61.	Barcelona	1501	3994	533
64.	Manchester	429	3976	540
69.	Milan	1241	3822	524
70.	Berlin	3417	3755	1889

Note: In the case of Madrid and Milan, data on the population of the conurbation differ significantly from the data indicated in other sources.

Source: Patrick Le Galès, *European Cities: Social Conflicts and Governance,* Oxford: Oxford University Press, 2002, 26.

Urban renewal

European cities strove to adapt to new demands caused by social change and globalization, with urban regeneration and development programs embracing both economic and social objectives. Both in the inner cities and in suburban districts of larger cities, urban management carried out and supported extensive real estate projects, which were preeminently important for the dynamically advancing sectors, such as financial services, research, or telecommunication and information technology. In the most successful cases of urban development, cities were enriched with new symbols or with sights that strengthened their touristic attractiveness further. Paris, again, can be cited among the best examples. In the French capital, already in the 1970s, a cultural complex, the Pompidou Centre, was established, which was almost as highly frequented as major historical sites. However, the list of sights also grew larger in the following decades: the renovated Louvre, the d'Orsay Museum, and the gigantic arch-like building of La Défense (*Arche de la Défense*), all belonged to this group. In fact, the new business district, La Défense, is an apt example of systematic and ambitious urban development. The renewal of this area began in the 1980s, in the longitudinal extension of the Louvre–Champs-Élysées–Arc de Triomphe axis, thus connecting the new district with the historical urban centre. La Défense principally included office blocks with vast floor space, but numerous conference and shopping centres, hotels, as well as exhibition halls were also established. Office building complexes were also erected in the outer urban parts of Paris, especially in Bercy, located over one of the western meanders of the Seine. Other European cities launched similar programs as well. In London, local decision makers even modified restrictions on the height of buildings and the density of building up in order to encourage the construction of inner-city office blocks. In Berlin, vast reconstructions took place in the Potsdamer Platz and its surroundings. This area had been the busiest site of the city in the interwar period, but was destroyed in its entirety in the Second World War and by the East Berlin authorities in the aftermath of the war. Subsequently, for decades it was a desolated no man's land near the Berlin Wall, and the ambitious construction works served to foster the integration of the two parts of the reunited Berlin.

Because many large European cities were founded on the shore of a river, by the sea, or, in some cases, on a bay, the rehabilitation of waterfront urban areas gained particular importance in recent decades, because the majority of the industrial establishments and storehouses in these areas were abandoned during post-war deindustrialization. The modernization of sea transport demanded wharfs capable of servicing larger vessels, including container ships: in the case of London, for instance, this meant that the port was relocated closer to the sea, rendering the majority of the existing docks unnecessary. Redundant buildings and territories stood unoccupied in all Europe for a considerable period, and they called the attention of urban planners and other experts only in the last two decades of the twentieth century, when they were transformed into high-quality loft residences, office blocks, shops or public institutions. A good example of the latter is the Amsterdam site of the International Institute of Social History, one of the biggest international research centres and archives of social history worldwide, which moved to a stately renovated old cocoa warehouse. The Aker Brygge business and trade centre in Oslo and the Olympic village in Barcelona were established in the same way, as well as Canary Wharf in London, which already ranks as the most formidable of these types of renewals still in progress.[69]

Because a highly qualified workforce became the decisive factor in the establishment of business centres and their best paid units, cities attempted to increase their appeal for qualified employees in various ways. Several municipalities endeavoured to create a new, more dynamic image, emphasizing their role as a centre of research and innovative technology. In this respect, university towns had a particularly advantageous position, because they could offer an attractive environment for a young and highly qualified workforce. Urban research indicates that the settling of high-tech companies has many preconditions, but the vicinity of a larger university or a national research centre is a crucial factor.[70] New developments, often designated with such a self-important name as 'technopolis', were carried out in big university cities, including Valencia, Barcelona, Toulouse, Montpellier, Torino and Milan, to mention examples only from the southern regions of the continent.

Conservation of urban heritage

The previously cited examples of post-war urban planning were expansionist, mostly focusing on the development and allocation of new functions to the peripheral parts of cities. In this way, these projects endeavoured to relieve the city cores, but at the same time they attended less to the changing conditions of the inner cities, assuming that these districts would continue to thrive. At the end of the twentieth century, inner cities began to attract more attention on the part of planners and decision makers, as well as civil society. Development began to focus more on protecting the existing architectural and historical heritage than on establishing new urban structures and buildings. Revitalization and rehabilitation projects included the often costly renovation of historical urban centres and heritage sites, the creation and preservation of parks and other green areas and the continuous improvement of the system of public transport.

In the last decades of the century, there was a shift in the relation of urban planning towards motorization. Whereas previously, city designers often tried to adjust the urban structure and the functions of the city to car traffic, by this time, they started to banish cars from the inner cities and to create pedestrian zones. Germany, the Netherlands and Denmark were particularly innovative in this respect, but they were soon followed by France as well: the first French pedestrian street was created in 1970 in Rouen; however, ten years later, similar streets existed in some 200 French cities.

In most European countries, the first legal foundations for the protection of certain architecturally or historically prominent buildings had already been laid at the end of the nineteenth century, but the protection of entire groups of houses or even districts evolved into a general practice only in the last third of the twentieth century. Among the diverse European conservation programs, hereby only a few can be highlighted. In the Netherlands, laws were passed that made possible not only the protection of buildings and districts but also the landscape around them. In France, exigent architectural renovations were carried out in Avignon, Chartres, Lyon and many other cities. In order to retain the population of the old town, urban authorities in Bruges had to take steps to complete an internal modernization of approximately 2000 protected buildings. By the 1960s, Venice was seriously threatened, among other reasons because the extraction of water and gas in the surrounding regions caused the city to sink 6 millimetres each year. The complex program elaborated to save the city stabilized the number of the population, and restored the greatest damages. In Great Britain, the historical districts of Bath, Chester and York and the Georgian New Town in Edinburgh underwent considerable and comprehensive renovations as well.[71]

Nonetheless, it cannot be stated that the conflicts between conservationists and business interests always, or at least, in the majority of cases, ended with the triumph of the former. Modernization endeavours destroyed entire architecturally valuable districts in Dublin, Madrid, and other cities. In this respect, Brussels is also a well-known example. The city achieved the position of an important economic and political centre after the foundation of the EEC, and apart from the numerous institutions of European integration, by 1968, 165 American and European companies had set up their headquarters in the city. The building boom created by the enormous demand for new offices led to the demolition of valuable parts of the inner city in the 1960s to 1970s. Although it was difficult to correct former errors, considerably more circumspect urban development decisions have been made since the 1970s, paying more attention to the needs of the local residents as well.[72]

Segregation, alienation, violence

The transformation of the employment structure, the increase in income inequalities and migration along with similar factors resulted in mounting social segregation in many Western and Southern European cities by the end of the twentieth century. Of course, segregation within urban areas was not a new phenomenon at all; it has always been present, albeit in different forms. Before the First World War, when housing building projects were run almost exclusively by private entrepreneurs, the location and the quality of the apartments reflected the social and financial status of the lodgers, which led to a strong social differentiation within the cities. In certain countries, already during the interwar period, but principally after the Second World War, numerous factors (especially state and communal housing projects, the rise in the living standards, and conscious communal policies addressing these issues) led to the moderation of segregation. However, the last decades of the twentieth century brought about another reversal of the trend, as urban segregation started to increase again, which was also expedited by some of the urban trends outlined above.[73] Because the majority of well-remunerated jobs were offered in the inner city, and major parts of the centre underwent gentrification in several cities, the upper middle class found the exigently renovated central areas appealing. After urban reconstruction programs, increasing real-estate prices in the gentrified neighbourhoods drove potential tenants with lower incomes to move to other districts. However, in other inner areas with less favourable economic potential, former working-class districts also survived, the states of which often deteriorated further.

At the end of the twentieth century, ethnic segregation also appeared in Western and Southern Europe. Social polarization in urban areas was heightened from the 1970s by the increasing influx of immigrants and refugees, who settled down primarily in cities. As pointed out in chapter 2, contrary to earlier periods, the majority of guest workers also brought their families to the recipient country. Immigrants and guest workers from the 1970s arrived primarily from North Africa, Turkey, the former colonies and other countries outside Europe, and their generally low level of qualification and foreign-language skills, as well as further cultural differences, rendered their integration more difficult. Although authorities usually aimed at avoiding the spatial segregation of these groups and the ghettoization of certain urban districts, integrationist policy failed even in Germany, where it was applied in the most systematic way. Sooner or later, the majority of the immigrants moved to large cities, and strove to join their own community. Consequently, districts with a majority of immigrant population were gradually forming into sharply distinct units in Western European cities. Although by the end of the twentieth century, immigration laws became prohibitive in most of the European countries, because the fertility rate of the immigrant population was usually higher than the average, these urban districts expanded. Urban areas with a predominantly immigrant population are also prominent because they are often located in the vicinity of the city centre, or other frequented urban districts.

As discussed earlier, the modernization and the partial renewal of the cities, along with the parallel increase in segregation, had an ambivalent effect on the inner neighbourhoods and densely built outer housing districts of many Western European cities. Besides the specific issues created by urbanization, these areas were also affected by more general social problems. In the inner cities, the ratio of single-parent families, low-income old-age pensioners or immigrant families with many children has been high. In the 1990s the income levels of families in the inner districts of Western and Southern European cities with one million inhabitants or more, except for Madrid and Lyon, remained below the national average.[74] In many cases, these conditions generated a vicious circle: poverty and the high rate of socially underprivileged residents brought about urban decay, which in turn devalued real-estate prices in the area, thus further strengthening the social disadvantages of the population. These conditions often led to anomie, vandalism, the spread of crime and other forms of social deviance.[75] The street disturbances that broke out in many Western European cities were dramatic manifestations of urban problems. The unrests started in Amsterdam, West Berlin and Zurich in 1980 and 1981, and later on appeared in numerous British and French cities, including London, Liverpool, Manchester, Lyon and Paris. Although all episodes of violence were sparked by specific reasons, some general causes can still be identified. The riots usually started out from neglected inner city areas or from densely built suburban districts, with a predominance of residents in a socially underprivileged position, including a considerable ratio of young unemployed, first- and second-generation immigrants. As a consequence of these incidents, extended government and local programs were initiated in Britain and France in the 1980s to improve housing and urban living conditions. Considerable efforts were made to strengthen local communities by the creation of community houses and by other means, such as improving the physical appearance of large housing projects, or increasing the availability of social benefits and services.[76] Even though these efforts yielded positive results, the several waves of street violence that broke out in Paris after the turn of the millennium (probably more violent than ever) also indicated the perseverance of these problems.

East Central European cities at the end of the twentieth century

As previously observed, urbanization after the Second World War progressed rapidly in East Central and South-Eastern Europe. Still, many urban trends that characterized Western Europe from the 1970s were hardly perceivable in this region until the collapse of communism. Besides the immediate reconstruction, which aimed at alleviating the damages of the Second World War, efforts to revitalize inner cities or to create new business centres were conspicuously lacking in the concepts of urban planning.[77] Therefore, by the time of the democratic transitions, the appearance of Western European and East Central European urban centres were fundamentally different. Not only were the latter more neglected, with their dilapidated housing conditions, but they also had considerably fewer modern and attractive office buildings, department stores, shops and catering establishments. Compared with the situation in Western Europe, the social polarization of residential districts remained a minor issue because, among other reasons, immigration was essentially non-existent in the region.

With the democratic transition, many differences in the urban development of East Central Europe and other parts of the continent started to level off, but the urban transformation of the region also included particular tendencies.[78] Probably the most substantial change in this area was caused by the establishment of the housing and real-estate market, because it allowed for commercial estate development. In addition, the opening up of the real-estate market had a positive effect on the reconstruction of historical cores as well. This was also encouraged by the upturn of tourism, which in certain cities, most notably in Prague, became significant even in an international context. It is without doubt that urban diversity, the lack of which had been previously pinpointed by many observers as the most typical characteristic of communist cities, increased rapidly, both with positive and negative implications.[79] The number of commercial and service establishments boomed, and their spatial distribution was also transformed: following the patterns of market economies, more frequented areas were occupied by specialist and luxury retail stores, foreign companies, banks and hotels. Consequently, residential areas in the inner cities decreased, although in the European context, urban floor area per person in the region was already low at the time of the regime change transitions: it amounted to 18–20 m^2, in contrast to the Western European average of 32 m^2.[80] As a further fundamental change in the real-estate market, after an initial transitional period, the majority of council flats and rents were privatized (tenants were granted preferential treatment in the process) and a significant raise was introduced in the rent and utilities.[81] Still, compared with the transformation of trade, the liberalization of the housing market did not bring about similarly rapid improvements. The change was probably the most perceptible in relation to poverty and social deviance, particularly in the large cities of the region.[82] Ethnic diversity increased as well, which was predominantly caused by immigration, because in many cases Central European cities proved to be considerably easier to access for immigrants, either legally or illegally, than similar Western European destinations. By the end of the 1990s, the presence of Chinese and Turkish restaurants, market vendors and Arabian money-changers became a familiar part of the urban landscape of Warsaw or Budapest. The increase of urban marginality was noticeable as well. Not only did poverty grow in East Central European cities, it also became more visible: the traditional harsh approach of the police no longer functioned in keeping beggars and homeless people away from frequented areas. Crime and other forms of social deviance spread in particular during the first years of the democratic transition, when international organized crime, including Russian and Ukrainian groups, also gained a foothold in the region. By the millennium, crime rates had been falling and public safety improved in East Central Europe, although this was not always the case in South-Eastern Europe.

Obviously, urban structure changed at a slower pace than other aspects of urban life. With the appearance of the *nouveau riche,* members of this class often purchased and renovated old villas in the traditional wealthy districts, or constructed their (frequently ostentatious) homes in the same areas. A belated suburbanization also began to unfold in larger cities at the turn of the millennium. Deprivation, crime, air pollution and other social and environmental problems degraded the quality of life in the inner cities, motivating an exodus towards suburban areas, also attractive because of their relatively lower real-estate prices. Nevertheless, the process of suburbanization was hindered to a great extent by the underdevelopment of the transport system, particularly, of the road infrastructure. For example, the lack of adequate transport facilities impeded the development of smaller suburban settlements around Budapest, such as Solymár or Piliscsaba, which in turn triggered a small-scale reversal of the movement of population, back towards the urban centres after the turn of the millennium. At the same time, both the physical and social conditions in the large housing estates, built principally during the 1960s and 1970s, were rapidly deteriorating. The prefabricated building technology applied in the construction of these blocks itself makes their conversion or renovation complicated. Therefore, the better-off populaces left these districts. Especially in declining former centres of heavy industry, processes similar to the scenario in the dilapidating urban parts in Western Europe unfolded: the proportion of disadvantaged social groups increased, projecting a further decay of these urban areas. Finally, the national urban hierarchy of the East Central European region was not affected by significant transformations either. Capitals preserved their privileged positions, also enhanced by the fact that they enjoyed a share well above their population ratio not only in redistribution, but also in the inflow of foreign capital.

9

EDUCATION, RELIGION AND CULTURE

The abundance of theoretical approaches and historical interpretations related to the present subject has already been referred to several times in earlier chapters. However, the diversity of approaches should be even more strongly highlighted concerning the historical study of culture and the term itself, which is generally known to be one of the most difficult concepts to define.[1] First and foremost, the notion of culture in everyday usage primarily includes what is often called high culture, such as the works and ideas of outstanding composers, great philosophers, writers, painters, architects or sculptors. This commonsensical notion of culture mainly reflects the humanistic definition emerging in the eighteenth century, mostly representing artistic dimensions, as well as carrying the connotation of being spiritual and free of purpose, that is, arts have not only educational or moral but also a transcendental value. In contemporary social science, the concept of culture is broader and incorporates everything that is transmitted by way of social but not biological processes in human society, such as norms of family behaviour, eating habits, clothing or national and religious symbols. The standard interpretation used in social sciences originates in the nineteenth-century anthropological meaning that encompasses the entirety of human activities. Edward Burnett Tylor is mostly recognized as the initiator of the anthropological definition, contending in 1871 that culture 'is that complex whole which includes knowledge, belief, art, morals, law, customs, and any other capabilities and habits acquired by man as a member of society'.[2] In this sense, culture is broadly equivalent to civilization, which corresponds more to French and Anglo-Saxon scholarly traditions of the nineteenth century, rather than to the classic German understanding. The latter holds *Kultur* to be the representation of human excellence and perfection, as often explicitly opposed to civilization, which incorporates the creations and habits of man as a natural being. Such dualistic contraposition surfaced in other understandings of culture as well. Karl Marx and his followers viewed culture as being determined, or, at least decisively conditioned, by the economic 'superstructure', thus essentially attributing the meaning of ideology to culture.

In the course of the twentieth century, the French and Anglo-Saxon tradition prevailed in the treatment of culture in international scholarly discourse, yet both the research on, and the interpretation of, culture became highly differentiated. One of the most important developments in the field was the emergence of a dichotomy between the concepts of culture and social structure. Several researchers in the cultural anthropological tradition, such as Franz Boas, Bronislaw Malinowski and Margaret Mead, regarded culture as a central notion in the social sciences, and the major determinant of human behaviour that should play a prior role in social theories as well. In contrast, researchers in the structuralist tradition, such as Alfred R. Radcliffe-Brown and Claude Lévi-Strauss, held that social structure should be the focus of social theories because this structure determines human interaction and beliefs. Unfolding the distinct relationship between social structure and culture became the subject of academic controversy. Predictably, structuralists maintain that the interaction of social actors is empirically prior to the emergence and operation of cultural patterns. In turn, culturalists contend that interaction between social actors is at least partly a cultural phenomenon, and cultural patterns have existed preliminary to the emergence of prevailing social relationships. Because both social structure and culture clearly operate interdependently, scholarly attempts to separate them and prove the causal priority of one over the other have brought little success. In the latter half of the twentieth century, several attempts were made to overcome the structure–culture division, or to more exactly elucidate their relationship. Talcott Parsons intended to settle the debate by arguing that societies are built of networks of institutions (social structure), whereas culture represents the integrative force that provides the cohesion of this structure. Despite these efforts, the exact boundaries of the concept of culture, even within the functionalist framework, are still controversial. Nevertheless, the differentiation of structure and culture still serves as a point of reference for many social scientists and historians. Accordingly, the concept of culture provides one of the most fundamental perspectives in investigating past and present societies. As a clear indication, the study of corresponding issues, such as popular or mass culture, has become a highly important subject of social history and social research in general.[3]

As shown above, the concept of culture is highly complex as well as contested, and its use looks back on a variety of scholarly and everyday traditions. Therefore, it is evident that only some selected aspects of the twentieth-century history of culture can be discussed here. The elements chosen are related to three major dimensions of culture: knowledge, identity and values. Although it is impossible to fully separate culture from the social sphere, there are some social domains that can be understood as cultural systems, because they have the objectives and functions of pursuing, mediating and transmitting culture. Such are the institutions of educational systems as well as religions and churches, and thus their twentieth-century development constitutes the first two subjects of the chapter. Social identity is often not considered as a constituent of the concept of culture. At the same time, it is associated with a number of major historical processes and problems in twentieth-century Europe, such as the development of class consciousness, national and ethnic identity, nationalisms and the relationship between nation states and the European integration process. Of these phenomena, historical changes in national identity as one of the major forms of social identity are addressed here. Finally, major perspectives of contemporary social science interpret values as an integral part of culture. However, as systematic historical research on this subject has not been carried out so far at a European level, the present work can only highlight value changes in the late twentieth century.

Schools, universities and society: highways and byways in education

The crucial social effects of education and instruction, generally considered beneficial, are long known, even if various ages and societies put diverse emphases on them. Early Protestant schools in sixteenth-century Europe regarded literacy as essential primarily from the perspective of religious life; the absolutist state of the seventeenth century wanted to raise loyal subjects by schooling; during the age of Enlightenment, the beneficial effects of curricular contents on personality development were emphasized; later, in the nineteenth century, the school system became a distinguished institution for facilitating the process of nation building, and the army required conscripts and soldiers to be literate as well. In the twentieth century, schooling was highly valued for the role of facilitating social integration and equal opportunity for citizens, necessary for the proper functioning of democratic systems. Moreover, a new demand for effective education emerged from perceiving schooling and learning as key factors of economic and technological development and competitiveness. Yet, the educational system has not been a source of beneficial social effects only. In the authoritarian regimes of the twentieth century, it also served as a sphere of political manipulation and indoctrination, and it has arguably contributed to the reproduction of social inequalities even in contemporary European societies.[4]

Beginning in the second half of the nineteenth century, the development of the European school systems broadly took place in three major, partly overlapping stages.

- The initial phase lasted approximately from the 1870s to the First World War, with state control gradually established over the system of education. In the preceding centuries, school systems were dominated by the churches; in the modern age beginning from the late nineteenth century, denominational schools continued to exist in various degrees but their significance clearly lessened. The heightened state involvement was manifest in several areas. Laws prescribed compulsory schooling, and the number of elementary schools was multiplied in order to achieve the major goal of eliminating illiteracy. The state created its educational bureaucracy in order to enforce compulsory schooling, to improve the educational system as well as to define and unify curricular contents.

- After the First World War, higher levels of schooling expanded to reach a wider range of social groups. This process was facilitated by efforts to discontinue the dual institutional system, in which, at the elementary level, schools focusing on the basics existed in parallel with schools explicitly preparing their pupils for higher levels of education. The abandonment of this dual structure and the emergence of the general primary school brought about the opportunity of progress to higher-level institutions, such as the *Gymnasium* (secondary grammar school) in Germany. However, the ratio of students in secondary education increased considerably only in the post-Second World War decades. The latter period was also the time when lower secondary education was unified, albeit not in every European country.
- From the mid-twentieth century, tertiary education underwent a major expansion. The entrance requirements to universities changed, and, at the same time, the elite character of higher education also disappeared. The structure of academic disciplines at universities was transformed, partly because of the proliferation of various new fields of study offered by the institutions.[5]

Elementary education

Some form of compulsory schooling at the elementary level had already been introduced in the nineteenth century in almost every European country. Protestant countries led the way in establishing schools and initiating compulsory schooling. Laws regulating children's school attendance had already been implemented in the first half of the nineteenth century in Prussia, Denmark, Sweden and Norway. Spain, Romania, Hungary, Austria, Scotland, Switzerland, Italy and England/Wales introduced compulsory schooling in the 1860s and 1870s. France followed suit in 1882, as did Ireland and Finland later in the century. The Netherlands and Belgium committed themselves to compulsory elementary education later, in 1900 and in 1914, respectively, because of the debates concerning the organization of state and denominational schools.

State schooling was a nineteenth-century innovation across Europe. Although denominational schools had advanced elementary education, especially in Protestant countries, from the age of the Enlightenment on, monarchs and governments tried to displace denominational schools, primarily in Catholic countries. This process was often burdened with heavy conflicts throughout the nineteenth century. In most countries, compromises were finally made, thus religious schooling was completely abolished only in France. Still, the ratio of church schools undoubtedly dropped compared with state administered and maintained institutions. The increasing state activity in education was a major factor in the emergence of universal and free elementary schooling by the end of the nineteenth century in a number of European countries. By 1910, the ratio of regular school attendance reached figures ranging from 62% to 85% in a wider age group, among the 5–14-year-olds in Western European societies (Table 9.1).

The spread of elementary schooling significantly advanced the educational, and, in particular, the literacy levels of the population all across Europe. Up until the

TABLE 9.1 The ratio of pupils as the percentage of their age group in European countries, 1880–1975

	Attendance at primary school among 5–14-year-olds						Attendance at secondary school among 10–19-year-olds					
	1880	1910	1920/1940	1950/1955	1960/1965	1970/1975	1880	1910	1920/1940	1950/1955	1960/1965	1970/1975
United Kingdom	46.7	78.6	81	68	63	65			6.4	34.3	43.4	51.1
France	81.6	85.3	74	82	71	56	1.2	1.4	4.9	11.3	29.3	45.9
Netherlands	62.2	70.3	74	70	64	61	0.9	1.6	6.4	14.5	21.1	29.0
Belgium	29.1	61.8	73	75	70	64	0.5	0.5	5.0	13.2	22.4	31.5
Ireland	44.2		86	87	88	82	1.6	3.2	5.4	10.7	16.5	29.9
Germany/FRG	75.0	71.9	75	72	69	67	2.7	5.0	6.6	11.8	18.3	30.0
Austria	56.1	69.9	78	73	74	74	1.2	1.8	5.1	7.2	9.3	14.8
Switzerland	75.0	70.2	78	76	79	80		2.9	5.5	7.3	7.6	9.2
Sweden	72.2	67.7	63	63	62	59		1.1	7.1	15.5	26.3	40.7
Denmark		66.5	66	63	71	70		0.8	8.0	14.7	18.5	31.4
Norway	55.5	68.6	73	75	74	62	2.5	2.3	5.5	10.1	22.1	40.8
Finland	6.7	26.3	59	69	66	62		2.8	6.6	16.8	26.8	42.2
Italy	34.6	43.3	54	59	55	55	0.3	0.5	2.6	9.2	22.7	43.0

Notes: Secondary schools 1920–1975: lower and upper secondary levels together, general and specialized schools included; 1920–1975: mean values of the given years; United Kingdom 1880–1910: England and Wales; United Kingdom 1920–1975: Great Britain; Denmark secondary school students 1910: in the 15–19 age group; Ireland secondary school students 1910: 1901; Belgium elementary school pupils 1880: unreliable data because of the conflicts between the state and the Catholic church; Germany 1880: Prussia; Austria 1880–1910: Cisleithania.

Sources: Wolfram Fischer, 'Wirtschaft und Gesellschaft Europas, 1850–1914', in Wolfram Fischer et al., eds., *Handbuch der europäischen Wirtschafts- und Sozialgeschichte*, Bd. 5, Stuttgart: Klett-Cotta, 1985, 96 (1880–1910); Wolfram Fischer, 'Wirtschaft, Gesellschaft und Staat in Europa, 1914–1980', in Wolfram Fischer et al., eds., *Handbuch der europäischen Wirtschafts- und Sozialgeschichte*, Bd. 6, Stuttgart: Klett-Cotta, 1987, 77 (1920–1975).

middle of the nineteenth century, schools had not played a central role in the teaching of reading. Even in Sweden, a leader in literacy, until 1858, authorities presumed that children were taught to read at home. At the same time, the diffusion of elementary schooling brought along fast changes in families in which the preconditions of home instruction were missing. Thus, in the second half of the nineteenth century, the prevalence of literacy increased rapidly all across Europe. However, regional differences were still considerable before the First World War, depending on how long compulsory education had been established in the given country and how efficiently regulations were enforced. In this respect, a north-to-south and a west-to-east slope was clearly manifest. In the Scandinavian countries and Germany, illiteracy was practically abolished by 1910. At the same time, there were significant differences in the prevalence of reading and writing, because in Germany, in France and in some parts of Scandinavia, the teaching of reading preceded the teaching of writing until the end of the nineteenth century, as opposed to the two skills being simultaneously taught in other countries.[6] In Finland, the ratio of readers was 99% among adults by 1910, yet in the same population those who could write amounted to only 50%. In the Austro-Hungarian monarchy divergences were evident in literacy. The majority of the Czech, German and Hungarian adult population could read and write; however, the ratio of literates was low in other ethnic groups. This did not only entail regional differences, because in regions with ethnically heterogeneous populations, ethnic disparities in literacy prevailed as well. Many were illiterate in Southern Europe, where regional differences were also salient. In 1910, among those over the age of ten, only about two-thirds of the Italian, half of the Spanish and one-third of the Portuguese population could read and even less could write (Figure 9.1).[7]

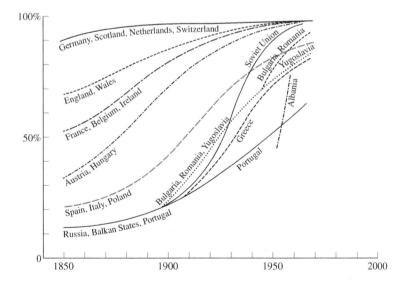

FIGURE 9.1 Literacy in Europe, 1850–1970

Source: R. A. Houston, 'Literacy', in Peter Stearns, ed., *Encyclopedia of European Social History*, vol. 5, New York: Scribner's, 2001, 393.

The elimination of illiteracy was remarkably rapid in the first decades of the twentieth century in those countries where it had been high at the turn of the century. Consequently, by the mid-twentieth century, illiteracy had diminished in these countries as well. In Italy, about three-quarters of the population over the age of six years was literate in 1930, a ratio that reached 86% by 1950. Still, at the mid-century, in addition to the most underdeveloped Albania, illiteracy was still wide-spread in Portugal (44%), Yugoslavia (27%), Greece (26%), Bulgaria (24%) and Romania (23%). In the following decades, considerable success was achieved in Southern and South-Eastern Europe. Nevertheless, there remained regions in Europe where illiteracy was still not uncommon at the end of the twentieth century. In particular, the Balkans and certain parts of the Iberian Peninsula were struggling with this problem. Fourteen percent of the population in Greece could still not read in 1971. In 1985, 9% of Yugoslavians were illiterate, and this figure included one-third of Kosovo's population and 23% of Bosnia and Herzegovina's. In the 1960s, 6% of Spanish and 30% of Portuguese people were not familiar with the alphabet, and in the latter, 16% were still illiterate even in 1985. Albania was the only country that had an even worse figure at the time.[8] Of course, these averages certainly included not only persisting regional differences in literacy but also excessive generational gaps, because the share of illiterates was usually negligible among the young, although it was over the average among the elderly population. However, the expectations concerning literacy also changed remarkably. Although in the eighteenth and nineteenth centuries, those who could spell their names were classified as literate, at the end of the twentieth century, there emerged the concept of residual or functional illiteracy, referring to those who cannot use their knowledge appropriately in everyday situations. Thus classified, a UNESCO calculation put the ratio of those with deficient literacy to 15–20% of the French and 15–30% of the Portuguese population, for instance, at the end of the twentieth century.[9]

Secondary education

By the end of the nineteenth century, similar structures of elementary and secondary public education had evolved all around Europe. Children obliged to attend school essentially had three options for continuing their studies after the elementary level (usually at the age of ten or eleven years, sometimes at twelve). The secondary schools of the highest prestige, which attracted mainly the children of the upper middle class and the upper classes, had curricula centred around classical knowledge, yet incorporated modern languages, mathematics and sciences as well. This type of secondary grammar school was called lyceum in France and Italy (*lycée; liceo*) and *Gymnasium* in Germany, Austria and Hungary. Corresponding to the ideal of classical education, the instruction of classical languages (Latin and classical Greek) had a great emphasis in this stream, with the intention that these transmit the high culture of classical antiquity to the students and also habituate them to intellectual discipline. These schools educated the social elite, because they were the only path to higher education for a long period. For example, in Germany, the final examination of secondary education (*Abitur*), a prerequisite of university entrance, was exclusively attainable in these institutions. The second type of secondary school of the time was more practically oriented. Arts and humanities were taught to a lesser degree there and classical languages were emphasized even less. In contrast, students had access to more instruction in science and also to more 'down-to-earth' knowledge in mathematics and other subjects. Those completing this stream usually did not go to university (and would not be accepted there upon completing this stream, actually, for a long time), yet they could attend tertiary-level technical and commercial/business schools. The third type of secondary school took only three to four years to finish after the elementary school, and the two were sometimes administratively joined. Thus, students who opted for this stream often finished their studies by the age of thirteen or might have entered into apprenticeship afterwards.

As early as the beginning of the twentieth century, structural changes were taking place in the education system, one major direction of which was intended to improve the links between secondary and university education.[10] From 1902 in Germany, universities were open to students completing the other two types of secondary schools besides *Gymnasium*, provided these students satisfied certain criteria. France made similar provisions in the very same year, and other countries followed suit. Thus, the changes primarily targeted the unification of parallel school streams that offered different qualifications, because not each of them had originally been intended to enable students to enter tertiary education. Although unification was achieved in many countries to some degree, in most, no ground-breaking trans-formations occurred between the two World Wars. Scandinavia was an exception, where after elementary education, all students attended a general school (lower secondary level) and could proceed from there to the secondary grammar school or to the other streams at this level. This system emerged before the First World War in Norway, Denmark and Sweden, and after the Second World War in Finland.

Parallel to elementary education embracing the entire respective age group, secondary education (broadly the age group of 10–19) began to expand. At the turn of the century, few continued their studies beyond the elementary level in Europe. The ratio of active students in the 10–19-year age group reached 3% in few countries. In 1910, this figure was 5% in Germany and around 3% in Norway, Finland, Switzerland, and in what later became Ireland.[11] From these low levels, the ratio of students in secondary education in Western Europe at least doubled in the 1920s and 1930s, and in some cases it grew even higher. This phenomenon was facilitated by the trend that the finishing age of compulsory education had been continuously raised since the beginning of the century, as a result of which students stayed in school until they were fourteen, fifteen, or even older (Table 9.1).[12]

The efforts to improve education in the interwar period can be shown by the considerable decline in the number of pupils per class and the better provision of teachers in several countries. For instance, in Belgium the teacher–student ratio was 1:46 in 1913, and only 1:29 in 1929. However, most countries improved significantly in this area only after the Second World War. In Germany and in the Netherlands, the teacher–student ratio was around 1:40 in the interwar period and changed considerably only by the 1970s, reaching 1:27 and then decreasing further to 1:18 by 1983. This figure was better than the Western European average of the time.[13]

Despite the achievements in secondary education in the interwar period, its growth, which could involve masses of the appropriate cohorts, was accomplished only after the Second World War in the European countries. It was all the more urgent because even the countries leading in this field in Europe were lagging far behind the United States, where high ratios participated in secondary education already in the era of the First World War, with 28% of 14–17-year-olds studying in such institutions in 1920. After the Second World War, the expansion did begin rapidly indeed in most European countries. For example, in Italy and Norway, the number of those attending school in the 10–19-year-old cohort doubled during the 1950s and doubled once again in the following decade. The Western European average increased two and a half times in the same period (Table 9.1).

With regard to the structural changes of education, unified secondary education was most successfully implemented in the Scandinavian countries, but similar policies proceeded at a slower rate elsewhere in Western Europe in the post-war decades. Great Britain, France and Germany provide noteworthy examples for the strong path-dependency of educational systems and reform efforts.

In Great Britain, impressive plans were formulated concerning the restructuring and democratization of the school system during the course of the Second World War. However, the Education Act of 1944 did not introduce unified secondary education. Instead, it defined three types of schools: the already existing secondary grammar school, the secondary technical school and an additional general type, the secondary modern school. Yet few schools of the new types were actually established, because communities found their parallel maintenance demanding financially. Furthermore, many students finished their studies in the new school types without graduating, or without a useful certificate. Then, in the 1960s, the idea of unified secondary education appeared again in Great Britain, as considerations of social justice became more stressed in governmental policies. As a result of the new reforms, already 83% of students attended comprehensive secondary schools by 1979.[14]

In France, the *Langevin-Wallon Report* of 1947, which proposed unified secondary education, was accepted by the major political actors, but the corresponding Debré Act was not passed until 1959. This law followed the English reform principles formulated in 1944 and aimed at providing further educational opportunity to those students who were not admitted in the strongly selective *lycées* after having completed their primary education. At the same time, these new schools meant only four additional years spent in formal education, until the age of 15, without any preparation for higher education. Thus, *lycées* preserved their elite character. However, some years later, more radical reforms were introduced in France. The Fouchet Decree in 1963 fundamentally changed the structure of education. All children completing their primary schooling at the age of 11 continued to study in the local general secondary school (*collegè d'enseignement secondaire*) for an additional

4 years. The *lycée* became a school type at the next level that prepared the students for higher education and issued the certificate necessary for university admission (*baccalauréat*). Those who did not intend to proceed to higher education could learn a trade in one of the newly established technical *lycées* (*lycées techniques*). For a long time, *lycées* continued to run various specialized classes, the unification of which was the last measure of the French educational reform in 1975.[15] However, this step still did not solve all the problems: although *lycées* had been unified, graduates of the highest-quality ones continued to monopolize entrance to the most prestigious universities and colleges, and thus the issue of social justice in education was raised again in the 1980s. Consequently, considerable efforts were made to standardize the quality of instruction in *lycées* as well as to make the other streams converge to these standards regarding instructional methods and levels as well as curricular contents.

Germany stands out in Western Europe with its relatively stable educational system after the Second World War. The American occupational authorities proposed the establishment of a comprehensive secondary school in the immediate post-war years, but this plan was not realized. The German school system maintained its fragmented nature, which had emerged by the beginning of the twentieth century. There were three alternatives after completion of the unified elementary school (*Grundschule*), which consisted of four grades. The most prestigious stream was the classic *Gymnasium* (grades 5–13), with its uninterrupted tradition since the end of the nineteenth century. This type offered high-quality education, including the foundations of academic disciplines, and occasionally offered training in a classical language in addition to English and one other modern foreign language. It concluded in a final examination (*Abitur*), automatically granting admittance to higher education, except for a few special university majors in which *numerus clausus* existed. The second stream was the *Realschule* (grades 5–10), which combined practical, vocational knowledge with academic instruction, placing great emphasis on foreign languages and mathematics. This type was traditionally the choice of those who considered taking up commercial or other business jobs. Studies in the *Realschule* could be continued in the *Berufsfachschule* (grades 11–12), which in itself did not qualify one to enter higher education; for this, additional studies were necessary. The third stream of secondary education was the *Hauptschule* (grades 5–9), which provided the general and practical knowledge necessary for blue-collar jobs. The only possible continuation of this type was the three-year vocational school (*Berufsschule*). This system was not much different from those implemented in Great Britain in 1944 and in France in 1959. Nonetheless, in the latter countries, significant structural reforms took place from the 1960s, whereas in Germany, this system has remained essentially unaltered up to the present day. It is obvious that the German approach forces the students and their parents to make a very early decision regarding school choice (after the first four years of education), a choice that is difficult to change later. This characteristic elicited criticism, and consequently several governments undertook to address the necessary reforms in education. Comprehensive secondary schools (*Gesamtschule*) were established in some federal states run by the Social Democrats (Bremen, Hamburg, Hesse and West Berlin) from the 1960s, but this stream did not become dominant even in these areas. Remarkably enough, after the unification of Germany, the majority of East German states adopted the selective West German system instead of keeping their unified, ten-grade general schools. Therefore the most significant structural change in the German school system pertained to the distribution of students among different school types. In the 1940s, approximately 10% of students attended the *Gymnasium*, whereas by the 1980s, this ratio exceeded 30%. Corresponding with this, attendance in the *Hauptschule* decreased, yet even in the 1990s, more than 40% of students entered this stream after completing their elementary studies. One of the main reasons for the lack of reforms was that almost every level of educational policy was assigned, and still belongs, to the jurisdiction of individual federal states in post-war West Germany. An additional factor of the conservation of the system was that students completing *Hauptschule* stood good chances in the labour market, because employers highly valued the solid and practical knowledge that they acquired there. This also indicates that the lack of structural reforms did not necessarily mean low quality in education. In fact, West German elementary and secondary education provided one of the highest-quality schoolings in Europe in the post-war era.[16]

As shown above, although the main endeavour in most of Europe in the first half of the century was the quantitative expansion of secondary education, which lasted well into the 1950s, the focus of the debate shifted in the 1960s. The issue was not merely to open up secondary education for the masses any more, but to implement fundamental educational reforms to create unified education from the elementary to the secondary levels that were accessible to every social group. In most Western and Southern European countries, comprehensive frameworks were indeed created at the lower secondary level at least. Naturally, there were national differences. For example, whereas comprehensive schools were established for 11–18-year-olds in Great Britain, in France only 14–16-year-old students were educated in a general setting and further educational instruction was specialized, with separate schools for practical training and preparation for higher education. Moreover, in Germany and some other countries, such as the Netherlands, Austria, Switzerland, and Luxembourg, the selective post-elementary school types were maintained.[17]

As regards vocational training, the changes were more moderate everywhere after the Second World War. According to the nineteenth-century German model, which was the most successful, students primarily acquire practical knowledge in factories. The British model was similar, only less thoroughly organized, whereas in France, vocational training was relegated to public schools to a greater extent. The adaptation of the German model in other countries was not easy, because employers' willingness to cooperate in the educational process was a crucial factor in its effectiveness, and in this respect other countries fell behind Germany.

Until 1945, the structure of the school systems in the countries in East Central and South-Eastern Europe was similar to that of Western European countries, i.e. different school types were characterized by marked differences in their curriculum as well as in the socioeconomic background of their students. Still, some reform endeavours emerged already before or during the Second World War. For example, in Hungary an eight-grade general school was introduced, which integrated the elementary and the lower secondary levels of education. This type of school did not become exclusive, but was widely established before the communist takeover. Communist governments nationalized basically the whole school system (though in Poland a limited number of private institutions could continue to function as institutions of education). This step subsequently enabled communists to begin thorough structural reforms in education: as a major element of this policy, general schools (usually covering the first eight grades, or the first ten, such as in East Germany) became the exclusive type at the elementary and lower secondary level.

The curricular contents were altered remarkably as well in communist Europe. Besides the national language, literature and history, great attention was now paid to Russian and Soviet literature and history, together with the history of the labour movement, and every subject possible was presented from a Marxist-Leninist perspective. Science was also given greater emphasis in education than before, or than in Western Europe generally. The first foreign language taught in schools was Russian, except in Romania and Yugoslavia, where French and English prevailed. As a result, although formerly dominant in the region, the German language lost its ground; Latin even more so. Religious education in schools was abolished.

After the initial eight or ten years of schooling in the general school, students had three options to continue their studies, which were similar to the alternatives discussed in Western European education. The general academic stream aiming at preparing for higher education was present in this region as well and mostly followed a path similar to the French *lycée* and the German *Gymnasium*. The second stream showed more independent features, offering practical knowledge in economics, health care, education, agriculture, or specific fields of technology. It also offered its students the option to acquire the certificate necessary for admittance to tertiary education. In time, it attracted more and more students and became the most popular stream of secondary education in certain countries. However, the number of students proceeding to higher education from here remained limited, because of the small capacity of universities and colleges. The third stream of secondary education was vocational training schools, which provided practical and applied theoretical training that lasted, depending on the country, one to three years.

Schools were also important institutions for political education and socialization, which was realized through both curricular content and the organization of extracurricular activities. Age-specific youth organizations aimed to align students' world view and behaviour to official ideologies. Nevertheless, the extent and manner of indoctrination changed over time and individual countries differed remarkably with respect to the directness and the claim for exclusivity in the mediation of official ideologies in schools and by youth organizations. Church institutions and religious communities could preserve a much higher level of autonomy and were able to have an impact on the youth in Poland, more so than in any other country in the region. In Hungary, communist youth organizations essentially maintained their monopolistic position until the democratic transformation and they had a strong presence in the schools as well, incorporating a huge majority of the students as members. However, their influence both on the world view of students and the organization of their leisure activities had been decreasing; thus, by the 1980s, only opportunism and leadership ambitions kept them alive. In contrast, in East Germany and Romania, indoctrination remained powerful, and communist youth organizations were active and exclusive even in the 1980s.

Higher education

By the nineteenth century, universities were one of the oldest institutions existing in Europe, with some of the traditional university structures from the early modern period surviving particularly in the British Isles and in Southern and Northern Europe.[18] Yet at the beginning of the century, two novel university models emerged in Europe that brought about the renewal of the past structures. The French model was rooted in earlier periods but was fully implemented by the Revolution and perfected by Napoleon. It was characterized by fragmented, specialized colleges strictly controlled by the central government, including the content of teaching, the awarding of degrees and several other aspects of university life. The model remained intact for some time and began to erode only in the final decades of the nineteenth century under the pressure of the German model. This model can be traced back to the educational reforms implemented in Prussia in the early nineteenth century and the ideas and activity of Wilhelm von Humboldt, who managed to persuade the King of Prussia to found a university in Berlin in 1810 based on liberal and humanistic principles of the freedom of teaching and study, the autonomy of universities, and comprehensive erudition and self-improvement. Equally importantly, Humboldt regarded the function of the university not as passing on practical skills, but rather as introducing students to the discovery of knowledge by linking scientific research and instruction through seminars and laboratory work. These ideals were not fully realized, but the reforms produced considerable results, nonetheless.[19] Hence the model diffused across the German states and the whole of continental Europe, and influenced the other universities across Europe. The flourishing of German universities was also fostered by their highly structured, decentralized system. Every German state aspired to have its own university, an ambition that promoted competition among academic institutions. If a talented young scholar did not manage to receive professorship at one university, he was very likely to get it in another state. Even though the guild-like behaviour of professors did result in a certain rigidity of the system by the end of the century, German universities still unquestionably represented the cutting edge of higher education in the world at the time. British universities did not constitute a 'model' in a strict sense in the nineteenth century, because there were a variety of types of institutions in higher education. The Scottish universities resembled more their counterparts in the continent. Oxford and Cambridge in England also adhered themselves to reforms, transforming their evaluation system during the century, abolishing religious examinations, and introducing new subjects besides the traditional ones in the natural sciences and technology. These last subjects were central to the newly established British universities (Sheffield, Birmingham, etc.) as well.[20]

Based on these foundations, European higher education kept expanding in the first half of the twentieth century, meeting the increasing demand of the economy and public services for highly qualified white-collar labour. Yet, on the whole, university entrance was still the privilege of only a minor segment of the youth all over Europe, students mostly coming from the relatively narrow middle classes. Before the First World War, university students represented 1–2% of the 20–24-year-old population in Western Europe on the average; in the 1920s, the ratio of those involved in higher education reached 4% of the 20–24-year-olds only in Austria, and even here there was a decrease during the years of the Great Depression (Table 9.2). Along with wars and the economic crisis, a major obstacle to further expansion was the limited number of students completing secondary education.[21]

With few exceptions, European states financed and controlled universities in the interwar era. At the same time, the freedom of research and instruction broadly prevailed: once appointed, professors essentially were irremovable, which was considered by universities as a guarantee of independence and the high quality of research and teaching. Even the authoritarian regimes could not ignore university autonomy. The most important exception was Nazi Germany, where higher education and research were subject to primarily racist blacklisting. Universities were mostly involved in purely scientific research, disregarded applied research, and put great emphasis on the transmission of general knowledge. Besides the classical universities covering a wide range of academic fields, new, specialized institutions were established in several countries including the *École Polytechnique* in Paris, the Imperial College of Science, Technology and Medicine in London, the technical and agricultural colleges in several German cities and similar technical and other colleges in the Netherlands and Scandinavia. In some countries, such as France, Switzerland and Spain, the prestige of these institutions even exceeded that of the traditional universities, but generally they had an inferior position in the hierarchy of higher education.[22]

After the Second World War, the number of students in tertiary education increased abruptly. During the war, many had been compelled to give up or postpone their studies, and they wished to continue learning when peace came. In Western European societies, the ratio of students involved in higher education reached 4–6% on the average. After a temporary decline around the end of the 1940s that surfaced in some of these countries, figures were on the rise again in the 1950s (Table 9.2).

However, the real boom took place in the 1960s and 1970s in Western Europe. Besides factors discussed elsewhere in this volume, such as the demands of economy or the considerations of social openness and mobility, the development of universities from the 1960s was promoted by the reforms introduced in secondary education (also covered earlier in the chapter), which contributed to the creation of

TABLE 9.2 The ratio of university students in their age group (20–24) in Europe, 1910–1995 (%)

	1910	1920	1930	1940	1950	1960	1970	1980	1990	1995
United Kingdom	1	2	2	1	3	9	14	19	30	50
France	1	2	2	3	4	7	16	25	40	51
Netherlands	1	2	3	3	8	13	20	29	40	49
Belgium	1	1	2	2	3	9	18	26	40	54
Ireland		2	2	2	4	9	14	18	29	39
Germany/FRG	1	2	2	1	4	6	14	26	34	44
Austria	4	4	4	2	5	8	12	22	35	47
Switzerland	2	2	2	3	4	6	8	18	26	33
Sweden	1	1	2	2	4	9	21	31	32	46
Denmark	1	2	3	2	6	9	18	28	37	45
Norway	1	1	2	2	3	7	16	26	42	59
Finland	1	1	2	3	4	7	13	32	49	70
Italy	1	2	1	4	4	7	17	27	31	41
Spain	1	1	2	2	2	4	9	23	37	49
Portugal	0	1	1	1	2	3	8	11	23	37
Greece	0	0	1	1	3	4	13	17	25	43
GDR					2	10	14	23	22	
Poland		1	2	2	6	9	11	18	22	25
Czechoslovakia		2	2	3	4	10	10	18	16	22
Hungary	2	2	2	2	3	7	10	14	14	24
Romania	1	1	2	2	3	5	10	12	10	23
Yugoslavia		1	1	2	4	9	16	28	16	18
Albania						5	8	8	10	10
Bulgaria	1	1	1	2	5	11	15	16	31	39

Note: United Kingdom: Great Britain.

Sources: Hartmut Kaelble, *Sozialgeschichte Europas: 1945 bis zur Gegenwart,* München: C. H. Beck, 2007, 392–393 (1950–1995); Hartmut Kaelble, *Soziale Mobilität und Chancegleichheit im 19. und 20. Jahrhundert,* Göttingen: Vandenhoeck, 1983, 200 (1910–1940).

a wider recruitment base. Entrance requirements were moderated, and the institutions themselves began offering more diverse training programmes, as a result of which tertiary education became more attractive for wide social groups. The ratio of women in higher education institutions grew constantly. The impressive increase of enrolments also showed that universities were increasingly characterized by their openness: in West Germany, from 247,000 in 1960 to 412,000 in 1970 and to 791,000 in 1980; in France, from 241,000 in 1960 to 694,000 in 1970 and 884,000 in 1980; in the United Kingdom, from 81,000 in 1950 to 258,000 in 1970 and 340,000 in 1980. In Italy, 268,000 students attended university in 1960, whereas in the middle of the 1980s their number reached well over one million.[23] The student enrolment ratios not only show the increase vis-à-vis the interwar era, or the early 1950s, but also enable the comparison of particular societies and regions. By applying a relatively narrow definition of higher education, we can see that the share of university and college students in the age cohort of 20–24 was well above the European average in the Scandinavian countries (26–32%), in the Netherlands (29%) and in Italy (27%) in 1980. Considering a broader approach, including the various institutions that offer tertiary level professional training, the actual increase would be even more remarkable: in Sweden, for example, the level was 4 percentage points higher at the end of the 1970s (Table 9.2).

One difficulty in comparing communist and other industrialized countries, including Western Europe, is that the former considered such institutions as parts of the higher education that are traditionally viewed as providing secondary education in Western Europe. First of all, some of the fields in technical colleges and teacher training constitute this ambiguous category. Nevertheless, even accepting their broad definition, the development of communist countries in higher education was far behind that of Western Europe in the post-war decades. In the 1950s, the gap was not yet significant, but in the following period East Central Europe and South-Eastern Europe kept steadily falling behind. By the 1980s, Hungary, Romania and Albania had the lowest ratio of students in higher education (around 10% of the respective age cohort). Statistics were only favourable in Yugoslavia and East Germany, though the above-mentioned inadequacies of comparison were evidently present in these countries. However, the divergence of communist countries seems more moderate when the ratio of higher education qualifications throughout the entire population is examined, rather than the actual ratios of university and college attendance in given age groups. This is because, on the one hand, students were not allowed to prolong their studies, as a result of which the average length of university studies was significantly shorter here than in the West, and, on the other hand, the drop-out rate was lower in these countries. In other words, if one was admitted to university, one was more likely to acquire the diploma within the expected 3 to 5 years, as opposed to Western Europe, where longer completion times were normal (sometimes even 7–8 years), especially from the 1970s, and where many students never managed to graduate.

Responding to the increase in the number of students, the capacity of existing institutions was expanded all across Europe. With hundreds of years of tradition behind them, prestigious universities that had mainly conducted elite instruction now shifted to mass education quickly. Often institutions of lower standards, such as technical or teacher training colleges, were developed into colleges of higher standards, with considerable investment, offering a wide variety of study programmes. Finally, many new universities were also established.

Different countries were characterized by individual mixtures of these three alternative ways of development. In Germany, old and distinguished universities, such as the ones in Göttingen, Heidelberg and Marburg, lost their elite character because of the booming number of students. This was, from another aspect, the result of a conscious public policy that intended to prevent the separation of the future elite by educating them together with other layers of society. Also in West Germany, some teacher training colleges were developed into universities, for instance, in Erlangen, but the foundation of new institutions was even more important. A few cases in point are Bielefeld, Stuttgart, Bochum and Cologne. In Great Britain, traditionally respected universities like Oxford and Cambridge maintained their elite character, and expansion essentially meant the establishment of eight new institutions in the 1960s (Sussex, York, Stirling, etc.), though several colleges of technology were also upgraded (Bath, Strathclyde, etc.). 'Greenfield' universities not only increased the number of institutions and thus academic competition, but, lacking any traditions and vested interest of researchers, also provided good chances for the formation of innovative scientific schools and research directions.

Despite often impressive investments, the development of university buildings and other infrastructure could generally not keep up with the growth in the number of students; nor could the administrative structure of universities. Moreover, the methods of instruction also seemed to become obsolete and received more and more criticism in the 1960s. Crowdedness, rigidity of university hierarchy, and dissatisfaction with curricular contents, along with other factors, such as fear of possible problems in finding jobs, diffusion of radical political views and protests against the Vietnam War, resulted in the 1968 student revolts, as seen earlier in Chapter 7. Initiatives of university reforms and social change emerged in Paris, Frankfurt, West Berlin and elsewhere in Western Europe, supported by many professors as well. These actions were not wholly without success because university autonomy was increased in France, Germany, Italy, the Netherlands, Spain and Scandinavian countries, instruction was modernized, and the administration of institutions became more democratic, even though some of the measures were later withdrawn. For instance, the Sorbonne University in Paris, swollen to an enormous size, was now divided into eight separate units; a decision obviously motivated, among others, by its being one of the centres of the student movements in 1968 and an institution too difficult to handle by public administration.

The student body multiplying manifold within only a few decades presented serious problems regarding selection as well. In the United States, in a hierarchical system of higher education, the selection of students was regulated by the great differences in the quality and prestige of universities and colleges as well as the corresponding amount of tuition fees that they charged. In contrast, higher education in Western Europe was primarily provided by public institutions charging no tuition. Among these institutions, except for a few exceptions, no clear-cut quality rank existed. Students entered higher education in various ways. One of them was the Italian solution, where the right to study was highly respected, and thus students could freely choose the universities they wished to attend. This strategy caused extreme overload in some faculties, which other countries tried to avoid. In Sweden and Germany, centralized nationwide systems were introduced that distributed students among universities according to predefined criteria, most eminently academic achievement at the secondary level and place of residence. A wide variety of transitional systems existed between these two types of student recruitment, which limited the number of those admissible in certain subjects and fields but not everywhere.

In addition, a *numerus clausus* was widely applied in Sweden in the 1980s to avoid the mass production of graduates in superfluous numbers in universities. Educational authorities tried to forecast future labour market demand in every field and determined the admission quotas and even curricular contents on this basis. Several other countries experimented along this line; however, quotas and centralized distribution strongly clashed with the principles of educational freedom and university autonomy; moreover, changes in the labour market rendered it impossible to foresee future needs. Also, the direct enforcement of labour market demand in university training occasionally even resulted in the reduction of the quality of instruction. There were similar efforts to directly connect the university curriculum to the needs of the economy in France in 1976 and 1987, but these attempts led to the decline of formerly high-quality programmes and to the emergence of poor-quality training; the provisions were in both cases withdrawn as a result of protests.[24] Similar endeavours created a severe conflict between the Thatcher government and universities in Great Britain, exemplified by the episode of Oxford University rejecting to endow the prime minister, formerly an Oxford student, with the title *Doctor honoris causa* in 1984. Sacrificed to financial considerations, several elements of university autonomy were lost in the period of the Thatcher governments, but in the 1990s, the previous conditions were mostly restored. From the 1980s, budget restrictions and the reinforcement of state control also transpired elsewhere in Europe as well as the direct adaptation to the needs of the economy appearing in the training programmes. These attempts presented formerly unknown obstacles to the realization of the freedom of instruction and research.[25]

Meanwhile the number of students continued to rise throughout the final two decades of the century as well. This was the time of spectacular development in the Southern European countries, for example in Portugal, where the ratio of university and college students in the 20–24-year-old population tripled from 1980 to 1995. A similar boom took place in East Central Europe after the democratic transformation. Student ratios tripled and quadrupled in a number of countries within a few years, and thus these countries essentially managed to catch up with other regions of Europe in this respect in the 1990s (Table 9.2).

Aspirations to create the European Higher Education Area

Although the expansion of school systems took place within the borders of nation states all around Europe in the twentieth century, international influences had always been present in education, especially in the university sphere. At the end of the century, the European integration process, slowly expanding beyond economic cooperation, gave a new impulse to the internationalization of European education. The administration of education was to remain a largely national affair, but a specific educational policy of the EU began to take shape at this time. The EU had already regulated a few aspects of the school systems of the member states in some subsidiary fields mostly related to the unified internal market (such as the working conditions of students in vocational schools), but the first real steps towards the recognition of EU competences for education were taken by the Maastricht Treaty (1992) and the Amsterdam Treaty (1997). Several programmes were funded by the EU with the explicit goal of developing cross-border cooperation between educational institutions, their teachers and, most importantly, their students. The Erasmus Programme, launched in 1987, has been particularly successful, with the participation of over two thousand colleges and universities all over Europe by the new millennium. By 2004, altogether 1.2 million students had taken the opportunity to study abroad with the assistance of the programme. For example, in Germany, 7% of all the country's students participated in exchanges at universities in other countries via the initiative. The EU has also been active in fostering the mutual acknowledgement of school certificates, although this has not become part of the acquis and thus has had no binding obligation on the member states yet. One of the key programmes of the structural and curricular advancement of European higher education was launched in 1999 in Bologna, where ministers of education from 29 European countries signed a declaration fostering student mobility and employability by the harmonization of the national university systems, including the implementation of a system based on undergraduate and postgraduate studies with easily comparable curricula and transferable degrees. The starting point of the reforms known as the Bologna Process was constituted by intergovernmental agreements rather than EU initiatives, but soon the EU adapted these objectives and urged the member states towards their speedy and complete realization. However, the means at the disposal of the EU for impelling national governments to act are not many in this area.[26] Hence its influence is indirect: for instance, the unified European Research Area surfaced in the programme approved by the 2000 Lisbon Summit, aimed at improving the competitiveness of the EU, as one of the important prerequisites for the achievement of common goals. Later, in 2010, the European Higher Education Area was officially launched by the EU, which meant that most of the objectives set at the Bologna Declaration in 1999 were accomplished and in the new stage the consolidation of the results was needed. These initiatives endeavoured to further reduce the segmentation of the European higher education sector. Nonetheless, at universities, the negative consequences of these measures were often alarmingly visible on the quality of programmes, and, paradoxically, the EU plans might even foster certain divergences. Since the decisions made in Lisbon, discussions often featured university centres of excellence and the establishment of elite universities, which were intended to increase European competitiveness in a global perspective. If realized, these plans would actually reinforce the internal differentiation of higher education in Europe.

Explanations for the development of schooling

Throughout the twentieth century, a remarkable expansion of the educational system took place, as a result of which the average number of years spent in school and higher education was multiplied in European societies. Although differences between nations persisted, the process of growth has been undoubtedly universal, which in turn gave rise to several interpretations. The classic economic approach primarily considers education as an investment. On the one hand, learning involves various costs (time, money and effort), and on the other hand, it brings benefits. The latter is garnered by individuals, whose higher qualification secures a better position when selling their labour on the market (they may obtain a higher income and better working conditions), which constitutes a major incentive for the expansion of schooling. However, beyond the perspective of the individual, there is a social rate of returns to education as well, because societies also benefit from the dividends of schooling in several ways: educated citizens work more effectively, their ratio of unemployment is usually lower, they pay more taxes, their health is better, etc.

For a long time, there has been broad agreement among policymakers and economists that education and economic prosperity are intertwined. Early economists, such as Adam Smith and John Stuart Mill, recognized this correlation. The argument that a literate workforce is more valuable had already appeared when compulsory elementary schooling was established in the nineteenth century. Yet it was later, after the Second World War, when economics began to systematically examine the effects of education on economy. As a major breakthrough, in the 1960s, the concept of human capital was introduced in economics, considering the stock of skills and the knowledge possessed by people as a form of capital and, as such, a principal input into production.[27] Even if mainstream neoclassical theories of economics have found it difficult to fit human capital into their models, from the post-war decades on, economists have generally acknowledged that education is an important factor of the competitiveness of countries. Accordingly, governments have also been determined to enhance the people's motivation and opportunities to learn, mainly by expanding schools and universities. However, measuring the benefits of human capital investments proved to be difficult, because returns are contingent on many variables, most of which are difficult to isolate. Early theories of human capital that proposed straightforward and linear relationships between education and economic growth have been substantially modified, also in view of the experiences of communist countries, and scholars proposed more modest claims for the effect of education on economic growth. In parallel, by the 1980s, growing concerns emerged in many countries about the creeping and uncontrollable costs of public education. Policymakers advocated for new priorities, including the more or less systematic assessment of educational outcomes in order to reduce costs through a more effective targeting of spending.

Economists have not only addressed the links between education and economic growth but also looked at numerous other aspects of schooling. An important direction of research emphasizes the limits of the demand for a highly educated labour force. If the expansion of the highly qualified labour pool outstrips the supply of jobs requiring such high levels of formal education, the benefits offered by schooling decrease. Those in jobs requiring the highest qualifications continue to earn the most, but their income advantage diminishes. Moreover, some university graduates have to accept positions that require only lower-level skills and consequently offer smaller incomes. It has also been argued that the rate of returns in education is diminishing or, in other words, an additional year of education results in lower returns than the previous years. Both are propositions that explain why income differences between groups of higher and lower educational levels were compressed in twentieth-century Europe, as shown in chapter 4.

Another explanation considers the effects of market mechanisms when interpreting education as a sort of consumption, satisfying personal needs. Learning in this model is given an enjoyment value that might emerge instantly (for instance, at a lecture on European social history), but benefits are more typically realized with a delay, when one applies the acquired knowledge and skills at one point later in life. This aspect of learning gained significance with the robust economic growth in post-war Europe, because rising incomes decreased the relative proportion of household expenditures on basic necessities, and thus a higher ratio of resources was allocated to satisfying the 'higher' needs for non-material goods, preeminently produced by the cultural and educational sectors.

The explanations that focus on social and political rather than economic processes do not simply connect the expansion of education to employment and production. According to these approaches, mass education originating in the nineteenth century and expanding in the twentieth century is related to the demands of modern states that aim at social and political integration. The expansion of education offered various benefits to nation states. Educated citizens could fulfil their duties better, by way of military service, obedience to law or taxation. In addition, they usually used their civic and political rights more actively, which in turn legitimized the political systems of modern democratic societies. Public schools took on a direct role in the transmission of the national cultural heritage, an integrative role *per se*. The modern state primarily realized these aims by compulsory education and the unification of curricular contents, which guaranteed that nearly the entire society acquired the knowledge, norms and beliefs fostering social integration, at least at a minimum level.

A further argument links the expansion of education to bureaucratization, because along with the diffusion of bureaucratic organizations in the economy, the number of vacant positions to be filled according to formal criteria increased as well in politics and elsewhere in society. Thus, this expansion resulted in a growing need for a qualified workforce with standardized degrees. Modern school systems responded to this need by tending to operate in a strongly formal and hierarchical manner, using the categories of classes, educational levels, curricula, timetables, examinations and grades.[28]

A related view suggests that extended formal, school-based instruction mainly has a screening or signalling function. Specialized knowledge can be acquired only in the workplace; therefore what the school actually does is the selection and labelling of students in the educational process. Employers often face situations in which they cannot easily observe the performance of workers, but the credential acquired is an indicator of the individual's diligence, abilities and other characteristics relevant to the employer in the hiring decision.[29]

An ambiguous aspect of education is emphasized by the conflict theory approach, suggesting that the school system and its development do not, or do not necessarily, serve social integration.[30] According to this view, the expansion of education was largely driven by the aspirations of the elite. The dominant social groups seek to continually increase the level of qualifications required in the elite positions, because together with family background, property and religion, exclusive schooling is a factor that allows the members of the social elite to distinguish themselves from others and maintain their superior status.[31] Most notably, Pierre Bourdieu elaborated on those 'fine distinctions' of a cultural nature that allow the higher classes to demarcate themselves from the rest of society and thus to reproduce themselves. These subtle differences surface in rules of social intercourse and language usage, and the school system, or, more precisely, the best schools, plays an important role in the acquisition of sophisticated social behaviour (an issue that is discussed below in more detail).

Social inequalities in education

As seen above, several individual benefits and social returns are associated with schooling, including, for example, higher income and longer life expectancy. Even if differences among individuals in schooling are partially attributable to biological factors, research has identified social, cultural and economic elements that also condition the level of individually attainable educational levels to a great extent.[32] Of the several types of educational disparities, the twentieth-century changes in gender and social inequalities are addressed, although such important dimensions as regional or ethnic differences cannot be discussed here.

One of the most visible manifestations of inequalities in education at the beginning of the twentieth century was related to gender differences, which mainly originated from the positions that men and women occupied within the family as well as in the labour market. Women, on the one hand, were less likely to attain higher educational levels, and, on the other hand, their choice of which degree to attain during their studies diverged from that of men. Remarkable changes took place in the course of the twentieth century in both respects that lessened gender disparities, and, in some respects, completely eliminated women's disadvantages. This process is well illustrated by the development of tertiary education.

The ratio of women in higher education significantly increased during the twentieth century. At the time of the First World War, the variance among European countries was great in this regard; for example, the share of female students already reached 27% in Great Britain and 20% in Italy, but it was still only 4% in Spain. From this point on, the convergence of gender ratios proceeded steadily in every society, and the differences between individual countries also decreased consistently. Also, it was remarkable that in most of the East Central European and South-Eastern European countries, the ratio of female students rose above the European average by the end of the 1930s. As suggested earlier, Poland was among the leading countries of the continent in this respect. Moreover, this tendency continued even after the Second World War. Thus, by 1980, the ratios of female students caught up with those of males in the Scandinavian and the communist countries; in some of these societies, the number of female students even exceeded the number of male students. By this time, only Switzerland was left behind, its higher education still being dominated by male students by a ratio of two-thirds (Table 9.3). The process of emancipation continued in the final decades of the century. A similar picture emerges when graduates are examined. In the youngest age groups, men and women had usually identical chances of graduating from higher education by the end of the century in most European countries. Only Swiss women suffered a significant disadvantage, and smaller, but not negligible inequalities were present in Great Britain, Germany and Belgium. In contrast, in Portugal, Spain, Denmark, Austria and several East Central European countries, women even left men behind in this respect.[33]

TABLE 9.3 The ratio of women in higher education in Europe, 1910–1995 (%)

	1910	1920	1930	1940	1950	1960	1970	1980	1990	1995
United Kingdom		27	26	27	22	23	33	46	48	50
France	9	13	26	34	34	41	45	50	53	55
Netherlands	14	15	18	14	21	26	28	40	44	47
Belgium			10	14	16	26	36	44	48	50
Ireland			29	23	30	28	34	41	46	51
Germany/FRG	4	9	18	14	16	23	27	41	41	45
Austria	8	14	17	24	21	23	29	42	46	48
Switzerland	22	12	12	13	13	17	24	30	35	
Sweden	8	10	15	24	23	36	42	52	54	56
Denmark	12	14	16	20	24	35	36	49	52	54
Finland			32	33	37	46	48	48	52	53
Norway			15	15	16	34	30	48	53	55
Italy	17	20	15	20	26	27	38	43	50	53
Spain	3	4	7	12	14	24	27	44	51	53
Portugal			12	20	26	30	46	48	56	57
Greece			8	11	24	26	32	41	49	48
GDR					23	32	43	58	52	
Poland					36	41	47	56	56	57
Czech R.						34	36	40	44	47
Hungary					24	33	43	50	50	52
Romania					33	33	43	43	47	53
Yugoslavia					33	29	39	45	52	53
Albania					33	18	33	50	52	53
Bulgaria					33		51	56	51	61

Note: 1910–1940: university data only. 1950–1995: data from every kind of higher education institution, unless indicated otherwise; United Kingdom: Great Britain. Belgium 1950, France 1950, 1970, Great Britain 1950, Italy, Norway 1950, Austria 1950, Portugal 1950, Sweden 1950, Switzerland 1950–1960: university data; Different periods: Denmark 1915, 1925, 1935; Spain 1917; Portugal 1935; East Germany 1951; 1980: France 1985, Great Britain 1985, Sweden 1985.

Sources: Hartmut Kaelble, *Sozialgeschichte Europas: 1945 bis zur Gegenwart,* München: C. H. Beck, 2007, 396 (1950–1995); Hartmut Kaelble, *Soziale Mobilität und Chancegleichheit im 19. und 20. Jahrhundert,* Göttingen: Vandenhoeck, 1983, 222 (1910–1940).

However, the levelling process was not of the same scale regarding faculties and programmes and, consequently, future job prospects. For instance, graduates of technical and natural sciences were mostly men throughout the century. Even in 1992, three to four times more men than women chose such studies in Western European countries. In contrast, in other areas, such as teacher training, women dominated. However, the highest gender differences in this field were present in Scandinavian countries, which had a successful emancipation policy. This phenomenon can be explained by the highly developed welfare services opening career opportunities for women in the caring professions.[34]

All through the century, gender differences in schooling were considerably outweighed by other types of social inequalities, that is, disparities resulting from the economic, social and cultural position of students' parents. Children of working class and peasant parents were underrepresented in every country at all but the elementary level of education, compared with the children of white-collar parents. The importance of the social dimension of educational inequality is indicated by the example of Germany, where men's chances of graduating from higher education were four times higher than women's in the mid-twentieth century, whereas the chances of children of white-collar employees being in high positions and of freelance intellectuals were about 50 times higher than that of children of unskilled or semiskilled workers.[35] Furthermore, as shown, gender differences in schooling mostly levelled off by the end of the century, whereas other social inequalities in schooling prevailed to a considerable extent. However, it is a matter of debate how educational inequalities changed in twentieth-century Europe and how the transformation of school systems, especially the expansion of education and structural changes in the school system in the twentieth century, affected educational disparities.[36]

Even the most adamant proponents of the class reproduction theory acknowledge that education is not fully responsible for the formation and prolongation of the existing class structure in industrial societies. There is a broad consensus in the literature that social inequalities in education declined in the course of the twentieth century, especially in the two or three post-war decades.[37] However, all school systems did not function the same way in this respect. In Germany, for example, social background was more important regarding educational achievement than in Sweden, which was certainly related to the overall characteristics of class structure, and the welfare state discussed in chapters 4 and 5.

A major strand of research indicates that the structure of the school system is an even more relevant factor than class or income difference in explaining international variations in educational inequality. The role of family background is stronger if the transition between levels of education is tied to strict achievement criteria; if the choice of school stream should be made at a relatively early age; and if stream selection definitively determines students' prospects. These problems and the attempts to solve them are considered in this chapter. It is argued that several countries (most notably Germany and Austria) were characterized by a system of early branching in the twentieth century, even if it was modified in the post-war era. Others have completely departed from early branching (such as the communist countries, Sweden, England and France) to allow an easier change between streams at the upper secondary level. These reforms, which were implemented in the post-war decades, and the expansion of schooling were intended to abolish unequal access to education.

However, empirical research has questioned whether egalitarian school reforms produced the expected results. The revolutionary transformations in communist countries, including 'reverse' or 'positive' discrimination of children of working-class origin, have not resulted in permanent change. The new elite largely replaced the old one. However, members of the new ruling class could transfer social advantages to their children. It is thus worth pointing out that educational reforms did not eliminate all means by which the old elite guaranteed their children favoured position in education, including, most importantly, bequeathing forms of human capital, and evading discriminatory measures by relying on personal networks or even corruption.[38] Empirical research also confirmed the assumption that East Central European countries with their early school reforms successfully dismantled barriers to social mobility, and showed lower educational inequality.[39] Another comparative survey conducted in the final decades of the twentieth century, which included 13 societies from both Western and Eastern Europe, found no improvement regarding social inequalities in education in 11 of the 13 cases examined.[40] The exceptions were Sweden and the Netherlands, where social inequalities did significantly decrease in education during the period surveyed. One of the major reasons why egalitarian school reforms usually did not eliminate class disadvantages in education was that once the admission to a particular level of schooling increased, the proportion of children from more affluent or educated families attending that level of education also increased, and thereby the class balance was hardly affected. Even more importantly, if the formerly disadvantaged groups had more access to a specific type of education, the next level of schooling became the major field in which class differences prevailed. There is a significant body of evidence showing that the high level of social disparities in educational outcomes could be moderated only if egalitarian school reforms were accompanied by complex social policy measures alleviating inequalities in the living conditions of families as well as in employment opportunities. That was obviously the case in Sweden and the Netherlands, which might account for the relative success of school reforms in these countries. In contrast, some studies suggested similar positive changes in other countries and divergences between the inequalities for measured competences and final educational attainment.[41] Thus, considering the present state of research, it is difficult to draw any clear-cut conclusions on the recent tendencies in educational inequality across Europe and the exact role of school structure in the emergence of these disparities.[42]

Religious practice: faith and community

Although numerous new small sects and religious factions appeared during the twentieth century in Europe, the religious map of the continent did not change significantly in this period. Building on a history of almost two thousand years, Catholicism was strongly represented and it was fully dominant in several countries (for example, in France, Italy, Spain, Portugal, Poland, Ireland, and Austria), while encompassing a smaller or greater majority of Christians in others (for instance, in Czechoslovakia and Hungary). Protestant churches represented another significant bloc, maintaining their status as the state church in Scandinavia and Great Britain and their members also constituting the major Christian denomination in Germany until the 1949 division of the country, and then in the GDR. Moreover, Protestants were present as minorities in other societies (Hungary and Romania). Members of the Orthodox Church dominated in major regions of South-Eastern Europe and in Greece. The Jewish religion was scattered. Partially as a consequence of the Second World War, instead of constituting a significant minority in some regions (East Central Europe and Germany), the Jewish population became a marginal group everywhere. Beyond this, the only other visible alteration in the distribution of denominations in the continent was the moderate growth of Islam, as a result of immigration in the last third of the twentieth century, mainly in Western and Southern Europe. The number of Buddhists and Hindu believers increased less significantly. Real transformation concerning religious life was brought about by secularization (or, in certain cases, by anti-religious policies), which also had their roots in earlier times, as early as the eighteenth century in France. Consequently, the ratio of those who considered themselves detached from any religion substantially increased by the end of the twentieth century.

The following section investigates the twentieth-century history of religion and churches in Europe primarily by tracing the changing relationship between religions and churches on the one hand, and society on the other, and simultaneously pays attention to the secularization process referred to above.

The relationships of religion, church and society in the twentieth century

The most comprehensive change in the role of church and religion in twentieth-century Europe is often described with the concept of secularization. Secularization denotes the process through which religious thinking, practices and institutions lose social significance.[43] Churches lost much of their influence among the working class in the second half of the nineteenth century; however, this decline affected other social groups less severely. The social and cultural role of churches still remained significant in Europe at the beginning of the twentieth century.[44] The political and social changes taking place during and after the First World War produced further considerable challenges for churches. The collapse of the monarchy in Germany and Austria–Hungary weakened the position of the churches in the region. The revolutions in Germany and elsewhere in Central and East Central Europe challenged churches more radically than ever before, but the positions of the churches were often considered unjustly privileged in established democratic societies as well. Consequently, churches, especially the Catholic Church, frequently showed reservation towards or even rejection of democracy and particularly opposed the rolling back of denominational schools as well as such novel phenomena of modern societies as, for instance, divorce. Secularization accelerated in the course of the twentieth century; however, the change in the relationship of religion or churches and society did not follow a linear path, and was more intricate than a simple loss in the social influence of religious institutions and ideas.

Although a systematic and detailed analysis of the links between church, state and society cannot be offered here, the chapter still attempts to outline the major types and directions of change in a concise manner. Applying David Martin's approach, four main paths of development are distinguished in terms of the above-mentioned relationship in Europe. The first category concerns countries with Protestant dominance (Great Britain and the Scandinavian countries). The second category involves societies in which Protestant majorities live together with a sub-stantial Catholic minority (the Netherlands, Germany, Switzerland and Northern Ireland). The third type consists of countries with Roman Catholic dominance (France, Italy, Austria, Ireland, Spain and Portugal). And finally, societies ruled by left-wing and right-wing authoritarian regimes and dictatorships constitute a separate category, where governments systematically persecuted the church and officially preferred atheism (post-war East Central Europe and South-Eastern Europe).[45]

1. The first path is that of purely Protestant countries, which, following the Reformation, did not have any Catholic minority at all (Scandinavia) or where Catholic communities were present as a result of immigration after the most important characteristics of the system had already been established in a purely Protestant era (Great Britain). Besides state churches, no significant Protestant dis-sent was present in the Scandinavian countries. In contrast, the state church was not so dominant in England, where smaller Protestant churches had considerable influence. Anti-religious and anti-clerical sentiments are not significantly present in this type, and are inversely related to the strength of the dissent churches. It is a fundamental principle of Protestantism that individuals make decisions on religious and political issues according to their own conscience and not according to ecclesiastical views. This principle was most pervasive where nineteenth century liberalism deeply permeated society, that is, much rather in Great Britain than in Scandinavia. As another important Protestant principle, churches as institutions do not claim social dominance, especially in non-religious issues. This makes Protestant state churches in a sense even more conservative than the Catholic Church, because it abolishes the independence of church institutions and transforms church structure to become isomorphic with prevailing social structures, at least in the sense that the clerical elite is recruited from the social elite.

However, there were deviations from this pattern. At first, Scandinavian Lutheran state churches opposed social democracy, but later, in the interwar period, they came to accept it. Moreover, they even tolerated the prospect of social democracy gaining hegemony in the region. A further, telling example comes from Norway, in union with Sweden until 1905. Religiosity was the strongest in the

Bergen area, and it was initially intertwined with the left, as opposed to semi-secularized Oslo and the Swedish dominance originating from there. That is, national and democratic emancipation efforts were joined in a religious party, thus separating religiosity from conservatism.

In Great Britain democratic endeavours and religious dissent were attached to liberalism in the nineteenth century. However, because political liberalism harboured big business, the *petit bourgeoisie* and craftsmen as well, the Conservative Party could gain support in the lower classes. This was because conservatives acted against the unlimited laissez-faire ideology supported by the liberals and materializing, for example, in factory legislation, which made workers largely defenceless. Consequently, conservatives took into consideration the needs of wider social classes in religious issues as well. Some of the groups of the Anglican Church, recalling the medieval traditions of organic solidarity, were solidaristic with the working class, which brought along a form of Anglo-Catholic socialism within the state church. Although the British situation was essentially different from the Scandinavian, the results were similar in one important aspect: anti-clericalism could not gather considerable strength here either because the liberals enjoyed the support of the free churches, whereas Catholic and Jewish minority communities supported the Labour Party, which in turn also relied on the radical factions of the free churches, and even on some groups within the state church. Consequently, churches were not in the focus of major social conflicts either in the nineteenth or the twentieth century in Protestant European countries. Secularization, being an issue for individuals, did not cause such conflicts, either.[46]

2. In the societies belonging to the second category, a significant Catholic minority existed alongside the Protestant majority. In the early twentieth century, Germany, Switzerland and the Netherlands conformed to this pattern. Later, the number of adherents to Catholicism overcame Protestants in all these countries; however, the social and cultural patterns determining the status of religion and church in society had been shaped at the time of major Protestant influence. In these societies, Catholics had rather inferior positions in economy, military and state administration during that period. Hence they supported political factions striving for emancipation.

In this constellation, no direct and unambiguous connection emerged between religion and politics, because Catholics did not associate with the conservative parties of the elites, because of their disadvantaged position. At the same time, in the Netherlands neither orthodox Calvinists nor Catholics could form an alliance with liberalism. The former had ideological reasons for keeping their distance, whereas the latter could not agree with the liberals on the question of religious education. Consequently, both opposing blocs established their separate systems of social and cultural institutions and tolerated the other, as a compromise resulting from the recognition of the state of balance. This phenomenon is called pillarization (*verzuiling*) or columnization in the literature. Socialism gaining strength at the end of the nineteenth century had to face this system in the Netherlands. As a result, it could obtain popularity in the lower classes only if it avoided strong anti-religious or anti-clerical rhetoric. The system of quasiautonomous institutions essentially remained unchanged for the greater part of the twentieth century, and began to diminish only when religious loyalty started to wane as a result of social mobility, urbanization and secularization.

Similarities appeared in Switzerland and Germany, although pillarization did not take place in these countries. Catholics were socially and politically disadvantaged in both countries, and thus they could not identify with the conservative elite. Politically, they tended to position themselves in the centre and were also characterized by cultural segregation, although not to the same extent as in the Netherlands. Nevertheless, a serious conflict emerged between church and state in Germany at the beginning of the 1870s, which is widely known as *Kulturkampf*. Bismarck considered Catholicism as a danger to national unity, and, with the support of the liberals, he openly attacked Catholic institutions. The measures included the expulsion of the Jesuits from the country as well as the introduction of state supervision of denominational schools and the attempt to control the appointment of new priests and remove uncooperative clergymen. By 1876, all Catholic bishops in Prussia were detained or banished, and a third of the Catholic parishes were vacant. The conflicts lasted only a few years, and within a decade, almost all of the anti-Catholic legislation was revoked. The Catholic Centre Party became a large voting bloc in the Reichstag. However, Catholicism collided with the state in Germany again between the two World Wars. The Nazi regime conducted an explicitly anti-Catholic policy, whereas it could reach agreement with the Lutheran church, which was abandoned only by a smaller dissenting group (*Bekennende Kirche*) because of the Nazi racist policy. In 1933, Hitler and the Vatican concluded a concordat, but later in 1937, the encyclical letter *Mit brennender Sorge* (written in German despite centuries-old traditions) condemned racism, although failing to address Nazism directly. The Nazi regime responded with a fierce anti-Catholic campaign, deporting a number of priests to concentration camps. Thus the relationship of the Catholic Church and the Nazi state remained tense, even if the Church attempted to reach an agreement with the Nazis later and the behaviour of Pope Pius XII (1939–58) *vis-à-vis* the Holocaust was also controversial. The church had a close relationship with the CDU in the immediate post-war years, but it loosened later. In sum, religious conflicts were present in these societies. However, both major religious blocs had enough power to encourage a politics of compromise all throughout the twentieth century in the Netherlands and Switzerland, and primarily in the second half of the century in Germany.[47]

In both types addressed thus far, two major factors in the nineteenth and twentieth centuries determined the relationship between religion and church, on the one hand, and society on the other. One of these was how closely religion and the churches were related to political movements, and especially whether religion and church were situated exclusively at one point on the political scale. If there was a strong connection with right-wing politics, churches alienated a significant proportion of society, hence religion could not be a symbol of unity or an integrative force in society anymore. However, if religion and church were not affiliated with any definite segment of the political spectrum, such alienation could not occur. In Great Britain, the position of religious minorities (Catholics and Protestant dissenters) prevented them from affiliating themselves exclusively with the conservative elite, but they were bonding with the political left, which, in turn, had a moderating effect on the anti-religious sentiments of the latter. In most of Scandinavia, anticlericalism did exist among Social Democrats, more in Sweden, Finland and Denmark and the least in Norway. However, on the one hand, the state churches were Protestant and refrained from actively participating in politics, and, on the other hand, they considered the political stance of individuals to be their own matter of conscience. All these prevented the escalation of political conflicts between the rival blocs. In Switzerland, the Netherlands and Germany, the situation diverged, because Catholics were in a relatively disadvantaged position in society, and thus they were interested in social emancipation and were not strongly affiliated with the conservative elites.

The other principal factor, not independent of the previous one, was the power relation or the pluralism of the denominations. If the Protestant state church was in a dominant position, it preserved its strong attachment to the social elite, weakening its ties with the lower classes. At the same time, the workers' withdrawal occurred only from church institutions, although Christianity did sustain a strong cultural influence among the working classes, based on associations and ecclesiastical religious activity, especially in Scandinavia. In the type emerging in Germany, Switzerland and the Netherlands, the Protestant and the Catholic churches represented two rival blocs, originally with a Protestant majority, although not domination. In these societies, religions became the protectors of regional interests and cultural positions and, as in the Netherlands, were able to mobilize large masses, including working-class elements within their own bloc. At the same time, among those outside the two blocs, a marked withdrawal from religious institutions can be observed. Furthermore, when Catholicism was emancipated, by approximately the last third of the twentieth century, the Catholic Church abandoned explicit political activity and focused more on the cultural domain. This is suggested by the fact that in Germany the relationship between the Catholic Church and the CDU loosened from the 1960s, and the weakening of the political activities of the Catholics was reflected in the decline of the Dutch and Swiss Catholic parties from the same period.[48]

3. The next group includes societies with a great Catholic majority. In these countries, the Church became an important point of reference, with many defining their place in politics and society in relation to it. This situation clearly facilitated the emergence of a dual opposition. Whereas in the previous types, the Catholic minority played what may be considered a balancing or stabilizing role, in this type great political and societal schisms and conflicts developed, often with extreme anti-clericalism and secularist dogmas on one side and the offensive behaviour of the Catholic Church on the other. Such conflicts occurred in France primarily between 1870 and 1905, in Italy from the mid-nineteenth century, in Portugal after 1910, and in Spain and Austria in the 1930s. Among the causes for conflict

emphasis should be placed on the strong integrating and unifying aspiration of the Catholic Church, which itself was organized and operated as an organic society. Religiousness and the observation of faith are connected to the ecclesiastical institution of the church to a higher degree for Catholics than for Protestants. Consequently, in the countries with Catholic dominance the Church became intertwined with society, and especially so regarding cultural issues. Therefore societal schisms endangered the Church as well, and vice versa, church-related problems appeared as challenges to the unity of the society. Social divides were strongly associated with religious issues, such as the regulation of marriage and divorce or denominational schools.

Conflicts focusing on education became especially sharp in France, where the state favoured the Catholic Church under the Second Empire, although it encouraged the anti-clerical movement under the Third Republic. Catholics desired to raise the next generations as Catholics, whereas Republicans demanded that children not be educated in the monarchist spirit. The struggle climaxed in 1905 with the complete separation of church and state. The First World War brought the opponents closer to each other, but their relationship remained tense. In 1925, French cardinals and archbishops issued a declaration condemning laicity and call-ing on the faithful not to obey laws that offend the church. Relations were sig-nificantly more structured between the Church and the Vichy government, which aimed at fostering traditional moral rules in social life.[49] At the same time, the Second World War discredited the right wing for collaborating with the Germans, thus pushing Catholicism toward the centre. A similar process took place after the Second World War not only in France but elsewhere in Western Europe, not only stabilizing democracies in particular nation states, but also shaping politics at the European level. As pointed out earlier, several Catholic parties and statesmen became major initiators of European integration.

Naturally, besides several important similarities, there are features different from French development in the other Catholic countries. The unification of Italy took place against the papal will and Catholics abandoned politics for some time in Italy, giving room primarily to the Liberals, but returned to political activity by the First World War. The continuing mutual suspicions between Catholics, Liberals and Socialists contributed to the Fascist takeover. The Lateran Treaty of 1929 aimed at the formation of a *modus vivendi* between Mussolini and the Church, but the Church did by no means surrender. Pius XI (1922–31) condemned the pagan worship of the Fascist state and declared its organizing principles incompatible with Catholic doctrine. Thus, the Church could assume its activities with credibility after the war, and it played an active, often pioneering role in addressing social problems in the following decades.

In Austria in the interwar period, there also emerged two bitterly opposing political blocs, which even commanded paramilitary units. The antagonism of the 'reds' (Social Democrats) and the 'blacks' (Christian Socialists) led to an open conflict in 1934, which eventually resulted in the establishment of a Catholic cor-poratist regime that lasted for a few years, until the *Anschluss* in 1938. At the same time, after the war, the parties did not move towards sharp polarization; rather, they favoured cooperation, although the blocs preserved their distinctiveness and separate positions. This was facilitated by Austria's becoming a democratic state late, because the open and ruthless antagonism in political life lasted only for a short time in the interwar era. Similarly to post-war Germany, the wing, refraining from direct political involvement, gained ground in the Catholic Church, in contrast to the interwar practice. Finally, even though there was an ideological link between the Austrian People's Party (*Österreichische Volkspartei* [ÖVP]) playing a major role in the post-war decades and the Catholic Church, because this party aspired for the support of lower classes (including peasants, the *petit bourgeoisie*, and even certain groups of workers), it could not establish a marked position in relation to the church, and thus the need for coalition building prevailed.

Twentieth-century Spain, Portugal and Greece comprise a subcategory of this group. Here, the polarization inherent in Catholicism appeared under authoritarian and military regimes aiming at the vertical integration of society. In Spain, the relationship between the Church on the one hand, and society and state on the other, was burdened with conflicts as early as the First Republic (1868–74), but even more so during the Second Republic (1931–36). The 1931 Constitution separated state from church, expropriated church property, and constrained the religious orders, excluding them from education completely. The conflict heightened in the Civil War, during which approximately seven thousand priests, nuns and monks were murdered by republicans, churches were vandalized and the bodies of clergymen were exhumed from their graves.[50] The dire atrocities against the church also turned significant social groups against the Republic. The church supported Franco in return for the reinstatement of its rights, but did not refrain from criticizing the regime from the 1960s. Thus, the Franco regime became increasingly suspicious of the Catholic Church and entered into more and more conflicts with the Vatican. Characteristically, in the early 1970s it was even proposed that education be a state monopoly in Spain.

4. The last type is represented by post-Second World War East Central and South-Eastern European communist countries. In the right-wing authoritarian regimes of the interwar and post-war period, such as the ones in Spain, Portugal and Greece, rulers intended to establish the concord of church and state, so that they could rely on the former and stabilize their positions. In contrast, communist regimes aimed at the complete separation of church and state as well as supplanting the social influence of the church. This can obviously be interpreted as these regimes aspiring to ideological monopoly and therefore persecuting all rival ideologies and institutions. In this regard, churches did not differ from other independent institutions, although they were undoubtedly considered a prime target because of their traditionally high organization, intellectual capacity and spiritual attractiveness.

Following Soviet examples, physical terror, administrative control over church activities, infiltration of secret agents, and the manipulation of the appointments of church officials were used in order to restrict religion and church activities. It was obvious that allowing any form of religious life was considered a simple compromise by the communist regimes, and their long-term goal was the eradication of religious-ness. The control over churches was usually delegated to some high-level government organization, such as the State Secretariat for Church Affairs in Czechoslovakia and the GDR. Churches were allowed to conduct activities reduced to religious service, and all their public engagements were not tolerated. The only exceptions regarding public activities were the state-sponsored associations of the clergy, such as the *Pacem in Terris* in Czechoslovakia, condemned by the Vatican in 1982, the so-called peace conferences coordinated by the Christian Peace Conference based in Prague and participation in international ecumenical organizations. The first were easily inte-grated into the propaganda of communist regimes that presented the 'peace camp' in opposition to Western imperialism. The last provided a kind of blackmailing potential, with conformism or at least cooperation with the regime as the price East Central European churches had to pay for being allowed to participate, although Western churches had to refrain from criticizing the communist regimes.

In supplanting religious faith, practices other than control and more or less open political violence were also resorted to. The regimes tried to compete at the ideolo-gical level as exemplified in East Germany by the slogan 'Socialism is the Gospel in action'. Secular equivalents of religious and church holidays and ceremonies were established, especially as regards birth, christening, confirmation, wedding and funeral. Again in East Germany, *Jugendweihe*, the state celebration of entering young adulthood, was a thinly veiled rite of passage to replace confirmation. In addition, the same way as in Western Europe, industrialization and urbanization also contributed to the diminishing influence of the church and, in particular, to the population increasingly becoming non-observant. The process of secularization is discussed in detail later.

The coercive policies also had significant consequences regarding the social relations of the church. Because communist regimes effectively controlled the recruitment for leading positions in society, the political, the economic, and even the cultural elite became mostly comprised of unreligious people, often committed atheists. Thus the majority of the actively religious people came from the numbers of the disadvantaged, the less educated, the elderly, and the rural population.

What characterized numerous public policy fields and social structure in the communist countries featured in the religious conditions of these states as well: even if there existed major commonalities in political objectives and practice, there were considerable divergences both in space and in time. The spectrum of policies ranges from the complete ban on religious life (Albania) to the relative independence of churches (Poland in the 1980s). In the late 1940s and early 1950s, the persecu-tion of the clergy was present everywhere in a ruthless form, although later, relative tolerance also appeared in the region. At the same time, a more considerate policy began only when repression had mostly succeeded in marginalizing churches, again, similar to other independent institutions and forms of civic opposition.

Religious and church independence was the highest in Poland, but even there, different periods can be distinguished, with waves of repression and concession following each other. According to the periodization of J. Lovenduski and

J. Woodall, the state aimed at annihilating the Catholic Church as an independent institution between 1948 and 1956, thus the Church focused on preserving its mere existence. Then between 1956 and 1970, the Church achieved certain successes in its conflicts with the state that relaxed restrictions in such areas as religious education and jurisdiction over church property. After 1970, the Church was increasingly confident of its social role and claimed rights regarding religion and belief, thus becoming the pool of opposition movements.[51] The Primate of Poland, Cardinal Stefan Wyszynski (1901–81), was the key figure in protecting the independence of the Church for several decades. The first half of the 1980s, an era of intensified social unrest, brought more vigorous acts of repression and the harassment of priests again, which provoked serious conflicts between the state and the Church. Their social embeddedness and high degree of organization enabled the Catholic Church to harbour many dissidents and play the role of a marginally tolerated opposition from time to time. The Church was able to draw on its past history of relative autonomy and the respect for the institution, which were deeply rooted in the past, when Catholicism became associated with the notion of national independence. The Church was also effectively supported by the Vatican (a factor obviously lacking in the case of Protestant churches in the region). In general, communist regimes were the least able to pacify the Catholic Church and they were more successful in eliciting the cooperation of Protestant churches, and even more so with Orthodox churches.[52]

Secularization

The horrors of the Second World War and the poverty and social problems of the years that followed it turned many people to religion again in European societies. The churches themselves also considered the lessons concerning their previous roles and attempted to direct their activities in ways that they thought more appropriate to the needs of society. They established organizations, including explicitly religious ones and others reaching out to wider strata of society. In this regard, the Second Vatican Council (1962–65), convened by Pope John XXIII (1958–63), was an event with decisive consequences. This council was crucial in modernizing Catholic doctrine and ritual practice, and in opening up the Church toward secular society and especially the world outside Europe.

However, neither the religious renewal nor the modernization efforts of churches were sufficient to halt the edging away of church from other social institutions or to stem the diminishing significance of religion as a source of individual identity in the post-war decades, that is, the process of secularization, already under way for a long time by then. This is not surprising insofar as the founding fathers of sociology, including Émile Durkheim and Max Weber, equally agreed that the significance of Christianity had already been waning around the turn of the century, and this view later turned dominant in Western social theory. During the 1960s, the secularization thesis became integrated into modernization theory, which diagnosed a decline of religious faith in the nineteenth and twentieth centuries in industrialized societies, and even assumed the continuation of this trend in the future.[53]

The most obvious indicator of the dynamics of secularization is the change in religious adherence and the ratio of those without religious affiliation. At the mid-century, the number of non-adherents was low everywhere in Southern and Western Europe. In 1960, only in France, the Netherlands and in the United Kingdom was the number of those not adhering to any denomination higher than the 0–5% observed elsewhere in Western and Southern Europe. In the following decades, a decline can be seen in every country in the numbers of those professing to be religious, except Norway and Greece, although considerable differences between societies prevailed regarding the dynamics of the change. In Belgium, France and Austria, the number of self-declared Roman Catholics dropped significantly in this period, whereas in Ireland, the change was only minimal. Protestant churches lost fewer adherents, except in the Netherlands, where low initial religious observance ratios diminished further, especially among Calvinists. In 1990, there were several countries (seven at least in Western and Southern Europe) with more than 5% of the population not adhering to any religion, and among them the Netherlands stood out, with 35% (Table 9.4).

Participation in church events requires the time and activity of the adherents and thus provides important information on the strength of belief and commitment to denominations. Several of these events mark important turning points or rites of passage in the individual's life (such as birth, adolescence, marriage, death), and they appear in similar forms not only in Christianity but in other religions as well. As regards baptism, data are available for only a few countries from the second half of the twentieth century, thus a comprehensive comparison cannot be attempted. Still, in Belgium, Roman Catholic parents christened 94% of their newborn children in 1960, but only 82% in 1990. A greater decline took place in the United Kingdom, where this ratio dropped from one-half to one-third of the infants of Anglican parents. In contrast, in Southern Europe, almost all children were baptised even at the end of the century. Similar tendencies are found for religious weddings, though, initial ratios themselves were lower. Still, in 1990 in most countries, half of the couples marked the beginning of their life together with a church service; the majority of couples did so in Southern Europe and in the Scandinavian countries (Table 9.5).

Because celebrating the above-mentioned events in the church can be a single, formal act, it is important to consider the frequency of attendance at religious services when determining the level of religious participation. The available data show significantly lower ratios in this regard both in the middle and at the end of the century than what was seen in the previous cases. In addition, there exists a marked gap between Catholic and Protestant communities in religious observance: the Catholic and Calvinist Church attract more attendances than the state churches of Anglicism in the United Kingdom and Lutheranism in Scandinavia. Outside France, at least one-third of the Catholics went to church once a month, and over one-fourth attended weekly even in 1990. What is more, more than half of the

TABLE 9.4 Declared religious adherence by the adult population in European countries, 1960–1990 (%)

	Year	Roman Catholic	Lutheran	Calvinist	Anglican	Other Protestant	Orthodox	Jewish	Islam	Hindu	Other	Without denomination and unknown
United Kingdom	1960	12.0		4.4	66.6	7.4	0.9	0.9	0.9	0.7	2.1	6.1
	1975	11.7		3.1	55.9	6.9	1.1	0.6	2.3	0.8	4.0	
France	1960	90.0		1.6			0.3	1.0	0.6		0.2	
	1990	67.0		1.7			5.2	1.6	7.8			7.9
Netherlands	1960	40.4		37.6								18.4
	1990	32.0		22.0		6.6			3.7	0.5	3.6	35.2
Belgium	1960	96.0										
	1990	65.0										
Ireland	1960	94.9			3.7	0.9		0.1			0.2	0.2
	1990	91.6			0.7	0.5		0.0				0.0
FRG	1960	44.1	50.5			3.1		0.1			1.3	0.9
	1990	41.6	42.9			0.6		0.1	2.7		2.0	8.0
Austria	1960	89.0	6.0								0.4	3.8
	1990	78.0	5.0	0.2		0.4		0.2			4.9	8.6
Switzerland	1960	45.4		52.7		0.5		0.4				1.0
	1990	40.0		46.1		2.1		0.3	2.2		0.4	7.4
Sweden	1960		98.3			2.0						
	1990	1.8	86.5			1.8						0.5
Denmark	1960		95.0									5.0
	1990	0.6	87.4			1.0		0.1			0.0	10.9
Norway	1960	0.2	96.2			2.7					0.6	0.2
	1990	0.7	95.3			1.0			0.5		0.5	0.1

TABLE 9.4 (continued)

	Year	Roman Catholic	Lutheran	Calvinist	Anglican	Other Protestant	Orthodox	Jewish	Islam	Hindu	Other	Without denomination and unknown
Finland	1960		92.4				1.4					6.2
	1990		88.0									
Italy	1960											
Spain	1981	93.0									1.0	6.0
	1960	99.9										0.1
	1990	86.0									1.0	13.0
Greece	1951	0.4				0.2	97.9	0.1				0.0
	1990						99.4		1.4		0.6	
GDR	1983	7.0	46.0									
Poland	1983	95.0										
Czech Republic	1983	70.0	10.0									
Hungary	1983	56.0	5.0	19.0								
Romania	1983	10.0					70.0					
Yugoslavia	1983	31.0					40.0		16.0			
Bulgaria	1983	1.0					70.0		10.0			

Notes: Czechoslovakia 1983: all Protestant churches together; East Germany 1983: all Protestant churches together.

Sources: Colin Crouch, *Social Change in Western Europe*, Oxford: Oxford University Press, 1999, 462–463 (Western Europe and Southern Europe); Joni Lovenduski and Jean Woodall, eds., *Politics and Society in Eastern Europe*, Bloomington: Indiana University Press, 1987, 333 (East Central Europe and Southern Europe).

TABLE 9.5 Changes in the ratio of baptisms and religious marriages in European countries, 1960–1990 (%)

	Denomination	Baptisms		Religious marriages	
		1960	*1990*	*1960*	*1990*
United Kingdom	Anglican	50.0	33.3	47.4	45.0
France	Roman Catholic	82.0	64.0	78.0	50.0
Netherlands	Roman Catholic			40.0	20.0
	Calvinist				3.0
Belgium	Roman Catholic	93.6	82.0	86.1	57.0
FRG	Roman Catholic		35.0	40.0	28.0
	Lutheran		35.0	38.0	25.0
Austria	Roman Catholic			75.0	55.0
Switzerland	Roman Catholic			55.0	38.0
	Calvinist			45.0	31.0
Sweden	Lutheran		72.0	94.0	72.0
Denmark	Lutheran	67.0	73.4		57.0
Norway	Lutheran			82.0	69.0
Finland	Lutheran	89.0	82.0		80.0
Italy	Roman Catholic		98.0	98.0	83.0
Spain	Roman Catholic		95.0		
Portugal	Roman Catholic		93.0		82.0
Greece	Greek Orthodox			100.0	91.5

Notes: The ratio of christened children to all children born; the ratio of religious marriages as proportions of total weddings.

Source: Colin Crouch, *Social Change in Western Europe,* Oxford: Oxford University Press, 1999, 267–268.

members of Catholic communities in Italy, Ireland and Great Britain did attend at least once a month. In contrast, except for the active Dutch Calvinists and Swiss Lutherans, only 10% of Protestants counted as regular church-goers (Table 9.6). Thus, in this regard the difference between the types of Christianity is greater than what surfaced for baptisms and weddings.

The proponents of the secularization theory refer to the above tendencies (that is, the long-term decline in religious practice and, in particular, church attendance) as major evidence of the process.[54] However, several researchers have questioned the classic interpretation of secularization, arguing that diminishing church attendance does not necessarily signal a real change in religious attitudes. The role of religion in the life of individuals and societies cannot be bound to activities that are historically specific. The frequency of church visits has undoubtedly decreased, but so did, in parallel, the participation in other, non-religious mass events. As the argument goes, people now follow these events, including church services, from their homes, on television, and also find other forms of practicing belief.[55]

Data on religious observation and the process of secularization in general must be interpreted with caution because the significance of specific activities or other phenomena may vary in the course of history and in different religions. For

TABLE 9.6 The frequency of attendance of religious services by denomination in European countries, 1960–1990 (%)

		1960				1990					
		Roman Catholic	Lutheran	Calvinist	Anglican	Roman Catholic	Lutheran	Calvinist	Anglican	Jewish	Islam
United Kingdom	Monthly	40.0				51.2			21.2		
	Weekly	20.0			15.0	14.9					
France	Monthly					25.4		5.0		22.0	10.0
Netherlands	Weekly	64.4		20.0		37.5		59.1			
	Monthly										
Belgium	Weekly	34.0				22.9					
	Monthly					47.7					
Ireland	Monthly					87.0					
FRG	Weekly					55.3	11.7				
	Monthly					40.9	14.0				
Austria	Weekly	34.5									
Switzerland	Weekly					33.0	33.0				
	Monthly										
Sweden	Monthly						11.6				
Denmark	Monthly		5.3				11.0				
Norway	Monthly						9.4				
Finland	Weekly		10.0								
	Monthly		5.0								
Italy	Weekly					35.0					
	Monthly					53.0					
Spain	Weekly					29.7					
	Monthly					38.7					
Portugal	Weekly	15.0									
	Monthly					36.9					

Source: Colin Crouch, *Social Change in Western Europe*, Oxford: Oxford University Press, 1999, 270.

Catholics, religious faith can be expressed only via the church, whereas for most Protestants, the role of the religious community is important, but not in the way or to the degree seen among Catholics, because in Protestantism the emphasis is on the relationship between the individual and God. Jan-Erik Lane and Svante O. Ersson, for example, found that to be a devout Catholic implied one church attendance a week, whereas for a Protestant believer one church attendance a month showed devoutness in most Western European countries in the last decades of the twentieth century.[56] Therefore the decline of church-going is a more sensitive indicator for Catholics than for Lutherans. This argument also supports the importance of asking for information on the intensity of religious belief and of adherence to one's church in surveys.[57]

The survey of the strength of religious belief does not only concern belief in God, but also faith in otherworldly phenomena important in Western Christianity, such as life after death or heaven. Long-term data available with respect to a few societies (the British, the French and the Dutch) showed that between 1947 and 2000, the ratio of those believing in God decreased, but the change was not dramatic and certainly was not linear. For instance, in France, the ratio of those who believed that God existed in some form began to rise in the middle of this period. As for faith in other types of phenomena, belief was weaker in these countries, but the available data do not support a claim of monotonous decrease in Southern or Western European societies. Rather, at the end of the century, a strengthening in different forms of religious belief can be found (Table 9.7).[58]

The advocates of the secularization thesis also point to other well-documented developments of the nineteenth-century and twentieth-century social history of industrialized countries. Religious institutions undoubtedly suffered a loss of social functions, including the expansion of secular institutions in the area of social protection and education. The official doctrines of the churches often diverged from popular opinions and behaviour, as shown by several plebiscites and other social developments. Despite the Catholic Church opposing the legalization of divorce, in Italy, a referendum endorsed it in 1974, and the same happened in the case of abortion in 1981. Divorce rates in Great Britain were among the highest in Europe in the decades after the Second World War, even though the Anglican Church gave up its disapproval of divorce only in the 1990s. Another telling example is that Spanish and Italian birth rates entered the group of the lowest figures in the continent by the end of the century, even though several indicators referred to above suggested that the social influence of the Catholic Church was relatively strong in these countries and the Church continued to oppose all forms of birth control. Ireland was the country where the majority of the population supported the stance of the Catholic Church in these issues the longest. For example, several popular votes rejected the legalization of abortion and the 'yes' votes in the 1997 referendum on divorce gained only a light majority, with 50.28%.

Secularization progressed considerably in East Central and South-Eastern Europe after the Second World War: all available data, such as the dropping frequency of church attendance or the lowering ratios of baptism, support this thesis. Religious indifference

TABLE 9.7 Religiosity in European countries, 1947–2000

Believing in (%)	UK				France				Netherlands				FRG			Belgium		Ireland		Spain		Denmark		Italy	
	1947	1968	1981	2000	1947	1968	1981	2000	1947	1968	1981	2000	1968	1981	2000	1981	2000	1981	2000	1981	2000	1981	2000	1981	2000
God	84	77	76	72	68	73	62	62	80	79	65	61	81	72	68	77	71	95	96	87	87	58	69	84	94
A soul			59	67			46				59			61		52		82		64		33		63	
Sin		38	69	58	59	35	42	40	38	50	49	40	41	59	41	44	44	85	86	58	51	29	21	63	73
Life after death	49		45	56		39	35	45		54	42	50	43	39	39	37	46	76	79	55	50	26	38	47	73
Heaven	54		57			17	27	31		29	39	37	25	31	31	33	34	83	85	50	51	17	18	41	59
The Devil	21		30			22	17			28	21		25	18		20		57		33		12		30	
Hell	23		27				15	20			15	14	25	14	20	18	19	54	53	34	33	8	10	31	49
Reincarnation	18		27			23	22			10	10		25	19		13		26		25		11		21	
Personal God			31				26				34			28		39		73		55		24		26	
Some sort of spirit or life force			39				26				29			40		24		16		23		24		50	
Don't really know what to think			19				22				17			17		15		6		12		22		11	
Don't think there is any sort of spirit, God or life force			9				19				12			13		8		2		6		21		6	

Source: Stephen Harding, David Phillips and Michael Fogarty, Contrasting Values in Western Europe: Unity, Diversity and Change, London: Macmillan, 1986, 46–47 (Western Europe 1947–1981); Grace Davie, Europe: The Exceptional Case – Parameters of Faith in the Modern World, London: Darton, Longman and Todd, 2002, 7 (Western Europe 2000).

in these regions reached its peak most probably in the 1970s, and from that time onwards, a moderate religious invigoration took place. At the same time, differences were large within the region and religious attitudes also showed substantial intergenerational differences. Religious adherence and participation became the lowest in Eastern Germany and Hungary by the end of the century, and they remained most intense in Poland. In the early 1990s in Hungary, the ratio of consistent believers (that is, those who are classified as adherents of churches from several aspects) among adults younger than forty years old was only 41.5% of the adherents among those sixty years old and older. In contrast, in Poland, the ratio of consistent believers among people under forty did almost equal the level found among over-sixties (90.1%). The great disparities within the region are also evidenced by a comparison of 13 Western and East Central European countries. Religious decline was by far the strongest in Hungary among these societies, whereas the ratio of adherents of the church in Poland decreased to a smaller degree than even that of Ireland's.[59]

The changes in the religious attitudes of the European population at the end of the twentieth century gave rise to two opposing interpretations. As Grace Davie claims, a mismatch between belief and religious practice emerged; religion as an institutional practice declined, but 'belief not only persists, but becomes increasingly personal, detached and heterogeneous particularly among young people'.[60] In other words, such attitudes prevailed that can be described with the notion of 'believing without belonging'.[61] Another view claims that the feeling of belonging to a religious community survived in large population groups in Europe, whereas the influence of church teachings on everyday life decreased considerably by the end of the twentieth century, and therefore the state of religion in Western Europe is best described by the phrase 'belonging without believing'.[62]

As shown above, proponents of both lines of argumentation can rely on empirical evidence to support their stance. The belief in God continues to characterize the majority of Europeans, and therefore it would be exaggerating to postulate the disappearance of belief. At the same time, it is also obvious that this belief is often fuzzy or diffuse and does not necessarily conform to the teachings of the church. As an observer of the French situation put it, belief is often transformed into 'religion à la carte' especially among the younger generations, and takes the form of an element of lifestyle, making it difficult to relate to any church and thus sustain and pass on one's religious faith to the next generations.[63]

Similarly, there is no doubt that the social influence of the churches declined in the second half of the twentieth century all over Europe, though it was still considerable at the end of the century. Especially in the Catholic countries, certain events of the individual's life, such as baptism and marriage, were unimaginable without church involvement for the vast majority of people. Churches were also important actors in education and the welfare systems. However, religious decline appears in a distinct perspective if we consider that secularization movements have been around for more than two centuries and that in the twentieth century several totalitarian regimes (both Nazi and communist ones) aimed at the annihilation of church and religion. It is remarkable that, in the course of the century, each regime of explicit atheism perished, and the manifestly anti-religious communist and socialist parties also began to decline or revise their attitudes towards the church from the 1960s in Western and Southern Europe. Thus, the losses of the radical proponents of secularization were greater than those of the churches at the end of the twentieth century. By then, the adversaries of the churches were no longer militant political movements or governments, instead originating from social indifference, which affected several other cultural, political and social organizations and institutions similarly.[64] Furthermore, it is notable that secularization does not appear to be an irreversible process. Religious subcultures, providing the main source of the reproduction of religion and churches, survived everywhere. In some countries, such as Denmark, the rising popularity of the church is seen in the last decades of the twentieth century. In others, including Italy, Portugal, West Germany and Austria, religious beliefs strengthened among the younger generations between 1981 and 1999.[65] A similar process took place before and especially after the collapse of communism in East Central and South-Eastern Europe. At the same time, the recurrent growth in religious adherence and participation could only compensate for some of the previous decline in these regions as well.

Causes and constraints of secularization

Classical secularization theories portray traditional institutionalized religions as flourishing mostly in pre-modern societies, before the emergence of science and under the conditions of predominantly agricultural production.[66] In his 1966 work on secularization, Bryan Wilson suggested that traditional values, beliefs and practices inevitably decline in modern societies. In industrial societies, there is no need any more for religion to help answer questions regarding the meaning of life, and churches lose several of their functions. These are replaced by spreading rationalism, science, and well-organized, differentiated and bureaucratized societies. Traditional thinking is more of an obstacle to, than an instrument of, solving modern social problems.[67] With regard to Europe, this argument undoubtedly has explanatory power, because the decline of the influence of the church proceeded in parallel with industrialization, urbanization and the progress of other components of modernization in ever newer regions. However, as seen above, the decline of religion was not a linear process, and outside Europe (such as in the United States and the Muslim world) the relation between the factors mentioned above cannot be observed.[68]

A more differentiated explanation was proposed by David Martin, which has already been evoked earlier in the chapter in several respects. As noted, he claimed that the main problems for European churches arose from their often strong relationship with the state. In order to survive, churches often sought or accepted political support from governments. However, the relationship was selective in the sense that the states and, with them, the churches formed stronger ties with particular social classes, milieus and geographical regions, whereas they neglected or discriminated against others. During the struggles for social emancipation and democracy, churches often sided with the elite and the old order. As a consequence, major segments of the population could not rely on the church and religion as a constituent factor of their social identity, and even turned hostile to them. In other words, this thesis insists that many social groups refused not religion itself but the association of religion with specific social preferences. In the United States, where no state church has existed, nor even an association between the state and the many small churches, the level of religious activity remained higher than in Europe.[69] Thus, the argument is appropriate to explain the progress of secularization in twentieth-century Europe, and its slower pace elsewhere. At the same time, it implies that the loosening of the link between religion and politics results in a growing influence of religious belief and the church, that is, the process of secularization is neither unilinear nor inevitable.[70]

Others pointed out that although religious and church activities declined, many people adhere to at least some elements of religion and spiritual beliefs in modern societies, despite the uninterrupted progress of science. The spread of religious sects did contribute to the fragmentation of churches, but this diffusion also reflects a continuous quest of humankind, the desire to find the meaning of life and eternal moral truths even in the highly materialistic Western societies. Furthermore, at the end of the twentieth century, scepticism for science also grew tangibly throughout Europe, which may facilitate a revival of religious life. Finally, the appearance and spread of Islam in Western Europe has already heightened attention to Christianity as a force shaping European identity, which leads us to the next theme of the chapter.[71]

Aspects of identity: nations, nationalisms and minorities

Identity is a fairly pervasive and contested aspect of culture. The concept of identity refers to the understanding that individuals and groups have about who they are. At the same time, it implies a differentiation from others; it has been suggested that it is boundaries that primarily define a group. Furthermore, identity formation is largely dependent on whether and how others acknowledge the distinctive characteristics of individuals or groups.[72]

Identities may take several forms and among the particular identity types a distinction is usually made between personal and social identities. Personal identity commonly relates to the special characteristics of an individual, including inherited or chosen values and physical traits. Social identity refers to an individual's social roles, such as gender, religious, ethnic, national, political or occupational group memberships. These roles and memberships usually imply that a person shares similarities with others, such as having the same language, culture, religion or social status. Usually several identities coexist, and one does not necessarily have to choose between them; however, some of these identities might be more important for the individual than others. In addition, social identities are historically conditioned, and subsequently underwent significant transformations in modern and contemporary Europe. This section cannot do justice to the full complexities of the subject. Rather, a historically eminent form of social identity is the focus, namely national identity and major aspects of its transformations in the continent during the twentieth century.

The nation: approaches in the literature

Traditionally, the concept of nation is attributed specific meanings in different cultures of Europe. In Western Europe, and especially in English-speaking and French-speaking countries, 'nation' encompasses everybody living in a bordered area and subject to the same government. Thus, here the concept has a primarily geographical and political meaning, and not an ethnic or a linguistic one, and its defining feature is the state as a political-territorial formation. The important characteristic of this understanding, as well as its wide diffusion in the twentieth century, is explicitly referred to and expressed by the use of 'nation' in the official name of the League of Nations, and later the United Nations, where membership was and is given exclusively to states; that is, nation and state were used as synonyms. In contrast, in Central and East Central Europe, and most notably in Germany, 'nation' is traditionally related to shared language and culture, as well as to common historical experience. The concepts of state and nation are separated from each other. The subjects of the state are those who hold citizenship, but the citizens of the state do not necessarily belong to the same nation. At the same time, members of a nation may live in several, neighbouring or even more distant states, independent of their citizenship. It must be noted that in recent decades the differences between the concepts of nation have faded, and the concept itself has become more complex. In Western Europe, ethnic and linguistic diversity and ambitions have gained importance again. In contrast, in Central Europe, the separate existence of the state emerged as a basis for national identity, independent of linguistic and cultural characteristics as exemplified by post-war German-speaking countries (Germany and Austria).[73]

The diverging public perceptions of nation in particular European societies obviously rendered any scholarly definition of the nation difficult, albeit arriving at a plausible scholarly agreement was not without major obstacles in other respects as well within this subject area. The systematic study of nation and national identity began in the mid-nineteenth century, and almost from the onset, there were two major strands in the research. One of the directions claimed that the nation was an objective entity, the characteristics of which can be studied empirically. These characteristics primarily included cultural and linguistic features, but also other factors, such as political links, territorial ties and economic relations.[74] As early as the beginning of the twentieth century, it became obvious that it was unfeasible to establish a universally relevant definition that would include all entities regarded as nations and that could be applied for all periods.[75] Therefore, the view emerged that there were different concepts of nation, such as the state-nation and the cultural nation mentioned before. The second major direction of research defined nation by subjective criteria: all those who were aware of their attachment to a nation and wished to belong to it were considered as members of that particular nation. In line with this concept, Ernest Renan regarded the existence of a nation as 'an everyday plebiscite' by the citizens concerning whether they want to be part of an existing national community.[76]

The fatal political consequences of nationalisms in the interwar period and during the Second World War had a profound impact on the study of nation and national identity. After the Second World War, the nation and nationalism were often presented as some kind of distortion that needed to be overcome or corrected, especially in Central and Eastern Europe. Some former research traditions also survived. The influence of both the war and the traditional state-nation and cultural-nation distinctions was obvious in the categorization that differentiated a rational, liberal, civic, constitutional and democratic 'Western' nationalism (France and Great Britain) from an irrational, mythical, illiberal, racist and authoritarian nationalism prevailing in Central and Eastern Europe but also in parts of Asia.[77] Even though most historians and social scientists continued to understand the nation as an objective entity, many researchers turned to a subjective concept again. The latter trend promoted an interest in nationalism because scholars could easily interpret this phenomenon as an ideology that facilitated the emergence and diffusion of the subjective feeling of belonging to a nation.[78]

As a result, in recent decades it has become customary to distinguish between two main interpretations of the historical development of nation and nationalism. One, the so-called modernist or constructivist paradigm, is based on the idea that the nation is a construct, an invention, and therefore the result of nationalism.[79] The other, the so-called primordialist school, considers the nation to be the product of an objective formative process.[80] For the modernists, the emergence of the nation is the result of the nationalist policy of the state, or, rather, the activity of the elites, who aim to secure their power through creating allegiance to the idea of the nation.[81] Moreover, modernization facilitated this endeavour: the shift from an agrarian to an industrial society is a process that demolishes old social hierarchies and commitments, and advances linguistic and cultural homogenization within the boundaries of the state. The homogenization furthers the emergence of industrial society because it makes workers' mobility and mass production possible. At the same time, the dissolution of old hierarchies and social ties creates a need for new relationships between the individual and the community. Nationalism serves the satisfaction of this need.[82] Therefore the nation and the myths and symbols evoking the emotions surrounding it can be seen as modern inventions.[83] Using Benedict Anderson's related phrase, nations are mere 'imagined communities'.[84] The history of nations reaches back to the times before the beginnings of modernization (in Europe, practically to the times before the nineteenth century); however, these antecedents are only of little importance regarding the emergence of modern nations when compared with the effects of modernization.

Primordialists refuse the equation of nation with modernity. Rather, they trace ethnic identity centuries back, if not millennia, even if not fully associating it with the modern notion of nation. In a classic formulation of this position, Clifford

Geertz identifies a chronic tension in the emerging modern states between the struggle for progress, associated with the modern civic state, and the need to maintain personal identity that is recognized as distinctive. The latter is considered to be a primordial sentiment, arousing, among others, from ties of language, region, culture and religion.[85] Primordialists insist that the key to the understanding of the emergence of the nation and the nation-state is the analysis of their historical roots. Myths, symbols and other phenomena related to nationalisms can be interpreted only in historical context. Only this procedure can explain why some forms of nationalism are virulent and aggressive, whereas others are not.[86]

As shown above, the antecedents of both scholarly approaches were present in the nineteenth century, and the borders between them began to disappear already in the early twentieth century. Proponents of the objectivist definition increasingly realized that a nation cannot exist without some form of national identity. At the same time, those focusing on subjective factors did not necessarily exclude the role of objective circumstances in the emergence of national identity either. Recently, Miroslav Hroch has also argued for the compatibility of the two approaches. In his view, when Ernest Gellner, as the best known representative of the modernists, claims that nationalism creates the nation, he simply shifts the causal explanation to a different level. From this point on, we should understand why nationalism could generate stronger or less pervasive mass effects, which is possibly only if we analyse objective social and cultural factors. Similarly, the 'invention' of national traditions and the formation of 'imagined communities' could take place only because specific social preconditions were present. Thus, the contrasting of the nation-formation process and nationalism (or the objective processes and subjective factors) is not inevitable when interpreting causal relationships. When taking all this into consideration, the differences between the two approaches do not seem to be dramatic. Rather, they lie in the diverging emphases placed on individual elements of the causal relationships.[87]

Nations and nation-states: trends in the twentieth century

In the nineteenth century, nation-state formation progressed considerably in Europe but was only partially completed. The German and the Italian unifications were accomplished and Belgium, Greece, Bulgaria and Romania, along with Norway, became independent as well. Yet at the beginning of the twentieth century, a few nations existed without their own state. Except for Italy, in each of the European great powers, several nations coexisted. In the course of the twentieth century, Europe made further steps towards the realization of the political self-determination of ethnic groups.

Nationalism as the instrument of national self-assertion diffused all over Europe in the nineteenth century, and it either gradually took over a considerable amount of the integrative role of religion and dynastic loyalty or, on the contrary, it played a disintegrative role in society. The integrative role itself was ambiguous. On the one hand, the principles of the nation–state and nationalisms alike carried emancipatory and democratic potential. On the other hand, they occasionally also had major oppressive and aggressive potential. The significance of national identity and nationalisms in contrast to other identities and ideologies was apparent already in the early period of the First World War, when governments all over Europe were able to mobilize such social groups for national objectives (most notably organized labour) that previously had seemed immune to nationalisms. The idea that all sizeable ethnic groups have a right to their own states gained ground during the war. Five of the famous fourteen points of Woodrow Wilson, the President of the USA, targeted the realization of national self-determination, although they were implemented selectively at the peace settlements ending the First World War.

The treaties after the war did indeed take important steps in that direction even if they also created new contradictions.[88] In Europe, outside Russia, before the First World War there were eleven ethnic groups with a considerable population size and highly developed national identity, but lacking their own state or an acceptable degree of autonomy that would include the whole group, namely Albanians, Basques, Bretons, Catalans, Croatians, the Czech, the Irish, the Polish, Slovaks and the Welsh. After the First World War, most of them established their own states, with the exception of Basques, Bretons, Catalans and the Welsh. In 1910, before the two Balkan wars, there were three nations on the continent the majority of whose members did not live in their respective nation-states, but in different other states: most of the Greeks, the Serbians and the Romanians were living under either the Ottoman or the Habsburg empires. Regarding these two empires, in each case the ruling nation was in fact a minority within the whole population of the lands they ruled. After the First World War, no nation still lived under these conditions any more. Likewise, by 1920, no empire or other bordered entity existed any more in Europe in which the largest nation occupied the position of a relative minority.

The primary means of realizing national self-determination was the redrawing of borders, but the creation of homogeneous nation-states was also promoted by population exchange. After the First World War, the changing borders affected 36 million people in the former Austro-Hungarian monarchy, 6.5 million in Germany, 6 million in Turkey and 3 million in the United Kingdom (Ireland). About 2 million people were affected by population exchange, which took place in the highest proportions between Greece and Turkey as well as Greece and Bulgaria. Consequently, after the First World War, peoples' right for self-determination was considered to a greater degree in the peace talks than later, after the Second World War. In a few cases (for example, in Northern Schleswig, Masuria, Upper Silesia, Southern Carinthia and the Sopron region) referenda were held, although this was considered an exceptional measure even at that time. Nevertheless, as a result of new borders and population exchange, the ratio of nations without state or a reasonable degree of self-government decreased considerably.[89]

However, the state borders delineated after the First World War were still questionable in several respects. On the one hand, especially in East Central Europe, it was sometimes impossible to draw borders in territories of highly ethnically mixed populations in a way that would result in ethnically homogeneous states. An even greater problem was that the victorious countries often denied the right of self-determination to the nations of the defeated states even if it could have been implemented. In the course of establishing the new borders, the greatest anomalies arguably occurred in the case of Hungary, because several of the territories populated largely, or even exclusively, by Hungarians were annexed to neighbouring countries by the new borders. Similar border issues emerged between Poland and Lithuania, as well as Italy and Slovenia/Yugoslavia. Thus, despite the redrawing of borders, several ethnic groups lived in the territories of the newly created or re-established states. In Poland and Romania, the Polish and the Romanians amounted to only two-thirds of the whole population. Furthermore, in Czechoslovakia and Yugoslavia (the Kingdom of Serbs, Croats and Slovenes until 1929) not only were there considerable ethnic groups, there also existed several nations that constituted the state itself.

Thus, one of the most important sources of political conflict in interwar Europe was the ethnic problem. Although the peace treaties defined the obligation to respect minority rights, these hardly came to any effect, especially in South-Eastern Europe. Former minorities, newly risen to the status of constituting a nation state, often used greater discrimination against their own present minorities than they had had to endure in the Austro-Hungarian monarchy and elsewhere. It would have been the obligation of the League of Nations to guard the clauses of the peace treaties protecting the minorities, but there were neither means nor will to do so. The new states enforced assimilation policies. Because the new borders replaced old ones that had not been changed for hundreds of or even almost a thousand years, contemporaries often could not regard the changes as final, and those suffering national grievances were expecting the opportunity for revision.

The assertion of national interests at the expense of other nations was not only present in the activities of the victorious countries during the peace talks. It was observable also in the practices rooted in economic nationalism, such as high import taxes, and the introduction of import restrictions in East Central European states in the 1920s and 1930s, which replaced rational economic exchange and cooperation.[90] The destructive potentials of nationalism in their most obvious form surfaced in the Fascist movements and National Socialism. These reached extremities in placing the nation into the centre of their political doctrine. Especially in the case of National Socialism, the definition of nation relied heavily on racial features, and the idea that these could provide the foundation for a hierarchy among nations, that is, that there were superior races and nations and inferior, less worthy ones. This idea, originating in social Darwinism, was not novel, but was represented more consistently than ever before and thus became the basis of an aggressive and expansive foreign policy and the persecution of other races and nations.

After the Second World War, Europe continued in the direction of nation-states, but taking different routes than after the First World War. The ratio of nations and minorities without their independent nation-state or autonomy further decreased. However, whereas between 1913 and 1923, the redrawing of borders was the main means, now, after the Second World War, it was the large-scale relocation of ethnic populations, or, to use a phrase from the end of the twentieth century, ethnic cleansing. As a result of the post-war settlements, about 20 million people were relocated, roughly half of whom were Germans. The large-scale population movement after the Second World War is discussed in chapter 2.

During the Second World War, the crimes committed in the name of the nation also discredited the nation-state to a considerable degree. In Western Europe, the idea of addressing a number of economic and political problems in the continent by creating supranational institutions that transcend national boundaries gained wide popularity. The realization of these ambitions primarily targeted economic integration, but obviously needed the political cooperation of the participating states as well.

Although the EC and its predecessor institutions initially encompassed only six countries, they brought about great changes in Europe even in the short run. Former rivalry between nations and aggressive nationalisms, present most of all in the French–German relationship, were replaced by a climate of cooperation. All this did not mean the disappearance of the pursuit of national interests at the European level. As Alan Milward argued, it was exactly Western European integration that could guarantee the survival of the crisis-stricken framework of the nation-state in the long run.[91] However, a clear sign of the changes was that during the economic depression of the 1970s, Western European countries did not search for recovery within narrowly defined national frameworks and at the expense of other nations, as they had done during the years of depression between the World Wars. Rather, they continued and soon deepened their economic cooperation, which helped to escape the economic turmoil.

In the communist countries, internationalism rose to the level of official ideology: this initially meant a realization of Soviet interests for most of them. However, in Yugoslavia, the notion of a national way of socialism appeared early, and later other countries also began to discuss national peculiarities among the reasons why deviating from the Soviet model was justified. As regards foreign policy, Albania and, to a smaller extent, Romania also distanced themselves from the Soviet Union. However, except for Yugoslavia, differences were moderate only in the handling of the issues of nation and nationality. Because of the mandate to prosecute nationalism, expressions of national sentiment by minorities were usually repressed. In other respects, internationalism did not prohibit the emergence or even encouragement of national sentiments provided that these inclinations conformed to the internal and foreign policy of the communist party. Thus, with the exception of East Germany, national identity proved to be a major factor of social cohesion and an origin of political loyalty in European communist countries, but a disintegrative force in other periods (a problem that is discussed later).[92]

Ethnic problems after the Second World War

The scale of post-war ethnic problems compared with the first half of the century was undoubtedly smaller in Europe. As a result of the developments discussed above, the number of those living in minority decreased, and the Second World War discredited national aspirations for years to come, making supranational institutions appear more desirable. Also, the antagonism of the superpowers left little room for the ambitions of smaller nations for self-determination; any change in the status quo was considered futile and even hazardous because it endangered the balance between the military blocs. In the eastern and southern regions of Europe, dictatorial regimes did not allow any space for the explicit articulation of national aspirations.

However, this did not mean that national minorities would have fully given up their ambitions for independence or autonomy. After the Second World War, there still lived about 6 million people in minority status in Europe, and their situation as regards self-determination and autonomy deteriorated compared with the pre-war conditions. This affected mostly Hungarians, Turks and Germans, but there were other, long-persisting and newly arising ethnic concerns as well. Following Jaroslav Krejci, the ethnic problems in Europe after the Second World War can be categorized into four groups.[93]

1. In the post-war decades, there existed six ethnic groups in Europe that did not have any state or self-government (even if only until the 1970s for some of them), despite their considerable population size and despite their occupying a compact territory as a result of which granting their self-government would have been a realistic option. These groups included the Alsatians, Basques, Bretons, Catalans, Corsicans and the Welsh, approximately 13 million people altogether in the 1970s. All these minorities lived in nation-states of great historical past and with old, solid borders (that is, France, Spain and Great Britain), which made it difficult for them to aspire to self-government. More importantly, the English, French and Spanish languages and cultures in general occupy a unique position in Europe, because they are extremely rich and attractive. These countries also have remarkable economic potential. Therefore the emancipation of the Bretons or Basques seemed unreasonable or even absurd to many. In Wales, it was an obstacle to gaining autonomy that at least three-fourths of the population of this ethnic group did not speak Welsh, only English. Thus their national identity was a kind of a mixture of Welsh and British elements. Still, the law guaranteeing the wide use of the Welsh language was passed in 1967 and later autonomy was granted as well. The Basques and Catalans had enjoyed small-scale autonomy for a few years in the 1930s, at the time of the republic. At the end of the Franco era, a little progress occurred as regards language rights, which were further widened in 1975. In 1977, Catalonia and in 1980, the Basque Country received wide territorial autonomy. However, in the latter, ETA (*Euskadi Ta Askatasuna* [Basque Homeland and Freedom]), a long-existing armed underground organization, continued its activities in order to fight for full independence.

Gaining similar autonomies was the most difficult in France, where the Breton, Corsican and Alsatian languages were held to be only dialects even at the end of the twentieth century and their use was neglected in schools and in public administration alike. In France, the revival of Corsican nationalism took place in the 1960s after Algerian French emigrants had arrived in the island. The emigrants occupied key positions in the local economy, which the indigenous Corsicans found to be unjust; as a result, they began to take steps for their own self-government.[94] However, granting the autonomy rights of the minorities referred to above was hardly compatible with the concept of the nation and political traditions prevailing in France, and therefore this did not occur by the end of the century or even beyond.

2. Another group included ethnic minorities that enjoyed a certain degree of self-government but were not content with these rights. In Western Europe, Scotland belonged to this category, the claims of which were based on a long historical tradition. Focusing its programme on Scottish autonomy, the Scottish National Party achieved major success for the first time at elections in the 1970s, when the large oil reserves discovered off the Scottish coast transformed the attitudes of many locals towards England. None of the British parties opposed the gradual widening of Scottish autonomy, but in 1979, the local referendum to approve it did not reach the required high participation level and was thus unsuccessful. After another, successful referendum in the 1990s, Scotland's independence increased significantly, and (as a major stage of the devolution process in the United Kingdom) an independent parliament was formed in 1999.

In many respects Yugoslavia had the most intricate ethnic relationships in Europe after the Second World War. Its nations had belonged to several states in the course of history and even in the early twentieth century, including the Ottoman Empire, Hungary and Austria. In addition, there were three major religious groups within its borders, namely Greek Orthodox, Catholic and Muslim. Yugoslavia comprised six federal states (Serbia, Croatia, Bosnia and Herzegovina, Slovenia, Macedonia, and Montenegro) and from 1945, Vojvodina and Kosovo enjoyed a limited autonomy. From 1974, these regions obtained more extensive autonomy and even became subjects of the Yugoslav Federation, preserving their status until 1989. Five different languages were spoken in the country (Serbo-Croatian, Slovenian, Macedonian, Albanian and Hungarian), but Serbs used Cyrillic whereas Croatians had the Latin alphabet, which presented yet another linguistic divide. The national and cultural diversity was coupled with extreme and often widening gaps in social and economic development. In 1975, the per capita GDP was six times higher in Slovenia than in Albanian-populated Kosovo, whereas the ratio of population growth in Kosovo was six times higher than in Slovenia, which was the result of a significant post-war divergence between the two regions in both respects.[95] The striking differences functioned as a centrifugal force. The cohesion was meant to be strengthened by institutions such as the unified Communist Party, and by a distinct Yugoslavian identity, sometimes even called Yugoslavian nationalism. This did not replace Slovenian, Croatian and other national identities in the country; rather, it complemented and partly counterbalanced them. In shaping and sustaining the unified Yugoslavian identity, the feeling of outside threats contributed considerably. The threat came from Soviet supremacist ambitions, which affected all communist countries and which Yugoslavia opposed from the late 1940s on. In addition to national aspirations, economic and social disparities, the ceasing of the Soviet threat, which was clearly manifest in the 1980s, facilitated the disintegration of the country. From the early 1990s, Yugoslavia gradually fell apart. This process was paralleled by bloody conflicts unseen in Europe since the end of the Second World War, mostly in Bosnia and Herzegovina, in certain regions of Croatia and in Kosovo.

In Czechoslovakia the almost complete post-war expulsion of the considerable body of ethnic Germans and the cleansing of a smaller number of ethnic Hungarians did greatly diminish ethnic heterogeneity. Nevertheless, Slovakian-Czech disagreement did not cease. Dividing the country into two republics of equal rights, the Czech and the Slovak Republics, in 1968 provided an acceptable framework for the unity of the state, but, after the regime change, proponents of independence gained ground, especially in Slovakia, and in 1992, two independent countries were created.

In Belgium, after the establishment of the state in 1830, the dominant language was French, spoken by the Walloon population, as well as the elites of the nineteenth-century industrialization who dominated public life, and the speakers of the regional Flemish dialects were at an acute disadvantage. The ratio of the Walloon and the Flemish populations was roughly equal at the beginning of the twentieth century, but then differing fertility levels gradually shifted the balance in favour of the Flemings, and gradually the Flemish national identity emerged, which was also facilitated by the economic emancipation of Flanders because of its faster growth. As a result of the growing divergences within the country and the waning of the Belgian national elite, conflicts began to sharpen over the language issue. Then, a long process of reform began to overcome the conflicts between Flemings and French speakers, because, specifically, a Walloon identity has not fully emerged alongside the Flemish identity. Rather, a Belgian Francophone identity has evolved, nurtured primarily by the linguistic conflict with the Flemings. To minimize tensions, in 1962–63, the country was divided into four linguistic regions, the full implementation of which took a further decade.[96] In the mid-1970s, the Flemish area was home to about 56% of the population, the French speaking Wallonia to 32%, the German-speaking region to 1% and the bilingual capital and the surrounding areas to 11%. In addition, the borders within Belgium became not simply linguistic but also political and administrative. Wallonia and Flanders gained considerable autonomy, and although their rivalry continued, the status quo was questioned only by a minority on either side. This situation began to change after the turn of the millennium, when conflicts between the two sides sharpened and even led to serious deadlocks in the functioning of governments.

3. Yet another type is constituted by ethnic groups living contiguously in specific territories which were, without their consent, separated from the body of their main national group so that they became citizens of other nation-states.[97] Several such ethnic minorities existed in interwar Europe, but their number dropped significantly after the Second World War. The largest of these groups remained the Hungarians (about 3 million). The majority became Romanian citizens, living

partly in one block by the Hungarian border and partly in the mixed population regions of Transylvania as well as in an ethnically rather homogeneous enclave, Székely Land. In the latter, an autonomous region was created after the Second World War that existed until 1956. After the termination of autonomy, the conditions for the Hungarian minority worsened with regard to language use, cultural activities and education; this situation deteriorated even further in the final years of the Ceauşescu regime. A considerably smaller Hungarian population lived in Czechoslovakia, the Soviet Union, Yugoslavia and their respective successor states. Concerning the use of language and education, the rights of the Hungarian and other minorities were the widest in Yugoslavia in the post-war era.

The other major minority groups in East Central and South-Eastern Europe included Germans (in Poland, Romania, Czechoslovakia and Yugoslavia) and Turks (in Bulgaria, Greece and Yugoslavia). After the expulsions following the Second World War, the decline of the German population in the region took a momentum in the 1970s and 1980s, because the Polish and then the Romanian governments agreed to let their ethnic German citizens emigrate more freely, in return for the economic compensations offered by West Germany, such as preferential credits and per capita payment after those allowed to emigrate from Romania.[98] These population movements are considered in chapter 2.

The longest-running and hottest ethnic conflict in Europe after the Second World War emerged in Northern Ireland. The province was established as a result of pressure from British Unionists who refused to belong to Ireland as it gained independence in 1920. The borders between the two Irelands were not delineated to correspond to the ethnic and religious composition; instead they were drawn according to the preferences of Great Britain. Consequently, there remained a considerable Irish population in Northern Ireland. The Protestants managed most of the economy and housing, and discriminated against the Catholic minority, which comprised about one-third of the population. Catholics suspected that this Protestant policy would change the status quo as well. Because ethnic and religious identities merged in the case of the opposing parties, a tension that was difficult to handle emerged, leading to almost war-like conditions at times. Negotiations to resolve the conflict led to partial results in the 1990s, including the announcement of a cessation of military operations by the IRA (Irish Republican Army) in 1994. This has not proved to be lasting and negotiations produced several stalemates; still, the conflict in Northern Ireland was relieved significantly after the turn of the millennium.

Yet another ethnic conflict occurred in South Tyrol, surfacing more acutely after the war but controlled more successfully. The territory, populated partly by Germans and formerly under Austrian rule, was annexed to Italy in 1919. The Italianization measures initiated under Fascism aimed at changing the region's ethnic composition and fuelled local hostility toward the Italian state. After the Second World War, Austria wished a part of the region to be returned, but was unsuccessful in its efforts. In 1948, the combined region of Trentino and South Tyrol received an autonomous status. German became the second official language and German-language education was allowed once more. However, because the combined region had an Italian dominance, the self-government of the German minority could not materialize, leading to strong dissatisfaction among South Tyroleans and even to terrorist incidents. The *Südtirolfrage* (South Tyrol question) was largely resolved by a new autonomous status introduced from 1972 onwards, which granted further rights to the region and the German-speaking population, including language rights and financial self-governance.

Even though many of the Albanians living in Kosovo felt repressed and discriminated in Yugoslavia after the Second World War, they did not put forward strong claims for secession for a long time. The Serb-dominated police prevented such actions, and prospects improved when a relatively wide cultural autonomy of Kosovo within Yugoslavia was recognized in the 1974 constitution. Albania, with its extreme regime of oppression, has not attracted the Kosovo Albanians, and Albania itself did not support aspirations for secession, either, because similar to Yugoslavia, the country followed policies considered dissident among communist countries and felt threatened by Soviet ambitions.[99] After the death of Marshal Tito, autonomy was restricted and Kosovo was soon fully integrated into Serbia. This turn became all the more irritating for Albanians, because their relative size in the Kosovo population had increased from about 70% in 1946 to about 90% in the 1980s. Tensions increased during the Bosnian War and violence spread over to Kosovo. To prevent the escalation of hostilities NATO launched a military campaign of air strikes against Serbia. Under these circumstances, Albanians felt encouraged to set up political institutions, initially with limited scope, then, in 2000, aiming at full independence.

Several other ethnic minorities also existed in post-Second World War Europe, such as Slovenians in Austria, Turks in Greece, Sorbs in East Germany and Swedes in Finland. The Romani, living in the largest numbers in East Central Europe and South-Eastern Europe, can also be classified as belonging to this type. Because of their specific lifestyle and sociocultural background, their assimilation was mostly unsuccessful, even though they gradually gave up a nomadic life. Because they belonged to the most disadvantaged social groups in every society, and they mostly spoke the language of the majority with all its implications to identity formation, the Roma problem was most often seen as social issue, not primarily an ethnic one. Because their fertility was higher everywhere than that of the neighbouring nationalities, the social inclusion of the Roma population had become one of the most important objectives of public policy in several countries of the region by the turn of the millennium.

4. Finally, ethnic problems also arose as a consequence of migration processes (within Europe as well as targeting Europe from other continents) in the second half of the century. Because migration is discussed in chapter 2, only selected aspects related to the present subject are outlined here.

After the Second World War, the first wave of refugees arriving in Western Europe from communist countries did not cause any ethnic problems because their numbers were small and their assimilation into the receiving societies progressed rapidly.

Immigration from colonies or former colonies to the 'mother' countries followed rather different paths. Great Britain treated the colonial population generously for a long time as far as immigration was concerned. Other countries, such as France, granted citizenship based on a hybrid system of rights, including elements of both descent and territorial principles, but still, it was relatively easy to obtain citizenship for children of immigrants. It was more difficult to obtain citizenship in Germany, where citizenship law was based on the principle of descent. From the 1960s, the countries with the most permissive regulation tightened citizenship laws, but still offered relatively favourable conditions for immigration for people from their former colonies. For Great Britain and the Netherlands, the numbers arriving from the colonies were especially high, but this movement also affected France, Italy and Portugal. In Great Britain and the Netherlands, racial, cultural and religious tolerance had long traditions, and thus in these, at least until the final decade of the century, immigration created little friction. The first to arrive to France and Portugal were mainly returning settlers and descendants of settlers, which also diminished the difficulties of their integration. However, in time, in most countries of Western and Southern Europe, other forms of overseas migration, most eminently economic and political migration, grew in scale, and, as a combined effect, conflicts of ethnic character became more vigorous.

Although in Germany, it was not easy for those without German ancestry to obtain citizenship, remarkably, it was here where the most foreigners lived at the end of the twentieth century. This was the result of partly a generous German asylum policy toward political refugees, and partly, and more importantly, the country being an attractive destination for economic migrants, including guest workers. As shown in the section on migration in chapter 2, guest workers arrived in several other countries in Western Europe from the Mediterranean in the prosperous post-war decades and at first mostly returned to their homelands. However, from the 1980s, Turkish, Algerian, Moroccan and other guest workers increasingly opted for settling down with their families in the host countries.[100]

Overseas migration has never proceeded without social frictions; however, it led to the emergence of more serious ethnic conflicts in most Western and Southern European countries by the end of the century, especially because assimilation was making only little progress for a series of reasons, including the hardships of the labour market, and the markedly diverging sociocultural background of the immigrants. Nevertheless, the differences were great within Western Europe in this regard. In Sweden, the assimilation of immigrants proceeded with relatively few problems mainly as a result of systematic governmental efforts of inclusion, whereas in France, it escalated into a considerable social problem, offering a starting point for the most massive anti-immigration political movement in Western Europe.[101]

Nations and nation-states at the turn of the millennium

In the last decade of the twentieth century, the number of European nation-states grew considerably. Disregarding the Soviet successor states, there exist half a dozen more states now than a decade and a half ago, primarily as a consequence of the dissolution of Yugoslavia. This process was not restricted to Europe, because the number of the member states of the United Nations has been continually increasing. At the end of the twentieth century, nationalisms revived in several regions of Europe, especially in the Balkans. The nation obviously remained an important institution and reference point for identity formation, even in recent Europe.[102]

At the same time, it is obvious that contemporary nation-states and concepts of nation undergo many major changes. Most eminently, the process of growing interdependence or globalization presents considerable challenges to nation-states. The power of the governments of nation-states originates in an almost unrestrained control of bordered political space, which also established the basis for national and ethnic identity. This system, sometimes called the system of territoriality, had fully developed by around 1860 and prevailed in most of the twentieth century, but began to decompose in the 1960s and continued to erode in the following decades.[103] The change has primarily surfaced in economic issues. In parallel with the expansion of economic relations, a growing proportion of economic decisions affecting national interests are not made within the competence of the nation-state any more, but in centres outside the control of nation-states, or in other nation-states commanding greater power to realize their interests in economic policy. New actors have also appeared on the international scene. In addition to the classic international organizations with nation-states as members, multinational companies and non-governmental organizations clearly gained significance. Some authors also count international terrorist and criminal groups as belonging to actors putting constraints on the authority of governments.

All this has great influence on the legitimization and the viability of the nation-state. Citizens of individual countries expect the representation of their interests primarily from their own governments, and these governments have fewer means than before to realize their objectives. At the same time, it is important to note that globalization has been unfolding mostly as a result of decisions made within the competence of nation-states, such as enabling an easier movement of capital. Furthermore, globalization has been progressing in different ways and at diverging paces in particular social and economic areas. For example, in jurisdiction, it hardly touched the competence of nation-states.

European economic integration is a process similar to globalization in several respects, but one controlled by nation-states to a higher degree. In the course of European unification, nation-states gradually liberalized trade, the movement of capital and finally the movement of labour. All this has become the most advanced form of supranational integration in the world, which, as Alan Milward argued, largely contributed to the consolidation of European nation-states after the Second World War, and can be seen as the answer that European nation-states gave to the challenge of globalization.[104] From this aspect, it is characteristic that the member states of the EU, although implementing large-scale economic integration, have been anxiously guarding their sovereignty in other areas such as education, which are fundamental in preserving national identity.

Despite the revival of national sentiments in some regions, nationalism on the whole has weakened in Western and Southern Europe in recent decades. Studies show that 'national pride', which researchers consider to be one of the indicators of nationalist sentiments, has been significantly moderated since the 1980s. Of the Europeans asked in 1982, 41% said that they were proud of their nationality, and in 1994, only 28% felt the same way. Only citizens of Ireland and Greece (and Poland in East Central Europe) preserved relatively high levels of national pride (Table 9.8).[105] However, the formation of European identity did not progress in a parallel way, even if it significantly diffused between 1970 and 2000 in most countries.[106]

Globalization is often considered to be a threat to the nation-states, which leads to their disintegration and to new regimes of supranational integration. As another possible developmental route, it was proposed that nationalist and protectionist defensive mechanisms would gain dominance in the threatened nation-states. From this perspective, European institutions of integration offer an alternative by preserving major elements of the sovereignty of the nation-state and addressing the need for the creation of economic units transcending national borders.

TABLE 9.8 Changes in national pride in Europe, 1970–1990 (%)

	1970	*1980*	*1990*
Great Britain		53	53
France	66	31	35
Netherlands	54	20	23
Belgium	70	29	31
Ireland		67	77
FRG	38	21	17
Austria			53
Sweden		30	41
Denmark		30	42
Norway		41	45
Finland			38
Italy	62	40	40
Spain		51	45
Portugal		33	42
Greece		76	72
GDR			29
Poland			69
Czechoslovakia			25
Hungary		67	47
Bulgaria			39

Notes: The percentage of respondents answering 'very proud' to the question targeting their attitudes to their national belongings. Different dates: Greece 1983, 1985.

Sources: Ronald Inglehart, *Culture Shift in Advanced Industrial Society*, Princeton: Princeton University Press, 1990, 411 (1970–1980); *World Values Survey, 1990–1991*, Question 322, www.worldvaluessurvey.org (1990).

Values of the turn of the millennium: post-materialism and individualism

Values, often called social or cultural values, are cultural principles expressing what is considered to be good and desirable, and what is recognized to be bad and rejected.[107] The judgements of what is desirable surface in individual preferences, but specific values are also shared by groups and societies. Values are often distinguished from attitudes: attitudes are manifestations of values, but values are strong, mostly stable even if not necessarily conscious, whereas attitudes are temporary, often shifting views or opinions. Thus, research generally focuses on the changes in values. At the same time, values are more difficult to study directly; they are mostly identified through attitudes; this is why we do not strictly differentiate them in the discussion that follows. Furthermore, values are not identical with norms, which are the behavioural rules of a society and adherence to which is generally sanctioned. Norms appear in more practical ways than the more abstract values and tend to conform behaviour and commitments to the values expressed. Individuals learn both values and norms in the process of socialization, which encompasses all influences from the outside world and the social environment, including the family and formal education, the work environment as well as the political life and the media. Therefore, values have great significance when studying twentieth-century social transformations. On the one hand, they are important determinants of the social behaviour of the individuals, and, on the other, they link the individuals and social change. In the following discussion, the main trends in value orientations are discussed in Europe in the last decades of the twentieth century.

Materialism and post-materialism

The most systematic comparative analysis of the value changes occurring in Western industrial societies after the Second World War was carried out by Ronald Inglehart and his colleagues. Inglehart identified the major thrust of the process in a shift from materialist to post-materialist values, which he called a 'silent revolution'.[108] He maintained that the social changes following the Second World War (especially increasing economic prosperity, improving opportunities to gain education, widening access to information and relative international stability) transformed the value orientations of extensive groups of the population in Western societies. The values of the population have been shifted from a strong emphasis on material well-being and physical security toward a new set of preferences, in which individual freedom and self-expression, new ways of participating in public life and the quality of life in general were prominent. Inglehart explained the value change primarily through two hypotheses. The first proposes that the priority of values is determined by relative scarcity. Human needs have a hierarchy, and people tend to first satisfy material needs and those related to physiological necessities, such as shelter and food. When this is achieved, the satisfaction of further, higher-order wants becomes possible, such as social and cultural needs, or what Abraham Maslow called 'self-actualization needs'. After the Second World War, an unprecedented large proportion of the Western population grew up under conditions of economic prosperity and existential security. Already satisfied material needs gave way to the satisfaction of non-material needs. By itself, this is not enough for an appropriate explanation of long-term value changes, which made it necessary for Inglehart to introduce the socialization hypothesis as well, proposing that the most important value priorities are formed in youth, in the first two decades of life. Values firmly rooted in youth change little over the life span, and thus these serve as points of reference later when judging social and political phenomena. Therefore the generations born and growing up during the Second World War and the immediately following period of distress and insecurity, would hold material values significantly more important than those born in the period of relative material security, who, in turn, are characterized by a reverence of post-materialist values.[109]

Inglehart also developed an indicator (the post-materialist values index) to assess differences in value orientations over time and between societies. It also provides a more accurate account of the respective dispositions of the materialist and post-materialist types. This index is constructed on the basis of how people rank different values as regards their perceived importance. Materialist values include, for example, a high rate of economic growth, maintaining order in the nation, the stability of prices, guaranteeing the safety of the country by a strong army, and the fight against crime. Post-materialist values include giving citizens more say in important government decisions, progress towards greater influence of employees on decisions at the workplace, the protection of freedom of speech, the protection of the man-made and natural environment, the move towards a society where ideas are more important than money, and international cooperation.[110] Inglehart and his colleagues later modified the approach, but the change concerned less the substance than the terminology, because they replaced the materialist/post-materialist dichotomy with the survival and self-expression dimensions complemented by the traditional/religious and the rational/secular dimensions, already referred to when discussing the changes in religious dispositions.[111]

As to the dynamics of changes, the shift between post-materialist and materialist values began in the 1960s and proceeded slowly in Western societies. Between 1970 and 1990, the ratio of those preferring materialist values dropped from approximately 40% to 25% in the Western countries, whereas the share of those embracing post-materialist values rose from 10% to 20% on the average. The remaining proportion of the population could not be classified unambiguously because their responses were not consistent. When analysing the temporal changes more closely, it appears that until about the early 1970s, significantly more people were materialist, but the ratio was gradually decreasing. In the mid-1970s, the importance of material values increased again for the respondents, but already from the late 1970s, the former, declining trend returned. In the mid-1980s, the ratios of those with materialist and with post-materialist values stabilized at around similar levels with respect to the whole of Western and Southern Europe (Table 9.9).

TABLE 9.9 The ratio of those with post-materialist value orientation among the adult population in European societies, 1970–2000 (%)

	Approximately 1970	Approximately 1980	Approximately 1990	Approximately 2000
Great Britain	8	14	19	19
France	12	20	25	18
Netherlands	13	20	34	23
Belgium	14	13	24	22
FRG	8	20	28	17
Austria	5		26	28
Ireland	8	9	19	13
Sweden		13	23	
Denmark	7	28	16	11
Norway		9	10	
Italy	9	10	24	28
Spain		10	21	18
GDR/FRG Eastern prov.			23	12
Poland		16		
Hungary		3		

Note: Periods for Western European data may be different from the years indicated in the table.

Source: Russell J. Dalton, 'Vergleichende Werteforschung', in Dirk Berg-Schlosser and Ferdinand Müller-Rommel, eds., *Vergleichende Politikwissenschaft,* Wiesbaden: VS Verlag für Sozialwissenschaften, 2003, 160 (Western Europe 1970–2000); Ronald Inglehart, *Culture Shift in Advanced Industrial Society,* Princeton: Princeton University Press, 1990, 442 (Hungary 1982 and Poland 1980, author's calculation).

Thus, the ratio of those with post-materialist value preferences roughly doubled in Western European countries between 1970 and 1990 (Table 9.9). Naturally, in individual societies, the dynamics of transformation diverged from the overall trends. In the Netherlands, West Germany and Austria, the ratio of the population with non-material value priorities was outstanding in that period. In addition to surveys, other evidence also supports the occurrence of value changes, including the emergence of new political movements and parties embracing post-materialist values and the proliferation of alternative culture reflecting the new values, such as alternative places for entertainment, or stores specializing in natural products.

Generational differences clearly manifested themselves in the surveys. In the oldest generations, born between 1886 and 1905, the ratio of those with post-materialist values was significantly lower than among younger generations. At the same time, the growth was neither continuous nor linear. The greatest break was found between the cohorts mentioned, those born during and immediately after the war and those in their youth in the prospering 1950s and 1960s. Later, the generational changes slowed down.

Inglehart's views received many criticisms, for considering values and needs as the same, and for his variables being strongly dependent on the actual socio-economic situation. For example, judging the stability of prices as a material value might be radically different in a period of inflation from at other times. More importantly, many question the direct link between the socioeconomic settings and the value priorities of the population. It has also been highlighted that value change might be more strongly affected by the actual economic situation (prosperity or stagnation) than by the economic conditions of the time the individual had been socialized.[112] If the latter modification is accepted, intergenerational value shifts, because the main source of value change would lose much of its weight. A further line of criticism claims that distinguishing between only a materialist and a post-materialist world of values is an oversimplification, as is an explanation of changes with only two hypotheses. For example, the inclusion of authoritarian and liberal values in the study as new dimensions of value changes was suggested.

However, it was widely accepted that community-related values increasingly lost ground from the 1960s in favour of values related to the self-expression or the self-realization of the individual. Because the latter orientations can take forms other than the post-materialist one described by Inglehart, several other social scientists prefer labelling the change as individualization. Individualization means, on the one hand, a separation from the respective social milieu, like leaving behind the value orientations of industrial workers, the *petit bourgeoisie*, or the peasantry. The influence of traditional communities and social institutions on the individual also weakened, be they the family, kinship, nation, church or trade union. The concrete forms that this process took have been shown previously, such as the dissolution of traditional roles within the family or the process of secularization.

Individualization and the departure from traditional values emerged as a growing acceptance of behaviours formerly considered as deviant or at least condemned by society. Value studies, mostly focusing on Western Europe, found that the population, and mostly the younger generations, were increasingly less hostile in judging phenomena like divorce, marital infidelity, abortion, euthanasia, homosexuality and prostitution. This did not necessarily mean that they would fully accept or follow these types of behaviour, only that they were more tolerant, and expressed a less negative opinion if other people behaved that way.[113] Tolerance towards minorities was already high in the 1960s among the citizens of Western European countries, and this did not change fundamentally later either. The question addressing this issue in surveys is whether respondents would accept a foreigner or a person of different colour or religion as their neighbour; in the 1980s, the great majority of respondents answered yes.

Turning to another aspect of social values and attitudes, the high level of trust between the members of society is considered to be a crucial factor regarding the functioning of society by several recent social theories and empirical studies. Trust is especially closely connected to the activity and potential of civil society, because it has favourable effects on cooperation between individuals, and contributes to the flourishing of civil organizations and other initiatives.[114] The level of trust in fellow citizens increased in the period between approximately 1960 and 1990, but trends are less straightforward afterwards in Western European countries. However, great intergenerational differences were present in this regard as well. In several surveys, the majority of the members of generations who survived the war believed that

TABLE 9.10 Changes in interpersonal trust in European countries, 1959–1997 (%)

	1959	1981–1983	1985	1990	1995–1997
Great Britain	56	43	40	44	30
Netherlands		45	50	54	
FRG	24	32	43	38	42
Austria				32	31
Switzerland				43	37
Sweden		57		66	60
Norway		62		65	65
Italy	8	27	30	35	
Spain		35	34	34	30
GDR/FRG Eastern prov.				26	25
Poland				35	18
Hungary		34		25	

Note: The ratio of those agreeing with the statement, 'Most people can be trusted'.

Source: Oscar W. Gabriel, Volker Kunz, Sigrid Roßteutscher and Jan W. van Deth, *Sozialkapital und Demokratie. Zivilgesellschaftliche Ressourcen im Vergleich,* Wien: WUV Universitätsverlag, 2002, 58.

one cannot trust most people outside one's family. However, younger generations gave positive responses in a higher ratio. Differences between societies were also rather remarkable in this respect. In the 1980s in the Scandinavian countries and in the Netherlands, the majority of the population claimed that they trusted their fellow citizens, whereas elsewhere (especially in Italy, Germany, France and Austria), fewer people thought so (Table 9.10).[115] For the level of trust in East Central European countries, the first comprehensive surveys are available from the period of the regime change. Evidence suggests that communism already left a strong mark on interpersonal relationships, and then, after the regime change, the initially low levels of trust continued to decline. This has been arguably the consequence of the more insecure and rapidly changing social environment, the rising crime rate and the increasing difficulty in earning a living.[116]

It is also worth noting that trust in public institutions had started to erode earlier, from the 1960s, even in democratic countries. In the 1980s in Western Europe, the greatest trust was given to the institutions responsible for keeping law and order: the police, the army and the courts. Schools and universities, as well as churches, were also largely trusted by the public, whereas people found big companies, the media and trade unions to be the least trustworthy.[117]

Even though researchers have not yet arrived at a full consensus regarding the nature of the value change in post-war Europe, and the most plausible theoretical frameworks for discussing the process are also controversial, it is hardly disputable that the transformation had a remarkable impact on social and political development. The growing need for self-expression and the decline of loyalty to social institutions are straightforward trends. The social consequences (such as the impact on family and religious life between the 1960s and 1980s) have already been presented in previous parts of this volume. However, value changes also affected other areas, including politics, in several respects. For post-materialists, environmental protection and the resolution of international conflicts through negotiations are fundamentally important values, ones that democratic governments cannot overlook. In addition, value changes influenced political participation and the political activity of citizens. However, this consequence was ambiguous. On the one hand, citizens' expectations toward political institutions heightened. In all surveys, post-materialists are found to show greater interest in public affairs than the rest of the population. However, this interest is different from traditional engagement in public issues based on parliamentarism. The civil society and the need for the involvement of civic initiatives in political processes are emphatic among post-materialist preferences, and thus direct political participation is stressed more, such as demonstrations, petitioning, referenda or boycotting companies that harm the environment. As has already been pointed out, the shift began in Western Europe from the late 1960s also in the shape of the foundation of many political movements and the proliferation of non-parliamentary political activities. On the other hand, the waning loyalty to traditional institutions also affected the parties, being less successful than before in attaching voters over long periods, and thus political processes became less calculable.[118] All in all, however, changes pointed not in the direction of the weakening of the democratic political system; rather, it was the frameworks of political activity that changed and became more complex.

The 1990s brought several rifts in the transformation of values, proving that change is not linear and not irreversible in this respect, either. The most obvious change was the decrease in the ratio of post-materialists in a number of Western European countries (Table 9.9). In this regard, the slowing down of secularization in several European countries was an important development, as discussed earlier. Trust levels were specifically rearranged. Whereas in previous decades, the degree of interpersonal trust had increased, from the 1990s, it began to decline in most Western European countries, such as in Great Britain, France and Italy. A consistently high level of trust persisted only in Scandinavia. At the same time, trust in public institutions was on the rise in most Western European countries. In post-communist countries, lacking in trust from the onset, the situation continued to worsen in both respects but especially as regards institutions, a trend continuing into the new millennium.[119]

As pointed out in chapter 3, there emerged shifts in attitudes related to family life as well at the turn of the millennium. However, earlier priorities prevailed to a great extent, among others, in spouse selection and childrearing. Continuity is seen not only regarding values related to family relations but other aspects of the value system as well, showing that the break was not complete. Tolerance for behaviours and lifestyles deviating from the traditional or the dominant social norms grew in most European societies in the 1990s, with the exception of only a few countries, such as Hungary and Finland. Tolerance was also on the increase toward minorities: people accepted living beside a neighbour of a different ethnic or religious group in ratios even higher than before. What made this remarkable was that at the same time, the level of interpersonal trust was decreasing, as shown above. However, recent studies suggest that tolerance began to erode after the turn of the millennium all over Europe, especially towards Muslims.

Several factors surfaced in the explanations of the value changes that occurred since the 1960s. As Inglehart's argument has shown, increasing material prosperity is the primary factor, which includes rising standards of living, a relative stability of employment and an improvement in access to schooling and information.[120] Later, this was complemented by the effects of post-industrialization, the transition to a service society, which, in this line of argument, liberates people with its new and more flexible forms of work organization.[121] Others stressed the role of the welfare state in facilitating the process of individualization, because it weakens family and other ties and turns the maintenance of such relationships into a matter of individual choice.[122] Yet another argument claims that it was primarily the political elite, the intellectuals and the experts, social movements and the media that prompted the change of values with their catchy messages and even propaganda hostile to traditional value orientations. A great deal of the changes in trends in the 1990s can be convincingly explained within Inglehart's framework. After the oil crisis of the 1970s, the economic climate greatly changed: the improvement of the standard of living slowed down, unemployment increased significantly and the perspectives of the generations entering the labour market were undoubtedly worse than before. Economic hardship had already surfaced in the communist countries in the 1980s, and a dire decline unfolded during the transformation crisis. All these developments gave a new appreciation to materialist values and gave emphases to individual life strategies, even if to diverging degrees in particular societies. At the same time, the changes cannot be described simply as a reversal of the direction of the attitudinal transformation (during which European societies proceed from post-materialist to materialist values), because values related to individualization or self-expression still continued to gain ground in several respects. Furthermore, there are attitudes, including trust, that do not receive enough attention in Inglehart's theory, even though several recent studies have shown that they are major aspects of value orientations. This calls attention to the fact that the materialist/post-materialist dimension alone, or even the revised version of the concept, cannot fully grasp the process of value change in late twentieth-century European societies.

10

CONCLUSIONS: THE SOCIETIES OF EUROPE AND EUROPE AS A SOCIETY IN THE TWENTIETH CENTURY

By way of concluding this volume, it is obviously not possible to provide a condensed and accurate but easily digestible version of the hundreds of preceding pages. Rather, an attempt is made to address some of the major problems related to the interpretations of the social history of twentieth-century Europe. First, the temporal ruptures of the last century and the spatial structure of the continent are considered. Then, we deal with several key accounts of the theme. Finally, we provide an overview of the lessons of this volume with regard to the possibilities and limits of writing a social history of contemporary Europe.

Rhythms of time and configurations of space: on periodization and the unity of the continent

Europe never came to constitute a clearly defined entity with stable outer limits, internal divisions and unambiguous structures, and thus the history of the continent (even from a social historical perspective) can be narrated in many ways. The definition of Europe and its external and internal boundaries in many respects depends on the perspective that one chooses for the historical analysis and narration. The preferred perspective decisively influences not only spatialities but also the dynamics of change, and thus the temporal structure of historical narration. That is, the analysis of certain aspects of history often results in distinct rhythms of time and spatial configurations, which above all originate from the logic of the given subfield, but at the same time, are shaped by the methods used during the analyses. Different aspects of social history are also characterized by the process outlined above: for example, the main spatial structures and temporal ruptures of twentieth-century European family history do not coincide with those of the patterns of social inequalities. In this section, first we look at what major possibilities the temporal division of twentieth-century European social history does have, where its most significant landmarks were, and into what more comprehensive framework of periodization they can be placed. Second, we discuss the twentieth-century formation of the spatial division of Europe, and the possibilities it yields for interpretation, focusing on the question of whether Europe can be considered as a unit from a social historical point of view.

The twentieth century in Europe: ruptures and continuities

Contrary to the multiple potential periodizations, one can see some remarkably strong cleavages in twentieth-century European history, which cannot be matched with similar ones in the nineteenth century or earlier.[1] On the one hand, this is the consequence of the process when, as opposed to previous periods, national periodizations coincide to a greater extent in the twentieth century. One of the reasons for this process is that the World Wars (as we will see) fundamentally marked the end of the old and the beginning of a new era in most societies. In addition, diffusion processes and entanglements strengthened even further during the century to the point that the dynamics of change of national societies became similar in many respects. On the other hand, one can also observe that during the twentieth century, the temporal layers of different social fields coalesced to a greater extent than earlier. Although Fernand Braudel in his famous history of the Mediterranean described the economic changes of the fifteenth to eighteenth centuries as long-term waves, he also clearly distinguished economic and political history as short-term changes. Obviously, short-term political changes did not cease to exist in the twentieth century, but with the acceleration of economic and social structural changes, and with the growth of the state's economic and social intervention, the epochal boundaries of political and social history became less and less differentiated.

On the basis of this, it is not surprising that although there have been significant scholarly controversies with respect to the periodization of earlier centuries (for example, the debated question of the beginning and ending of the Renaissance), one can see more consensus concerning the epochal division of the twentieth century in international historiography. In almost all European countries, the most important such turning points are constituted by both or one of the World Wars, and the fall of the European communist systems is also usually seen as another common temporal landmark. In order to illustrate this periodization scheme, some important syntheses of the last two decades are relevant: Harold James begins his work on European history with 1914 and basically continues his narration up until today; the synthesis of Tony Judt, which received considerable acclaim, investigates the history of Europe from the end of the Second World War; Eric Hobsbawm, in his widely known work that surveys twentieth-century history, considered the fall of Eastern European socialist systems as the end point of his work, and thus gave rise to the popular concept of the 'short twentieth century' (1914–91).[2] Syntheses using a social or economic historical perspective are dominated by these concepts of periodization as well.[3]

However, there are periodizations that locate the greatest ruptures of the recent past beyond the twentieth century. One of these was suggested by Giovanni Arrighi, who elaborated the concept of the 'long twentieth century', which begins at the end of the nineteenth century, with the onset of globalization, and leads to the indefinite future.[4] Charles Maier argues for a new kind of periodization as well; according to Maier, the internal breaks of the twentieth century (the beginnings and ends of wars, the rise and fall of Nazism and communism, the Great Economic Depression) are so numerous that the century shows little structural unity.[5] Instead of these events, Maier focuses on the formation, dominance and crisis of territoriality. Territoriality means a potentiality (mainly of political power) yielded by a bordered space, which was the base for national identity and the nation-state until recently. According to the argument, the dominance of territoriality started around 1860, and towards the end of the 1960s, this system began to fall apart and a new era sprang up.

Thus, it is difficult to say to which of the three major temporal divisions of the twentieth century we can attribute greatest credence, or whether we might perhaps search for the most significant ruptures of historical time beyond the century.

The advantage of applying the two World Wars as turning points is that these are important dividing lines not only across Europe but also beyond the continent. This circumstance is especially significant because there are generally established periodical concepts in Europe, such as classical antiquity, or the Middle Ages, with beginnings and endings, which cannot be easily interpreted beyond the continent.

Within this periodization scheme, there are considerable arguments in favour of highlighting 1914 as a prominent point of time, which cannot be fully enumerated here. The First World War brought about the crisis of liberalism both in a political and an economic sense. Moreover, the 'Old Europe' had been destroyed during the war: whole empires were dissolved, and a new plethora of nation-states was created or strengthened. The war also gave rise and popularity to those ideas that were later realized in authoritarian regimes (especially in Central and Eastern Europe), and that survived the interwar period and occasionally even the Second World War itself. Among the causes of the Great Depression, the First World War counted as one of the most prominent, but the colonial system began to collapse with the First World War as well. The period of the war brought about changes with respect to many social historical processes in a narrower sense as well. For example, the sizeable wave of transatlantic migration that set in around 1880 (when the European continent lost one-fifth of its natural increase by way of migration) was ended by the First World War. However, the war and the ensuing peace treaties initiated the first waves of forced migration as well. Social cleavages and the system of political parties assumed the form that eventually persisted in European democracies until the last third of the century. There were similar tendencies as well that seemed to alter during the course of the First World War, but they did not prove to be lasting. The war without doubt brought about a considerable change in the political and social mobilization of masses, and subsequently the activity of social movements significantly increased in the immediate post-war years, which manifested in the increased tendency to call a strike, although this turned out to be short-lived. At the same time, several socioeconomic tendencies of the pre-war period continued. For instance, the First World War (contrary to general suppositions) did not end in substantial long-term alteration in the rate of economic growth, and thus the change of the level and patterns of consumption went on without any significant ruptures. Similarly, urbanization advanced at a relatively continuous pace, even if it produced some obviously novel phenomena in the interwar period, such as the appearance of more systematic urban planning and the growing appreciation of green areas.

Therefore, the First World War could be plausibly considered a major historical turning point. However, one might find even more plausible arguments to prove that Second World War (and the mid-century) was the main rupture in twentieth-century European history. The space limitation of this section of this book hinders the systematic discussion of all the arguments, so only a couple of examples can be offered in order to shed light on the process. After the war, relations among the European states underwent fundamental change. On the one hand, there emerged a new antagonism between the western and the eastern half of the continent. On the other hand, economic and political integration started on an unprecedented scale in wider Western Europe. Moreover, the pace of economic growth increased manifold from the 1950s, and it reached a level that was without precedent in the history of the continent. What is more, this growth persisted on this high level for a long time. This change in itself had a significant impact on the living standard and the lifestyle of the population. The structural change of economy accelerated, which above all manifested itself in the rapid decline of agriculture. Numerous elements of the traditional peasant lifestyle existed even in many Western European regions in the mid-century, whereas two or three decades later, it could be seen only as marginal local entities in the eastern and southern fringe of the continent. However, lifestyle was far from being formed only by economic determinants; social and cultural factors had their share as well. The mid-century brought about a stronger rupture with respect to the demographic characteristics of the population and the forms of the family than in the early part of century, even if these changes (for instance, the increase of fertility) were only temporary in many respects. The expansion of the welfare state can be dated back to the mid-century as well, even if the most rapid growth of the level of coverage and expenditures of the welfare programmes began later. Although the formation of consumer society started before the twentieth century in Europe, only the period after the Second World War brought about its new or mature form, usually termed mass consumption society. However, mass consumption society was not omnipresent in Europe, which emphasizes that the social processes referred to above ensued with considerable temporal shifts on the continent. This is particularly evident in East Central and South-Eastern Europe, where one can see not only the lack (or different form) of the consumer society in the post-war decades but also of numerous other phenomena, which existed at the same time in the western half of the continent, such as the baby boom. There were some social historical processes (for example, the increase in female employment and in the number of divorces, or secularization), which in turn surfaced in this region in a more drastic manner.

Finally, the third potential temporal boundary, the collapse of the communist systems (the years of 1989–91) is obviously a significant rupture in Eastern and East

Central Europe, which led not only to the birth of democratic political systems in most of the countries but also the transition to a market economy, and initiated a series of social changes, from occasionally dramatic alterations in the marriage patterns to the belated arrival of the consumer society.

Nevertheless, one can enumerate such arguments that relativize the importance of 1989–91 as the end of the modern period of European history: the attractiveness of communist ideology evaporated early; the communist systems lost the economic race with the West even before that; in some respects the divergences between Western European and East Central European societies had already begun to fade before that (for example, as far as the institutions of the welfare state are concerned); as a result of the transformation crisis, East Central Europe diverged from rather than converged on Western Europe for a couple of years in several respects; with the collapse of the Soviet Union, the position of Russia remained unclear for a time in international politics.

However, these considerations themselves are insufficient to argue against the suggested periodization. Despite its importance, the disappearance of East-West opposition opened up a new perspective for the whole continent, but it is a less significant division in Western European or Southern European political life than it is in the eastern part of the continent, and especially seems to be secondary when compared with the World Wars. For example, integration had already started earlier, in the mid-century, in Western Europe, and gradually expanded later. In addition, previous chapters have already addressed those social processes that either accelerated in the mid-century, or took a different path. That is, from a social historical perspective the *annus mirabilis* of 1989 (or the years of 1989–91) cannot be interpreted as a turning point in Europe, because the historiography of Western Europe decisively influences European periodization. The end of the century, although not one particular year, from other perspectives (especially as a result of the advance of globalization and the subsequently induced social transformations) brought about significant changes with regard to the whole of Europe. However, without the proper historical distance and perspective, it is difficult to assess how significantly this period can be regarded as a turning point in European history.

The latter issue also leads to the notion of the 'long twentieth century', which is directly linked to the process of globalization. Hence, the question arises whether this could provide a basis for creating a more plausible periodization than earlier alternatives. In the following discussion, we examine this question with regard to the other novel interpretation of periodization (as discussed earlier), which is based on the process of territorialization.

The processes of globalization and territorialization worked in parallel for a long time. As the most significant element of globalization, economic relations between countries and continents (i.e., international trade and monetary transactions) boomed at the end of the nineteenth century. A further feature of this process is that it was also the period when international institutions such as the Universal Postal Union and the Geneva Protocols were established. Territorialization, which had its beginnings earlier, around the 1860s, was linked to the expansion of nation-states and nationalism, which were obviously major determinants of twentieth-century political changes as well. Globalization and territorialization were highly important processes of nineteenth-century to twentieth-century European history; however, their more direct impact on societies was not so significant in the nineteenth century as to make it possible to point out any date in the second half of the century as a watershed from the perspective of social history. In contrast, the new phase of globalization that ensued at the end of the twentieth century seems to exercise a more profound influence on European societies.[6] The same applies to the end point of the expansion phase of territorialization as well, which we would rather locate in the mid-century in Europe. As a repercussion of the Second World War, the advance of nationalism and the primacy of the idea of the nation-state came to an end, because a new European peace system was created, nation-states started to weaken, and at the same time, the new position of the United States as a world power solidified.[7] In addition, it is not difficult to recognize that the expansion of both globalization and territorialization conflicted with each other, which also shows that one could attribute these processes to the first half of the century only with strong limitations. Consequently, these phenomena cannot form the basis of the interpretation and periodization of twentieth-century European history.

Concluding what has been said so far, it seems doubtless that the First World War, the Second World War and the years around 1990 were the most important turning points in twentieth-century European history. Moreover, on the basis of highly plausible arguments, it seems reasonable to assume that the Second World War or the mid-century could be regarded as the real watershed from both the perspectives of political as well as social and economic history. Still, there also exist further boundaries, nonetheless, that demarcate subperiods that are worth investigating as well. In the first half of the century, it was the Great Depression that meant an additional break, whereas in the second half of the century, several scholars argue for and emphasize the 1960s, and others the 1970s, as the decade of substantial changes.

The world economic crisis that started in 1929 and intensified in Europe some years later brought significant shifts in the social relations of European countries, to the extent that it eventually became a strong catalyst of political changes, especially in Central Europe, where it largely contributed to political radicalism. The intensification of the economic and social intervention of the state had consequences in the long run, although most of the social changes (such as the dramatically high level of unemployment and the decrease in the standard of living) did not last long, which evidently moderates the importance of this temporal divide. Furthermore, the economic crisis was largely entangled with the wars: on the one hand, the social movements brought about by the First World War barely subsided; on the other hand, the crisis itself had lasted in many European countries until the mid-1930s and occasionally to the end of that decade. This circumstance also adds to the difficulty of interpreting the Great Depression as a historical turning point.

With respect to the internal breaks in the post-war period, European historiography has paid great attention to the 1960s ('the sixties') for a long time, which many scholars interpret not only as a historical watershed but as a specific, distinct period.[8] It is in this sense that the boundaries of the 1960s usually did not coincide with the calendar beginning and ending of the decade. For instance, Arthur Marwick supports the concept of the 'long sixties', which takes in the period between 1958 and 1974. As he impressively describes it, among the changes occurring in this period in Western countries, the best-known and most important change happened in youth culture (and more generally in popular culture), the central element of which was rock music, which also evolved internationally into a kind of universal language for youth. In relation to this, the influence of the younger generations increased within the society with respect to determining fashion, lifestyle and public discourse. The youth possessed more and more purchasing power, and created a huge market of their own, ranging from clothes to rock records, and thus they became a distinguished marketing target. In addition, considerable changes occurred in race and family relationships in the sixties, but they also reflected a general pattern of emancipation efforts and challenge to established authorities and social hierarchies. New subcultures and social movements also expanded, which usually had a critical approach towards the existing capitalist order. They often led to explicit protest movements, which culminated in 1968. Furthermore, significant changes ensued in interpersonal relationships and sexual behaviour, which can also be described by the term 'permissiveness', and included changes in public and private morals, more openness in personal relations and modes of expression, and especially sexual liberation.[9] The often impressive social changes of the 1960s were not exclusively characteristic of Western Europe. In many communist countries (above all in Czechoslovakia and Hungary), a palpably more open political climate began to unfold. What is more, economic and political reforms were implemented in these countries, most of which, however, did not prove to be lasting.

The 1960s were a particular turning point in the twentieth century, because, unlike other internal temporal boundaries, they were not linked to any war, or even to any economic or social crisis, but primarily to cultural and subsequently evolving social changes. Moreover, the 1960s are a distinct subject of historical research because the assessment of their significance diverges in the wider public opinion to a great extent: not independent of political factions, there are those for whom the 1960s were the period of social emancipation and progressive social changes (or at least the hope of these), whereas for others, it was the era of the disintegration of the old and stable framework of morality, authority and values of restraint. Although these diverging opinions suggest that this was the period of considerable social and political upheavals, a more critical assessment has to emphasize, as well, that political changes were superficial or were not even realized. The Cold War remained a continuing and primary organizing process of political life in most countries. Social transformations were more significant, but the 1960s brought about cultural rather than socioeconomic shifts. Moreover, changes during the 1960s were more significant in the USA than in Europe: great society, civil rights, black power, the Cuban Missile Crisis, the Vietnam War, the New Left and the New Right were concepts and events (to mention only those with direct links to politics) that had no similar counterparts in Europe.[10]

Although for a long time, the 1960s appeared to be the turning point or turning period in the second half of the century, recently, more and more historians have argued that the 1970s were the period when social changes assumed new characteristics and qualities in Europe.[11] Above all, the early 1970s brought about the abrupt end of the *Trente Glorieuses*, that is, the spectacular economic growth of the post-war era disappeared, and even occasionally negative growth set in. As a result of the first oil crisis in 1973 and then the second in 1979, economic growth did not simply slow down but inflation plummeted and considerable changes ensued on the labour market as well: the full employment that was characteristic of the 1960s in many Western European states turned into high-rate unemployment. Economic difficulties put hard pressure on public expenditures, arresting the previously unimpeded growth of the welfare state. These developments led to such repercussions as increasing social inequalities and poverty and expanding social deviances. The increase in income inequalities broke a long trend of decrease in the previous decades of the century, although not in every country.

The decade (or 'the long 1970s' starting in 1968) could also be regarded as a turning point because of the invigoration of political violence. Although after the First World War, political violence prevailed in numerous European countries, it almost disappeared after the Second World War. The decade in question marked a significant break in this respect. The terrorist attacks of the *Rote Armee Fraktion* (RAF) in Germany, ETA in Spain, the *Brigate Rosse* in Italy, and the conflicts between Catholics and Protestants in Northern Ireland can be considered as manifestations of this change.

Although, as has already been pointed out, the 1960s can be seen as the period of substantial cultural changes in Europe, the 1970s also brought about significant cultural alterations. On the one hand, these can be interpreted as the period of 'the end of confidence', that is, the shaking of faith of the previous decades in the unimpeded economic growth, technological development, and even social development, and in the continuous increase of the standard of living and other positive social changes.[12] Related to this disillusionment but also to other factors, the 1970s also witnessed the emergence of new types of movements across Europe. Environmentalists are emblematic among these new movements, not least because the green movements achieved direct political representation in many countries. However, movements with old traditions, such as the feminist movement, were invigorated as well. Nevertheless, it is not clear which decade led to greater changes or turns in lifestyle and values. For example, the pluralization of family forms began in the 1960s in Western Europe, a fact which by itself represented important value changes. However, this change expanded only in a few Scandinavian countries at that time, and what is called individualization (which extended far beyond family relations) began to diffuse in the next decade.

The 1970s is regarded by many as the period of democracies consolidating in Europe. The Southern European authoritarian regimes (preeminently Spain and Portugal) and the Greek military dictatorship transformed into democracies. The 1970s were a turning point in East Central Europe as well, because the sources of extensive economic growth began to finally deplete at that time, and could be replenished only by running into increasing debt in many countries, and other societies witnessed the deterioration of the supply of consumer goods. This was the period when communist systems started to finally lose their attraction both internally and externally, which stimulated the formation of political opposition. This region embraced cultural changes in a different manner from the western half of Europe: here, it was not the preference towards post-materialist values, but rather the strengthening of materialism and the spread of anomie.

The 1970s were a watershed not only in European history, although they had more considerable economic and social repercussions for the old continent than for the USA. The financial consequences of the crisis, such as the collapse of the Bretton Woods system, were Western and not simply European affairs, even if European crisis management was more problematic because of the often conflicting national economic policies. However, the crisis affected Europe more than other industrialized regions of the world partly because of its greater dependence on resources, partly because of its specificities of economic structures. Cultural changes, such as the often quoted silent revolution, also manifested more vigorously in Western Europe than in the USA.

Among the turning points addressed in this chapter (the First World War, the Great Depression, the Second World War, the 1960s, the 1970s and around 1990 with the collapse of the communist systems and the acceleration of globalization), we can regard the Second World War as the most prominent one from a social historical but also from a wider perspective. Therefore, this turning point divides the twentieth century into two major periods. However, the starting point of the pre-war period and the end point of the post-war era are more controversial yet. This study interprets the First World War as the potential starting point of the first period of the twentieth century, and thus the interwar era is accepted as a subperiod of European social history. As for the ending point of the second period, its designation is hindered by a lack of proper historical perspective, yet it seems plausible to assume that the golden age or *Trente Glorieuses* approximately between 1950 and 1973 was one of the subperiods, and the subsequent period between 1973 and around 1990 can be considered as a further subperiod of the post-war era.

Europe in the twentieth century: divisions and unity

There is no other major region of the world, the unity or the disunity of which has been so intensively and so long a subject of discussion, as Europe. This discourse on Europe's character and inner diversity has been going on since the times of classical antiquity, and was broadened in the last decades by the debate on the political and material implications of Europe's shared heritage.[13] No one can seriously question that a significant body of common heritage exists. Yet the interpretation of this shared history and legacy in Europe is contested nonetheless because the European heritage is of a complex nature and, thus, difficult to grasp. Furthermore, many fear that narratives on Europe serve an instrumentalization of history to legitimize and promote the European integration project, and some even downright refute them as an invented or imagined past.

The problem of European unity and disunity increasingly leads us to pose the question whether a European society exists or not, and if it indeed does, what its characteristics are, which historical processes led to its formation, and what its future perspectives are. At first glance, the answer to this question seems to be straightforward. If society is meant in its traditional and most widely used sense, then one cannot or could not speak about European society either today or at any time in the past. Although society has numerous definitions, most of them generally consider society as a group of people who are related to each other by sharing a dominant culture, inhabiting a particular geographical area, being subject to the same political authority, and believing that they represent a unified and separate entity. Europe obviously does not confirm to this, because Europe is not an entity where the congruence of power, space and identity emerge. It is not a state with extensive control over bounded territories that regulates the social and economic life of a unitary society or nation. Instead of this unified notion, today Europe is, and during the whole twentieth century was, constituted of a multiplicity of competing nation-states. Moreover, in a strict sense, Europeans do not have a common culture, which is manifested, for instance, in linguistic diversity. Last, in relation to the previous discussion, the citizens of Europe, or at least most of them, do not believe that they constitute a single and distinct entity; in other words, they do not possess a common identity. Moreover, Europe cannot be regarded as a federative state like the United States either. Europe consists of separate and more or less homogeneous nation-states, which have never been conjoined during their history by such a strong legal bond as the otherwise diverse member states of the USA.[14]

These circumstances are indeed significant and those who argue against the plausibility of the concept of the European society rightly emphasize them. Nonetheless, further considerations should also be regarded when investigating the question. On the one hand, the concept of society referred to above reflects the prominence of the nation-state as a basic unit of social organization, and thus it is often regarded as methodological nationalism. This concept of society emerged at the time that the bordered and guarded national territory, the political sovereignty and domination by the nation-state, and the national or ethnic identity based on the national language and culture developed as well, which was often created by force.

Nevertheless, reflecting the social changes during the twentieth century, especially in its second half, alternative ideas appeared that made the concept of society more dynamic and took into consideration that the factors constituting societies might also change. These more recent concepts did not focus on common values, solidarity, identity and culture in general and their accompanying emotions. Rather, they characteristically regard communication as well as (after Max Weber) rationality, economic performance and the institutional order framing these elements as the cohesive forces of modern society. A series of twentieth-century European social processes undoubtedly strengthen the plausibility of the alternative concepts. Because these ideas go beyond the concepts of national societies, so the European integration unfolding from the mid-twentieth century transcended national societies in several instances. It can also be seen that, in the form of a learning process, rationality as a factor constituting society was among the most significant factors of the European integration process, which is of key importance with regard to the question of European society. The acceleration of the flow of information at the end of the twentieth century also challenged the boundaries of national societies. Thus, it is far from imperative to approach European society only on the basis of the analogy of national societies. However, for the time being, these alternative concepts of society in themselves are not fully sufficient for the conceptualization of European society, and their application in historical studies is hindered by even more obstacles. Therefore, in the following discussion, when addressing the problem of European unity, we focus on the considerations of traditional concepts of society, with a special emphasis on the factors and directions of the transformations of national societies as well.

The social diversity of Europe is a reality that can be easily supported throughout the twentieth century. The differences between the individual national societies are discussed from multiple perspectives in earlier chapters. Thus, it is enough to refer to only two examples here. The division between Eastern Orthodox Christianity and Western variations of Christianity has been central to establishing a separation between Eastern and Western Europe. The division of Europe into a wealthy and industrialized north and a relatively underdeveloped south has also been a traditional separation. The dynamics of diversity were often also peculiar: the religious cleavages were reinforced by the Cold War but the secularization process moderated its significance, and the north–south socioeconomic gap was lessened during the post-war decades.

However, it is insufficient if only the signs of heterogeneity in Europe are taken into consideration, because this variety is a specific one. This particular diversity can be conceptualized in several ways. For instance, Colin Crouch (as discussed later) speaks about the existence of 'structured diversity' in post-war Western Europe: in other words, there is social heterogeneity but this is an ordered and limited diversity, also constituting a kind of unity in the region. If we use this concept, then the question arises as to which factors eventually structured diversity in Europe, and particularly, what are the characteristics and marks of the social unity of Europe in its distant and more recent history, as well as in the present?

The social unity of Europe can be approached in various ways, and there is a huge literature on the subject. We can highlight here only those aspects of the unity that we regard as most important. These partly overlapping aspects include European cultural traditions and values; the historical and personal experiences gained from the European space; the specificities of social institutions and social structures; the institutions of European cooperation and integration; and finally, identity, which might follow from the previous elements.

Before addressing these issues, it seems necessary to comment on the discourse on Europe; all the more so, because some express their opinion that Europe should primarily be understood as a narrative or an idea.[15] The notion that Europe is a community where states intensively communicate with other independent entities was born relatively early. According to some scholars, the intensive exchange of technical, artistic and scientific innovations in the European space had been going on since the age of the great migrations. There appeared the need to unify, which culminated under Charles the Great, but the discourse persisted and emphasized those elements among European peoples and their diversity that bound them together, sought for unity and which they preeminently found in Christianity. Obviously, in early medieval times, Europe did not mean the same as we usually understand it today, but something more constrained, loosely encompassing Western European areas.

It is without doubt that the spatial dimension that culturally or in other senses is commonly regarded as Europe expanded in the Middle Ages and later. However, the development of the idea of Europe (and for that matter, the history of European unity) cannot be interpreted as a linear process in which Europe covered an ever-widening geographical area and was characterized by an increasing cooperation between the peoples and societies constituting it. On the one hand, the endeavour to seek out unity (especially from the late Middle Ages) was exchanged for another approach in which the consciousness of religious and cultural bonding did not vanish, yet the dividing and dissimilar features came to the foreground. However, Europe was subsequently more and more conceived as a system of independent states, which had to cooperate for the sake of their own interests.[16] In addition, the historical development of the concept of Europe in turn also included the exclusion of certain regions, as was convincingly proved in relation to the Balkans and Eastern Europe.[17]

Consequently, the idea of European unity can be found in the distant past; however, this surfaced on the continent fragmented both in space and time. We cannot see the continuous and constant presence of the idea of Europe in the twentieth century either, because these thoughts and institutions appeared differently in the eastern part of Europe after the Second World War from in Western Europe. Therefore, what today we call European integration (that is, the institutional representation of the unity) relied on these traditions, yet it is not plausible to regard a political unity or integration emerging out of European cultural legacies. Rather, it is more suitable to approach it as one of the primary repercussions of twentieth-century historical experiences. The mid-century beginnings of integration originated primarily from the experiences of the previous period of the 'European civil war' and the subsequent East–West confrontation. Then, the development of integration in the following post-war decades was primarily based on the edifying experiences of peace and socioeconomic prosperity. Thus, the long historical traditions are important when studying European unity, but one has to see the ruptures and turns of trends as well, and subsequently the openness of the European integration process in order to avoid arriving at teleological interpretations.

After these precautions, we can turn to the manifestations of European unity. To begin with the first set of characteristics, Europe as a cultural community formed by traditions has demanded significant attention for a long time: the most persuasive writings on Europe in the last centuries considered Europe as an idea and ideal that can be realized in a more concrete form. Some conceptualize these common features as cultural traditions or values.[18] Among the numerous concepts, we can refer to one in particular, because the advantages and questions raised by it are both edifying. Hans Joas regards Europe as a community based on shared culture and values, which manifest partly normatively, partly in the everyday life of European societies: this set of values includes freedom, which originates from Greek and Roman traditions, and its representation as an ideal was considerably influenced by the experiences of slavery; the acceptance of plurality, which appeared during the long digestion of religious conflicts in the modern age; rationality, which acquired a distinct status in Europe with the rise of Protestantism and the Enlightenment; the idea of inwardness, which demarcates the individual's personal, inner life from the external social reality, and thus creates the basis for individualism; self-realization, which is the high stage of individualism, is directly related to the latter process, which was crystallized as a self-conscious value and aim late, at the end of the eighteenth century, and became widespread only in the second half of the twentieth century; and finally, the appreciation of everyday life, which stemmed from the fourteenth century, preeminently means the respect of work, money, meals and love, and was an important elevator of the individual's emancipation from the churches, and subsequently of individualism and secularization in general.[19]

Obviously, this rough, headword survey cannot reflect the real and whole depth of the original reasoning. It indeed sheds light on substantial elements of European cultural traditions; however, one also has to pay attention to the pitfalls, which are often inherent in such claims. On the one hand, we might misleadingly regard the particular elements of the heritage as a European cultural trait that is independent of time and space, and thus we may arrive at some kind of European essentialism, although the heritage of classical antiquity had clearly influenced only one part of Europe directly, whereas in several other regions, only the nineteenth and twentieth centuries brought about its expansion, usually through mediation. Moreover, it is not clear what the temporal dynamics of these values were, for example, when they accelerated during the twentieth century, and when they were broken by ruptures. An additional pitfall might occur if one forgets that these cultural characteristics can be found outside Europe as well, and that they did not come into being in an altogether autochthon way, but had external sources of origin as well. Furthermore, the question might be raised whether it would be perhaps more reasonable to propose these as Western values. This problem is aptly shown by the spread of the concept of freedom as an ideal and value, because one might rightfully emphasize the role of the USA in the adoption and particularly in the universalization of this value. Finally, the above-mentioned conceptualization did not reflect the tensions among these and possibly other cultural values, which, for instance, resulted in colonialism, and the formation of totalitarian ideologies along with ultraviolence in Europe in the first half of the twentieth century.

Besides the controversial yet undoubtedly existing set of common European cultural values, the common past and the experiences gained about the European space are also candidates for the elevators of European unity. However, the nature of historical and personal experiences is bifurcated: these can equally bind and separate. From a historical perspective, Europe was characterized by a competition of relatively small units (this feature is regarded by Michael Mann and others as one of the most important European characteristics), which was often conjoined with hegemonic pursuits, and repetitively ended in conflicts and wars.[20] Obviously, these conflicts and their memories rather divide Europeans than link them; the statues and other memorials of famous men of the intra-European wars stand in some elevated space in almost every European city. Nevertheless, since the beginning of the modern age, the endeavour to regulate and limit conflicts has also appeared in European history, which included the rules of civilized warfare and compromised peace-making, as well as the goal of preventing wars, which is a recurrent motive in contemporary works on European unity. After the dramatic failures of these efforts in the twentieth century, the need and will to prevent future conflicts appeared with reinforced strength. The endeavour to critically assess war and violence occupied a central place in European historical memory after the Second World War. According to recent surveys, a majority of European citizens attributed importance to European unity at the millennium because of its role in maintaining peace in the continent.[21] These developments testify that the historical learning process already mentioned strongly manifested in Europe during the twentieth century, and had tangible results as well.

Experiences directly gained of other societies might be similarly contradictory, as evidently represented by the developments of the twentieth century. The European population acquired such experiences already in the first half of the twentieth century, mainly through wars by being a soldier, prisoner of war, refugee, depor-tee, or emigrant; in other words, often in a traumatic way. This pattern dramati-cally changed in the second half of the twentieth century, when those encounters that took place in a more positive context were overrepresented, and involved tourists, guest workers and students, among others. Moreover, the number of those gaining personal experiences in this manner and the intra-European entanglements, transfers and communication in general greatly increased, especially in Western Europe, and after the system changes, the eastern regions of Europe also joined in these processes intensively.[22] Besides the phenomena referred to above, the process occasionally called the 'Europeanization of Europe' involved the expansion of trade, academic and cultural relations and the movement of labour, but also the wider usage of European symbols, such as the anthem, the flag, the passport and then the common currency. All this had gradually promoted Europe into an everyday reality for most European citizens by the millennium. However, the restraints of this process also remained obvious in many respects: it is particularly remarkable that the European public sphere was only marginally realized even at the very beginning of the new millennium, which had fundamental consequences on the legitimacy and functioning of the institutions of European integration.[23]

Cultural traditions and historical experiences can achieve the status of becoming real shaping forces of the society only if they are embedded into a proper structural framework of institutions. As Hans-Peter Müller argued, the most important

institutional innovation of Europe was the productive separation of different institutions and spheres of society.[24] The institutional differentiation process manifested
itself in many ways. The separation of powers might have been the most significant
element of the latter, but much before this, the separation of the ecclesiastical and
secular spheres also appeared, which subsequently brought about the separation of
the ecclesiastical and national language, theology and philosophy, canonical law
and secular law, as well as that of religion and science. There are numerous other
examples beyond the realm of church and religion, such as the separation of capital
and work, or of household and economic functions. These processes of differentiation
added specific dynamics to European societies. For instance, the demarcation between
religion and politics was an indispensable condition for the formation of democracy
and constitutionalism; the dualism of wage work and capital became the basis of
the market economy; the separation of religion and science led to dynamic technological progress. Although we have referred to processes thus far that had been
going on for centuries, still the separation and therein the autonomy of spheres
(especially within the field of politics and law) were extended with full consistency
relatively late, from the mid-twentieth century. The latter happened after the
Second World War in the western part of Europe, whereas in East Central Europe
it ensued only after the fall of communism.

Beyond the similarities of the abstract institutional arrangements in Europe, one
can also see similarities among European societies with regard to certain social
institutions and respective social spheres, even in a global perspective. These can be
more easily grasped empirically in the twentieth century. This study also touches
upon these processes in earlier chapters, and we emphasize the peculiarities and
similarities of the development of European societies particularly with respect to the
welfare state and urbanization. However, even beyond these, one can see further
evidence for the commonalities, and indeed, convergences of European societies,
or many of them, in the twentieth century. The most systematic analysis of social
convergences in the continent was carried out by Hartmut Kaelble, which is
addressed in the following discussion of major interpretations of twentieth-century
European social history.

Besides all these factors facilitating unity, there has existed for a couple of decades what is sometimes called the 'official Europe', that is, the supranational institutions of the European integration. The EU and its predecessors, such as the
European Steel and Coal Community, decisively contributed to the situation in
which the question of the existence of a European society could be raised at all.
The institutions of European integration created increasingly concise frameworks
for supporting political and economic harmonization. What is more, they regarded
economic and social homogenization (or to use the official EU terminology,
cohesion) as their explicit political aim. The EU, as many have already pointed out,
is a peculiar entity: it does not function like the nation-states, and nobody can
reasonably expect it to do so in the near future; at the same time, it cannot be regarded
as a federative state; yet it is more than a simple intergovernmental organization.
Nevertheless, besides the EU, there are intergovernmental organizations in

considerable numbers in Europe, which usually extend beyond the circle of EU member states. These include the Council of Europe, which was founded in 1946 and which involves practically all European countries, together with its European Commission of Human Rights and the European Court of Human Rights.

The phenomena that have been previously touched upon, such as common historical experiences, similarities of social structure and institutions and the institutions of European integration, facilitated the emergence of European identity, even if this has remained limited and contradictory thus far. The cultural identification with Europe, as has already been suggested, has a long history, although until recently, it mostly included the ecclesiastical and cultural elite, and from the beginning, involved altering and usually smaller territories of the continent than today. This kind of identity can be mostly witnessed in literary works, artworks and other cultural representations of the intellectual elite, and dominated concepts about Europe until the European unity was institutionalized from the mid-century.

With the appearance of the EU and its predecessors from the 1950s, European identity was vested into a new, more concrete and at the same time more complex form, which in turn began to involve a larger share of the population of Europe. In the first decade of the twenty-first century, the EU included most of the societies of Europe, and offered new possibilities of European identification, besides the already existing cultural one, to the citizens of the recently joined countries. Moreover, as the EU and its predecessors gradually deepened the integration, and as it expanded to other areas beyond the economy, the EU gained more potential for inviting identification, and the EU itself made strenuous efforts from the 1970s to intensify European identity as well.

Nonetheless, the European identity remained limited and contradictory. In the 1990s, the results of the successive waves of Eurobarometer surveys showed that although there was a considerable variation across societies, in most EU countries, a small minority of citizens (on the average around 5%) had an exclusive European identity.[25] The remaining 95% dispersed in almost equal proportion among those who did not have any sense of European identity and those having some degree of European identity. However, even more important was the fact that in the last few decades, the ratio of those having a firm European identity did not increase lastingly. Even for those who have already shown such inclination, Europe and the EU bore mostly instrumental value, such as free movement and travel, or economic advantages, and could excite less emotional identification. This sheds light on considerable differences compared with national identities, and in itself refers to the limits of the European identity. In addition, one can also observe in this respect that the history of European unity is far from being unidirectional: it was precisely the extension of the EU that contributed to the erosion of the European identity in considerable segments of Western European societies.

Others find contradictions in the European identity not only in the fact that attitudes towards Europe have differed across European societies and that views on Europe diverge within given nations along various lines such as class, gender and age but also because during the formation of national identities, a separation from

Europe also plays a key role, opposed to an identification with Europe: Europe has appeared as 'the Other' within Europe as well.[26]

Concluding what has been said so far, we can speak about a European society in none of the periods of the twentieth century, provided the concept is understood in the traditional sense. However, it is conspicuous that Europe possesses a stronger cultural and social coherence when compared with other continents with similar geographical structure and ethnic diversity. The different elements of the unity, particularly the discursive one, also have a long history. Besides this, the dynamics of the unity are remarkable as well: the twentieth century witnessed considerable changes in this respect. Whereas the wars of the first half of the century (contrary to the social convergences that surfaced in many ways) alienated the citizens of the continent from each other, the mid-century can already be seen as the starting period of the institutionalization of unity in Western and Southern Europe and of the increase in similarities, and finally at the millennium, these processes also expanded to the eastern part of the continent. It is true nonetheless that the unification of Europe advanced to the greatest extent in the economy, although it is less tangible socially and culturally.

Interpretations of twentieth-century European social history: social integration, social compromise and modernity

As elaborated in the Introduction, our intention was to write a social history of Europe by balancing grand theories of social change and normative approaches, largely ignoring empirical facts or the issue of historical relevance on the one hand, with highly specialized, purely empirical studies in which it is hard to find some more general knowledge in the wider context. However, we do not deny the importance of broad interpretations, all the more because there exist accounts that are able to offer a comprehensive social history or historical sociology of twentieth-century Europe with an overarching narrative and at the same time rely on systematic empirical evidence. It is edifying to consider these nonetheless, and thus, we present a short overview and assessment of the three accounts (by Hartmut Kaelble, Colin Crouch and Göran Therborn) that arguably qualify as the most significant accounts in this respect.

Social integration in Europe

The starting point of Hartmut Kaelble is that European integration after the Second World War was not only the result of the visions and efforts of politicians or the cost-benefit calculation of economic actors, but also that of less obvious social changes. The far-sighted decisions of statesmen, such as Monnet, Schuman, Adenauer, De Gasperi and Spaak, were undoubtedly indispensable for the offset of the integration process, just as those of their successors were required to maintain its dynamics. Similarly, the economic interests of large corporations and the everyday decisions of millions of European consumers (to purchase imported products or to travel abroad) also contributed to the deepening of integration. These factors were significant (or even the most important) determinants of the integration process, but the process was also facilitated by the increasing similarity between European (or rather Western European) societies and their growing interdependence. This process of social integration within Europe did not necessarily appear in particular treaties on economic and political cooperation, but it arguably contributed to the success of integration in the long run. However, this was also a case of inter-dependence: the long existence and activity of the EEC and its successor organizations itself advanced the process of social integration in Europe.[27]

The most promising approach to the analysis of European social integration for Kaelble is to examine the peculiarities of European societies in order to identify those structures and social practices that separate them from other advanced industrial societies in North America or Asia. Obviously, these common characteristics of European societies do not necessarily prevail in every country and region to the same extent. However, if such a peculiarity appears in most of the societies (as Kaelble maintains), whereas it is absent in other industrial countries (such as the United States, Canada or Australia), then it can be considered a distinctive European feature nonetheless.

The next major step is to identify the convergent and divergent tendencies between twentieth-century European societies, possibly together with regional disparities and similarities. Not only the post-war period, when political integration emerged, but also the trends in the first half of the century are to be considered here so that the longevity of trends can be determined.

Kaelble also argues (especially in his recent works) that the interdependence and mutual influence of European societies should be examined: in addition to economic relations, what kind of other (scientific, intellectual-cultural, touristic, educational) connections and transfers emerged among European societies or their citizens, and how these affected the process of European integration along with the formal and informal institutions in the continent as well as the attitudes to Europe among the citizens.

Kaelble synthesizes the relevant results of historical and social research and also carries out his own empirical analysis. He finds distinct Western European patterns in a number of areas in twentieth-century social development that clearly separate these societies from the North American, Japanese or Soviet societies. One set of these peculiarities is related to family structure and family life, where these patterns prevailed during most of the twentieth century but faded away by the end of the millennium (dominance of nuclear families, high age at first marriage, high per-centage of lifelong celibacy, intensive emotional ties between partners based on the ideal of romantic love). For most of the century, the primacy of industrial employment can be considered another European trait, together with its numerous consequences (for instance, the power of trade unions, or stricter regulation of working hours). Compared with the USA, the level of social mobility was lower but social inequalities were more moderate. This was primarily the result of the early formation of the welfare state at the end of the nineteenth century in Europe and a subsequent expansion and diffusion process. The dynamics of urbanization in Europe were not as stormy in the twentieth century as in many other parts of the world, and hence, did not create insurmountable problems for urban development: traditional urban structures and the quality of urban life could be preserved.

As has been pointed out before, Kaelble also suggests that the similarities among European societies increased during the century. The convergence was especially marked after the Second World War. As a sign of diminishing differences, industrialization expanded to the peripheries of Europe, including Scandinavia and Southern Europe. Consequently, the employment structure of particular countries or even regions became similar to each other, except for the share of agricultural workforce that considerably decreased by the end of the century. In the area of education, in addition to the closing of gaps in literacy between the northern and the southern regions, gender gaps and differences between students' social background were also mitigated within Europe. As far as urbanization is concerned, not only did the ratio of urban population converge in Western European countries but the urban structure became more similar as well. Finally, the welfare state is the area where there emerged not only significant European peculiarities, but certain structural features also converged in the second half of the twentieth century, such as the size and distribution of social welfare expenditures, or the social security coverage of the population. However, Kaelble also points out divergences in certain areas (like unionization and strike patterns) but he considers these to be significantly less substantial than the opposing social trends, indicating the integration among Western European societies in the twentieth century.

Social compromise and the resurgence of capitalism

Leaving behind the Second World War, Western Europe consisted of a set of countries where different social conditions prevailed. However, Colin Crouch claims that this diversity was limited, ordered and structured. He observes that Western Europe had a certain unity, mainly because a distinct balance emerged among the major institutions of societies in this part of the continent in the post-war era. Crouch defines the four sets of these institutions in the following manner: the economic activities; the system of ownership and control over resources; the traditional community, such as family, religion, ethnic group and nation; and the political society, that is, the organization of interests and the rights of citizenship.[28]

These elements have practically been in a constant tension with each other in European history. The French Revolution caused severe hostilities between citizenship rights and traditional community, and the industrial revolution created a friction between both of these and the economy. There were conflicts within the particular sets of institutions themselves, such as the clash of interests between parties and various organized interests in the world of politics. However, after the complete exhaustion of societies in the Second World War, most of the conflicts were replaced by a form of 'structured tolerance', meaning that people typically joined one of the major poles and then sought compromise with old enemies.

Employees and employers gathered in their respective interest organizations and managed to agree on wages and other working conditions; the different denominations and churches (although maintaining their independence and their distinctive doctrines) also moved towards each other; political parties governed in coalitions, or at least accepted the principles of parliamentarism; nation-states that had often fought each other in wars created institutions of integration in post-war Europe.

As a consequence, a unique system emerged in the post-Second World War decades in Western Europe in which a balance was established between the different sets of institutions. The balance was based on the following structures and features prevailing in every Western European country: the societies were characterized by industrial employment; capitalist private property dominated in economy; the rights of traditional communities were respected by other institutions but communities also accepted if someone wanted to leave them. It also became generally accepted to grant rights to individuals as citizens, ranging from civic rights to social rights. Consequently, a subtle mixture of separation and cooperation was realized, which created the society of 'mid-century compromise' that became dominant by the beginning of the 1960s. Nevertheless, this does not mean that all of the elements of the model had fully developed by this time (the welfare state, for instance, achieved its full size later), but in general, the formation of the model took place around 1960.

The essence of the mid-century compromise was the equilibrium among the four potentially opposing elements. The advance of any of them could be possible only at the expense of the others, and that would obviously jeopardize the balance. This had been the case before as well, when the existence of the traditional community was threatened by the advance of modern capitalism during nineteenth-century industrialization, resulting in changes that disturbed its functioning, and the relations between people were increasingly influenced by market transactions. Then, the conflicts of capitalism and citizenship rights came to the foreground; yet another tendency was when the advocates of capitalism and those of expanding citizenship rights joined forces against the traditional community.

In this sense, the mid-century compromise can be interpreted as a distinct moment in the changing balance between various social forces. It is not surprising, therefore, to witness the shift of this previous balance in the last decades of the century. According to Crouch, the first and most apparent among these changes was the expansion of citizenship rights, especially social rights. This originates in the post-Second World War years, when as result of the diffusion of the Fordist model of mass production, employees, especially industrial workers performing manual labour, became major actors in the functioning of the economy. With massive economic growth and full employment, the social position of workers improved and their political influence continuously strengthened. As a result, in the 1960s in most Western European countries, welfare expenditures radically increased, significantly changing the distribution of national product for the benefit of the employees. This development, as Crouch argues, disturbed the existing equilibrium in several ways. The expansion of education, health care and social care resulted in the growth of the service sector at the expense of industry, thus giving impetus to the emergence of post-industrial society. Moreover, a significant number of the new jobs were filled by women, which weakened the previous family model. The robust social policy weakened the capitalist element of the model because it decreased the capitalists' ratio of production and redistribution of the national product.

However, from the 1980s, a new and, in many respects, opposing turn started to take place, which is referred to by Crouch as the 'resurgence of capitalism'. The rate of unemployment increased after the oil crisis of the 1970s, and in order to defend themselves against the significant effects of inflation, governments started to set up deflationary goals, instead of the previous Keynesian economic policy, which limited their room for manoeuvring both in the areas of labour market and social policy. At the same time, the proportion of industrial employment radically decreased, affecting the organizational strength and political weight of the workers. Moreover, by the 1980s, globalization increased the independence of capital from national governments and from the indigenous workforce. Thus, power relations significantly changed in favour of capitalism and its main beneficiaries, the class of capital owners and managers. The shift affected not only social rights but the traditional community as well. For instance, the spread of overtime and the increasing commonness of weekend working hours in services and industry encroached on the time that was previously spent on attending churches, or that had traditionally been reserved for families being together.

Modernity and its aftermath

Göran Therborn put modernity in the focus of his work on European societies in the second half of the twentieth century. He maintains that the concept of modernity has several advantages compared with other epochal terms, such as 'industrial society' or 'capitalism', because it has a number of varieties and connects to current debates in social research. Modernity and its related concepts (such as the modern and modernization) are central to the scholarly and public discourse on contemporary European societies, as well as culture, and their twentieth-century transformations. The same applies to the concepts and phenomena that are usually contrasted with these changes, such as tradition, stagnation, underdevelopment and religious fundamentalism. With the help of the conceptual toolbar belonging to modernity, these topics can all be covered and included in the research. Therborn suggests that there is no other way to conceptualize the twentieth century that would entail a similar range of concerns.[29]

However, the subject of Therborn's book is not modernity in general but European modernity as a historical era, together with its manifestation, importance and historical meaning. Modernity, he argues, is an epoch that is oriented towards the future, which is regarded as different from the past and the present in a positive sense. The idea of a better future appears in science, politics, the arts, and the everyday discourse about public affairs. Modernity emerged victorious in the second half of the eighteenth century in Western Europe. Despite all of their creativity and innovation, the Renaissance and the Reformation relied on the traditions of the past that they regarded as their model, and that they intended to revitalize. However, from the eighteenth century onward, the idea of progress and the accumulation of knowledge, as well as social evolution, emerged and subsequently began to be widely used in the continent. The beginning of industrialization, the expansion of trade, the advancement of science, and the French revolution all served as starting points of this process. Modernity as an era, Therborn continues, ends when this orientation towards the future ceases to be a dominant one, when the dichotomies of traditional-modern and developed-undeveloped lose their centrality in discourses on society. To put it differently, modernity lasts as long as the differentiation between the past and the future is no longer of central significance in the discourse about society and culture, and until the change of society and culture is regarded as desirable. Whereas 'modern man' was looking into the future by planning, anticipating and building it, the post-modern era puts an end to the sense of controllability and predictability and denies any 'sense of time direction'.

Therborn also claims that different routes of social development characterized the era of modernity. One of the four major models was represented by Europe, where both the advocates and the adversaries of modernity emerged and were endogenous, which materialized in civil wars, revolutions and intense internal conflicts, whereas in the New Worlds, for example, the enemies mostly came from outside. Therborn tries to give account of the characteristics of European modernity in the second half of the twentieth century by a thorough empirical enquiry into European societies and cultures, including major dimensions of social life from labour and education to consumption patterns. Based on this analysis, he aims at answering several questions related to modernity, most importantly whether modernity still exists or has already been replaced by post-modernity.

His results indicate that the second half of the twentieth century did not constitute a complete break from the previous period; it was instead a kind of climax and the start of the exit from it, that is, a turning point. It was a distinct era because it brought about a number of turning points in Europe: for instance, the spectacular economic growth starting after 1950 ended around 1973; the long period of emigration was replaced by immigration; industrialization permeated the continent but soon gave way to services; the working class reached the peak of its political influence at this time, as did the welfare state; women appeared in the labour market in great numbers; and secularization was also given a major impetus.

European modernity, Therborn concludes, started to fade at the end of the century. Concepts like progress, development, emancipation, and liberation lost their appeal. Economic growth still remained an objective of governments and desirable for the public, but with strict limitations. However, if modernity originally had several versions, then it also seems plausible that there are various passages leading out of it. That is why Therborn hesitates, beyond the necessary precaution of the social scientist, to claim that the peak of modernity will be followed by a universal, global post-modern age, or that it has already arrived.

The merits of interpretations

As indicated in the previous section and elsewhere in the book, conceptualizing the unity and the diversity of the continent is one of the fundamental difficulties that studies of the history and sociology of Europe have to face. This truly sweeping and vital issue had already been the focus of a number of historical and sociological studies. However, Hartmut Kaelble set out to examine the development of similarities and differences among European societies, applying a systematic approach with regard to the selected areas of the survey and a long-run analysis covering the whole twentieth century.

There exist many signs indicating increasing similarity among twentieth-century European societies. We have presented a number of these, several of which Kaelble's studies had already suggested; others point beyond the scope of his work. Just to mention a few, there are longer periods of diminishing differences among Western European societies in the areas of mortality, marriage patterns, welfare expenditures, social security coverage, economic growth, consumer habits and patterns of consumption, and the structure of employment.

Social convergence was not a universal and especially not a linear trend in Western Europe. There were societies that participated in this process to a lesser degree. Significant evidence suggests that the process of convergence that was accelerated during the 'great boom' (in the third quarter of the century) generally came to a halt in the 1970s, and was replaced by divergences in several areas (such as economic growth and income inequality), even in Western Europe.

It is especially striking that during a great part of the century, convergence did not affect the societies in the eastern and south-eastern parts of Europe. In the first decades of the century these societies (or at least the societies of East Central Europe) also participated in processes of unification that were actually rather limited even in Western Europe at that time. We have provided ample evidence to show that the communist takeover put an end to this trend, first in areas directly related to politics, and then as divergence became stronger in other respects as well. Although certain characteristics did not show the same trend, these are less significant than the divergent processes. After the regime change, a number of patterns formerly limited to Western Europe appeared in various social segments in East Central Europe at a surprising pace: the most obvious examples are to be found in demography and family life.

The dynamics of social divisions lead us to the related subject of social differences between Europe and the other continents, especially between Europe and other advanced industrial societies. Although we only touched upon this topic, the unique patterns of family formation, the extensive welfare state, the distinct quality of urban life and a low level of social inequalities are undoubtedly among the particular features of European societies.

As to the criticism of Kaelble's thesis, the focus on convergences and divergences, or social integration, excludes other important aspects of social history. Moreover, in the original formulation of his thesis, Kaelble dealt in detail only with

Western and Southern Europe and especially with the core countries of the EU, even though, in his later works, he devoted more attention to East Central Europe.[30] More importantly, he tends to make generalizations and thus identifies Western European or European tendencies on the basis of trends in a limited number of Western European countries. One may also claim that over-emphasizes the convergent trends in Europe because of the limited number of aspects included in the analysis. These methodological and conceptual problems are all the more relevant, because social research arrived at conflicting results about the convergences and divergences of European societies, especially in the period starting from the 1970s.

All in all, however, our study confirmed that Hartmut Kaelble's approach can be plausibly and productively applied in considering the social history of Europe in the modern age. Kaelble explicates a genuine European perspective: it is a *par excellence* interpretation of European social history, because the entire continent can plausibly be integrated into the framework, which is not bound to any particular era or social formation. No comprehensive approach to the social history of twentieth-century Europe can ignore the analysis of temporal changes and the dynamics of the diversities and commonalities of particular societies, which con-forms to Kaelble's approach focusing on the assessment of the social peculiarities of Europe in the world and the analysis of social convergences and divergences.

Studying the characteristics and relations of various social groups or classes and institutions is the most fundamental task in dealing with twentieth-century European social history. Thus, we also introduced in this volume the major trends in social inequalities, the emergence and transformation of the welfare state, as well as the changes in the trade union movement, working conditions and political institutions, which are also major themes in Colin Crouch's analysis of the 'mid-century social compromise'. Crouch suggests that the social constellation in Western Europe during the two or three decades after the middle of the century is to be regarded as exceptional in several respects, which found support in our study. In family life, a return to former, traditional roles can be witnessed in several respects, fertility underwent a sudden increase, the rate of economic growth reached a historical high, institutions of social solidarity were being established extensively, income differences declined, consumption in every social class showed a dynamic growth and new consumption patterns emerged in the region.

Our study also substantiates Crouch's claim that there were essential changes in the relations among the most important social institutions in Western Europe in the second half of the century. We presented evidence in the relevant chapters for the weakening of traditional social institutions, such as the family and the churches. The pluralization of family forms, that is, the increase in the ratio of extramarital births and cohabitation, constitutes an important piece of evidence, together with the galloping number of divorces and people remaining unmarried. We also addressed the decreasing social influence of religion and the church during the century. In parallel, the transformation of social structure together with other factors resulted in the weakening of the relative social position of labour.

Crouch views the creation of ordered, limited and structured diversity as essential to the birth of the Western European social compromise. In East Central Europe, these conditions obviously did not emerge in the middle of the century. On the contrary, the newly established communist systems explicitly intended to eliminate the prevailing balances between social institutions, because they limited their own political ambitions. For this reason, they quickly launched a frontal attack on the churches, but a number of measures and transformation processes also contributed to the rapid weakening of the traditional arrangements of the family. Thus, although Crouch does not directly deal with social divergences between the East and the West, his work provides a framework to address the issue, as well as further evidence for the intensification of divergences after the Second World War.

Because of the prevailing lack of systematic research, it is still unclear how the decline of the system of social compromise in Western Europe at the end of the twentieth century affected the differences between the eastern and western parts of Europe. Although a series of institutions were established in East Central Europe after the regime change that pointed towards the emergence of a system of balances between social institutions, even two decades after the fall of communism, there was not a single country that showed the signs of a 'social compromise', that is, a balance between capitalism, traditional society and citizenship rights. However, in the light of the recent changes in Western Europe, this can plausibly be interpreted as an element of social convergence in Europe.

The most remarkable feature of Crouch's approach is its ability to grasp a central problem of contemporary European social history, namely the shifts in the balance of social forces and their effects on the character of the entire society. At the same time, the categories that Crouch relies on seem to be static. Although social changes stand in the focus of his work, he is able to convincingly present only those transformations that took place in the relations between certain major sets of institutions: in the case of several other institutions, such as the family, he cannot properly account for the fact that these evolved in the period examined as well.

As we saw earlier, Göran Therborn claims that modernity implies positive expectations for the future, an appreciation of human capabilities and possibilities, a dramatic shift in our concepts about the individual and his or her relation to society, and a series of other similar cultural transformations. He does not neglect aspects of culture; however, he carries out the analysis of post-war European modernity by concentrating more on social and economic dimensions. Some of these areas did undergo changes that conform to the modernity–post-modernity divide. One may convincingly argue, for instance, that the transformation of the family structure starting in the 1960s transcends the family relations of modernity. The modernity–post-modernity shift may also be applied (as shown in the relevant chapter of this book) in the interpretation of social inequalities and the transformation of social structure at the end of the twentieth century, even though there are other theories to explain new developments, most eminently the theory of post-industrial society.

Perhaps the most important weakness in the approach that Therborn took in his interpretation of twentieth-century European social history is that it does not allow him to plausibly account for the differences within Europe. While presenting evidence, the Swedish sociologist greatly relies on the analysis of the 'glorious years' that he understands as the parallel prosperity in democratic–capitalist Western Europe and communist Eastern Europe. Therborn suggests that economic growth and the increase in living standards equally (or at least to a similar degree) prevailed in both halves of Europe. Whereas Crouch regards the common existence of institutional factors among the prerequisites to the social compromise in the middle of the century, Therborn rather relies on a limited number of economic and social divisions in his argument on parallel modernities in Europe.

Our survey did not support Therborn's claim about the parallel existence of the glorious years in Western and Eastern Europe. Even if we disregard the obvious deficit in the area of civil rights that was especially striking in the first period of the communist systems, other factors, such as economic growth, patterns of mass consumption or rates of mortality do not verify the claim either that East Central Europe (or Eastern Europe, for that matter) showed social and economic prosperity comparable with that in Western Europe. On the contrary, we have seen that as the communist system had strong detrimental influence on the quality of life, the region was increasingly left behind by not only North-Western or Central Europe but also by Southern Europe in these areas.

Therborn's other, more convincing argument concerns the common elements of value orientations within Europe: scepticism towards religion, the nation-state and science are claimed to be shared characteristics, along with a marked preference for public welfare measures. Our perspective on these areas led to similar observations and provided further arguments for the existence of common features shared by European societies, even though we could not systematically examine how these characteristics were related to trends outside Europe. Despite these conformities, Therborn's interpretation exaggerates the similarities and convergences within post-war Europe. The culturalist definition of modernity seems to account for this result because modernity in that sense was a process that both the West and the East went through.

In sum, the distinct value of Therborn's work is the wide thematic range and geographical scope, and the sensitivity towards cultural changes, in addition to transformations in social structure. In his definition of modernity, Therborn primarily focuses on cultural elements, and from this aspect, the second half of the twentieth century can be plausibly considered a turning point in history. However, the trajectories of various social areas that he reveals do not always convincingly qualify this claim. Thus, Therborn's assumption requires further confirmation, especially with regard to the question of whether the turning points he uncovered in the second half of the twentieth century were more significant than the changes that had occurred in earlier periods of modernity. The evaluation of the economic and social performance of communist Eastern Europe can be considered problematic even though these assessments are crucial for the thesis of a common European boom and shared modernity in this period. Consequently, his narrow concept of modernity and the associated theoretical framework is highly relevant for the interpretation of twentieth-century European social history, yet it is arguably less plausible than the other two approaches presented and assessed here.

Finally, it has to be emphasized again that the three studies revisited here bear prominent value because, besides the fact that they convey a comprehensive interpretation and provide a coherent narrative of the social changes that Europe underwent in the twentieth century, these works also build their investigations on extensive empirical analyses encompassing almost the entire continent. Each of the three approaches undoubtedly carries remarkable values for the analysis of twentieth-century European social history that other interpretations cannot provide to such extent or in such a form. Therefore, the above three approaches can be equally beneficial for those studying twentieth-century European social history, despite the critical points we raised.

The parallel existence of the above approaches also indicates both the necessity for and the difficulties of comprehensive accounts of European social history. This ambiguity was also explicitly present in the previous chapters, which offered some lessons regarding the writing of the social history of twentieth-century Europe. These lessons are outlined next.

Writing a social history of Europe: promises and constraints

After addressing some of the most acclaimed and valuable interpretations of social development in contemporary Europe, it seems expedient to outline the difficulties and lessons that emerged during the writing of a social history of the continent, together with the possible benefits such an undertaking yields. Out of the alternatives regarding the organization of the volume, we decided to follow a thematic structure, and chronological considerations were observed only within that framework. This option enabled us to offer a long-term presentation of how particular social areas and institutions changed. This perspective made it easier to consider the twentieth century as a whole in the selected dimensions than would have been the case by giving preference to chronological considerations. It also allowed us to offer a coherent account covering mortality trends, changes in family structure, trajectories of income inequality, changes in patterns of consumption, the development of social welfare institutions and a number of other phenomena for the entire twentieth century. In addition, we gained insight into the most important research results, and assessed the often conflicting concepts and interpretations in the research literature of these areas of social history and social sciences in a systematic way. We also studied the most important periods or phases of such various fields as the development of family, social inequalities, cities and education, which often overlapped one another, together with the characteristics of these changes. Furthermore, the thematic structure permitted us to present, in a detailed manner, the long-term factors behind the particular social transformations.

However, it is obvious that this preferred structure implied a couple of undesirable side effects as well. The primacy assigned to the thematic approach prevented us from offering a coherent picture of the different historical periods and it often made it difficult to introduce the connections between the various aspects of social history, even if we attempted to do so within the thematic chapters. This weakness could only be slightly moderated by the section on periodization in this Conclusion. The thematic organization of the book had an impact on the mode of presentation as well: inconsistencies and deficiencies in the argumentation became more conspicuous compared with the chronological presentation prevailing in traditional historical works. In this study, the thematic approach also necessitated the application of the same perspectives to a particular phenomenon when discussing the different regions and historical eras. Although this requirement could not be met to its full extent for practical reasons, including the unavailability of sources or a simple lack of space, still it sometimes resulted in a rather airtight structure that did not allow for detours that might have made the text more lively.

Studies in demography, political science, economy and especially sociology have proved highly applicable in mapping out twentieth-century European social history. The data and perspectives offered by these disciplines assisted us in identifying the questions and objectives necessary for a problem-oriented presentation of the different aspects of social history and the systematization of knowledge, and contributed to establishing the connections between various phenomena as well as the causes of changes. The use of the results of social sciences allowed us, for instance, to systematize the consequences of long-term demographic changes, to identify the factors facilitating migration, to isolate the types of welfare systems emerging in the second half of the twentieth century or to present the social cleavages defining crucial political institutions.

However, for reasons outlined in the Introduction, we did not present social changes in twentieth-century European social history from a single theoretical perspective. Instead, we selected a particular approach for the introduction of each major aspect of social history and the relations among them. The lack of an all-encompassing, comprehensive theoretical framework and overarching narrative resulted in a fragmented line of argumentation, but in our view, this choice enabled us to provide more substantial information about the particular areas of study in social history.

Another conclusion that we may draw highlights the importance of the quantitative approach in writing the twentieth-century social history of Europe. Such a comprehensive work must deal with many societies and social phenomena, which is uncommon in historical studies, and requires conducting long-term analyses so that various historical periods can be discussed in parallel. If the work intends to take a scholarly approach to its subject and to provide evidence for its claims, then it not only has to process a large amount of material but also to present these to the readers. However, the requirements of comprehensible arguments and a manageable size of the book make it necessary to compress relevant information; and this practically obliges us to widely apply the quantitative approach, including statistics. Even if we use statistics in a competent manner, this once again entails certain costs. When using historical statistics, we are faced with the risk that they do not properly reflect the historical context. Important information might disappear or be disregarded when condensed into numbers, sometimes during the work of collecting and processing material at the statistical office, that is, even before the historian could attempt to correct these mistakes.

After these conclusions are drawn from the possibilities and difficulties arising in a comprehensive presentation of European social history, we make two remarks directly linked to the twentieth-century social history of the continent: the first concerns the East–West division, whereas the other refers to the periods of social history. In our study, the relation between East and West has proved to be a main concern, because not only the logic of the historical material, but also the comparative approach repeatedly compelled us to contrast these regions, especially when discussing the second half of the century. As could be clearly seen, the twentieth century was not only the century of political but also of social divisions. Social integration also visited East Central Europe between the two World Wars, but it was followed by a divergence from Western Europe in such areas as population development, economy, consumption and the quality of life. Some of the elements of the Western European social compromise seemed to appear in the East as well: labour was granted extensive social rights after the Second World War. At the same time, there was a loss in terms of civil rights, and the relations between important institutions took a different course of development than in Western Europe. Modernity also appeared in East Central Europe but in a significantly different form from in the western part of the continent, and from around the middle of the century, its negative side began to manifest more, including the use of the state's increased potential for oppression and the rapid disintegration of traditional communities.

The disappearance of the East–West political division became an important event at the turn of the millennium. European social and economic divergence accelerated even further after the fall of communism, but differences within Europe soon started to diminish in many respects. This process is likely to continue in areas directly related to economy (such as consumption patterns), but in other respects the future is more uncertain.

The study of twentieth-century European social history that we undertook is expected to fulfil a number of functions. The comparative perspective assumed a major role in the volume, even if we could not venture to apply the comparative method in an explicit and fully systematic manner (all the more so because the comparative analysis of so many societies is hardly possible in a still accessible and manageable manner).[31] However, similarly to systematic comparative analyses, we attempted to address the important differences and similarities among European societies in the periods examined and we also integrated the results of comparative research in history and related disciplines.[32] Thus, the purpose of the study largely resembles that of the comparative method in historical studies.

A wider European perspective in study and research may help us with a more accurate description, and thus a better understanding of the characteristics of particular national societies. The basis of this function is that without a comparison with other societies, it is obviously hardly possible to identify those features of a given society that deserve special attention. The comparison may focus on finding differences, that is, the presentation of the distinctive features of the cases under examination. For instance, in the analysis of the qualitative aspects of consumption, we identified the shortage economy emerging in the communist countries of East Central Europe and South-Eastern Europe as a characteristic that clearly distinguished these countries from other societies on the continent, and based on that, refuted the concept of 'socialist consumer society'. However, as a result of a parallel investigation of several societies, we not only encounter differences but also similarities. In the previous chapters, we often referred to historical examples illustrating the increasing similarities among Western European societies in the whole or in specific periods of the twentieth century, including mortality patterns and income inequalities.

The contrasting of different societies may fulfil a heuristic function as well: it may focus our attention to phenomena and characteristics otherwise overlooked or not treated according to their significance in research. Thereby it contributes to discovering thus far unknown factors of change and arriving at novel explanations.

Analytical objectives also surfaced in the volume that were best reflected in the attempts to verify the claims about or accounts of twentieth-century European societies. These claims can be of general relevance, in which case our task is to test the formulations and scientific hypotheses about the development of societies. In addition, the assessment of accounts of special cases or particular phenomena also becomes possible.[33] The comparison of societies may help us in the analysis of historical causality or in establishing typologies of various social phenomena.

The search for the factors underlying historical phenomena is one of the most complex tasks of the historian. By means of comparison, historians and social scientists can indirectly carry out experiments, thus taking a step closer to the methodology of natural sciences. Besides, creating typologies is another important analytical tool, and, in fact, itself a form of theorizing. For instance, one of the most influential typologies in the past decades that had a historical relevance classified the welfare states. This typology (as discussed in the relevant chapter) differentiated among 'three worlds of welfare' in the second half of the twentieth century. The formulation of this typology required the systematic application of comparison that enabled the clustering of various welfare institutions into distinct types.[34]

Studying non-native societies is also beneficial in that it provides the historians with new perspectives, unknown in the discourse of their own national historiography, and thereby 'distances' them from the object of the research.[35] Historical research is often characterized by ethnocentrism, which means that the argumentation is resting on assumptions rooted in the national culture without the author or the reader even realizing it. When a wider, international perspective is applied, these premises become more explicit. The experience of our own nation or society, as well as the research results referring to it, often turn out geographically and historically specific, that is, they become relativized and lose their supposed universal validity. The distance may be especially constructive in the case of national historiographies that are isolated for particular reasons, such as small size or language barriers.

The distancing effect of a European perspective facilitates research and study in other ways as well: it can contribute to more grounded assessments of historical events, processes or persons. Historians are generally characterized by an ambivalent attitude towards assessment or evaluation because they tend to see themselves as the representatives of scholarly neutrality, preventing them from evaluating historical processes. Despite this, evaluation appears in most historical accounts because historians evidently talk about successful or less successful developments, institutions, politicians, periods, etc. Moreover, in international historiography the idea of value neutrality (which clearly contributed to the emergence of history as a discipline in the nineteenth century) has been challenged for a long time, and it is now generally accepted that value preferences inevitably surface in historical studies; the choice of topic, for example, is already defined by such values. However, the manner of evaluation clearly influences the quality of the work. The European perspective helps us clarify and present our preferences in an explicit manner, and most importantly it provides a solid methodology for the assessment, because we do not rely on artificial and abstract ideas in our evaluations but rather on the reality of other societies.

Finally, intended or not, historical works largely contribute to the formation (invention, strengthening or transformation) of social identities. At the end of the nineteenth century and even beyond, contribution to the formation of national identity was a more obvious and endorsed goal of historical study than it is today, but the function is still present nonetheless. Moreover, historical writing contributes not only to the making of national identity but to the formation of other (such as local, ethnic or European) identities as well. From this perspective, understanding the social history of Europe is of great significance, because, as a result of the distancing effect mentioned above, it may contribute to the emergence of national identities based on more solid foundations. Some features of the national past that are considered unique may appear elsewhere and may turn out to be not so distinct. Last but not least, well-founded knowledge about our own national past and the history of Europe may also contribute to the reconciliation of different, such as national and European, identities.

NOTES

1 Introduction

1 Neil Fligstein, *Euroclash: The EU, European Identity, and the Future of Europe*, Oxford: Oxford University Press, 2008, 1–6.
2 Frank B. Tipton and Robert Aldrich, *An Economic and Social History of Europe*, vol. 1–2, Baltimore: The John Hopkins University Press, 1987.
3 Gerold Ambrosius and William H. Hubbard, *A Social and Economic History of Twentieth-Century Europe*, Cambridge, MA: Harvard University Press, 1989.
4 Hartmut Kaelble, *A Social History of Western Europe, 1880–1980*, Dublin: Gill and Macmillan, 1989. (In German: Hartmut Kaelble, *Auf dem Weg zu einer europäischen Gesellschaft*, München: C. H. Beck, 1987.); Hartmut Kaelble, *Sozialgeschichte Europas – 1945 bis zur Gegenwart*, München: Beck, 2007.
5 Göran Therborn, *European Modernity and Beyond: The Trajectory of European Societies, 1945–2000*, London: Sage, 1995.
6 Colin Crouch, *Social Change in Western Europe*, Oxford: Oxford University Press, 1999.
7 Jan-Erik Lane and Svante O. Ersson, *Politics and Society in Western Europe*, London: Sage, 1991; Percy Allum, *State and Society in Western Europe*, Cambridge: Polity Press, 1995.
8 J. Klausen and L. A. Tilly, eds., *European Integration in Social and Historical Perspective*, Lanham: Rowman and Littlefield, 1997; J. Bailey, ed., *Social Europe*, London: Longman, 1998; T. P. Boje, B. van Sterbergen and S. Walby, eds., *European Societies: Fusion or Fission?* London: Routledge, 1999; Mary Fulbrook, ed., *Europe Since 1945*, Oxford: Oxford University Press, 2001; Hartmut Kaelble, ed., *The European Way: European Societies during the Nineteenth and Twentieth Centuries*, New York: Berghahn, 2004; Gianfranco Bettin Lattes and Ettore Recchi, eds., *Comparing European Societies: Towards a Sociology of the EU*, Bologna: Monduzzi Editore, 2005; Jens Alber, Tony Fahey and Chiara Saraceno, eds., *Handbook of Quality of Life in the Enlarged European Union*, London and New York: Routledge, 2008.
9 Peter Stearns, ed., *Encyclopedia of European Social History, 1350–2000*, vol. 1–6, New York: Scribner's, 2001.
10 See Robert Bideleux and Ian Jeffries, *A History of Eastern Europe*, 2nd edition, London: Routledge, 2007.
11 Daniel Bell, *The Coming of Post-Industrial Society*, New York: Basic Books, 1974.
12 Manuel Castells, *The Rise of the Network Society*, Oxford: Blackwell, 1996.

13 Axel Schulte, 'Multikulturelle Gesellschaft: Chance, Ideologie oder Bedrohung?', *Aus Politik und Zeitgeschichte*, vol. 23–24 (1990) 16–23.

14 James Coleman, *Foundations of Social Theory*, Cambridge, MA: The Belknap Press, 1990.

15 William Kornhauser, *The Politics of Mass Society*, Glencoe, IL: The Free Press, 1959.

16 Horst Opaschowski, *Soziologie der Freizeit*, Leverkusen: Leske und Budrich, 1994.

17 Ulrich Beck, *Die Risikogesellschaft*, Frankfurt/M.: Suhrkamp, 1986.

18 Anthony Giddens, *The Consequences of Modernity*, Cambridge: Polity Press, 1990, 36.

19 Jean-François Lyotard, *La Condition Postmoderne: Rapport sur le Savoir*, Paris: Minuit, 1979. (In English: *The Postmodern Condition: A Report on Knowledge*, Minneapolis: University of Minnesota Press, 1984.)

20 Therborn, *European Modernity and Beyond*, 13.

2 Population

1 For major concepts and methods of demography, see Paul Demeny and Geoffrey McNicoll, eds., *Encyclopedia of Population*, vol. 1–2, New York: Thomson and Gale, 2003; Jacob S. Siegel and David A. Swanson, eds., *The Methods and Materials of Demography*, San Diego etc.: Elsevier, 2004; Graziella Caselli, Jacques Vallin and Guillaume Wunsch, eds., *Demography: Analysis and Synthesis*, vol. I–IV, Amsterdam: Elsevier, 2006.

2 John C. Caldwell, 'History of Demography', in Demeny and McNicoll, eds., *Encyclopedia of Population*, vol. 1, 216–21; Dennis Hodgson, 'Contemporary Population Thought', in Demeny and McNicoll, eds., *Encyclopedia of Population*, vol. 2, 765–72.

3 Tony Fahey, 'Population', in Göran Therborn and Stefan Immerfall, eds., *Handbook of European Societies*, Berlin: Springer, 2010, 413–14.

4 For the most important indicators of demography, see Huw Jones, *Population Geography*, London: Paul Chapman, 1990, 96–98; Dirk J. van de Kaa, 'Europe and its Population: The Long View', in Dirk J. van de Kaa et al., ed., *European Population: Unity and Diversity*, Dordrecht, Boston and London: Kluwer Academic Publishers, 1999, 1–49.

5 As noted earlier, for practical reasons the present volume deals with a limited number of countries, appearing in Table 2.1, and the term Europe refers to these societies. However, no claim is made to exclude countries not surfacing in the text from the notion of Europe.

6 As indicated earlier, throughout the book Russia, the Soviet Union and its successor states are not considered.

7 Wolfram Fischer, 'Wirtschaft, Gesellschaft und Staat in Europa, 1914–80', in Wolfram Fischer et al., eds., *Handbuch der europäischen Wirtschafts- und Sozialgeschichte*, Bd. 6, Stuttgart: Klett-Cotta, 1987, 17. For details on population size, see Brian R. Mitchell, *European Historical Statistics, 1750–1975*, London: Macmillan, 1980, 29–37; Franz Rothenbacher, *The European Population, 1850–1945*, Basingstoke: Palgrave, 2002; Franz Rothenbacher, *The European Population since 1945*, Basingstoke: Palgrave, 2005.

8 Fischer, 'Wirtschaft, Gesellschaft und Staat in Europa, 1914–80', 19–20.

9 Rothenbacher, *The European Population since 1945*, 14; Zsolt Spéder, 'Childbearing Behaviour in the New EU Member States: Basic Trends and Selected Attitudes', in Wolfgang Lutz, Rudolf Richter and Chris Wilson, eds., *The New Generations of Europeans: Demography and Families in the Enlarged European Union*, London and Sterling, VA: Earthscan, 2006, 59–82.

10 Jean-Claude Chesnais, *The Demographic Transition: Stages, Patterns, and Economic Implications – A Longitudinal Study of Sixty-Seven Countries Covering the Period 1720–1984*, Oxford: Oxford University Press, 1992; D. Kirk, 'Demographic Transition Theory', *Population Studies*, vol. 50 (1996), no. 3, 361–87; Jacques Vallin, 'Europe's Demographic Transition, 1740–1940', in Caselli, Vallin and Wunsch, eds., *Demography: Analysis and Synthesis*, vol. III, 41–66.

11 Ansley J. Coale, 'The Demographic Transition', in United Nations, ed., *The Population Debate*, New York: United Nations, 1975, 347–55.

12 The model has other versions, with three or with more than four stages.

13 Jean-Claude Chesnais, *The Demographic Transition*, Oxford: Oxford University Press, 1992.

14 A. J. Coale and S. C. Watkins, eds., *The Decline of Fertility in Europe*, Princeton: Princeton University Press, 1986.

15 Vallin, 'Europe's Demographic Transition, 1740–1940', 43–49.

16 François Höpflinger, *Bevölkerungssoziologie*, Weinheim und München: Juventa Verlag, 1997, 40–42.

17 András Klinger, 'A megyék termékenységi arányszámai az utolsó 150 évben', *Statisztikai Szemle*, vol. 58 (1980), no. 1, 74–85; György Acsády and András Klinger, *Magyarország népesedése a két világháború között*, Budapest: KJK, 1965, 9.

18 Coale and Watkins, *The Decline of Fertility in Europe*; Susan Cotts Watkins, *From Provinces into Nations: Demographic Integration in Western Europe, 1870–1960*, Princeton: Princeton University Press, 1991, 55–83.

19 Jean-Louis Rallu and Alain Blum, 'European Population', in Alain Blum and Jean-Louis Rallu, eds., *European Population II.: Demographic Dynamics*, Paris: John Libbey Eurotext, 1993, 3–6, 11–14, 18–28.

20 Tomas Sobotka, 'Is Lowest-low Fertility in Europe Explained by the Postponement of Childbearing?', *Population and Development Review*, vol. 30 (2004), 195–220.

21 Paul Demeny, 'Early Fertility Decline in Austria–Hungary: A Lesson in Demographic Transition', in D. V. Glass and Roger Revelle, eds., *Population and Social Change*, London: Arnold, 1972, 153–72; Dezső Dányi, 'Regionális fertilitási sémák Magyarországon a 9. század végén', *Demográfia*, vol. XX (1977), no. 1, 56–87.

22 Jean-Paul Sardon, 'Generation Replacement in Europe since 1900', *Population: An English Selection*, vol. 3 (1991), 22.

23 David Coleman, 'New Patterns and Trends in European Fertility: International and Sub-National Comparisons', in David Coleman, ed., *Europe's Population in the 1990s*, Oxford: Oxford University Press, 1996, 11.

24 David Coleman, 'European Demographic Systems of the Future: Convergence or Diversity?, in *Human Resources in Europe at the Dawn of the 21st Century*, Luxembourg: Office for Official Publications of the European Community, 1992, 141–79.

25 Acsády and Klinger, *Magyarország népesedése a két világháború között*, 25.

26 Rallu and Blum, 'European Population', 13–14.

27 Béla Tomka, *Családfejlődés a 20. századi Magyarországon és Nyugat-Európában*, Budapest: Osiris, 2000, 130.

28 For a catalogue of determinants, see Rudolf Andorka, *Determinants of Fertility in Advanced Societies*, London: Methuen, 1978.

29 Charles Tilly, 'Historical Study of Vital Processes', in Charles Tilly, ed., *Historical Studies of Changing Fertility*, Princeton: Princeton University Press, 1978, 18–20.

30 Richard A. Easterlin, 'The Economics and Sociology of Fertility: A Synthesis', in Tilly, ed., *Historical Studies of Changing Fertility*, 57–133.

31 Deborah Sporton, 'Fertility: the Lowest Level in the World', in Daniel Noin and Robert Woods, eds., *The Changing Population of Europe*, Oxford: Blackwell, 1993, 58.

32 Heather Joshi and Patricia David, 'The Social and Economic Context of Fertility', in Caselli, Vallin and Wunsch, eds., *Demography: Analysis and Synthesis*, vol. I, 509.

33 Michael R. Haines, 'The Population of Europe: The Demographic Transition and After', in Peter Stearns, ed., *Encyclopedia of European Social History*, vol. 2, 163.

34 See e.g. Richard A. Easterlin, *Growth Triumphant: The Twentieth Century in Historical Perspective*, Ann Arbor, MI: University of Michigan Press, 1996.

35 Michael Anderson, 'British Population History, 1911–91', in Michael Anderson, ed., *British Population History: From the Black Death to the Present Day*, Cambridge: Cambridge University Press, 1996, 390.

36 M. Murphy, 'Economic Models of Fertility in Post-War Britain – A Conceptual and Statistical Reinterpretation', *Population Studies*, vol. 46 (1992), 235–57.

37 Ronald Inglehart, 'The Silent Revolution in Europe: Intergenerational Change in Post-industrial Societies', *American Political Science Review*, vol. 65 (1971), no. 4, 991–1017.
38 P. Ariès, 'Two Successive Motivations for the Declining Birth Rate in the West', *Population and Development Review*, vol. 6 (1980), 645–50.
39 Dirk J. van de Kaa, 'The Past of Europe's Demographic Future', *European Review*, vol. 7 (1999), no. 4, 537.
40 R. Lesthaeghe and J. Surkyn, 'Cultural Dynamics and Economic Theories of Fertility Change', *Population and Development Review*, vol. 14 (1988), 1–45.
41 Tony Fahey and Zsolt Spéder, *Fertility and Family Issues in an Enlarged Europe*, Luxembourg: Office for Official Publications of the European Communities, 2004, 48.
42 Andorka, *Determinants of Fertility in Advanced Societies*.
43 Jerzy Berent, 'Causes of Fertility Decline in Eastern Europe and the Soviet Union II: Economic and Social Factors', *Population Studies*, vol. 24 (1970), no. 2, 282–85.
44 Demeny, 'Early Fertility Decline in Austria–Hungary', 170; Rudolf Andorka, 'A regionális termékenység-különbségeket befolyásoló gazdasági és társadalmi tényezők', *Demográfia*, vol. 12 (1969), no. 1–2, 114–24.
45 S. Jay Olshansky and Bruce A. Carnes, 'The Future of Human Longevity', in Peter Uhlenberg, ed., *International Handbook of Population Aging*, Berlin: Springer, 2009, 741.
46 Arthur E. Imhof, 'Von der unsicheren zur sicheren Lebenszeit. Ein folgeschwerer Wandel im Verlaufe der Neuzeit', *Vierteljahresschrift für Sozial-und Wirtschaftsgeschichte*, vol. 71 (1984), no. 2, 175–98.
47 Josef Ehmer, *Bevölkerungsgeschichte und historische Demographie, 1800–2000*, München: Oldenbourg, 2004, 34–35.
48 For demographic tendencies in general, see Rothenbacher, *The European Population, 1850–1945*, 3–73.
49 Daniel Noin, 'Spatial Inequalities in Mortality', in Noin and Woods, eds., *The Changing Population of Europe*, 46–47.
50 Rothenbacher, *The European Population since 1945*, 172; Willian C. Cockerham, *Health and Social Change in Russia and Eastern Europe*, New York: Routledge, 1999, 174.
51 Guang Guo, 'Mortality Trends and Causes of Deaths: A Comparison Between Eastern and Western Europe, 1960s–1980s', *European Journal of Population*, vol. 9 (1993), no. 3, 287–312.
52 Péter Józan, 'Epidemiológiai válság Magyarországon a kilencvenes években', I–II, *Statisztikai Szemle*, vol. 72 (1994), no. 1, 5–20, and vol. 72 (1994), no. 2, 101–23.
53 Marek Okolski, 'East-West Mortality Differentials', in Blum and Rallu, eds., *European Population II*, 165–89.
54 France Mesle, 'Mortality in Eastern and Western Europe: A Widening Gap', in Coleman, ed., *Europe's Population in the 1990s*, 132–33.
55 For details, see Tomka, *Családfejlődés a 20. századi Magyarországon és Nyugat-Európában*, 30–32.
56 Differences between European countries did not only decrease with regard to extreme values, as clearly shown by the dynamics of change in the coefficient of variation. Although the coefficient of variation was 8–8% for female and male life expectancy in 1990, this dropped to 5% and 3%, respectively, by 1950, and to 2% and 1%, respectively, by 1990. Tomka, *Családfejlődés a 20. századi Magyarországon és Nyugat-Európában*, 130–31.
57 Coleman, 'European Demographic Systems of the Future', 175.
58 Béla Tomka, 'Demographic Diversity and Convergence in Europe, 1918–90: The Hungarian Case', *Demographic Research*, vol. 6 (2002), no. 2, 17–48.
59 Mesle, 'Mortality in Eastern and Western Europe', 127.
60 Daniel Noin, 'Spatial inequalities of mortality in the European Union', in Ray Hall and Paul White, eds., *Europe's Population Towards the Next Century*, London: UCL Press, 1995, 58; Johan Mackenbach et al., 'Socioeconomic Inequalities in Mortality Among Women and Among Men: An International Study', *American Journal of Public Health*, vol. 89 (1999), no. 12, 1800–806.

61 For a classic formulation of this view, see Thomas McKeown, *The Modern Rise of Population*, New York and London: Arnold, 1976.

62 John Burnett, 'Housing and the Decline of Mortality', in R. Schofield, D. Reher and A. Bideau, eds., *The Decline of Mortality in Europe*, Oxford: Clarendon Press, 1991, 158–76.

63 Robert Woods, 'Public Health and Public Hygiene: The Urban Environment in the Late Nineteenth and Early Twentieth Centuries', in Schofield, Reher and Bideau, eds., *The Decline of Mortality in Europe*, 233–47.

64 Abdel Omran, 'The Epidemiologic Transition: A Theory of the Epidemiology of Population Change', *Milbank Memorial Fund Quarterly*, vol. 49 (1971), 509–38; R. Spree, 'Der Rückzug des Todes. Der epidemiologische Übergang in Deutschland während des 19. und 20. Jahrhunderts', *Historical Social Research*, vol. 23 (1998), 4–43; James N. Gribble and Samuel H. Preston, eds., *The Epidemiological Transition: Policy and Planning Implications for Developing Countries: Workshop Proceedings*, Washington, DC: National Academy Press, 1993.

65 Ehmer, *Bevölkerungsgeschichte*, 38–41.

66 Cockerham, *Health and Social Change in Russia and Eastern Europe*, 23.

67 For the East–West divergence and especially as regards cardiovascular and cancerous diseases, see Guang Guo, 'Mortality Trends and Causes of Deaths: A Comparison Between Eastern and Western Europe, 1960s–1970s', *European Journal of Population*, vol. 9 (1993), no. 3, 287–312.

68 Marek Okolski, 'East–West Mortality Differentials', in Blum and Rallu, eds., *European Population II*, 165–89; Mesle, 'Mortality in Eastern and Western Europe', 140–41.

69 Cockerham, *Health and Social Change in Russia and Eastern Europe*, 245–51.

70 László Hablicsek, *Az első és a második demográfiai átmenet Magyarországon és Közép-Kelet-Európában*, Budapest: KSH, 1995, 39.

71 Robert Woods and Naomi Williams, 'Must the Gap Widen before it Can Be Narrowed? Long-term Trends in Social Class Mortality Differentials', *Continuity and Change*, vol. 10 (1995), no. 1, 105–37.

72 Michael Anderson, 'The Social Implications of Demographic Change', in F. M. L. Thompson, ed., *The Cambridge Social History of Britain, 1750–1950*, vol. 2, Cambridge: Cambridge University Press, 1990, 23.

73 Höpflinger, *Bevölkerungssoziologie*, 161; Tapani Valkonen, 'Social Inequalities in Mortality', in Caselli, Vallin and Wunsch, eds., *Demography: Analysis and Synthesis*, vol. II, 195–206.

74 Jacques Vallin, 'Mortality, Sex, and Gender', in Caselli, Vallin and Wunsch, eds., *Demography: Analysis and Synthesis*, vol. II, 177–94.

75 For a historical overview, see Klaus J. Bade, *Migration in European History*, Oxford: Blackwell, 2003; For post-war trends, see Klaus F. Zimmermann, 'Introduction: What We Know About Migration', in Klaus F. Zimmermann, ed., *European Migration: What Do We Know?*, Oxford: Oxford University Press, 2005, 1–14.

76 For typologies of migration, see Dirk Hoerder, Jan Lucassen and Leo Lucassen, 'Terminologien und Konzepte in der Migrationsforschung', in Klaus J. Bade et al., Hrsg., *Enzyklopädie: Migration in Europa vom 17. Jahrhundert bis zur Gegenwart*, Paderborn and München: Ferdinand Schöningh and Wilhelm Fink, 2008, 37.

77 Dudley Baines, *Emigration from Europe, 1815–1930*, Cambridge: Cambridge University Press, 1991, 2–5.

78 Akis Kalaitzidis, 'Immigration to the United States during the 1920s and 1930s', in Thomas Cieslik, David Felsen and Akis Kalaitzidis, eds., *Immigration: A Documentary and Reference Guide*, Westport, CT: Greenwood Press, 2009, 61.

79 Massimo Livi-Bacci, *A Concise History of World Population*, Malden, MA: Blackwell, 1997.

80 Ian R. G. Spencer, *British Immigration Policy Since 1939*, London: Routledge, 1997, 129–51.

81 Joanne van Selm, 'Forced Migration', in Demeny and McNicoll, eds., *Encyclopedia of Population*, vol. 1, 435–38.

82 Bade, *Migration in European History*, 199–206.
83 For ethnic cleansing, see Philipp Ther, *Die dunkle Seite der Nationalstaaten: 'Ethnische Säuberungen' im modernen Europa*, Göttingen: Vandenhoeck & Ruprecht, 2011.
84 Höpflinger, *Bevölkerungssoziologie*, 115; Graziella Caselli, 'International Migration in the 20th Century: The Case of the Western Countries', in Caselli, Vallin and Wunsch, eds., *Demography: Analysis and Synthesis*, vol. II, 274.
85 Ehmer, *Bevölkerungsgeschichte und historische Demographie*, 31.
86 Sarah Collinson, *Europe and International Migration*, New York: Pinter Publishers, 1993, 40.
87 Peter Marschalck, *Bevölkerungsgeschichte Deutschlands im 19. und 20. Jahrhundert*, Frankfurt/ M.: Suhrkamp, 1984, 87.
88 Rainer Ohliger and Cătălin Turliuc, 'Minorities into Migrants: Emigration and Ethnic Unmixing in Twentieth-Century Romania', in Rainer Ohliger, Karen Schönwälder and Triadafilos Triadafilopoulos, eds., *European Encounters: Migrants, Migration and European Societies since 1945*, Aldershot: Ashgate, 2003, 64.
89 Heinz Fassmann and Rainer Münz, 'European East–West Migration, 1945–92', in Robin Cohen, ed., *The Cambridge Survey of World Migration*, Cambridge: Cambridge University Press, 1995, 473–74.
90 Leslie Page Moch, 'Moving Europeans: Historical Migration Practices in Western Europe', in Cohen, ed., *The Cambridge Survey of World Migration*, 126–30.
91 Stephen Castles and Mark J. Miller, *The Age of Migration: International Population Movements in the Modern World*, New York: The Guilford Press, 1993, 57–60; Philip E. Ogden, 'International Migration in the Nineteenth and Twentieth Centuries', in Philip E. Ogden and Paul E. White, eds., *Migrants in Modern France: Population Mobility in the Later Nineteenth Centuries*, London: Unwin Hyman, 1989, 46.
92 Anthony M. Messina, *The Logics and Politics of Post-Second World War Migration to Western Europe*, Cambridge: Cambridge University Press, 2007, 20–30.
93 Dudley Baines, 'European Immigration since 1945', in Max-Stephan Schulze, ed., *Western Europe: Economic and Social Change since 1945*, London: Longman, 1999, 179–80.
94 Bade, *Migration in European History*, 246.
95 For a review of theories, see Örn B. Bodvarsson and Hendrik Van den Berg, *The Economics of Immigration: Theory and Policy*, Berlin: Springer, 2009, 59–77.
96 Heinz Fassmann and Rainer Münz, 'Patterns and Trends of International Migration in Western Europe', in Heinz Fassmann and Rainer Münz, eds., *European Migration in the Late Twentieth Century: Historical Patterns, Actual Trends, and Social Implications*, Aldershot: Edward Elgar, 1994, 16–18.
97 Castles and Miller, *The Age of Migration*, 19–26.
98 Peter Stalker, *The Work of Strangers: A Survey of International Labour Migration*, Geneva: ILO, 1994, 91.
99 Baines, 'European Immigration since 1945', 188.
100 Höpflinger, *Bevölkerungssoziologie*, 138.
101 Mike Philips and Trevor Philips, *Windrush: The Irresistible Rise of Multi-Racial Britain*, London: Harper and Collins, 1999.
102 Christian Joppke, *Immigration and the Nation-State: The United States, Germany, and Great Britain*, Oxford: Oxford University Press, 1999, 147–259.
103 Ceri Peach, Alisdair Rogers, Judith Chance and Patricia Daley, 'Immigration and Ethnicity', in A. H. Halsey and Josephine Webb, eds., *Twentieth-Century British Social Trends*, London: Macmillan, 2000, 166–67.
104 Stalker, *The Work of Strangers: A Survey of International Labour Migration*, 95.
105 For current trends, see David Coleman, 'Facing the 21st Century: New Developments, Continuing Problems', in M. Macura, A. L. MacDonald and W. Haug, eds., *The New Demographic Regime: Population Challenges and Policy Responses*, New York and Geneva: United Nations, 2005, 11–43; Wolfgang Lutz, Rudolf Richter and Chris Wilson, *The New Generations of Europeans: Demography and Families in the Enlarged European Union*, London and Sterling, VA: Earthscan, 2006; Fahey, 'Population', 413–37.

106 Dirk J. van de Kaa, 'Europe's Second Demographic Transition', *Population Bulletin*, vol. 42 (1987), no. 3, 3–57.

107 R. L. Cliquet, 'The Second Demographic Transition: Fact or Fiction?', *Council of Europe: Population Studies*, No. 23, 1991.

108 Coleman, 'New Patterns and Trends in European Fertility', 15; David Coleman, 'Why We Don't Have to Believe without Doubting in the "Second Demographic Transition" – Some Agnostic Comments', in *Vienna Yearbook of Population Research, 2004*, Vienna: Austrian Academy of Sciences, 2004, 11–24.

109 John Salt, 'Migration Pressures on Western Europe', in Coleman, ed., *Europe's Population in the 1990s*, 92–126.

110 R. Münz, 'Immigration Trends in Major Destination Countries', in P. Demeny and G. McNicol, eds., *Encyclopedia of Population*, New York: Thomson and Gale, 2003, 519–23.

111 *World Migration 2005: Costs and Benefits of International Migration*, Geneva: International Organization for Migration, 2005, 141.

112 Salt, 'Migration Pressures on Western Europe', 100.

113 Hartmut Kaelble, *Sozialgeschichte Europas: 1945 bis zur Gegenwart*, München: C. H. Beck, 2007, 240; Paul White and Deborah Sporton, 'East-west Movement: Old Barriers, New Barriers?', in Hall and White, eds., *Europe's Population*, 107–21.

114 Salt, 'Migration Pressures on Western Europe', 120.

115 Dušan Drbohlav, 'International Migration Patterns in the New EU Member States', in Lutz, Richter and Wilson, eds., *The New Generations of Europeans*, 223–45.

116 On population ageing and its implications, see David J. Ekerd, ed., *Encyclopedia of Aging*, vol. 1–4, New York: Thomson and Gale, 2002; Steven A. Nyce and Sylvester J. Schieber, *The Economic Implications of Aging Societies*, New York: Cambridge University Press, 2005; Miriam Bernard and Thomas Scharf, eds., *Critical Perspectives on Ageing Societies*, Bristol: Policy Press, 2007.

117 Emily Grundy, 'Population Ageing in Europe', in Coleman, ed., *Europe's Population in the 1990s*, 291.

3 Families and households

1 For a similar definition, see John Scott and Gordon Marshall, eds., *A Dictionary of Sociology*, Oxford: Oxford University Press, 2005, 212.

2 For an introduction to family history, see Michael Anderson, *Approaches to the History of the Western Family, 1500–1914*, London and Basingstoke: Macmillan, 1980; Michael Mitterauer and Reinhard Sieder, *The European Family: Patriarchy to Partnership from the Middle Ages to the Present*, Chicago: University of Chicago Press, 1982; Tamara K. Hareven, 'Historical Analysis of the Family', in Marvin B. Sussmann and Suzanne K. Steinmetz, eds., *Handbook of Marriage and the Family*, New York: Plenum Press, 1987, 37–57; Göran Therborn, *Between Sex and Power: Family in the World, 1900–2000*, London: Routledge, 2004.

3 Different types of households can be differentiated on the basis of the composition of the household. Peter Laslett distinguished the following types in his well-known typology: (1) solitaries: widows or widowers; single people; (2) no family households: households no two members of which belong to the same family; (3) simple family households: nuclear family households, with only the couple and their dependent children without any other type of relative or non-relative present; (4) extended family households: nuclear families plus one or more relatives, such as a parent, a sibling or siblings, who do not form other couples; (5) multiple family households: households comprised of more than one couple, who are closely related in some way, such as nuclear families living together; most often parents and their married child with his/her spouse (*stem family*); parents with more married children and their spouses (*joint family*); or married siblings with their spouses. Peter Laslett, 'Introduction: The History of the

Family', in Peter Laslett and Richard Wall, eds., *Household and Family in Past Time*, Cambridge: Cambridge University Press, 1972, 1–89.

4 Peter Laslett, *The World We Have Lost*, London: Methuen, 1965.

5 Philippe Ariès, *Centuries of Childhood*, London: Jonathan Cape, 1962.

6 For similar categorization of impetuses, see Tamara K. Hareven, 'Family', in Peter Stearns, ed., *Encyclopedia of Social History*, New York: Garland, 1994, 258–59.

7 John Hajnal, 'European Marriage Patterns in Perspective', in D. V. Glass and D. E. C. Eversley, eds., *Population in History*, London: Edward Arnold, 1965, 101–43.

8 In his classic work on the subject, John Hajnal (and others in his wake) defined the ratio of lifelong celibacy based on those people in the cohort of 45–49-year-olds who never married (Hajnal, 'European Marriage Patterns in Perspective', 101–4). In the following discussion, because of a greater availability of data, the ratio is usually based on the cohort of 45–54-year-olds. However, this difference does not alter the results significantly.

9 John C. Haskey, 'Formation and dissolution of unions in the different countries of Europe', in Alain Blum and Jean-Louis Rallu, eds., *European Population, II: Demographic Dynamics*, Paris: John Libbey Eurotext, 1993, 214–15.

10 Béla Tomka, 'Social Integration in Twentieth Century Europe: Evidence from Hungarian Family Development', *Journal of Social History*, vol. 35 (2001), no. 2, 327–48.

11 Hajnal, 'European Marriage Patterns in Perspective', 103; Demeny, 'Early Fertility Decline in Austria–Hungary: A Lesson in Demographic Transition', 164–68; Máire Ni Bhrolchain, 'East–West Marriage Contrasts, Old and New', in Blum and Rallu, eds., *European Population II*, 461–79.

12 *Patterns of First Marriage: Timing and Prevalence*, New York: United Nations, 1990, 9–10.

13 *Patterns of First Marriage: Timing and Prevalence*, 224.

14 Kathleen E. Kiernan, 'Partnership Behaviour in Europe: Recent Trends and Issues', in Coleman, ed., *Europe's Population in the 1990s*, 62–64.

15 Józsefné Csernák, 'Házasodási szokások Finnországban és Magyarországon', *Statisztikai Szemle*, vol. 71 (1993), no. 10, 801.

16 Michael Mitterauer, 'A "European Family" in the Nineteenth and Twentieth Centuries?', in Hartmut Kaelble, ed., *The European Way: European Societies during the Nineteenth and Twentieth Centuries*, New York: Berghahn, 2004, 146–47.

17 Michael Mitterauer, 'Europäische Familienformen in interkulturellen Vergleich', in Michael Mitterauer, *Historisch-anthropologische Familienforschung: Fragestellungen und Zugangsweisen*, Wien: Böhlau, 1990, 38.

18 John Hajnal, 'Two Kinds of Preindustrial Household Formation System', *Population and Development Review*, vol. 8 (1982), 449–94.

19 Michael Anderson, *Approaches to the History of the Western Family*, London: Macmillan, 1980; Franz Rothenbacher, *The European Population, 1850–1945*, Houndmills: Palgrave, 2002, 36.

20 *Patterns of First Marriage: Timing and Prevalence*, 41.

21 Anderson, *Approaches to the History of the Western Family*, 66–68.

22 *Patterns of First Marriage: Timing and Prevalence*, 260–61.

23 Peter Laslett, 'Mean Household Size in England since the Sixteenth Century', in Peter Laslett and Richard Wall, eds., *Household and Family in Past Time*, Cambridge: Cambridge University Press, 1972, 125–58.

24 From the rich literature on pre-twentieth century development, see e.g. Anderson, *Approaches to the History of the Western Family, 1500–1914*; Michael Mitterauer and Reinhard Sieder, *The European Family*, Chicago: University of Chicago Press, 1982.

25 Laslett, 'Mean Household Size in England since the Sixteenth Century', 126.

26 Rothenbacher, *The European Population, 1850–1945*, 51; Franz Rothenbacher, *The European Population since 1945*, Houndmills: Palgrave, 2005; Lajos Thirring, 'Magyarország népessége 1869–1949 között', in József Kovacsics, ed., *Magyarország történeti demográfiája*, Budapest: KJK, 1963, 295.

27 Rothenbacher, *The European Population since 1945*, 45; The distribution of dwellings in Hungary in 1930 by the number of habitants in settlements over 10,000 inhabitants.

Tamás Faragó, *Nemek, nemzedékek, családok és rokonok a XVIII–XX. században* (Doctoral dissertation), Budapest: MTA Kézirattár, 1994, Appendix 49.

28 Mitterauer and Sieder, *The European Family: Patriarchy to Partnership*, 55.

29 K. Schwarz, 'Household Trends in Europe after World War II', in Nico Keilman, Anton Kuijsten and Ad Vossen, eds., *Modelling Household Formation and Dissolution*, Oxford: Clarendon Press, 1988, 74.

30 Schwarz, 'Household Trends in Europe after World War II', 73–76.

31 Faragó, *Nemek, nemzedékek, családok és rokonok*, Melléklet 38.

32 Richard Wall, 'Introduction', in Richard Wall, ed., *Family Forms in Historic Europe*, Cambridge: Cambridge University Press, 1983, 48.

33 For this issue in a Balkan context, see Michael Mitterauer, 'Family Contexts: The Balkans in European Comparison', *History of the Family*, vol. 1 (1996), no. 4, 387–406.

34 Judit Morvay, 'The Joint Family in Hungary', in *Europa et Hungaria*, Budapest: Akadémiai Kiadó, 1965, 231, 239; Edit Fél and Tamás Hofer, *Proper Peasants*, Chicago: Aldine Publishing, 1969, 103.

35 In 1970 in Hungary, the ratio of households with relatives in the ascending line was 6.4% in villages, 3.6% in the capital Budapest, and 3.8% in towns in the country. Cseh-Szombathy László, 'A mai magyar család legfőbb jellegzetességei', in Cseh-Szombathy László, ed., *A változó család*, Budapest: Kossuth, 1978, 46.

36 Statistical distortion may also have increased the ratio of complex family households. Because of the special system of allocating council apartments, in larger towns relatives would often register as living in the same dwelling (e.g. grandchildren with grandparents) as a measure to keep or gain the right to rent it.

37 Tamás Faragó, 'Housing and Households in Budapest, 1850–1944', in *History and Society in Central Europe*, vol. 1 (1991), no. 1, 29–63.

38 Ambrosius and Hubbard, *A Social and Economic History of Twentieth-Century Europe*, 23.

39 *Time Series of Historical Statistics, 1867–1992*, vol. I. Budapest: KSH, 1993, 163.

40 Ambrosius and Hubbard, *A Social and Economic History of Twentieth-Century Europe*, 23–24; Rudolf Andorka, *Determinants of Fertility in Advanced Societies*, London: Methuen, 1978.

41 Schwarz, 'Household Trends in Europe after World War II', 76.

42 Sibylle Meyer and Eva Schulze, 'Nichteheliche Lebensgemeinschaften – Alternativen zur Ehe? Eine internationale Datenübersicht', *Kölner Zeitschrift für Soziologie und Sozialpsychologie*, Jg. 35 (1983), 735–54; Kathleen Kiernan, 'Leaving Home: Living Arrangements of Young People in Six West European Countries', *European Journal of Population*, vol. 2 (1986), no. 2, 177–84.

43 Nico Keilman, 'Recent Trends in Family and Household Composition in Europe', *European Journal of Population*, vol. 3 (1987), 304–5.

44 Hall, 'Family Structures', in Noin and Woods, eds., *The Changing Population of Europe*, 104.

45 For these changes, see Martine Segalen, *Historical Anthropology of the Family*, Cambridge: Cambridge University Press, 1996, 201–56.

46 Michael Young and Peter Willmott, *The Symmetrical Family*, New York: Pantheon Books, 1973.

47 John Ermisch, 'The Economic Environment for Family Formation', in Coleman, ed., *Europe's Population in the 1990s*, 144–62.

48 For a summary of female employment, see Kaelble, *A Social History of Western Europe*, 129. For different countries until the mid-twentieth century, see E. Boserup, ed., *Female Labour before, during and after the Industrial Revolution* (8th International Economic History Congress), Budapest: Akadémiai Kiadó, 1982.

49 Katja Boh, 'European Family Life Patterns – A Reappraisal', in Katja Boh et al., eds., *Changing Patterns of European Family Life: A Comparative Analysis of 14 European Countries*, London and New York: Routledge, 1989, 271–72.

50 Riitta Jallinoja, 'Women between Family and Employment', in Boh et al., eds., *Changing Patterns of European Family Life*, 118.

51 Manfred G. Schmidt, 'Gendered Labour Force Participation', in Francis G. Castles, ed., *Families of Nations: Patterns of Public Policy in Western Democracies*, Aldershot: Dartmouth, 1993, 182.

52 Kaelble, *A Social History of Western Europe*, 130–33.

53 Boh, 'European Family Life Patterns', 269.

54 Wolfram Fischer, 'Wirtschaft, Gesellschaft und Staat in Europa, 1914–80', in Wolfram Fischer et al., eds., *Handbuch der europäischen Wirtschafts-und Sozialgeschichte*, Bd. 6, Stuttgart: Klett-Cotta, 1987, 82.

55 André Michel, 'The Impact of Marriage and Children on the Division of Gender Roles', in Boh et al., eds., *Changing Patterns of European Family Life*, 183.

56 Kaelble, *A Social History of Western Europe*, 129; S. Harding, D. Philips and M. Fogarty, *Contrasting Values in Western Europe: Unity, Diversity and Change*, London: Macmillan, 1986, 129.

57 R. Inglehart, M. Basáñez and A. Moreno, eds., *Human Values and Beliefs: A Cross-Cultural Sourcebook*, Ann Arbor, MI: University of Michigan Press, 1998, Table V223.

58 Harding, Philips and Fogarty, *Contrasting Values in Western Europe*, 128.

59 Harding, Philips and Fogarty, *Contrasting Values in Western Europe*, 120–21; Inglehart, Basáñez and Moreno, eds., *Human Values and Beliefs: A Cross-Cultural Sourcebook*, Tables V198–V210.

60 Alexander Szalai, ed., *The Use of Time*, The Hague: Mouton, 1972, 643, 662.

61 Therborn, *European Modernity and Beyond*, 64–65.

62 Szalai, *The Use of Time*, 643.

63 Rudolf Andorka, Tamás Kolosi and György Vukovich, eds., *Social Report*, Budapest: TÁRKI, 1992, 136.

64 Inglehart, Basáñez and Moreno, eds., *Human Values and Beliefs: A Cross-Cultural Sourcebook*, Tables V198–V210.

65 In addition to the cited studies by Ariès, see: Lloyd DeMause, ed., *The History of Childhood*, New York: Psychohistory Press, 1974; Lawrence Stone, *The Family, Sex, and Marriage in England, 1500–1800*, New York: Harper and Row, 1979; Edward Shorter, *The Making of the Modern Family*, New York: Basic Books, 1976. For a more recent publication, see Joseph M. Hawes and N. Ray Hiner, eds., *Children in Historical and Comparative Perspective*, New York and London: Greenwood Press, 1991.

66 Stone, *The Family, Sex, and Marriage in England*, 423.

67 Anne Hélène Gauthier, *The State and the Family: A Comparative Analysis of Family Policies in Industrialized Countries*, Oxford: Oxford University Press, 1996, 50–58, 73–82.

68 Hoóz István, *Népesedéspolitika és népességfejlődés Magyarországon a két világháború között*, Budapest: Akadémiai Kiadó, 1970, 161.

69 Gauthier, *The State and the Family*, 74, 166.

70 Gauthier, *The State and the Family*, 53–56, 107–9.

71 Gauthier, *The State and the Family*, 107–9, 181.

72 Linda Clark, 'France', in Hawes and Hiner, eds., *Children in Historical and Comparative Perspective*, 294.

73 Göran Therborn, 'The Politics of Childhood: The Rights of Children in Modern Times', in Francis G. Castles, ed., *Families of Nations: Patterns of Public Policy in Western Democracies*, Aldershot: Dartmouth Publ., 1993, 241–91.

74 Therborn, 'The Politics of Childhood', 254–55.

75 Colin Heywood, *A History of Childhood: Children and Childhood in the West from Medieval to Modern Times*, Cambridge: Polity Press, 2006, 39.

76 Therborn, 'The Politics of Childhood', 255.

77 Nigel Lowe and Gillian Douglas, eds., *Families Across Frontiers*, The Hague: Martinus Nijhoff, 1996.

78 Therborn, 'The Politics of Childhood', 257.

79 For similar developments, see Bob Franklin, 'Children's Rights and Media Wrongs: Changing Representations of Children and the Developing Rights Agenda', in Bob

Franklin, *The New Handbook of Children's Rights: Comparative Policy and Practice*, London: Routledge, 2002, 15–42.

80 Gauthier, *The State and the Family*, 157.

81 Therborn, 'The Politics of Childhood', 264.

82 Therborn, 'The Politics of Childhood', 276–77.

83 Kaelble, *A Social History of Western Europe*, 135; Harding, Philips and Fogarty, *Contrasting Values in Western Europe*, 19–24; the study included Belgium, Denmark, Spain, France, Great Britain, the Netherlands, Ireland, Italy, West Germany and Northern Ireland.

84 Inglehart, Basáñez and Moreno, eds., *Human Values and Beliefs: A Cross-Cultural Sourcebook*, Tables V226–V236.

85 Harding, Philips and Fogarty, *Contrasting Values in Western Europe*, 19–24.

86 Therborn, *European Modernity and Beyond*, 292–93.

87 Inglehart, Basáñez and Moreno, eds., *Human Values and Beliefs: A Cross-Cultural Sourcebook*, Tables V224–V236; for similar results of another, more limited survey, see Rossella Palomba and Hein Moors, 'Attitudes towards Marriage, Children, and Population Policies in Europe', in Rossella Palomba and Hein Moors, eds., *Population, Family and Welfare: A Comparative Survey of European Attitudes*, vol. I, Oxford: Clarendon Press, 1995, 245–53.

88 Mitterauer and Sieder, *The European Family*, 70–92.

89 See e.g. Talcott Parsons, *Structure and Process in Modern Societies*, Glencoe: Free Press, 1960, 302; Mitterauer and Sieder, *The European Family*, 78–90.

90 Mitterauer and Sieder, *The European Family: Patriarchy to Partnership*, 94.

91 Philippe Ariès, *Centuries of Childhood*, London: Jonathan Cape, 1962; Stone, *The Family, Sex, and Marriage in England, 1500–1800*, 21–22; Shorter, *The Making of the Modern Family*.

92 Shorter, *The Making of the Modern Family*, 205.

93 Shorter, *The Making of the Modern Family*, 191–99.

94 Stone, *The Family, Sex, and Marriage in England*, 223.

95 Philippe Ariès, *Centuries of Childhood*, London: Jonathan Cape, 1962.

96 Anderson, *Approaches to the History of the Western Family, 1500–1914*, 61–64.

97 Kaelble, *A Social History of the Western Europe*, 133.

98 Robert Chester, 'Conclusion', in Robert Chester, ed., *Divorce in Europe*, Leiden: Martinus Nijhoff, 1977, 288.

99 Francis G. Castles and Michael Flood, 'Why Divorce Rates Differ: Law, Religious Belief and Modernity', in Castles, ed., *Families of Nations*, 300–301.

100 For family dissolutions in different Western European countries, see Chester, ed., *Divorce in Europe*.

101 Józsefné Csernák, 'Házasság és válás Magyarországon', 350, 362.

102 On major trends of family formation, see Therborn, *Between Sex and Power*, 192–225.

103 Höpflinger, 'Haushalts- und Familienstrukturen im intereuropäischen Vergleich', in Stefan Hradil and Stefan Immerfall, *Die westeuropäischen Gesellschaften im Vergleich*, Opladen: Leske und Budrich, 1997, 105.

104 On this issue, see also Meyer and Schulze, 'Nichteheliche Lebensgemeinschaften – Alternativen zur Ehe?', 735–54; Kathleen Kiernan, 'Leaving Home: Living Arrangements of Young People in Six West-European Countries', *European Journal of Population*, vol. 2 (1986), 182; Nico Keilman, 'Recent Trends in Family and Household Composition in Europe', *European Journal of Population*, vol. 3 (1987), 309–12.

105 Catherine Villeneuve-Gokalp, 'From Marriage to Informal Union: Recent Changes in the Behaviour of French Couples', *Population: An English Selection*, vol. 3 (1991), 81–111.

106 Höpflinger, 'Haushalts- und Familienstrukturen im intereuropäischen Vergleich', 105.

107 Schwarz, 'Household Trends in Europe after World War II', 78.

108 Höpflinger, 'Haushalts- und Familienstrukturen im intereuropäischen Vergleich', 106.

109 Höpflinger, 'Haushalts- und Familienstrukturen im intereuropäischen Vergleich', 109.

110 Elwood Carlson and Andras Klinger, 'Partners in Life: Unmarried Couples in Hungary', *European Journal of Population*, vol. 3 (1987), no. 1, 85–99; Szűcs Zoltán, *Az élettársi kapcsolatban élő családok társadalmi-demográfiai jellemzői*, Budapest: KSH, 1996, 7.

111 Ron Lesthaeghe and Guy Moors, 'Living Arrangements, Socio-economic Position, and Values among Young Adults: A Pattern Description for France, West-Germany, Belgium, and the Netherlands, 1990', in Coleman, ed., *Europe's Population in the 1990s*, 211–12; Höpflinger, 'Haushalts- und Familienstrukturen im intereuropäischen Vergleich', 110.

112 Franz Rothenbacher, 'Social Change in Europe and Its Impact on Family Structures', in John Eekelaar and Thandabantu Nhlapo, eds., *The Changing Family: Family Forms and Family Law*, Oxford: Hart Publ., 1998, 5–10.

113 Elina Haavio-Mannila and Anna Rotkirch, 'Sexuality and Family Formation', in Immerfall and Therborn, eds., *Handbook of European Societies*, 465–97.

114 Hana Maříková, 'The Czech Family at Present and in the Past', in Mihaela Robila, ed., *Families in Eastern Europe*, Amsterdam etc.: Elsevier, 2004, 33.

115 Tiziana Nazio, *Cohabitation, Family and Society*, New York and London: Routledge, 2008, 16–22.

116 Jacqueline Scott, 'Family Change: Revolution or Backlash in Attitudes?', in Susan McRae, ed., *Changing Britain: Families and Households in the 1990s*, Oxford: Oxford University Press, 1999, 98.

117 Spéder Zsolt, 'Az európai családformák változatossága. Párkapcsolatok, szülői és gyermeki szerepek az európai országokban az ezredfordulón', *Századvég*, vol. 22, (2005) no. 3, 3–48.

118 Kathleen Kiernan, 'Partnership Behaviour in Europe', in Coleman, ed., *Europe's Population in the 1990s*, 67–68; Zsolt Spéder, 'Változások az ezredfordulón', in Andorka, *Bevezetés a szociológiába*, 416.

119 Kiernan, 'Partnership Behaviour in Europe', 74–75.

120 Kiernan, 'Partnership Behaviour in Europe', 71.

121 In family history, the concept of life course was also introduced, because it is arguably more flexible and is thus more appropriate to describe historically changing family forms. See Tamara K. Hareven, 'Historical Analysis of the Family', in Marvin B. Sussman and Suzanne K. Steinmetz, eds., *Handbook of Marriage and the Family*, New York: Plenum Press, 1987, 45–49.

122 Mitterauer and Sieder, *The European Family*, 49–62; Josef Ehmer, *Sozialgeschichte des Alters*, Frankfurt/M.: Suhrkamp, 1990, 187–93.

123 Michael Anderson, 'The Emergence of the Modern Life Cycle in Britain', *Social History*, vol. 10 (1985), no. 1, 69–87.

124 Martin Kohli, 'Die Institutionalisierung des Lebenslaufs: Historische Befunde und theoretische Argumente', *Kölner Zeitschrift für Soziologie und Sozialpsychologie*, vol. 37 (1985) 1–29; for a similar experience of a communist country, see Hartmut Wendt, 'The Former German Democratic Republic: the Standardized Family', in Franz-Xaver Kaufmann et al., ed., *Family Life and Family Policies in Europe, Vol. I: Structures and Trends in the 1980s*, Oxford: Clarendon Press, 1997, 114–54.

125 Michael Mitterauer, 'A "European Family"?', in Kaelble, ed., *The European Way*, 149–51.

126 Trutz von Trotha, 'Zum Wandel der Familie', *Kölner Zeitschrift für Soziologie und Sozialpsychologie*, vol. 42 (1990), 452–73.

4 Social stratification and social mobility

1 David. B. Grusky, 'The Past, Present and Future of Social Inequality', in David B. Grusky, *Social Stratification: Class, Race and Gender in Sociological Perspective*, Boulder, CO: Westview Press, 2001, 4.

2 Ralf Dahrendorf, *Class and Class Conflict in Industrial Society*, Stanford, CA: Stanford University Press, 1959, 170–72.

3 Grusky, 'The Past, Present and Future of Social Inequality', 7; David B. Grusky and Jesper B. Sørensen, 'Can Class Analysis Be Salvaged?', *American Journal of Sociology*, vol. 103 (1998), 1187–1234.

4 Dahrendorf, *Class and Class Conflict in Industrial Society*, 170; Frank Parkin, *Class Inequality and Political Order: Social Stratification in Capitalist and Communist Societies*, New York: Praeger, 1971, 25; Erik O. Wright, *Class Counts: Comparative Studies in Class Analysis*, Cambridge: Cambridge University Press, 1997; Robert Erikson and John H. Goldthorpe, *The Constant Flux: A Study of Class Mobility in Industrial Societies*, Oxford: Clarendon Press, 1992.

5 Grusky, *The Past, Present and Future of Social Inequality*, 7.

6 Simon Kuznets, 'Economic Growth and Income Inequality', *American Economic Review*, vol. XLV (1995), no. 1, 1–28.

7 Hartmut Kaelble, 'Introduction', in Hartmut Kaelble and Mark Thomas, eds., *Income Distribution in Historical Perspective*, Cambridge and Paris: Cambridge University Press and Maison des Sciences de l'Homme, 1991, 1–56.

8 Peter H. Lindert and Jeffrey G. Williamson, 'Growth, Equality and History', *Explorations in Economic History*, vol. 22 (1985), no. 4, 341–77; Peter H. Lindert, 'Three Centuries of Inequality in Britain and America', in Anthony B. Atkinson and François Bourguignon, eds., *Handbook of Income Distribution*, vol. 1, Amsterdam: Elsevier, 2000, 167–216.

9 Ambrosius and Hubbard, *A Social and Economic History of Twentieth-Century Europe*, 70.

10 Hartmut Kaelble, 'Der Wandel der Einkommensverteilung während der zweiten Hälfte des 20. Jahrhunderts', in Stefan Ryll and Alparslan Yenal, eds., *Politik und Ökonomie: Problemsicht aus klassischer, neo-und neuklassischer Perspektive*, Marburg: Metropolis-Verlag, 2000, 230–31.

11 Franz Kraus, 'The Historical Development of Income Inequality in Western Europe and the United States', in Peter Flora and Arnold J. Heidenheimer, eds., *The Development of Welfare States in Europe and America*, New Brunswick and London: Transaction, 1981, 203.

12 Kraus, 'The Historical Development of Income Inequality', 203–4.

13 Wolfram Fischer, 'Wirtschaft, Gesellschaft und Staat in Europa, 1914–80', in Wolfram Fischer et al., eds., *Handbuch der europäischen Wirtschafts- und Sozialgeschichte*, Bd. 6, Stuttgart: Klett-Cotta, 1987, 61.

14 János Kornai, *The Socialist System: The Political Economy of Communism*, Princeton: Princeton University Press, 1992, 322–23.

15 Anthony B. Atkinson, Lee Rainwater and Timothy M. Smeeding, *Income Distribution in OECD Countries: Evidence from the Luxembourg Income Study*, Paris: OECD, 1995, 39–58.

16 Anthony B. Atkinson, 'Income Distribution in Europe and the United States', *Oxford Review of Economic Policy*, vol. 12 (1996), no. 1, 15–28.

17 Bennett Harrison and Barry Bluestone, *The Great U-Turn*, New York: Basic Books, 1988.

18 Arthur S. Alderson and François Nielsen, 'Globalization and the Great U-Turn: Income Inequality Trends in 16 OECD Countries', *American Journal of Sociology*, vol. 107 (2002), no. 5, 1248.

19 Anthony B. Atkinson, 'Distribution of Income and Wealth', in A. H. Halsey and Josephine Webb, eds., *Twentieth-Century British Social Trends*, London: Macmillan, 2000, 363.

20 A. B. Atkinson, *The Changing Distribution of Earnings in OECD Countries*, Oxford: Oxford University Press, 2008, 48–51.

21 Anthony B. Atkinson, 'Income Distribution in Europe and the United States', *Oxford Review of Economic Policy*, vol. 12 (1996), no. 1, 15–28.

22 Guy Routh, *Occupation and Pay in Great Britain, 1906–1979*, London and Basingstoke: Macmillan, 1980, 59–132.

23 Jürgen Kocka, *Die Angestellten in der deutschen Geschichte, 1850–1980*, Göttingen: Vandenhoeck und Ruprecht, 1981.

24 Walter D. Connor, *Socialism, Politics, and Equality: Hierarchy and Change in Eastern Europe and the USSR*, New York: Columbia University Press, 1979, 231.

25 Rachel A. Rosenfeld and Arne L. Kalleberg, 'A Cross-national Comparison of the Gender Gap in Income', *American Journal of Sociology*, vol. 96 (1990), no. 1, 69–106;

Tanja van der Lippe and Liset van Dijk, 'Comparative Research on Women's Employment', *Annual Review of Sociology*, vol. 28 (2002), 221–41.

26 Edward N. Wolff, 'International Comparisons of Wealth Inequality', *Review of Income and Wealth*, vol. 4 (1996), 433–51.

27 James B. Davies and Anthony Shorrocks, 'The Distribution of Wealth', in Atkinson and Bourguignon, eds., *Handbook of Income Distribution*, 637.

28 Anthony B. Atkinson and A. J. Harrison, 'Trends in the Distribution of Wealth in Britain', in Anthony B. Atkinson, ed., *Wealth, Income, and Inequality*, Oxford: Oxford University Press, 1980, 218; W. D. Rubinstein, 'Modern Britain', in W. D. Rubinstein, ed., *Wealth and The Wealthy in the Modern World*, London: Croom Helm, 1980, 57; Davies and Shorrocks, 'The Distribution of Wealth', 639.

29 Adeline Daumard, 'Wealth and Affluence in France since the Beginning of the Nineteenth Century', in Rubinstein, ed., *Wealth and The Wealthy in the Modern World*, 115.

30 Crouch, *Social Change in Western Europe*, 158.

31 Rainer Geißler, *Die Sozialstruktur Deutschlands*, Opladen: Westdeutscher Verlag, 1992, 58–59.

32 Gerhard Lenski, *Power and Privilege: A Theory of Social Stratification*, Chapel Hill: The University of North Carolina Press, 1984 [1966], 313–18.

33 Kraus, 'The Historical Development of Income Inequality', 213.

34 Kaelble, 'Der Wandel der Einkommensverteilung während der zweiten Hälfte des 20. Jahrhunderts', 233.

35 Martin Schnitzer, *Income Distribution: A Comparative Study of the United States, Sweden, West Germany, East Germany, the United Kingdom, and Japan*, New York: Praeger, 1974, 81.

36 Kornai, *The Socialist System*, 316–32.

37 Jan Tinbergen, *Income Distribution: Analysis and Policies*, Amsterdam: North-Holland Publishing Company, 1975, 97; 103.

38 Kaelble, 'Der Wandel der Einkommensverteilung während der zweiten Hälfte des 20. Jahrhunderts', 234.

39 Simon Kuznets, *Economic Growth and Income Inequality*, 1–28.

40 Routh, *Occupation and Pay in Great Britain, 1906–1979*, 178–79.

41 Kaelble, 'Der Wandel der Einkommensverteilung während der zweiten Hälfte des 20. Jahrhunderts', 236–40.

42 Atkinson, 'Distribution of Income and Wealth', 359.

43 Bart van Ark, 'Sectoral Growth Accounting and Structural Change in Post-War Europe', in Bart van Ark and Nicholas Crafts, eds., *Quantitative Aspects of Post-War European Economic Growth*, Cambridge: Cambridge University Press, 1996, 84–164.

44 From the literature on employment structure: Joachim Singelmann, *From Agriculture to Services: The Transformation of Industrial Employment*, Beverly Hills, CA and London: Sage, 1978; Gerold Ambrosius, 'Wirtschaftsstruktur und Strukturwandel: Gesamt-wirtschaft', in Gerold Ambrosius, Dietmar Petzina and Werner Plumpe, eds., *Moderne Wirtschaftsgeschichte*, München: Oldenbourg, 1996, 175–91.

45 Of the classic literature: Colin G. Clark, *The Conditions of Economic Progress*, London: Macmillan, 1940.

46 Therborn, *European Modernity and Beyond*, 66; Paul Bairoch, ed., *La Population active et sa Structure*, Bruxelles: Université Libre de Bruxelles, 1968, 83–120.

47 Hartmut Kaelble, 'Was Prometheus Most Unbound in Europe? Labour Force in Europe during the Late XIXth and XXth Centuries', *Journal of European Economic History*, vol. 18 (1989), no. 1, 66–85.

48 Therborn, *European Modernity and Beyond*, 69.

49 Kaelble, *A Social History of Western Europe*, 27.

50 Therborn, *European Modernity and Beyond*, 69–73.

51 Therborn, *European Modernity and Beyond*, 72–73.

52 Singelmann, *From Agriculture to Services*, 31.

53 Singelmann, *From Agriculture to Services*, 72–84; Manuel Castells, *The Information Age: Economy, Society and Culture, Vol. I, The Rise of the Network Society*, Oxford: Blackwell, 2000, 227–30.

54 Clark, *The Conditions of Economic Progress*.

55 Victor Fuchs, *The Service Economy*, New York: Columbia University Press, 1968, 46–76.

56 Grusky, 'The Past, Present, and Future of Social Inequality', 7.

57 Ambrosius and Hubbard, *A Social and Economic History of Twentieth-Century Europe*, 62.

58 Max Haller, 'Klassenstruktur und Arbeitslosigkeit – Die Entwicklung zwischen 1960 und 1990', in Stefan Hradil and Stefan Immerfall, eds., *Die westeuropäischen Gesellschaften im Vergleich*, Opladen: Leske und Budrich, 1997, 390.

59 Ambrosius and Hubbard, *A Social and Economic History of Twentieth-Century Europe*, 62.

60 Ambrosius and Hubbard, *A Social and Economic History of Twentieth-Century Europe*, 62–63.

61 Ambrosius and Hubbard, *A Social and Economic History of Twentieth-Century Europe*, 64.

62 For comprehensive discussions of the changes in social stratification, see P. Nolte, 'Social Inequality in History: Stratification and Classes', in N. Smelser and P. Baltes, eds., *International Encyclopedia of the Social and Behavioral Sciences*, vol. 21, 2001 14313–20; for antecedents, see Hans-Ulrich Wehler, ed., *Klassen in der europäischen Geschichte*, Göttingen: Vandenhoeck, 1979.

63 For a similar classification: Hartmut Kaelble, *Sozialgeschichte Europas: 1945 bis zur Gegenwart*, München: C. H. Beck, 2007, 155.

64 Anthony L. Cardoza, *Aristocrats in Bourgeois Italy: The Piedmontese Nobility, 1861–1930*, Cambridge: Cambridge University Press, 1997, 212–19.

65 David Cannadine, *The Decline and Fall of the British Aristocracy*, New Haven: Yale University Press, 1990, 695.

66 T. Iván Berend and György Ránki, *Közép-Kelet-Európa gazdasági fejlődése a 19–20. században*, Budapest: KJK, 1976, 535–36.

67 Wolfram Fischer, 'Wirtschaft, Gesellschaft und Staat in Europa, 1914–80', in Wolfram Fischer et al., eds., *Handbuch der europäischen Wirtschafts-und Sozialgeschichte*, Bd. 6, Stuttgart: Klett-Cotta, 1987, 59.

68 Peter Stearns, *European Society in Upheaval: Social History since 1750*, New York: Macmillan, 1975, 294.

69 Margaret Scotford Archer and Salvador Giner, 'Social Stratification in Europe', in Margaret Scotford Archer and Salvador Giner, eds., *Contemporary Europe: Class, Status and Power*, New York: St Martin's Press, 1971, 43.

70 Archer and Giner, 'Social Stratification in Europe', 43.

71 Max Haller, Tamás Kolosi and Péter Róbert, 'Social Mobility in Austria, Czechoslovakia, and Hungary', in Max Haller, ed., *Class Structure in Europe: New Findings from East–West Comparisons of Social Structure and Mobility*, Armonk and London: M. E. Sharpe, 1990, 191.

72 Carmen González Enriquez, 'Elites and Decommunization in Eastern Europe', in John Higley, Jan Pakulski and Wlodzimierz Weselowski, *Postcommunist Elites and Democracy in Eastern Europe*, London: Macmillan, 1998, 277–79.

73 John Higley, Jan Pakulski and Wlodzimierz Weselowski, 'Introduction: Elite Change and Democratic Regimes in Eastern Europe', in Higley, Pakulski and Weselowski, *Postcommunist Elites and Democracy in Eastern Europe*, 1–33.

74 Jürgen Kocka, 'The Middle Classes in Europe', in Kaelble, ed., *The European Way*, 17–19.

75 Percy Allum, *State and Society in Western Europe*, Cambridge: Polity Press, 1995, 68.

76 John Scott, 'Class and Stratification', in Geoff Payne, ed., *Social Divisions*, Houndmills: Macmillan, 2000, 47.

77 Allum, *State and Society in Western Europe*, 73–74.

78 Geoffrey Crossick and Heinz-Gerhard Haupt, *The Petite Bourgeoisie in Europe, 1780–1914: Enterprise, Family and Independence*, London: Routledge, 1995, 1–15; Geoffrey Crossick, 'The Petite Bourgeoisie and Comparative History', in Kaelble, ed., *The European Way*, 89–114.

79 Kocka, 'The Middle Classes in Europe', 33–35.

80 Jürgen Kocka, 'Bürgertum und bürgerliche Gesellschaft im 19. Jahrhundert: Europäische Entwicklungen und deutsche Eigenarten', in Jürgen Kocka and Ute Frevert, eds., *Bürgertum im 19. Jahrhundert*, Bd. 1, München: Deutscher Taschenbuch Verlag, 1988, 58–63.

81 A verbatim translation of the German *Wirtschaftsbürgertum* is 'economic bourgeoisie', and that of *Bildungsbürgertum* is 'educated bourgeoisie'.

82 For the society of East Central Europe in the pre-Second World War period, see Andrew C. Janos, *East Central Europe in the Modern World: The Politics of the Borderland from Pre- to Post-Communism*, Stanford, CA: Stanford University Press, 2000, 65–217.

83 Kocka, 'The Middle Class in Europe', 19–24; Waclaw Dlugoborski, 'Das polnische Bürgertum vor 1918 in vergleichender Pesrpektive', in Kocka and Frevert, eds., *Bürgertum im 19. Jahrhunder*, Bd. 1, 266–99.

84 David Lane, 'Structural and Social Change in Poland', in David Lane and George Kolankiewicz, eds., *Social Groups in Polish Society*, London and Basingstoke: Macmillan, 1973, 17.

85 Valuch Tibor, *Magyarország társadalomtörténete a XX. század második felében*, Budapest: Osiris, 2001, 171–72.

86 Gerhard Schildt, *Die Arbeiterschaft im 19. und 20. Jahrhundert*, München: Oldenbourg, 1996, 76.

87 Dick Geary, 'Protest and Strike: Recent Research on "Collective Action" in England, Germany, and France', in Klaus Tenfelde, ed., *Arbeiter und Arbeiterbewegung im Vergleich*, München: Oldenbourg, 1986, 363–87.

88 Therborn, *European Modernity and Beyond*, 74.

89 Kaelble, *Sozialgeschichte Europas*, 188.

90 Gøsta Esping-Andersen, *The Three Worlds of Welfare Capitalism*, Cambridge: Polity Press, 1990, 99.

91 Béla Tomka, 'Western European Welfare States in the 20th Century: Convergences and Divergences in a Long-Run Perspective', *International Journal of Social Welfare*, vol. 12 (2003), no. 4, 249–60.

92 Ralf Dahrendorf, *Class and Class Conflict in Industrial Society*, Stanford: Stanford University Press, 1959 [1957], 48–51.

93 Archer and Giner, 'Social Stratification in Europe', 36.

94 Peter Saunders, *Social Class and Stratification*, London: Routledge, 1990, 118–27.

95 Gábor Gyáni and György Kövér, *Magyarország társadalomtörténete a reformkortól az első világháborúig*, Budapest: Osiris, 1998, 280, 294–95.

96 Joni Lovenduski and Jean Woodall, *Politics and Society in Eastern Europe*, Bloomington, IN: Indiana University Press, 1987, 150–51.

97 Lane, *Structural and Social Change in Poland*, 24.

98 Stefan Houpt, Pedro Lains and Lennart Schön, 'Sectoral Developments, 1945–2000', in Stephan Broadberry and Kevin H. O'Rourke, eds., *The Cambridge Economic History of Modern Europe, Vol. 2: 1870 to the Present*, Cambridge: Cambridge University Press, 2010, 334–42.

99 Anne Moulin, *Peasantry and Society in France since 1789*, Cambridge: Cambridge University Press, 1988, 192–97.

100 Archer and Giner, 'Social Stratification in Europe', 29.

101 Paul Lewis, 'The Peasantry', in Lane and Kolankiewicz, eds., *Social Groups in Polish Society*, 87.

102 Valuch, *Magyarország társadalomtörténete a XX. század második felében*, 188–212.

103 Anthony Giddens, *The Class Structure of the Advanced Societies*, London: Hutchinson, 1973, 107.

104 D. V. Glass, ed., *Social Mobility in Britain*, London: Routledge and Kegan Paul, 1954.

105 Pitirim A. Sorokin, *Social Mobility*, Glencoe, IL: Free Press, 1959 [1927], 152–54.

106 Seymour M. Lipset and Reinhard Bendix, eds., *Social Mobility in Industrial Society*, Berkeley, CA: University of California Press, 1962 [1959], 251–53; John J. Goldthorpe,

Social Mobility and Class Structure in Modern Britain, Oxford: Clarendon Press, 1980, 17–20.

107 Hartmut Kaelble, 'Social Mobility', in Stearns, ed., *Encyclopedia of European Social History*, vol. 3, 19–20.

108 Kaelble, 'Social Mobility', 20.

109 Richard Breen, 'The Comparative Study of Social Mobility', in Richard Breen, ed., *Social Mobility in Europe*, Oxford: Oxford University Press, 2004, 3–4.

110 Hartmut Kaelble, 'Eras of Social Mobility in 19th and 20th Century Europe', *Journal of Social History*, vol. 17 (1984), no. 3, 491.

111 Anthony Heath, *Social Mobility*, Glasgow: Fontana, 1981, 78–106.

112 Wolfram Fischer, 'Wirtschaft, Gesellschaft und Staat in Europa, 1914–80', in Wolfram Fischer et al., eds., *Handbuch der europäischen Wirtschafts-und Sozialgeschichte*, Bd. 6, Stuttgart: Klett-Cotta, 1987, 65–66.

113 Fischer, 'Wirtschaft, Gesellschaft und Staat in Europa, 1914–80', 66.

114 Peter Stearns, 'The Unskilled and Industrialization: A Transformation of Consciousness', *Archiv für Sozialgeschichte*, vol. 16 (1976), 249–82.

115 Kaelble, *A Social History of Western Europe*, 33–34.

116 Heath, *Social Mobility*, 88–94.

117 Fischer, 'Wirtschaft, Gesellschaft und Staat in Europa, 1914–80', 64; in addition to the British example, similar conclusions are drawn regarding the French, German and Swedish business elite. Hartmut Kaelble, *Social Mobility in the 19th and 20th Centuries: Europe and America in Comparative Perspective*, Leamington Spa: Berg, 1985, 114.

118 For the origin of the term 'trendless fluctuation', see Pitirim A. Sorokin: *Social Mobility*, Glencoe, IL: Free Press, 1959 [1927], 152–54.

119 Heath, *Social Mobility*, 83–87. In order to eliminate the effect of age, researchers examined the social position of individuals included in the sample every ten years after they started their career, because older age increased the probability of changing occupations.

120 Although Erikson and Goldthorpe based their study on a data survey conducted between 1970 and 1978, they examined cohorts born between 1905 and 1940 and working between the 1920s and the 1960s, which means that their data mostly refer to the middle of the century.

121 Robert Erikson and John H. Goldthorpe, *The Constant Flux: A Study of Class Mobility in Industrial Societies*, Oxford: Clarendon Press, 1992, 65–106, 141–81.

122 Erikson and Goldthorpe, *The Constant Flux*, 381.

123 Richard Breen and Ruud Luijkx, 'Social Mobility in Europe between 1970 and 2000', in Breen, ed., *Social Mobility in Europe*, 47–50.

124 Breen and Luijkx, 'Social Mobility in Europe between 1970 and 2000', 50–73.

125 Erikson and Goldthorpe, *The Constant Flux*, 395.

126 Rudolf Andorka, *A társadalmi mobilitás változásai Magyarországon*, Budapest: Gondolat, 1982, 56.

127 Albert Simkus, 'Cross-National Comparisons of Social Mobility', *International Journal of Sociology*, vol. 25 (1995), no. 4, 70; Marek Boguszak, 'Transition to Socialism and Intergenerational Class Mobility: The Model of Core Social Fluidity Applied to Czechoslovakia', in Max Haller, ed., *Class Structure in Europe: New Findings from East-West Comparisons of Social Structures and Mobility*, London: M. E. Sharpe, 1990, 253.

128 Albert Simkus, 'Class Divisions in East-Central Europe, 1949–88', *International Journal of Sociology*, vol. 25 (1995), no. 4, 120.

129 Simkus, 'Cross-National Comparisons of Social Mobility', 68.

130 Boguszak, 'Transition to Socialism', 245.

131 Karin Kurz and Walter Müller, 'Class Mobility in the Industrial World', *Annual Review of Sociology*, vol. 13 (1987), 426.

132 The formulation of the thesis: J. Kelley and H. S. Klein, 'Revolution and the Rebirth of Inequality: A Theory of Stratification in Postrevolutionary Society', *American Journal of Sociology*, vol. 83 (1977), 78–99.

133 Max Haller, Tamás Kolosi and Péter Róbert, 'Social Mobility in Austria, Czechoslovakia, and Hungary: An Investigation of the Effects of Industrialization, Socialist Revolution, and National Uniqueness', in Haller, ed., *Class Structure in Europe: New Findings from East-West Comparisons of Social Structures and Mobility*, 191.

134 Talcott Parsons, *Structure and Process in Modern Societies*, Glencoe, IL: Free Press, 1960, Ch. 3–4; C. Kerr et al, eds., *Industrialism and Industrial Man*, Cambridge, MA: Harvard University Press, 1960.

135 Seymour Martin Lipset and Reinhard Bendix, eds., *Social Mobility in Industrial Society*, Berkeley, CA: University of California Press, 1959, 75; David L. Featherman, F. Lancaster Jones and Robert M. Hauser, 'Assumptions of Mobility Research in the United States: The Case of Occupational Status', *Social Science Research*, vol. 4 (1975), 340.

136 Significant difference was also found by Max Haller, *Klassenstrukturen und Mobilität in fortgeschrittenen Gesellschaften*, Frankfurt/M.: Campus, 1989, 291.

137 Simkus, 'Cross-National Comparisons of Social Mobility', 68.

138 David Grusky and Robert M. Hauser, 'Comparative Social Mobility Revisited: Models of Convergence and Divergence in 16 Countries', *American Sociological Review*, vol. 49 (1984) 33; Erikson and Goldthorpe, *The Constant Flux*, 388.

139 Walter Müller and Reinhard Pollak, 'Social Mobility in West Germany: The Long Arms of History Discovered?', in Breen, ed., *Social Mobility in Europe*, 77–114.

140 David B. Grusky, 'The Past, Present, and Future of Social Inequality', in David B. Grusky, ed., *Social Stratification: Class, Race, and Gender in Sociological Perspective*, Boulder, CO: Westview Press, 2001, 32–36.

141 Daniel Bell, *The Coming of Post-Industrial Society: A Venture in Social Forecasting*, London: Heinemann, 1974; Alain Touraine, *The Post-Industrial Society*, London: Wildwood, 1974.

142 Bell, *The Coming of Post-Industrial Society*, 301–37.

143 Alvin W. Gouldner, *The Future of Intellectuals and the Rise of the New Class*, New York: Continuum Publishing Service, 1979, 1–29.

144 James Burnham, *The Managerial Revolution*, Bloomington, IN: Indiana University Press, 1962, 71–76.

145 Gil Eyal, Iván Szelényi and Eleanor Townsley, *Making Capitalism without Capitalists: Class Formation and Elite Struggles in Post-Communist Central Europe*, London: Verso Press, 1998, 113–58.

146 Zygmunt Bauman, *Intimations of Postmodernity*, London: Routledge, 1992, xvii–xxii., 191–204.

147 Stephen Crook, Jan Pakulski and Malcolm Waters, *Postmodernization*, London: Sage, 1992, 222.

148 Jan Pakulski and Malcolm Waters, *The Death of Class*, London: Sage, 1996, 4.

149 David Ashley, *History without a Subject: The Postmodern Condition*, Boulder, CO: Westview, 1997, 225–35.

150 Gøsta Esping-Andersen, *Social Foundations of Postindustrial Economies*, Oxford: Oxford University Press, 1999.

151 Castells, *The Information Age: Economy, Society and Culture, Vol. 1: The Rise of the Network Society*, 28–76.

152 Eurostat, ed., *Eurostat Yearbook, 2002*, Luxembourg: Eurostat, 2002, 295; http://epp.eurostat.ec.europa.eu/cache/ITY_OFFPUB/KS-QA-09-046/EN/KS-QA-09-046-EN.PDF (Retrieved 30.03.2011), http://www.internetworldstats.com/top25.htm (Retrieved 30.03.2011).

153 Stefan Hradil, *Sozialstrukturanalyse in einer fortgeschrittenen Gesellschaft*, Opladen: Leske und Budrich, 1987, 40–46.

154 Ulrich Beck, *Risikogesellschaft: Auf dem Weg in eine andere Moderne*, Frankfurt/M.: Suhrkamp, 1986.

155 Beck, *Risikogesellschaft*, 116.

156 Jonathan Gershuny, *After Industrial Society?*, London: Macmillan, 1978.

157 Crouch, *Social Change in Western Europe*, 78–120.

158 Castells, *The Information Age: Economy, Society and Culture*, Vol. *1, The Rise of the Network Society*, 285; Daniel C. Vaughan-Whitehead, *EU Enlargement versus Social Europe? The Uncertain Future of the European Social Model*, Cheltenham: Edward Elgar, 2003, 35–108.

159 OECD, *Society at a Glance: OECD Social Indicators. 2002*, Paris: OECD, 2002, 33.

160 Gøsta Esping-Andersen, Zina Assimakopoulou and Kees van Kersbergen, 'Trends in Contemporary Class Structuration: A Six-Nation Comparison', in Gøsta Esping-Andersen, ed., *Stratification and Mobility in Post-industrial Societies*, London: Sage, 1993, 39–40.

161 Richard Breen and David. B. Rottmann, *Class Stratification: A Comparative Perspective*, New York and London: Harvester Wheatsheaf, 1995, 154–55.

162 Gordon Marshall, *Repositioning Class: Social Inequality in Industrial Societies*, London: Sage, 1997, 17.

163 Crouch, *Social Change in Western Europe*, 411–14.

164 Crouch, *Social Change in Western Europe*, 425, see also 420–24.

5 The welfare state

1 For the origin and interpretation of the welfare state, social state, social security state and similar concepts, see Peter Flora and Arnold J. Heidenheimer, 'The Historical Core and Changing Boundaries of the Welfare State', in Peter Flora and Arnold J. Heidenheimer, eds., *The Development of Welfare States in Europe and America*, New Brunswick and London, 1981, 17–34; Gerhard A. Ritter, *Der Sozialstaat: Entstehung und Entwicklung im internationalen Vergleich*, Munich: Oldenbourg, 1991, 4–29.

2 Ritter, *Der Sozialstaat*, 7–10; Bent Greve, *The Historical Dictionary of the Welfare State*, Lanham, MD. and London: Scarecrow Press, 1998, 129–32.

3 For a recent comprehensive account of the welfare state, see Francis G. Castles et al., eds., *The Oxford Handbook of the Welfare State*, Oxford: Oxford University Press, 2010.

4 Paul Johnson, 'Welfare States', in Max-Stephan Schulze, ed., *Western Europe: Economic and Social Change Since 1945*, London and New York: Longman, 1999, 123.

5 ILO, *The Cost of Social Security*, Geneva: ILO, 1949ff. (Different volumes.)

6 OECD, *Social Expenditure Statistics of OECD Member Countries*, Labour Market and Social Policy Occasional Papers. No. 17, Paris: OECD, 1996, 3–7; Johnson, *Welfare States*, 123.

7 Commission of the European Communities, *Social Protection in Europe, 1993*, Luxembourg: Commission of the European Communities, 1994, 44.

8 Johnson, *Welfare States*, 123–27; Walter Korpi, *The Democratic Class Struggle*, London: Routledge and Kegan Paul, 1983, 183–93.

9 Adalbert Evers, 'Shifts in the Welfare Mix – Introducing a New Approach for the Study of Transformations in Welfare and Social Policy', in A. Evers and H. Wintersberger, eds., *Shifts in the Welfare Mix*, Frankfurt/M.: Campus, 1990, 7–30; Christoph Conrad, 'Mixed Incomes for the Elderly Poor in Germany, 1880–1930', in Michael B. Katz and Christoph Sachsse, eds., *The Mixed Economy of Social Welfare*, Baden-Baden: Nomos, 1996, 340–67.

10 For recent overviews of the history of the welfare state in Europe, see Stein Kuhnle and Anne Sander, 'The Emergence of the Western Welfare State', in Francis G. Castles, Stephan Leibfried, Jane Lewis and Herbert Obinger, eds., *The Oxford Handbook of the Welfare State*, Oxford: Oxford University Press, 2010, 61–80; Frank Nullmeier and Franz Xaver Kaufmann, 'Post-War Welfare State Development', in Castles, Leibfried, Lewis and Obinger, eds., *The Oxford Handbook of the Welfare State*, 81–101.

11 Gerhard A. Ritter, *Social Welfare in Germany and Britain: Origins and Development*, Leamington Spa and New York: Berg, 1986, 134.

12 For social security legislation in Western countries, see Peter Flora and Jens Alber, 'Modernization, Democratization and the Development of the Welfare States in Western Europe', in Peter Flora and Arnold J. Heidenheimer, eds., *The Development of Welfare States in Europe and America*, New Brunswick and London: Transaction, 1981, 48–70; Detlev Zöllner,

'Landesbericht Deutschland', 83–92; Saint-Jours, 'Landesbericht Frankreich', 209–12; Ogus, 'Landesbericht Grossbritannien', 334–42; Herbert Hofmeister, 'Landesbericht Österreich', 533–88; Maurer, 'Landesbericht Schweiz', in Peter A. Köhler and Hans F. Zacher, eds., *Ein Jahrhundert Sozialversicherung in der Bundesrepublik Deutschland, Frankreich, Grossbritannien, Österreich und der Schweiz*, Berlin: Duncker und Humblot, 1981, 780–88.

13 Jens Alber, *Vom Armenhaus zum Wohlfahrtsstaat: Analysen zur Entwicklung der Sozialversicherung in Westeuropa*, Frankfurt/M.: Campus, 1987, 28.

14 Alber, *Vom Armenhaus zum Wohlfahrtsstaat*, 27; Flora and Heidenheimer, 'The Historical Core and Changing Boundaries of the Welfare State', 27; Peter Flora, 'Solution or Source of Crises? The Welfare State in Historical Perspective', in W. J. Mommsen, ed., *The Emergence of the Welfare State in Britain and Germany, 1850–1950*, London: The German Historical Institute, 1981, 388; Arnold J. Heidenheimer, Hugh Heclo and Carolyn Teich Adams, *Comparative Public Policy: The Politics of Social Choice in America, Europe, and Japan*, New York: St Martin's Press, 1990, 229.

15 Saundra K. Schneider, 'The Sequential Development of Social Programs in Eighteen Welfare States', *Comparative Social Research*, vol. 5 (1982), 195–219.

16 Manfred G. Schmidt, *Sozialpolitik*, Opladen: Leske und Budrich, 1988, 119–20.

17 Alber, *Vom Armenhaus zum Wohlfahrtsstaat*, 47.

18 Alber, *Vom Armenhaus zum Wohlfahrtsstaat*, 43.

19 As regards arguments for analysing additional factors too, not only expenditures, see Gøsta Esping-Andersen, *The Three Worlds of Welfare Capitalism*, Cambridge: Polity Press, 1990, 19.

20 Flora, 'Solution or source of crises?', 359.

21 For social insurance and social security expenditures in Western Europe, see Peter Flora, ed., *State, Economy, and Society in Western Europe, 1815–1975*, vol. I, Frankfurt/M.: Campus, 1983, 456; ILO, *The Cost of Social Security: Fourteenth International Inquiry, 1987–1989*, Geneva: ILO, 1996, 108–65, and other volumes of the series; Flora, 'Solution or source of crises?', 359; Statistisches Bundesamt, ed., *Bevölkerung und Wirtschaft, 1872–197*, Stuttgart: Statistisches Bundesamt, 1972, 219–60; Wolfram Fischer, ed., *Handbuch der europäischen Wirtschafts-und Sozialgeschichte*, Bd. 6, Stuttgart: Klett-Cotta, 1987, 217; Alber, *Vom Armenhaus zum Wohlfahrtsstaat*, 60.

22 Our own computation based on the following work: Statistisches Bundesamt, ed., *Bevölkerung und Wirtschaft, 1872–1972*, 219–24, 260; according to the data of Jens Alber, in 1930, social insurance expenditures accounted for 7.8% of GDP in Germany. See Alber, *Vom Armenhaus zum Wohlfahrtsstaat*, 60.

23 For sources of related statistics, see ILO, *The Cost of Social Security: Eleventh International Inquiry, 1978–1980*, Geneva: ILO, 1985, 57–58; ILO, *The Cost of Social Security: Fourteenth International Inquiry, 1987–1989*, Geneva: ILO, 1996, 74–75; ILO, *World Labour Report 2000: Income Security and Social Protection in a Changing World*, Geneva: ILO, 2000, 313; Flora, ed., *State, Economy, and Society in Western Europe*, vol. I, 456; in the case of certain countries, the ILO statistics underestimate expenditures by a few percentage points in relation to other data collections along similar principles. Differences in the taxation of welfare allowances can also bias the level of net social allowances by several percentage points. For similar methodological dilemmas, see Willem Adema, 'Uncovering Real Social Spending', *The OECD Observer*, vol. 37 (1998), no. 211, 20–23.

24 However, OECD figures do not include special welfare allowances for public servants on the grounds that these constitute their income. For OECD data, see Peter Flora, ed., *Growth to Limits: The Western European Welfare States Since World War II*, vol. 4, Berlin and New York: De Gruyter, 1987, 325–815; OECD, *Social Expenditure, 1960–1990*, Paris: OECD, 1985, 80; OECD, *Social Expenditure Statistics of OECD Member Countries*, Labour Market and Social Policy Occasional Papers, No. 17, Paris: OECD, 1996, 19; UNESCO, *Statistical Yearbook, 1993*, Paris: UNESCO, 1993, 416–18; OECD, *National Accounts: Main Aggregates, 1960–1997*, vol. I, Paris: OECD, 1999.

25 Christopher Pierson, *Beyond the Welfare State?*, Cambridge: Polity Press, 1991, 111.

26 Maciej Zukovski, 'Pension Policy in Poland after 1945: Bismarck and Beveridge Traditions', in John Hills, John Ditch and Howard Glennerster, eds., *Beveridge and Social Security: An International Perspective*, Oxford: Clarendon Press, 1994, 155–56.

27 Francis G. Castles, 'Whatever Happened to the Communist Welfare State?', *Studies in Comparative Communism*, vol. XIX (1986), no. 3/4, 216–19.

28 Béla Tomka, 'Western European Welfare States in the Twentieth Century: Convergences and Divergences in a Long-Run Perspective', *International Journal of Social Welfare*, vol. 12 (2003), no. 4, 249–60.

29 Margaret Gordon, *Social Security Policies in Industrial Countries*, Cambridge: Cambridge University Press, 1988, 199–204.

30 Peter A. Köhler and Hans F. Zacher, 'Sozialversicherung: Pfade der Entwicklung', in Köhler and Zacher, eds., *Ein Jahrhundert Sozialversicherung*, 37.

31 Alber, *Vom Armenhaus zum Wohlfahrtsstaat*, 55.

32 Alber, *Vom Armenhaus zum Wohlfahrtsstaat*, 169–70.

33 Zöllner, 'Landesbericht Deutschland', in Köhler and Zacher, eds., *Ein Jahrhundert Sozialversicherung*, 157.

34 Jens Alber, 'Germany', in Flora, ed., *Growth to Limits*, vol. 2, 42–47; Richard Perry, 'United Kingdom', in Flora, ed., *Growth to Limits*, vol. 2, 83–188; Hans Günter Hockerts, 'Die Entwicklung vom Zweiten Weltkrieg bis zur Gegenwart', in Peter A. Köhler and Hans F. Zacher, eds., *Beiträge zur Geschichte und aktueller Situation der Sozialversicherung*, Berlin: Duncker und Humblot, 1983, 158–59.

35 Crouch, *Social Change in Western Europe*, 371–73, 482–87.

36 Zukovski, 'Pension Policy in Poland after 1945: Bismarck and Beveridge Traditions', 154–70; Rudolf Andorka and István György Tóth, 'A szociális kiadások és a szociálpolitika Magyarországon', in Rudolf Andorka, Tamás Kolosi and György Vukovich, eds., *Társadalmi riport, 1992*, Budapest: TÁRKI, 1992, 413.

37 For more on the ratio of those eligible, see Flora, ed., *State, Economy, and Society in Western Europe, 1815–1975*, 460–61; ILO, *The Cost of Social Security: Fourteenth International Inquiry, 1987–1989*, Geneva: ILO, 1996, 201–16; ILO, *Yearbook of Labour Statistics, 1995*, Geneva: ILO, 1996, 164–69.

38 Peter Flora, 'On the History and Current Problems of the Welfare State', in S. N. Eisenstadt and Ora Ahimeir, eds., *The Welfare State and its Aftermath*, London and Sydney: Croom Helm, 1985, 19.

39 Flora, 'Solution or Source of Crises?', 343–89; Alber, *Vom Armenhaus zum Wohlfahrtsstaat*, 52.

40 Alber, *Vom Armenhaus zum Wohlfahrtsstaat*, 52; Hans Günter Hockerts, 'Die Entwicklung vom Zweiten Weltkrieg bis zur Gegenwart', in Köhler and Zacher eds., *Beiträge zur Geschichte und aktueller Situation der Sozialversicherung*, 155.

41 Therborn, *European Modernity and Beyond*, 90.

42 Palme, 'Pension Rights in Welfare Capitalism', 52; for more on the requirements for eligibility between the two World Wars and in the 1980s, see: ILO, *International Survey of Social Services*, Studies and Reports, Series M, No. 11, Geneva: ILO, 1933, 42–618; US Department of Health and Human Services, ed., *Social Security Throughout the World, 1981*, Washington, DC: US Department of Health and Human Services, 1982, 12–261.

43 Ritter, *Der Sozialstaat*, 152.

44 Hans Hansen, *Elements of Social Security*, Copenhagen: The Danish National Institute of Social Research, 1998, 9–11.

45 Flora and Alber, 'Modernization, Democratization', 53; Harold L. Wilensky, *The Welfare State and Equality*, Berkeley, CA: University of California Press, 1975, 39.

46 Christoph Conrad, 'The Emergence of Modern Retirement: Germany in an International Comparison, 1850–1960', *Population: An English Selection*, vol. 3 (1991), 191; Hockerts, 'Die Entwicklung vom Zweiten Weltkrieg', 156–57.

47 Conrad, 'The Emergence of Modern Retirement', 192.

48 Ritter, *Der Sozialstaat*, 160.

49 Hockerts, 'Die Entwicklung vom Zweiten Weltkrieg', 157–58.
50 Author's own calculations based on Esping-Andersen, *The Three Worlds of Welfare Capitalism*, 99.
51 Palme, *Pension Rights in Welfare Capitalism*, 49.
52 Commission of the European Communities, *Comparative Tables of the Social Security Schemes in the Member States of the European Communities*, Luxembourg: European Commission, 1989, 46–47.
53 Therborn, *European Modernity and Beyond*, 94.
54 Esping-Andersen, *The Three Worlds of Welfare Capitalism*, 47.
55 Esping-Andersen, *The Three Worlds of Welfare Capitalism*, 28.
56 Esping-Andersen, *The Three Worlds of Welfare Capitalism*, 26–28.
57 Gøsta Esping-Andersen, *Social Foundations of Postindustrial Economies*, Oxford: Oxford University Press, 1999, 73; Francis G. Castles and Deborah Mitchell, 'Worlds of Welfare and Families of Nations', in Francis G. Castles, ed., *Families of Nations: Patterns of Public Policy in Western Democracies*, Aldershot: Dartmouth, 1993, 93–128.
58 Maurizio Ferrera, 'The "Southern Model" of Welfare in Social Europe', *Journal of European Social Policy*, vol. 6 (1996), no. 1, 17–37; Stephan Leibfried, 'Towards a European Welfare State? On Integrating Poverty Regimes into the European Community', in Zsuzsa Ferge and Jon Eivind Kolberg, eds., *Social Policy in a Changing Europe*, Frankfurt/M. and Boulder, CO: Campus, 1992, 245–79.
59 Manfred Schmidt, 'Wohlfahrtsstaatliche Regime: Politische Grundlagen und politischökonomisches Leistungsvermögen', in Stephan Lessenich and Ilona Ostner, eds., *Welten des Wohlfahrtskapitalismus: Der Wohlfahrtsstaat in vergleichender Perspektive*, Frankfurt am Main: Campus, 1998, 179–200; Kees van Kersbergen, *Social Capitalism: A Study of Christian Democracy and the Welfare State*, London: Routledge, 1995, 23–26.
60 Esping-Andersen, *Social Foundations*, 88–94.
61 Esping-Andersen, *Social Foundations*, 47–72.
62 Joh Grahl and Paul Teague, 'Is the European Social Model Fragmenting?', *New Political Economy*, vol. 2 (1997), no. 3, 405–26; Ian Gough, 'Social Aspects of the European Model and Its Economic Consequences', in Wolfgang Beck, Laurent van der Maesen and Alan Walker, eds., *The Social Quality of Europe*, Bristol: Policy Press, 1998, 89–108.
63 Esping-Andersen, *Social Foundations*, 47–72.
64 Hartmut Kaelble, 'Wie kam es zum Europäischen Sozialmodell?', *Jahrbuch für Europa und Nordamerikastudien*, vol. 4 (2000), 45.
65 Francis G. Castles, 'The Future of the Welfare State: Crisis Myths and Crisis Realities', *International Journal of Health Services*, vol. 32 (2002), no. 2, 255–77.
66 Bernhard Ebbinghaus, 'Does the European Social Model Exist and Can it Survive?', in Gerhard Huemer, Michael Mesch and Franz Traxler, eds., *The Role of Employer Associations and Labour Unions in the EMU*, Aldershot: Ashgate, 1999, 1–26.
67 Richard Hauser, 'Soziale Sicherung in westeuropäischen Staaten', in Hradil and Immerfall, eds., *Die westeuropäischen Gesellschaften im Vergleich*, 521–45.
68 Zsuzsa Ferge, 'The Changing Hungarian Social Policy', in Else Oyen, ed., *Comparing Welfare States and Their Futures*, Aldershot: Gower, 1986, 152; for the use of the concept, see: Lynne Haney, 'Familial Welfare: Building the Hungarian Welfare Society, 1948–68', *Social Politics*, vol. 7 (2000), no. 1, 101–22.
69 Manfred G. Schmidt, *Sozialpolitik der DDR*, Wiesbaden: VS Verlag für Sozialwissenschaften, 2004, 34.
70 János Kornai, *The Socialist System: The Political Economy of Communism*, Princeton, NJ: Princeton University Press, 1992, 204.
71 Schmidt, *Sozialpolitik der DDR*, 43–47.
72 Rudolf Andorka and István György Tóth, 'A szociális kiadások és a szociálpolitika Magyarországon', in Rudolf Andorka, Tamás Kolosi and György Vukovich, eds., *Társadalmi riport, 1992*, Budapest: TÁRKI, 1992, 442.
73 Therborn, *European Modernity and Beyond*, 95.

74 For main representatives of the approach, see Harold L. Wilensky, *The Welfare State and Equality: Structural and Ideological Roots of Public Expenditures*, Berkeley: University of California Press, 1975; Frederick Pryor, *Public Expenditure in Capitalist and Communist Nations*, Homewood, IL: R. D. Irwin, 1968.

75 Wilensky, *The Welfare State and Equality*, 47.

76 Harold L. Wilensky et al., *Comparative Social Policy: Theories, Methods, Findings*, Berkeley, CA: University of California Press, 1985, 8; Philips Cutright, 'Political Structure, Economic Development, and National Social Security Programs', *American Journal of Sociology*, vol. 70 (1965), 537–50.

77 Cf. Peter Baldwin, *The Politics of Social Solidarity*, Cambridge: Cambridge University Press, 1990, 288–99.

78 Esping-Andersen, *The Three Worlds of Welfare Capitalism*, 32.

79 Heidenheimer, Heclo and Teich Adams, *Comparative Public Policy*, 223–24.

80 Esping-Andersen, *The Three Worlds of Welfare Capitalism*, 32.

81 For representatives of this approach, see Walter Korpi, 'Social Policy and Distributional Conflict in the Capitalist Democracies', *West European Politics*, vol. 3 (1980), no. 3, 296–316; Michael Shalev, 'The Social Democratic Model and Beyond', *Comparative Social Research*, vol. 6 (1983), 315–51.

82 Flora and Alber, 'Modernization, Democratization, and the Development of Welfare States', 65–68.

83 Pierson, *Beyond the Welfare State?*, 35.

84 Gaston V. Rimlinger, *Welfare Policy and Industrialization in Europe, America and Russia*, New York: John Wiley, 1971.

85 Alber, *Vom Armenhaus zum Wohlfahrtsstaat*, 126–33.

86 On the special impact Catholic players had on welfare, see Harold L. Wilensky, 'Leftism, Catholicism, and Democratic Corporatism: The Role of Political Parties in Recent Welfare State Development', in Flora and Heidenheimer, eds., *The Development of Welfare States*, 356–58, 368–70; for the same in the Netherlands, see Robert H. Cox, *The Development of the Dutch Welfare State*, Pittsburgh: Pittsburgh University Press, 1993, 58–95.

87 Hugh Heclo, 'Toward a New Welfare State?', in Flora and Heidenheimer, eds., *The Development of Welfare States*, 383–406.

88 Wilensky, 'Leftism, Catholicism, and Democratic Corporatism', 345–82.

89 Esping-Andersen, *The Three Worlds of Welfare Capitalism*, 31–33.

90 See Franz-Xaver Kaufmann and Lutz Leisering, 'Demographic Challenges in the Welfare State', in Else Oyen, ed., *Comparing Welfare States and their Futures*, Aldershot: Gower, 1986, 96–113.

91 Crouch, *Social Change in Western Europe*, 370.

92 David Collier and Richard Messick, 'Prerequisites Versus Diffusion: Testing Alternative Explanations of Social Security Adoption', *American Political Science Review*, vol. 69 (1975), 1299–1315; Wilensky et al., *Comparative Social Policy*, 12–15.

93 Stein Kuhnle, 'The Growth of Social Insurance Programs in Scandinavia: Outside Influences and Internal Forces', in Flora and Heidenheimer, eds., *The Development of Welfare States*, 125–50; Hugh Heclo, *Modern Social Politics in Britain and Sweden: From Relief to Income Maintenance*, New Haven, CT: Yale University Press, 1974.

94 Harold L. Wilensky, 'Leftism, Catholicism, and Democratic Corporatism', 345–82.

95 J. Baldock, 'Culture: The Missing Variable in Understanding Social Policy?', *Social Policy and Administration*, vol. 33 (1999), no. 4, 458–73; Carsten G. Ullrich, *Wohlfahrtsstaat und Wohlfahrtskultur*, Working Papers Nr. 67, Mannheim: Mannheimer Zentrum für Europäische Sozialforschung, 2003; A. B. Sørensen, 'On Kings, Pietism and Rent-seeking in Scandinavian Welfare States', *Acta Sociologica*, vol. 41 (1998), no. 4, 363–75.

96 Schmidt, *Sozialpolitik*, 147.

97 For a recent overview of the major critiques, see Desmond King and Fiona Ross, 'Critics and Beyond', in Francis G. Castles, Stephan Leibfried, Jane Lewis and Herbert

Obinger, eds., *The Oxford Handbook of the Welfare State*, Oxford: Oxford University Press, 2010, 45–57.

98 Friedrich Hayek, *Law, Legislation and Liberty*, vol. 2, London: Routledge, 1993 [1973], 62–100.

99 Thomas H. Marshall, *Class, Citizenship, and Social Development*, New York: Anchor Books, 1965 [1964], 71–134.

100 Uriel Rosenthal, 'Welfare State or State of Welfare? Repression and Welfare in the Modern State', in Richard F. Tomasson, ed., *The Welfare State, 1883–1983*, Greenwich, CT and London: JAI Press, 1983, 279–97.

101 Wilensky, *Rich Democracies*, 335; for a comprehensive account of the link between inequalities in income and welfare models, see Walter Korpi and Joakim Palme, 'Robin Hood, St Matthew, or Simple Egalitarian Strategies of Equality in Welfare States', in Patricia Kennett, ed., *A Handbook of Comparative Social Policy*, Cheltenham: Edward Elgar, 2004, 153–79.

102 S. Scarpetta, 'Assessing the Role of Labour Market Policies and Institutional Settings on Unemployment: A Cross-Country Study', *OECD Economic Studies*, vol. 26 (1996), 43–98; Gøsta Esping-Andersen, 'The State and the Economy', in Neil J. Smelser and Richard Swedberg, eds., *The Handbook of Economic Sociology*, Princeton, NJ: Princeton University Press, 1994, 721.

103 Ian Gough, 'Social Aspects of the European Model and Its Economic Consequences', in Beck, van der Maesen and Walker, eds., *The Social Quality of Europe*, 101; Ian Gough, 'The Needs of Capital and the Needs of People: Can the Welfare State Reconcile the Two?', in Ian Gough, *Global Capital, Human Needs and Social Policies*, Houndmills: Palgrave, 2000, 3–29.

104 Angus Maddison, *Dynamic Forces in Capitalist Development: A Long-Run Comparative View*, Oxford: Oxford University Press, 1991, 128–66; Nicholas Crafts and Gianni Toniolo, eds., *Economic Growth in Europe since 1945*, Cambridge: Cambridge University Press, 1996; Bart van Ark and Nicholas Crafts, eds., *Quantitative Aspects of Post-War European Economic Growth*, Cambridge: Cambridge University Press, 1996; for welfare expenditures, see Béla Tomka, *Welfare in East and West*, Berlin: Akademie Verlag, 2003, 35–48.

105 Angus Maddison, *Monitoring the World Economy, 1820–1992*, Paris: OECD, 1995, 25.

106 Peter Lindert, *Growing Public: Social Spending and Economic Growth Since the Eighteenth Century*, vol. 2, Cambridge: Cambridge University Press, 2004, 94–99; Peter H. Lindert, 'The Rise of Social Spending, 1880–1930', *Explorations in Economic History*, vol. 31 (1994), 1–37; Peter H. Lindert, 'What Limits Social Spending?', *Explorations in Economic History*, vol. 33 (1996), 1–34.

107 UN Population Division, *World Population Prospects: The 1998 Revision*, vol. I: Comprehensive Tables; vol. II: Sex and Age, New York: United Nations, 1999.

108 Francis G. Castles, 'The Future of the Welfare State: Crisis Myths and Crisis Realities', *International Journal of Health Services*, vol. 32 (2002), no. 2, 264.

109 Castles, 'The Future of the Welfare State: Crisis Myths and Crisis Realities', 255.

110 Neil Gilbert, *Transformation of the Welfare State: The Silent Surrender of Public Responsibility*, Oxford: Oxford University Press, 2002, 61–89.

111 Gilbert, *Transformation of the Welfare State*, 112.

112 Gilbert, *Transformation of the Welfare State*, 104–6.

113 Castles, 'The Future of the Welfare State: Crisis Myths and Crisis Realities', 263.

114 Herbert Obinger and Uwe Wagschal, 'Social Expenditure and Revenues', in Castles et al., ed., *The Oxford Handbook of the Welfare State*, 333–52.

115 Wilensky, *Rich Democracies*, 223–26, 232.

116 Thomas Bahle, Jürgen Kohl and Claus Wendt, 'Welfare State', in Stephan Immerfall and Göran Therborn, eds., *Handbook of European Societies: Social Transformations in the 21st century*, New York: Springer, 2010, 621.

117 Bob Deacon, 'Developments in East European Social Policy', in Catherine Jones, ed., *New Perspectives on the Welfare State in Europe*, London and New York: Routledge, 1993, 196.

118 Gøsta Esping-Andersen, 'After the Golden Age? Welfare State Dilemmas in a Global Economy', in Gøsta Esping-Andersen, ed., *Welfare States in Transition*, London: Sage, 1996, 1–31; Zsuzsa Ferge, 'Social Policy Regimes and Social Structure', in Zsuzsa Ferge and J. E. Kolberg, eds., *Social Policy in a Changing Europe*, Frankfurt/M. and Boulder, CO: Campus, 1992, 220.

119 Ferge, 'Social Policy Regimes and Social Structure', 219.

120 Zsuzsa Ferge, 'Welfare and "Ill-Fare" Systems in Central-Eastern Europe', in Robert Sykes, Bruno Palier and Pauline M. Prior, eds., *Globalization and European Welfare States: Challenges and Change*, Houndmills and Basingstoke: Palgrave, 2001, 151.

121 Tomasz Inglot, 'Historical Legacies, Institutions, and the Politics of Social Policy in Hungary and Poland, 1989–99', in Grzegorz Ekiert and Stephen E. Hanson, eds., *Capitalism and Democracy in Central and Eastern Europe: Assessing the Legacy of Communist Rule*, Cambridge: Cambridge University Press, 2003, 243.

122 Bob Deacon, 'Eastern European Welfare States: The Impact of the Politics of Globalization', *Journal of European Social Policy*, vol. 10 (2000), no. 2, 151.

6 Work, leisure and consumption

1 Josef Ehmer, 'History of Work', in Neil J. Smelser and Paul B. Baltes, eds., *International Encyclopedia of the Social and Behavioral Sciences*, vol. 24, Elsevier: Oxford, 2001, 16569–75.

2 For comprehensive accounts of the history of consumption, see Robert Bocock, *Consumption*, London: Routledge, 1993; Peter Stearns, *Consumerism in World History: The Global Transformation of Desire*, London: Routledge, 2001; Gary Cross, 'Consumerism', in Stearns, ed., *Encyclopedia of European Social History*, vol. 5, 77–88; John Brewer and Roy Porter, eds., *Consumption and the World of Goods*, London: Routledge, 1993; on the historiography of the research into consumption, see Daniel Miller, 'Consumption as the Vanguard of History', in Daniel Miller, ed., *Acknowledging Consumption: A Review of New Studies*, London: Routledge, 1995, 1–57.

3 Peter N. Stearns, *Lives of Labour: Work in a Maturing Industrial Society*, London: Croom Helm, 1975, 19–117; Jürgen Kocka, 'Work as a Problem in European History', in Jürgen Kocka, ed., *Work in a Modern Society: The German Historical Experience in Comparative Perspective*, New York: Berghahn, 2010, 1–15.

4 ILO, *Yearbook of Labour Statistics*, Geneva: ILO, 1939–98.

5 Kaelble, *Sozialgeschichte Europas*, 67–68; B. Lutz, *Der kurze Traum immerwährender Prosperität – eine Neuinterpretation der industriell-kapitalistischen Entwicklung im Europa des 20. Jahrhunderts*, Frankfurt/M.: Campus, 1984, 115–41, 246.

6 Harry Braverman, *Labour and Monopoly Capital*, New York: Monthly Review Press, 1974.

7 Keith Grint, *The Sociology of Work*, Cambridge: Polity Press, 2005, 299–301.

8 Åke Sandberg, 'The Uddevalla Experience in Perspective', in Åke Sandberg, *Enriching Production: Perspectives on Volvo's Uddevalla Plant as an Alternative to Lean Production*, Aldershot: Avebury, 2004, 1–33.

9 George Ritzer, *The McDonaldization of Society*, Thousand Oaks, CA: Pine Forge Press, 1993.

10 Bernhard Ebbinghaus and Jelle Visser, *Trade Unions in Western Europe since 1945*, London: Macmillan, 2000, 35–36.

11 Ambrosius and Hubbard, *A Social and Economic History of Twentieth-Century Europe*, 92.

12 Ebbinghaus and Visser, *Trade Unions in Western Europe since 1945*, 36.

13 George Sayers Bain and Robert Price, *Profiles of Union Growth*, Oxford: Blackwell, 1980, 163.

14 Colin Crouch, *Industrial Relations and European State Traditions*, Oxford: Clarendon Press, 1993, 176–292.

15 Jelle Visser, 'Trade Unions from a Comparative Perspective', in Joris Van Ruysseveldt, Rien Huiskamp and Jacques van Hoof, eds., *Comparative Industrial and Employment Relations*, London: Sage, 1995, 55.

16 Ebbinghaus and Visser, *Trade Unions in Western Europe since 1945*, 43–44.

17 Ebbinghaus and Visser, *Trade Unions in Western Europe since 1945*, 36–37.

18 Bernhard Ebbinghaus and Jelle Visser, 'Der Wandel der Arbeitsbeziehungen im westeuropäischen Vergleich', in Stefan Hradil and Stefan Immerfall, eds., *Die westeuropäischen Gesellschaften im Vergleich*, Opladen: Leske und Budrich, 1997, 336–38; Colin Crouch, *Industrial Relations and European State Traditions*, Oxford: Clarendon Press, 1993, 176–292.

19 Ebbinghaus and Visser, 'Der Wandel der Arbeitsbeziehungen im westeuropäischen Vergleich', 336–38; Crouch, *Industrial Relations and European State Traditions*, 176–292.

20 Kornai, 'The Socialist System', 461–73.

21 Paul Blyton, *Changes in Working Time: An International Review*, London: Croom Helm, 1985, 19.

22 Gary S. Cross, 'Work Time', in Stearns, ed., *Encyclopedia of European Social History*, vol. 4, 504–5; Michael Huberman, 'Working Hours of the World Unite? New International Evidence of Worktime, 1870–1913', *Journal of Economic History*, vol. 64 (2004), 964–1001.

23 Gerhard Bosch, Peter Dawkins and François Michon, 'Working Time in 14 Industrialized Countries: An Overview', in Gerhard Bosch, Peter Dawkins and François Michon, eds., *Times Are Changing: Working Time in 14 Industrialized Countries*, Geneva: ILO, 1993, 1–5.

24 Michael Huberman and Chris Minns, 'The Times They Are Not Changin': Days and Hours of Work in Old and New Worlds, 1870–2000', *Explorations in Economic History*, vol. 44 (2007), 545–47.

25 Cross, 'Work Time', 505.

26 Huberman and Minns, 'The Times they are not Changin'', 546.

27 Jesse H. Ausubel and Arnulf Grübler, 'Working Less and Living Longer: Long-Term Trends in Working Time and Time Budgets', *Technological Forecasting and Social Change*, vol. 50 (1995), 205.

28 David S. Landes, *The Unbound Prometheus: Technological Change and Industrial Development in Western Europe from 1750 to the Present*, Cambridge: Cambridge University Press, 1969, 373.

29 Stearns, *Lives of Labour*, 90–91.

30 Derek H. Aldcroft, *From Versailles to Wall Street, 1919–1929*, Berkeley: University of California Press, 1977, 191–93.

31 W. R. Garside, *British Unemployment, 1919–1939: A Study in Public Policy*, Cambridge: Cambridge University Press, 1990, 5.

32 Charles H. Feinstein, Peter Temin and Gianni Toniolo, eds., *The European Economy Between the Wars*, Oxford: Oxford University Press, 1997, 125–45.

33 Barry Eichengreen, *The European Economy since 1945: Coordinated Capitalism and Beyond*, Princeton: Princeton University Press, 2007, 264.

34 Crouch, *Social Change in Western Europe*, 70.

35 Crouch, *Social Change in Western Europe*, 72.

36 Crouch, *Social Change in Western Europe*, 78–82.

37 Kornai János, *A hiány*, Budapest: KJK, 1982, 247–79; Kornai, *A szocialista rendszer*, 231–42.

38 Pascal Paoli et al., *Working Conditions in Candidate Countries and the European Union (in 2001)*, Dublin: European Foundation for the Improvement of Living and Working Conditions, 2002.

39 Daniel Vaughan-Whitehead, *EU Enlargement Versus Social Europe?*, Cheltenham: Edward Elgar, 2003, 56–81.

40 Cf., for example, Norman J. G. Pounds, 'Standards of Living', in Stearns, ed., *Encyclopedia of European Social History*, 451; Angus Maddison, *Economic Growth and Standards of Living in the Twentieth Century*, Research Memorandum 576 (GD-15); Groningen, 'Groningen Growth and Development Centre, 1994', 18; there are authors who consider such factors as life expectancy, quality of the environment, education, political democracy, etc., as parts of the standard of living, in other words several of those factors that are

regarded as elements of the quality of life by others. Richard A. Easterlin, 'The Worldwide Standard of Living since 1800', *Journal of Economic Perspectives*, vol. 14 (2000), no. 1, 7–26; Wolfram Fischer, 'Nord und Süd – Ost und West: Wirtschafts-systeme und Lebensstandard in Europa', in Wolfram Fischer, ed., *Lebensstandard und Wirtschaftssysteme*, Frankfurt/M.: Fritz Knapp Verlag, 1995, 213–57; Peter von der Lippe: 'Die Messung des Lebensstandards', in Fischer, ed., *Lebensstandard und Wirt-schaftssysteme*, 57–102.

41 Heinz-Herbert Noll, 'Wohlstand, Lebensqualität und Wohlbefinden in den Ländern der Europäischen Union', in Hradil and Immerfall, eds., *Die westeuropäischen Gesell-schaften im Vergleich*, 440.

42 For the historical aspects of the standard of living, see Pounds, 'Standards of Living', 451–60; R. Floud, 'Standards of Living and Industrialization', in Anne Digby and Charles Feinstein, eds., *New Directions in Economic and Social History*, Chicago: Lyceum Books, 1989, 117–29; Hannes Siegrist, Hartmut Kaelble and Jürgen Kocka, eds., *Europäische Konsumgeschichte: Zur Gesellschafts-und Kulturgeschichte des Konsums (18. bis 20. Jahrhundert)*, Frankfurt/M.: Campus Verlag, 1997; H. Baudet and M. Bogucka, eds., *Types of Consumption, Traditional and Modern*, Budapest: Akadémiai Kiadó, 1982; More recently: Stearns, *Consumption in World History*.

43 Maddison, *Economic Growth and Standards of Living in the Twentieth Century*, 18; Jeffrey G. Williamson, *Evolution of Global Labor Markets Since 1830: Background Evidence and Hypotheses*, Working Paper 36, Cambridge, MA: National Bureau of Economic Research, 1992.

44 Ambrosius and Hubbard, *A Social and Economic History of Twentieth-Century Europe*, 252–53.

45 A. S. Deaton, 'The Structure of Demand in Europe, 1920–70', in Carlo M. Cipolla, ed., *The Fontana Economic History of Europe: The Twentieth Century*, Part One, Glasgow: Collins/Fontana Books, 1976, 92–94.

46 Tamás Bauer, *Tervgazdaság, beruházás, ciklusok*, Budapest: KJK, 1981, 197; the link between investment decisions of the central economic management and the standard of living is underlined by Bogdan Mieczkowski, *Personal and Social Consumption in Eastern Europe: Poland, Czechoslovakia, Hungary, and East Germany*, New York: Praeger, 1975, 59–63.

47 Bauer, *Tervgazdaság, beruházás, ciklusok*, 70.

48 Mária Barát, *A magyar gazdaság vargabetűje*, Budapest: Aula, 1994, 435, 194.

49 Barát, *A magyar gazdaság vargabetűje*, 176–77.

50 Maddison, *The World Economy in the 20th Century*, 55.

51 Elements of private consumption can be classified by the following categories: (1) food and drinks (tobacco); (2) clothing and footwear; (3) home and energy; (4) furniture, household equipment and appliances; (5) health; (6) transport and communication; (7) leisure and culture; (8) others.

52 Secretariat of the United Nations Economic Commission for Europe (UNECE), 'Consumption Trends and Prospects in the ECE Region', *Economic Bulletin for Europe*, vol. 39 (1987), no. 2, 249; regarding the expenditure ratio of individual countries, it has to be noted that the calculation of expenditure ratios is based on various price ratios, instead of common prices. Preeminently this is the reason why the lower price level of certain product groups may lead to the lower' expenditure ratio of these products.

53 Eurostat, ed., *Consumers in Europe: Facts and Figures, 1999–2004*, Luxembourg: Eurostat, 2005, 24.

54 Deaton, 'The Structure of Demand in Europe, 1920–70', 107.

55 Eurostat, ed., *Consumers in Europe: Facts and Figures, 1999–2004*, Luxembourg: Eurostat, 2004, 112–13.

56 On trends in consumption ratios, see Kovács Ilona, 'Fogyasztási szerkezetek nemzetközi összehasonlításban', *Statisztikai Szemle*, vol. 65 (1987), 979.

57 Ben Fine, Michael Heasman and Judith Wright, *Consumption in the Age of Affluence: The World of Food*, London: Routledge, 1996.

58 D. J. Oddy, 'Food, Drink and Nutrition', in F. M. L. Thompson, ed., *The Cambridge Social History of Britain, 1750–1950*, vol. 2, Cambridge: Cambridge University Press, 1990, 276.

59 Oddy, 'Food, Drink and Nutrition', 278.

60 Deaton, 'The Structure of Demand in Europe, 1920–70', 113–14.

61 Eurostat, ed., *Consumers in Europe: Facts and Figures, 1999–2004*, 98.

62 Peter Corrigan, *The Sociology of Consumption*, London: Sage, 1997, 161.

63 Corrigan, *The Sociology of Consumption*, 168.

64 Deaton, 'The Structure of Demand in Europe, 1920–70', 115–17.

65 M. J. Daunton, 'Housing', in Thompson, ed., *The Cambridge Social History of Britain, 1950–1950*, 219.

66 Eurostat, ed., *Consumers in Europe: Facts and Figures, 1999–2004*, Luxembourg: Eurostat, 2004, 112–13.

67 Cf. 'Consumption Trends and Prospects in Selected ECE Countries', 284.

68 John Brewer, 'Was können wir aus der Geschichte der frühen Neuzeit für die moderne Konsumgeschichte lernen?', in Siegrist, Kaelble and Kocka, eds., *Europäische Konsumgeschichte*, 52–53.

69 Heinz-Gerhard Haupt, *Konsum und Handel: Europa im 19. und 20. Jahrhundert*, Göttingen: Vandenhoeck and Ruprecht, 2003, 118.

70 Michael B. Miller, *The Bon Marché: Bourgeois Culture and the Department Store, 1869–1920*, Princeton: Princeton University Press, 1981, 21–22.

71 Miller, *The Bon Marché*, 183–89.

72 Peter Eigner, '(Detail)Handel und Konsum in Österreich im 20. Jahrhundert: Die Geschichte einer Wechselbeziehung', in Susanne Breuss and Franz X. Eder, eds., *Konsumiren in Österreich: 19. und 20. Jahrhundert*, Innsbruck: StudienVerlag, 2006, 65.

73 Robert C. Ostergren and John G. Rice, *The Europeans: A Geography of People, Culture, and Environment*, New York: The Guilford Press, 2004, 334.

74 Peter Scholliers, 'The Transformation from Traditional to Modern Patterns of Demand in Belgium (Nineteenth and Twentieth Centuries)', in H. Baudet and M. Bogucka, eds., *Types of Consumption, Traditional and Modern*, Budapest: Akadémiai Kiadó, 1982, 58.

75 Sabine Haustein, 'Westeuropäische Annäherungen durch Konsum seit 1945', in Hartmut Kaelble and Jürgen Schriewer, eds., *Gesellschaften im Vergleich*, Frankfurt/M.: Peter Lang, 1999, 353–90; according to the survey carried out by F. Gardes, which included four countries (France, German Federal Republic, the Netherlands, and the United Kingdom), differences in the structure of consumption decreased by 2–4% yearly between 1960 and 1978 (based on the average of multilateral distance between percentage ratios of consumer product categories). A more comprehensive survey including 14 Western European countries indicated a similar 1–3% yearly convergence between 1960 and 1982, with a break in 1973 lasting a few years, resulting in the divergence of countries. Other researchers argue in favour of convergence within Western Europe in the three decades after 1960, based on ratios of the structure of consumption, and especially proportions within food consumption. F. Gardes, 'International convergence of consumption patterns', *Economic Bulletin for Europe*, vol. 39 (1987), no. 2, 280–82.

76 Fine, Heasman and Wright, *Consumption in the Age of Affluence*, 205; Ostergren and Rice, *The Europeans: A Geography of People, Culture, and Environment*, 337–38.

77 Hartmut Kaelble, 'Europäische Besonderheiten des Massenkonsums, 1950–90', in Siegrist, Kaelble and Kocka, eds., *Europäische Konsumgeschichte*, 192.

78 Gardes, 'International Convergence of Consumption Patterns', 276–77.

79 A classic study of the system: Kornai János, *A hiány*, Budapest: KJK, 1980.

80 Andrzej K. Kozminski, 'Consumers in Transition from the Centrally Planned Economy to the Market Economy', *Journal of Consumer Policy*, vol. 14 (1992), 352–54.

81 Stephen Merl, 'Staat und Konsum in der Zentralverwaltungswirtschaft', in Siegrist, Kaelble and Kocka, eds., *Europäische Konsumgeschichte*, 206–13.

82 János Kornai, *The Socialist System*, 234–36.

83 Ádám György, *Az orvosi hálapénz története Magyarországon*, Budapest: Magvető, 1986.

84 Peter Burke, 'The Invention of Leisure in Early Modern Europe', *Past and Present*, vol. 146 (1995), 136–50.

85 Charles Rearick, 'Consumer Leisure', in Stearns, ed., *Encyclopedia of European Social History*, vol. 5, 208.

86 Rearick, 'Consumer Leisure', 210.

87 Eli Noam, *Television in Europe*, New York: Oxford University Press, 1991, 116–17.

88 Donald Sassoon, *The Culture of the Europeans: From 1800 to the Present*, London: Harper and Collins, 2006, 1147–69.

89 Peter Dahlgren, 'Key Trends in European Television', in Jan Wieten, Graham Murdock and Peter Dahlgren, eds., *Television Across Europe: A Comparative Introduction*, London: Sage, 2000, 23–34.

90 John Urry, *The Tourist Gaze*, London: Sage, 2002, 17–26; Hasso Spode, 'Der Aufstieg des Massentourismus im 20. Jahrhundert', in Haupt and Torp, eds., *Die Konsumgesellschaft in Deutschland, 1890–1990*, 114–28.

91 Ostergren and Rice, *The Europeans: A Geography of People, Culture, and Environment*, 341–47.

92 Jafar Jafari, ed., *Encyclopedia of Tourism*, London: Routledge, 2000, 208, 334, 550.

93 Ostergren and Rice, *The Europeans: A Geography of People, Culture, and Environment*, 349.

94 Roberta Sassatelli, *Consumer Culture: History, Theory and Politics*, London: Sage, 2007, 2.

95 Jan de Vries, 'Between Purchasing Power and the World of Goods', in J. Brewer and R. Porter, eds., *Consumption and the World of Goods*, London: Routledge, 1993, 85–132; Colin Campbell, *The Romantic Ethic and the Spirit of Modern Consumerism*, Oxford: Blackwell, 1987; Neil McKendrick, 'Die Ursprünge der Konsumgesellschaft: Luxus, Neid und soziale Nachahmung in der englischen Literatur des 18. Jahrhunderts', in Siegrist, Kaelble and Kocka, eds., *Europäische Konsumgeschichte*, 75–107.

96 Paul Glennie, 'Consumption within Historical Studies', in Daniel Miller, ed., *Acknowledging Consumption*, London: Routledge, 1995, 167.

97 Peter Kramper, *From Economic Convergence to Convergence in Affluence?*, LSE Working Paper No. 56/00, London: LSE, 2000, 4.

98 For a similar account, see Nicholas Abercrombie, Stephen Hill and Bryan S. Turner, eds., *The Penguin Dictionary of Sociology*, London: Penguin Books, 2000, 71.

99 For the critique of consumer culture and society, see Stearns, *Consumerism in World History*, 61–64; Max Horkheimer and Theodor W. Adorno, *Dialektik der Aufklärung*, München: Fischer Taschenbuch Verlag, 1971 [1944], 108–50; John K. Galbraith, *The Affluent Society*, London: Penguin, 1991 [1958], 126–33; Jean Baudrillard, *The Consumer Society: Myths and Structures*, London: Sage, 1998 [1970], 77–86; Roberta Sassatelli, *Consumer Culture: History, Theory and Politics*, London: Sage, 2007, 74–77.

100 Stearns, *Consumerism in World History*, 61–64.

101 Reinhold Wagnleitner, *Coca-Colonization and the Cold War: The Cultural Mission of the United States in Austria after the Second World War*, Chapel Hill & London: The University of North Carolina Press, 1994.

102 Max Horkheimer and Theodor W. Adorno, *Dialektik der Aufklärung*, München: Fischer Taschenbuch Verlag, 1971 [1944], 108–50.

103 John K. Galbraith, *The Affluent Society*, London: Penguin, 1991 [1958], 126–33.

104 Jean Baudrillard, *The Consumer Society: Myths and Structures*, London: Sage, 1998 [1970], 77–86.

105 Sassatelli, *Consumer Culture: History, Theory and Politics*, 117.

106 Sassatelli, *Consumer Culture: History, Theory and Politics*, 74–77.

107 Alexander Stephan, ed., *The Americanization of Europe: Culture, Diplomacy, and Anti-Americanism after 1945*, New York: Berghahn, 2006; Anselm Doering-Manteuffel, 'Amerikanisierung und Westernisierung', Version: 1.0, in *Docupedia-Zeitgeschichte*, 18. 1.2011, https://docupedia.de/zg/Amerikanisierung_und_Westernisierung?oldid=76659.

108 Victoria de Grazia, *Irresistible Empire: America's Advance through Twentieth-Century Europe*, Cambridge, MA: The Belknap Press, 2005.

109 Volker R. Berghahn, 'The Debate on "Americanization" among Economic and Cultural Historians,' *Cold War History*, vol. 10 (2010), no. 1, 107–30; Kaelble, 'Europäische Besonderheiten des Massenkonsums, 1950–90', 188–89.

110 Avner Offer, 'Economic Welfare Measurements and Human Well-Being', in Paul A. David and Mark Thomas, eds., *The Economic Future in Historical Perspective*, Oxford: Oxford University Press, 2003, 372.

111 Ronald Inglehart, *Modernization and Postmodernization: Cultural, Economic and Political Change in 43 Societies*, Princeton: Princeton University Press, 1997.

112 For example, William D. Nordhaus and James Tobin, *Is Growth Obsolete?*, New York: National Bureau of Economic Research, 1972; Robert Eisner, 'Extended Accounts for National Income and Product', *Journal of Economic Literature*, vol. 26 (1988), 1611–84.

113 For comprehensive accounts, see Frank Ackerman et al., ed., *Human Well-being and Economic Goals*, Washington, DC: Island Press, 1997; Ruut Veenhoven, 'Quality-of-Life Research', in Clifton D. Bryant and Dennis L. Peck, eds., *21st Century Sociology: A Reference Handbook*, vol. 2, London: Sage, 2007, 54–62; Martha Nussbaum and Amartya Sen, eds., *The Quality of Life*, Oxford: Oxford University Press, 1993; Heinz-Herbert Noll, 'Wohlstand, Lebensqualität und Wohlbefinden in den Ländern der Europäischen Union', in Hradil and Immerfall, eds., *Die westeuropäischen Gesellschaften im Vergleich*, 431–73.

114 Amartya Sen, *The Standard of Living*, Cambridge: Cambridge University Press, 1987.

115 OECD, *The Well-being of Nations: The Role of Human and Social Capital*, Paris: OECD, 2001, 10–11.

116 Tim Jackson and Nick Marks, *Measuring Sustainable Economic Welfare: A Pilot Index, 1950–1990*, Stockholm: Stockholm Environment Institute, 1994.

117 Offer, 'Economic Welfare Measurements', 372.

118 Xenophon Zolotas, *Economic Growth and Declining Social Welfare*, Athens: Bank of Greece, 1981.

119 Michael Argyle, 'Subjective Well-Being', in Avner Offer, ed., *In Pursuit of the Quality of Life*, Oxford: Oxford University Press, 1996, 18–45.

120 Such items included in the GPI are the following: value of domestic work and raising children, value of voluntary and charitable work, value of free time, damages of non-renewable natural resources, costs of family breakdown, level of environmental damage, costs of commuting to work, costs of crime, costs of noise pollution, etc. Clifford Cobb, Ted Halstead and Jonathan Row, *The Genuine Progress Indicator: Summary of Data and Methodology*, San Francisco: Redefining Progress, 1995, 13–39.

121 Cf. webpages of the organization *Friends of the Earth*: http://www.foe.org.uk/campaigns/sustainable_development/progress. Retrieved 10.07.2008.

122 United Nations Development Programme, *Human Development Report. 1998*, New York: Human Development Report Office, 1998; Arne Melchior, Kjetil Telle and Henrik Wiig, *Globalisation and Inequality: World Income Distribution and Living Standards, 1960–1998*, Oslo: The Norwegian Institute of International Affairs, 2000, 23–32; Nicholas Crafts, 'The Human Development Index and Changes in Standards of Living: some Historical Comparisons', *European Review of Economic History*, vol. 1 (1997), 299–322.

123 www.foe.org.uk/campaigns/sustainable_development/progress. Retrieved 10.07.2008.

124 Offer, 'Economic Welfare Measurements', 374, 393.

7 Politics and society

1 Seymour M. Lipset and Stein Rokkan, 'Cleavage Structures, Party Systems, and Voter Alignments: An Introduction', in Seymour M. Lipset and Stein Rokkan, eds., *Party Systems and Voter Alignments: Cross-National Perspectives*, New York: Free Press, 1967, 1–64; Stein Rokkan, *Citizens, Elections, Parties: Approaches to the Comparative Study of the Processes of Development*, New York: David McKay, 1970, 72–144.

2 Talcott Parsons, *Politics and Social Structure*, New York: Free Press, 1969; Niklas Luhmann, 'Soziologie des politischen Systems', in Niklas Luhmann, *Soziologische Aufklärung: Aufsätze zur Theorie sozialer Systeme*, Köln and Opladen: Westdeutscher Verlag, 1970, 154.

3 Gabriel Almond and Sidney Verba, *The Civic Culture: Political Attitudes and Democracy in Five Nations*, Princeton, NJ: Princeton University Press, 1963; Ronald Inglehart, *The Silent Revolution: Changing Values and Political Styles among Western Publics*, Princeton, NJ: Princeton University Press, 1977.

4 Giovanni Sartori, 'From Sociology of Politics to Political Sociology', in Seymour M. Lipset, ed., *Politics and the Social Sciences*, New York: Oxford University Press, 1969, 65–100.

5 Jan-Erik Lane and Svante O. Ersson, *Politics and Society in Western Europe*, London: Sage, 1991, 55–101; Stein Rokkan, *Citizens, Elections, Parties: Approaches to the Comparative Study of the Processes of Development*, 72–144; Stein Rokkan, *Staat, Nation, und Demokratie in Europa*, Frankfurt/M.: Suhrkamp, 2000, 335–66.

6 Enyedi Zsolt and Körösényi András, *Pártok és pártrendszerek*, Budapest: Osiris, 2004, 55–74.

7 Rokkan, *Citizens, Elections, Parties: Approaches to the Comparative Study of the Processes of Development*, 72–144; Rokkan, *Staat, Nation, und Demokratie in Europa*, 335–66.

8 Lipset and Rokkan, *Cleavage Structures, Party Systems, and Voter Alignments*, 1–64.

9 Lane and Ersson, *Politics and Society in Western Europe*, Table 2.20 and 2.21.

10 Lane and Ersson, *Politics and Society in Western Europe*, 75–79.

11 Ralf Dahrendorf, *Class and Class Conflict in Industrial Society*, Stanford, CA: Stanford University Press, 1959.

12 John H. Goldthorpe, 'Class and Politics in Advanced Industrial Societies', in D. J. Lee and B. S. Turner, eds., *Conflicts about Class: Debating Inequality in Late Industrialism*, London: Longman, 1996, 196–208.

13 Mark N. Franklin, 'The Decline of Cleavage Politics', in Mark N. Franklin, Thomas T. Mackie and Henry Valen et al., *Electoral Change: Responses to Evolving Social and Attitudinal Structures in Western Countries*, Cambridge: Cambridge University Press, 1992, 383–405.

14 Enyedi and Körösényi, *Pártok és pártrendszerek*, 73–74.

15 Yves Mény, *Government and Politics in Western Europe: Britain, France, Italy, Germany*, Oxford: Oxford University Press, 1994, 19–47.

16 Raffaele Romanelli, 'Electoral Systems and Social Structures: A Comparative Perspective', In Raffaele Romanelli, ed., *How Did They Become Voters?* The Hague: Kluwer Law International, 1998, 1–36; Richard S. Katz, *Democracy and Elections*, New York: Oxford University Press, 1997, 100–106.

17 Richard Rose, *What Is Europe? A Dynamic Perspective*, New York: Harper Collins, 1996, 25.

18 Stefano Bartolini, 'Franchise Expansion', in Richard Rose, ed., *International Encyclopedia of Elections*, Washington, DC: CQ Press, 2000, 117–29.

19 Rose, *What is Europe?* 25.

20 Wilma Rule, 'Women: Enfranchisement', in Rose, ed., *International Encyclopedia of Elections*, 345–48.

21 Püski Levente, *A Horthy-rendszer*, Budapest: Pannonica, 2006, 99–100.

22 Rose, *What is Europe?*, 33–34.

23 Thomas H. Marshall, *Class, Citizenship, and Social Development*, New York: Anchor Books, 1965 [1950], 71–134.

24 Thomas Poguntke, 'Internationale Vergleichende Parteienforschung', in Dirk Berg-Schlosser and Ferdinand Müller-Rommel, eds., *Vergleichende Politikwissenschaft*, Opladen: Leske und Budrich, 2003, 189–206.

25 Percy Allum, *State and Society in Western Europe*, Cambridge: Polity Press, 1995, 176–79.

26 Michael Keating, *The Politics of Modern Europe: The State and Political Authority in the Major Democracies*, Cheltenham: Edward Elgar, 1999, 49–70.

27 Lane and Ersson, *Politics and Society in Western Europe*, 113–31.

28 Enyedi and Körösényi, *Pártok és pártrendszerek*, 75.

29 Dick Richardson, 'The Green Challenge: Philosophical, Programmatic and Electoral Considerations', in Dick Richardson and Chris Roots, eds., *The Green Challenge: The Development of Green Parties in Europe*, London: Routledge, 1995, 4–22.

30 Stefan Immerfall, *Einführung in den europäischen Gesellschaftsvergleich*, Passau: Wissenschaftsverlag Rote, 1995, 123.

31 Mark N. Franklin, Thomas T. Mackie and Henry Valen et al., *Electoral Change: Responses to Evolving Social and Attitudinal Structures in Western Countries*, Cambridge: Cambridge University Press, 1992, 383–405; Russell J. Dalton, Paul Allen Beck and Scott C. Flanagan, 'Electoral Change in Advanced Industrial Democracies', in Dalton, Beck and Flanagan, eds., *Electoral Change in Advanced Industrial Democracies: Realignment or Dealignment?*, Princeton: Princeton University Press, 1984, 3–22; Ronald Inglehart, 'The Changing Structure of Political Cleavages in Western Society', in Dalton, Beck and Flanagan, eds., *Electoral Change in Advanced Industrial Democracies*, 30.

32 Mark N. Franklin, 'The Decline of Cleavage Politics', 404.

33 Donatella della Porta and Mario Diani, *Social Movements: An Introduction*, Oxford: Blackwell, 2006, 20; Sidney Tarrow, *Power in Movement: Social Movements, Collective Action and Politics*, Cambridge: Cambridge University Press, 1994, 3–4.

34 Charles Tilly, Louise Tilly and Richard Tilly, *The Rebellious Century, 1830–1930*, Cambridge, MA: Harvard University Press, 1975.

35 The next sections largely rely on the following work: Joachim Raschke, *Soziale Bewegungen: Ein historisch-systematischer Grundriß*, Frankfurt/M.: Campus, 1988, 22–67.

36 Raschke, *Soziale Bewegungen*, 22–75.

37 Hanspeter Kriesi et al., *New Social Movements in Western Europe: A Comparative Analysis*, London: UCL Press, 1995.

38 Stefan Berger, 'Labour Movements', in Stefan Berger, ed., *A Companion to Nineteenth-Century Europe, 1789–1914*, Oxford: Blackwell, 2006, 166–67.

39 Raschke, *Soziale Bewegungen*, 87.

40 Tarrow, *Power in Movement*, 5–6.

41 L. Olsson, 'History of Labor Movements', in Smelser and Baltes, eds., *International Encyclopedia of the Social and Behavioural Sciences*, vol. 12, 8194–99.

42 Laura E. Nym Mayhall, 'Feminism', in Stearns, ed., *Encyclopedia of European Social History*, vol. 4, 45–54.

43 For a similar inventory of factors related to the stability and vulnerability of interwar democracies, see Dirk Berg-Schlosser and Jeremy Mitchell, 'Introduction', in Dirk Berg-Schlosser and Jeremy Mitchell, eds., *Conditions of Democracy in Europe, 1919–39: Systematic Case Studies*, Houndmills: Macmillan, 2000, 1–17; Michael Mann, *Fascists*, Cambridge: Cambridge University Press, 2004, 13.

44 Jürgen Kocka, 'German History before Hitler: The Debate about the German "Sonderweg"', *Journal of Contemporary History*, vol. 23 (1988), no. 1, 3–16; David Blackbourn and Geoff Eley, *The Peculiarities of German History: Bourgeois Society and Politics in Nineteenth-Century Germany*, Oxford: Oxford University Press, 1984.

45 Raschke, *Soziale Bewegungen*, 56–59.

46 Raschke, *Soziale Bewegungen*, 60–64.

47 Hanspeter Kriesi et al., *New Social Movements in Western Europe: A Comparative Analysis*, xvii–xxii.

48 Klaus Eder, 'Social Movements and Democratization', in Gerald Delanty and Engin F. Isin, eds., *Handbook of Historical Sociology*, London: Sage, 2003, 280–81.

49 Craig Calhoun, 'New Social Movements of the Early Nineteenth Century', *Social Science History*, vol. 17 (1993), no. 3, 385–427.

50 Abigail Halcli, 'Social Movements', in Gary Browning, Abigail Halcli and Frank Webster, *Understanding Contemporary Society: Theories of the Present*, London: Sage, 2000, 468–70.

51 Kristina Schulz, 'Studentische Bewegungen und Protestkampagnen', in Ronald Roth and Dieter Ruch, eds., *Die sozialen Bewegungen in Deutschland seit 1945*, Frankfurt/M.: Campus, 2008, 442.

52 Gisela Kaplan, 'New Social Movements', in Stearns, ed., *Encyclopedia of European Social History*, vol. 3, 297.
53 Wolfgang Eichwede, 'Archipel Samizdat', in Wolfgang Eichwede, ed., *Samizdat: Alternative Kultur in Zentral-und Osteuropa*, Bremen: Temmen, 2000, 8–19.
54 Ivan T. Berend, *Europe since 1980*, Cambridge: Cambridge University Press, 2010, 33.
55 Jan-Erik Lane and Svante O. Ersson, *European Politics*, London: Sage, 1996, 175.
56 Gabriel Almond, 'Comparative Political Systems', *Journal of Politics*, vol. 18 (1956), no. 2, 391–409.
57 Almond and Verba, *The Civic Culture*.
58 Russell J. Dalton, *Politics in Germany*, New York: Harper Collins, 1993, 108.
59 Dalton, *Politics in Germany*, 120–21.
60 Alan R. Ball and B. Guy Peters, *Modern Politics and Government*, Houndmills: Palgrave, 2000, 89.
61 Ronald Inglehart, *Culture Shift in Advanced Industrial Society*, Princeton: Princeton University Press, 1990; Ronald Inglehart, *Human Values and Beliefs: A Cross-Cultural Sourcebook*, Ann Arbor: University of Michigan Press, 1998. The European Community initiated the public opinion polls called Eurobarometer in 1973, in which data of this type have been published regularly since then. Another important source was launched in 1981. The first wave of the *European Values Survey* included 10 countries, and it was replicated in several additional ones in the following years. The *World Values Survey* built on this research first. Then it vastly broadened the geographic scope of value research, and it has been repeated several times. Thus, it has become the most important database of its kind by now. *The New Democracies Barometer* conducted regular research into the public opinion of communist countries after the regime change.
62 Richard Topf, 'Electoral Participation', in Hans-Dieter Klingemann and Dieter Fuchs, eds., *Citizens and the State*, Oxford: Oxford University Press, 1995, 41.
63 Lane and Ersson, *European Politics*, 186.
64 Francis Fukuyama, *Trust*, London: Penguin Books, 1996.
65 Lane and Ersson, *European Politics*, 187–89; Richard Rose and Neil Munro, *Elections and Parties in New European Democracies*, Washington, DC: CQ Press, 2003, 34–70.
66 Lane and Ersson, *European Politics*, 190.
67 Gábor Tóka, 'Political Support in East-Central Europe', in Hans-Dieter Klingemann and Dieter Fuchs, eds., *Citizens and the State*, 376.
68 Ambrosius and Hubbard, *A Social and Economic History of Twentieth-Century Europe*, 112.
69 Winand Gellner, 'Massenmedien', in Oscar W. Gabriel and Frank Brettschneider, eds., *Die EU-Staaten im Vergleich*, Opladen: Westdeutscher Verlag, 1994, 286.
70 Dalton, *Politics in Germany*, 166–67.
71 Winand Gellner, 'Massenmedien', in Gabriel and Brettschneider, eds., *Die EU-Staaten im Vergleich*, 290.
72 Rose, *What is Europe?*, 151.
73 Rose, *What is Europe?*, 153.

8 Urbanization

1 For its first conceptualization, see Georg Simmel, 'Die Großstädte und das Geistesleben', in Otthein Rammstedt, ed., *Georg Simmel Gesamtausgabe, Bd. 7: Aufsätze und Abhandlungen, 1901–1908*, Frankfurt/M: Suhrkamp, 1995 [1903], 116–31. Louis Wirth, 'Urbanism as a Way of Life', *American Journal of Sociology*, vol. XLIV (1938), no. 1, 1–24.
2 A classic example of this approach: E. W. Burgess, 'The Growth of a City', in R. E. Park, E. W. Burgess and R. D. McKenzie, eds., *The City*, Chicago: Chicago University Press, 1925, 42–62.
3 Bácskai Vera, 'Várostörténet', in Bódy Zsombor and Ö. Kovács József, *Bevezetés a társadalomtörténetbe*, Budapest: Osiris, 2003, 246–50.

4 Paul M. Hohenberg and Lynn Hollen Lees, *The Making of Urban Europe, 1000–1950*, Cambridge, MA and London: Harvard University Press, 1985, 218–20.

5 Peter Flora, *Indikatoren der Modernisierung: Ein historisches Datenhandbuch*, Opladen: Westdeutscher Verlag, 1975, 28–29.

6 William H. Frey and Zachary Zimmer, 'Defining the City', in Ronan Paddison, ed., *Handbook of Urban Studies*, London: Sage, 2001, 14.

7 Wolfram Fischer, 'Wirtschaft, Gesellschaft und Staat in Europa, 1914–80', in Wolfram Fischer, ed., *Handbuch der europäischen Wirtschafts-und Sozialgeschichte*, vol. 6, Stuttgart: Klett-Cotta, 1987, 53.

8 F. E. Ian Hamilton, 'Urbanization in Socialist Eastern Europe: The Macro-Environment of Internal City Structure', in R. A. French and F. E. Ian Hamilton, eds., *The Socialist City: Spatial Structure and Urban Policy*, Chichester: John Wiley, 1979, 171.

9 United Nations, *World Urbanization Prospects: The 2003 Revision*, New York: United Nations, 2003, 168 (as quoted in Kaelble, *Sozialgeschichte Europas*, 368–69).

10 Paul C. Cheshire, 'Some Causes of Western European Patterns of Urban Change', in Anita A. Summers, Paul C. Cheshire and Lanfranco Senn, eds., *Urban Change in the United States and Western Europe: Comparative Analysis and Policy*, Washington, DC: The Urban Institute Press, 1999, 179–84.

11 L. H. Klaassen and G. Scimemi, 'Theoretical issues in urban dynamics', in L. H. Klaassen, W. T. M. Molle and J. H. P. Paelinck, eds., *Dynamics of Urban Development*, Aldershot: Gower, 1981, 18; L. van der Berg, R. Drewett, L. H. Klaassen, A. Rossi and C. H. T. Vijverberg, *Urban Europe, Vol. 1: A Study of Growth and Decline*, Oxford: Pergamon, 1982, 36.

12 A. J. Fielding, 'Migration and Urbanization in Western Europe since 1950', *Geographical Journal*, vol. 155 (1989), no. 1, 60–69.

13 Richard Lawton, 'An Age of Great Cities', *Town Planning Review*, vol. 43 (1972), no. 3, 199–224.

14 L. S. Bourne, 'Reinventing the Suburbs: Old Myths and New Realities', *Progress in Planning*, vol. 46 (1996), no. 3, 163–84.

15 Peter Hall and Dennis Hay, *Growth Centres in the European Urban System*, Berkeley and Los Angeles: University of California Press, 1980, 225–31.

16 Tony Champion, 'Urbanization, Suburbanization, Counterurbanization and Reurbanization', in Paddison, ed., *Handbook of Urban Studies*, 150.

17 A. J. Fielding, 'Counterurbanization in Western Europe', *Progress in Planning*, vol. 17 (1982), no. 1, 1–52.

18 Robert Fishmann, 'Megapolis Unbound: Decentralisation and the End of Metropolitan Culture', in Theo Barker and Anthony Sutcliffe, eds., *Megapolis: The Giant City in History*, New York: St Martin's Press, 1993, 195.

19 A. J. Fielding, 'Migration and Urbanization in Western Europe since 1950', *Geographical Journal*, vol. 155 (1989), no. 1, 60–69.

20 William Lever, 'Urbanization', in Max-Stephan Schulze, ed., *Western Europe: Economic and Social Change since 1945*, London and New York: Longman, 1999, 235–39.

21 Fielding, 'Counterurbanization in Western Europe', 1–52; A. G. Champion, ed., *Counterurbanization: The Changing Pace and Nature of Population Deconcentration*, London: Edward Arnold, 1989.

22 A. G. Champion, 'Geographical Distribution and Urbanization', in Noin and Woods, eds., *The Changing Population of Europe*, 30–36.

23 Rainer Mackensen, 'Urban Decentralization Processes in Western Europe', in Summers, Cheshire and Senn, eds., *Urban Change in the United States and Western Europe: Comparative Analysis and Policy*, Washington, DC: The Urban Institute Press, 1999, 322.

24 P. Cheshire, 'A New Phase of Urban Development in Western Europe? The Evidence for the 1980s', *Urban Studies*, vol. 32 (1995), no. 7, 1045–63.

25 Champion, 'Urbanization, Suburbanization, Counterurbanization and Reurbanization', 154.

26 Fielding, 'Migration and Urbanization in Western Europe since 1950', 68–69; Paul C. Cheshire, 'A Postscript: Exurbia or Islington?', in Summers, Cheshire and Senn, eds., *Urban Change in the United States and Western Europe: Comparative Analysis and Policy*, 590.
27 Lever, 'Urbanization', 242–44.
28 Lever, 'Urbanization', 242–44.
29 Alexander Cowan, 'Urbanization', in Stearns, ed., *Encyclopaedia of European Social History*, vol. 2, 240–42.
30 Leonardo Benevolo, *A város Európa történetében*, Budapest: Atlantisz, 1994.
31 Leonardo Benevolo, *The European City*, Oxford: Blackwell, 1993.
32 A. Burtenshaw, M. Bateman and G. Ashworth, *The European City: A Western Perspective*, London: David Fulton, 1991, 38.
33 Burtenshaw, Bateman and Ashworth, *The European City*, 38–41.
34 Hough Clout, Mark Blacksell, Russell King and David Pinder, *Western Europe: Geographical Perspectives*, Burnt Mill: Longman, 1989, 127.
35 Hartmut Kaelble, 'Die Besonderheiten der europäischen Stadt im 20. Jahrhundert', in Lenger and Tenfelde, eds., *Die europäische Stadt im 20. Jahrhundert: Wahrnehmung – Entwicklung – Erosion*, 25–44; for other, more concise conceptualizations of it, see Kaelble, *A Social History of Western Europe, 1880–1980*, 59–74; Hartmut Kaelble, 'Europäische Vielfalt und der Weg zu einer europäischen Gesellschaft', in Hradil and Immerfall, eds., *Die westeuropäischen Gesellschaften im Vergleich*, 38–40.
36 For a detailed elaboration, see G. J. Ashworth, 'The Conserved European City as Cultural Symbol: The Meaning of the Text', in Brian Graham, ed., *Modern Europe: Place, Culture, Identity*, London: Arnold, 1998, 261–86.
37 Patrick Le Galès, *European Cities: Social Conflicts and Governance*, Oxford: Oxford University Press, 2002, 66–67.
38 Kaelble, 'Die Besonderheiten der europäischen Stadt im 20', Jahrhundert, 33–44.
39 Iván Szelényi, *Urban Inequalities under State Socialism*, Oxford: Oxford University Press, 1983.
40 R. A. French and F. E. Ian Hamilton, eds., *The Socialist City: Spatial Structure and Urban Policy*, Chichester: John Wiley and Sons, 1979; David M. Smith, 'The Socialist City', in Gregory Andrusz, Michael Harloe and Ivan Szelenyi, eds., *Cities after Socialism: Urban and Regional Change and Conflict in Post-Socialist Societies*, Oxford: Blackwell, 1996, 70–99; György Enyedi, 'Urbanization under Socialism', in Andrusz, Harloe and Szelenyi, eds., *Cities after Socialism*, 100–118; Ivan Szelenyi, 'Cities under Socialism – and After', in Andrusz, Harloe and Szelenyi, eds. *Cities after Socialism*, 286–317.
41 Jiří Musil, 'Changing Urban Systems in Post-Communist Societies in Central Europe', *Urban Studies*, vol. 30 (1993), no. 6, 901–2.
42 R. A. French and F. E. Ian Hamilton, 'Is There a Socialist City?', in French and Hamilton, eds., *The Socialist City*, 6.
43 Hartmut Häussermann, 'From the Socialist to the Capitalist City: Experiences from Germany', in Andrusz, Harloe and Szelenyi, eds., *Cities after Socialism*, 219.
44 F. E. Ian Hamilton, 'Spatial Structure in East European Cities', in French and Hamilton, eds., *The Socialist City*, 201–7; Enyedi György, 'Urbanization under Socialism', in Andrusz, Harloe and Szelenyi, eds., *Cities after Socialism*, 111.
45 French and Hamilton, *Is There a Socialist City?*, 15–16.
46 Iván Szelényi, 'East European Cities: How Different Are They?', in Greg Guldin and Aidan Southall, eds., *Urban Anthropology in China*, Leiden: E. J. Brill, 1993, 53.
47 Hanák Péter, 'Polgárosodás és urbanizáció. Bécs és Budapest városfejlődése a 19. században', in Hanák Péter, *A Kert és a Műhely*, Budapest: Gondolat, 1988, 39; Gyáni Gábor, *Az utca és a szalon. Társadalmi térhasználat Budapesten, 1870–1940*, Budapest: Új Mandátum, 1999, 40.
48 Grzegorz Weclawowicz, 'The Structure of Socio-economic Space in Warsaw in 1931 and 1970: A Study in Factorial Ecology', in French and Hamilton, eds., *The Socialist City*, 387–423.

49 György Konrád and Iván Szelényi, *Az új lakótelepek szociológiai problémái*, Budapest: Akadémiai Kiadó, 1969.

50 David M. Smith, 'The Socialist City', in Andrusz, Harloe and Szelenyi, eds., *Cities after Socialism*, 86–88, 96–99.

51 Hohenberg and Lees, *The Making of Urban Europe*, 226–29.

52 Therborn, *European Modernity and Beyond*, 185–86.

53 Mark Jefferson, 'The Law of the Primate City', *Geographical Review*, vol. 29 (1939), 226–32.

54 G. Champion, ed., *Counterurbanization: The Changing Pace and Nature of Population Deconcentration*, London: Edward Arnold, 1989.

55 J. L. Berry, ed., *Urbanization and Counterurbanization*, Beverly Hills, CA: Sage, 1976.

56 Paul L. Knox, *The Geography of Western Europe: A Socio-Economic Survey*, London: Croom Helm, 1984, 167.

57 Much of the following discussion is based on Burtenshaw, Bateman and Ashworth, *The European City*, 248–71.

58 Burtenshaw, Bateman and Ashworth, *The European City*, 278; Luther A. Allen, British and French New Towns Programs, *Comparative Social Research*, vol. 5 (1982), 269–98.

59 Arnold J. Heidenheimer, Hugh Heclo and Carolyn Teich Adams, *Comparative Public Policy: The Politics of Social Choice in America, Europe and Japan*, New York: St Martin's Press, 1990, 272–73.

60 Heidenheimer, Heclo and Teich Adams, *Comparative Public Policy*, 273–74; Burtenshaw, Bateman and Ashworth, *The European City*, 256–57.

61 Dieter Schott, 'London and its "New Towns" and Randstad Holland: Metropolitan Planning on Both Sides of the Channel after 1945', in Lenger and Tenfelde, eds., *Die europäische Stadt im 20. Jahrhundert*, 298–304; Burtenshaw, Bateman and Ashworth, *The European City*, 259.

62 Frans M. Dieleman and Andreas Faludi, 'Randstad, Rhine-Ruhr and Flamand Diamond as one Polynucleated Macro-Region?', *Tijdschrift voor Economische en Sociale Geografie*, vol. 89 (1998), no. 3, 320–27.

63 György Enyedi, 'Urbanization under Socialism', in Andrusz, Harloe and Szelenyi, eds., *Cities after Socialism*, 113–15.

64 Douglas V. Shaw, 'The Post-Industrial City', in Paddison, ed., *Handbook of Urban Studies*, 284–95.

65 Saskia Sassen, 'Cities and Communities in the Global Economy: Rethinking Our Concepts', *American Behavioral Scientist*, vol. 39 (1996), no. 5, 629–39; Le Galès, *European Cities*, 131–43.

66 Ostergren and Rice, *The Europeans*, 279.

67 Lars Nilsson, 'Main Trends in Modern Nordic Urbanization', in Lenger and Tenfelde, eds., *Die europäische Stadt im 20. Jahrhundert*, 114.

68 Manuel Castells, *The Informational City*, Oxford: Oxford University Press, 1989; Saskia Sassen, *The Global City: New York, London, Tokyo*, Princeton: Princeton University Press, 1991.

69 Ostergren and Rice, *The Europeans*, 280–84.

70 Peter Hall, 'Priorities in Urban and Economic Development', in Summers, Cheshire and Senn, eds., *Urban Change in the United States and Western Europe*, 60.

71 Hugh Clout, Mark Blacksell, Russell King and David Pinder, *Western Europe: Geographical Perspectives*, Burnt Mill: Longman, 1989, 129–31.

72 Clout, Blacksell, King and Pinder, *Western Europe*, 130–32.

73 Hartmut Häussermann, 'Sozialräumliche Polarisierung und Exklusion in der "europäischen Stadt": Politische Chancen für eine "soziale Stadt"?', in Lenger and Tenfelde, eds., *Die europäische Stadt im 20. Jahrhundert*, 516–19.

74 Annick Magnier, 'Large Urban Systems', in Gianfranco Bettin Lattes and Ettore Recchi, eds., *Comparing European Societies: Towards a Sociology of the EU*, Bologna: Monduzzi Editore, 2005, 305.

75 Paul White, 'Urban Life and Social Stress', in David Pinder, ed., *The New Europe: Economy, Society and Environment*, Chichester: John Wiley, 1998, 315–18.

76 Clout, Blacksell, King and Pinder, *Western Europe*, 135–37.
77 Jiří Musil, 'Changing Urban Systems in Post-Communist Societies in Central Europe', *Urban Studies*, vol. 30 (1993), no. 6, 900–902.
78 G. Andrusz, 'Post-socialist Cities', in Smelser and Baltes, eds., *International Encyclopedia of the Social and Behavioral Sciences*, vol. 3, 1835–40.
79 Szelenyi, 'East European Cities: How Different Are They?', 53–54.
80 Grigoriy Kostinskiy, 'Post-Socialist Cities in Flux', in Paddison, ed., *Handbook of Urban Studies*, 455.
81 Raymond J. Struyk, 'Housing Privatization in the Former Soviet Bloc to 1995', in Andrusz, Harloe and Szelenyi, eds., *Cities after Socialism*, 202–3.
82 Szelenyi, 'Cities under Socialism – and After', 312–14.

9 Education, religion and culture

1 For aspects of culture, see Ludgera Vogt, 'Culture and Civilization', in Georg Ritzer, ed., *Encyclopedia of Social Theory*, vol. 1, Thousand Oaks and London: Sage, 2005, 181–82; Chris Baker, *The Sage Dictionary of Cultural Studies*, London: Sage, 2004, 44–45; Samuel Gilmore, 'Culture', in Borgetta and Borgetta, eds., *Encyclopedia of Sociology*, vol. 1, 404–11.
2 Edward Burnett Tylor, *Primitive Culture*, Gloucester, MA: Smith, 1924 [1871], 1; as cited by Samuel Gilmore, 'Culture', in Borgetta and Borgetta, eds., *Encyclopedia of Sociology*, vol. 1, 405.
3 Peter Burke, 'Popular Culture', in Stearns, ed., *Encyclopedia of Social History*, vol. 5, 3–13.
4 Fritz Ringer, *Education and Society in Modern Europe*, Bloomington: Indiana University Press, 1979; Mary Jo Maynes: *Schooling in Western Europe: A Social History*, Albany: State University of New York Press, 1985.
5 Walter Müller, Susanne Steinmann and Reinhart Schneider, 'Bildung in Europa', in Hradil and Immerfall, eds., *Die westeuropäischen Gesellschaften im Vergleich*, 178.
6 R. A. Houston, 'Literacy', in Stearns, ed., *Encyclopedia of European Social History*, vol. 5, 394.
7 David Vincent, *The Rise of Mass Literacy: Reading and Writing in Modern Europe*, Cambridge: Polity, 2000, 1–26; Wolfram Fischer, 'Wirtschaft und Gesellschaft Europas, 1850–1914', in Fischer et al., eds., *Handbuch der europäischen Wirtschafts-und Sozialgeschichte*, Bd. 5, 86.
8 Peter Flora, *State, Economy, and Society in Western Europe, 1815–1970*, vol. I, Frankfurt/M.: Campus, 1983, 80; *UNESCO Yearbook. 1985*, Paris: UNESCO, 1985.
9 Houston, 'Literacy', 405.
10 The term 'primary education' generally refers to the first four or five grades following kindergarten. The next level, 'secondary education', refers to the lower (grades five–eight) and upper secondary (grades nine–twelve) levels.
11 Fischer, 'Wirtschaft und Gesellschaft Europas, 1850–1914', 93.
12 Paul F. Grendler, 'Schools and Schooling', in Stearns, ed., *Encyclopedia of European Social History*, vol. 5, 339–41.
13 Fischer, 'Wirtschaft, Gesellschaft und Staat in Europa, 1914–80', 75.
14 Martin McLean, 'Education', in Schulze, ed., *Western Europe: Economic and Social Change since 1945*, 204–9.
15 McLean, 'Education', 194–95.
16 Isabell van Ackeren and Klaus Klemm, *Entstehung, Struktur und Steuerung des deutschen Schulsystems*, Wiesbaden: VS Verlag für Sozialwissenschaften, 2009, 11–46.
17 Lynne Chisholm, 'A Crazy Quilt: Education, Training and Social Change in Europe', in J. Bailey, ed., *Social Europe*, London: Longman, 1998, 131–34; McLean, 'Education', 192.
18 For the most updated surveys on the history of universities in Europe, see Walter Rüegg, ed., *A History of the University in Europe, Vol. III: Universities in the Nineteenth and Early Twentieth Centuries (1800–1945)*, Cambridge: Cambridge University Press, 2004; Walter Rüegg, ed., *A History of the University in Europe, Vol. IV: Universities since 1945*, Cambridge: Cambridge University Press, 2011.

19 Rüegg, 'Themes', in Rüegg, ed., *A History of the University in Europe, Vol. III*, 4–6.
20 Christopher Charle, 'Patterns', in Rüegg, ed., *A History of the University in Europe, Vol. III*, 33–57.
21 Fritz Ringer, 'Admission', in Rüegg, ed., *A History of the University in Europe, Vol. III*, 233–46.
22 Charles R. Day, 'Higher Education', in Stearns, ed., *Encyclopedia of European Social History*, vol. 5, 355–58.
23 Guy Neave, 'Patterns', in Rüegg, ed., *A History of the University in Europe, Vol. IV*, 42; A. H. Halsey, 'Admission', in Rüegg, ed., *A History of the University in Europe, Vol. IV*, 208.
24 Heidenheimer, Heclo and Teich Adams, *Comparative Public Policy*, 49–51.
25 Day, 'Higher Education', 362–63.
26 Stefan Immerfall, *Europa – politisches Einigungswerk und gesellschaftliche Entwicklung*, Berlin: VS Verlag für Sozialwissenschaften, 2006, 70–74.
27 Theodor W. Schultz, 'Investment in Human Capital', *American Economic Review*, vol. 51 (1961), 1–17; G. S. Becker, *Human Capital: A Theoretical and Empirical Analysis with Special Reference to Education*, New York: National Bureau of Economic Research, 1964.
28 Talcott Parsons, 'The School Class as a Social System: Some of Its Functions in American Society', *Harvard Educational Review*, vol. 29 (1959), 297–318; R. Collins, 'Some Comparative Principles of Educational Stratification', *Harvard Educational Review*, vol. 47 (1977), 1–27.
29 A. Spence, *Market Signaling*, Cambridge, MA: Harvard University Press, 1974.
30 Pierre Bourdieu and Luc Boltanski, 'Changes in Social Structure and Changes in the Demand for Education', in Salvador Giner and Margaret S. Archer, eds., *Contemporary Europe: Social Structures and Cultural Patterns*, London: Routledge, 1978, 197–227.
31 R. Collins, 'Functional and Conflict Theories of Educational Stratification', *American Sociological Review*, vol. 36 (1971), 1002–19.
32 Pierre Bourdieu, 'Cultural Reproduction and Social Reproduction', in J. Karabel and A. H. Halsey, eds., *Power and Ideology in Education*, New York: Oxford University Press, 1977, 487–510.
33 Walter Müller, Susanne Steinmann and Reinhart Schneider, 'Bildung in Europa', in Hradil and Immerfall, eds., *Die westeuropäischen Gesellschaften im Vergleich*, 214–16.
34 Müller, Steinmann and Schneider, 'Bildung in Europa', 217–18.
35 Müller, Steinmann and Schneider, 'Bildung in Europa', 219.
36 Walter Müller and W. Karle, 'Social Selection in Educational Systems in Europe', *European Sociological Review*, vol. 9 (1993), 1–23.
37 Hartmut Kaelble, *Soziale Mobilität und Chancengleichheit im 19. und 20. Jahrhundert*, Göttingen: Vandenhoeck und Ruprecht, 1983, 227.
38 P. Barnhouse Walters, 'Social Inequality and Schooling', in Smelser et al., ed., *International Encyclopedia of Social and Behavioural Sciences*, 14309–13; P. Barnhouse Walters, 'The Limits of Growth: School Expansion and School Reform in Historical Perspective', in M. Hallinan, ed., *Handbook of the Sociology of Education*, New York: Kluwer Academic–Plenum Press, 2000, 241–64.
39 Walter Müller, Paul Lüttinger, Wolfgang König and Wolfgang Karle, 'Class and Education in Industrial Nations', in Max Haller, ed., *Class Structure in Europe: New Findings from East-West Comparisons of Social Structure and Mobility*, Armonk and London: M. E. Sharpe, 1990, 61–91.
40 Y. Shavit and H.-P. Blossfeld, eds., *Persistent Inequalities: Changing Educational Stratification in Thirteen Countries*, Boulder, CO: Westview Press, 1993.
41 Walter Müller and Irena Kogan, 'Education', in Immerfall and Therborn, eds., *Handbook of European Societies*, 257.
42 U. Henz and I. Maas, 'Chancengleichheit durch Bildungsexpansion?', *Kölner Zeitschrift für Soziologie und Sozialpsychologie*, Jg. 47 (1995), 605–33.
43 Bryan Wilson, *Religion in Secular Society*, London: Watts, 1966, xiv.

44 Henk van Dijk, 'Religion Between State and Society in Nineteenth-Century Europe', in Kaelble, ed., *The European Way*, 263–65.
45 The section largely relies on the following work: David Martin, 'The Religious Condition of Europe', in Giner and Archer, eds., *Contemporary Europe*, 237–62. This typology does not include Greek Orthodoxy; for a similar framework, see John T. S. Madeley, 'A Framework for the Comparative Analysis of Church-State Relations in Europe', in John T. S. Madeley and Zsolt Enyedi, eds., *Church and the State in Contemporary Europe: The Chimera of Neutrality*, London and Portland, OR: Frank Cass, 2003, 22–48.
46 David Martin, 'The Religious Condition of Europe', in Giner and Archer, eds., *Contemporary Europe: Social Structures and Cultural Patterns*, 237–39.
47 Martin 'The Religious Condition of Europe', 239–41.
48 Martin: 'The Religious Condition of Europe', 239–44.
49 Keith P. Luria, 'Catholicism', in Stearns, ed., *Encyclopedia of European Social History*, vol. 5, 296; Nicholas Atkin, '*Ralliés* and *résistants*: Catholics in Vichy France, 1940–44', in Kay Chadwick, ed., *Catholicism, Politics and Society in Twentieth-Century France*, Liverpool: Liverpool University Press, 2000, 97–118.
50 Luria, 'Catholicism', 297.
51 Joni Lovenduski and Jean Woodall, *Politics and Society in Eastern Europe*, Bloomington: Indiana University Press, 1987, 338.
52 Martin, 'The Religious Condition of Europe', 257–61; David Turnock, *Eastern Europe: An Economic and Political Geography*, London and New York: Routledge, 1989, 26–30, 117–21.
53 Philip S. Gorski, 'Historicizing the Secularization Debate', in Michele Dillon, ed., *Handbook of the Sociology of Religion*, Cambridge: Cambridge University Press, 2003, 111–13.
54 Malcolm Hamilton, *The Sociology of Religion: Theoretical and Comparative Perspectives*, London and New York: Routledge, 1995, 193–94.
55 S. Burne, ed., *Religion and Modernization: Sociologists and Historians Debate the Secularization Thesis*, Oxford: Clarendon Press, 1992.
56 Lane and Ersson, *Politics and Society in Western Europe*, 71.
57 Crouch, *Social Change in Western Europe*, 259.
58 Grace Davie, *Europe: The Exceptional Case – Parameters of Faith in the Modern World*, London: Darton, Longman and Todd, 2002, 7.
59 Tomka Miklós, 'Vallás és vallásosság', in Rudolf Andorka, Tamás Kolosi and Györgi Vukovich, eds., *Társadalmi riport. 1996*, Budapest: TÁRKI–Századvég, 1996, 609.
60 Grace Davie, 'God and Caesar: Religion in a Rapidly Changing Europe', in Bailey, ed., *Social Europe*, 233; Davie, *Europe: The Exceptional Case*, 8.
61 Davie, 'God and Caesar: Religion in a Rapidly Changing Europe', 8; Malcolm Hamilton, *The Sociology of Religion: Theoretical and Comparative Perspectives*, London and New York: Routledge, 1995, 185–214.
62 Eva Hamberg's phrase as quoted by Crouch, *Social Change in Western Europe*, 277–78.
63 Crouch, *Social Change in Western Europe*, 278.
64 Crouch, *Social Change in Western Europe*, 273.
65 Marco Bontempi, 'Religious Pluralism and the Public Sphere', in Bettin Lattes and Recchi, eds., *Comparing European Societies: Towards a Sociology of the EU*, 163.
66 James A. Beckford, *Social Theory and Religion*, Cambridge: Cambridge University Press, 2003, 33–43.
67 Bryan Wilson, *Religion in a Secular Society*, London: Watts, 1966.
68 Philip Jenkins, *God's Continent: Christianity, Islam, and Europe's Religious Crisis*, New York: Oxford University Press, 2007, 47–48.
69 David Martin, *A General Theory of Secularization*, Oxford: Gregg Revivals, 1993 [1978], 100–167.
70 David Martin, 'The Secularization Issue: Prospect and Retrospect', *British Journal of Sociology*, vol. 42 (1991), no. 3, 465–74.
71 Jenkins, *God's Continent*, 283–89.
72 Therborn, *European Modernity and Beyond*, 10; 229–33.

73 Jaroslav Krejci, 'Ethnic Problems in Europe', in Archer and Giner, eds., *Contemporary Europe*, 125; For a literature review, see Gerard Delanty, 'The Persistence of Nationalism: Modernity and Discourses of the Nation', in Gerard Delanty and Engin F. Insin, eds., *Handbook of Historical Sociology*, London: Sage, 2003, 287–300.
74 Miroslav Hroch, 'Historical Aspects of Nationalism: The West', in Smelser and Baltes, eds., *International Encyclopedia of the Social and Behavioural Sciences*, vol. 15, 10357–65.
75 Miroslav Hroch, *Das Europa der Nationen: Die moderne Nationsbildung im europäischen Vergleich*, Göttingen: Vandenhoeck, 2005, 11–26.
76 Ernest Renan, 'What is a Nation?', in H. K. Bhabha, ed., *Nation and Narration*, London: Routledge, 1990 [1882], 8–22.
77 Hans Kohn, *The Idea of Nationalism: A Study in its Origins and Background*, New York: Macmillan, 1946, 18–20, 329–31; on 'good' and 'bad' nationalisms, see Philip Spencer and Howard Wollman, *Nationalism: A Critical Introduction*, London: Sage, 2002, 94–106.
78 Miroslav Hroch, 'Historical Aspects of Nationalism: The West', in Smelser and Baltes, eds., *International Encyclopedia of the Social and Behavioral Sciences*, vol. 15, 10358–59.
79 Ernest Gellner, 'Scale and Nation', *Philosophy of the Social Sciences*, vol. 3 (1973), 1–17; Benedict R. Anderson, *Imagined Communities: Reflections on the Origin and Spread of Nationalism*, London: Verso, 1991, 37–46.
80 John A. Armstrong, *Nations before Nationalism*, Chapel Hill: University of North Carolina Press, 1982, 3–13, 283–99.
81 Ernest Gellner, *Nations and Nationalism*, Oxford: Oxford University Press, 1983.
82 Ernest Gellner, 'Adam's Navel: "Primordialists" versus "Modernists"', in E. Mortimer, ed., *People, Nation and State: The Meaning of Ethnicity and Nationalism*, London: Tauris, 1999, 31–35.
83 Eric J. Hobsbawm and Terrence Ranger, eds., *The Invention of Tradition*, Cambridge: Cambridge University Press, 1983.
84 Anderson, *Imagined Communities*, 37–46.
85 Clifford Geertz, 'The Integrative Revolution: Primordial Sentiments and Civic Politics in the New States', in Clifford Geertz, ed., *Old Societies and New States: The Quest for Modernity in Asia and Africa*, New York: Free Press, 1963, 107–13.
86 Anthony D. Smith, *The Ethnic Origin of Nations*, Oxford: Blackwell, 1986.
87 Hroch, *Historical Aspects of Nationalism*, 10361; Hroch, *Das Europa der Nationen*, 13–40.
88 The argument of this section largely relies on the following study: Jaroslav Krejci, 'Ethnic Problems in Europe', in Archer and Giner, eds., *Contemporary Europe*, 141–62.
89 Regarding the whole of Europe, i.e. now including Russia and the Soviet Union, the ratio of the population of the nations without an independent state or self-government dropped from 25% in 1910 to 4% in 1930 (Krejci, 'Ethnic Problems in Europe', 141).
90 For economic nationalism in interwar East Central Europe, see Ágnes Pogány, Eduard Kubu and Jan Kofman, eds., *Für eine nationale Wirtschaft: Ungarn, die Tschechoslowakei und Poland vom Ausgang des 19. Jahrhunderts bis zum Zweiten Weltkrieg*, Berlin: Berliner Wissenschaftsverlag, 2006.
91 Alan S. Milward, *The European Rescue of the Nation-State*, London: Routledge, 1993.
92 Krejci, 'Ethnic Problems in Europe', 150.
93 Krejci, 'Ethnic Problems in Europe', 143.
94 Michael Hechter and Margaret Levi, 'The Comparative Analysis of Ethnoregional Movements', *Ethnic and Racial Studies*, vol. 2/3 (1979), 262–74.
95 Andrew C. Janos, *East Central Europe in the Modern World: The Politics of the Borderlands from Pre- to Postcommunism*, Stanford, CA: Stanford University Press, 2000, 275, 278.
96 Robert B. Howell, 'The Low Countries: A Study in Sharply Contrasting Nationalisms', in Stephen Barbour and Catherine Carmichael, eds., *Language and Nationalism in Europe*, Oxford: Oxford University Press, 2000, 149; Sébastien Dubois, 'The Making of Nations in Belgium and Western Europe in Historical Perspective (Fifteenth–Twentieth Century): National Ideology, Ethnicity, Language and Politics', in Nikki Slocum-Bradley, ed., *Promoting Conflict or Peace through Identity*, Aldershot: Ashgate, 2008, 35.

97 The ethnic groups of Switzerland and Belgium do not belong to this type, because the former country is a federal state, and Belgium was a state where nations had long enjoyed equal rights and became a federal state in 1993.

98 Bernhard Schäfers, *Gesellschaftlicher Wandel in Deutschland*, Stuttgart: Enke, 1995, 103–4.

99 Krejci, 'Ethnic Problems in Europe', 154–60.

100 Huw Jones, *Population Geography*, London: Paul Chapman, 1990, 246.

101 Klaus J. Bade, *Migration in European History*, Oxford: Blackwell, 2003, 221–27, 241.

102 Craig Calhoun, 'Is It Time to Be Postnational?', in Craig Calhoun, ed., *Nations Matter: Culture, History, and the Cosmopolitan Dream*, London and New York: Routledge, 2007, 11–26.

103 Charles Maier, 'Consigning the Twentieth Century to History: Alternative Narratives for the Modern Era', *American Historical Review*, vol. 105 (2000), no. 3, 807–31.

104 Alan S. Milward, *The European Rescue of the Nation-State*, London: Routledge, 1993.

105 A.-P. Frognier, 'Nation: Sociological Aspects', in Smelser and Baltes, eds., *International Encyclopedia of the Social and Behavioral Sciences*, 10294–98.

106 Philip Schlesinger, '"Europeanness": A New Cultural Battlefield?', *Innovation*, vol. 5 (1992), no. 1, 12–22; Michael Bruter, *Citizens of Europe? The Emergence of a Mass European Identity*, Houndmills: Palgrave, 2005, 138.

107 Harding, Phillips and Fogarty, *Contrasting Values in Western Europe*, 2.

108 Ronald Inglehart, 'The Silent Revolution in Europe', *American Political Science Review*, vol. 4 (1971), 991–1017; Ronald Inglehart, *The Silent Revolution*, Princeton: Princeton University Press, 1977; for other recent value surveys in Europe, see Loek Halman, ed., *The European Values Study: A Third Wave, Source Book of the 1999/2000 European Values Study Surveys*, Tilburg: Tilburg University, 2001; Peter Ester, Michael Braun, and Peter Mohler, eds., *Globalization, Value Change, and Generations: A Cross-National and Inter-generational Perspective*, Leiden and Boston: Brill, 2006.

109 Ronald Inglehart, *Culture Shift in Advanced Industrial Society*, Princeton: Princeton University Press, 1990, 67–74.

110 Inglehart, *Culture Shift in Advanced Industrial Society*, 130–44.

111 Ronald Inglehart and Christian Welzel, *Modernization, Cultural Change, and Democracy*, Cambridge: Cambridge University Press, 2005, 63.

112 Russell J. Dalton, 'Vergleichende Wertewandelforschung', in Dirk Berg-Schlosser and Ferdinand Müller-Rommel, eds., *Vergleichende Politikwissenschaft*, Wiesbaden: VS Verlag für Sozialwissenschaften, 2003, 154.

113 S. Ashford and N. Timms, *What Europe Thinks: A Study of Western European Values*, Aldershot: Dartmouth, 1995, 126.

114 A classic treatise on the topic: Robert D. Putnam, *Making Democracy Work: Civic Traditions in Modern Italy*, Princeton: Princeton University Press, 1993.

115 Stefan Immerfall, 'Soziale Integration in den westeuropäischen Gesellschaften: Werte, Mitgliedschaften und Netzwerke', in Hradil and Immerfall, eds., *Die westeuropäische Gesellschaften im Vergleich*, 148.

116 Oscar W. Gabriel, Volker Kunz, Sigrid Roßteutscher and Jan W. van Deth, *Sozialkapital und Demokratie: Zivilgesellschaftliche Ressourcen im Vergleich*, Wien: WUV Universitätsverlag, 2002, 58.

117 Harding, Phillips and Fogarty, *Contrasting Values in Western Europe*, 65–96; Ashford and Timms, *What Europe Thinks*, 16, 132.

118 Jan-Erik Lane and Svante O. Ersson, *European Politics*, London: Sage, 1996, 128–32.

119 Adam B. Seligman and Katalin Füzer, 'The Problem of Trust and the Transition from State Socialism', *Comparative Social Research*, vol. 14 (1994), 216.

120 Inglehart, *Culture Shift in Advanced Industrial Society*, 6.

121 Inglehart and Welzel, *Modernization, Cultural Change, and Democracy*, 26–31.

122 Ulrich Beck, 'Losing the Traditional: Individualization and "Precarious Freedoms"', in Ulrich Beck and Elisabeth Beck-Gernsheim, eds., *Individualization*, London: Sage, 2002, 1–21.

10 Conclusions

1 The literature on historical periodization is not abundant: Peter Stearns, 'Periodization in Social History', in Peter Stearns, ed., *Encyclopedia of European Social History, 1350–2000*, vol. 1, New York, 2001, 125–30; Ludmilla Jordanova, *History in Practice*, London: Arnold, 2000, 114–40; Johan Hendrik Jacob V. Pot, *Sinndeutung und Periodisierung der Geschichte: Eine Systematische Übersicht der Theorien und Auffassungen*, Leiden: Brill, 1999; William A. Green, 'Periodizing World History', *American Historical Review*, vol. 101 (1996), no. 3, 749–70; Lawrence Besserman, 'The Challenge of Periodization: Old Paradigms and New Perspectives', in Lawrence Besserman, ed., *The Challenge of Periodization*, New York: Garland, 1996, 3–28.

2 Harold James, *Europe Reborn: A History, 1914–2000*, Harlow: Pearson, 2003; Tony Judt, *Postwar: A History of Europe since 1945*, New York: Penguin, 2005; Eric Hobsbawm, *The Age of Extremes: The Short Twentieth Century, 1914–1991*, London: Abacus, 1995, xxi.

3 This can be exemplified by the work of Gerold Ambrosius and William H. Hubbard, which discusses the social and economic history of Europe after 1914, or the volume on the economic history of post-war Western Europe edited by Max-Stephan Schulze. The same applies to Hans-Ulrich Wehler's five-volume work on the history of Germany after 1750: the third volume examines the period between 1849 and 1914, the fourth between 1914 and 1949, and the fifth between 1949 and 1990. Gerold Ambrosius and William H. Hubbard, *A Social and Economic History of Twentieth-Century Europe*, Cambridge, MA: Harvard University Press, 1989; Max-Stephan Schulze, ed., *Western Europe: Economic and Social Change since 1945*, London: Longman, 1999; Hans-Ulrich Wehler, *Deutsche Gesellschaftsgeschichte*, vol. 3–5, München: C. H. Beck, 1995–2008.

4 Giovanni Arrighi, *The Long Twentieth Century: Money, Power, and the Origins of Our Times*, London: Verso, 1994.

5 Charles Maier, 'Consigning the Twentieth Century to History: Alternative Narratives for the Modern Era', *American Historical Review*, vol. 105 (2000), no. 3, 807–31.

6 Ronald Findlay and Kevin H. O'Rourke, *Power and Plenty: Trade, War, and the World Economy in the Second Millennium*, Princeton: Princeton University Press, 2007, 378–425.

7 For a different assessment of the impact of integration on nation states in Western Europe, see Alan S. Milward, *The European Rescue of the Nation-State*, London: Routledge, 1993.

8 Arthur Marwick, *The Sixties: Cultural Revolution in Britain, France, Italy, and the United States, c. 1958–1974*, Oxford: Oxford University Press, 1998; Arthur Marwick, 'The Cultural Revolution of the Long Sixties: Voices of Reaction, Protest, and Permeation', *The International History Review*, vol. 27 (2005), no.4, 780–806.

9 For a catalogue of developments, see Marwick, *The Sixties*, 17–20.

10 M. J. Heale, 'The Sixties as History: A Review of the Political Historiography', *Review in American History*, vol. 33 (2005), 133–52.

11 Hartmut Kaelble, *The 1970s in Europe: A Period of Disillusionment or Promise?*, German Historical Institute, The 2009 Annual Lecture, London: The German Historical Institute, 2009.

12 Konrad H. Jarausch, 'Verkannter Strukturwandel. Die siebziger Jahre als Vorgeschichte der Probleme der Gegenwart', in Konrad H. Jarausch, ed., *Das Ende der Zuversicht? Die siebziger Jahre als Geschichte*, Göttingen: Vandenhoeck, 2008, 9–26.

13 There is a vast body of literature on the problem of Europe's cultural and social unity. For some recent related works with further references, see Gerard Delanty, 'The European Heritage: History, Memory, and Time', in Chris Rumford, ed., *The SAGE Handbook of European Studies*, London: SAGE, 2009, 36–51; Gerard Delanty and Chris Rumford, *Rethinking Europe: Social Theory and the Implications of Europeanization*, London: Routledge, 2005; Hartmut Kaelble, 'Eine europäische Gesellschaft?', in

Gunnar Volke Schuppert et al., ed., *Europawissenschaft*, Baden-Baden: Nomos, 2005, 299–330; Jacques Le Goff, *The Birth of Europe*, Oxford: Blackwell, 2005; Mikael af Malmborg and Bo Stråth, eds., *The Meaning of Europe*, Oxford and New York: Berg, 2002; Anthony Pagden, ed. *The Idea of Europe: From Antiquity to the European Union*, Cambridge: Cambridge University Press, 2002.

14 The ensuing sections largely rely on the argument of the following article: Hans-Peter Müller, 'Auf dem Weg in eine europäische Gesellschaft', *Berliner Journal für Soziologie*, vol. 17 (2007), no. 1, 7–31.

15 Catherine Lee and Robert Bideleux, '"Europe": What Kind of Idea?,' *The European Legacy*, vol. 14 (2009), no. 2, 163–76.

16 Manfred Fuhrmann, *Der europäische Bildungskanon*, Frankfurt/M.: Insel Verlag, 2004, 17–28.

17 Maria Todorova, *Imagining the Balkans*, Oxford: Oxford University Press, 1997.

18 Two examples of works dealing with this question in long-term temporal perspectives: Shmuel Noah Eisenstadt, *European Civilization in a Comparative Perspective: A Study in the Relations between Culture and Social Structure*, Oslo: Norwegian University Press, 1987; Michael Mitterauer, *Warum Europa? Mittelalterliche Grundlagen eines Sonderwegs*, München: Beck, 2003.

19 Hans Joas, 'Die kulturellen Werte Europas', in Hans Joas and Klaus Wiegandt, eds., *Die kulturellen Werte Europas*, Frankfurt/M.: Fischer, 2005, 17–39.

20 Michael Mann, *The Sources of Social Power*, 2 vols., Cambridge: Cambridge University Press, 1986.

21 'Values of Europeans', *Eurobarometer*, vol. 69 (2008), no. 1, 14.

22 Neil Fligstein, *Euroclash: The EU, European Identity, and the Future of Europe*, Oxford: Oxford University Press, 2008.

23 Martin Conway and Kiran Klaus Patel, eds., *Europeanization in the Twentieth Century: Historical Approaches*, Houndmills: Palgrave, 2010; Kaelble, 'Eine europäische Gesellschaft?', 308–10.

24 Hans-Peter Müller, 'Auf dem Weg in eine europäische Gesellschaft', 18.

25 Josep R. Llobera, 'What Unites Europeans?', in Montserrat Guibernau, ed., *Governing European Diversity*, London: SAGE, 2001, 175.

26 Bo Stråth, 'A European Identity: To the Historical Limits of a Concept,' *European Journal of Social Theory*, vol. 5 (2002), no. 4, 387–401.

27 Kaelble, *A Social History of Western Europe, 1880–1980*, especially 1–11, 150–61; Hartmut Kaelble, 'Social Peculiarities of Nineteenth- and Twentieth-Century Europe', in Kaelble, ed., *The European Way*, 276–317.

28 Crouch, *Social Change in Western Europe*, especially 32–47, 410–23.

29 Therborn, *European Modernity and Beyond*, especially 1–15, 348–59.

30 Hartmut Kaelble, *Sozialgeschichte Europas: 1945 bis zur Gegenwart*, München: C. H. Beck, 2007.

31 From the rich literature on the methodology of comparison, see Else Oyen, ed., *Comparative Methodology*, London: Sage, 1990; Mattei Dogan and Ali Kazancigil, eds., *Comparing Nations: Concepts, Strategies, Substance*, Oxford: Blackwell, 1994; for historical comparisons, see Hartmut Kaelble, *Der historische Vergleich*, Frankfurt/M. and New York: Campus, 1999; Heinz-Gerhard Haupt and Jürgen Kocka, eds., *Geschichte und Vergleich: Ansätze und Ergebnisse international vergleichender Geschichtsschreibung*, Frankfurt/M. and New York: Campus, 1996; Heinz-Gerhard Haupt, 'Comparative History,' in Smelser and Baltes, eds., *International Encyclopedia of the Social and Behavioral Sciences*, vol. 4, 2397–2403; Heinz-Gerhard Haupt, 'Comparative History – a Contested Method', *Historisk Tidskrift*, vol. 12 (2007), no. 4, 697–716; Larry J. Griffin, 'Comparative-Historical Analysis', in Edgar F. Borgetta and Marie L. Borgetta, eds., *Encyclopedia of Sociology*, vol. 1, New York: Macmillan, 1992, 263–71; Philipp Ther, 'Beyond the Nation: The Relational Basis of a Comparative History of Germany and Europe', *Central European History*, vol. 36 (2003), no. 1, 45–73.

32 For the major functions of historical comparison, see Theda Skocpol and Margaret Somers, 'The Uses of Comparative History in Macrosocial Inquiry', *Comparative Studies in Society and History*, vol. 22 (1980), no. 2, 174–97; Charles Tilly, *Big Structures, Large Processes, Huge Comparisons*, New York: Russel Sage, 1984; A. A. van den Braembussche, 'Historical Explanation and Comparative Method: Towards a Theory of the History of Society', *History and Theory*, vol. XXVIII (1989), no. 1, 1–24. We argued elsewhere for the relevance of the joint typologies of Heinz-Gerhard Haupt and Haupt and Jürgen Kocka, as well as that of Hartmut Kaelble. See Haupt, 'Comparative History', 2397–2403; Haupt and Kocka, 'Historischer Vergleich', 9–45; Kaelble, *Der historische Vergleich*, 35–78. Jürgen Kocka and Heinz-Gerhard Haupt divide the relevant studies on the basis of their functions into four types of comparison. Comparisons may fulfil a 'heuristic', 'descriptive' (or 'contrastive' as Haupt puts it), 'analytical', or 'alienating' (or 'distancing' as in Haupt) function. See Haupt and Kocka, 'Historischer Vergleich' 12–14; Haupt, 'Comparative History', 2397–2403; Kaelble applies similar categories when he writes about 'analytical', 'evaluating', 'understanding' and 'identity comparison'. See, Kaelble, *Der historische Vergleich*, 49–78.
33 Chris Lorenz, 'Comparative Historiography: Problems and Perspectives', *History and Theory*, vol. 38 (1999), 25–39.
34 Esping-Andersen, *The Three Worlds of Welfare Capitalism*, 21–22; Esping-Andersen, *Social Foundations of Postindustrial Economies*, 73–94.
35 On this aspect, see Mattei Dogan and Dominique Pelassy, *How to Compare Nations*, Chatham, NJ: Chatham House, 1990, 5–14.

SELECTED BIBLIOGRAPHY

Full references appear throughout the main text; thus, the titles listed here are but a small selection of the literature that might be most interesting or helpful for the reader who may want to further explore specific topics.

1. General works

Alber, Jens, Fahey, Tony and Saraceno, Chiara, eds., *Handbook of Quality of Life in the Enlarged European Union*, London and New York: Routledge, 2008.

Allum, Percy, *State and Society in Western Europe*, Cambridge: Polity Press, 1995.

Ambrosius, Gerold and Hubbard, William H., *A Social and Economic History of Twentieth-Century Europe*, Cambridge, MA: Harvard University Press, 1989.

Bailey, J., ed., *Social Europe*, London: Longman, 1998.

Bell, Daniel, *The Coming of Post-Industrial Society*, New York: Basic Books, 1974.

Castells, Manuel, *The Information Age: Economy, Society and Culture, Vol. I: The Rise of the Network Society*, Oxford: Blackwell, 2000.

Crouch, Colin, *Social Change in Western Europe*, Oxford: Oxford University Press, 1999.

Fischer, Wolfram, et al., eds., *Handbuch der europäischen Wirtschafts- und Sozialgeschichte*, Bd. 6, Stuttgart: Klett-Cotta, 1987.

Fulbrook, Mary, ed., *Europe since 1945*, Oxford: Oxford University Press, 2001.

Hradil, Stefan and Immerfall, Stefan, eds., *Die westeuropäischen Gesellschaften im Vergleich*, Opladen: Leske und Budrich, 1997.

Kaelble, Hartmut, *A Social History of Western Europe, 1880–1980*, Dublin: Gill and Macmillan, 1989.

Kaelble, Hartmut, ed., *The European Way: European Societies during the Nineteenth and Twentieth Centuries*, New York: Berghahn, 2004.

Kaelble, Hartmut, *Sozialgeschichte Europas: 1945 bis zur Gegenwart*, München: C. H. Beck, 2007.

Lattes, Gianfranco Bettin and Recchi, Ettore, eds., *Comparing European Societies: Towards a Sociology of the EU*, Bologna: Monduzzi Editore, 2005.

Schulze, Max-Stephan, ed., *Western Europe: Economic and Social Change since 1945*, London: Longman, 1999.

Stearns, Peter, ed., *Encyclopedia of European Social History, 1350–2000*, vol. 1–6, New York: Scribner's, 2001.

Therborn, Göran, and Immerfall, Stefan, eds., *Handbook of European Societies*, New York: Springer, 2010.
Therborn, Göran, *European Modernity and Beyond: The Trajectory of European Societies, 1945–2000*, London: Sage, 1995.
Tipton, Frank B., and Aldrich, Robert, *An Economic and Social History of Europe*, vol. 1–2, Baltimore: The John Hopkins University Press, 1987.
Wilensky, Harold L., *Rich Democracies*, Berkeley: University of California Press, 2002, 335.

2. Population

Andorka, Rudolf, *Determinants of Fertility in Advanced Societies*, London: Methuen, 1978.
Bade, Klaus J. et al., eds., *Enzyklopädie: Migration in Europa vom 17. Jahrhundert bis zur Gegenwart*, Paderborn and München: Ferdinand Schöningh and Wilhelm Fink, 2008, 37.
Bade, Klaus J., *Migration in European History*, Oxford: Blackwell, 2003.
Baines, Dudley, *Emigration from Europe, 1815–1930*, Cambridge: Cambridge University Press, 1991.
Blum, Alain and Rallu, Jean-Louis, eds., *European Population II: Demographic Dynamics*, Paris: John Libbey Eurotext, 1993.
Caselli, Graziella, Vallin, Jacques and Wunsch, Guillaume, eds., *Demography: Analysis and Synthesis*, vol. I–IV, Amsterdam: Elsevier, 2006.
Chesnais, Jean-Claude, *The Demographic Transition: Stages, Patterns, and Economic Implications – A Longitudinal Study of Sixty-Seven Countries Covering the Period 1720–1984*, Oxford: Oxford University Press, 1992.
Coale, A. J. and Watkins, S. C., eds., *The Decline of Fertility in Europe*, Princeton: Princeton University Press, 1986.
Coleman, David, 'Facing the 21st Century: New Developments, Continuing Problems', in M. Macura, A. L. MacDonald and W. Haug, eds., *The New Demographic Regime: Population Challenges and Policy Responses*, New York and Geneva: United Nations, 2005, 11–43.
Coleman, David, ed., *Europe's Population in the 1990s*, Oxford: Oxford University Press, 1996.
Demeny, Paul and McNicoll, Geoffrey, eds., *Encyclopedia of Population*, vol. 1–2, New York: Thomson and Gale, 2003.
Ekerdt, David J., ed., *Encyclopedia of Aging*, vol. 1–4, New York: Thomson and Gale, 2002.
Imhof, Arthur E., 'Von der unsicheren zur sicheren Lebenszeit. Ein folgeschwerer Wandel im Verlaufe der Neuzeit', *Vierteljahresschrift für Sozial-und Wirtschaftsgeschichte*, vol. 71 (1984), no. 2, 175–98.
McKeown, Thomas, *The Modern Rise of Population*, New York and London: Arnold, 1976.
Noin, Daniel and Woods, Robert, eds., *The Changing Population of Europe*, Oxford: Blackwell, 1993.
Omran, Abdel, 'The Epidemiologic Transition: A Theory of the Epidemiology of Population Change', *Milbank Memorial Fund Quarterly*, vol. 49 (1971), 509–38.
Rothenbacher, Franz, *The European Population, 1850–1945*, Basingstoke: Palgrave, 2002.
Ther, Philipp, *Die dunkle Seite der Nationalstaaten: 'ethnische Säuberungen im modernen Europa'*, Göttingen: Vandenhoeck & Ruprecht, 2011.
van de Kaa, Dirk J., 'Europe's Second Demographic Transition', *Population Bulletin*, vol. 42 (1987), no. 3, 3–57.
Watkins, Susan Cotts, *From Provinces into Nations: Demographic Integration in Western Europe, 1870–1960*, Princeton: Princeton University Press, 1991, 55–83.

3. Family

Anderson, Michael, *Approaches to the History of the Western Family, 1500–1914*, London and Basingstoke: Macmillan, 1980.
Ariès, Philippe, *Centuries of Childhood*, London: Jonathan Cape, 1962.

Hajnal, John, 'European Marriage Patterns in Perspective', in D. V. Glass and D. E. C. Eversley, eds., *Population in History*, London: Edward Arnold, 1965, 101–43.

Keilman, Nico, 'Recent Trends in Family and Household Composition in Europe', *European Journal of Population*, vol. 3 (1987), 297–325.

Kiernan, Kathleen, 'Leaving Home: Living Arrangements of Young People in Six West European Countries', *European Journal of Population*, vol. 2 (1986), no. 2, 177–84.

Laslett, Peter and Wall, Richard, eds., *Household and Family in Past Time*, Cambridge: Cambridge University Press, 1972.

Laslett, Peter, *The World We Have Lost*, London: Methuen, 1965.

Mitterauer, Michael and Sieder, Reinhard, *The European Family: Patriarchy to Partnership from the Middle Ages to the Present*, Chicago: University of Chicago Press, 1982.

Therborn, Göran, *Between Sex and Power: Family in the World, 1900–2000*, London: Routledge, 2004.

United Nations, *Patterns of First Marriage: Timing and Prevalence*, New York: United Nations, 1990.

4. Social stratification

Alderson, Arthur S. and Nielsen, François, 'Globalization and the Great U-Turn: Income Inequality Trends in 16 OECD Countries', *American Journal of Sociology*, vol. 107 (2002), no. 5, 1244–1300.

Atkinson, Anthony B. and Bourguignon, François, eds., *Handbook of Income Distribution*, vol. 1, Amsterdam: Elsevier, 2000.

Atkinson, Anthony B., Rainwater, Lee and Smeeding, Timothy M., *Income Distribution in OECD Countries: Evidence from the Luxembourg Income Study*, Paris: OECD, 1995.

Breen, Richard, ed., *Social Mobility in Europe*, Oxford: Oxford University Press, 2004.

Broadberry, Stephan and O'Rourke, Kevin H., eds., *The Cambridge Economic History of Modern Europe, Vol. 2: 1870 to the Present*, Cambridge: Cambridge University Press, 2010.

Clark, Colin, *The Conditions of Economic Progress*, London and New York: MacMillan, 1957.

Crossick, Geoffrey and Haupt, Heinz-Gerhard, *The Petite Bourgeoisie in Europe, 1780–1914: Enterprise, Family and Independence*, London: Routledge, 1995.

Dahrendorf, Ralf, *Class and Class Conflict in Industrial Society*, Stanford, CA: Stanford University Press, 1959.

Erikson, Robert and Goldthorpe, John H., *The Constant Flux: A Study of Class Mobility in Industrial Societies*, Oxford: Clarendon Press, 1992.

Eyal, Gil, Szelényi, Iván and Townsley, Eleanor, *Making Capitalism without Capitalists: Class Formation and Elite Struggles in Post-Communist Central Europe*, London: Verso Press, 1998.

Grusky, David B., *Social Stratification: Class, Race and Gender in Sociological Perspective*, Boulder, CO: Westview Press, 2001.

Haller, Max, ed., *Class Structure in Europe: New Findings from East–West Comparisons of Social Structure and Mobility*, Armonk and London: M. E. Sharpe, 1990.

Kaelble, Hartmut and Thomas, Mark, eds., *Income Distribution in Historical Perspective*, Cambridge: Cambridge University Press, 1991.

Kaelble, Hartmut, *Social Mobility in the 19th and 20th Centuries: Europe and America in Comparative Perspective*, Leamington Spa: Berg, 1985.

Kocka, Jürgen and Frevert, Ute, eds., *Bürgertum im 19. Jahrhundert*, Bd. 1, München: Deutscher Taschenbuch Verlag, 1988.

Kocka, Jürgen, *Die Angestellten in der deutschen Geschichte, 1850–1980*, Göttingen: Vandenhoeck und Ruprecht, 1981.

Kraus, Franz, 'The Historical Development of Income Inequality in Western Europe and the United States', in Peter Flora and Arnold J. Heidenheimer, eds., *The Development of Welfare States in Europe and America*, New Brunswick–London: Transaction, 1981, 187–236.

Lipset, Seymour Martin and Bendix, Reinhard, eds., *Social Mobility in Industrial Society*, Berkeley: University of California Press, 1959.

Rubinstein, W. D., ed., *Wealth and the Wealthy in the Modern World*, London: Croom Helm, 1980.

Singelmann, Joachim, *From Agriculture to Services: The Transformation of Industrial Employment*, Beverly Hills, CA and London: Sage, 1978.

Tenfelde, Klaus, eds., *Arbeiter und Arbeiterbewegung im Vergleich*, München: Oldenbourg, 1986.

van Ark, Bart, 'Sectoral Growth Accounting and Structural Change in Post-War Europe', in *Economic Growth*, Cambridge: Cambridge University Press, 1996, 84–164.

Wolff, Edward N., 'International Comparisons of Wealth Inequality', *Review of Income and Wealth*, vol. 4 (1996), 433–51.

5. The welfare state

Alber, Jens, *Vom Armenhaus zum Wohlfahrtsstaat: Analysen zur Entwicklung der Sozialversicherung in Westeuropa*, Frankfurt/M.: Campus, 1987.

Castles, Francis G., ed., *Families of Nations: Patterns of Public Policy in Western Democracies*, Aldershot: Dartmouth, 1993.

Castles, Francis G., Leibfried, Stephan, Lewis, Jane and Obinger, Herbert, eds., *The Oxford Handbook of the Welfare State*, Oxford: Oxford University Press, 2010.

Castles, Francis G., 'Whatever Happened to the Communist Welfare State?', *Studies in Comparative Communism*, vol. XIX (1986), no. 3/4, 213–26.

Esping-Andersen, Gøsta, *Social Foundations of Postindustrial Economies*, Oxford: Oxford University Press, 1999.

Esping-Andersen, Gøsta, *The Three Worlds of Welfare Capitalism*, Cambridge: Polity Press, 1990.

Flora, Peter and Heidenheimer, Arnold J., eds., *The Development of Welfare States in Europe and America*, New Brunswick and London, 1981.

Flora, Peter, ed., *State, Economy, and Society in Western Europe, 1815–1975*, vol. I, Frankfurt/M.: Campus, 1983.

Heidenheimer, Arnold J., Heclo, Hugh and Adams, Carolyn Teich, *Comparative Public Policy: The Politics of Social Choice in America, Europe, and Japan*, New York: St. Martin's Press, 1990.

Korpi, Walter, *The Democratic Class Struggle*, London: Routledge and Kegan Paul, 1983.

Lindert, Peter, *Growing Public: Social Spending and Economic Growth since the Eighteenth Century*, vol. 1–2, Cambridge: Cambridge University Press, 2004.

Pierson, Christopher, *Beyond the Welfare State?*, Cambridge: Polity Press, 1991.

Ritter, Gerhard A., *Der Sozialstaat: Entstehung und Entwicklung im internationalen Vergleich*, München: Oldenbourg, 1991.

Tomka, Béla, *Welfare in East and West*, Berlin: Akademie Verlag, 2003.

Tomka, Béla, 'Western European Welfare States in the 20th Century: Convergences and Divergences in a Long-run Perspective', *International Journal of Social Welfare*, vol. 12 (2003), no. 4, 249–60.

van Kersbergen, Kees, *Social Capitalism: A Study of Christian Democracy and the Welfare State*, London: Routledge, 1995.

6. Work, leisure and consumption

Bosch, Gerhard, Dawkins, Peter and Michon, François, eds., *Times Are Changing: Working Time in 14 Industrialized Countries*, Geneva: ILO, 1993.

Crouch, Colin, *Industrial Relations and European State Traditions*, Oxford: Clarendon Press, 1993.

Deaton, A. S., 'The Structure of Demand in Europe, 1920–70', in Carlo M. Cipolla, ed., *The Fontana Economic History of Europe: The Twentieth Century*, Part One, Glasgow: Collins–Fontana Books, 1976, 89–131.

Ebbinghaus, Bernhard and Visser, Jelle, *Trade Unions in Western Europe since 1945*, London: Macmillan, 2000.

Eichengreen, Barry, *The European Economy since 1945: Coordinated Capitalism and Beyond*, Princeton: Princeton University Press, 2007.

Feinstein, Charles H., Temin, Peter and Toniolo, Gianni, eds., *The European Economy Between the Wars*, Oxford: Oxford University Press, 1997.
Haupt, Heinz-Gerhard, *Konsum und Handel: Europa im 19. und 20. Jahrhundert*, Göttingen: Vandenhoeck and Ruprecht, 2003.
Huberman, Michael, 'Working Hours of the World Unite? New International Evidence of Worktime, 1870–1913', *Journal of Economic History*, vol. 64 (2004), 964–1001.
Kocka, Jürgen, ed., *Work in a Modern Society: The German Historical Experience in Comparative Perspective*, New York: Berghahn, 2010.
Kornai, János, *The Socialist System: The Political Economy of Communism*, Princeton: Princeton University Press, 1992.
Nussbaum, Martha and Sen, Amartya, eds., *The Quality of Life*, Oxford: Oxford University Press, 1993.
Offer, Avner, ed., *In Pursuit of the Quality of Life*, Oxford: Oxford University Press, 1996.
Sassatelli, Roberta, *Consumer Culture: History, Theory and Politics*, London: Sage, 2007.
Sassoon, Donald, *The Culture of the Europeans: From 1800 to the Present*, London: Harper and Collins, 2006.
Siegrist, Hannes, Kaelble, Hartmut and Kocka, Jürgen, eds., *Europäische Konsumgeschichte: Zur Gesellschafts-und Kulturgeschichte des Konsums (18. bis 20. Jahrhundert)*, Frankfurt/M.: Campus Verlag, 1997.
van der Linden, Marcel, *Transnational Labour History: Explorations*, Aldershot: Ashgate, 2003.

7. Politics and society

Allum, Percy, *State and Society in Western Europe*, Cambridge: Polity Press, 1995.
Almond, Gabriel and Verba, Sidney, *The Civic Culture: Political Attitudes and Democracy in Five Nations*, Princeton, N.J.: Princeton University Press, 1963.
Conway, Martin, 'Democracy in Post-War Western Europe: The Triumph of a Political Model', *European History Quarterly*, vol. 32 (2002), 59–84.
Gabriel, Oscar W. and Brettschneider, Frank, eds., *Die EU-Staaten im Vergleich*, Opladen: Westdeutscher Verlag, 1994.
Inglehart, Ronald, *Culture Shift in Advanced Industrial Society*, Princeton: Princeton University Press, 1990.
Inglehart, Ronald, *Human Values and Beliefs: A Cross-Cultural Sourcebook*, Ann Arbor: University of Michigan Press, 1998.
Inglehart, Ronald, *The Silent Revolution: Changing Values and Political Styles among Western Publics*, Princeton: Princeton University Press, 1977.
Lane, Jan-Erik and Ersson, Svante O., *Politics and Society in Western Europe*, London: Sage, 1991.
Lipset, Seymour M. and Rokkan, Stein, eds., *Party Systems and Voter Alignments: Cross-National Perspectives*, New York: Free Press, 1967.
Rokkan, Stein, *Staat, Nation, und Demokratie in Europa*, Frankfurt/M.: Suhrkamp, 2000.

8. Urbanization

Andrusz, Gregory, Harloe, Michael and Szelenyi, Ivan, eds., *Cities after Socialism: Urban and Regional Change and Conflict in Post-Socialist Societies*, Oxford: Blackwell, 1996.
Champion, A. G., ed., *Counterurbanization: The Changing Pace and Nature of Population Deconcentration*, London: Edward Arnold, 1989.
French, R. A. and Hamilton, F. E. Ian, eds., *The Socialist City: Spatial Structure and Urban Policy*, Chichester: John Wiley, 1979.
Hohenberg, Paul M. and Lees, Lynn Hollen, *The Making of Urban Europe, 1000–1950*, Cambridge, MA and London: Harvard University Press, 1985.
Le Galès, Patrick, *European Cities: Social Conflicts and Governance*, Oxford: Oxford University Press, 2002.

Lenger, Friedrich and Tenfelde, Klaus, eds., *Die europäische Stadt im 20. Jahrhundert: Wahrnehmung – Entwicklung – Erosion*, Köln and Wien: Böhlau, 2006.

Musil, Jiří, 'Changing Urban Systems in Post-Communist Societies in Central Europe', *Urban Studies*, vol. 30 (1993), no. 6, 899–905.

Paddison, Ronan, ed., *Handbook of Urban Studies*, London: Sage, 2001.

Summers, Anita A., Cheshire, Paul C. and Senn, Lanfranco, eds., *Urban Change in the United States and Western Europe: Comparative Analysis and Policy*, Washington, DC: The Urban Institute Press, 1999.

9. Education, religion and culture

Anderson, Benedict R., *Imagined Communities: Reflections on the Origin and Spread of Nationalism*, London: Verso, 1991.

Ashford, S. and Timms, N., *What Europe Thinks: A Study of Western European Values*, Aldershot: Dartmouth, 1995.

Calhoun, Craig, ed., *Nations Matter: Culture, History, and the Cosmopolitan Dream*, London and New York: Routledge, 2007.

Davie, Grace, *Europe: The Exceptional Case – Parameters of Faith in the Modern World*, London: Darton, Longman and Todd, 2002.

Dillon, Michele, ed., *Handbook of the Sociology of Religion*, Cambridge: Cambridge University Press, 2003.

Gabriel, Oscar W., Kunz, Volker, Roßteutscher, Sigrid and van Deth, Jan W., *Sozialkapital und Demokratie: Zivilgesellschaftliche Ressourcen im Vergleich*, Wien: WUV Universitätsverlag, 2002.

Gellner, Ernest, *Nations and Nationalism*, Oxford: Oxford University Press, 1983.

Harding, S., Philips, D. and Fogarty, M., *Contrasting Values in Western Europe: Unity, Diversity and Change*, London: Macmillan, 1986.

Hobsbawm, Eric J. and Ranger, Terrence, eds., *The Invention of Tradition*, Cambridge: Cambridge University Press, 1983.

Hroch, Miroslav, 'Historical Aspects of Nationalism: The West', in Smelser and Baltes, eds., *International Encyclopedia of the Social and Behavioural Sciences*, vol. 15, 10357–65, 2001.

Hroch, Miroslav, *Das Europa der Nationen: Die moderne Nationsbildung im europäischen Vergleich*, Göttingen: Vandenhoeck, 2005.

Inglehart, Ronald, *Culture Shift in Advanced Industrial Society*, Princeton: Princeton University Press, 1990.

Inglehart, Ronald, *Modernization and Postmodernization: Cultural, Economic and Political Change in 43 Societies*, Princeton: Princeton University Press, 1997.

Krejci, Jaroslav, 'Ethnic Problems in Europe', in Margaret Scotford Archer and Salvador Giner, eds., *Contemporary Europe: Class, Status and Power*, New York: St. Martin's Press, 1971, 124–71.

Martin, David, 'The Religious Condition of Europe', in Archer and Giner, eds., *Contemporary Europe: Class, Status and Power*, New York: St. Martin's Press, 1971, 228–87.

Ringer, Fritz, *Education and Society in Modern Europe*, Bloomington: Indiana University Press, 1979.

Rüegg, Walter, ed., *A History of the University in Europe, Vol. III: Universities in the Nineteenth and Early Twentieth Centuries (1800–1945)*, Cambridge: Cambridge University Press, 2004.

Rüegg, Walter, ed., *A History of the University in Europe, Vol. IV: Universities since 1945*, Cambridge: Cambridge University Press, 2011.

Shavit, Y. and Blossfeld, H.-P., eds., *Persistent Inequalities: Changing Educational Stratification in Thirteen Countries*, Boulder, CO: Westview Press, 1993.

Vincent, David, *The Rise of Mass Literacy: Reading and Writing in Modern Europe*, Cambridge: Polity, 2000.

10. Conclusions: the societies of Europe and Europe as a society in the 20th century

Conway, Martin and Patel, Kiran Klaus, eds., *Europeanization in the Twentieth Century: Historical Approaches*, Houndmills: Palgrave, 2010.

Delanty, Gerard, 'The European Heritage: History, Memory, and Time', in Chris Rumford, ed., *The SAGE Handbook of European Studies*, London: SAGE, 2009.

Delanty, Gerard and Rumford, Chris, *Rethinking Europe: Social Theory and the Implications of Europeanization*, London: Routledge, 2005.

Fligstein, Neil, *Euroclash: The EU, European Identity, and the Future of Europe*, Oxford: Oxford University Press, 2008.

Joas, Hans and Klaus Wiegandt, eds., *Die kulturellen Werte Europas*, Frankfurt/M.: Fischer, 2005.

Kaelble, Hartmut, 'Eine europäische Gesellschaft?', in Gunnar Volke Schuppert et al., ed., *Europawissenschaft*, Baden-Baden: Nomos, 2005, 299–330.

Kocka, Jürgen, 'Die Grenzen Europas: Ein Essay aus historischer Perspektive', in Gunnar Volke Schuppert et al., ed., *Europawissenschaft*, Baden-Baden: Nomos, 2005, 275–87.

Malmborg, Mikael af and Stråth, Bo, eds., *The Meaning of Europe: Variety and Contention within and among Nations*, Oxford: Berg Publishers, 2002.

Mitterauer, Michael, *Warum Europa? Mittelalterliche Grundlagen eines Sonderwegs*, München: Beck, 2003.

Outhwaite, William, *European Society*, Cambridge: Polity, 2008.

Stråth, Bo, ed., *Europe and the Other, Europe as the Other*, Brussels: P.I.E.–Peter Lang, 2000.

INDEX

Printed in Great Britain
by Amazon

19557236R00316